AutoCAD® 2015 for Interior Design and Space Planning

Beverly L. Kirkpatrick

James M. Kirkpatrick

Hossein Assadipour

Boston   Columbus   Indianapolis   New York   San Francisco   Hoboken
Amsterdam   Cape Town   Dubai   London   Madrid   Milan   Munich   Paris   Montreal   Toronto
Delhi   Mexico City   São Paulo   Sydney   Hong Kong   Seoul   Singapore   Taipei   Tokyo

Executive Editor: Lisa McClain
Cover Designer: Sandra Schroeder
Full-Service Project Management:
  Mohinder Singh, Aptara®, Inc.

Composition: Aptara®, Inc.
Printer/Binder: Edwards Brothers Malloy
Cover Printer: Edward Brothers Malloy
Text Font: ITC Bookman

Certain images and materials contained in this publication were reproduced with the permission of Autodesk, Inc. © 2015. All rights reserved. Autodesk, AutoCAD, Revit, DWG, and the DWG logo are registered trademarks of Autodesk, Inc., in the U.S.A. and certain other countries.

Credits and acknowledgments borrowed from other sources and reproduced, with permission, in this textbook appear on appropriate page within text.

Disclaimer

The publication is designed to provide tutorial information about AutoCAD® and/or other Autodesk computer programs. Every effort has been made to make this publication complete and as accurate as possible. The reader is expressly cautioned to use any and all precautions necessary, and to take appropriate steps to avoid hazards, when engaging in the activities described herein.

Neither the author nor the publisher makes any representations or warranties of any kind, with respect to the materials set forth in this publication, express or implied, including without limitation any warranties of fitness for a particular purpose or merchantability. Nor shall the author or the publisher be liable for any special, consequential or exemplary damages resulting, in whole or in part, directly or indirectly, from the reader's use of, or reliance upon, this material or subsequent revisions of this material.

Many of the designations by manufacturers and sellers to distinguish their products are claimed as trademarks. Where those designations appear in this book, and the publisher was aware of a trademark claim, the designations have been printed in initial caps or all caps.

Library of Congress Cataloging-in-Publication Data

Kirkpatrick, Beverly L.
  AutoCad 2015 for interior design and space planning / Beverly L. Kirkpatrick, James M. Kirkpatrick, Hossein Assadipour.
    pages cm
  Includes bibliographical references and index.
  ISBN 978-0-13-314485-7 (alk. paper)—ISBN 0-13-314485-2 (alk. paper)
  1. Interior decoration—Computer-aided design. 2. Interior architecture—Data processing. 3. Space (Architecture)—Computer-aided design. 4. Industrial floor space—Planning—Data processing. 5. Office layout—Planning—Data processing. I. Kirkpatrick, James M. II. Assadipour, Hossein. III. Title.
  NK2114.K57 2014
  729.0285'536—dc23
                                                              2014035175

10 9 8 7 6 5 4 3 2 1

ISBN 10:   0-13-314485-2
ISBN 13: 978-0-13-314485-7

Features of *AutoCAD® 2015 for Interior Design and Space Planning*

This text uses the new features of AutoCAD® 2015 in a variety of exercises specifically for interior design and architecture. Features include:

Chapter Objectives with a bulleted list of learning objectives at the beginning of each chapter provide users with a roadmap to the commands, concepts, and practices to be introduced.

CHAPTER OBJECTIVES

* Describe the AutoCAD user interface and begin using parts of the screen.
* Modify and save a worksp

TUTORIAL 2-1
Part 1, Beginning an AutoCAD Drawing: Saving Your Work; Setting Units, Limits, Grid, and Snap; Creating Layers

Beginning an AutoCAD Drawing

When you click **New...** from the **Quick Access** toolbar or **New** from the application menu button, or **Start Drawing** (Get Started) from the **New Tab** window, AutoCAD allows you to select a template file from the **Template**

Because users need lots of practice, a **Quick-Start Tutorials** chapter (provided right after the introductory chapter) challenges the user to make 2D drawings. These tutorials are designed with special step-by-step instructions that will walk the reader through the entire development process while raising interest in mastering the content to come in the rest of the chapters.

The first appearance of each **key term** is bold and italic within the running text and accompanied by a brief definition in the margin. The glossary at the end of the book contains a complete list of the key terms and more detailed definitions to help students understand and use the language of the computer-aided drafting (CAD) world.

Drawing Window and Graphics

user interface: All the elements such as the AutoCAD screen that make up the interface between the user and the AutoCAD program.

The AutoCAD *user interface* (Figure 1-4) contai access to commands. The drawing window is wh played. The graphics cursor (or crosshairs) follow mouse when points of a drawing are entered or a box at the center of the crosshairs is called a *pic*

OPTIONS	
Application Menu:	Options
Shortcut Menu:	Right-click the command window, and click Options
Menu Bar:	Tools/Options
Type a Command:	OPTIONS
Command Alias:	OP

* Status Bar
* Command Line

   The size of the graphics cursor and pick modate individual preferences. The colors of window also can be changed.
   Information regarding commands is att turned on or off using the **DYN** toggle in the in this chapter.

Step 1. Locate the **Options** dialog box, whe cursor, the colors of the elements ir pickbox can be changed, as describ

---

Command Grids appear in the margin alongside the discussion of the command or the particular exercise in which it is demonstrated. These grids provide specific information about the ways of invoking each command, including any of the following:

* Toolbar icon
* Ribbon panel
* Pull-down menu
* Command line
* Command alias

Tip, **Note**, and **For More Details** boxes highlight additional helpful information for the student. Such information may contain dos and don'ts, facts, warnings, and alternative ways of proceeding, as well as cross-references to other chapters and topics.

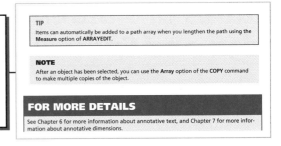

New to AutoCAD® 2015 icons indicate the commands and tools that are new to the program. This feature allows instructors and other users to quickly identify topics that are completely new, saving them a good amount of research time. It also demonstrates to students the recent improvements to the AutoCAD software, as well as the valuable updated information contained in this textbook.

 tcount command and with Starting nu as prefix:

Text sample line one

Text sample line two

Text sample line three

Text sample line four

Text sample line five

End-of-Chapter material can easily be located by the shading on the page edges. This material will help students evaluate and practice the knowledge they've acquired about the most important concepts explained in the chapter. This material's content includes:

- Chapter Summary
- Chapter Test Questions
  - Multiple Choice
  - Matching
  - True or False
  - List (Five different ways of executing commands in AutoCAD 2015)

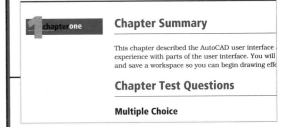

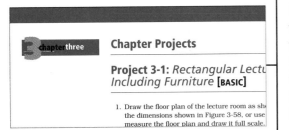

Chapter Projects are additional assignments located at the end of each chapter in which students are directed to solve particular tasks on their own. The projects are labeled as basic, intermediate, and advanced according to the degree of complexity. Students will use the knowledge acquired throughout the chapter as well as in previous chapters in completing these assignments.

Instructor Resources

The **Online Instructor's Manual** provides answers to unit exercises and tests, solutions to end-of-chapter questions, and lecture-supporting Power-Point® slides.

To access supplementary materials online, instructors need to request an instructor access code. Go to **www.pearsonhighered.com/irc**, where you can register for an instructor access code. Within 48 hours after registering, you will receive a confirming e-mail, including an instructor access code. Once you have received your code, go to the site and log on for full instructions on downloading the materials you wish to use.

Preface

AutoCAD has become the industry-standard graphics program for interior design and space planning. This program is used to complete the many contract documents (CDs) that make up a design project. Many design firms have adopted AutoCAD as their standard because:

- It saves time.

- Affiliated professions have chosen it so that they can exchange files and work on the same drawing.

- Their competitors use it.

- Their clients expect it.

To be successful in design today, students must be proficient in the use of AutoCAD as it relates to interior design and space planning. The need for an AutoCAD textbook geared specifically to this field is what led us to write *AutoCAD® 2015 for Interior Design and Space Planning*.

This text, newly updated for AutoCAD® 2015, is divided into three parts:

- Part I: Preparing to Draw with AutoCAD (Chapter 1).

- Part II: Two-Dimensional AutoCAD (Chapters 2–13).

- Part III: Three-Dimensional AutoCAD (Chapters 14–15).

This new edition includes many features designed to help you master AutoCAD® 2015:

- The prompt-response format is clearly defined with numbered steps. This step-by-step approach is used in the beginning exercises of all chapters and then moves to an outline form in projects at the end of most chapters. This allows students to learn commands in a drawing situation and then practice applying them on their own.

- Lineweights have been carefully assigned to provide line contrast in all drawing exercises.

- Plotting is used in Chapter 2 to allow students to plot their first drawings.

- Chapter 5 has been reworked. Students can plot drawings containing different scales with plot styles and multiple viewports.

- Exercises are geared to architects, interior designers, and space planners, allowing students to work with real-world situations.

- More than 600 illustrations (many printed to scale) support the text and reinforce the material.

- Screen shots and command grids help the user locate AutoCAD commands within the AutoCAD menus and ribbon.

- "Tip," "Note," and "For More Details" boxes give students additional support and information.

- Practice projects at the end of every chapter review the commands learned.

- Learning objectives and review questions in every chapter reinforce the learning process.

- An online Instructor's Manual is available to support the text.

Organized around architectural and interior design–related projects, *AutoCAD® 2015 for Interior Design and Space Planning* gives students an understanding of the commands and features of AutoCAD® 2015 and demonstrates how to use the program to complete interior design and space planning projects. The book is appropriate for self-paced and lecture classes and covers both two-dimensional and three-dimensional drawings.

Throughout the exercises in this book, steps numbered in color provide instructions. **Prompt** and **Response** columns in the numbered steps provide step-by-step instructions for starting and completing a command. The **Prompt** column text repeats the AutoCAD prompt that appears in the command area of the AutoCAD screen. The **Response** column text shows how you should respond to the AutoCAD prompt. Screen shots of menus and command grids show you how to locate the command you are using.

Using numerous illustrations, the text captures the essence of this powerful program and the importance it plays in the interior design, architecture, and space planning professions.

Most importantly, this text was written to help you, the reader, master the AutoCAD program, which will be a valuable tool in your professional career.

Hallmark Features

Progresses from Basic Commands to Complex Drawing Exercises

- Builds confidence and basic skills before moving on to more complex assignments.

- Ensures students have mastered the fundamental features and commands of the AutoCAD program before they apply it to more complex problems.

- Guides readers step-by-step through each new AutoCAD command.

- Encourages students to learn commands and features on their own.

Provides More Than 100 Exercises and Projects

- Gives students the opportunity to work with a variety of real-world situations, including both commercial and residential projects.

Highlights Seven Projects Appropriate for Interior Design, Space Planning, and Architecture Students

- Projects are a tenant space, hotel room, wheelchair-accessible commercial restroom, bank, log cabin, and two houses.

- Includes project floor plans, dimension plans, elevations, furniture plans, reflected ceiling plans, and voice/data/power plans, as well as isometric drawings, a presentation sheet, and the sheet set command that combines multiple plans.

- Includes a 15-unit condominum building as an exercise in Appendix C.

Includes More Than 600 Figures

- Helps students by allowing them to compare their work and progress with the many figures available.

- Shows many drawings to scale so students can assess and check their understanding of chapter material.

Introduces the AutoCAD DesignCenter

- The **DesignCenter** is used to import blocks, layers, and dimension styles from other drawings into existing drawings.

Covers Solid Modeling in Two Chapters

- Splits solid modeling material into two chapters: Chapter 14, Solid Modeling; and Chapter 15, Advanced Modeling.

- Uses the **3DWALK** and **Animation Motion** commands to create walk-through presentations.

New to This Edition

The **new AutoCAD® 2015 interface** and commands include the following:

- **New Tab**
- **Enhanced Help (to locate tools in AutoCAD)**
- **(View) Ribbon Enhancements**
- **Layer Sort**
- **Trim and Extend Enhancements**
- **MText Enhancements**
- **Isometric Drawing (ISODRAFT)**

Acknowledgments

We would like to acknowledge those who contributed ideas and drawings: Dr. David R. Epperson, the CAD students at Eastfield College, Tech Art, Benjamin Puerte, Jr., Paul Flournoy, Center Line Design and Drafting, Dr. Stephanie Clemons, Stephen Huff, Laura Clark, and Kelly McCarthy, McCarthy Architecture. Thank you also to Pei Cobb Freed & Partners for cover art. We would like to thank Autodesk, Inc. Finally, we would like to thank Dr. H. Assadipour who undertook the task of upgrading the textbook to AutoCAD 2015.

B.L.K.
J.M.K.

Style Conventions in *AutoCAD® 2015 for Interior Design and Space Planning*

Text Element	Example
Key Terms—**Boldface** and italic on first mention (first letter lowercase, as it appears in the body of the text). Brief definition in margin alongside first mention. Full definition in Glossary at back of book.	Views are created by placing ***viewport*** objects in the paper space layout.
AutoCAD commands—Bold and uppercase.	Start the **LINE** command.
Ribbon and panel names, palette names, toolbar names, menu items, and dialog box names—Bold and follow capitalization convention in AutoCAD toolbar or pull-down menu (generally first letter cap).	The **Layer Properties Manager** palette The **File** menu
Panel tools, toolbar buttons, and dialog box controls/buttons/input items—Bold and follow the name of the item or the name shown in the AutoCAD tooltip.	Choose the **Line** tool from the **Draw** panel. Choose the **Symbols and Arrows** tab in the **Modify Dimension Style** dialog box. Choose the **New Layer** button in the **Layer Properties Manager** palette. In the **Lines and Arrows** tab, set the **Arrow size:** to **.125**.
AutoCAD prompts—Dynamic input prompts are set in a different font to distinguish them from the text. Command window prompts are set to look like the text in the command window, including capitalization, brackets, and punctuation. Text following the colon of the prompts specifies user input in bold.	AutoCAD prompts you to *Specify first point: Specify center point for circle or [3P 2P Ttr (tan tan radius)]:* **3.5**
Keyboard Input—Bold with special keys in brackets.	Type **3.5 <Enter>**

Contents

Contents **xv**

New to AutoCAD 2015

Introducing the AutoCAD User Interface

CHAPTER OBJECTIVES

- Describe the AutoCAD user interface and begin using parts of the screen.

- Modify and save a workspace.

Introduction

Before you start using the exercises in this book, you need to understand their structure and purpose. Throughout the exercises in this book:

- Numbered steps provide instructions.

- **Prompt** and **Response** columns within the numbered steps provide step-by-step instructions for starting and completing a command.

- The **Prompt** column text repeats the AutoCAD prompt that appears in the command line area of the AutoCAD screen.

- The **Response** column text shows your response to the AutoCAD prompt.

- Command grids in the margins and menu screens show you how to locate the command you are using.

EXERCISE 1-1
Examine the AutoCAD User Interface and Save a Workspace

As you launch AutoCAD 2015, it displays the interface shown in Figure 1-1, with the **New Tab**. It displays as a file tab when there are no drawings open, and when you create a new tab. The New Tab contains two sliding content frames: Learn and Create.

Figure 1-1
The **New Tab** of AutoCAD 2015

Create

The Create page is displayed by default. It serves as a launchpad where you can access sample files, recent files, templates, product updates, and the online community.

If you click *Get Started*, Drawing1, created from a default template, opens and there is still a tab at the top. You can click the **New Tab** button (it looks like the New Tab button on your browser) to get the same 3-column screen (Figure 1-1) you see when you open AutoCAD. There you can start a new drawing or open an existing one. By the way, layout tabs similarly have a **New Layout** button. Figure 1-2 shows the list of available drawing templates organized by groups. The last template used becomes the default template.

The real advantage is that each drawing that you open, whether from a tab or by using the **OPEN** command, has its own tab. Now it's really easy to switch among drawings.

The third column displays *Notifications* such as hardware acceleration, trial period, and where to download offline help. It also enables you to sign into Autodesk® 360 cloud-based service and send feedback directly to Autodesk. **Autodesk 360** is a secure set of online servers. The *Get Started* button takes you to a window where you can sign in for an **Autodesk 360**

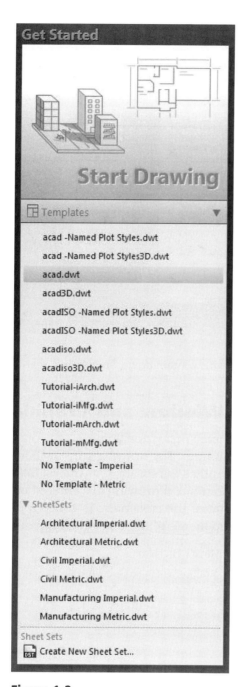

Figure 1-2
List of available drawing templates in AutoCAD 2015

account. **Autodesk 360** is your connection to the **Cloud** where you can store, share, and view drawings.

Learn

If you slide to the Learn page by clicking the **Learn** content frame, located to the left of **Create** at the bottom of the page, you will see Figure 1-3, which provides you tools to help you learn AutoCAD 2015. It's divided into three columns: **What's New**, **Getting Started Videos**, and **Tip/Online Resources**. The **NEWTABMODE** system variable specifies whether clicking the plus (+) button on the file tab displays a **New Tab** or a new drawing.

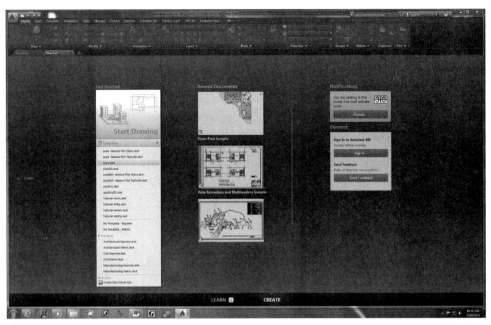

Figure 1-3
Learn content frame, containing getting started, learning, and tips/online resources

Drawing Window and Graphics Cursor

user interface: All the elements such as the AutoCAD screen that make up the interface between the user and the AutoCAD program.

The AutoCAD **user interface** (Figure 1-4) contains the drawing window and access to commands. The drawing window is where your drawing is displayed. The graphics cursor (or crosshairs) follows the movement of a mouse when points of a drawing are entered or a command is selected. The box at the center of the crosshairs is called a *pickbox*.

Other components of the user interface, as shown in Figure 1-4, are:

- Application Menu Button
- Quick Access Toolbar
- Info Center
- Ribbon and Its Tabs and Panels
- ViewCube
- Navigation Bar
- User Coordinate System Icon
- Status Bar
- Command Line

The size of the graphics cursor and pickbox can be changed to accommodate individual preferences. The colors of the elements in the drawing window also can be changed.

Information regarding commands is attached to the cursor. This can be turned on or off using the **DYN** toggle in the status bar, as described later in this chapter.

Step 1. Locate the **Options** dialog box, where the size of the graphics cursor, the colors of the elements in the drawing window, and the pickbox can be changed, as described next:

OPTIONS	
Application Menu:	Options
Shortcut Menu:	Right-click the command window, and click Options
Menu Bar:	Tools/Options
Type a Command:	OPTIONS
Command Alias:	OP

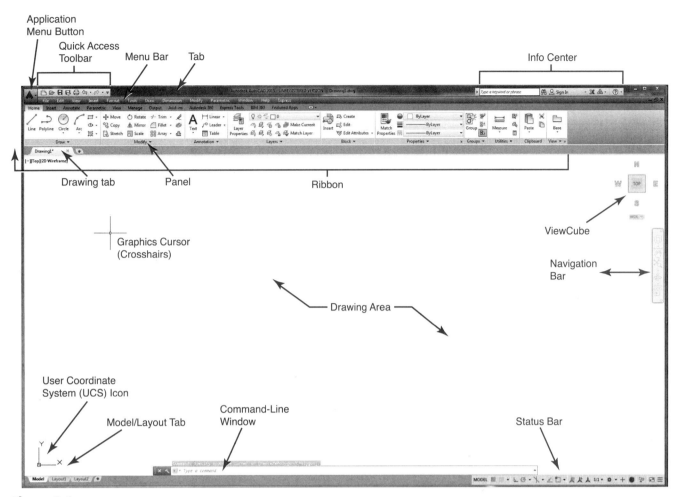

Figure 1-4
The AutoCAD user interface

Prompt	Response
Type a command:	Type **OP <Enter>** (in this book, **<Enter>** means to press the **<Enter>** key or press the right mouse button to enter a command)
The **Options** dialog box appears	Click the **Display** tab
The **Display** tab appears (Figure 1-5):	Click the **Crosshair size** slider in the lower right to decrease or increase the size of the crosshairs
	Click the **Colors...** button on the left
The **Drawing Window Colors** dialog box (Figure 1-6) appears:	This is where you can change colors of the elements in the drawing window
	Click **Cancel** to exit the **Drawing Window Colors** dialog box
	Click the **Selection** tab
The **Selection** tab appears:	Click the **Pickbox size** slider in the upper left to decrease or increase the size of the pickbox
	Click **Cancel** to exit the **Options** dialog box

Figure 1-5
Options dialog box—
Display tab

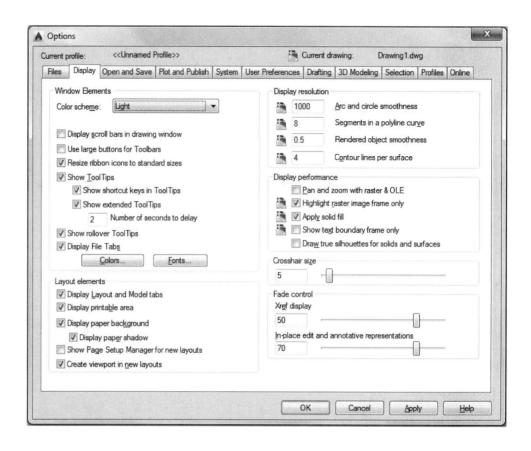

Figure 1-6
Drawing Window Colors
dialog box

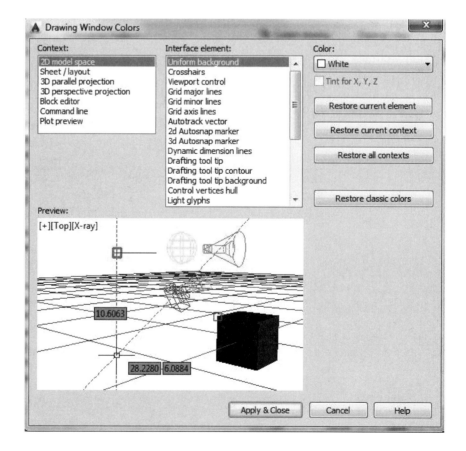

Application Menu Button

When you click (quickly press and release the left mouse button) on the **Application** menu button, the application menu opens. The application menu commands (Figure 1-7) can be used to:

- Create a new drawing
- Open an existing drawing
- Save a drawing
- Save a drawing as
- Export your drawing to a different format
- Share a drawing
- Print or plot a drawing
- Access tools to maintain your drawing
- Close a drawing

At the top of the application menu, you can enter key words in the text box to search for additional menu items.

Step 2. Click the application menu button with your left mouse button to open it. Hold your mouse over each command to see the brief descriptions of the command options. Press the **<Esc>** key to exit the application menu (Figure 1-7).

Figure 1-7
Application menu

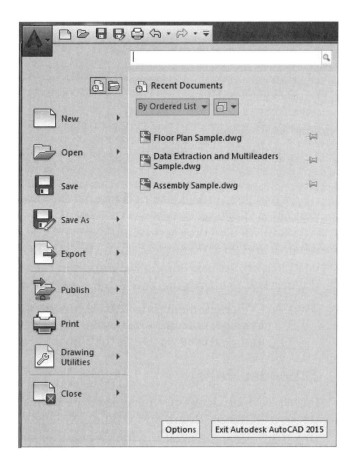

Major Ways to Input/Select a Command

AutoCAD provides four major ways to input/select a command:

1 Select a command icon from the ***ribbon***.

2 Type a full command name or command alias (e.g., **L** for **line**) at the ***command line window***.

3 Use the **Quick Access** toolbar customization button to show the menu bar. You can then select an icon/command from the ***menu bar***.

4 Use the **Tools** menu on the menu bar to access the AutoCAD toolbars. You can then select a command icon from a ***toolbar***.

Ribbon

The ribbon displays the commands used to make a drawing. If you right-click (quickly press and release the right mouse button) on any menu tab, you will get a right-click menu (Figure 1-8) that has commands to hide or show tabs, panels, and panel titles. This right-click menu also has commands to close the ribbon or undock it. If you close the ribbon, type **RIBBON <Enter>** at the command prompt to reopen it.

Figure 1-8

Display the right-click menu by right-clicking on a ribbon tab

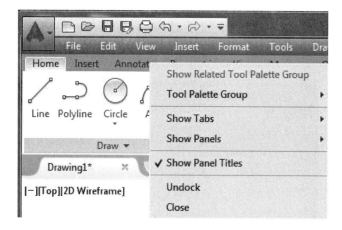

When you undock the ribbon, you can drag it to display as horizontal, vertical, or floating.

You can also drag individual panels of the ribbon into your drawing window and float them. You can drag them back into the ribbon, or you can click on **Return Panels to Ribbon** in the upper right corner grab bar (Figure 1-9) to return the panel to the ribbon.

Step 3. Click each menu tab—**Home, Insert, Annotate, Parametric, View, Manage, Output, Add-ins, Autodesk 360, Express Tools, BIM 360,** and **Featured Apps**—in the ribbon to view the commands available.

Expanded Panels

Panels with an arrow to the right of the panel title can be expanded to display additional commands. When you click the left mouse button on the arrow, the panel will expand. When the panel is expanded, you can use the pushpin icon to the left of the panel title to keep the panel expanded (Figure 1-10).

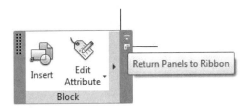

Figure 1-9
Return Panels to Ribbon option in the upper right corner of a floating panel

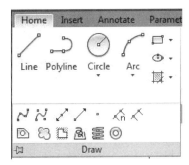

Figure 1-10
Expanded panel

Dialog Boxes and Palettes

Panels with a diagonal arrow in the lower right corner of the panel title have dialog boxes or palettes. When you click the left mouse button on the diagonal arrow, a dialog box or palette will appear, as shown in Figure 1-11.

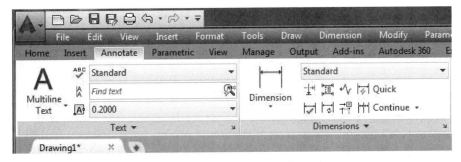

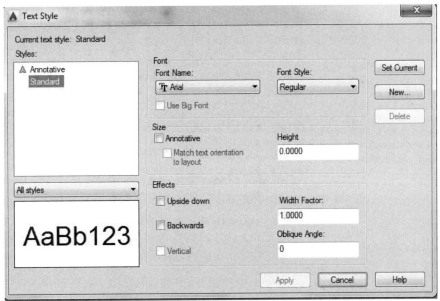

Figure 1-11
Clicking the diagonal arrow in the lower right corner of a panel will display a dialog box or palette

Tooltips

When you hold the mouse pointer steady (do not click) on any command in the ribbon, a tooltip displays the name of the command, and a text string gives a brief description of the command (Figure 1-12).

Flyouts

Commands with a small arrow have flyouts. When you click the left mouse button on the arrow, the flyout will appear, as shown in Figure 1-13. When you click on a command in the flyout, a command is activated.

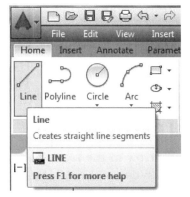

Figure 1-12
Tooltips

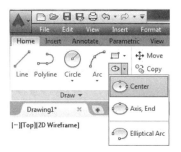

Figure 1-13
Flyouts

Command Line Window (<Ctrl>+9)

The command line window shown at the bottom of the screen may be moved and resized or turned off. The command line window is where you can see AutoCAD respond to a command you have started. After a command is started, AutoCAD prompts you to enter specific information. Always watch the command line to make sure you and AutoCAD are communicating.

AutoComplete command entry: When you start to type a command (e.g., **L** for **line**) at the *command line window*, AutoCAD provides a list of commands that start with L, command aliases, and system variables (Figure 1-14). You can scroll through the list and select the command you want. When you right-click on the command line, the right-click menu shown in Figure 1-14 appears. You can turn off **AutoComplete** (delete the check beside the suggestion list) and also change the amount of time it takes for the list to appear.

Quick Access Toolbar

This toolbar contains the **New, Open, Save, Save As…, Cloud Options, Plot, Undo, Redo,** and **Workspace Switching** commands.

When you right-click on the **Quick Access** toolbar, the right-click menu shown in Figure 1-15 appears:

The First Option: Allows you to remove commands from the **Quick Access** toolbar

The Second Option: Allows you to add a separator line between command icons in the **Quick Access** toolbar

The Third Option: Allows you to add frequently used commands to the **Quick Access** toolbar

The Fourth Option: Allows you to move the **Quick Access** toolbar to below the ribbon

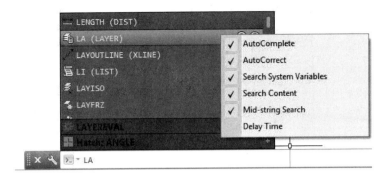

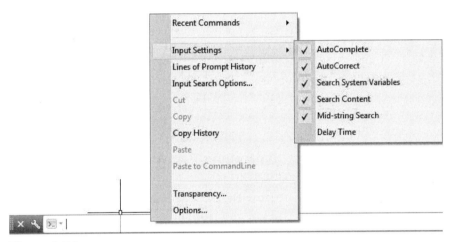

Figure 1-14
AutoComplete command entry list and right-click menu

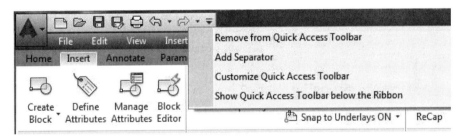

Figure 1-15
Right-click on the **Quick Access** toolbar

Customize Quick Access Toolbar Down Arrow and Show Menu Bar

When you click the **Customize Quick Access Toolbar** down arrow to the right of the **Quick Access** toolbar, the menu shown in Figure 1-16 appears:

> **Commands:** Clicking a command to display the check mark adds the command icon to the **Quick Access** toolbar.

> **More Commands....** Takes you to the **Customize User Interface Editor** and allows you to add frequently used commands to the **Quick Access** toolbar.

Figure 1-16
Customize Quick Access
Toolbar

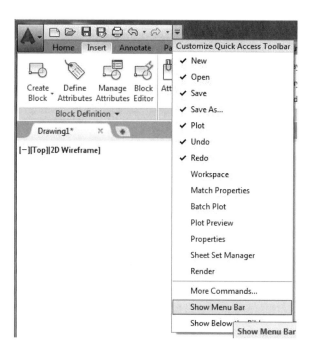

Show Menu Bar: Allows you to display the menu bar shown in Figure 1-17.

Show Below the Ribbon: Allows you to move the **Quick Access** toolbar below the ribbon.

Step 4. Hold your mouse steady over each icon in the **Quick Access** toolbar to see the text string that gives a brief description of each command.

Step 5. Right-click on the **Quick Access** toolbar (Figure 1-15) to view the right-click menu. Press the **<Esc>** key to exit the right-click menu.

Step 6. Click on the **Customize Quick Access Toolbar** down arrow to view the menu shown in Figure 1-16. This is where you select **Show Menu Bar** to add the menu bar and the commands you can use to make a drawing (Figure 1-17). Press the **<Esc>** key to exit the menu.

Menu Bar

Figure 1-17
Display the menu bar

AutoCAD Toolbars

The AutoCAD toolbars have buttons that start commands you can use to make a drawing. You can display, hide, dock, and resize toolbars. You can create your own toolbars and turn a toolbar into a ribbon panel.

Step 7. Click the ribbon **View** from the pull-down menu, and then select **Toolbars** (Figure 1-18) to view the list of available toolbars.

Figure 1-18
Available toolbars

Chapter 1

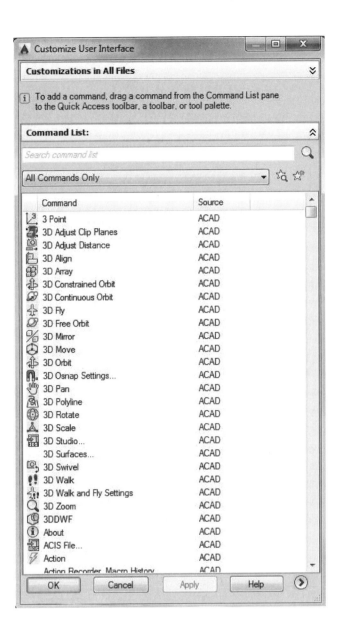

User Coordinate System Icon

user coordinate system icon: An icon showing the orientation of the *X-, Y-,* and *Z*-axes of the current coordinate system. In two-dimensional drawings only the *X-* and *Y*-axes are used. The UCS icon is located at the origin of the current UCS (0,0).

All AutoCAD drawings are made on a coordinate system (Figure 1-19). The ***user coordinate system (UCS) icon*** in the lower left corner of the drawing window shows the orientation of the *X-*, *Y-*, and *Z*-axes of the current coordinate system. In 2D drawings, only the *X-* and *Y*-axes are used. The UCS icon is located at the origin of the UCS (0,0). In this figure, the lines (grid marks) are spaced ½″ apart. The crosshairs of the cursor are located 3″ to the right (the X direction) and 2″ up (the Y direction) from 0,0. The numbers in the gray area show the cursor coordinate values (the location of the crosshairs).

Advantage of Using the UCS   The origin (0,0) of the UCS can be moved to any point on a drawing; when the origin is relocated, you can easily draw from that point. When a drawing contains dimension information from a specific location, relocating the origin to that specific location makes drawing much easier.

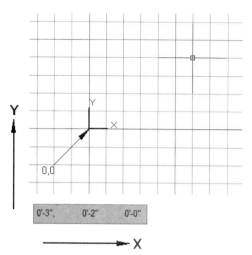

Figure 1-19
The AutoCAD user coordinate system—
Cartesian coordinates

Viewport Label Menus

The drawing window can be divided into multiple viewports. The **Viewport Label Menus** in the upper left drawing area can be used in the current single viewport or in multiple viewports. The **Viewport Label Menus** consist of the following:

    Viewport Controls: When you click on the **Viewport Controls** icon, the menus shown in Figure 1-20 open. You can change from a single viewport to a multiple viewport configuration and use the display options **ViewCube, SteeringWheels**, and the navigation bar for each viewport.

Figure 1-20
Viewport controls

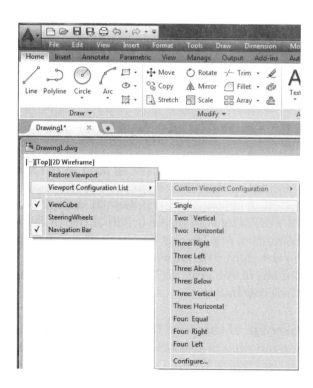

View Controls: The menu shown in Figure 1-21 provides a list of all the standard and custom views available to use in each viewport.

Visual Style Controls: The menu shown in Figure 1-22 provides access to all the visual styles available to use in each viewport.

These menus can be turned OFF. Type and enter **VPCONTROL** at the command line; type **OFF** to respond to the prompt *Enter new value for VPCONTROL <ON>*.

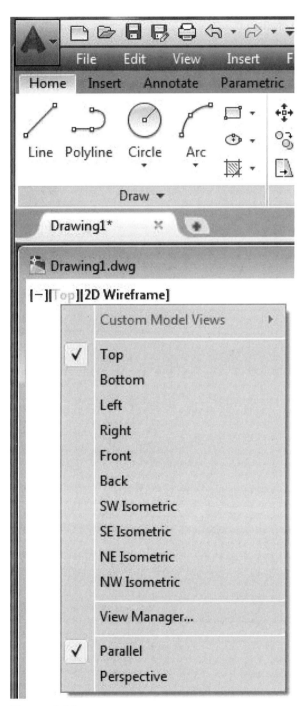

Figure 1-21
View controls

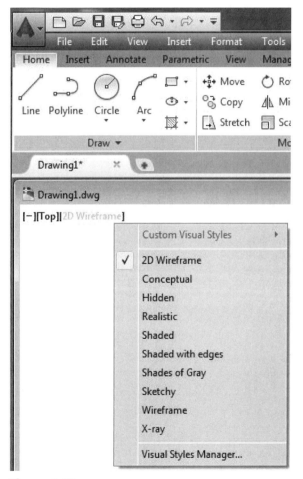

Figure 1-22
Visual style controls

ViewCube

ViewCube: A three-dimensional viewing tool that can be used to switch from one view of a model to another.

ViewCube: Used to navigate the 3D drawing.

UCS Menu: Used in 2D and 3D drawing to change the origin of the UCS (user coordinate system). WCS stands for *world coordinate system,* the AutoCAD fixed-coordinate system, which is common to all AutoCAD drawings.

Step 8. Right-click in the ViewCube area to display the right-click menu (Figure 1-23). Click **ViewCube Settings...** on the right-click menu to access the **ViewCube Settings** dialog box (Figure 1-24), where you can change the display of the ViewCube and the **UCS** menu. Press the **<Esc>** key to exit the dialog box.

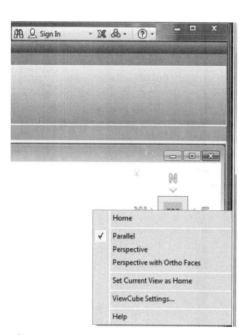

Figure 1-23
Right-click **ViewCube** menu

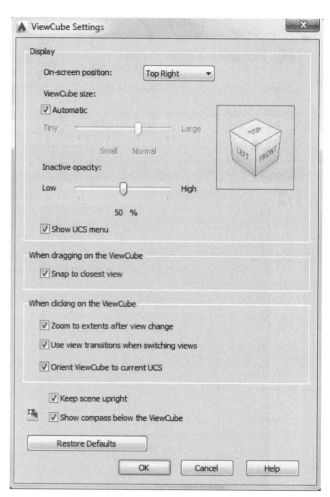

Figure 1-24
ViewCube Settings dialog box

Navigation Bar

navigation bar: An area in the AutoCAD user interface that contains navigation tools that are common across multiple Autodesk programs. The unified navigation tools include Autodesk ViewCube, SteeringWheels, ShowMotion, and 3Dconnexion.

Tools on the *navigation bar* with a small down arrow can be expanded to display additional tools. The **NAVBAR** system variable controls appearance of the navigation bar (ON or OFF).

Similarly, the system variable **DISPLAYVIEWCUBEIN2D** (ON or OFF) controls the display of the ViewCube.

SteeringWheels: Used by experienced 3D users to navigate the 3D drawing. There is also a 2D wheel.

Pan: Used in 2D and 3D drawing. Analogous to panning with a camera, using this tool allows you to maintain the current display magnification and see parts of the drawing that may be off the screen and not visible in the drawing window.

Zoom: Used in 2D and 3D drawing, the **Zoom** commands help you control how you view the drawing area on the display screen.

Orbit: Rotates the view in 3D space.

Show Motion: Used in 3D to record animation.

Step 9. Click on the button in the bottom right of the navigation bar to view the menu shown in Figure 1-25. Clicking a command to display the check mark adds the command icon to the navigation bar; clicking to remove the check mark removes the command icon from the navigation bar. Press the **<Esc>** key to exit the menu.

You can click on the button in the top right of the navigation bar to close it. You can click the ribbon, **View** tab, **Viewport Tools** panel, and change the display of the ViewCube and the navigation bar (Figure 1-26).

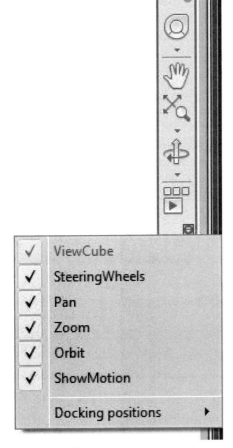

Figure 1-25
Click on the button in the bottom right of the navigation bar to view a menu

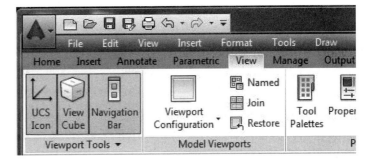

Figure 1-26
You can change the display of the **ViewCube** and the navigation bar

Infocenter

Text Input Box: You can enter a word or phrase in the **Infocenter** text box to search for information (Figure 1-27). Click on the **Search** button to the right of the text box to display the search results in **Autodesk Exchange – AutoCAD. Autodesk Exchange** connects you to the AutoCAD help content, instructional videos, and downloads. You can collapse the text input box by clicking the arrow to the left of the box.

Figure 1-27
Infocenter Search

Autodesk 360: This is where you can sign in for an **Autodesk360** account.

Autodesk Exchange Apps: Displays the **Autodesk Exchange Apps** website.

Stay Connected: This provides access to Autodesk product services, support, and the AutoCAD online community.

Help: Displays the help menu in **Autodesk Exchange**. The down arrow to the right has additional help information. If you have closed the **Welcome Screen**, you can turn it on here.

Status Bar

The status bar (Figure 1-28) at the bottom of the screen contains the following options. This feature is a bit different from the previous versions of AutoCAD. In AutoCAD 2015 the **Drawing Tools** status toggles, and the tools under the status bar tray are combined together at the lower right corner of the graphical user interface. The **Customization** tool at the rightmost end of the status bar allows you to show the tools you want to see on the status bar.

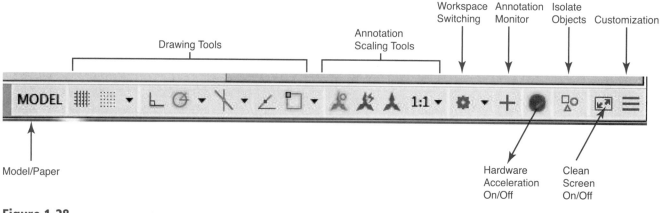

Figure 1-28
Status bar

Drawing Coordinates Values (<Ctrl>+I)

This is not shown by default, but can be turned on using the **Customization** tool of the status bar. Using an *X*- and *Y*-axis system, the drawing coordinate display value in the lower left corner tells you where the cursor on the screen is located in relation to 0,0 (the lower left corner). Clicking on the coordinates turns them on and off.

The drawing tools status toggles (snap, grid, ortho, polar tracking, etc.) are at the bottom right corner of the screen and are represented by icons (Figure 1-28). Click the **Customization** tool at the lower right end of the status bar to see the current set of icons on the status bar (Figure 1-29). For example, the cursor coordinates, which traditionally were on the lower left end of the status bar, now are not shown by default.

The drawing tools status toggles at the bottom of the screen allow you to turn on or off drawing tools that affect your drawing. You can also turn many of the tools off and on using the function keys. The tools and the function keys are as follows:

> **INFER (Infer Constraints) (<Ctrl>+<Shift>+I):** When on, this controls the application and visibility of geometric constraints such as horizontal, vertical, and perpendicular while you are drawing (Figure 1-30). It also controls the display of dimensional constraints between geometric objects or points on objects and the order in which constraints are applied to your drawing.

> **SNAP (Snap Mode) (<F9>):** When a command is active and you are specifying points, your graphics cursor (crosshairs) snaps to invisible snap points as you move the cursor across the screen when **SNAP** is on. You set the size between snap points.

Coordinates

✓ Model Space

✓ Grid

✓ Snap Mode

Infer Constraints

Dynamic Input

✓ Ortho Mode

✓ Polar Tracking

✓ Isometric Drafting

✓ Object Snap Tracking

✓ 2D Object Snap

LineWeight

Transparency

Selection Cycling

3D Object Snap

Dynamic UCS

Selection Filtering

Gizmo

✓ Annotation Visibility

✓ AutoScale

✓ Annotation Scale

✓ Workspace Switching

✓ Annotation Monitor

Units

Quick Properties

✓ Graphics Performance

✓ Clean Screen

Figure 1-29
Drawing tool buttons displayed on the status bar

Figure 1-30
Constraint Settings dialog box

GRID (Grid Display) (<F7>): A visible grid that you see on the screen when **GRID** is on. You set the size of the grid and can set the appearance of the grid to lines or dots.

ORTHO (Ortho Mode) (<F8>): Restricts you to draw only horizontally and vertically when on.

POLAR (Polar Tracking) (<F10>): Shows temporary alignment paths along polar angles when on (Figure 1-31). While the default increment for **PolarSnap** is 90 degrees, one can change it easily to 60, 45, 30, 15, and so on as shown in Figure 1-32. The system variable **POLARANG** can be used to reset **PolarSnap**.

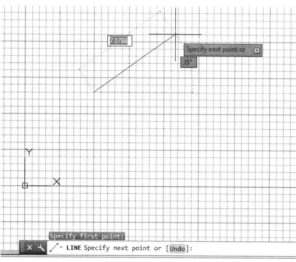

Figure 1-31
Polar angles with **POLAR** on

Figure 1-32
PolarSnap angles set from status bar

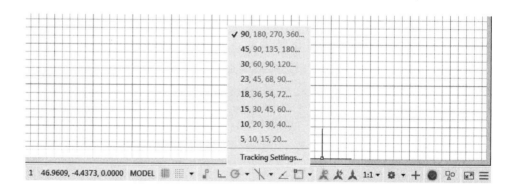

Isometric Drawing (<ISODRAFT>): Allows easy switching between the isoplanes for those who use isometric drawings (e.g., piping and instrumentation diagrams [Figure 1-33]).

OSNAP (Object Snap) (<F3>): Contains command modifiers that help you draw very accurately.

3DOSNAP (3D Object Snap) (<F4>): Object snap setting for drawing in 3D. It contains command modifiers for drawing very accurately in 3D.

OTRACK (Object Snap Tracking) (<F11>): Shows temporary alignment paths along object snap points when on.

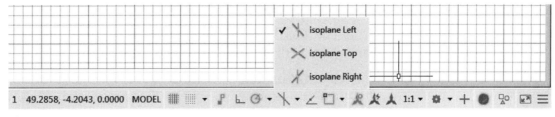

Figure 1-33

Isometric Drawing toggle to switch between isoplanes

DUCS (Allow/Disallow Dynamic UCS) (<F6>): Used in 3D to move the user coordinate system.

DYN (Dynamic Input) (<F12>): Gives you information attached to the cursor regarding commands, coordinates, and tooltips. This is the same information that AutoCAD displays in the command line window.

LWT (Show/Hide Lineweight): You can assign varying lineweights (widths) to different objects in a drawing. When this toggle is on, the lineweights are displayed on the screen.

TPY (Show/Hide Transparency): You can assign varying transparency levels to an object. When this toggle is on, the transparency is displayed on the screen.

QP (Quick Properties) (<Ctrl>+<Shift>+P): Every drawing object that you draw has properties such as color, layer, and linetype. When this button is on, the **Quick Properties** window appears when you select an object and allows you to view and change the settings for the properties of the object.

SC (Selection Cycling) (<Ctrl>+W): When two drawing objects lie very close to each other or one on top of the other, this helps you select one of the objects. When this toggle is on, you can hold down **<Shift>**+space bar and cycle through the objects.

AM (Annotation Monitor): Associative is a property that belongs to dimensions. Associative dimensions are linked to association points on the object dimensioned. When the association point on the object moves (the object is made larger or smaller), the dimension location, orientation, and text value of the dimension change. When this button is on, dimensions that are disassociated will have a badge beside them.

Model or Paper Space

These buttons control the visibility of the model and paper space (layout) working environments.

Model space is the drawing window where your drawing is displayed. **Paper space** (layout) is the area where you can annotate, lay out, and preview your drawing for printing or plotting.

model space: One of the two primary spaces in which objects are made.

paper space: One of the two spaces in which objects are made or documented. Paper space is used for making a finished layout for printing or plotting. Often, drawings are restored in paper space in a drawing title block and border.

Quick View Tools

Quick View Layouts: Allows you to preview and switch between the current drawing and its layouts

Quick View Drawings: Allows you to preview and switch between open drawings and their layouts

Annotation Scaling Tools

These buttons affect annotative objects such as text and dimensions that are added to drawings and need to be scaled when plotted.

Annotation Scale: This button allows you to control how annotative text and dimensions appear on the drawing.

Annotation Visibility: When you have annotative objects on your drawing that support different scales, this button controls their visibility. When it is off, only the annotative objects with the current annotation scale are visible.

Auto Scales: When this button is on and the annotation scale is changed, the annotative objects change on the screen to reflect the new scale size. The object then supports two scales.

Workspace Switching

A **workspace** is the environment in which you work. It is defined by the menus, toolbars, or palettes that appear on the workspace. This button allows you to switch between defined workspaces.

Lock/Unlock Toolbar and Window Positions

Toolbars and windows can be added to your workspace. This button allows you to lock and unlock the location of these toolbars and windows.

On/Off Hardware Acceleration

When you are working with large drawings or rendering and hiding models, hardware acceleration enhances the graphic performance in AutoCAD.

The area of the status bar, which was formerly named **Status Bar Tray**, does not exist anymore, and tools such as annotation monitor and **Isolate Objects** have been rearranged on the status bar.

- **Annotation Monitor:** The **AM toggle (Annotation Monitor)** in the drawing tools area of the status bar keeps track of associated and disassociated dimensions. When the **AM toggle** is **ON**, a cross appears in the tray area of the status bar.

- **Isolate Objects:** You can isolate objects in a drawing or hide them regardless of layer. When objects have been isolated or hidden in the drawing, the light bulb is red. When all objects in the drawing are visible, the light bulb is yellow.

Clean Screen (<Ctrl>+0 [Zero])

When on, this button clears the screen of the ribbon, toolbars, and dockable windows, excluding the command line, as shown in Figure 1-34.

Figure 1-34
Clean Screen tool on the status bar

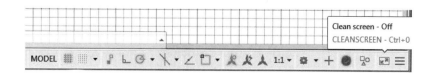

Modify and Save a Workspace

AutoCAD provides you with four different workspaces to choose from when making your own workspace:

Drafting & Annotation: This workspace has the ribbon displayed by default, and the menu bar, toolbars, and tool palettes are off by default.

3D Basics: This workspace is used when you make basic 3D solid models. The basic 3D commands are available. The ribbon containing these basic commands is on by default.

3D Modeling: This workspace is used when you make complex 3D solid models. All the commands and settings used to make, assign materials to, and render solid models are on by default. The ribbon is on by default.

AutoCAD Classic: This is the traditional workspace. The ribbon is turned off by default, and the menu bar, toolbars, and tool palettes are displayed by default.

Step 10. Make sure the **Drafting & Annotation** workspace is current, as described next:

Prompt	Response
Type a command:	Click the **Workspace Switching** button on the status bar
The **Workspace Switching** menu appears (Figure 1-35):	If there is a check mark beside **Drafting & Annotation**, it is active
	If it is active, press **<Esc>** to exit the menu
	If it is not active, click **Drafting & Annotation** to make it the active workspace

Figure 1-35
Workspace switching menu

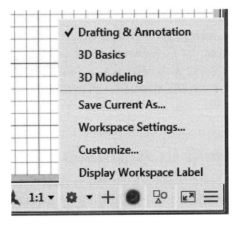

Step 11. Add the menu bar to the AutoCAD screen, as described next:

Prompt	Response
Type a command:	Click the customization button (the down arrow at the right end of the **Quick Access** toolbar)
	Click **Show Menu Bar** (the menu bar appears as shown in Figure 1-36)

Figure 1-36
Show Menu Bar option

Step 12. Save your workspace, as described next:

Prompt	Response
Type a command:	Click the **Workspace Switching** button
The **Workspace Switching** menu appears:	Click **Save Current As...**
The **Save Workspace** text box appears:	Type your name in the **Name:** text box <**Enter**>

As you become familiar with AutoCAD, you may want to add menus, toolbars, or palettes to your drawing display and keep that display. Click **Save Current As...**, locate your name in the **Name:** text box, and save the modified drawing display as your named workspace again.

Getting Help in AutoCAD 2015

The AutoCAD Help system includes a new way to help you locate tools in the AutoCAD user interface (UI) directly from the relevant Help content. In the **Help** window, click the tool you want to use or the **Find** link next to it. An animated arrow points you directly to that tool in the AutoCAD ribbon. For example, Figure 1-37 shows how the **Find** link locates help on the **Arc** command.

If the tool is not accessible from the current workspace or is located in a hidden tab or panel, a tooltip in the **Help** window tells you on which ribbon tab and panel you can find it, as shown in Figure 1-38, looking for the **UCS** command.

Figure 1-37

Help on the **Arc** command

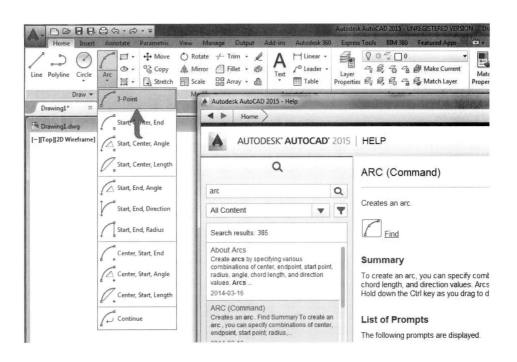

Figure 1-38

Help on the **UCS** (user coordinate system) command

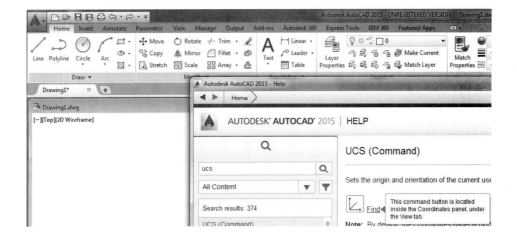

Close AutoCAD

For now, you will not name or save this exercise. The new workspace is already saved.

Step 13. Click the **Close** button (the **X**) in the upper right corner of the AutoCAD screen if you want to exit AutoCAD.

Chapter Summary

This chapter described the AutoCAD user interface and gave you some experience with parts of the user interface. You will now be able to modify and save a workspace so you can begin drawing effectively.

Chapter Test Questions

Multiple Choice

Circle the correct answer.

1. Which of the following is **not** one of the commands in the application menu?

   a. **Delete** c. **Close**

   b. **Open** d. **Publish**

2. Which of the following is a ribbon panel?

   a. **Home** c. **Draw**

   b. **File** d. **Save**

3. Which of the following icons on the **Modify** panel of the ribbon has a flyout?

   a. **Move** c. **Scale**

   b. **Copy** d. **Trim**

4. Ribbon panels with a diagonal arrow in the lower right corner display which of the following when the diagonal arrow is clicked?

   a. Flyouts c. The **Help** menu

   b. A dialog box or palette d. Options

5. Which of the following display the name of the command and give other information relating to it?

   a. Tooltips c. Dialog boxes

   b. Flyouts d. Palettes

Matching

Write the number of the correct answer on the line.

a. **Workspace Switching** _____

b. **Application Status Bar Menu** _____

c. **Quick Access** toolbar _____

d. **Quick View Layouts and Drawings** _____

e. **Selection Cycling** _____

1. Allows you to switch between defined workspaces

2. Allows you to preview and switch between layouts and drawings

3. A menu that allows you to turn off and on the visibility of the buttons in the status bar

4. A means of choosing one object when two objects lie directly one on top of the other

5. Contains the **New, Open, Save, Save As..., Cloud Options, Plot, Undo, Redo**, and **Workspace Switching** commands

True or False

Circle the correct answer.

1. **True or False:** The **Quick Access** toolbar can be customized.

2. **True or False:** The **Selection** tab on the **Options** dialog box allows you to change the size of the crosshairs.

3. **True or False:** The **Display** tab on the **Options** dialog box allows you to change the size of the pickbox.

4. **True or False:** The menu bar can be added to the AutoCAD screen by clicking the down arrow to the right of the **Quick Access** toolbar and clicking **Show Menu Bar**.

5. **True or False:** The navigation tools on the right side of the screen allow you to zoom and pan.

List

1. Five components of AutoCAD's graphical user interface.

2. Five tools from **Drawing Tools** toggles on the status bar.

3. Five tabs from the ribbon.

4. Five panels under the **Home** tab of the ribbon.

5. Five commands accessible through the **Application** menu.

6. Five tools from the **Quick Access** toolbar

7. Five tools under the **Modify** panel, under the **Home** tab of the ribbon.

8. Five tools under the **Draw** panel, under the **Home** tab of the ribbon.

9. Five items that can be added to the status bar using the **Customization** tab.

10. Five ways of executing AutoCAD commands.

Questions

1. How are the tutorials in this book structured?

2. What is the purpose of the **Options** dialog box?

3. What are the four means of inputting or selecting a command?

4. What is the structure of the ribbon?

5. Why would you want to drag a panel from the ribbon, and how do you drag it off and return it to the ribbon?

2 chapter two

Quick-Start Tutorials: Basic Settings and Commands

CHAPTER OBJECTIVES

- Begin a new AutoCAD drawing and make settings for units, limits, grid, and snap.
- Make layers and assign color, linetype, and lineweight to each layer.
- Use function keys to control grid and snap.
- Use the commands **Save** and **Save As** to save work.
- Use grips to modify objects.
- Use **ORTHO** mode to control drawing horizontal and vertical lines.
- Use annotation scale to control how text and other annotative objects appear on drawings and plots.
- Print/plot drawings from a **Model** tab.

- Correctly use the following commands and settings:

ARC	**MOVE**
CIRCLE	**PAN**
DONUT	**REDO**
DYN	**REDRAW**
ELLIPSE	**REGEN**
ERASE	**SCALE**
GRIDDISPLAY	**Single Line Text**
Highlight	**UNDO**
LINE	**ZOOM**
LTSCALE	

- Correctly use selection set option
- Draw using absolute, relative, polar coordinates, and direct distance entry.

Introduction

The following is a hands-on, step-by-step procedure to complete your first drawing using AutoCAD:

- Tutorial 2-1, Part 1, describes the *settings* that must be made before starting a drawing.

- Tutorial 2-1, Part 2, describes *how to draw using basic commands.*

- Tutorial 2-2 describes *how to print* your drawing.

When you have completed Tutorial 2-1 your drawing will look similar to Figure 2-1.

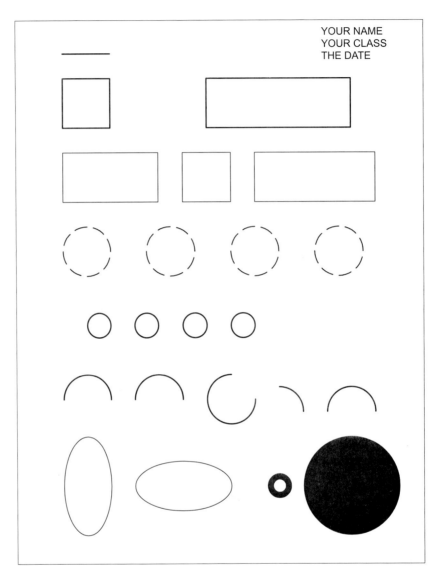

Figure 2-1
Tutorial 2-1 complete

Following the Tutorials in This Book

You are probably using a mouse with a small scroll wheel between the buttons. The left button is the pick button used to select commands and click points on the drawing. The **Response** column item used in the tutorials describes the location of points on the drawing that are clicked by the left button on your mouse. Figures are provided throughout the chapters to show the location of the points. The points are indicated in bold type in the **Response** column by a **P→**. The **P** is followed by a number; for example, **P1→, P2→**. Look at the figure referenced in the step to locate the numbered point on the figure, and click a point in the same place on your drawing.

TUTORIAL 2-1
Part 1, Beginning an AutoCAD Drawing: Saving Your Work; Setting Units, Limits, Grid, and Snap; Creating Layers

Beginning an AutoCAD Drawing

When you click **New...** from the **Quick Access** toolbar or **New** from the application menu button, or **Start Drawing** (Get Started) from the **New Tab** window, AutoCAD allows you to select a template file from the **Template** folder or use the default template file. A template file has settings already established. These settings can include units, limits, grid, snap, and a border and title block. *Templates save time because the settings are already made.*

If you click **New...** and select the **acad.dwt** template, as shown in Figure 2-2, you are in the same drawing environment as when you simply open the AutoCAD program and begin drawing. AutoCAD uses the acad.dwt template for the drawing settings if no other template is selected.

You do not need to click **New...** from the **File** menu. You can stay in the drawing environment that appeared when you started AutoCAD.

NEW	
Application Menu:	New
Quick Access Toolbar	
Menu Bar:	File/New...
Type a Command:	New

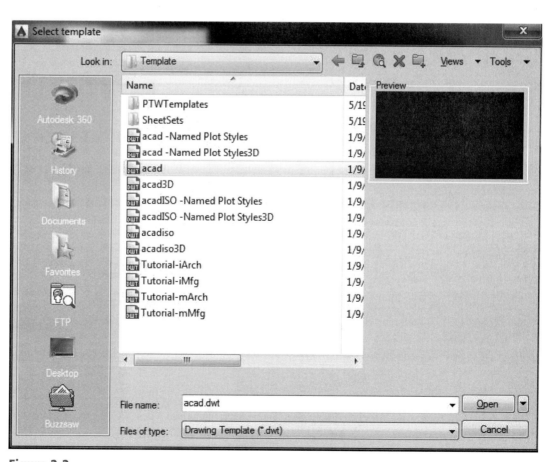

Figure 2-2
Select the **acad.dwt** template for a new drawing

Step 1. If your named workspace is not active, you can select it by using the **Workspace Switching** button in the status bar or in the **Quick Access** toolbar. You can modify your workspace and save it again as often as you like.

Saving the Drawing

SAVE	
Application Menu:	💾 Save
Quick Access Toolbar	Save
Menu Bar:	File/Save
Type a Command:	SAVE

You must understand two commands, **Save** and **Save As**, and their uses to name and save your work in the desired drive and folder.

Save

When the **Save** command is clicked for a drawing that *has not been named*, the **Save Drawing As** dialog box is activated. You may name the drawing by typing a name in the **File name:** input box. You also select a drive and folder where you want the drawing saved.

When the **Save** command is clicked and the drawing *has been named* and already saved, no dialog box appears, and the drawing is saved automatically to the drive and folder in which you are working. At this time, the existing drawing file (.dwg) becomes the backup file (.bak), and a new drawing file is created.

SAVE AS	
Application Menu:	📝 Save As...
Quick Access Toolbar	💾
Menu Bar:	File/ Save As...
Type a Command:	SAVEAS

Save As

Save As activates the **Save a copy of the drawing** selection box (Figure 2-3) *whether or not the drawing has been named* and allows you to save your drawing to **Save Drawing As** (Figure 2-4) to any drive or folder you choose with a new name if you choose so.

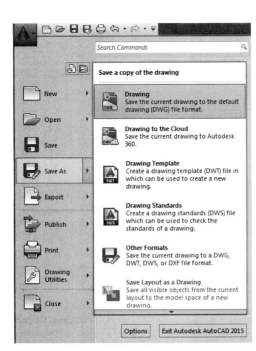

Figure 2-3
Save a copy of the drawing selection box from **Application** menu

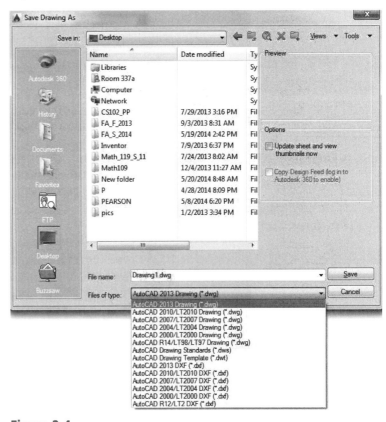

Figure 2-4
Save Drawing As dialog box with file types shown

Some additional features of the **Save As** command are as follows:

1 If the default drive is used (the drive on which you are working), and the drawing has been opened from that drive, .dwg and .bak files are created when **Create backup copy with each save** is checked on the **Open and Save** tab of the **Options** dialog box as shown in Figure 2-5. To access the **Options** dialog box, type **OP <Enter>**.

Figure 2-5
Options dialog box, **Open and Save** and **Online** tabs

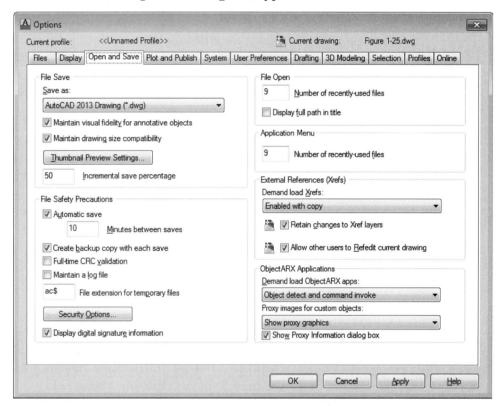

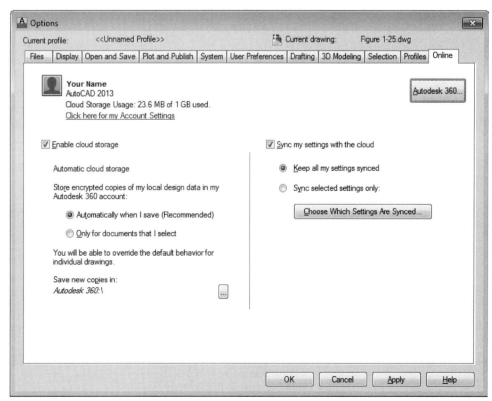

2 If a drive other than the default is specified, only a .dwg file is created.

3 To change the name of the drawing, you may save it under a new name by typing a new name in the **File name:** input box. The drawing is still saved under the original name as well as the new name. You can save the drawing under as many names as you need.

4 If the drawing was previously saved, or if a drawing file already exists with the drawing file name you typed, AutoCAD gives you the message *drawing name.dwg already exists. Do you want to replace it?* When you are updating a drawing file, the old .dwg file is replaced with the new drawing, so the answer to click is **Yes**. If an error has been made and you do not want to replace the file, click **No**.

5 A drawing may be saved to as many disks or to as many folders on the hard disk as you wish. You should save your drawing in two different places as insurance against catastrophe.

6 Drawings can be saved to an **Autodesk 360 Cloud Account**. This is where you can store, share, and view your drawings online from any computer, mobile phone, or tablet. **AutoCAD WS** is a cloud-based CAD editor from Autodesk that allows you to view, edit, and share your drawings.

On the **Online** tab of the **Options** dialog box, Figure 2-5, when the **Enable cloud storage** box is checked and the **Automatically when I save (Recommended)** radio button is selected, your drawings are automatically saved by default to the cloud. You can change this setting for each drawing individually, using the **Save Drawing As** dialog box, Figure 2-4, when you click the **Keep a copy of this document in my cloud account** box to delete the check mark. The **Set Online Options...** button on the **Save Drawing As** dialog box takes you to the **Online** tab of the **Options** dialog box.

7 Any drawing may be saved as other file types (Figure 2-4):

DWT

This is a drawing template file. Settings are already established in a template file. Just as you opened the **acad.dwt** template file to start a drawing, you can make settings for a drawing that are unique to your work situation and save those settings as a template file. This saves time, because settings such as units, limits, grid, snap, and layers (which you will learn in this chapter) will already be set.

DWS

This is a drawing standards file. It defines standards for layers, dimension styles, linetypes, and text styles. You can associate the standards file with another drawing, audit the drawing to see if the standards differ, and automatically change any differing standards to match the DWS file.

> **NOTE**
> AutoCAD automatically names your drawings, using the names **Drawing1, Drawing2,** and so on, if you do not type a name in the **File name:** input box. The name you save the drawing as appears in the AutoCAD title bar.

DXF

This is a drawing interchange format file. It is used to share drawing data among other CAD programs. You can open a DXF file, save it as a DWG file, and work with the drawing.

Step 2. Name and save Tutorial 2-1 on the drive and/or folder you want (Figure 2-6), as described next:

SAVE	
Application Menu:	💾 Save
Quick Access Toolbar	Save
Menu Bar:	File/Save
Type a Command:	SAVE

Prompt	Response
Type a command:	**Save**
The **Save Drawing As** dialog box appears with the file name highlighted:	Type **CH2-TUTORIAL1**
The **Save Drawing As** dialog box appears, as shown in Figure 2-6:	Select the drive and/or folder in which you want to save **CH2-TUTORIAL1** Click **Save**

Figure 2-6
Save Drawing As dialog box; save **CH2-TUTORIAL1**

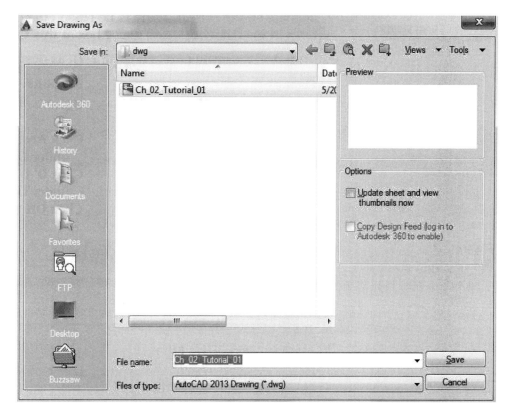

Drawing Name and File Name Extension

The drawing name can be up to 255 characters long and can have spaces. The drawing name cannot have special characters that the AutoCAD or Microsoft® Windows programs use for other purposes. The special characters that cannot be used include the less-than and greater-than symbols (<>), forward slashes and backslashes (/ \), backquotes (`), equal signs (=), vertical bars (|), asterisks (*), commas (,), question marks (?), semicolons (;),

UNITS	
Application Menu:	Drawing Utilities/ Units
Menu Bar:	Format/ Units...
Type a Command:	UNITS
Command Alias:	UN

units: A setting referring to drawing units. For example, an inch is a drawing unit. Architectural units utilize feet and fractional units. Decimal, fractional, engineering, and scientific units are also available in the **Drawing Units** dialog box.

colons (:), and quotation marks ("). As you continue to learn AutoCAD, other objects will be also named, such as layers. These naming conventions apply to all named objects.

AutoCAD automatically adds the file extension .dwg to the drawing name and .bak to a backup file. The icon to the left of the file name in the **Save Drawing As** dialog box describes the file type.

> **TIP**
>
> If you lose a drawing file, the drawing's .bak file can be renamed as a .dwg file and used as the drawing file. Using Windows Explorer, right-click on the file name and select **Rename** from the menu. Simply keep the name, but change the file extension. If the .dwg file is corrupted, you may give the .bak file a new name and change the extension to .dwg. Don't forget to add the .dwg extension in either case, because *the file will not open without a .dwg extension.*

Units

Units refers to drawing units. For example, an inch is a drawing unit. In this book, architectural units, which utilize feet and fractional inches, are used. The **Precision:** input box in the **Drawing Units** dialog box allows you to set the smallest fraction to display when showing coordinates and defaults on the screen. There is no reason to change any of the other settings in the **Drawing Units** dialog box at this time.

Step 3. Set drawing units (Figure 2-7), as described next:

Prompt	Response
Type a command:	**Units...** (or type **UN <Enter>**)
The **Drawing Units** dialog box appears (Figure 2-7):	Click **Architectural** (for **Type:** under **Length**)
	Click **0'-0 1/16"** (for **Precision:** under **Length**)
	Click **OK**

Figure 2-7
Drawing Units dialog box

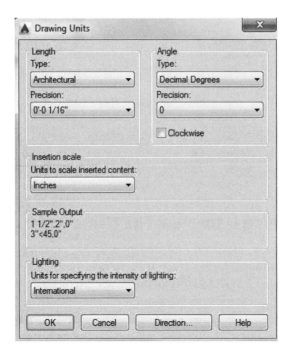

Controlling Your Drawing

When you begin drawing with AutoCAD, you may perhaps click a tab or drawing tool that you do not need. If you select the **Layout1** or **Layout2** tab at the bottom of your drawing window and are not sure where you are in the drawing, simply select the **Model** tab to return to your drawing. The **Layout** tabs are used for printing or plotting and will be described later.

NOTE

To cancel a command, press **<Esc>** (from the keyboard).

Step 4. Make sure **SNAP** and **GRID** are on in the status bar and that **INFER, ORTHO, POLAR, OSNAP, 3DOSNAP, OTRACK, DUCS, DYN, LWT, TPY, QP, SC,** and **AM** are off.

Drawing Scale

drawing scale: The scale at which drawings are made.

A **drawing scale** factor does not need to be set. When using AutoCAD to make drawings, always draw full scale, using real-world feet and inches. Full-scale drawings can be printed or plotted at any scale.

Drawing Limits and the Cartesian Coordinate System

Step 5. Set drawing limits, as described next:

LIMITS	
Menu Bar:	Format/Drawing Limits
Type a Command:	LIMITS
Command Alias:	None

Prompt	Response
Type a command:	Type **LIMITS <Enter>**
Specify lower left corner or [ON OFF] <0'-0", 0'-0">:	**<Enter>**
Specify upper right corner <1"-0', 0'-9">:	Type **8-1/2,11 <Enter>**

drawing limits: The user-defined rectangular area of the drawing covered by lines or dots (when specified) when the grid is on.

Cartesian coordinate system: A coordinate system that has three axes, *X*, *Y*, and *Z*. The *X*-axis value is stated first and measures left to right horizontally. The *Y*-axis value is stated second and measures from bottom to top vertically. The *Z*-axis value is stated third and is used in three-dimensional modeling.

TIP

Pressing the space bar is just like pressing the **<Enter>** key.

Think of **drawing limits** as your drawing area, sheet size, or sheet boundaries. This sheet of paper is also called the *workplane.* The workplane is based on a **Cartesian coordinate system**. A Cartesian coordinate system has three axes, *X*, *Y*, and *Z*. Here, 8-1/2,11 was set as the drawing limits.

In the Cartesian coordinate system, that value is entered as 8-1/2,11 using a comma with no spaces to separate the *X*- and *Y*-axis coordinates. The *X*-axis coordinate of a Cartesian coordinate system is stated first (8-1/2) and measures drawing limits from left to right (horizontally). The *Y*-axis coordinate is second (11) and measures drawing limits from bottom to top (vertically). You will be drawing on a vertical 8-1/2″ × 11″ workplane similar to a standard sheet of typing paper. The *Z*-axis is used in 3D.

The lower left corner, the origin point of the drawing boundaries, is 0,0 and is where the *X*- and *Y*-axes intersect. The upper right corner is 8-1/2,11 (Figure 2-8). These are the limits for Tutorial 2-1. To turn the 8-1/2″ × 11″ area horizontally, enter the limits as 11,8-1/2. With units set to Architectural, AutoCAD defaults to inches, so the inch symbol is not required.

Figure 2-8
Drawing limits

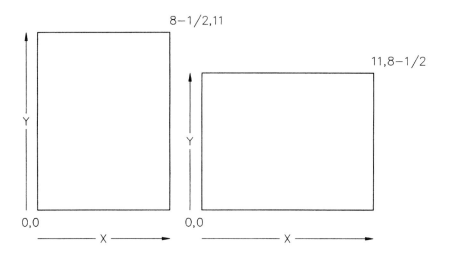

NOTE

The acad.dwt template provides 1′-0″,0′-9″ as the drawing limits for the upper right corner of the drawing. Remember, to change the upper right limits, you must type the *X*-axis coordinate first, a comma, and then the *Y*-axis coordinate second.

The coordinate display numbers in the extreme lower left corner of the AutoCAD screen tell you where the crosshairs on the screen are located in relation to the 0,0 origin. The display updates as you move the cursor.

If you need to change the drawing limits, you may do so at any time by entering new limits to the *Specify upper right corner:* prompt. Changing the drawing limits will automatically show the grid pattern for the new limits.

Grid

grid: An area consisting of evenly spaced dots or lines to aid drawing. The grid is adjustable. The grid lines or dots do not plot.

The **grid** is a visible pattern of lines or dots on the display screen. The grid is not part of the drawing, but it helps in visualizing the size and relationship of the drawing elements. It can also confirm where your limits are. It is never plotted. Pressing function key **<F7>** or **<Ctrl>+G** turns the grid on or off, as does clicking the **GRID** button at the bottom of the screen.

GRIDDISPLAY

GRIDDISPLAY is a system variable that controls the grid behavior using the following settings:

0 When **GRIDDISPLAY** is set to **0**, the grid is restricted to the limits that are set. Currently, the limits are set to **8-1/2,11** as shown in Figure 2-9.

1 When **GRIDDISPLAY** is set to **1,** the grid is not restricted to the limits set, as shown in Figure 2-10.

2 This setting turns on the adaptive grid display. That means when you are zoomed out, the density of the grid is limited. To see the difference between a 1″ line zoomed out with **GRIDDISPLAY** set to **0** and **GRIDDISPLAY** set to **2** with **GRID** set to ¼″, see Figure 2-11.

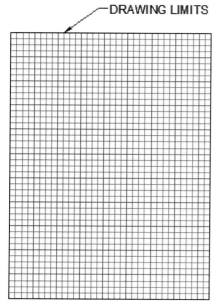

Figure 2-9
GRIDDISPLAY set to **0**

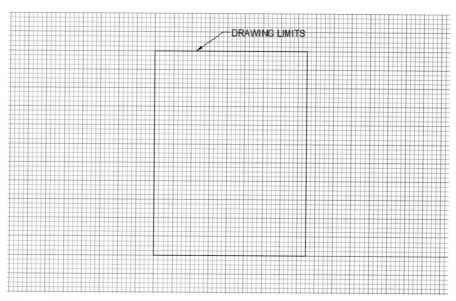

Figure 2-10
GRIDDISPLAY set to **1**

Figure 2-11
Difference between
GRIDDISPLAY set to **0** and **2**
when zoomed out, with
GRID set to ¼″

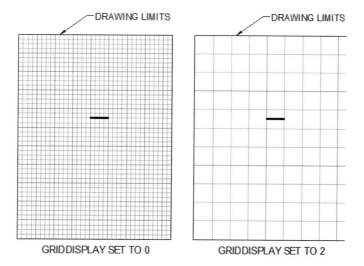

GRIDDISPLAY SET TO 0   GRIDDISPLAY SET TO 2

Step 6. Set **GRIDDISPLAY** to zero so the grid will be restricted to the area specified by the limits, as described next:

Prompt	Response
Type a command:	Type **GRIDDISPLAY <Enter>**
Enter new value for GRIDDISPLAY <3>:	Type **0 <Enter>**

Step 7. Set the grid spacing, as described next:

Prompt	Response
Type a command:	Type **GRID <Enter>**
Specify grid spacing(X) or [ON OFF Snap Major aDaptive Limits Follow Aspect] <0'-0 1/2">:	Type **1/4 <Enter>**
Type a command:	**<Enter>** (to repeat the **GRID** command)
Specify grid spacing(X) or [ON OFF Snap Major aDaptive Limits Follow Aspect] <0'-0 1/4">:	Type **M <Enter>**
Enter the number of grid divisions per major grid line <5>:	Type **4 <Enter>**

GRID	
Menu Bar:	Tools/ Drafting Settings...
Function Key	<F7>
Status Bar:	GRID/Right Click/Drafting Settings...
Type a Command:	GRID

> **NOTE**
> You can click the options in the command prompt line. Instead of typing **M** for the option **Major**, use your mouse to *click the option in the command prompt line.*

You have just set a grid spacing of 1/4", where each line is spaced 1/4" vertically and horizontally, with a major grid line every four spaces. By the way, if you see dots for the grid points instead of grid lines, you need to change your **Visual Styles** setting from **Wireframe 2D** to **Hidden** using **Visual Style** from the **View** pull-down menu.

Snap

Step 8. Set the snap spacing, as described next:

Prompt	Response
Type a command:	Type **SN <Enter>**
Specify snap spacing or [ON OFF Aspect Legacy Style Type] <0'-0 1/2">:	Type **1/8 <Enter>**

SNAP	
Menu Bar:	Tools/ Drafting Settings...
Function Key	<F9>
Status Bar:	SNAP/Right Click/Drafting Settings...
Type a Command:	SNAP
Command Alias:	SN

You have set 1/8" as the snap spacing. Snap is an invisible grid on the display screen. When a command is active and you are specifying points, the crosshairs will snap, or lock, to an invisible snap grid when snap is on. When snap is on and points are not being specified, the crosshairs do not snap to a grid. With a setting of 1/8", each snap point is spaced 1/8" horizontally and vertically.

Pressing function key **<F9>** or **<Ctrl>+B** turns the snap on or off. The snap can also be turned on or off by selecting either option in response to the prompt *Specify snap spacing or [ON OFF Aspect Style Type]* or by clicking the **SNAP** button at the bottom of the screen. Snap may be turned on and off while you are drawing.

It is helpful to set the snap spacing the same as the grid spacing or as a fraction of the grid spacing so the crosshairs snap to every grid point or to every grid point and in between. The snap can be set to snap several times in between the grid points.

Zoom

Step 9. View the entire drawing area, as described next.

Prompt	Response
Type a command:	**Zoom-All** (or type **Z <Enter>**)
Specify corner of window, enter a scale factor (nX or nXP), or [All Center Dynamic Extents Previous Scale Window Object] <real time>:	Type **A <Enter>**

The **Zoom-All** command displays the entire drawing limits or extents, whichever is larger. You already know what limits are by setting the limits of the drawing. Extents is anything you have drawn and may be within or outside your limits. In this instance, **Zoom-All** will provide a view of the drawing limits. With **GRIDDISPLAY** set to **0** the grid display shows the limits.

Drafting Settings Dialog Box

You can also set snap and grid by using the **Drafting Settings** dialog box (Figure 2-12).

zoom: The process of moving around the drawing. Zooming in shows you a close-up view of a drawing area. Zooming out shows you a larger viewing area.

ZOOM ALL	
Ribbon/Panel	View/ Navigate All
Zoom Toolbar:	
Navigation Bar:	Zoom/All
Menu Bar:	View/ Zoom/All
Type a Command:	ZOOM <Enter> ALL<Enter>
Command Alias:	ZA

Figure 2-12
Drafting Settings dialog box

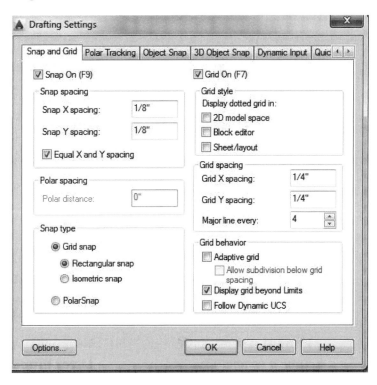

To access the **Drafting Settings** dialog box, right-click on **SNAP** or **GRID** in the status bar and click **Settings...** (or type DS for Drafting Settings and <Enter>). The dialog box is a handy tool to use in setting the snap and grid spacing, but if you are a fair typist, typing these commands from the keyboard is faster.

Layers

layer: A group of drawing objects that are like transparent overlays on a drawing. Layers can be viewed individually or in combination with other layers. Layers can be turned on or off, frozen or thawed, plotted or not plotted, and filtered.

Different parts of a project can be placed on separate *layers* (Figure 2-13). The walls may be on one layer, the fixtures on another, the electrical on a third layer, the furniture on a fourth layer, and so on. There is no limit to the number of layers you may use in a drawing. Each is perfectly aligned with all the others. Each layer may be viewed on the display screen separately, one layer may be viewed in combination with one or more of the other layers, or all layers may be viewed together. Each layer may also be plotted separately or in combination with other layers, or all layers may be plotted at the same time. The layer name can be from 1 to 255 characters in length.

Figure 2-13
Four separate layers

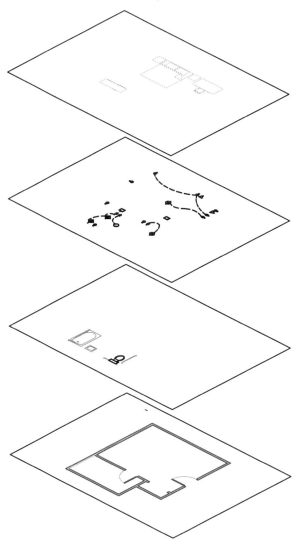

Step 10. Create layers using the **Layer Properties Manager** palette (Figures 2-14 and 2-15), as described next:

Prompt	Response
Type a command:	**Layer Properties** (or type **LA <Enter>**)
The **Layer Properties Manager** palette appears:	Click the **New Layer** icon three times (see Figure 2-14)
Layer1, Layer2, Layer3 appear in the **Layer Name** list (Figure 2-15):	Click the box under **Color**, beside **Layer1**

LAYER	
Ribbon/ Panel	Home/ Layers
Layers Toolbar:	
Menu Bar:	Format/ Layer...
Type a Command:	LAYER
Command Alias:	LA

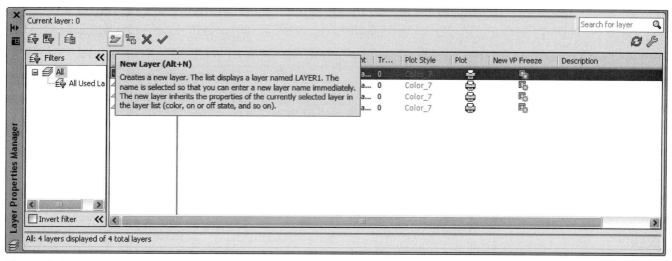

Figure 2-14
Layer Properties Manager palette

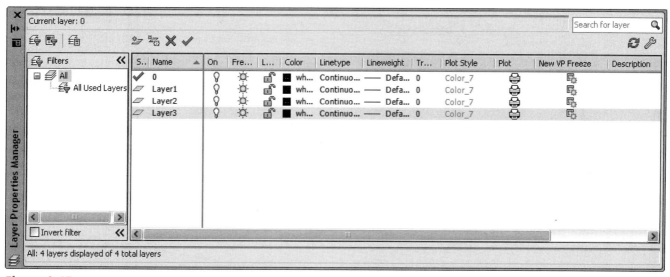

Figure 2-15
Layer1, Layer2, and **Layer3** appear in the **Layer Name** list

NOTE

The standard colors are 1 (red), 2 (yellow), 3 (green), 4 (cyan), 5 (blue), 6 (magenta), and 7 (white or black).

Layer Lists

Layer lists are now displayed using natural ordered sort. For example, the layer names 1, 4, 25, 16, 21, 2, 20, 10 are sorted as 1, 2, 4, 10, 16, 20, 21, 25 instead of 1, 10, 16, 2, 20, 21, 25, 4. Natural ordered sort applies to all layer lists including the Hatch Editor Ribbon tab and Quick Select just to name a few. You can restore the ASCII sort used in previous releases by changing the new **SORTORDER** system variable to **0**.

Step 11. Assign colors to layers (Figure 2-16), as described next:

Prompt	Response
The **Select Color** dialog box appears:	Click the color **white** (Color Index: 7) (Figure 2-16); click **OK**
The **Layer Properties Manager** palette appears:	Click the box under **Color**, beside **Layer2**
The **Select Color** dialog box appears:	Click the color **blue** (Index color: 5) Click **OK**
The **Layer Properties Manager** palette appears:	Click the box under **Color**, beside **Layer3**
The **Select Color** dialog box appears:	Click the color **red** (Index color: 1) Click **OK**

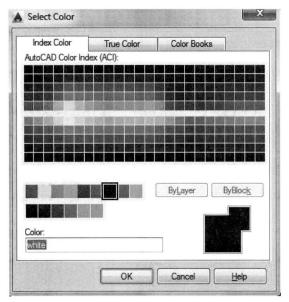

Figure 2-16
Select Color dialog box

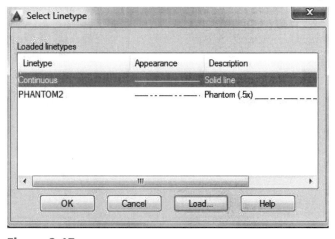

Figure 2-17
Select Linetype dialog box

Step 12. Assign linetypes to layers (Figures 2-17, 2-18, and 2-19), as described next:

Prompt	Response
The **Layer Properties Manager** palette appears:	Click the word **Continuous** under **Linetype**, beside **Layer2**
The **Select Linetype** dialog box appears (Figure 2-17):	Click **Load...** (to load linetypes so they can be selected)
The **Load or Reload Linetypes** dialog box appears:	Move the mouse to the center of the dialog box and click the right mouse button

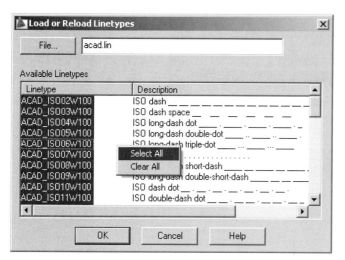

Figure 2-18
Load or Reload Linetypes dialog box

Figure 2-19
Click **Skip reloading the linetype, PHANTOM2**

Prompt	**Response**
	Click **Select All** (Figure 2-18)
	Click **OK**
The **Linetypes-Reload Linetypes** dialog box appears:	Click **Skip reloading the linetype, PHANTOM2** (Figure 2-19)

Linetypes

linetype: How a line, arc, polyline, circle, or other item is displayed. For example, a continuous line has a different linetype than a hidden line.

Linetypes must be loaded before they can be selected. You can load individual linetypes or you can load several by holding down the **<Shift>** key as you select. The AutoCAD library of standard linetypes provides you with three different sizes of each standard linetype other than continuous. For example, the DASHED line has the standard size called **DASHED**, a linetype half the standard size called **DASHED2(.5x)**, and a linetype twice the standard size called **DASHEDX2(2x)**.

Prompt	**Response**
The **Select Linetype** dialog box appears (Figure 2-20):	Click **DASHED**
	Click **OK**
	Click the close button **(X)** in the upper left corner of the **Layer Properties Manager** palette

Lineweights

lineweight: A width value that can be assigned to objects such as lines, arcs, polylines, circles, and many other objects that contain features that have width.

Lineweights are expressed in millimeters or inches. The default lineweight initially set for all layers is .25 mm, or .010 inch. Lineweights need to be varied, for example, to show thick lines for walls and thin lines for dimensions, to emphasize something on the drawing, to show existing and new construction, or to show existing and new furniture. Lineweight is an

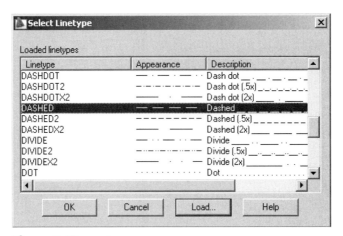

Figure 2-20
Select the **DASHED** linetype

important component for drawing legibility. Lineweights are displayed in pixels on the screen; they plot with the exact width of the assigned lineweight.

Lineweight Settings Dialog Box

To access the **Lineweight Settings** dialog box (Figure 2-21), right-click **LWT** in the status bar and click **Settings....** In this dialog box, you can change the **Units for Listing** from millimeters to inches or reset the default lineweight. You can also adjust the **Model** tab display scale of lineweights by moving the slider to change the scale.

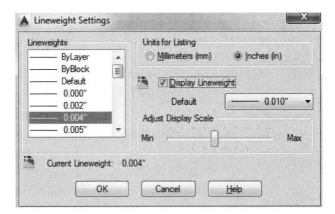

Figure 2-21
Change **Lineweight** settings to inches

Step 13. Set the **Units for Listing** in the **Lineweight Settings** dialog box to **Inches**. The lineweights will read in inches in the **Layer Properties Manager** palette instead of millimeters. If you prefer millimeters, set it to millimeters. Pick **OK** to exit the dialog box.

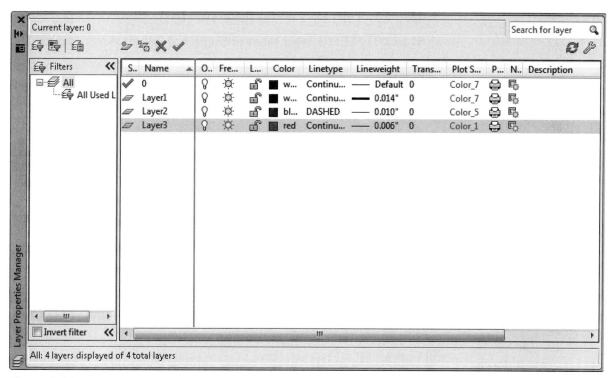

Figure 2-22
Assign lineweights to layers

Step 14. Assign lineweights to layers (Figure 2-22), as described next:

Prompt	Response
Type a command:	**Layer Properties** (or type **LA <Enter>**)
The **Layer Properties Manager** palette appears:	Click the word **Default** under **Lineweight,** beside **Layer1**
The **Lineweight** dialog box appears:	Click **0.014″** (.35mm) Click **OK**
The **Layer Properties Manager** palette appears:	Click the word **Default** under **Lineweight,** beside **Layer2**
The **Lineweight** dialog box appears:	Click **0.010″** (.25mm) Click **OK**
The **Layer Properties Manager** palette appears:	Click the word **Default** under **Lineweight,** beside **Layer3**
The **Lineweight** dialog box appears:	Click **0.006″** (.15mm) Click **OK**

LWT

The display of the lineweights in your drawing is controlled by clicking **LWT** on the status bar. Lineweights are not displayed unless **LWT** is on.

Step 15. Turn **LWT** on (in the status bar).

Step 16. Make a layer current (Figure 2-23), as described next:

Prompt	Response
The **Layer Properties Manager** palette appears with layer names, colors, and linetypes assigned:	Click **Layer1** (to select it) (Figure 2-23). Be sure to click on a layer name, not on one of the other properties such as lock or color.
	Click **Set Current** (the green check icon)
	Click the close button **(X)** in the upper left corner of the palette

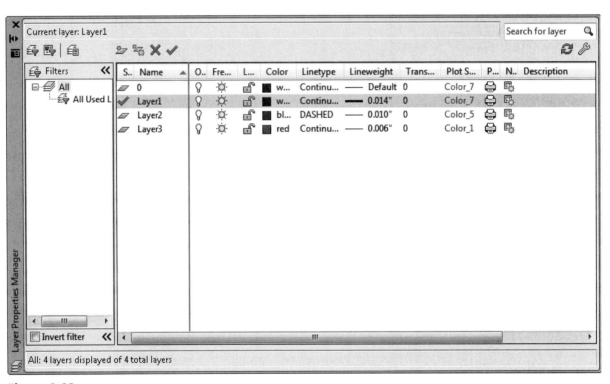

Figure 2-23
Layers with colors, linetypes, lineweights assigned, and Layer1 current

You can also double-click the layer name to set it current. Anything drawn from this point until another layer is set current will be on Layer1.

To change a layer name after using **New Layer** to create layers, click the layer name to highlight it, then slowly left-click the name again in the **Name:** input area, and type over the existing name. You can also click the layer name and then use **Rename** from the right-click menu to rename a layer. You can initially name the layers by clicking **New** and then typing the layer names separated by a comma. When you type the comma, you move to the next layer.

Additional layer control option icons on the **Layer Properties Manager** palette and **Layers** panel of the **Home** tab of the ribbon (Figure 2-24) that can be changed, reading from left to right, are as follows:

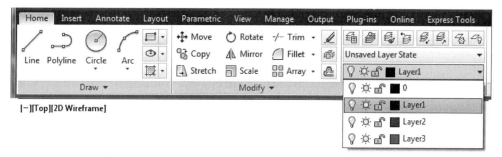

Figure 2-24
Layer status on the **Layers** panel of the **Home** tab of the ribbon

> **NOTE**
>
> When a layer is off or frozen and it aligns with other layers, it is important not to move objects that align with a frozen or off layer. Objects on the off or frozen layer do not move and will not be aligned with the moved items when you turn the off layer on or thaw the frozen layer. However, when all objects are selected (when you type **ALL <Enter>** to select objects), objects on a layer that is off and thawed will move.

Turn a Layer On or Off for Entire Drawing: This option pertains to the visibility of layers. When a layer is turned off, it is still part of the drawing, but any entity drawn on that layer is not visible on the screen and cannot be plotted. For instance, the building exterior walls layer, interior walls layer, and electrical layer are turned on and all other layers turned off to view, edit, or plot an electrical plan. One or more layers can be turned off and on as required.

Freeze or Thaw a Layer for Entire Drawing: This option also pertains to the visibility of layers. The difference between on/off and freeze/thaw is a matter of how quickly the drawing regenerates on the display screen. If a layer is frozen, it is not visible and cannot be plotted, and AutoCAD spends no time regenerating it. A layer that is turned off is not visible and cannot be plotted, but AutoCAD does regenerate it.

Lock or Unlock a Layer Globally for Entire Drawing: When a layer is locked, it is visible, and you can draw on it. You cannot use any of the **Edit** commands to edit any of the drawing entities on the layer. You cannot accidentally change any entity that is already drawn.

To change the state of any layer, pick the icon to select the alternative state. For example, Figure 2-24 shows that **Layer1** was turned off by picking the lightbulb to turn it off. Additional layer properties that are shown in the **Layer Properties Manager** palette are as follows:

transparency: A setting that makes an object more or less transparent.

Transparency: This option pertains to changing the *transparency* versus the opaqueness of objects on a layer. You can enter a transparency value between 0 and 90, inclusive.

Plot Style: Plot styles are created using a plot style table to define various properties such as color, grayscale, and lineweight. A layer's plot style overrides the layer's color, linetype, and lineweight. Plot styles are used when you want to plot the same drawing with different settings or different drawings with the same settings.

FOR MORE DETAILS

See Chapter 5 for more on plot styles.

Plot: Allows you to make visible layers nonplottable. For example, you may not want to plot a layer that shows construction lines. When a layer is nonplottable, it is displayed but not plotted.

New VP Freeze: Allows you to freeze layers in a newly created viewport.

Description: Allows you to type a general description of the layer in the area.

If you create some layers that you do not need, delete them by highlighting them and picking the **Delete** icon.

Annotation Scale

annotation scale: A setting that controls the size of text and other annotative objects on the drawing.

Annotation scale is a setting that controls how text and other annotative objects appear on a drawing. This setting affects annotative objects, such as text and dimensions, that are added to drawings that will be scaled when plotted (e.g., scale: $1/4'' = 1'-0''$). Each object, such as text or dimensions, *has an annotative property that it must be set to for this setting to apply.*

Step 17. Make sure your annotation scale located in the lower right corner of the AutoCAD screen is set to the default **1:1** (Figure 2-25).

Figure 2-25
Annotation scale is set to 1:1

Saving the Drawing

Step 18. Save the drawing, as described next:

Prompt	Response
Type a command:	**Save**
The drawing is saved in the drive and folder selected at the beginning of this exercise.	

> **NOTE**
> Make sure you save your drawing often, so you do not lose any of your work.

Using the Mouse and Right-Click Customization

The **Right-Click Customization** dialog box settings control what happens when you click the right mouse button (shown as **<Enter>** in this book). To access the **Right-Click Customization** dialog box, type **OP <Enter>**. Select the **User Preferences** tab of the **Options** dialog box (Figure 2-26). Click the **Right-click Customization...** button in the **Windows Standard Behavior** area, and the **Right-Click Customization** dialog box (Figure 2-27) appears.

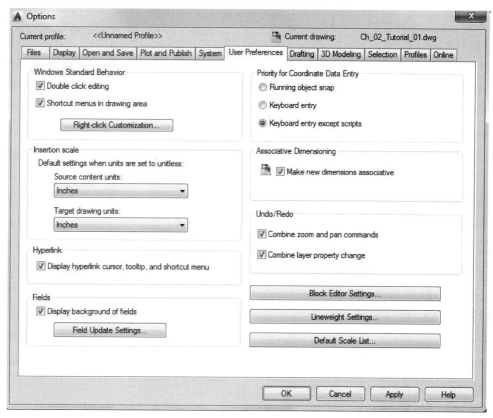

Figure 2-26
Options dialog box with **User Preferences** tab clicked

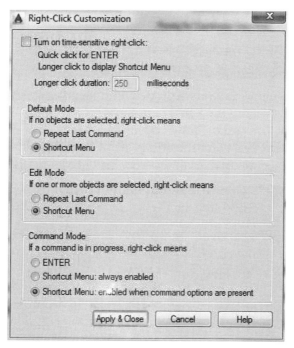

Figure 2-27
Right-Click Customization dialog box

In the **Response** columns of the exercises, **<Enter>** indicates that the right mouse button should be clicked. Notes in parentheses are used to clarify how **<Enter>** is used; for example, **<Enter>** (to return to the **Line** command prompt). Leave the **Right-Click Customization** dialog box set to the default as shown in Figure 2-27. As you become more familiar with AutoCAD, you may decide to change this setting.

TUTORIAL 2-1
Part 2, Drawing Lines, Circles, Arcs, Ellipses, and Donuts

Ortho

Ortho: A setting that limits pointing device input to horizontal or vertical (relative to the current snap angle and the user coordinate system).

Press the **<F8>** function key to turn *Ortho* mode on and off, or click **ORTHO** at the bottom of your screen. **Ortho** mode, when on, helps you draw lines perfectly, horizontally and vertically. It does not allow you to draw at an angle, so turn **Ortho** off and on as needed.

Step 19. Make sure that **SNAP, GRID, ORTHO,** and **LWT** are on and the remaining buttons in the status bar are off. Make sure **Layer1** is current.

Step 20. Complete a **Zoom-All** command to make sure you are looking at the entire 8-1/2 × 11 limits of your drawing.

ORTHO MODE	
Function Key	<F8>
Status Bar:	ORTHO or ⌊⌋
Type a Command:	ORTHO
Keyboard Alias:	<Ctrl>+L

> **TIP**
>
> When **Ortho** mode is on, drawing or editing a drawing part is restricted to horizontal and vertical movements only. Hold down the **<Shift>** key as a temporary override key to turn **ORTHO** off and on. See Appendix B for additional temporary override keys.

Drawing Lines Using the Grid Marks and Snap Increments

Use Figure 2-28 as a guide when locating the line, squares, and rectangles drawn using the **LINE** command.

Lines can be drawn by snapping to the grid visible on the screen. The snap is set at 1/8″, and the grid is set at 1/4″. The grid provides a visual cue for the snap points that snap on every grid mark and in between every grid mark.

Step 21. Draw a horizontal line 1″ long, using the snap increments and grid marks (Figure 2-28), as described next:

LINE	
Ribbon/ Panel	Home/ Draw
Draw Toolbar:	
Menu Bar:	Draw/Line
Type a Command:	LINE
Command Alias:	L

Prompt	Response
Type a command:	**Line** (or type **L <Enter>**)
Specify first point:	**P1→** (Do not type "P1." Look at Figure 2-28 and click the point P1→, approximately two grid spaces down (1/2″) and four grid spaces to the right (1″) of the upper left corner of the page.)

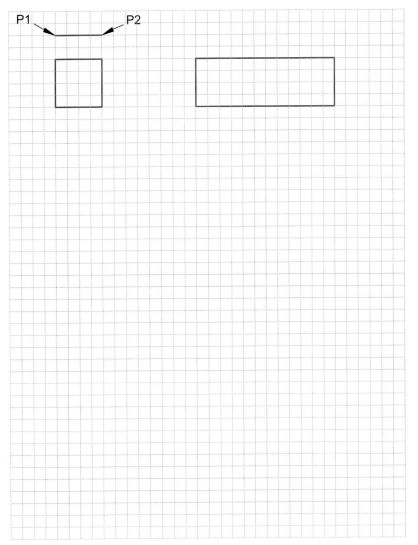

Figure 2-28
Draw a line, a square, and a rectangle

Prompt	Response
Specify next point or [Undo]:	**P2→** (move your mouse four grid marks to the right and click the point P2→)
Specify next point or [Undo]:	**<Enter>** When the right mouse button is used for **<Enter>**, a shortcut menu appears, and **<Enter>** must be clicked on the shortcut menu to complete the command. When the keyboard **<Enter>** key or the space bar is used, the command is completed, and the shortcut menu does not appear.

ERASE	
Ribbon/ Panel	Home/ Modify 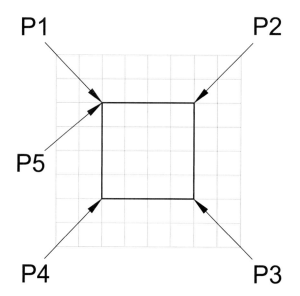
Modify Toolbar:	
Menu Bar:	Modify/Erase
Type a Command:	ERASE
Command Alias:	E

Erase and Undo

Step 22. Erase the line and bring it back again, as described next:

Prompt	Response
Type a command:	**Erase** (or type **E <Enter>**)
Select objects:	Position the small box that replaces the crosshairs anyplace on the line and click the line
Select objects: 1 found	
Select objects:	**<Enter>** (the line disappears)
Type a command:	Type **U <Enter>** (the line reappears)

> **NOTE**
>
> Use the **Undo** arrow in the **Quick Access** toolbar to reverse the most recent action. Click the arrow to the right of the **Undo** arrow to see a list of actions you can undo. The **Redo** arrow reverses the effect of the **Undo** arrow and also has a list of actions you can redo.

Do not be afraid to draw with AutoCAD. If you make a mistake, you can easily erase it using the **ERASE** command. The **UNDO** command will restore everything erased by the **ERASE** command. When you are using the **ERASE** command, a small box replaces the screen crosshairs. The small box is called the *pickbox*.

Step 23. Draw a 1″ square using the snap increments and grid marks and undo the last two lines (Figure 2-29), as described next:

Prompt	Response
Type a command:	**Line**
Specify first point:	**P1→** (click a point 1/2″ directly below the left end of the line just drawn)
Specify next point or [Undo]:	**P2→** (Figure 2-29)
Specify next point or [Undo]:	**P3→**
Specify next point or [Close Undo]:	**P4→**
Specify next point or [Close Undo]:	**P5→**

Figure 2-29

Draw a 1″ square using grid marks

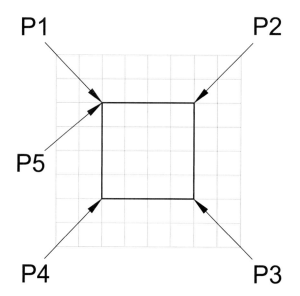

Prompt	Response
Specify next point or [Close Undo]:	Type **U <Enter>** (move your mouse to see that the line is undone)
Specify next point or [Close Undo]:	Type **U <Enter>**
Specify next point or [Close Undo]:	**<Enter>** (to stop and return to the command prompt)

While in the **LINE** command, if you decide you do not like the last line segment drawn, use the **UNDO** command to erase it and continue on with the *Specify next point or [Close Undo]:* prompt. Clicking more than one undo will backtrack through the line segments in the reverse order in which they were drawn.

Step 24. Complete the square (Figure 2-29), as described next:

Prompt	Response
Type a command:	**<Enter>** (to return the **Line** command prompt)
Specify first point:	**<Enter>** (to see the line attached, turn the grid off and back on).
Specify next point or [Undo]:	**P4→**
Specify next point or [Undo]:	**P5→**
Specify next point or [Close Undo]:	**<Enter>** (to stop)

The **LINE** command has a very handy feature: If you respond to the *Specify first point:* prompt by pressing the **<Enter>** key or the space bar, the line will start at the end of the most recently drawn line.

> **TIP**
> Pressing the **<Esc>** key cancels the command selection process and returns AutoCAD to the command prompt. Use **<Esc>** if you get stuck in a command.

Drawing Lines Using Absolute Coordinates

absolute coordinates: Coordinate values measured from an origin point or 0,0 point in the drawing.

Remember, 0,0 is the lower left corner of the page, the origin point of the Cartesian coordinate system. When you use ***absolute coordinates*** to draw, the X-axis coordinate is entered first and identifies a location on the horizontal axis. The Y-axis coordinate is entered second and identifies a location on the vertical axis. The page size is 8-1/2,11. A little adding and subtracting to determine the absolute coordinates will locate the rectangle on the page as follows.

Step 25. Draw a rectangle using absolute coordinates (Figure 2-30), as described next. Remember: **GRID, SNAP, ORTHO,** and **LWT** should be on.

Prompt	Response
Type a command:	**Line** (move the crosshairs to the center of the screen)
Specify first point:	Type **4,10 <Enter>** (the line begins)
Specify next point or [Undo]:	Type **7,10 <Enter>**
Specify next point or [Undo]:	Type **7,9 <Enter>**
Specify next point or [Close Undo]:	Type **4,9 <Enter>**
Specify next point or [Close Undo]:	Type **C <Enter>**

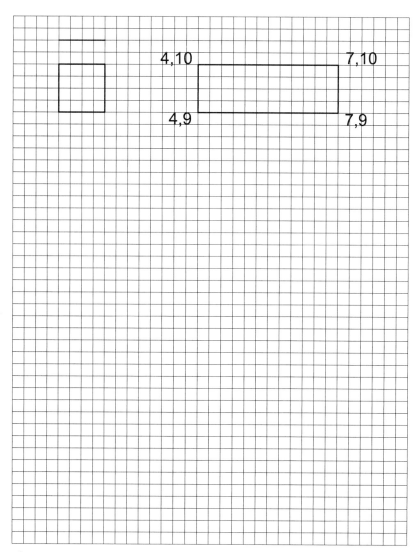

Figure 2-30
Draw a rectangle using absolute coordinates

Step 26. Click on the coordinate display to turn the screen coordinate display on (if needed) and move your pointer to each corner of the square. Watch how the screen coordinate display shows the X,Y coordinate position of each corner. Compare those coordinates with the coordinates you just typed and entered. They are the same.

NOTE

If you turn **DYN** on by clicking it on the status bar, you will see the dynamic input display attached to the cursor. The appearance of dynamic input display is controlled by the settings made in the **Drafting Settings** dialog box. Right-click on **DYN** in the status bar to access these settings.

Drawing Lines Using Relative Coordinates

relative coordinates: Coordinates specified in relation to a previous point picked. Relative coordinates are entered by typing @ followed by the X and Y coordinates. For example, after a point is entered to start a line, typing and entering @1,0 will draw the line 1″ in the X direction and 0″ in the Y direction.

Relative coordinates are used after a point is entered. (Relative to what? Relative to the point just entered.) After a point has been clicked on the drawing, relative coordinates are entered by typing @, followed by the X,Y coordinates. For example, after a point is entered to start a line, typing and entering @1,0 will draw the line 1″ in the X direction, 0″ in the Y direction.

Step 27. Set **Layer3** current. Layer3 has a .006″ (.15mm) lineweight.

Step 28. Draw a rectangle using relative coordinates (Figure 2-31), as described next:

Prompt	Response
Type a command:	**Line**
Specify first point:	Click a point on the grid **1/2″** below the lower left corner of the first square drawn
Specify next point or [Undo]:	Type **@2,0 <Enter>**
Specify next point or [Undo]:	Type **@0,–1 <Enter>**
Specify next point or [Close Undo]:	Type **@–2,0 <Enter>**
Specify next point or [Close Undo]:	Type **C <Enter>**

Figure 2-31

Draw a rectangle using relative coordinates, a square using polar coordinates, and a rectangle using direct distance entry

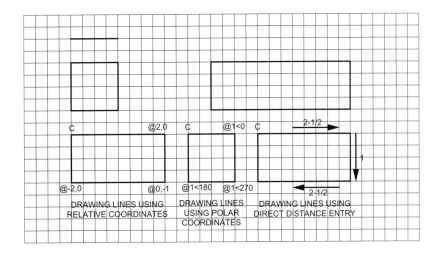

A minus sign (−) is used for negative line location with relative coordinates. Negative is to the left for the *X*-axis and down for the *Y*-axis.

TIP

Remember, you can change the colors of the elements in the drawing window. Type **OP <Enter>** to display the **Options** dialog box. Click the **Display** tab and the **Colors...** button to access the **Drawing Window Colors** dialog box.

Drawing Lines Using Polar Coordinates

Absolute and relative coordinates are extremely useful in some situations; however, for many design applications (for example, drawing walls) *polar coordinates* or direct distance entry is used. Be sure you understand how to use all types of coordinates.

Polar coordinates are also relative to the last point entered. They are typed starting with an @, followed by a distance and angle of direction. Figure 2-32 shows that the default direction for positive angles is counterclockwise. The angle of direction is always preceded by a < sign when polar coordinates are entered.

polar coordinates: Coordinate values that are entered relative to the last point picked. They are typed starting with an @ followed by a distance and angle of direction; the angle is preceded by a < sign.

Figure 2-32
Polar coordinate angles

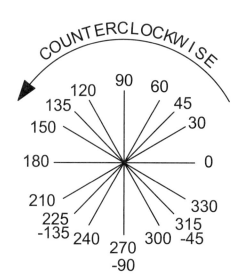

You can change the direction for positive angles to clockwise by clicking to add a check mark in the **Clockwise** box on the **Drawing Units** dialog box. We will use the default counterclockwise direction in this book.

Step 29. Draw a 1″ square using polar coordinates (Figure 2-31), as described next:

Prompt	Response
Type a command:	**<Enter>** (to return to the **Line** command prompt)
Specify first point:	Click a point on the grid **1/2″** to the right of the upper right corner of the last rectangle drawn
Specify next point or [Undo]:	Type **@1<0 <Enter>**
Specify next point or [Undo]:	Type **@1<270 <Enter>**
Specify next point or [Close Undo]:	Type **@1<180 <Enter>**
Specify next point or [Close Undo]:	Type **C <Enter>**

Drawing Lines Using Direct Distance Entry

direct distance entry: The process of specifying a second point by first moving the cursor to indicate direction and then entering a distance.

Direct distance entry is a quick, accurate, and easy way to draw lines. It can also be used with any other command that asks you to specify a point. Click on the screen first, then move your mouse in the direction you want to draw, type **the distance**, and press **<Enter>**.

Step 30. Draw a rectangle using direct distance entry (Figure 2-31), as described next:

Prompt	Response
Type a command:	**Line** (with **ORTHO** on)
Specify first point:	Click a point on the grid **1/2″** to the right of the upper right corner of the square just drawn
Specify next point or [Undo]:	Move your mouse to the right; type **2-1/2 <Enter>**
Specify next point or [Undo]:	Move your mouse down; type **1 <Enter>**

Prompt	Response
Specify next point or [Close Undo]:	Move your mouse to the left; type **2-1/2 <Enter>**
Specify next point or [Close Undo]:	Type **C <Enter>**

DYN	
Function Key	<F12>
Status Bar:	DYN/Right-Click/Drafting Settings...
Menu Bar:	Tools/ Drafting Settings...

DYN

As you gain more experience, you may want to use dynamic input to draw. Click **DYN** at the bottom of your screen to turn dynamic input on and off. When on, **DYN** mode displays three tooltips of command information near your cursor. These are *pointer input*, *dimension input*, and *dynamic prompts* (see Figure 2-33).

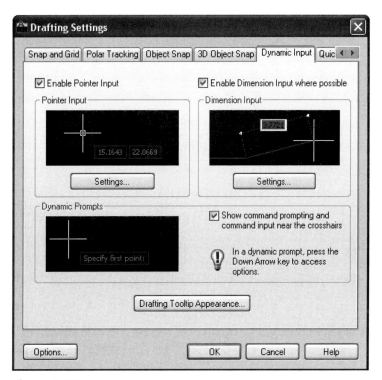

Figure 2-33
Drafting Settings dialog box, **Dynamic Input** tab

When **DYN** is on, you can enter coordinate values into the input fields instead of using the command line. They are entered as follows:

To enter *absolute coordinates* type the pound sign (#) prefix, then the absolute coordinates, and press **<Enter>** (example: **#4,4 <Enter>**).

Entering *relative coordinates* is the default. To enter relative coordinates type the relative coordinates without the @ sign, and press **<Enter>** (example: **5,3 <Enter>**).

To enter *polar coordinates:* type **the distance from the first point**, press **<Tab>** (to lock the value), then type the angle value, and press **<Enter>**.

Right-click **DYN** on the status bar, then click **Settings...** to access the **Dynamic Input** tab of the **Drafting Settings** dialog box (Figure 2-33). On this tab, you can control the display of the three tooltips near your cursor when **DYN** is on. Hold **<F12>** down to turn **DYN** off temporarily.

CIRCLE	
Ribbon/ Panel	Home/ Draw
Draw Toolbar:	
Menu Bar:	Draw/Circle
Type a Command:	CIRCLE
Command Alias:	C

Circle

Step 31. Look at Figure 2-34 to determine the approximate location of the four dashed-line circles you will draw.

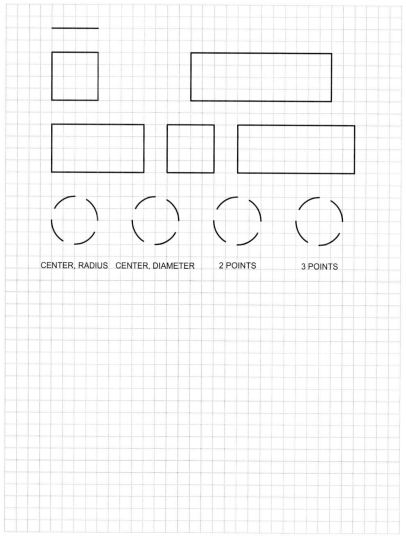

Figure 2-34
The locations of four circles

Step 32. Set **Layer2** current. Layer2 has a dashed linetype.

Step 33. Turn **ORTHO** off; **SNAP, GRID,** and **LWT** are on.

Center, Radius

Step 34. Draw a circle with a 1/2″ radius (Figure 2-35), as described next:

Prompt	**Response**
Type a command:	**Center, Radius** (or type **C <Enter>**)
Specify center point for circle or [3P 2P Ttr(tan tan radius)]:	**P1→** (Figure 2-35)
Specify radius of circle or [Diameter]:	Type **1/2 <Enter>** (the circle appears)

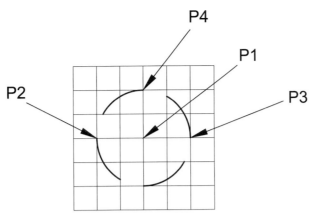

Figure 2-35
Draw the same-size circle using four different methods

Center, Diameter

Step 35. Draw a circle with a 1″ diameter (Figure 2-35), as described next:

Prompt	Response
Type a command:	**<Enter>** (to return to the **CIRCLE** command prompt)
Specify center point for circle or [3P 2P Ttr(tan tan radius)]:	**P1→** (Figure 2-35)
Specify radius of circle or [Diameter] <0′-0 1/2″>:	Type **D <Enter>** (to specify diameter)
Specify diameter of circle <0′-1″>:	**<Enter>** (the circle appears)

2 Points

Step 36. Draw a 1″-diameter circle by locating the two endpoints of its diameter (Figure 2-35), as described next:

Prompt	Response
Type a command:	**2 Point**
Specify center point for circle or [3P 2P Ttr(tan tan radius)]: _2p	
Specify first endpoint of circle's diameter:	**P2→** (on a grid mark, Figure 2-35)
Specify second endpoint of circle's diameter:	**P3→** (move four grid spaces to the right)

3 Points

Step 37. Draw a 1″-diameter circle by clicking three points on its circumference (Figure 2-35), as described next:

Prompt	Response
Type a command:	**3 Point**
Specify center point for circle or [3P 2P Ttr(tan tan radius)]: _3p	
Specify first point on circle:	**P2→** (Figure 2-35)
Specify second point on circle:	**P3→** (move four grid spaces to the right)
Specify third point on circle:	**P4→** (the center of the top of the circle)

You have just learned four different methods of drawing the same-size circle. You can watch the size of the circle change on the screen by moving the pointer, and you can select the desired size by clicking the point that indicates the size.

TTR

The next option of the **CIRCLE** command is **Tan, Tan, Radius**. This stands for tangent, tangent, and radius. A tangent touches a circle at a single point.

LTSCALE

AutoCAD provides a variety of linetypes that you may use. For example, the DASHED linetype provided by AutoCAD consists of 1/2″ line segments with 1/4″ spaces in between. The given line segment length (1/2″) and spacing (1/4″) for the DASHED linetype are drawn when the global linetype scale factor is set to 1 (the default).

To make the line segment length or spacing smaller, enter a linetype scale factor smaller than 1 but larger than 0 at the **LTSCALE** prompt. To make the line segment length and spacing larger, enter a linetype scale factor larger than 1. Look closely to see the circle's DASHED linetype scale change when the following is entered.

LTSCALE	
Type a Command:	LTSCALE
Command Alias:	LTS

Step 38. Use **LTSCALE** to change the size of the DASHED linetype, as described next:

Prompt	Response
Type a command:	Type **LTSCALE <Enter>**
Enter new linetype scale factor <1.0000>:	Type **1/2 <Enter>**
Regenerating model.	

ZOOM

The most commonly used **ZOOM** commands (**Extents, Window, Previous, Realtime,** and **All**) help you control how you view the drawing area on the display screen. While drawing the lines and circles for this chapter you have been able to view the entire 8-1/2″ × 11″ drawing limits on the screen. The **Zoom-All** command was used earlier to assure that view. The **ZOOM** commands are located on the navigation bar and the ribbon (Figure 2-36).

Zoom-Window

The **Zoom-Window** command allows you to pick two opposite corners of a rectangular window on the screen. The cursor changes to form a rubber band that shows the size of the window on the screen. The size of the window is controlled by the movement of the mouse. The part of the drawing inside the windowed area is magnified to fill the screen when the second corner of the window is clicked.

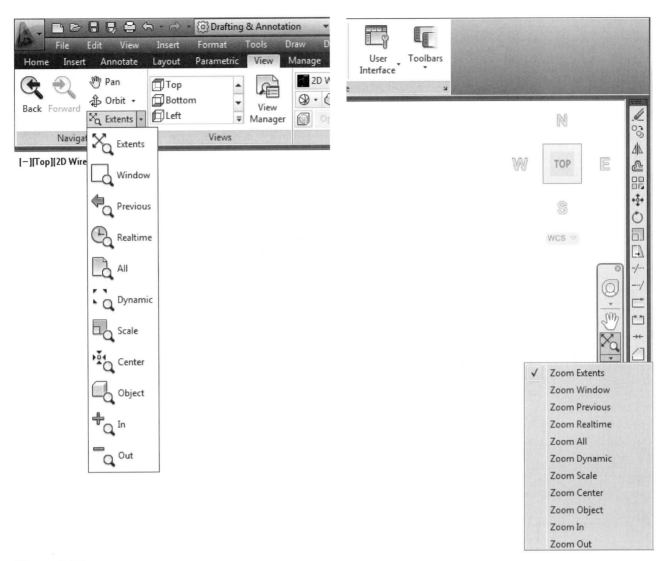

Figure 2-36
ZOOM commands on the ribbon and the navigation bar

Step 39. Use **Zoom-Window** to look more closely at the four circles (Figure 2-37), as described next:

Prompt	**Response**
Type a command:	Type **Z <Enter>**
Specify corner of window, enter a scale factor (nX or nXP), or [All Center Dynamic Extents Previous Scale Window Object] <real time>:	**P1→** (lower left corner of the window, Figure 2-37)
Specify opposite corner:	**P2→** (upper right corner of the window)

Zoom-All

Now that you have a windowed area of the drawing, how do you return to the entire drawing view? The drawing extents include whatever graphics are

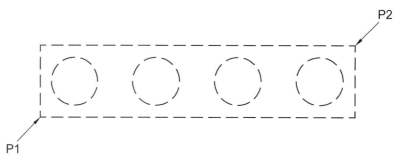

Figure 2-37
Use **Zoom-Window**

actually drawn on the page. If only half of the page is full of graphics, the extents will take up half of the page. Sometimes, graphics are drawn outside the limits; this, too, is considered the drawing extents. The limits of the drawing are set with the **Limits** command. *The **Zoom-All** command displays the entire drawing limits or extents, whichever is larger.* In this instance, **Zoom-All** will provide a view of the drawing limits.

Step 40. Use **Zoom-All** to view the entire drawing, as described next:

Prompt	Response
Type a command:	**Zoom-All** (or type **Z <Enter>**)
Specify corner of window, enter a scale factor (nX or nXP), or [All Center Dynamic Extents Previous Scale Window Object] <real time>:	Type **A <Enter>**

Zoom-Previous

Zoom-Previous is a very convenient feature. AutoCAD remembers up to 10 previous views. This is especially helpful and saves time if you are working on a complicated drawing.

Step 41. Use **Zoom-Previous** to see the last view of the tangent circles again, as described next:

Prompt	Response
Type a command:	**<Enter>** (to repeat the **ZOOM** command)
Specify corner of window, enter a scale factor (nX or nXP), or [All Center Dynamic Extents Previous Scale Window Object] <real time>:	Type **P <Enter>**

Zoom-Extents

The extents of a drawing include whatever graphics are actually drawn on the page. The **Zoom-Extents** command provides a view of all drawing entities on the page as large as possible to fill the screen.

Step 42. Use **Zoom-Extents** to view the extents of drawing **CH2-TUTORIAL1**.

Zoom-Object

Zoom-Object allows you to select an object or objects and press **<Enter>** to describe the area that will be displayed.

Zoom-Realtime

Press **<Enter>** at the **Zoom** prompt to activate **Zoom-Realtime**. After activating the command, to zoom in or out, hold down the left mouse button and move the mouse up or down to change the magnification of the drawing. Press **the right mouse button** to access a shortened **Zoom** and **Pan** menu. Click **Exit** or press **<Esc>** to exit the command.

Wheel Mouse   You can also zoom in and out by turning the wheel of a two-button mouse.

PAN REALTIME

PAN	
Ribbon/ Panel	View/ Navigate 2D
Navigation Bar:	PAN
Menu Bar:	View/Pan
Type a Command:	PAN
Command Alias:	P

The **Pan Realtime** command is located on the navigation bar and on the ribbon. **Pan** allows you to maintain the current display magnification and see parts of the drawing that may be off the screen and not visible in the display. Like panning with a camera, **Pan** does not change the magnification of the view.

You may also type **P <Enter>** to activate this command. To move the view of your drawing at the same magnification, hold down the left button on your mouse and move the mouse in any direction to change the view of your drawing.

Wheel Mouse   If you have a wheel mouse, you can pan by pressing down on the wheel and moving the mouse.

Transparent Commands

transparent command: A command that can be used while another command is in progress.

A *transparent command* is one that can be used while another command is in progress. It is convenient to be able to change the display while a command such as **Line** is in progress. All the **ZOOM** commands and the **PAN** command from the navigation bar and the ribbon may be used transparently; you can simply click them.

Commands that do *not* select objects, create new objects, or end the drawing session also usually can be used transparently. The grid and snap settings can be used transparently. After you have entered a command such as **Line**, you can type **'CAL <Enter>** to start the calculator command transparently, type **'P <Enter>** to start the **PAN** command, or type **'grid** to change the grid setting. An apostrophe (') must precede the command name. The >> preceding the command prompt in the command line window indicates the command is being used transparently.

REDRAW	
Function Key	<F7>
Menu Bar:	View/Redraw
Type a Command:	REDRAW
Keyboard Alias:	R

REDRAW

When you pick **Redraw** from the **View** menu or type **R <Enter>**, AutoCAD redraws and cleans up your drawing. Drawing entities affected by editing of other objects are redrawn. Pressing function key **<F7>** twice turns the grid off and on and also redraws the screen.

REGEN	
Menu Bar:	View/Regen
Type a Command:	REGEN
Keyboard Alias:	RE

REGEN

When you click **Regen** from the **View** menu, AutoCAD regenerates the entire drawing.

HIGHLIGHT

When you select any object such as a circle or line to erase or move or otherwise modify, the circle or line is highlighted. This highlighting is controlled by the **HIGHLIGHT** system variable. When you type **HIGHLIGHT <Enter>**, the **HIGHLIGHT** command has two responses: enter **1** to turn highlighting on, or **0** to turn highlighting off. You will need to have this variable on so the items selected are confirmed by the highlighting.

Move and Editing Commands Selection Set

You may want to move some of the items on your page to improve the layout of the page. The **MOVE** command allows you to do that.

Step 43. Set **Layer1** current.

Step 44. Use **Zoom-All** to view the entire drawing. Use **Zoom-Realtime** as needed to draw the circles in the next step.

Step 45. Draw a row of four 1/2″-diameter circles, 1″ on center (1″ from the center of one circle to the center of the next circle), as shown in Figure 2-38.

Step 46. Pick **Move** from the ribbon (or type **M <Enter>**).

Step 47. Select a circle by clicking a point on the circle, and move it (Figure 2-39), as described next:

MOVE	
Ribbon/ Panel	Home/ Modify Move
Modify Toolbar:	Move
Menu Bar:	Modify/Move
Type a Command:	MOVE
Command Alias:	M

Prompt	Response
Select objects:	**P1→** (any point on the circumference of the circle, as shown in Figure 2-39)
Select objects: 1 found Select objects:	**<Enter>** (you have completed selecting objects)
Specify base point or [Displacement] <Displacement>:	**P2→** (the center of the circle—be sure **SNAP** is on)
Specify second point or <use first point as displacement>:	Click a point three grid spaces (3/4″) to the right -or- with **ORTHO** on, move your mouse to the right; type **3/4 <Enter>**

NOTE

Keep snap on while moving a drawing entity. Snap from one grid point (base point or displacement) to another (second point).

Figure 2-38
Draw a row of four
1/2″-diameter circles, 1″ on
center

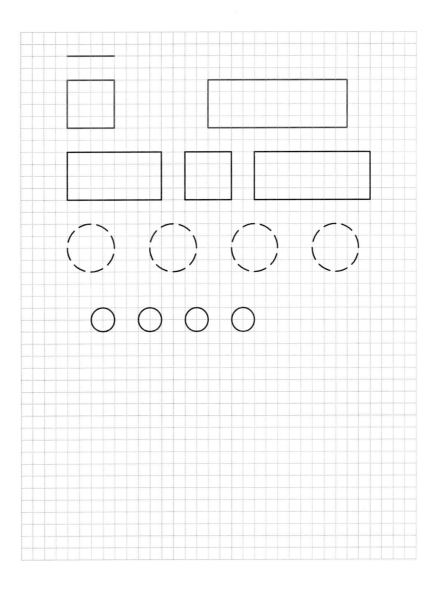

Figure 2-39
Select a circle by clicking a
point on the circle, and
move it

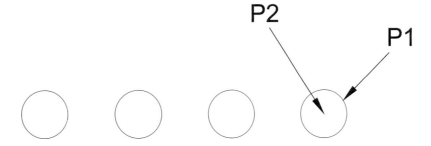

Step 48. Select a circle by clicking a point on the circle, and move it using
relative coordinates (Figure 2-40), as described next:

Prompt	Response
Type a command:	**<Enter>** (to repeat the **Move** command prompt)
Select objects:	**P1→** (Figure 2-40)
Select objects: 1 found	
Select objects:	**<Enter>**

Figure 2-40
Select a circle by clicking a point on the circle, and move it using relative coordinates

Prompt	Response
Specify base point or [Displacement] <Displacement>:	**P2→** (the center of the circle)
Specify second point or <use first point as displacement>:	Type **@–3/4,0 <Enter>**

> **NOTE**
> When you use the **MOVE** command, the base point can be anyplace on the drawing if you give a specific direction and distance for the second point.

You can give the second point of displacement by clicking a point on the screen or by using absolute, relative, or polar coordinates, or direct distance entry.

Step 49. Select items to be edited by using a window, and then remove an item from the selection set (Figure 2-41), as described next:

Prompt	Response
Type a command:	**<Enter>** (to repeat the **Move** command prompt)
Select objects:	**P1→** (Figure 2-41)
Specify opposite corner: 4 found	**P2→**
Select objects:	Type **R <Enter>** (or hold down the **<Shift>** key)
Remove objects:	**P3→**

Figure 2-41
Select items to be edited by using a window, and then remove an item from the selection set

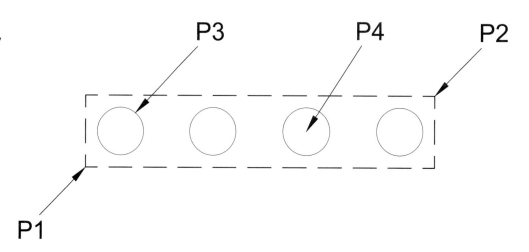

Prompt	Response
Remove objects:	**\<Enter\>**
Specify base point or	
[Displacement] \<Displacement\>:	**P4→** (the center of the circle or anyplace on the drawing)
Specify second point or \<use first point as displacement\>:	With **ORTHO** on, move your mouse down; type **1/2 \<Enter\>**

Options for Selecting Objects to Modify

After you pick **Move,** the prompt in the prompt line asks you to *Select objects:*. Also, a pickbox replaces the screen crosshairs. The pickbox helps you select the item or group of items to be moved by positioning the pickbox on the item. The item or group of items selected is called the *selection set.* Many of the AutoCAD **Modify** commands provide the same prompt, the pickbox, and also the same options used to select the object or objects to be edited. To view all the options used to select an object or objects, type and enter a **?** at the *Select objects:* prompt. The options are Window/Last/Crossing/Box/All/Fence/WPolygon/Cpolygon/Group/Add/Remove/Multiple/Previous/Undo/AUto/SIngle/Subobject/Object. We will cover some of the more commonly used options used to select objects.

Window (W) and Crossing Window (C)

The window selection (picking left to right) and crossing window selection (picking right to left) options allow you to pick two opposite corners of a rectangular window on the screen. The crosshairs of the pointer change to form a rubber band that shows the size of the window on the screen. The size of the window is controlled by the movement of the pointer.

With the window selection option, only the parts of the drawing that are *entirely contained within the window* are selected to be edited. If the window covers only a part of a drawing entity, that entity is not selected. You may also type **W \<Enter\>** at the *Select objects:* prompt to activate the Window response.

When you use the crossing window selection, any part of the drawing that is contained within or *crossed by the crossing window* is included in the selection set. With a crossing window, a drawing entity such as a line or circle does not have to be entirely contained within the window to be selected—it only has to be touched by the crossing window. The colors of both the crossing window and the window are controlled by the **Visual Effect Settings** on the **Selection** tab of the **Options** dialog box.

Picking an empty area on the drawing and moving your mouse to the right creates a window. Picking and moving to the left creates a crossing window.

TIP

Typing **W \<Enter\>** or **C \<Enter\>** to activate a window or a crossing window is helpful when the drawing area is dense and clicking an empty area is difficult or impossible.

Step 50. Return the circles to the approximate location as shown in Figure 2-38.

All (ALL)

Selects all objects on thawed layers.

Fence (F)

Allows you to click points that draw a line that selects any objects it crosses.

Remove (R) and Add (A)

The **Remove** option allows you to remove a drawing part from the selection set. If you are in the **Remove** mode and decide to add another drawing part to the selection set, type **A <Enter>** to return to the **Add** mode.

Last (L) and Previous (P)

The **Last** option selects the most recent drawing entity created. The **Previous** option selects the most recent selection set. Both are handy if you want to use several editing commands on the same drawing entity or the same selection set. You may also type and enter **L** or **P** from the keyboard while you are in a command and selecting objects.

Undo (U)

While in an editing command, if you decide you do not want something in a selection set, you may use the **UNDO** command to remove it and continue on with the *Select objects:* prompt. Typing **U <Enter>** backtracks through the selection sets in the reverse of the order in which they were selected.

Grips

grips: Small squares, rectangles, and triangles that appear on objects you select when no command is active. After selecting the grip, you can move, stretch, rotate, scale, copy, add a vertex, convert a line to an arc, convert an arc to a line, and mirror the objects without entering commands.

Grips are small squares that appear on an object if it is selected with no command active. Grips are very useful and can speed up your use of many of the **Modify** commands.

> **TIP**
> If grips appear when you do not want them, press the **<Esc>** key.

Step 51. Use grips to change the size of a circle; then move, scale, and rotate several circles at the same time, as described next:

Prompt	Response
Type a command:	With no command active, click on one of the ½″ diameter circles you have drawn
Small blue squares (grips) appear at each quadrant and at the center of the circle:	Click one of the grips at one of the quadrants of the circle
The grip changes color (becomes hot). Specify stretch point or [Base point Copy Undo eXit]:	Move your mouse to see that the size of the circle changes, then type **3/4 <Enter>**

Prompt	Response
The radius of the circle is now 3/4″	Click **Undo** (or type **U \<Enter\>**) to return the circle to its previous size
Type a command:	Using a window, select all four 1/2″ diameter circles
Grips appear at each quadrant and at the centers of all circles:	Click the grip at the far left quadrant
The grip changes color (becomes hot).	
STRETCH	
Specify stretch point or [Base point Copy Undo eXit]:	Press the space bar to advance to the **Move** grip mode in the command area
MOVE	
Specify move point or [Base point Copy Undo eXit]:	Move your mouse to the right to see that the circles move with your cursor. You can now type the distance to move the circles or you can click the destination point. For now, type **5 \<Enter\>** to move the circles 5″ to the right.
With all circles still displaying grips:	Click the grip at the far left quadrant
The grip changes color (becomes hot).	
STRETCH	
Specify stretch point or [Base point Copy Undo eXit]:	Press the space bar twice to advance to the **Rotate** grip mode
ROTATE	
Specify rotation angle or [Base point Copy Undo Reference eXit]:	Move your mouse so you can see that the circles are rotated. You can now type an angle or you can click a point to select the angle. For now, type **45 \<Enter\>** to rotate the circles 45°.
Type a command:	Click **Undo** twice (or type **U \<Enter\>** twice) to return the circles to their original position.

FOR MORE DETAILS

See Chapters 3 and 14 for more about grips.

NOTE

Hold down the **\<Shift\>** key to select multiple grips.

UNDO	
Quick Access Toolbar	←
Menu Bar:	Edit/Undo ←
Type a Command:	UNDO
Command Alias:	U

REDO	
Quick Access Toolbar	→
Menu Bar:	Edit/Redo →
Type a Command:	REDO

UNDO and REDO

Understanding how to use the **UNDO** command can be very helpful when drawing with AutoCAD.

When the **Undo** icon on the **Quick Access** toolbar is clicked, the most recent command is undone. To undo more than one command, click the **Undo** icon more than once or use the list provided under the down arrow to undo a group of commands. The **Redo** icon becomes active and *you can immediately use the Redo icon or list to redo as many commands as you need. If you resume drawing immediately after using the Undo icon, the Redo icon does not become active.*

When **U** is typed from the keyboard at the command prompt, and the **<Enter>** key is pressed, the most recent command operation is undone. Most of the time the operation that is undone is obvious, such as when a line that you have just drawn is undone. The most recent mode settings that are not obvious, such as **Snap**, will be undone also. *Typing **REDO** and pressing **<Enter>** will redo only one undo, and must immediately follow the **U** or **UNDO** command.*

When **U** is typed and entered from the keyboard, no prompt line appears. If you type **UNDO <Enter>**, the prompt *Enter the number of operations to undo or [Auto Control BEgin End Mark Back] <1>:* appears. The default is <1>. You may enter a number for the number of operations to be undone. For instance, if 5 is entered at the prompt, five operations will be undone. If you decide you went too far, you can type **REDO <Enter>** or select **Redo** from the **Standard** toolbar, and all five operations will be restored.

Typing **U** from the keyboard and pressing the **<Enter>** key is the same as entering the number **1** at the **Undo** prompt. In that instance, **Redo** *will redo only one undo, no matter how many times you typed and entered **U**.*

ARC	
Ribbon/ Panel	Home/ Draw
Draw Toolbar:	
Menu Bar:	Draw/Arc
Type a Command:	ARC
Command Alias:	A

ARC

There are many methods from which to choose when you are drawing arcs. Whatever the situation, you can select a method to suit your needs. Experiment with the different methods described next and decide which ones you prefer to use. Use Figure 2-42 as a guide when locating the approximate location of the arcs on your drawing.

3-Point

Using the **3-point** method, you can draw an arc clockwise or counterclockwise by specifying the start point, second point, and endpoint of the arc.

Step 52. Draw three arcs using the **3-point** method (Figure 2-43), as described next:

Prompt	Response
Type a command:	**3 Point** (or type **A <Enter>**)
Specify start point of arc or [Center]:	**P1→**
Specify second point of arc or [Center End]:	**P2→** (Figure 2-43)
Specify end point of arc:	**P3→**
Command:	**<Enter>** (repeat **ARC**)
Specify start point of arc or [Center]:	**P4→**
Specify second point of arc or [Center End]:	**P5→**
Specify end point of arc:	**P6→**

Figure 2-42
Draw arcs

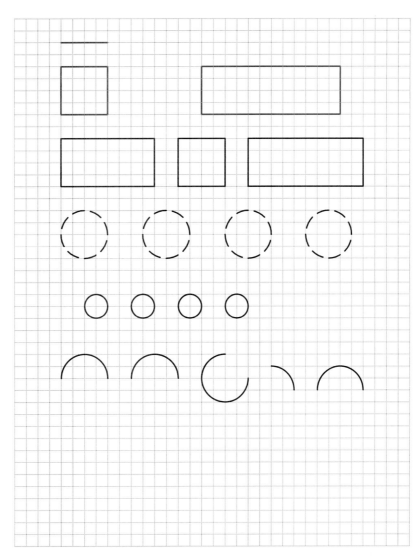

Figure 2-43
Draw arcs using the 3-point method

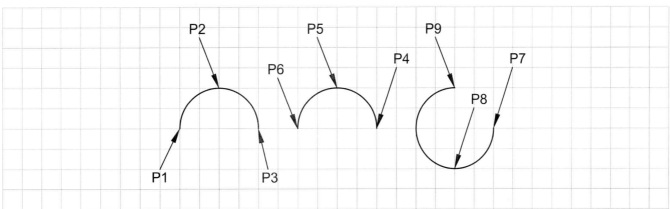

Prompt	Response
Command:	**<Enter>** (repeat **ARC**)
Specify start point of arc or [Center]:	**P7→**
Specify second point of arc or [Center End]:	**P8→**
Specify end point of arc:	**P9→**

Start, Center, End

The **Start, Center, End** method allows you to draw an arc only counter-clockwise, by specifying the start, center, and end.

Step 53. Draw two arcs using the **Start, Center, End** method (Figure 2-44), as described next:

Prompt	Response
Type a command:	**Arc-Start, Center, End**
Specify start point of arc or [Center]:	**P1→**
Specify second point of arc or [Center End]:_c Specify center point of arc:	**P2→** (Figure 2-44)
Specify end point of arc or [Angle chord Length]:	**P3→**
Command:	**Arc-Start, Center, End**
Specify start point of arc or [Center]:	**P4→** (Figure 2-44)
Specify second point of arc or [Center End]:_c Specify center point of arc:	**P5→**
Specify end point of arc or [Angle chord Length]:	**P6→**

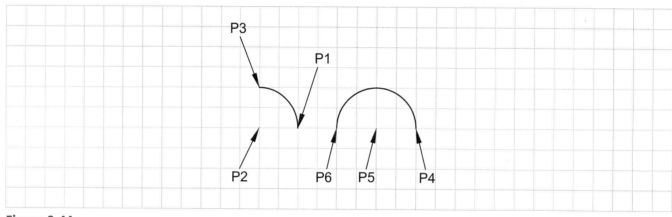

Figure 2-44
Draw arcs using the **Start, Center, End** method

Start, Center, Angle

In the **Start, Center, Angle** method, **A** is the included angle (the angle the arc will span). A positive angle will draw the arc counterclockwise; a negative angle will draw the arc clockwise.

Start, Center, Length

In the **Start, Center, Length** method, **L** is the chord length. A *chord* is a straight line that connects an arc's start point and endpoint. A positive chord length can be entered to draw a minor arc (less than 180°), and a negative chord length can be entered to draw a major arc (more than 180°). Both are drawn counterclockwise.

Start, End, Angle

With the **Start, End, Angle** method, after the start point and endpoint of the arc have been picked, a positive angle draws the arc counterclockwise; a negative angle keeps the same start and endpoints but draws the reverse arc or draws clockwise.

Start, End, Direction

In this method, **Direction** is the specified direction that the arc takes from the start point. The direction is specified in degrees. You can also specify the direction by pointing to a single point. Major, minor, counter-clockwise, and clockwise arcs can be drawn with the **Start, End, Direction** method.

Start, End, Radius

In the **Start, End, Radius** method, **Radius** is the arc radius. When you use this method, enter a positive radius to draw a minor arc (less than 180°), and enter a negative radius to draw a major arc (more than 180°). Both are drawn counterclockwise.

Continue

If **Continue** is picked, a new arc starts tangent at the endpoint of the last arc or line drawn. You need to pick only the endpoint of the new arc to complete it. If an arc is already drawn, pressing the **<Enter>** key has the same effect.

ELLIPSE

Look at Figure 2-45 to determine the approximate location of the ellipses drawn with the **ELLIPSE** command.

Axis, End

The minor axis of an ellipse is its smaller axis, and the major axis is the larger axis.

Step 54. Set **Layer3** current.

Step 55. Draw an ellipse by entering points for the minor axis of the ellipse (Figure 2-46), as described next:

Prompt	Response
Type a command:	**Ellipse-Axis, End** (or type **EL <Enter>**)
Specify axis endpoint of ellipse or [Arc Center]:	**P1→** (Figure 2-46)
Specify other endpoint of axis:	**P2→**—With **ORTHO** on, move your mouse to the right; type **1 <Enter>**
Specify distance to other axis or [Rotation]:	**P3→**—With **ORTHO** on, move your mouse up; type **1 <Enter>**

Figure 2-45
Draw ellipses and donuts

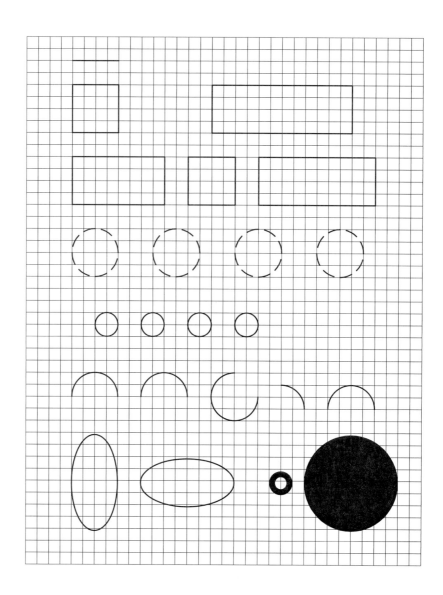

Figure 2-46
Draw an ellipse by entering
points for the minor and
major axes of the ellipse

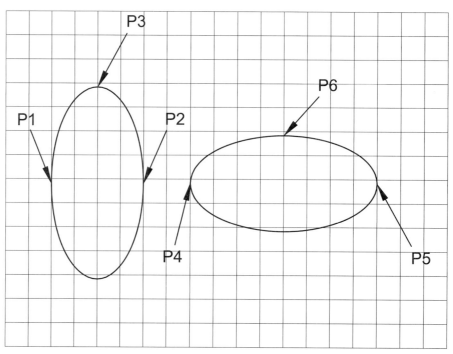

ELLIPSE	
Ribbon/ Panel	Home/Draw
Draw Toolbar:	Ellipse
Menu Bar:	Draw/Ellipse
Type a Command:	ELLIPSE
Command Alias:	EL

Step 56. Draw an ellipse by entering points for the major axis of the ellipse (Figure 2-46), as described next:

Prompt	Response
Type a command:	**Ellipse-Axis, End**
Specify axis endpoint of ellipse or [Arc Center]:	**P4→** (Figure 2-46)
Specify other endpoint of axis:	**P5→**—With **ORTHO** on, move your mouse to the right; type **2 <Enter>**
Specify distance to other axis or [Rotation]:	**P6→**—With **ORTHO** on, move your mouse up; type **1/2 <Enter>**

Center

You may also draw an ellipse by specifying the center point, the endpoint of one axis, and the length of the other axis. Type **C** and press **<Enter>** at the prompt *Specify axis endpoint of ellipse or [Arc Center]:* to start with the center of the ellipse. Entering the center point first is similar to the first two methods described, and either the minor or major axis may be constructed first. As with all methods of drawing an ellipse, you can specify the points by clicking a point on the drawing, by typing and entering coordinates, or by direct distance entry.

DONUT

DONUT	
Ribbon/ Panel	Home/Draw 
Draw Toolbar:	None
Menu Bar:	Draw/Donut
Type a Command:	DONUT
Command Alias:	DO

Look at Figure 2-45 to determine the approximate location of the solid ring and solid circle drawn using the **DONUT** command.

Step 57. Set **Layer1** current.

Step 58. Use the **DONUT** command to draw a solid ring (Figure 2-47), as described next:

Prompt	Response
Type a command:	**DONUT** (or type **DO <Enter>**)
Specify inside diameter of donut <default>:	Type **1/2 <Enter>**
Specify outside diameter of donut <default>:	Type **1 <Enter>**
Specify center of donut or <exit>:	Click a point on the drawing
Specify center of donut or <exit>:	**<Enter>**

Figure 2-47
Use the **DONUT** command to draw a solid ring and a solid circle

Step 59. Use the **DONUT** command to draw a solid circle (Figure 2-47), as described next:

Prompt	Response
Type a command:	**<Enter>** (repeat **DONUT**)
Specify inside diameter of donut <0'-0 1/2">:	Type **0 <Enter>** (so there is no center hole)
Specify outside diameter of donut <0'-1">:	**<Enter>**
Specify center of donut or <exit>:	Click a point on the drawing
Specify center of donut or <exit>:	**<Enter>**

The **DONUT** command can be used to draw solid dots of any size as well as solid rings with different inside and outside diameters.

SCALE

SCALE	
Ribbon/ Panel	Home/Modify
Modify Toolbar:	
Menu Bar:	Modify/Scale
Type a Command:	SCALE
Command Alias:	SC

The **SCALE** command lets you reduce or enlarge either drawing entities or an entire drawing. The **Copy** option of the **SCALE** command allows you to copy and enlarge or reduce the object at the same time.

<Scale factor>

Step 60. Use the **SCALE** command to reduce the solid ring (Figure 2-48), as described next:

Prompt	Response
Type a command:	**SCALE** (or type **SC <Enter>**)
Select objects:	Window the ring (or click the outside edge of the ring)
Select objects:	**<Enter>**
Specify base point:	Click the center of the ring
Specify scale factor or [Copy Reference]:	Type **.5 <Enter>**

The relative scale factor of .5 was used to reduce the solid ring. A relative scale factor of 2 would have enlarged the solid ring.

Reference

Step 61. Use the **SCALE** command to enlarge the solid donut (Figure 2-48), as described next:

Prompt	Response
Type a command:	**<Enter>** (repeat **SCALE**)
Select objects:	Window the solid donut
Select objects:	**<Enter>**
Specify base point:	Click the center of the solid donut
Specify scale factor or [Copy Reference] <default>:	Type **R <Enter>**
Specify reference length <0'-1">:	**<Enter>** (to accept **1** as the default)
Specify new length or [Points] <0'-1">:	Type **2 <Enter>**

The **Reference** option allows you to type and enter a number for the reference (current) length of a drawing entity. You can also enter the reference (current) length by picking two points on the drawing to show AutoCAD the reference (current) length. You can type and enter the new length by using a number, or you can enter it by picking two points on the drawing to show the new length.

YOUR NAME
YOUR CLASS
THE DATE

Figure 2-48
Tutorial 2-1, Part 2, complete

Adding Text

Step 62. Set **Layer3** current.

Step 63. Add your name, class, and date to the upper right corner of your drawing as described next:

SINGLE-LINE TEXT	
Ribbon/ Panel	Home/ Annotation **A**
Text Toolbar:	**A**
Menu Bar:	Draw/Text/ Single Line Text
Type a Command:	TEXT or DTEXT
Command Alias:	DT

Prompt	**Response**
Type a command:	**Single Line Text** (or type **DT <Enter>**)
Specify start point of text or [Justify Style]:	Click a point in the upper right corner to start typing your name as shown in Figure 2-48

Prompt	Response
Specify height <default>:	Type **1/8 <Enter>**
Specify rotation angle of text <0>:	**<Enter>** (to accept the 0 default rotation)
The **In-Place Text Editor** appears:	Type **YOUR NAME <Enter> YOUR CLASS <Enter> THE DATE <Enter>**
The **In-Place Text Editor**:	**<Enter>** (to close the **In-Place Text Editor**)

Command Lines of Prompt History

AutoCAD provides a record of the command history for the current session. Gray highlighted lines of this command history are shown in the floating command line. You can change the number of **Lines of Prompt History** displayed by using the command line right-click menu in Figure 2-49.

Figure 2-49
Command line right-click menu

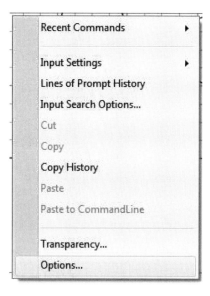

Clicking **<F2>** will show you a full command history of the current session that you can scroll through.

Step 64. When you have completed Tutorial 2-1, Part 2 (Figure 2-48), save your drawing in at least two places.

PLOT	
Ribbon/ Panel	Output/Plot 🖨
Quick Access Toolbar:	🖨
Menu Bar:	File/Plot...
Type a Command:	PLOT/PRINT
Command Alias:	<Ctrl>+P

TUTORIAL 2-2
Plot Responses for CH2-TUTORIAL1, Using the Model Tab

When you start a new drawing, AutoCAD provides a single **Model** tab and two **Layout** tabs at the bottom of the drawing window. Thus far you have been working on the **Model** tab in model space. Model space is the 2D (and also 3D) environment where you create your drawings. You can also plot (or print) from the **Model** tab. Tutorial 2-2 describes how to print from the **Model** tab.

The following is a hands-on, step-by-step tutorial to make a hard copy of **CH2-TUTORIAL1**.

Step 1. Open drawing **CH2-TUTORIAL1** and complete a **Zoom-All** command so it is displayed on the screen.

Step 2. Make sure the **Model** tab is current.

Step 3. Click the **Plot** command from the **Quick Access** toolbar or type **PLOT <Enter>** to access the **Plot** dialog box. Pressing **<Ctrl> + P** will also access the **Plot** dialog box.

Step 4. Click the **More Options** arrow in the lower right corner of the **Plot** dialog box to display the entire **Plot** dialog box (Figure 2-50).

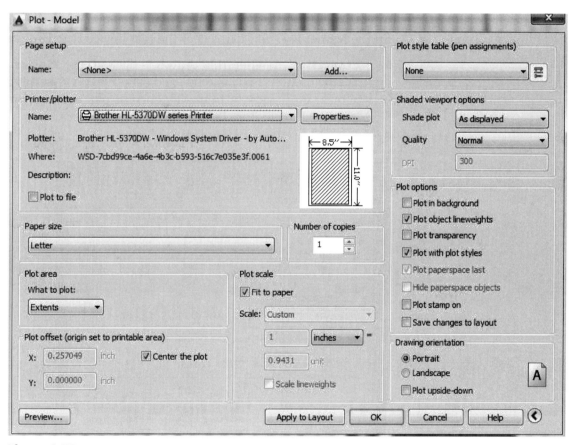

Figure 2-50
Plot dialog box

FOR MORE DETAILS

See Chapter 5 for advanced plotting.

Plot - Name

The strip at the top of the dialog box displays the current layout tab name or shows whether the **Model** tab is current. It shows **Model** now because the **Model** tab is current.

Page Setup

Name: The settings that control the final plot output are referred to as *page setups.* This list box displays any named or saved page setups that you can select to apply to the current page setup.

Add...: When this button is clicked, the **Add Page Setup** dialog box is displayed. You can specify a name for the new page setup.

Step 5. Set the **Page setup** to **None**.

Printer/Plotter

The **Name:** line displays the current plot device (plotter or printer). When the down arrow is clicked, a list of the available plotting devices is displayed in the **Name:** list. You can select the plot device that you want to use.

Properties...: When this button is clicked, the **Plotter Configuration Editor** (Figure 2-51) is displayed. The **Plotter Configuration Editor** allows you to view or to modify current plot device information. If **None** is in the **Name:** line, **Properties...** is grayed out.

Figure 2-51
Plotter Configuration Editor dialog box

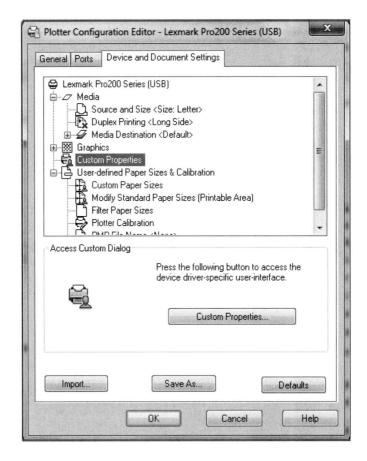

Custom Properties...: When this button of the **Plotter Configuration Editor** is clicked, a **Properties** dialog box for the configured plotter (or printer) appears. Each plotter (or printer) has a unique **Properties** dialog box; you can customize settings for the vector colors, print quality, and raster corrections for your plotter (or printer) using the **Properties** dialog box.

Step 6. Select the printer that you will use. If the **Name:** line does not show the correct plot device, click the down arrow and select the printer that you will use.

If you need to add a plot device, the **Plotter Manager** (under **File** in the menu bar) is used to add or modify plotter and printer configuration files.

Plot to File

If you do not check the **Plot to file** button, AutoCAD plots directly from your computer. If there is a cable leading from your computer to the printer or plotter, or if you are plotting from a network, do not check the **Plot to file** button.

If you do check the **Plot to file** button, a file is created with the extension .plt. You can save this plot file and transfer it to any computer connected to a plotter or printer.

Browse for Plot File...

When **Plot to file** is selected, and **OK** is clicked, the **Browse for Plot File** dialog box is displayed. This dialog box allows you to save the plot file.

Step 7. Select the correct setting for the **Plot to file** check box for your situation.

Plot Style Table (Pen Assignments)

plot style table: A collection of plot styles. Plot styles are made using plot style tables. They apply to objects only when the plot style table is attached to a layout or viewport.

Plot styles allow you to plot the same drawing in different ways. The ***plot style table*** (Figure 2-52) can be used to create, edit, or store plot style files.

Figure 2-52
Plot style table

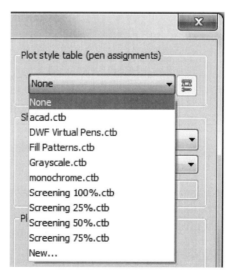

FOR MORE DETAILS

See Chapter 5 for more on plot styles.

Step 8. Set the **Plot style table** to **None**.

Paper Size

The **Paper size:** line displays the current paper size. When the down arrow is clicked, it lists the paper sizes the printer (Figure 2-53) or plotter (Figure 2-54) can accommodate; the current size is highlighted. An A, B, D, or E displayed

Figure 2-53
Paper sizes for a printer

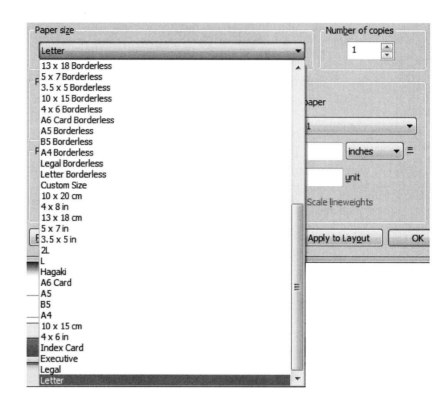

Figure 2-54
Paper sizes for a plotter

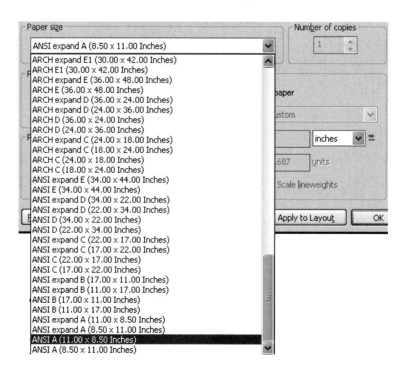

beside the size indicates a standard American National Standards Institute (ANSI) paper size. ARCH displayed beside the size indicates a standard architectural paper size.

Step 9. Select the **Letter** (8.5 × 11 in.) paper size, and **1** for the **Number of copies**.

Plot Area

When you click the down arrow, the following options are displayed (**View** will not be displayed because you have not named and saved a view in your drawing):

Display: This option plots the part of the drawing that is displayed on the screen at the time the plot is made.

Extents: This option plots the drawing extents. The drawing extents are whatever graphics are actually drawn, including any graphics that lie outside the limits of the drawing area.

Limits: This option plots the part of the drawing that lies within the drawing limits. The limits for drawing **CH2-TUTORIAL1** are 8-1/2,11.

Window: This selection allows you to pick two corners of a window and plot only the part of the drawing that is within the window. When the **Window** < button is clicked, it clears the **Plot** dialog box so you can view your drawing and use your mouse to click the two corners of a window. AutoCAD then returns to the **Plot** dialog box.

Step 10. Click **Extents** to select the drawing extents as part of the drawing that is to be printed.

Plot Scale

Scale: In model space, you draw full scale, so most drawings need to be plotted to scale. The **Scale:** line displays the scale at which the drawing will be plotted. If the scale list is gray, click the check mark in the **Fit to paper** check box so a scale may be selected. When the down arrow is clicked, a list of available scales is displayed. You can select the scale that you want to use. To be able to measure a plotted drawing accurately using a scale, you must enter a specific plotting scale.

Fit to paper: You may respond by selecting **Fit to paper** instead of entering a specific scale. When you select this option, AutoCAD scales the selected plot area as large as possible to fit the specified paper size.

Annotative Property and Annotation Scale

Objects such as text, dimensions, hatches, and leaders can be annotative. To make text annotative, you can turn the annotative property on in the **Text Style** dialog box. Also, before you add the text to your drawing, you must set the annotation scale, located in the lower right corner of the status bar.

When a drawing such as a large house or building is drawn full scale, the text that is added to the drawing also must be large. For instance, if you want the text of a drawing to be 1/8″ high when plotted at a scale of 1/4″ = 1′-0″, the text that you add while drawing full scale will need to be 6″ high, as shown in the 1/4″ = 1′-0″ scale in Figure 2-55.

ANNOTATION SCALE	TEXT SIZE ON SCALED PLOTTED DRAWINGS	SCALE FACTOR	TEXT SIZE ON FULL-SIZE DRAWINGS
1/8"=1'-0"	1/8"	96	12"
1/4"=1'-0"	1/8"	48	6"
1/2"=1'-0"	1/8"	24	3"
1"=1'-0"	1/8"	12	1-1/2"

Figure 2-55
Examples of annotation scales for text

Annotation scale controls how the text and other annotative objects appear on the drawing. When you make the text annotative and set the annotation scale of the drawing, AutoCAD automatically does the arithmetic for you and controls how the text looks on your screen. When adding the text, you have to enter only the size of the text you want in the plotted drawing, and AutoCAD automatically calculates the size of the text on the drawing using the annotation scale setting.

If you have annotative objects on your drawing and have set the annotation scale, it is usually best to plot your drawing at the same scale as the annotation scale that you have set. If there are no annotative objects on your drawing, the annotation scale does not affect anything. If the plot scale and the annotation scale differ, when the plot is initiated, AutoCAD prompts you with *The annotation scale is not equal to the plot scale. Do you wish to Continue?* You can answer with **OK** or **Cancel**.

Step 11. Select a scale of **1:1**, which is 1 plotted inch = 1 drawing unit.

FOR MORE DETAILS

See Chapter 6 for more information about annotative text, and Chapter 7 for more information about annotative dimensions.

Plot Offset (Origin Set to Printable Area)

Center the plot: To center the drawing on the paper, place a check in the **Center the plot** check box, and the plot will be automatically centered on the paper.

X and Y offset: The plot offset specifies the location of the plot, on the paper, from the lower left corner of the paper. The **X:** input line moves the plotted drawing in the X direction on the paper, and the **Y:** input moves the drawing in the Y direction. You can enter either positive or negative values.

Step 12. Place a check in the **Center the plot** check box.

Notice that the X and Y inputs are automatically calculated to center the selected plotting area (extents) in the paper size (8-1/2″ × 11″).

Shaded Viewport Options

These options relate to 3D drawings and control how shaded and rendered viewports are plotted. This is described in Chapters 14 and 15.

Plot Options

Plot in background: A check mark in this box allows you to continue working while your drawing is being plotted.

Plot object lineweights: A check mark in this box tells AutoCAD to plot the drawing using the lineweights you have assigned to any object in the drawing.

Plot transparency: You can enter a transparency value in the **Layer** dialog box. It is a setting that makes an object more or less transparent. If you have transparent objects in your drawing, this option determines whether the transparency is plotted.

Plot with plot styles: This option allows you to use a plot style. Because you are not using a plot style, this box will not be checked.

Plot paperspace last: When this option is checked, model space will be plotted first. Usually, paper space drawings are plotted before model space drawings.

Hide paperspace objects: The **Hide paperspace objects** check box refers to 3D objects only. When you use the **Hide** command, AutoCAD hides any surface on the screen that is behind another surface in 3D space. If you want to do the same on your paper space plot, you must click the **Hide paperspace objects** check box so that a check appears in the box. This shows only in the full plot preview window.

Another way to hide in paper space is to select the viewport in which you want to have hidden lines, click **Properties** under **Modify** in the menu bar, and turn **Shade plot** to **Hidden**.

Plot stamp on: A check mark here allows you to place signatures and other stamps on the drawing.

Save changes to layout: Checking this box allows you to save any changes you have made in the **Plot** dialog box.

Step 13. If there is a check in the **Plot with plot styles** box, remove the check. Put a check in the **Plot object lineweights** box. (**Plot paperspace last** and **Hide paperspace objects** are grayed out because no **Layout** tabs were used.)

Drawing Orientation

The paper icon represents the orientation of the selected paper size. The letter A icon represents the orientation of the drawing on the paper.

Portrait: This button allows you to specify a vertical orientation of the drawing on the page.

Landscape: This button allows you to specify a horizontal orientation of the drawing on the page. If a plot shows only half of what should have been plotted, the orientation may need to be changed.

Plot upside-down: This check box allows you to plot the drawing, in a portrait or landscape orientation, upside-down.

Step 14. Select the **Portrait** orientation.

Preview...

The **Preview...** button shows you exactly how the final plot will appear on the sheet.

Step 15. Click the **Preview...** button.

Preview your plot for **CH2-TUTORIAL1**, Part 2, Figure 2-56. If there is something wrong with the plot, press the space bar and make the necessary adjustments. If the preview looks OK, press the space bar to end the preview. You may also click the right mouse button to access the menu shown in Figure 2-57.

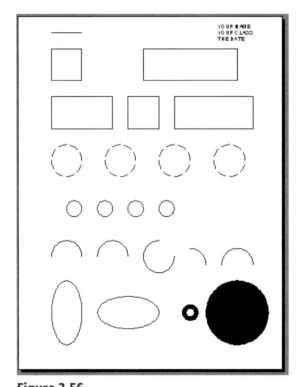

Figure 2-56
Plot preview

Figure 2-57
Preview right-click menu

Step 16. Click **OK** from the **Plot** dialog box (or click **Plot** from the right-click menu).

The plot proceeds from this point. If you have not created a plot file, remove the completed plot from the printer or plotter. If you have created a .plt file, take your disk to the plot station or send your plot via a network.

Chapter Summary

This chapter provided you the information necessary to set up and begin a new AutoCAD drawing. In addition you learned to make layers and assign color, linetype, and lineweight to each layer. You also learned how to use the **Save** and **Save as** commands, use basic drawing and editing commands, and print or plot your drawing. Now you have the skills and information necessary to set up and make basic drawings, save your drawings, and print or plot your drawings.

Chapter Test Questions

Multiple Choice

Circle the correct answer.

1. The function key **<F7>** described in this chapter does which of the following?

   a. Flips the screen from the text display

   b. Turns snap on or off

   c. Turns **ORTHO** on or off

   d. Turns grid on or off

2. Which of the following function keys is used to turn snap on or off?

   a. **<F2>**   c. **<F8>**

   b. **<F7>**   d. **<F9>**

3. How many layers may be used in a drawing?

   a. 1   c. 32

   b. 16   d. An unlimited number

4. AutoCAD provides how many sizes of each standard linetype (except continuous)?

   a. 1   c. 3

   b. 2   d. As many as you want

5. When the **MOVE** command is used with a window selection (click left, drag right — not a crossing window):

   a. Everything the window touches is selected

   b. Everything entirely within the window is selected

   c. The last item clicked is selected

   d. Nothing is selected

6. When the **MOVE** command is used with a crossing window selection (click right, drag left):

   a. Everything the window contains or touches is selected

   b. Everything entirely within the window is selected

   c. The last item clicked is selected

   d. Nothing is selected

7. Which of the following are small squares that appear on an object when it is selected with no command active?

   a. Grips   c. Squares

   b. Snaps   d. Rectangles

8. When you plot from the **Model** tab, which of the following will produce a plot of the part of the drawing that is displayed on the screen?

   a. **Display**   c. **Window**

   b. **Extents**   d. **Limits**

9. When you plot from the **Model** tab, which of the following will produce a plot of the entire drawing, even if part of it is outside the limits?

   a. **Display**   c. **Window**

   b. **Extents**   d. **Limits**

10. A drawing that is to be plotted using the **Model** tab so that it fits on a particular size sheet without regard to the scale requires which scale response?

   a. **1:1**   c. **1:2**

   b. **Full**   d. **Fit to paper**

Matching

Write the number of the correct answer on the line.

a. **Ortho** _____

b. **Ltscale** _____

c. **Save As...** _____

d. **Extents** _____

e. **GRIDDISPLAY** _____

1. A command that allows you to save drawings with a different name

2. A setting that changes the spacing between dashes in a hidden line

3. A setting that permits you to draw only horizontally or vertically

4. When this setting is zero the grid shows the limits of the drawing

5. When this area is selected all of the drawing is plotted even if part of it is outside the drawing limits

True or False

Circle the correct answer.

1. **True or False:** The default lower left corner of the drawing limits is 8-1/2,11.

2. **True or False:** To make the line segment length and spacing larger for a dashed linetype, enter a number larger than 1 at the **Ltscale** prompt *Enter new linetype scale factor <1.000>.*

3. **True or False:** Direct distance entry can be used only when drawing a line.

4. **True or False:** The **3-point** method of drawing arcs allows you to draw arcs clockwise or counterclockwise.

5. **True or False:** Pressing the **<Esc>** key cancels a command.

List

1. Five types of **Drawing Units** available in AutoCAD.

2. Five **Visual Styles** accessible from the **View** (pull-down) menu.

3. Five ways to access the **Plot** command.

4. Five color index numbers and their corresponding colors.

5. Five ways of drawing an arc.

6. Five options of the **ZOOM** command.

7. Five ways of accessing the **ELLIPSE** command.

8. Five commands and their respective aliases.

9. Five ways of accessing the **Layer Properties Manager** palette.

10. Five ways of accessing the single-line text command in AutoCAD.

General Questions

1. In what situations would you use the **Ortho** setting?

2. Why would you want to use the **Ltscale** setting?

3. How can the annotation scale be used to make it easier to draw and plot drawings?

4. Which settings on the status bar do you want to use in your workspace?

5. What are all the selection set options, and how can you use them effectively?

Chapter Projects

Project 2-1: *Drawing Shapes I* [BASIC]

Draw, full size, the shapes shown in Figure 2-58. Use the dimensions shown. Locate the shapes approximately as shown. Use your workspace to make the following settings:

Figure 2-58
Project 2-1: Drawing Shapes I

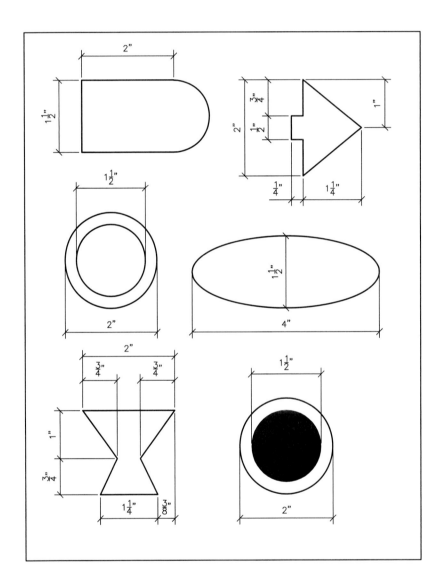

1. **Use Save As...** to save the drawing with the name **CH2-P1**.

2. Set drawing units: **Architectural**

3. Set drawing limits: **8-1/2,11**

4. Set **GRIDDISPLAY: 0**

5. Set grid: **1/4"**

6. Set snap: **1/8″**

7. Create the following layers:

LAYER NAME	COLOR	LINETYPE	LINEWEIGHT
Layer1	blue	continuous	.010″ (.25 mm)

Project 2-2: *Drawing a Pattern* [BASIC]

Draw the pattern shown in Figure 2-59. Use an architectural scale to measure the pattern and draw it full scale. Use your workspace to make the following settings:

1. Use **Save As...** to save the drawing with the name **CH2-P2**.

2. Set drawing units: **Architectural**

3. Set drawing limits: **8-1/2,11**

4. Set **GRIDDISPLAY**: **0**

5. Set grid: **1/4″**

6. Set snap: **1/8″**

7. Create the layers on your own.

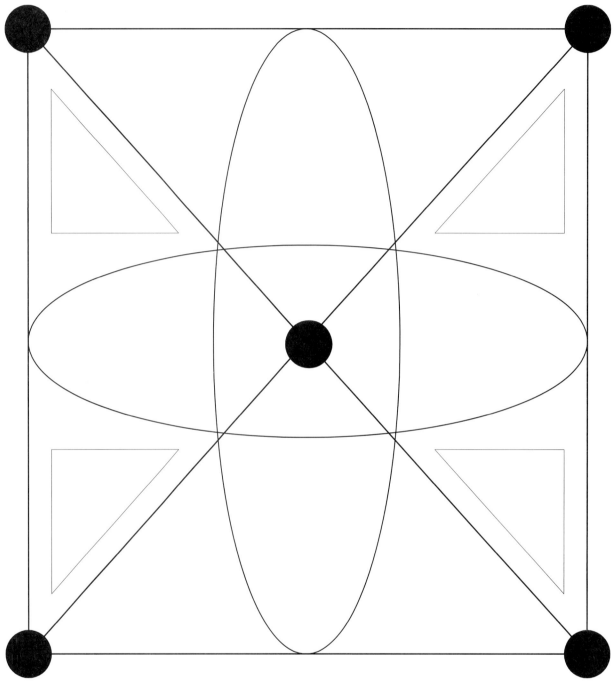

Figure 2-59
Project 2-2: Drawing a pattern (scale: 1″ = 1″)

Project 2-3: *Drawing Shapes II* [INTERMEDIATE]

Draw the shapes shown in Figure 2-60. Use an architectural scale to measure the shapes and draw them full scale. Your drawing will be the size shown in the figure. Use your workspace to make the following settings:

1. Use **Save As...** to save the drawing with the name **CH2-P3**.

2. Set drawing units: **Architectural**

3. Set drawing limits: **8-1/2,11**

4. Set **GRIDDISPLAY: 0**

5. Set grid: **1/4″**

6. Set snap: **1/8″**

7. Create the layers on your own.

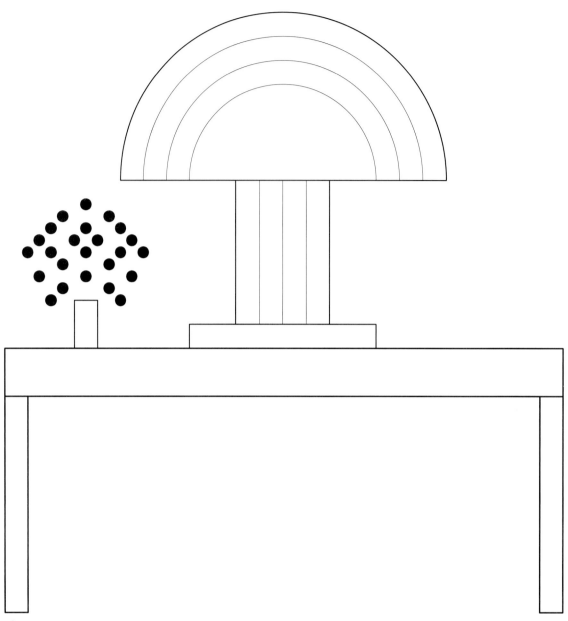

Figure 2-60
Project 2-3: Drawing Shapes II (scale: 1″ = 1″)

Project 2-4: *Drawing a Door* [INTERMEDIATE]

Draw the door shape shown in Figure 2-61. Use an architectural scale to measure the figure and draw it full scale. Use your workspace to make the following settings:

1. Use **Save As...** to save the drawing with the name **CH2-P4**.

2. Set drawing units: **Architectural**

3. Set drawing limits: **8-1/2,11**

4. Set **GRIDDISPLAY**: **0**

5. Set grid: **1/4″**

6. Set snap: **1/8″**

7. Create the layers on your own.

Figure 2-61
Project 2-4: Drawing a door
(scale: 1″ = 1″)

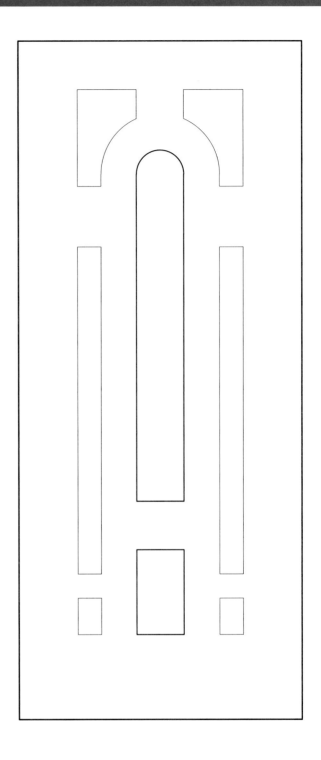

Project 2-5: *Drawing Shapes III* [ADVANCED]

Draw the shape shown in Figure 2-62. Use an architectural scale to measure the figure and draw it full scale. Use your workspace to make the following settings:

1. Use **Save As...** to save the drawing with the name **CH2-P5**.

2. Set drawing units: **Architectural**

3. Set drawing limits: **8-1/2,11**

4. Set **GRIDDISPLAY**: **0**

5. Set grid: **1/4″**

6. Set snap: **1/16″**

7. Create the layers on your own.

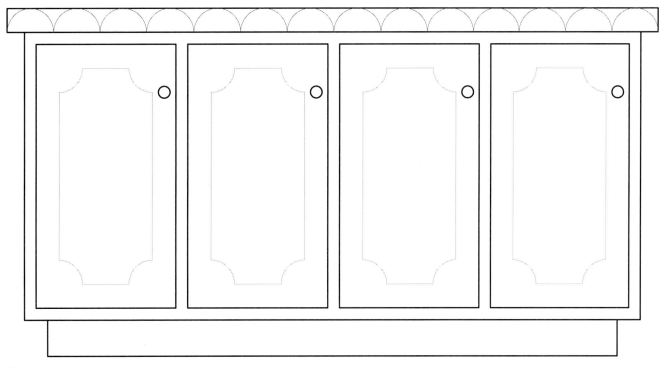

Figure 2-62
Project 2-5: Drawing Shapes III (scale: 1″ = 1)

3 chapter three

Drawing with AutoCAD: Conference and Lecture Rooms

CHAPTER OBJECTIVES

- Correctly use the following commands and settings:

BREAK	FILLET
CHAMFER	From
COPY	Grips
Distance	HATCH
DIVIDE	ID Point
Drawing Template	MEASURE
EXPLODE	MIRROR

OFFSET	Polyline Edit
OSNAP	Rectangle
POINT	RECTANGULAR ARRAY
POLAR ARRAY	ROTATE
POLYGON	Tracking
Polyline	TRIM

- Draw using polar tracking.
- Use Point Style to set the appearance of points.

EXERCISE 3-1

Drawing a Rectangular Conference Room, Including Furniture

A conference room, including walls and furnishings, is drawn in Exercise 3-1. When you have completed Exercise 3-1, your drawing will look similar to Figure 3-1.

Step 1. Use your workspace to make the following settings:

1. Use **Save As...** to save the drawing with the name **CH3 EXERCISE1**.
2. Set drawing units: **Architectural**

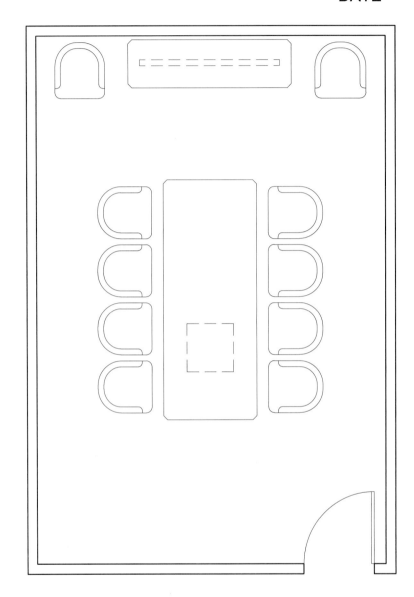

3. Set drawing limits: **25′,35′** (Don't forget the foot marks.)
4. Set **GRIDDISPLAY: 0**
5. Set grid: **12″**
6. Set snap: **6″**
7. Create the following layers:

Layer Name	Color	Linetype	Lineweight
a-anno-text	green	continuous	.006″ (.15 mm)
a-door	red	continuous	.004″ (.09 mm)
a-wall-intr	blue	continuous	.010″ (.25 mm)
i-eqpm-ovhd	red	hidden	.004″ (.09 mm)
i-furn	cyan	continuous	.004″ (.09 mm)

8. Set layer **a-wall-intr** current.
9. Use **Zoom-All** to view the limits of the drawing.
10. Turn **SNAP, GRID**, and **LWT** on. The remaining buttons in the status bar are off.

Drawing Template

drawing template: A drawing used to ensure consistency by providing standard styles and settings.

You will be able to use these settings for the remaining tutorials in this chapter. Making a ***drawing template*** of the settings will save you the time of setting up Exercises 3-2, 3-3, and 3-4.

Step 2. Save the drawing as a template on the drive and/or folder in which you want to save (Figures 3-2 and 3-3), as described next:

Prompt	Response
Type a command:	**Save As...**
The **Save Drawing As** dialog box appears:	Click the down arrow in the **Files of type:** input box and move the cursor to
	Click **AutoCAD Drawing Template (*.dwt)**
	Type **Ch3-conference-rm-setup** (in the **File name:** input box so the **Save Drawing As** dialog box appears as shown in Figure 3-2). Notice the text in the **Save in:** input box has changed to **Template.**
	Click the down arrow in the **Save in:** input box, and highlight the drive and folder in which you want to save
	Click **Save**
The **Template Options** dialog box appears (Figure 3-3):	Type **Setup for Ch3 conference rooms** (as shown in Figure 3-3)
	Click **OK**

Figure 3-2
Save the drawing as a
template

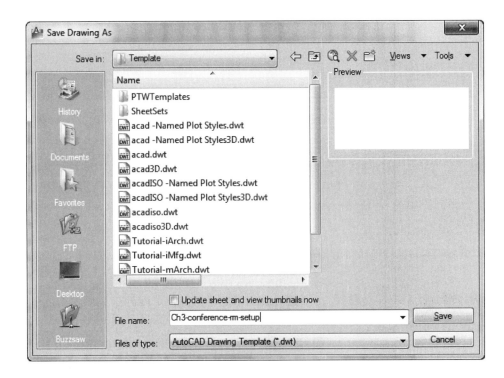

Figure 3-3
Template Options
dialog box

Step 3. The drawing remains as a template in the **Template** folder, so you must save it again as a drawing file. Save the drawing as a drawing file on the drive and/or folder in which you want to save, as described next:

Prompt	Response
Type a command:	**Save As...**
The **Save Drawing As** dialog box appears:	
	Click the down arrow in the **Files of type:** input box and move the cursor to
	Click **AutoCAD 2013 Drawing (*.dwg)**
	Click the down arrow in the **Save in:** input box, and highlight the drive and folder in which you want to save

Prompt	Response
	Click **CH3-EXERCISE1** (to appear in the **File name:** input box)
	Click **Save**
The **Save Drawing As** dialog box appears saying the drawing already exists. Do you want to replace it?	Click **Yes**

Polyline

polyline: A continuous line or arc composed of one or more segments, the width of which can be changed.

POLYLINE	
Ribbon/ Panel	Home/Draw
Draw Toolbar:	
Menu Bar:	Draw/Polyline
Type a Command:	PLINE
Command Alias:	PL

Begin by drawing the conference room walls using the **Polyline** command. A **polyline** is different from a regular line in that regardless of the number of segments that make up a polyline, AutoCAD treats a polyline drawn with one operation of the **Polyline** command as a single entity. This is especially helpful when you are drawing walls, because after you draw the outline of a single room or entire building, you can offset the entire polyline to show the thickness of the walls.

Step 4. Use **Polyline** to draw the inside lines of the conference room walls (Figure 3-4), as described next:

Prompt	Response
Type a command:	**Polyline** (or type **PL<Enter>**)
Specify start point:	Type **5′,5′ <Enter>**

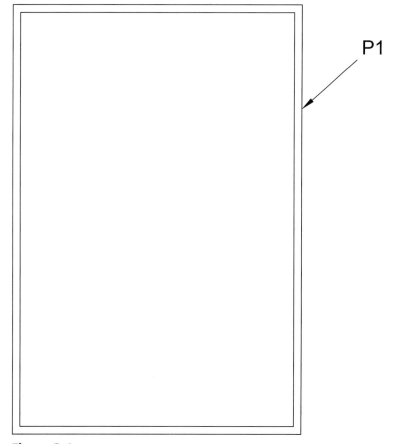

Figure 3-4
Draw the conference room walls

Prompt	Response
	(You have just entered absolute coordinates; the polyline starts 5′ to the right on the *X*-axis and 5′ up on the *Y*-axis.)
	Set **ORTHO** on (press **<F8>** or click **ORTHO**)
Current line-width is 0′-0″.	
Specify next point or [Arc Halfwidth Length Undo Width]:	Move your mouse to the right and type **15′ <Enter>** (direct distance entry)
Specify next point or [Arc Close Halfwidth Length Undo Width]:	Move your mouse up and type **22′ <Enter>**
Specify next point or [Arc Close Halfwidth Length Undo Width]:	Move your mouse to the left and type **15′<Enter>**
Specify next point or [Arc Close Halfwidth Length Undo Width]:	Type **C <Enter>**

Undo

The **Polyline Undo** option is similar to the **LINE** command. If you do not like the last polyline segment drawn, use the **Undo** option to erase it and continue with the *Specify next point or [Arc Close Halfwidth Length Undo Width]:* prompt.

You can enter any of the capitalized options in the **Polyline** prompt by typing the letters in either upper- or lowercase. The remaining options in the **Polyline** prompt will be described later in this chapter.

OFFSET

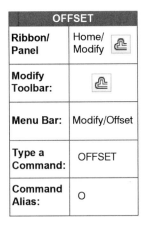

OFFSET	
Ribbon/ Panel	Home/ Modify
Modify Toolbar:	
Menu Bar:	Modify/Offset
Type a Command:	OFFSET
Command Alias:	O

Because the polyline is treated as a single entity, when you click one point on the polyline, you are able to offset the entire outline of the conference room at once. If the outline of the room had been drawn with the **LINE** command, using the **OFFSET** command would offset each line segment individually, and the corners would not meet.

Step 5. Use the **OFFSET** command to draw the outside line (showing depth) of the conference room walls (Figure 3-4), as described next:

Prompt	Response
Type a command:	**Offset** (or type **O <Enter>**)
Specify offset distance or [Through Erase Layer] <Through>:	Type **5 <Enter>**
Select object to offset or [Exit Undo] <Exit>:	Click anyplace on the polyline
Specify point on side to offset or [Exit Multiple Undo] <Exit>:	**P1→** (outside the rectangle, Figure 3-4)
Select object to offset or [Exit Undo] <Exit>:	**<Enter>**

There are four options in the **Offset** prompt: **offset distance, Through, Erase,** and **Layer.** To complete the conference room wall, 5″ was set as the offset distance. To use any of the other options, type and enter the capital letter shown for the option in the command line or press **<Enter>** to start the **<Through>** default option.

Through

When the **Through** option is started and the object to be offset has been selected, AutoCAD prompts: *Specify through point or [Exit Multiple Undo] <Exit>:*. You respond by clicking a point on the drawing through which you want the object to be offset.

Erase

When the **Erase** option is started, AutoCAD prompts: *Erase source object after offsetting? [Yes No] <No>:*. You can then respond with **Yes** or **No,** and AutoCAD continues by asking you to specify the offset distance, object to offset, and point on side to offset.

Layer

When the **Layer** option is started, AutoCAD prompts: *Enter layer option for offset objects [Current Source] <Source>:*. You can then respond with the selection of current or source layer, and AutoCAD continues by asking you to specify the offset distance, object to offset, and point on side to offset.

EXPLODE

Because the polyline is treated as a single entity, it must be "exploded" before individual line segments can be edited. The **EXPLODE** command splits the solid polyline into separate line segments. After the polyline is exploded into separate line segments, you will be able to add the conference room door.

Step 6. Use the **EXPLODE** command to split the two polylines that make the conference room walls, as described next:

Prompt	Response
Type a command:	**Explode** (or type **X <Enter>**)
Select objects:	Click anyplace on the outside polyline
Select objects:	Click anyplace on the inside polyline
Select objects:	**<Enter>**

After you use the **EXPLODE** command, the walls do not look different, but each line segment is now a separate entity.

ID Point

A very useful command, **ID Point** (located under **Utilities** panel of the **Home** tab on the ribbon) allows you to locate a point on a drawing and have the position of the point displayed in coordinates. AutoCAD remembers the coordinate location of the point. A command, such as **LINE,** can be initiated *immediately* after the **ID Point** command has located a point on the drawing. You can enter the start point of the **LINE** command by using relative or polar coordinates, or you may also use direct distance entry to specify a distance from the established ID point location. Alternatively, you can use the **From** option of the **Osnap** menu (shown later in Figure 3-16 and used in Step 39) to define a reference point and then define the x and y-offset from that point. This will be explained further in the upcoming steps. Let's continue with the exercise using ID Point.

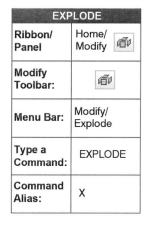

EXPLODE	
Ribbon/ Panel	Home/ Modify
Modify Toolbar:	
Menu Bar:	Modify/ Explode
Type a Command:	EXPLODE
Command Alias:	X

ID POINT	
Ribbon/ Panel	Home/ Utilities
Inquiry Toolbar:	
Menu Bar:	Tools/ Inquiry/ ID Point
Type a Command:	ID

Step 7. Use **Zoom-Window** to magnify the lower right corner of the conference room where the door will be located.

Step 8. Use **ID Point** to locate a point on the drawing. Use **LINE** to draw the right side of the door opening (Figure 3-5), as described next:

Prompt	Response
Type a command:	**ID Point** (or type **ID <Enter>**)
Specify point:	**P1→** (with **SNAP** on, snap to the inside lower right corner of the conference room, Figure 3-5)
Point: X = 20'-0" Y = 5'-0" Z = 0'-0"	
Type a command:	Type **L <Enter>**
Specify first point:	Type **@6<180 <Enter>** (you have just entered polar coordinates; move your mouse so you can see where the line is attached)
Specify next point or [Undo]:	Type **@5<–90 <Enter>** (using polar coordinates; the line 5") is extended downward
Specify next point or [Undo]:	**<Enter>**

Figure 3-5
Draw the door opening

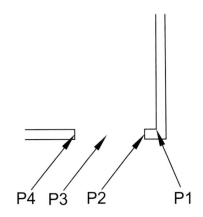

P4 P3 P2 P1

TIP

Instead of typing **@5<–90 <Enter>**, type **PER <Enter>** and draw the line down until it intersects at a 90° angle with the outside line of the wall. This is an **Object Snap** mode **(Perpendicular)**, which is described more fully later in this exercise.

Step 9. Offset the line 3' to the left to form the door opening, as described next:

Prompt	Response
Type a command:	**Offset** (or type **O <Enter>**)
Specify offset distance or [Through Erase Layer] <0'-5">:	Type **3' <Enter>**
Select object to offset or [Exit Undo]<Exit>:	**P2→** (the 5" line you just drew; Figure 3-5)
Specify point on side to offset or [Exit Multiple Undo]<Exit>:	**P3→** (pick to the left)
Select object to offset or [Exit Undo]<Exit>:	**<Enter>**

TRIM

TRIM	
Ribbon/ Panel	Home/ Modify -/---
Modify Toolbar:	-/---
Menu Bar:	Modify/ Trim
Type a Command:	TRIM
Command Alias:	TR

Watch the **Trim** prompts carefully. You cannot pick the objects to trim until all cutting edges (the edge to which the object is trimmed) have been selected and the **<Enter>** key has been pressed, so that the prompt *Select object to trim or shift-select to extend or [Fence Crossing Project Edge eRase Undo]:* appears. If you are unable to trim an object because it does not intersect a cutting edge, and you have selected **all** as the cutting edges, hold the **<Shift>** key down and click on the entity to extend while still in the **TRIM** command.

> **NOTE**
>
> Press <Enter> at the **Trim** prompt *Select objects or <select all>:* to select all objects as cutting edges.

Step 10. Use the **TRIM** command to trim the horizontal wall lines between the two 5″ vertical lines that represent the door opening (Figure 3-5), as described next:

Prompt	Response
Type a command:	**Trim** (or type **TR <Enter>**)
Current settings: Projection = UCS Edge = None	
Select cutting edges	
Select objects or <select all>:	**P2→** (the 5″ vertical line; Figure 3-5)
Select objects: 1 found	
Select objects:	**P4→** (the second 5″ vertical line)
Select objects: 1 found, 2 total	
Select objects:	**<Enter>**
Select object to trim or shift-select to extend or [Fence Crossing Project Edge eRase Undo]:	Click the two horizontal wall lines between **P2→** and **P4→** (Figure 3-5) **<Enter>** (to complete the command)

Step 11. Set layer **a-door** current.

Rectangle

RECTANGLE	
Ribbon/ Panel	Home/Draw
Draw Toolbar:	
Menu Bar:	Draw/ Rectangle
Type a Command:	RECTANGLE
Command Alias:	REC

Step 12. Draw a 1-1/2″-long by 3′-wide rectangle to represent the door (Figure 3-6):

Prompt	Response
Type a command:	**Rectangle** (or type **REC <Enter>**)
Specify first corner point or [Chamfer Elevation Fillet Thickness Width]:	**P1→** (be sure **SNAP** is on); snap to the upper right corner of the door opening to begin the rectangle
Specify other corner point or [Area Dimensions Rotation]:	Type **D <Enter>**
Specify length for rectangle <0′-1 1/2″>:	Type **1-1/2 <Enter>**

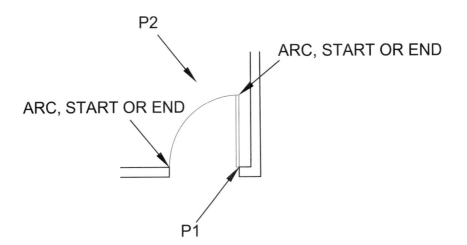

Figure 3-6
Draw the door using
Rectangle and **Arc-Start,
End, Direction** commands

P2

ARC, START OR END

ARC, START OR END

P1

Prompt	Response
Specify width for rectangle <3'-0">:	Type **3'<Enter>**
Specify other corner point or [Area Dimensions Rotation]:	**P2→** (pick any point to the left of the door symbol so the rectangle appears as shown in Figure 3-6)

Step 13. Use the **Arc-Start, End, Direction** method to draw the door swing arc. Be sure **SNAP** and **ORTHO** are on. The arc can be drawn clockwise or counterclockwise. Move your mouse so the direction of the arc appears as shown in Figure 3-6.

TIP

The default setting for the **Rectangle** command when the **Dimension** option is selected is:

Default Rotation setting of 0:
Length is the X direction value
Width is the Y direction value.

When the Rotation setting is changed to 90:
Length is the Y direction value
Width is the X direction value.

When the rectangle is visible and the prompt *Specify other corner point:* appears, you change the position of the rectangle by moving your mouse right or left, up or down.

Step 14. Set layer **i-furn** current. Use **Zoom-Extents.**

Step 15. Use the **Polyline** command to draw a credenza (84″ long by 24″ deep) centered on the 15′ rear wall of the conference room, 2″ away from the wall. Locate an ID point by snapping to the inside upper left corner of the conference room. Start the polyline **@48,–2** (relative coordinates) away from the point. Finish drawing the credenza by using direct distance entry. You can use feet or inches. Remember, AutoCAD defaults to inches in architectural units, so use the foot (′) symbol if you are using feet. Be sure to draw the credenza using one operation of **Polyline** so it is one continuous polyline. Use the **Close** option for the last segment of the polyline (Figure 3-7).

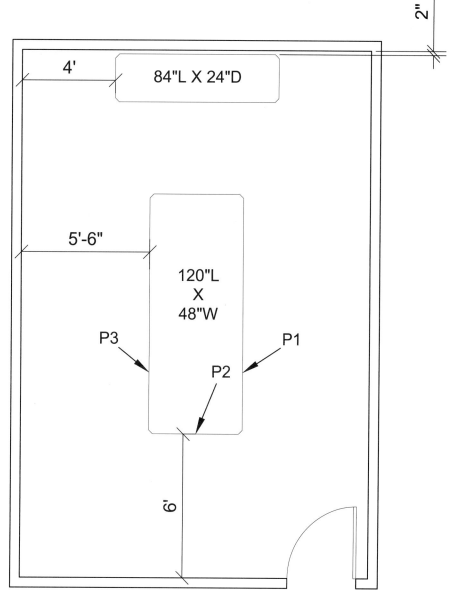

Figure 3-7
Draw a credenza and a conference table; chamfer the corners

Step 16. Draw a conference table 120″ long by 48″ wide using the **LINE** command. You can determine the location of the first point by using **ID Point** or by using grid and snap increments. Use direct distance entry to complete the table. Refer to Figure 3-7 for the location of the table in the room.

Step 17. Zoom in on the table.

CHAMFER

A **chamfer** is an angle (usually 45°) formed at a corner. The following steps will use the **CHAMFER** command to make the beveled corners of the conference table and credenza.

Step 18. Use the **CHAMFER** command to bevel the corners of the table (Figure 3-7), as described next:

CHAMFER	
Ribbon/ Panel	Home/ Modify
Modify Toolbar:	
Menu Bar:	Modify/ Chamfer
Type a Command:	CHAMFER
Command Alias:	CHA

Prompt	Response
Type a command:	**Chamfer** (or type **CHA <Enter>**)
(TRIM mode) Current chamfer Dist1 = 0'-0" Dist2 = 0'-0"	
Select first line or [Undo Polyline Distance Angle Trim mEthod Multiple]:	Type **D <Enter>**
Specify first chamfer distance <0'-0">:	Type **2 <Enter>**
Specify second chamfer distance <0'-2">:	**<Enter>**
Select first line or [Undo Polyline Distance Angle Trim mEthod Multiple]:	**P1→** (Figure 3-7)
Select second line or shift-select to apply corner or [Distance Angle mEthod]:	**P2→**
Type a command:	**<Enter>** (repeat **CHAMFER**)
(TRIM mode) Current chamfer Dist1 = 0'-2", Dist2 = 0'-2"	
Select first line or [Undo Polyline Distance Angle Trim mEthod Multiple]:	**P2→**
Select second line or shift-select to apply corner:	**P3→**

> **NOTE**
>
> Type **M <Enter>** (for **Multiple**) at the **Chamfer** prompt so you do not have to repeat the **CHAMFER** command.

Step 19. Chamfer the other corners of the table (Figure 3-7).

Step 20. Zoom in on the credenza.

Polyline

Because the credenza was drawn using one operation of the **Polyline** command, and the **Close** option was used to complete the credenza rectangle, it is treated as a single entity. The **CHAMFER** command **Polyline** option chamfers all corners of a continuous polyline with one click.

Undo

Allows you to undo the previous chamfer.

Angle

This option of the **CHAMFER** command allows you to specify an angle and a distance to create a chamfer.

Trim

This option of both the **CHAMFER** and **FILLET** commands allows you to specify that the part of the original line removed by the chamfer or fillet remains as it was. To do this, type **T <Enter>** at the **Chamfer** prompt and **N <Enter>** at the *Trim/No trim <Trim>:* prompt. Test this option on a corner of the drawing so you know how it works. Be sure to return it to the **Trim** option.

mEthod

The **mEthod** option of the **CHAMFER** command allows you to specify whether you want to use the **Distance** or the **Angle** method to specify how the chamfer is to be drawn. The default is the **Distance** method.

Multiple

Allows you to chamfer multiple corners without repeating the **CHAMFER** command.

Step 21. Use chamfer distance 2″ to chamfer the corners of the credenza (Figure 3-7), as described next:

Prompt	Response
Type a command:	**Chamfer**
(TRIM mode) Current chamfer Dist1 = 0′-2″, Dist2 = 0′-2″	
Select first line or [Undo Polyline Distance Angle Trim mEthod Multiple]:	Type **P <Enter>** (accept 2″ distances as previously set)
Select 2D polyline or [Distance Angle mEthod]:	Click anyplace on the credenza
4 lines were chamfered	

TIP

If the last corner of the credenza does not chamfer, this is because the **Close** option of the **Polyline** command was not used to complete the polyline rectangle. Explode the credenza and use the **CHAMFER** command to complete the chamfered corner.

NOTE

While in the **CHAMFER** command hold down the **<Shift>** key to select any two lines that do not meet, and you can make 90° corners of those two lines. This is the same as a 0 chamfer distance but will work regardless of the chamfer distance set.

When setting the chamfer distance you can set a different distance for the first and second chamfers. The first distance applies to the first line clicked, and the second distance applies to the second line clicked. You can also set the distance by clicking two points on the drawing.

You can set a chamfer distance of zero and use it to remove the chamfered corners from the table. Using a distance of zero will make 90° corners on the table. Then you can erase the old chamfer lines. This will change the table but not the credenza because it does not work with a polyline. If you have two lines that do not meet to form an exact corner or that overlap, use the **CHAMFER** command with 0 distance to form an exact corner. The **CHAMFER** command will chamfer two lines that do not intersect. It automatically extends the two lines until they intersect, trims the two lines according to the distance entered, and connects the two trimmed ends with the chamfer line.

Step 22. Zoom in on a portion of the grid outside the conference room walls.

Step 23. Draw a rectangle 26″ wide by 28″ deep using the **LINE** command (Figure 3-8). Be sure to have **SNAP** on when you draw the rectangle. Next, you will edit this rectangle using the **FILLET** command to create the shape of a chair.

Figure 3-8
Draw a rectangle 26″ wide × 28″ deep using the **LINE** command

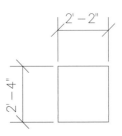

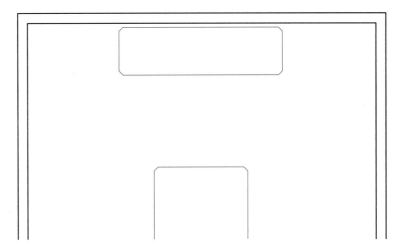

FILLET

The **FILLET** command is similar to **CHAMFER**, except the **FILLET** command creates a round instead of an angle.

Step 24. Use the **FILLET** command to edit the back of the rectangle to create the symbol of a chair (Figure 3-9), as described next:

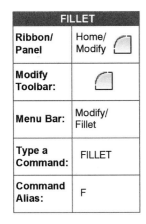

FILLET	
Ribbon/ Panel	Home/ Modify
Modify Toolbar:	
Menu Bar:	Modify/ Fillet
Type a Command:	FILLET
Command Alias:	F

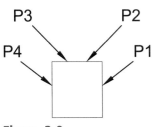

Figure 3-9
Use **FILLET** to create the chair symbol

Prompt	Response
Type a command:	**Fillet** (or type **F <Enter>**)
Current settings: Mode = TRIM, Radius = 0′-0″	
Select first object or [Undo Polyline Radius Trim Multiple]:	Type **R <Enter>**
Specify fillet radius <0′-0″>:	Type **12 <Enter>**
Select first object or [Undo Polyline Radius Trim Multiple]:	Type **T <Enter>**
Enter Trim mode option [Trim No trim]<Trim>:	Type **T<Enter>** (verify **Trim** option)

Prompt	Response
Select first object or [Undo Polyline Radius Trim Multiple]:	**P1→** (Figure 3-9)
Select second object or shift-select to apply corner or [Radius]:	**P2→**
Type a command:	**<Enter>** (repeat **Fillet**)
Current settings: Mode = TRIM, Radius = 1'-0"	
Select first object or [Undo Polyline Radius Trim Multiple]:	**P3→**
Select second object or shift-select to apply corner or [Radius]:	**P4→**

The **Polyline** option of **Fillet** automatically fillets an entire continuous polyline with one click. Remember to set the fillet radius first.

Fillet will also fillet two circles, two arcs, a line and a circle, a line and an arc, or a circle and an arc.

Step 25. Use the commands **OFFSET, TRIM,** and **FILLET** to complete the shape of the chair as shown in Figure 3-10.

COPY and Osnap-Midpoint

The **COPY** command allows you to copy any part of a drawing either once or multiple times. Object snap modes (***Osnap***), when combined with other commands, help you to draw very accurately. As you become more familiar with the object snap modes, you will use them constantly to draw with extreme accuracy. The following introduces the **Osnap-Midpoint** mode, which helps you snap to the midpoint of a line or arc.

> **NOTE**
>
> Save your drawing often so you do not lose your work.

Step 26. Use the **COPY** command, combined with **Osnap-Midpoint**, to copy the chair you have just drawn (Figure 3-11), as described next:

Prompt	Response
Type a command:	**Copy** (or type **CP <Enter>**)
Select objects:	Click the first corner of a window that will include the chair
Specify opposite corner:	Click the other corner of the window to include the chair
Select objects:	**<Enter>**
Specify base point or [Displacement mOde] <Displacement>:	Type **MID <Enter>**
Mid of	**P1→** (Figure 3-11) (Turn **SNAP** off as needed)
Specify second point or [Array] <use first point as displacement>:	**P2→** (be sure **SNAP** is on, and leave enough room to rotate the chair, Figure 3-12)
Specify second point or [Array Exit Undo]<Exit>:	**<Enter>**

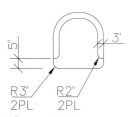

Figure 3-10
Use **OFFSET, TRIM,** and **FILLET** commands to complete the shape of the chair

Osnap: An abbreviation of *object snap*, which specifies a snap point at an exact location on an object.

COPY	
Ribbon/ Panel	Home/ Modify
Modify Toolbar:	
Menu Bar:	Modify/Copy
Type a Command:	COPY
Command Alias:	CO or CP

Figure 3-11
Copy the chair using **Osnap-Midpoint**

Figure 3-12
The rotated chair

The **Osnap-Midpoint** mode helped you snap very accurately to the midpoint of the line; you used the midpoint of the line that defines the front of the chair as the base point. When using the **COPY** command, carefully choose the base point so that it helps you easily locate the copies.

ROTATE

ROTATE	
Ribbon/ Panel	Home/ Modify
Modify Toolbar:	
Menu Bar:	Modify/ Rotate
Type a Command:	ROTATE
Command Alias:	RO

The **ROTATE** command rotates a selected drawing entity in the counter-clockwise direction; 90° is to the left, and 270° (or −90°) is to the right. You select a base point of the entity to be rotated, and the entity rotates about that base point.

> **TIP**
>
> The AutoCAD system variable **ANGDIR** sets the direction of positive angles. If the variable is set to 1, the direction is clockwise and is the same as adding a check mark in the **Clockwise** box on the **Drawing Units** dialog box. When **ANGDIR** is set to 0, the direction is counterclockwise, and the **Clockwise** box of the **Drawing Units** dialog box does not have a check in it.

Step 27. Use the **ROTATE** command to rotate CHAIR 2 (Figure 3-12), as described next:

Prompt	Response
Type a command:	**Rotate** (or type **RO <Enter>**)
Current positive angle in UCS: ANGDIR=counterclockwise ANGBASE=0	
Select objects:	Start the window to include CHAIR 2
Specify opposite corner:	Complete the window to include CHAIR 2
Select objects:	**<Enter>**
Specify base point:	Type **MID <Enter>**
Mid of	**P1→** (Figure 3-12)
Specify rotation angle or [Copy Reference]:	Type **90 <Enter>**

> **NOTE**
>
> If part of the entity that is to be rotated lies on the specified base point, that part of the entity remains on the base point while the entity's orientation is changed.

Reference

The **Reference** option of the **Rotate** prompt is sometimes easier to use, especially if you do not know the rotation angle. It allows you to select the object to be rotated and click the base point. Type **R <Enter>** for **Reference.** Then you can enter the *Reference angle:* (current angle) of the object by typing it and pressing **<Enter>**. If you don't know the current angle, you can show AutoCAD the *Reference angle:* by picking the two endpoints of the line to be rotated. You can specify the *New angle:* by typing it and pressing **<Enter>**. If you don't know the new angle, you can show AutoCAD the *New angle:* by picking a point on the drawing.

POINT

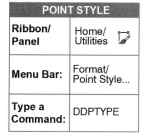

POINT	
Ribbon/ Panel	Home/Draw
Draw Toolbar:	
Menu Bar:	Draw/Point
Type a Command:	POINT
Command Alias:	PO

The **POINT** command allows you to draw points on your drawing. **Object Snap** recognizes these points as nodes. The **Osnap** mode **Node** is used to snap to points.

There are many different types of points to choose from. The appearance of these points is determined by the **PDMODE** (point definition mode) and **PDSIZE** (point definition size) options within the **POINT** command.

Step 28. Use the **Point Style...** command to set the appearance of points, as described next:

POINT STYLE	
Ribbon/ Panel	Home/ Utilities
Menu Bar:	Format/ Point Style...
Type a Command:	DDPTYPE

Prompt

Type a command:

The **Point Style** dialog box appears (Figure 3-13):

Response

Point Style... (or type **DDPTYPE <Enter>**)

Click the **X** box
Click **Set Size in Absolute Units**
Type **6″** in the **Point Size:** input box
Click **OK**

Figure 3-13
Point Style dialog box

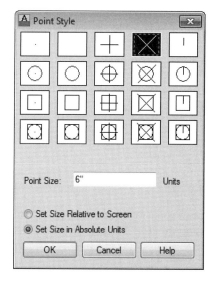

You have just set the points to appear as an X, and they will be 6″ high. The **Point Style** dialog box shows the different types of points available. The size of the point may be set in a size relative to the screen or in absolute units.

Step 29. Use the **OFFSET** command to offset the line that defines the long left side of the conference table. The chairs will be placed 6″ from the edge of the table, so set 6″ as the offset distance. Offset the line outside the table, as shown in Figure 3-14. This line will be used as a construction line to help locate the chairs.

DIVIDE

DIVIDE	
Ribbon/ Panel	Home/ Draw 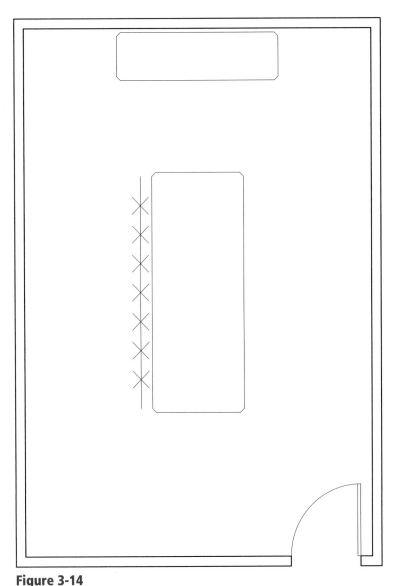
Menu Bar:	Draw/Point/ Divide
Type a Command:	DIVIDE
Command Alias:	DIV

The **DIVIDE** command divides an entity into equal parts and places point markers along the entity at the dividing points. The **PDMODE** variable has been set to 3 (an X point), so an X will appear as the point marker when you use **DIVIDE.**

Step 30. Use **DIVIDE** to divide the offset line into eight equal segments (Figure 3-14), as described next:

Prompt	**Response**
Type a command:	**Divide** (or type **DIV <Enter>**)
Select object to divide:	Click anyplace on the offset line
Enter the number of segments or [Block]:	Type **8 <Enter>** (the X points divide the line into eight equal segments)

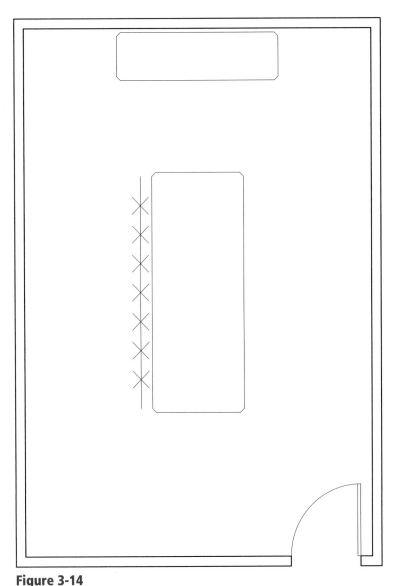

Figure 3-14
Offset the lines defining the long left side of the conference table; divide the line into eight equal segments

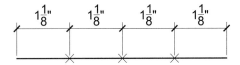

DIVIDE: Four equal parts of a 4-1/2" line

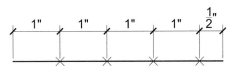

MEASURE: 1" lengths of a 4-1/2" line

Figure 3-15
Examples of the **DIVIDE** and **MEASURE** commands

MEASURE	
Ribbon/ Panel	Home/ Draw 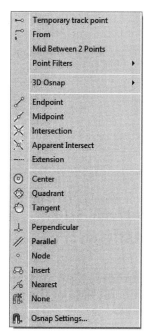
Menu Bar:	Draw/Point/ Measure
Type a Command:	MEASURE
Command Alias:	MEA

MEASURE

The **MEASURE** command is similar to the **DIVIDE** command (Figure 3-15) except that with **MEASURE** you specify the distance. **DIVIDE** calculates the interval to divide an entity into a specified number of equal segments. The **MEASURE** command places point markers at a specified distance along an entity.

The measurement and division of a circle start at the angle from the center that follows the current snap rotation. The measurement and division of a closed polyline start at the first vertex drawn. The **MEASURE** command also draws a specified block at each mark between the divided segments.

OSNAP

It is important that you become familiar with and use object snap modes in combination with **DRAW, MODIFY,** and other AutoCAD commands. When an existing drawing object is not located on a snap point, it is impossible to connect a line or other drawing entity exactly to it. You may try, and you may think that the two points are connected, but a close examination **(Zoom-Window)** will reveal that they are not. Object snap modes are used in combination with other commands to connect exactly to points of existing objects in a drawing. You need to use object snap modes constantly for complete accuracy.

Activating Osnap

An **Osnap** mode can be activated in the following ways:

1 Type the **Osnap** abbreviation (first three letters of the object snap mode).

2 Press **<Shift>** and right-click in the drawing area, then choose an object snap mode from the **Object Snap** menu that appears (Figure 3-16).

3 Right-click **OSNAP** on the status bar, then click **Settings...** (Figure 3-17) to access the **Drafting Settings** dialog box (Figure 3-18). Click a check mark beside the desired **Osnap** mode or modes.

Figure 3-16
Activate the **Osnap** menu by pressing **<Shift>** and right-click in the drawing area

Figure 3-17
Activate **OSNAP** by right-clicking **OSNAP** on the status bar, then clicking **Settings...** to access the **Drafting Settings** dialog box

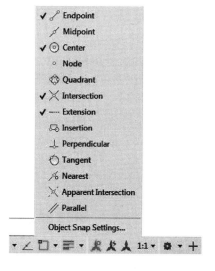

Figure 3-18
Drafting Settings dialog box
with only **Node** selected

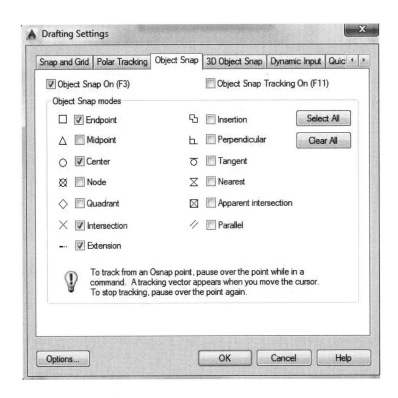

Copy, Osnap-Midpoint, Osnap-Node

Step 31. Right-click **OSNAP** on the status bar, then click **Settings...**, and set a running **Osnap** mode of **Node** (Figures 3-17 and 3-18).

Step 32. Make sure **ORTHO** and **SNAP** are off and **OSNAP** is on in the status bar.

Step 33. Use the **COPY** command (combined with **Osnap-Midpoint** and **Osnap-Node**) to copy CHAIR 2 four times on the left side of the conference table (Figure 3-19), as described next:

Prompt	Response
Type a command:	**Copy** (or type **CP <Enter>**)
Select objects:	Click below and to the left of CHAIR 2
Specify opposite corner:	Window CHAIR 2
Select objects:	**<Enter>**
Specify base point or [Displacement mOde] <Displacement>:	Type **MID <Enter>**
_mid of	**P1→** (anyplace on the straight line that forms the front of the chair symbol)
Specify second point or [Array] <use first point as displacement>:	**P2→, P3→, P4→, P5→ <Enter>** (Figure 3-19)

The points act as nodes (snapping exactly on the center of the X) when a running **Object Snap** is set.

Step 34. Type **PDMODE <Enter>** at the command prompt. Set the **PDMODE** to 1, and the drawing is regenerated. The Xs will disappear. You have set the **PDMODE** (point definition mode) to be invisible.

Step 35. Erase the offset line used to locate the chairs on the left side of the table. Use **<F7>** to redraw when it looks as if part of the chairs has been erased.

Figure 3-19
Copy CHAIR 2 four times
on the left side of the
conference table using
Osnap-Midpoint and
Osnap-Node

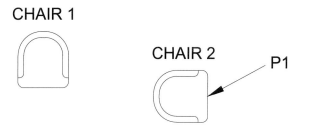

CHAIR 1

CHAIR 2

P1

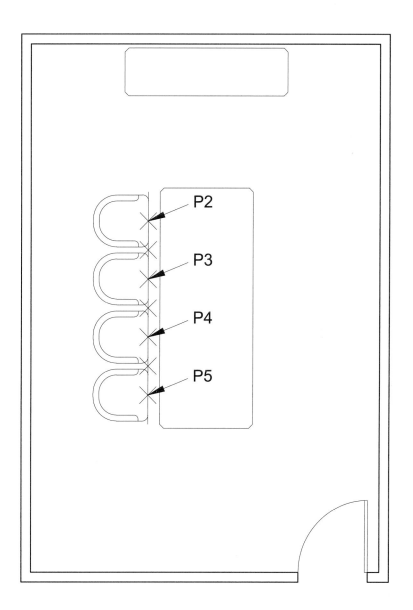

MIRROR	
Ribbon/ Panel	Home/ Modify
Modify Toolbar:	
Menu Bar:	Modify/Mirror
Type a Command:	MIRROR
Command Alias:	MI

MIRROR

The **MIRROR** command allows you to mirror about an axis any entity or group of entities. The axis can be at any angle.

Step 36. Draw the chairs on the right side of conference table using the **MIRROR** command (Figure 3-20), as described next:

Prompt	**Response**
Type a command:	**MIRROR** (or type **MI <Enter>**)
Select objects:	**P1→**

Figure 3-20
Use the **MIRROR** command to copy the four chairs on the left side to the right side, and copy CHAIR 1 to both sides of the credenza

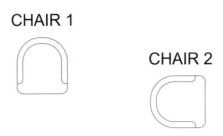

CHAIR 1

CHAIR 2

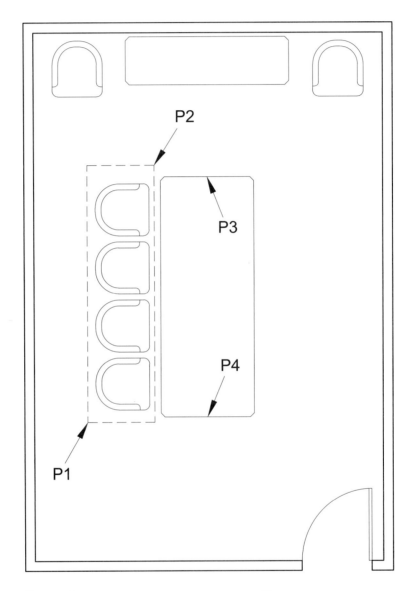

Prompt	Response
Specify opposite corner:	**P2→** (window the chairs on the left side of the conference table)
68 found	
Select objects:	**<Enter>**
Specify first point of mirror line:	Type **MID <Enter>**
mid of	**P3→**
Specify second point of mirror line:	Type **MID <Enter>**
mid of	**P4→**
Erase source objects? [Yes No] <N>:	**<Enter>**

Step 37. Add the chairs on each side of the credenza as shown in Figure 3-20.

Step 38. Set layer **i-eqpm-ovhd** current.

Step 39. Add the 72″ × 3″ recessed projection screen and the 24″ × 24″ ceiling-mounted projector to the plan as shown in Figure 3-21. Let's use the **From** option of the **OSNAP** menu to do this.

Start the **Rectangle** command, use **<Shift>** and right-click to open the **OSNAP** menu, select **From**, and then show the inner upper left corner of the room as the reference point. You will be prompted to define the x and y-offsets: 4′6″ and −1′, respectively. 72″ and 3″. This fixes one corner of the rectangle for the recessed projection screen. The second corner is fixed by typing in @72, −3

Figure 3-21
Add the projection screen and projector

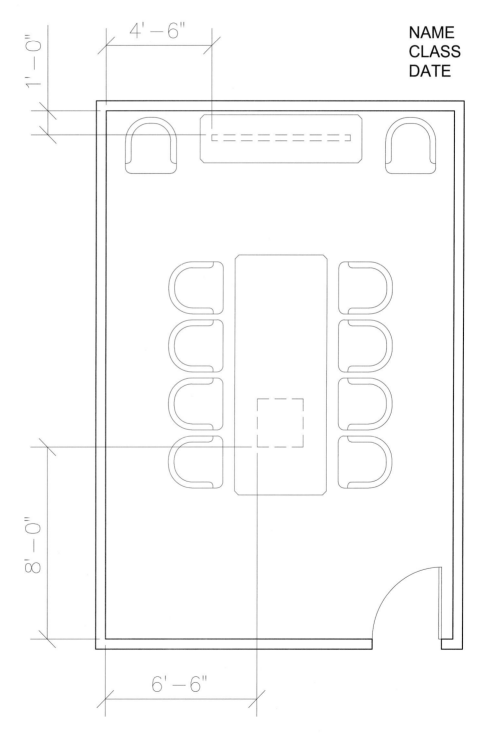

NAME
CLASS
DATE

and pressing **<Enter>**. As for the ceiling-mounted projector, use the inner lower left corner of the room as the reference, 6′6″ and 8′0″ as the x and y-offsets to fix the lower left corner of the rectangle, and @24, 24 to fix the second point of the rectangle.

Step 40. Erase the chairs you have drawn outside the conference room walls.

Step 41. Set layer **a-anno-text** current.

> **TIP**
>
> Remember to change the **LTSCALE** setting if your hidden linetype does not show as hidden. To make the line segment length or spacing smaller, enter a linetype scale factor smaller than 1 but larger than 0 at the **LTSCALE** prompt. To make the line segment length and spacing larger, enter a linetype scale factor larger than 1.

Step 42. Use the **Single Line Text** command (type **DT <Enter>**) to type your name, class number, and date, 6″ high in the upper right corner. When plotted to a scale of 1/4″ = 1′-0″, the 6″-high text will be 1/8″ high.

FOR MORE DETAILS

Annotative text is described and used in Chapter 6. When adding annotative text, you have to enter only the size of the text you want in the printed drawing, and AutoCAD automatically calculates the size of the text on the drawing.

Step 43. When you have completed Exercise 3-1 (Figure 3-22), save your work in at least two places.

Step 44. Print your drawing from the **Model** tab at a scale of **1/4″ = 1′-0″**.

FOR MORE DETAILS

In Chapter 5 you will use a color-dependent plot style to change layer colors 1 through 7 to the color black when printing and plotting.

Osnap Modes That Snap to Specific Drawing Features

You have already used **Osnap-Midpoint** and **Node.** They are examples of **Osnap** modes that snap to drawing features. **Midpoint** snaps to the midpoint of a line or arc, and **Node** snaps to a point entity.

The following list describes other **Osnap** modes that snap to specific drawing features. AutoCAD **Osnap** modes treat each edge of a solid and each polyline segment as a line. You will use many of these **Osnap** modes while completing the exercises in this book.

Mid Between 2 Points (M2P): Snaps to a point midway between two points that you pick on the drawing.

Endpoint (END): Snaps to the endpoint of a line or arc. The end of the line or arc nearest the point picked is snapped to.

Midpoint (MID): Snaps to the midpoint of a line or arc.

Figure 3-22
Exercise 3-1 complete

Chapter 3

NAME
CLASS
DATE

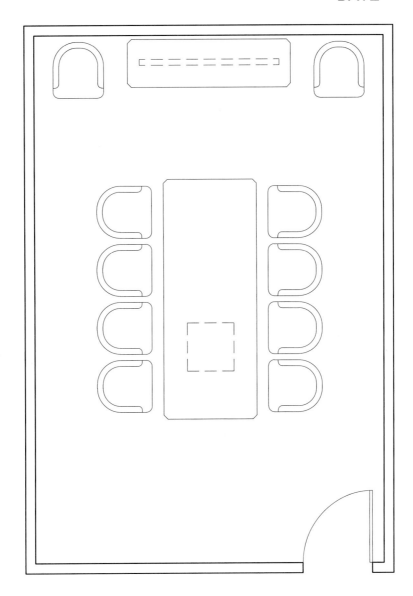

Center (CEN): Snaps to the center of an arc or circle.

Node (NOD): Snaps to a point (**POINT** command).

Quadrant (QUA): Snaps to the closest quadrant point of an arc or circle. These are the 0°, 90°, 180°, and 270° points on a circle, arc, or ellipse.

Intersection (INT): Snaps to the intersection of two lines, a line with an arc or circle, or two circles and/or arcs.

Extension (EXT): Extends a line or arc. With a command and the **Extension** mode active, pause over a line or arc, and after a small plus sign is displayed, slowly move along a temporary path that follows the extension of the line or arc. You can draw objects to and from points on the extension path line.

Insertion (INS): Snaps to the insertion point of text, attribute, or block. (These objects are described in later chapters.)

Perpendicular (PER): Snaps to the point on a line, circle, or arc that forms a 90° angle from that object to the last point. For example, if you are drawing a line, click the first point of the line, then use **Perpendicular** to connect the line to another line. The new line will be perpendicular to the first pick.

Tangent (TAN): Snaps to the point on a circle or arc that when connected to the last point entered forms a line tangent to (touching at one point) the circle or arc.

Nearest (NEA): Snaps to the point on a line, arc, or circle that is closest to the position of the crosshairs; also snaps to any point (**POINT** command) node that is closest to the crosshairs. You will use this mode when you want to be sure to connect to a line, arc, circle, or point, and cannot use another **Osnap** mode.

Apparent intersect (APP): Snaps to what appears to be an intersection even though one object is above the other in 3D space.

Parallel (PAR): Draws a line parallel to another line. With the **LINE** command active, click the first point of the new line you want to draw. With the **Parallel** mode active, pause over the line you want to draw parallel to, until a small parallel line symbol is displayed. Move the cursor away from but parallel to the original line, and an alignment path is displayed for you to complete the new line.

For the **LINE** command, you can also use the **Tangent** and **Perpendicular** modes when picking the first point of the line. This allows you to draw a line tangent to, or perpendicular to, an existing object.

Running Osnap Modes

You can use individual **Osnap** modes while in another command, as you did with **Midpoint**. You can also set a running **Osnap** mode, as you did with **Node**. A running **Osnap** mode is constantly in effect while you are drawing, until it is disabled. This saves time by eliminating your constant return to the **Osnap** setting.

Clicking **OSNAP** on in the status bar (or pressing function key **<F3>**) will activate any running **Osnap** modes you have set, and clicking it off will disable any running **Osnap** modes you have set.

> **NOTE**
>
> Be sure to disable a running **Osnap** mode when you are through using it. A running **Osnap** mode can interfere with your drawing if it snaps to a point to which you do not intend to snap.

Osnap Settings: Marker, Aperture, Magnet, Tooltip

Note the markers (small symbols) beside each **Object Snap** mode in the **Drafting Settings** dialog box, **Object Snap** tab (Figure 3-18). The display of the markers is controlled under the **Drafting** tab of the **Options** dialog box (Figure 3-23). A check mark beside **Marker** will add the marker symbol to the crosshairs. The **AutoSnap Marker Size** slider bar near the bottom of the dialog box specifies the size of the marker.

Figure 3-23
Options dialog box,
Drafting tab

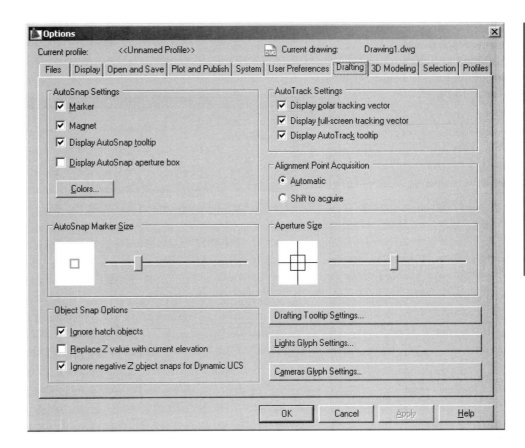

When **Osnap** is activated, a small target box called an *aperture* can also be added to the screen crosshairs. This small box shows the area within which AutoCAD will search for **Object Snap** candidates. The **Aperture Size** slider bar on the right side of the dialog box specifies the size of the box.

EXERCISE 3-2

Drawing a Rectangular Lecture Room, Including Furniture

A lecture room, including walls and furnishings, is drawn in Exercise 3-2. When you have completed Exercise 3-2, your drawing will look similar to Figure 3-24.

Step 1. Click **Open...**, change the **Files of type:** input box to **Drawing Template (*.dwt)**, and open template **Ch3-conference-rm-setup**, previously made at the beginning of Exercise 3-1.

Step 2. Click **Save As...**, change the **Files of type:** input box to **AutoCAD 2013 Drawing (.dwg)**, and save the template as a drawing file named **CH3-EXERCISE2**.

-or-

Step 3. Use your workspace to make the following settings:

1. Use **Save As...** to save the drawing with the name **CH3 EXERCISE2**.
2. Set drawing units: **Architectural**
3. Set drawing limits: **25',35'**
4. Set **GRIDDISPLAY: 0**

Figure 3-24

Exercise 3-2: Drawing a rectangular lecture room, including furniture (scale: 1/4″ = 1′-0″)

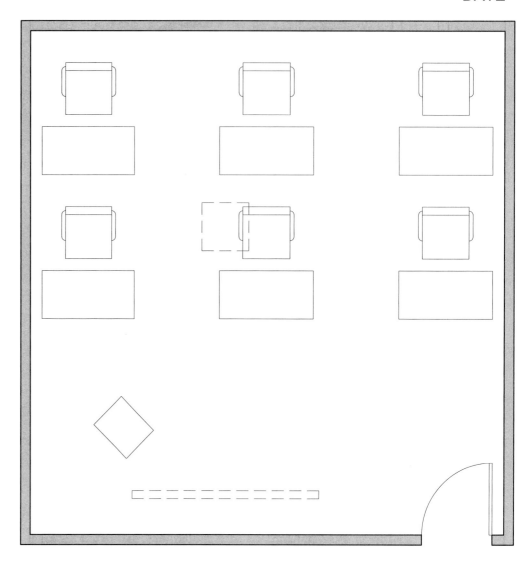

5. Set grid: **12″**
6. Set snap: **6″**
7. Create the following layers:

Layer Name	Color	Linetype	Lineweight
a-anno-text	green	continuous	.006″ (.15 mm)
a-door	red	continuous	.004″ (.09 mm)
a-wall-intr	blue	continuous	.010″ (.25 mm)
i-eqpm-ovhd	red	hidden	.004″ (.09 mm)
i-furn	cyan	continuous	.004″ (.09 mm)

Step 4. Set layer **a-wall-intr** current.

Step 5. Use **Zoom-All** to view the limits of the drawing.

Step 6. Turn **SNAP, GRID**, and **LWT** on. The remaining buttons in the status bar should be off.

Solid Walls Using Polyline and Solid Hatch

In Exercise 3-2 you will use the **LINE** command to draw the lecture room walls; then you will use the **Polyline Edit** command to change the lines to a polyline before you offset the walls. After you have completed drawing the walls, you will use the **HATCH** command to make the walls solid.

Step 7. Use **LINE** to draw the walls of the lecture room (Figure 3-25), as described next:

Prompt	Response
Type a command:	**Line** (or type **L <Enter>**)
Specify first point:	**Type 2′,7′ <Enter>**
Specify next point or [Undo]:	Turn **ORTHO** on
	Move your mouse to the right and type **20′4 <Enter>**
Specify next point or [Undo]:	Move your mouse straight up and type **21′ <Enter>**
Specify next point or [Close Undo]:	Move your mouse to the left and type **20′4 <Enter>**
Specify next point or [Close Undo]:	Type **C <Enter>**

Figure 3-25
Use the **LINE** command to draw the lecture room walls

Step 8. Use **Zoom-Window** to magnify the lower right corner of the lecture room where the door will be drawn.

From

From: A command modifier that locates a base point and then allows you to locate an offset point from the base point.

From is a command modifier that locates a base point and then allows you to locate an offset point from that base point. It is similar to **ID Point** but differs in that **From** is used within a command; **ID Point** must be used before the command is activated. **From** is used at a prompt that asks you to locate a point, and it does not work unless a command is active to issue that prompt. Both **From** and **ID Point** are usually used in combination with **Object Snap** modifiers when locating the initial base point.

BREAK

BREAK	
Ribbon/ Panel	Home/ Modify
Modify Toolbar:	
Menu Bar:	Modify/ Break
Type a Command:	BREAK
Command Alias:	BR

The **BREAK** command can be used to erase a part of a drawing object.

Step 9. Use the **BREAK** command to create an opening for the lecture room door (Figure 3-26), as described next:

Prompt	Response
Type a command:	**Break** (or type **BR <Enter>**)
Select object:	Click anyplace on the bottom horizontal line
Specify second break point or [First point]:	Type **F <Enter>** (for first point)
Specify first break point:	Type **FRO <Enter>** (abbreviation for **From**)
Base point:	**Osnap-Intersection**
int of	**P1→** (Figure 3-26)

Figure 3-26
Use the **BREAK** command to make an opening for the lecture room door

Prompt	Response
<Offset>:	Type **@6<180 <Enter>** (polar coordinate)
Specify second break point:	Type **@36<180 <Enter>** (polar coordinate)

First

When selecting an entity to break, you may use the point entered in the selection process as the first break point, or you may type **F <Enter>** to be able to select the first break point. Using **F <Enter>** allows you to start over in specifically selecting both beginning and ending break points.

@

Sometimes you need only to break an entity and not erase a section of it. In that case, use @ as the second break point. The line will be broken twice on the same point; no segments will be erased from the line.

Polyline Edit

Polyline Edit is a **Modify** command used to edit polylines or to change lines into polylines. It can join lines or arcs together and make them a single polyline. It can also be used to change the width of a polyline.

Step 10. Use **Polyline Edit** to change the lines into a polyline, as described next:

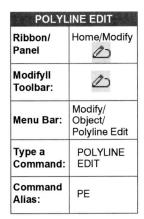

POLYLINE EDIT	
Ribbon/ Panel	Home/Modify
ModifyII Toolbar:	
Menu Bar:	Modify/ Object/ Polyline Edit
Type a Command:	POLYLINE EDIT
Command Alias:	PE

Prompt	Response
Type a command:	**Polyline Edit** (or type **PE <Enter>**)
Select polyline or [Multiple]:	Click any of the lines drawn
Object selected is not a polyline	
Do you want to turn it into one? <Y>	**<Enter>** (to tell AutoCAD yes, you want to turn it into a polyline)
Enter an option [Close Join Width Edit vertex Fit Spline Decurve Ltype gen Reverse Undo]:	Type **J <Enter>** (for **Join**)
Select objects:	
5 found	Type **ALL <Enter>** (to select all the lines)
Select objects:	**<Enter>**
4 segments added to polyline	
Enter an option [Open Join Width Edit vertex Fit Spline Decurve Ltype gen Reverse Undo]:	**<Enter>**

Step 11. Use the **OFFSET** command to offset the polyline 5″ to the **outside** of the current polyline.

Step 12. Use the **LINE** command with a running **Osnap Endpoint** to close the polyline. Type **L <Enter>**. Click **P1→, P2→ <Enter><Enter>**. Click **P3→, P4→ <Enter>** as shown in Figure 3-27.

Step 13. Use **Zoom-Extents** so you can see the entire drawing graphics.

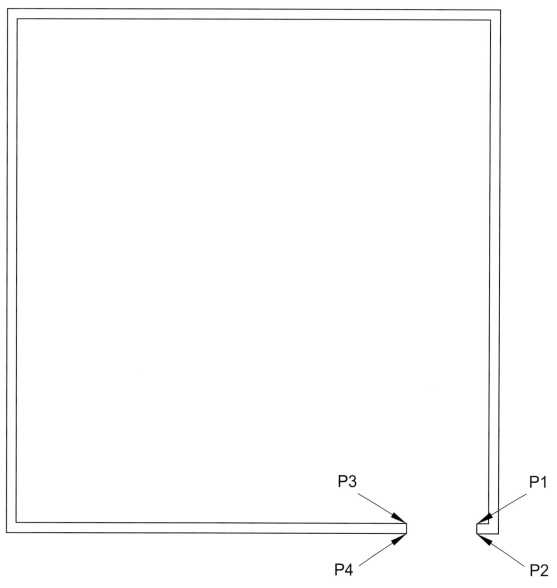

Figure 3-27
Use the **LINE** command to close the ends of the polylines

HATCH

hatch: The process of filling in a closed area with a pattern. Hatching can consist of solid filled areas, gradient-filled areas, or areas filled with patterns of lines, dots, or other objects.

You will use a single *hatch* pattern to create solid walls as shown in Figure 3-24.

FOR MORE DETAILS

See Chapters 8 and 13 for more about the **Hatch and Gradient** dialog box.

Step 14. Create the following new layer and set it as the current layer:

Layer Name	Color	Linetype	Lineweight
a-wall-patt-gray	gray (253)	continuous	.004″ (.09 mm)

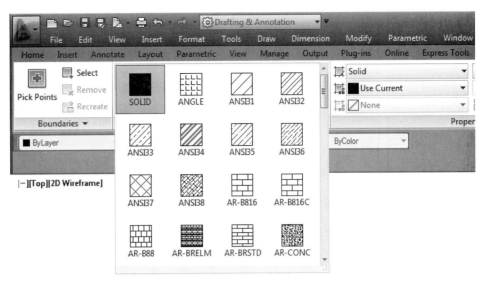

Figure 3-28
Hatch Pattern Gallery with **SOLID** hatch selected

HATCH	
Ribbon/ Panel	Home/Draw
Draw Toolbar:	
Menu Bar:	Draw/ Hatch...
Type a Command:	HATCH
Command Alias:	H

Step 15. Use the **HATCH** command to make the walls solid, as described next:

Prompt	**Response**
Type a command:	**Hatch** (or type **H <Enter>**)
The **Hatch Creation** ribbon tab appears:	Click the down arrow **button** of the **Hatch Pattern Gallery** (Figure 3-28)
Pick internal point or [Select objects seTtings]:	Click the **SOLID pattern**, as shown in Figure 3-28
Pick internal point or [Select objects seTtings]:	Click **P1→** (any point between the two polylines forming the wall, Figure 3-29—you may have to turn **SNAP** off)
Pick internal point or [Select objects seTtings]:	**<Enter>**

Step 16. Set layer **a-door** current.

Step 17. Draw a 1-1/2″-long by 3′-wide rectangle to represent the door (Figure 3-29). Be sure to use **Osnap-Endpoint** or **Osnap Intersection** to start the rectangle at the upper right corner of the door opening.

Step 18. Use the **Arc-Start, End, Direction** method to draw the door swing arc. Be sure **OSNAP** and **ORTHO** are on. The arc can be drawn clockwise or counterclockwise. Move your mouse so the arc appears as shown in Figure 3-29.

Step 19. Set layer **i-furn** current.

Step 20. Locate the table and chair symbols as shown in Figure 3-30. Use the **LINE** or **Rectangle** command to draw the 48″-long × 24″-wide table. Center a 24″-long × 26″-wide rectangle 6″ from the table to start the chair symbol, as shown in Figure 3-30.

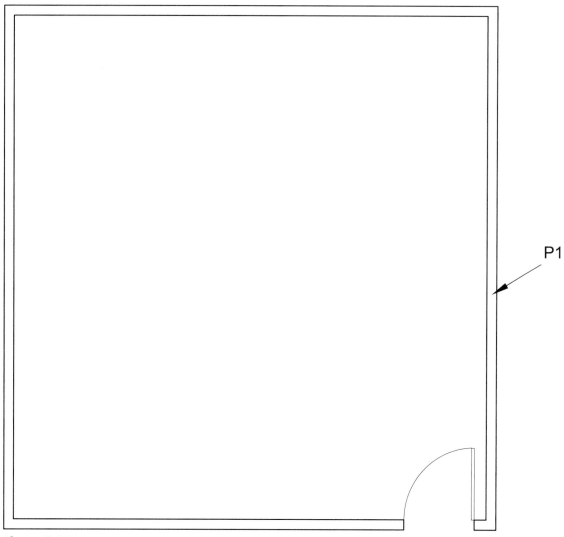

P1

Figure 3-29
Click any point between the two polylines forming the wall to make the walls solid; draw the door

Step 21. Complete the chair symbol as shown in Figure 3-31.

Step 22. Use **Zoom-Extents** after you finish drawing the chair symbol.

ARRAY

RECTANGULAR ARRAY	
Ribbon/ Panel	Home/Modify Array ▫▫ ▫▫
Modify Toolbar:	▫▫ ▫▫
Menu Bar:	Modify/Array/ Rectangular
Type a Command:	ARRAY
Command Alias:	AR

The **ARRAY** command allows you to make multiple copies of an object in a rectangular or polar (circular) array and along a path as shown in Figure 3-33. The **Rectangular** option is used in Exercise 3-2; the **Polar** option is described in Exercise 3-3.

> **NOTE**
> In the **ARRAY** command, include the original item in the number of rows and columns.

Step 23. Use the **ARRAY** command to make a rectangular pattern of six chairs and tables (Figures 3-32 and 3-33), as described next:

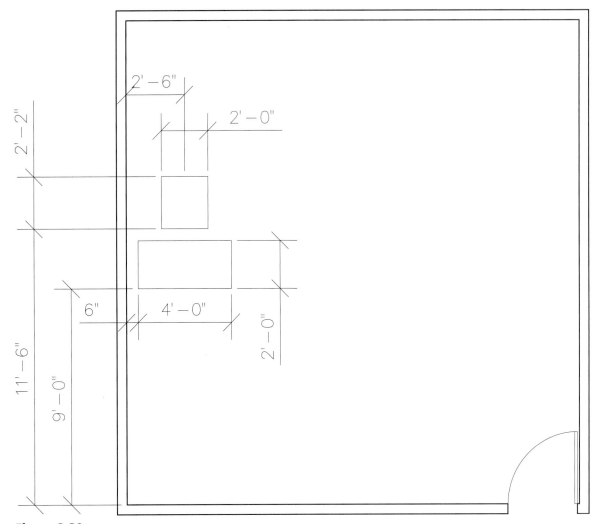

Figure 3-30
Locate the table and chair symbols

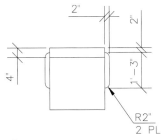

Figure 3-31
Complete the chair symbol

Prompt	Response
Type a command:	**Rectangular Array** (or type **ARRAYRECT <Enter>**)
Select objects:	Click **P1→** to locate the first corner of a window to include the entire chair and table
Specify opposite corner:	Click **P2→** to window the chair and table just drawn
Select objects:	**<Enter>**
An array preview of the table and chair is shown on the screen. Type = Rectangular Associative = Yes Select grip to edit array or [Associative Base point COUnt Spacing COLumns Rows Levels eXit]<eXit>:	Type **S <Enter>**
Specify the distance between columns or [Unit cell] <6'>:	Type **7'8<Enter>**

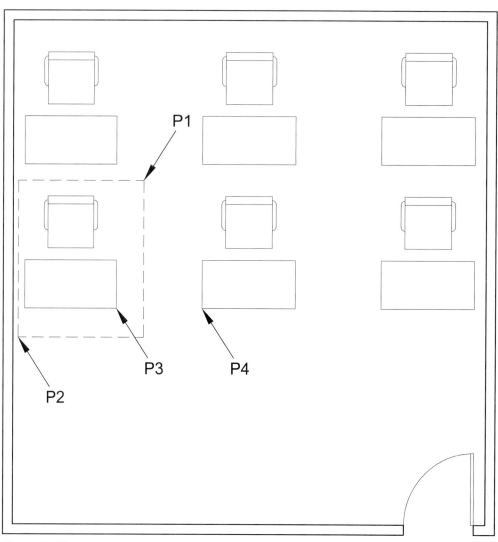

Figure 3-32
Array the tables and chairs; use **Distance** to measure the aisle width

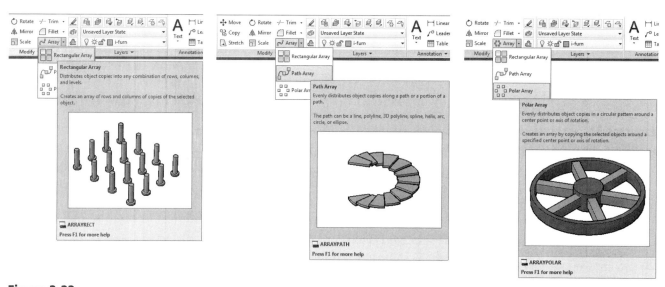

Figure 3-33
The three types of arrays

Prompt	Response
Specify the distance between rows <7'>:	Type **6'<Enter>**
Select grip to edit array or [Associative Base point COUnt Spacing COLumns Rows Levels eXit]<eXit>:	Type **COU<Enter>**
Enter the number of columns or [Expression] <4>:	Type **3<Enter>**
Enter the number of rows or [Expression] <3>:	Type **2<Enter>**
Select grip to edit array or [Associative Base point COUnt Spacing COLumns Rows Levels eXit]<eXit>:	**<Enter>**

Rectangular

The **Rectangular** option of **ARRAY** allows you to make multiple copies of an object in a rectangular array. The array is made up of horizontal rows and vertical columns. The direction and spacing of the rows and columns are determined by the distance you specify between each. In the previous example we used the table and chair as the cornerstone element in the lower left corner of the array. Positive numbers were used for the distance between the rows and columns, and the array went up and to the right. When a positive number is entered for the rows, they proceed up; when a negative number is entered, they proceed down. When a positive number is entered for the columns, they proceed to the right; when a negative number is entered, they proceed to the left.

Path

The **Path** option of **ARRAY** allows you to make multiple copies of an object evenly distributed along a path or part of a path. The path can be a line, polyline, arc, circle, or ellipse.

ARRAYEDIT

An array must be associative, an option in the array commands, for the **ARRAYEDIT** command to work. When an array is associative, it is treated as a single object and can be edited by using **grips, Properties**, or **ARRAYEDIT**.

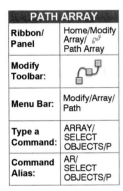

PATH ARRAY	
Ribbon/Panel	Home/Modify Array/ Path Array
Modify Toolbar:	
Menu Bar:	Modify/Array/Path
Type a Command:	ARRAY/SELECT OBJECTS/P
Command Alias:	AR/SELECT OBJECTS/P

ARRAYEDIT	
Ribbon/Panel	Home/Modify ArrayEdit
Modify Toolbar:	
Menu Bar:	Modify/Object/Array
Type a Command:	ARRAYEDIT
Command Alias:	AREDIT

TIP

Items can automatically be added to a path array when you lengthen the path using the **Measure** option of **ARRAYEDIT**.

NOTE

After an object has been selected, you can use the **Array** option of the **COPY** command to make multiple copies of the object.

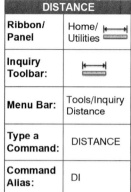

DISTANCE	
Ribbon/ Panel	Home/ Utilities
Inquiry Toolbar:	
Menu Bar:	Tools/Inquiry Distance
Type a Command:	DISTANCE
Command Alias:	DI

Distance

The **Distance** command can be used to determine measurements.

Step 24. Use the **Distance** command to measure a specified distance (Figure 3-32), as described next:

Prompt	Response
Type a command:	**Distance** (or type **DI <Enter>**)
Specify first point:	**Osnap-Intersection**
int of	**P3→** (Figure 3-32)

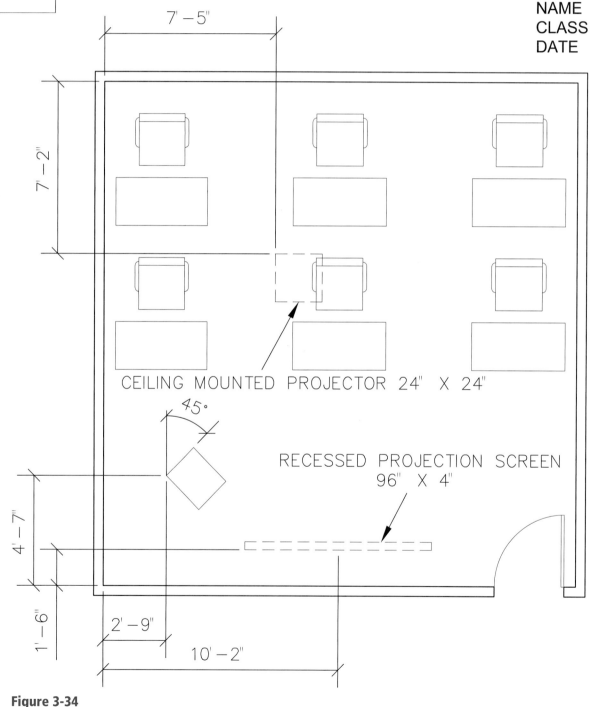

Figure 3-34
Draw the 24″ × 20″ lectern, the 24″ × 24″ ceiling projector, and the 96″ × 4″ recessed projection screen

Prompt	Response
Specify second point or [Multiple points]:	**Osnap-Intersection**
int of	**P4→** (Figure 3-32)
Distance = 3'8", Angle in XY Plane = 0, Angle from XY Plane = 0, Delta X = 3'-8", Delta Y = 0'-0", Delta Z = 0'-0"	

Step 25. Draw the 24" × 20" lectern as shown in Figure 3-34.

Step 26. Set layer **i-eqpm-ovhd** current.

Step 27. Draw the 24" × 24" ceiling-mounted projector and the 96" × 4" recessed projection screen as shown in Figure 3-34.

Step 28. Set layer **a-anno-text** current.

Step 29. Use the **Single Line Text** command (type **DT <Enter>**) to type your name, class number, and date, 6" high in the upper right corner.

Step 30. When you have completed Exercise 3-2 (Figure 3-35), save your work in at least two places.

Figure 3-35
Exercise 3-2 complete

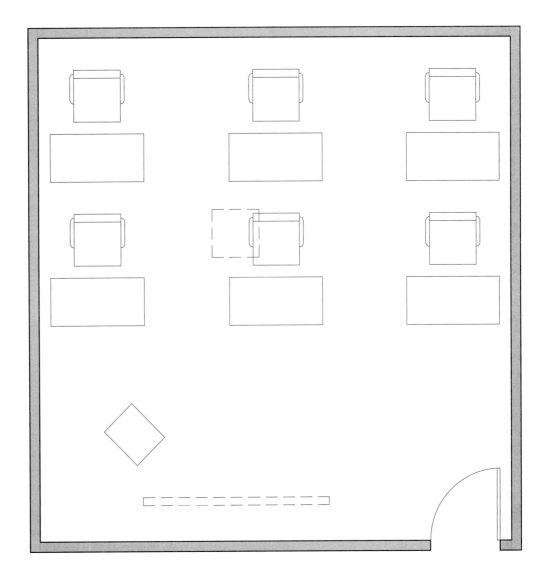

As for the dimensions and other annotations shown in Figure 3-34, dimension and multi-leader tools are needed and will be discussed in future exercises.

Step 31. Print your drawing from the **Model** tab at a scale of **1/4″ = 1′-0″**.

EXERCISE 3-3

Drawing a Curved Conference Room, Including Furniture

A conference room, including walls and furnishings, is drawn in Exercise 3-3. When you have completed Exercise 3-3, your drawing will look similar to Figure 3-36.

Figure 3-36

Exercise 3-3: Drawing a curved conference room, including furniture (scale: 1/4″ = 1′-0″)

NAME
CLASS
DATE

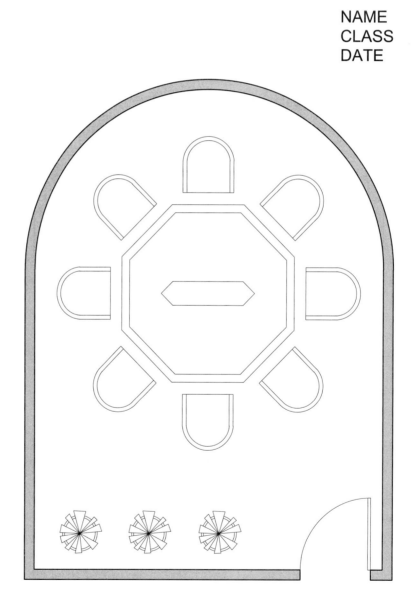

Step 1. Click **Open…**, change the **Files of type:** input box to **Drawing Template (*.dwt)**, and open the **Ch3-conference-rm-setup** template, previously made at the beginning of Exercise 3-1.

Step 2. Click **Save As...**, change the **Files of type:** input box to **AutoCAD 2013 Drawing (.dwg)**, and save the template as a drawing file named **CH3-EXERCISE3**.

-or-

Step 3. Use your workspace to make the following settings:

1. Use **Save As...** to save the drawing with the name **CH3 EXERCISE3**.
2. Set drawing units: **Architectural**
3. Set drawing limits: **25′,35′**
4. Set **GRIDDISPLAY: 0**
5. Set grid: **12″**
6. Set snap: **6″**
7. Create the following layers:

Layer Name	Color	Linetype	Lineweight
a-anno-text	green	continuous	.006″ (.15 mm)
a-door	red	continuous	.004″ (.09 mm)
a-wall-intr	blue	continuous	.010″ (.25 mm)
i-eqpm-ovhd	red	hidden	.004″ (.09 mm)
i-furn	cyan	continuous	.004″ (.09 mm)

Step 4. Set layer **a-wall-intr** current.

Step 5. Use **Zoom-All** to view the limits of the drawing.

Step 6. Turn **SNAP, GRID** and **LWT** on. The remaining buttons in the status bar should be off.

Polyline

Step 7. Use **Polyline, LINE,** and **ARC** to draw the inside lines of the conference room walls (Figure 3-37) as described next:

Prompt	Response
Type a command:	**Polyline** (or type **PL <Enter>**)
Specify start point:	Type **5′,5′<Enter>**
	Set **ORTHO** on
Current line-width is 0′-0″	
Specify next point or [Arc Halfwidth Length Undo Width]:	Move your mouse to the right and type **15′ <Enter>** (direct distance entry)
Specify next point or [Arc Close Halfwidth Length Undo Width]:	Move your mouse up and type **12′6 <Enter>**
Specify next point or [Arc Close Halfwidth Length Undo Width]:	Type **A <Enter>**
Specify endpoint of arc or [Angle CEnter CLose Direction Halfwidth Line Radius Second pt Undo Width]:	Move your mouse to the left and type **15′ <Enter>**

Figure 3-37
Use the **Polyline** command with **LINE** and **ARC** options to draw the inside lines of the conference room walls

Prompt	Response
Specify endpoint of arc or [Angle CEnter CLose Direction Halfwidth Line Radius Second pt Undo Width]:	Type **L <Enter>**
Specify next point or [Arc Close Halfwidth Length Undo Width]:	Type **C <Enter>**

> **NOTE**
> When a wide polyline is exploded, the width information is lost, and the polyline changes to a line segment.

Width

The **Polyline Width** option allows you to draw wide polylines. The starting and ending points of the polyline are the *center* of the polyline's width.

Half Width

This option specifies the width of the polyline from the center of the polyline to either edge.

Length

The **Length** option in the **Polyline** prompt allows you to draw a polyline segment at the same angle as the previously drawn polyline segment, by specifying the length of the new segment.

Close

It is always best to use the **Close** option when you are completing a wide polyline. The effect of using **Close** is different from clicking or entering a point to complete the polyline. With the **Close** option, the last corner is completely closed.

Step 8. Use the **OFFSET** command to offset the polyline 5″ to the **outside**, as shown in Figure 3-38.

Step 9. Set layer **a-door** current.

Step 10. Use the **Rectangle** command to draw a **1-1/2″**-long by **3′**-wide rectangle to represent the door (Figure 3-38).

Step 11. Draw the **3′** door opening as shown in Figure 3-38.

Step 12. Use the **Trim** command with the two vertical lines of step 11 as cutting edges and trim the 3′ wide opening in the wall as shown in Figure 3-38.

Step 13. Use the **Arc-Start, End, Direction** method to draw the door swing arc (Figure 3-38). Be sure **SNAP** and **ORTHO** are on.

Step 14. Set layer **i-furn** current.

Figure 3-38
Offset the polyline, explode the polylines, and draw the door opening and the door

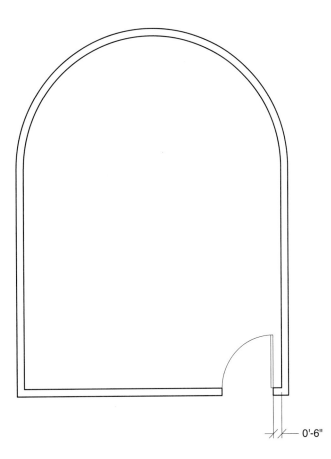

0'-6"

POLYGON

POLYGON: Command that draws a polygon with 3 to 1024 sides.

The **_POLYGON_** command draws a polygon with 3 to 1024 sides. After the number of sides is specified, the **Polygon** prompt is *Specify center of polygon or [Edge]:*. When the center of the polygon (default option) is specified, the polygon can then be inscribed in a circle or circumscribed about a circle.

POLYGON	
Ribbon/ Panel	Home/ Draw
Draw Toolbar:	
Menu Bar:	Draw/ Polygon
Type a Command:	POLYGON
Command Alias:	POL

When the polygon is inscribed in a circle, all the vertices lie on the circle, and the edges of the polygon are inside the circle. When the polygon is circumscribed about a circle, the midpoint of each edge of the polygon lies on the circle, and the vertices are outside the circle. A polygon is a closed polyline.

Step 15. Use the **POLYGON** command to draw the conference table (Figure 3-39), as described next:

Prompt	**Response**
Type a command:	**Polygon** (or type **POL <Enter>**)
Enter number of sides <4>:	Type **8 <Enter>**
Specify center of polygon or [Edge]:	**P1→** (Figure 3-39)
Enter an option [Inscribed in circle Circumscribed about circle]<I>:	Type **I <Enter>** (or just **<Enter>** if **I** is the default)
Specify radius of circle:	Type **48 <Enter>**

Figure 3-39
Locate the polygon

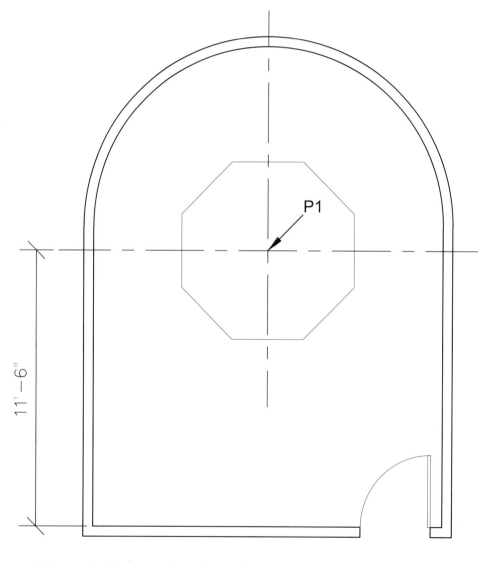

The method of specifying the radius controls the orientation of the polygon. When the radius is specified with a number, as in the preceding responses, the bottom edge of the polygon is drawn at the current snap angle—horizontal in the polygon just drawn. When the radius of an inscribed polygon is specified with a point, a vertex of the polygon is placed at the point location. When the radius of a circumscribed polygon is specified with a point, an edge midpoint is placed at the point's location.

Edge

When the **Edge** option of the prompt is selected, AutoCAD prompts *Specify first endpoint of edge:* and *Specify second endpoint of edge:*. The two points entered at the prompts specify one edge of a polygon that is drawn counterclockwise.

Step 16. Use the **Polyline** or **Rectangle** command to draw a rectangle 36″ long × 12″ wide in the center of the polygon just drawn (Figure 3-40A). This is a good exercise to learn how to specify the center of the polygon as reference point (use **From** followed by **Mid Between 2 Points** from the **Osnap** menu) to construct the rectangle. Once the center is defined as the reference point the upper-left and lower-right corners are defined with @–18, 6 and A38, −12, respectively. Try this on your own or ask your instructor to demonstrate it.

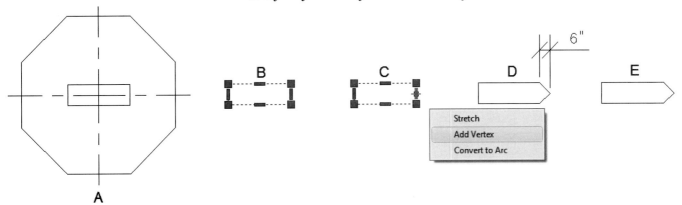

Figure 3-40
Steps for adding a 6″ vertex to the right side of the rectangle

> **NOTE**
> If you activate the grips on the vertex just added, you will get the grip option **Remove Vertex** when you hover over the vertex grip.

Grips—Add Vertex

The **Add Vertex** grip is for objects drawn using the **Polyline, Rectangle**, or **POLYGON** command. When you hover over a grip, a tooltip displays the options **Stretch, Convert to Arc, Convert to Line**, and **Add Vertex**, or you can right-click and get a menu that shows all the grip options.

Step 17. Use the **Add Vertex** grip to draw a vertex on the right side of the rectangle just drawn, as described next (Figure 3-40):

Prompt	Response
Type a command:	With no command active, click on the rectangle you have drawn
Small blue squares (grips) appear at each midpoint and intersection of the rectangle lines (Figure 3-40B):	Hover over the midpoint grip on the right side of the rectangle (Figure 3-40C)

Prompt	Response
A tooltip menu is displayed:	Click **Add Vertex**
A vertex appears (Figure 3-40D):	With **ORTHO** on, move your cursor to the right and type **6 <Enter>** (Figure 3-40E)
	Press **<Esc>** to clear the grips

Step 18. Use the **Add Vertex** grip to add a 6″ vertex on the left side of the rectangle (Figure 3-41).

Figure 3-41
Add a 6″ vertex on the left side of the rectangle

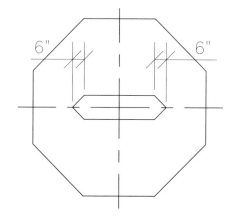

Step 19. To begin drawing the chair symbol, use the **Polyline** or **Rectangle** command to draw a rectangle 26″ long × 16″ wide (Figure 3-42A) and 6″ away from the outer edge of the table.

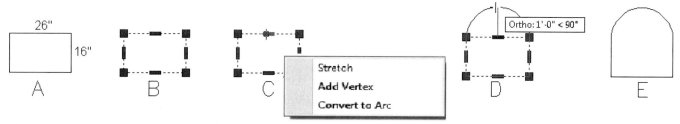

Figure 3-42
Steps in drawing the chair using **Convert to Arc**

Grips—Convert to Arc

The **Convert to Arc** grip is for objects drawn using the **Polyline, Rectangle,** or **POLYGON** command.

Step 20. Use the **Convert to Arc** grip to draw the back curved edge of the chair symbol as described next (Figure 3-42):

Prompt	Response
Type a command:	With no command active, click on the rectangle you have drawn
Small blue squares (grips) appear at each midpoint and intersection of the rectangle lines (Figure 3-42B):	Hover over the midpoint grip on the top line of the rectangle (Figure 3-42C)
A tooltip menu is displayed:	Click **Convert to Arc**

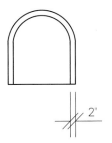

Figure 3-43
Explode the polylines and offset them

Prompt	Response
An arc appears (Figure 3-42D):	With **ORTHO** on, move your cursor up and type **12 <Enter>** Press **<Esc>** to clear the grips (Figure 3-42E)

Step 21. Use the **EXPLODE** command to split the polylines.

Step 22. Use the **OFFSET** command (offset 2″) to draw the **inside** lines of the chair symbol (Figure 3-43).

> **NOTE**
>
> If you activate the grips on the chair symbol arc, before it is exploded, you will get the grip option **Convert to Line** when you hover over the arc grip.

Step 23. The chairs are located 6″ out from the outside edge of the table. Use the **MOVE** command, **Osnap-Midpoint** (to the front of the chair), and **From** to locate the front of the chair 6″ outside the midpoint of an edge of the conference table polygon (Figure 3-44).

You could have avoided the use of the **Move** command in this step by using the .x, .y, and .z (x, y, z filters) to place the rectangle at its correct location 6″ away from the outer edge of the table. Use the Help system of AutoCAD to learn about coordinate filters or ask your instructor to demonstrate them in class.

Figure 3-44
Position the chair and offset the polygon

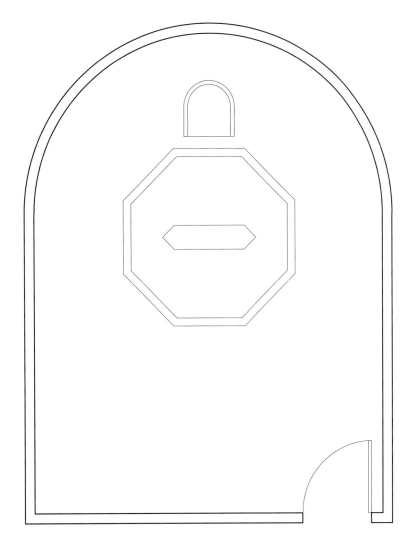

POLAR ARRAY	
Ribbon/ Panel	Home/ ▢ ▢ Modify ▢ ▢ Array ▢ ▢
Modify Toolbar:	▢ ▢ ▢ ▢ ▢ ▢
Menu Bar:	Modify/Array/ Polar
Type a Command:	ARRAY
Command Alias:	AR

Polar: The option of the **ARRAY** command that allows you to make multiple copies of an object in a circular array.

Step 24. Use the **OFFSET** command to offset the outside edge of the conference table 4″ to the **inside** to form the 4″ band (Figure 3-44).

Step 25. Use **Zoom-Extents** after you finish drawing the 4″ band.

ARRAY

Polar

The *Polar* option of the **ARRAY** command allows you to make multiple copies of an object in a circular array. The 360° **Angle to fill** can be specified to form a full circular array. An angle less than 360° can be specified to form a partial circular array. When a positive angle is specified, the array is rotated counterclockwise (+=ccw). When a negative angle is specified, the array is rotated clockwise (−=cw).

AutoCAD constructs the array by determining the distance from the array's center point to a point on the object selected. *If more than one object is selected, the reference point is on the last item in the selection set.*

Step 26. Use the **POLAR ARRAY** command to make a polar (circular) pattern of eight chairs (Figure 3-45), as described next:

Prompt	Response
Type a command:	**Polar Array** (or type **ARRAYPOLAR** **<Enter>**)

Figure 3-45
Array the chairs, draw the potted plant and copy it, and hatch the walls

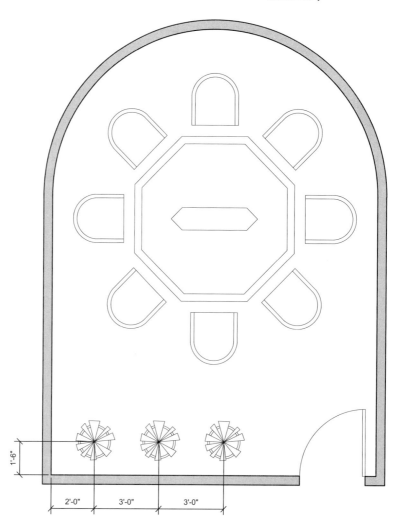

Prompt	Response
Select objects:	Click the first corner for a window to select the chair just drawn
Specify opposite corner:	Window the chair just drawn
Select objects:	**<Enter>**
Specify center point of array [or Base point Axis of rotation]:	Click the center point of the polygon
Select grip to edit array or [ASsociative Base point Items Angle between Fill angle ROWs Levels ROTate items eXit] <eXit>:	Type **I<Enter>**i
Enter number of items in array or [Expression] <6>:	Type **8<Enter>**
Select grip to edit array or [ASsociative Base point Items Angle between Fill angle ROWs Levels ROTate items eXit]<eXit>:	**<Enter>**

Step 27. Use **Zoom-Window** to zoom in on the area of the conference room where the plants and planters are located (Figure 3-45).

Step 28. Use the **CIRCLE** command, **9″** radius, to draw the outside shape of one planter.

Step 29. Use the **OFFSET** command, offset distance **1″**, offset to the **inside** of the planter, to give a thickness to the planter.

Step 30. Use the **LINE** command to draw multisegmented shapes (to show a plant) in the planter (Figure 3-45).

Step 31. Use the **TRIM** command to trim the lines of the pot beneath the plant leaves. Window the entire planter to select the cutting edges, and then select the lines to trim.

Step 32. Use the **COPY** command to draw the next two planters, as shown in Figure 3-45.

Step 33. Create the following new layer and set it as the current layer:

Layer Name	Color	Linetype	Lineweight
a-wall-patt-gray	gray (253)	continuous	.004″ (.09 mm)

Step 34. Use the **HATCH** command to make the walls solid (Figure 3-45).

Step 35. Set layer **a-anno-text** current.

Step 36. Use the **Single Line Text** command (type **DT <Enter>**) to type your name, class number, and date, 6″ high in the upper right corner.

Step 37. When you have completed Exercise 3-3 (Figure 3-46), save your work in at least two places.

Step 38. Print your drawing from the **Model** tab at a scale of **1/4″ = 1′-0″**.

Figure 3-46
Exercise 3-3 complete

NAME
CLASS
DATE

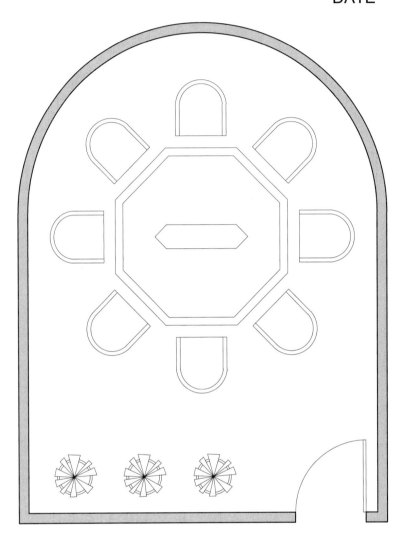

EXERCISE 3-4

Drawing a Conference Room Using Polar Tracking

In Exercise 3-4, polar tracking is used to draw lines at angles in 15° increments. When you have completed Exercise 3-4, your drawing will look similar to Figure 3-47.

Step 1. Click **Open...**, change the **Files of type:** input box to **Drawing Template (*.dwt)**, and open the **Ch3-conference-rm-setup** template, previously created at the beginning of Exercise 3-1.

Step 2. Click **Save As...**, change the **Files of type:** input box to **AutoCAD 2013 Drawing (.dwg)**, and save the template as a drawing file named **CH3-EXERCISE4**.

Figure 3-47
Exercise 3-4: Drawing a conference room using polar
tracking (scale 1/4″ = 1′-0″)

NAME
CLASS
DATE

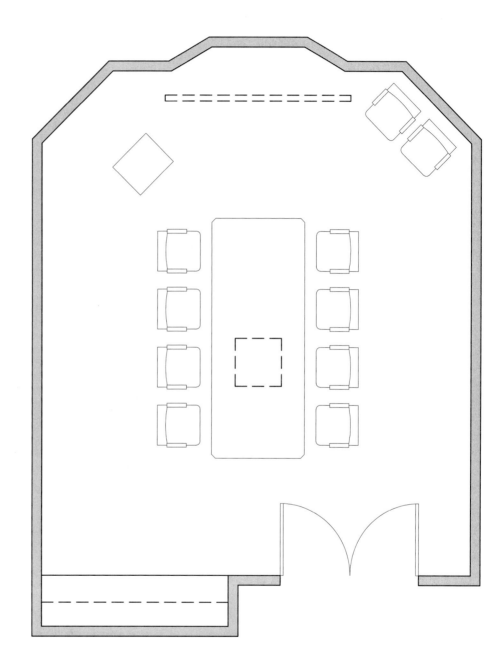

-or-

Step 3. Use your workspace to make the following settings:

1. Use **Save As...** to save the drawing with the name **CH3
   EXERCISE4**.
2. Set drawing units: **Architectural**
3. Set drawing limits: **25′,35′**
4. Set **GRIDDISPLAY: 0**
5. Set grid: **12″**
6. Set snap: **6″**

Chapter 3 | Drawing with AutoCAD: Conference and Lecture Rooms   **151**

7. Create the following layers:

Layer Name	Color	Linetype	Lineweight
a-anno-text	green	continuous	.006″ (.15 mm)
a-door	red	continuous	.004″ (.09 mm)
a-wall-intr	blue	continuous	.010″ (.25 mm)
i-eqpm-ovhd	red	hidden	.004″ (.09 mm)
i-furn	cyan	continuous	.004″ (.09 mm)

Step 4. Set layer **a-wall-intr** current.

Step 5. Use **Zoom-All** to view the limits of the drawing.

Step 6. Turn **SNAP, GRID,** and **LWT** on. The remaining buttons in the status bar should be off.

Polar Tracking

polar tracking: A means of specifying points (similar to using **ORTHO** to constrain screen pointing motion) using your own increment angle.

Step 7. Set *polar tracking* angles at 15°, as described next:

Prompt	Response
Type a command:	Place your mouse over **POLAR** on the status bar and right-click
	Click **Settings...**
A right-click menu appears:	
The **Drafting Settings** dialog box appears with the **Polar Tracking** tab selected:	Click the list under **Increment angle:** and click **15** (as shown in Figure 3-48)
	Click **OK**

POLAR (Polar Tracking) (<F10>): Shows temporary alignment paths along specific angles of interest (e.g., 15 degrees). While the default increment for PolarSnap is 90 degrees, one can change it easily to 60, 45, 30,

Figure 3-48
Set polar tracking angles

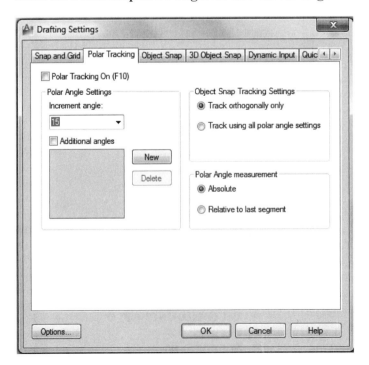

15, and so on as shown in Figure 1-32. The system variable **POLARANG** can be used to reset PolarSnap.

Step 8. Use the **LINE** command with direct distance entry and polar tracking to draw the inside lines of the conference room walls (Figure 3-49), as described next:

Prompt	Response
Type a command:	**Line** (or type **L <Enter>**)
Specify first point:	Type **11′6,4′ <Enter>**
Specify next point or [Undo]:	Turn **ORTHO** on
	Move your mouse down and type **2′ <Enter>**

Figure 3-49
Measurements for the walls

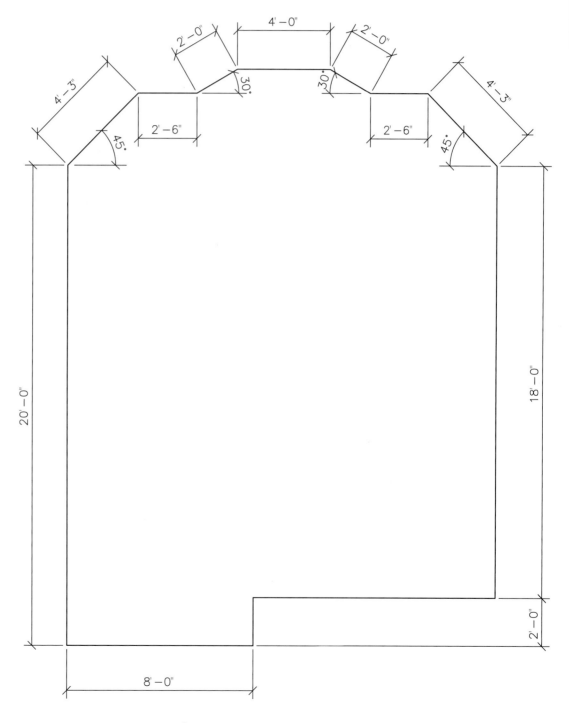

Prompt	Response
Specify next point or [Undo]:	Move your mouse to the left and type **8'<Enter>**
Specify next point or [Close Undo]:	Move your mouse straight up and type **20'<Enter>**
Specify next point or [Close Undo]:	Turn **POLAR** on (**ORTHO** turns off automatically)
	Move your mouse so that **45°** shows and type **4'3 <Enter>**
Specify next point or [Close Undo]:	Move your mouse so that **<0°** shows and type **2'6 <Enter>**
Specify next point or [Close Undo]:	Move your mouse so that **<30°** shows and type **2' <Enter>**
Specify next point or [Close Undo]:	Move your mouse so that **<0°** shows and type **4' <Enter>**
Specify next point or [Close Undo]:	Move your mouse so that **<330°** shows and type **2' <Enter>**
Specify next point or [Close Undo]:	Move your mouse so that **<0°** shows and type **2'6 <Enter>**
Specify next point or [Close Undo]:	Move your mouse so that **<315°** shows and type **4'3 <Enter>**
Specify next point or [Close Undo]:	Move your mouse straight down so that **<270°** shows and type: **18' <Enter>**
Specify next point or [Close Undo]:	Type **C <Enter>** (to complete the **LINE** command)

Polyline Edit

Step 9. Use **Polyline Edit** to join all lines into a single polyline, as described next:

Prompt	Response
Type a command:	**Polyline Edit** (or type **PE <Enter>**)
Select polyline or [Multiple]:	Click any of the lines
Object selected is not a polyline	
Do you want to turn it into one? <Y>	**<Enter>**
Enter an option [Close Join Width Edit vertex Fit Spline DecurveLtype gen Reverse Undo]:	Type **J <Enter>**
Select objects:	Type **ALL <Enter>** (or use a crossing window to select all)
12 found	
Select objects:	**<Enter>**
11 segments added to polyline	
Enter an option [Open Join Width Edit vertex Fit Spline Decurve Ltype gen Reverse Undo]:	**<Enter>**

Step 10. Use the **OFFSET** command to offset the polyline 5″ to the **outside**, as shown in Figure 3-50.

Step 11. To split the two polylines that make the conference room walls into separate line segments, place two vertical lines (length: wall thickness = 5″) and location as shown in Figure 3-50.

Figure 3-50
Offset the polyline 5″ to the outside, explode both polylines, make the 6′ door opening, and draw the two doors

> **Step 12.** Use the **Trim** command to create the 6′ door opening as shown in Figure 3-50. The two vertical lines of the previous step will be the cutting edges for the **Trim** command.
>
> **Step 13.** Set layer **a-door** current.
>
> **Step 14.** Use the **Rectangle** command to draw the two 1-1/2″ × 3′ door symbols (Figure 3-50).
>
> **Step 15.** Use the **Arc-Start, End, Direction** method to draw the door swing arcs (Figure 3-50).
>
> **Step 16.** Set layer **i-furn** current.

Tracking

tracking: A means of reducing if not eliminating the number of construction lines you draw by specifying points. Alternatively, use the **From** option of the **Osnap** menu (shown earlier in Figure 3-16) to define a reference point and then define the x- and y-offset from that point. This will be explained further in the upcoming steps. For now, let's continue with the exercise using ID Point.

Tracking, which is similar to the **ID Point** command, allows you to specify points, except that you can activate tracking whenever AutoCAD asks for a point. You can also specify as many points as you need until you arrive at the desired location. Then, you press **<Enter>** to end the tracking mode.

Step 17. Draw the table using **Rectangle** and **Osnap-Tracking** (Figure 3-51), as described next:

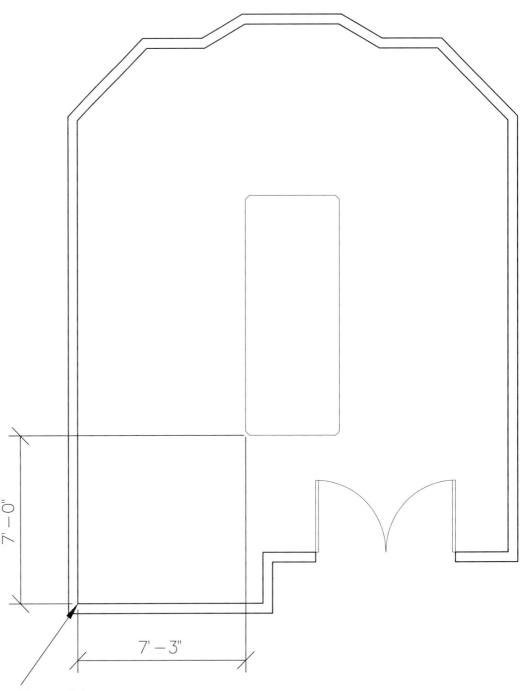

First tracking point

Figure 3-51
Draw the table using **Rectangle** and **Osnap-Tracking**

Prompt	Response
Type a command:	**Rectangle** (or type **REC <Enter>**)
Specify first corner point or [Chamfer Elevation Fillet Thickness Width]:	Type **C <Enter>**
Specify first chamfer distance for rectangles <0'-0">:	Type **2 <Enter>**
Specify second chamfer distance for rectangles <0'-2">:	**<Enter>**
Specify first corner point or [Chamfer Elevation Fillet Thickness Width]:	Type **TRACK <Enter>**
First tracking point:	Type **INT <Enter>** (with **ORTHO** off) the lower left inside corner of the room
Next point (Press ENTER to end tracking):	Move your mouse to the right (with **ORTHO** on and **OSNAP** off) and type **7'3 <Enter>**
Next point (Press ENTER to end tracking):	Move your mouse up and type **7' <Enter>**
Next point (Press ENTER to end tracking):	**<Enter>** (to end tracking)
Specify other corner point or [Area Dimensions Rotation]:	Type **@48,120 <Enter>** (relative coordinates)

Draw the Chairs around the Conference Table

Step 18. Zoom in on a portion of the grid so you can begin to draw the chair symbol.

Step 19. Draw a rectangle 20" wide by 22" deep (change chamfer distance to 0) using the **LINE** or **Rectangle** command (Figure 3-52A).

Step 20. Draw the 2" × 10" left chair arm using **Rectangle** and **Tracking** (Figure 3-52B).

Step 21. Use **MIRROR** and **TRIM** to place the right arm and trim the extra lines out (Figure 3-52C).

Figure 3-52
Draw the conference room chair

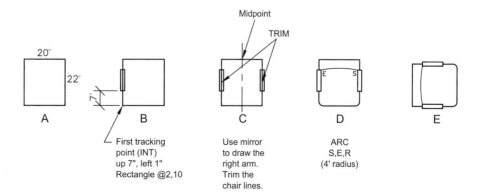

20"
22"

Midpoint
TRIM

A   B   C   D   E

First tracking point (INT) up 7", left 1"
Rectangle @2,10

Use mirror to draw the right arm. Trim the chair lines.

ARC
S,E,R
(4' radius)

Step 22. Draw a 2″ fillet on the bottom two corners of the chair (Figure 3-52D).

Step 23. Use **Arc-Start, End, Radius** (4′ radius) to complete the chair symbol (Figure 3-52D).

Step 24. Rotate the chair to appear as shown in Figure 3-52E.

Step 25. Explode the table, then offset the line that defines the long left side of the table 6″ to the outside of the table. Alternatively, place a line 6″ away from the edge of the table to the left, using the **Line** command and **From** option of **Osnap** as shown in Figure 3-53. Use **Explode** at a minimum, especially when it can be avoided.

Step 26. Set the **Point Style** to **X** and size to **6″**.

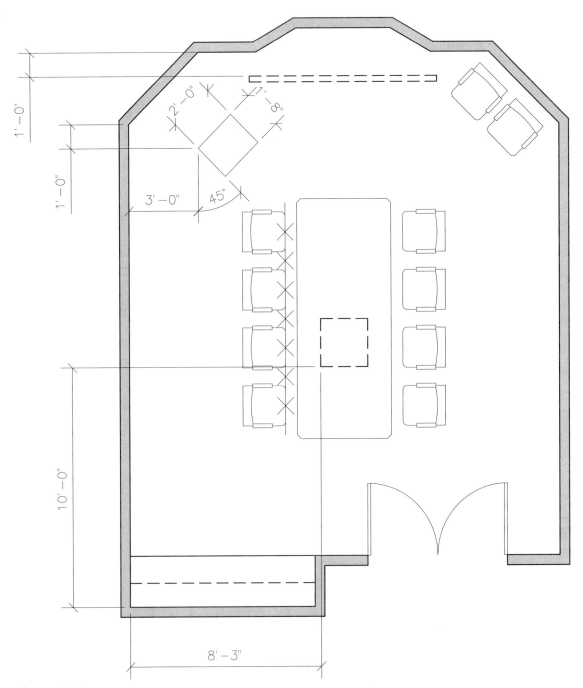

Figure 3-53
Complete the conference room

Step 27. Divide the offset line into eight equal segments.

Step 28. Use **COPY** and **Osnap-Midpoint** to pick up the chair and **Osnap-Node** to copy the chair on the points of the divided line (Figure 3-53).

Step 29. Use the **MIRROR** command to draw the chairs on the right side of the conference table (Figure 3-53).

Step 30. Set **PDMODE** to **1** (invisible).

Step 31. Erase the offset line used to locate the chairs.

Complete the Conference Room

Step 32. Draw the 24″ × 20″ lectern as shown in Figure 3-53.

Step 33. Set layer **i-eqpm-ovhd** current.

Step 34. Add the 96″ × 3″ recessed projection screen and the 24″ × 24″ ceiling-mounted projector to the plan as shown in Figure 3-53. Locating the 96″ × 3″ recessed projection screen will require use of the x, y, z-filters and the **Mid Between 2 Points** option of the **Osnap** menu. Ask your instructor to demonstrate it in class.

Step 35. Make the following new layers and draw the lines for the built-in upper and lower cabinets as shown in Figure 3-53:

Layer Name	Color	Linetype	Lineweight
a-flor-case	green	continuous	.006″ (.15 mm)
a-flor-case-uppr	red	hidden line	.004″ (.09 mm)

Step 36. Copy and rotate the two extra chairs in the room as shown in Figure 3-53.

Step 37. Create the following new layer and set it as the current layer:

Layer Name	Color	Linetype	Lineweight
a-wall-patt-gray	gray (253)	continuous	.004″ (.09 mm)

Step 38. Use the **HATCH** command to make the walls solid, as shown in Figure 3-53.

Step 39. Set layer **a-anno-text** current.

Step 40. Use the **Single Line Text** command (type **DT <Enter>**) to type your name, class number, and date, 6″ high in the upper right corner (Figure 3-54).

Step 41. When you have completed Exercise 3-4 (Figure 3-54), save your work in at least two places.

Step 42. Print your drawing from the **Model** tab at a scale of **1/4″ = 1′-0″**.

Sync my Settings

SYNC MY SETTINGS	
Ribbon/Panel	Online/Customization Sync/
Options Dialog Box:	Sync My Settings with Cloud

This command allows you to sync your computer settings to multiple computers using your **Autodesk 360 Cloud** account. When you sync your settings to the Cloud, you can sync the settings from the Cloud to other computers.

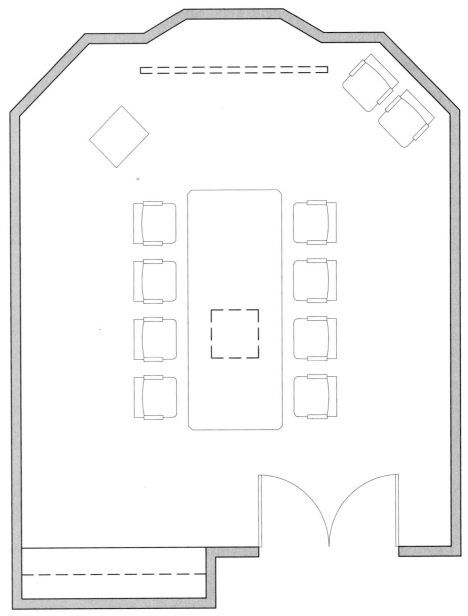

Figure 3-54
Exercise 3-4 complete

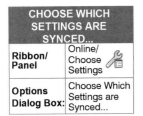

CHOOSE WHICH SETTINGS ARE SYNCED...	
Ribbon/ Panel	Online/ Choose Settings
Options Dialog Box:	Choose Which Settings are Synced...

On the **Online** tab of the **Options** dialog box (Figure 3-55), when the **Sync my settings with the cloud** box is checked and the **Keep all my settings synced** radio button is selected, all the settings shown in the **Choose Which Settings are Synced** dialog box are automatically saved to the Cloud. You can also use the **Sync selected settings only** radio button to choose individual settings.

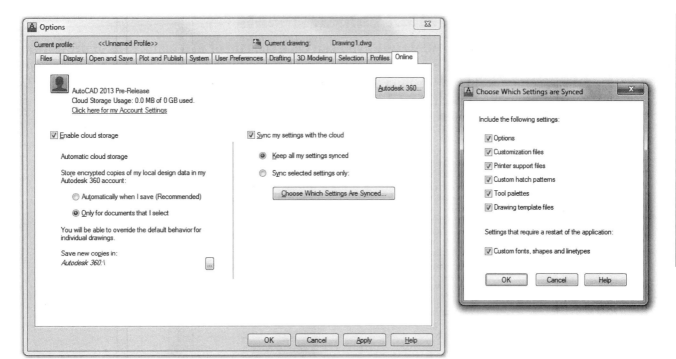

Figure 3-55
Options dialog box **Online** tab

Command Preview

NEW to AutoCAD 2015

A new command, **Preview control** on the **Selection** tab of the **Options** dialog box (Figure 3-56A), enables you to preview the results of **Trim**, **Extend**, **Lengthen**, **Break**, and **MatchProp** operations before actually selecting the objects. The new command also enables you to preview **Fillet**, **Chamfer**, and **Offset** operations.

For example, the **Trim** and **Extend** tools are enhanced in AutoCAD 2015 to provide a preview of the results before you commit the selection. After you select the cutting or boundary edges, you simply pass the cursor over the object you want to trim or extend. A preview of the resulting object is displayed. When trimming, the segment to be removed is dimly displayed and a cursor badge indicates that it will be deleted.

Figure 3-56A
Options dialog box, **Selection** tab – **Preview control** command

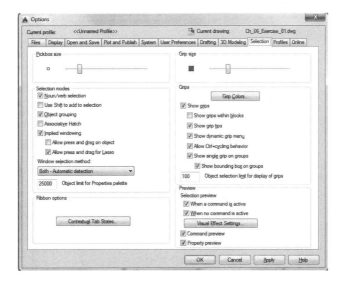

Selection Enhancements

In AutoCAD 2015 you can click the cursor in a blank area of the drawing and then drag around the objects to create a lasso selection. A new control in the **Options** dialog box on the **Selection** tab enables you to specify the lasso (Figure 3-56B). For a traditional rectangular window or crossing selection, click and release to pick each corner of the rectangle.

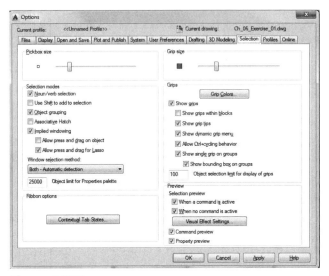

Figure 3-56B
Options dialog box, **Selection** tab – **Selection** enhancements

Chapter Summary

This chapter provided you the information necessary to set up and draw conference and lecture rooms. You learned how to use many of the **Draw, Inquiry,** and **Modify** commands. You also learned how to use the command options **Osnap, From, Tracking**, and **Polar Tracking,** and you learned the uses of a drawing template. Now you have the skills and information necessary to produce conference and lecture rooms.

Chapter Test Questions

Multiple Choice

Circle the correct answer.

1. When the outline of the walls of a room is drawn with a zero-width polyline, which of the following commands can be used to draw most quickly the second line that shows the depth of the walls?
   a. **Line**
   b. **Polyline**
   c. **OFFSET**
   d. **COPY**

2. Which of the following commands is used to split a solid polyline into separate segments?
   a. **ID Point**
   b. **OFFSET**
   c. **ARRAY**
   d. **EXPLODE**

3. Which of the following commands is used to locate a point on a drawing and to display the position of that point in absolute coordinates?
   a. **ID Point**
   b. **Inquiry**
   c. **First point**
   d. **Distance**

4. Which of the following commands can be used to draw a rounded corner?
   a. **CHAMFER**
   b. **FILLET**
   c. **OFFSET**
   d. **TRIM**

5. Which of the following **Osnap** modifiers is used to snap to a point entity?
   a. **Perpendicular**
   b. **Endpoint**
   c. **Node**
   d. **Midpoint**

6. Which of the following rotation angles is the same as −90°?
   a. 90
   b. 180
   c. 270
   d. 300

7. Which of the following controls the appearance of the markers used in the **DIVIDE** command?
   a. **Aperture Size (APBOX)**
   b. **Point Style (DDPTYPE)**
   c. **Osnap (OSNAP)**
   d. **Pickbox Size (PICKBOX)**

8. Which of the following is used to change the size of the target box that appears when **Modify** commands are used?

   a. **Aperture (APBOX)**   c. **Osnap (PICKBOX)**

   b. **Point Style (DDPTYPE)**   d. **Pickbox Size (PICKBOX)**

9. Which of the following commands can be used to join lines or arcs together and make them a single polyline?

   a. **EXPLODE**   c. **Polyline**

   b. **Polyline Edit (PEDIT)**   d. **CLOSE**

10. Which of the following command options allows you to chamfer the corners of a rectangle using only the **Rectangle** command?

   a. **C**   c. **P**

   b. **D**   d. **All**

Matching

Write the number of the correct answer on the line.

a. **Osnap** _____

b. **Polyline** _____

c. **TRIM** _____

d. **Tracking** _____

e. **From** _____

1. A setting option that allows you to start a line from the exact endpoint of an existing line

2. A command used to draw a rectangle that can be offset with a single click

3. A command modifier that locates a base point and then allows you to locate an offset point from that base point

4. A command that is used to cut off lines

5. A method of locating points before the start point of a line is specified

True or False

Circle the correct answer.

1. **True or False:** The **Chamfer** command will chamfer two lines that do not intersect.

2. **True or False:** All lines of a square drawn with a polyline can be offset with one use of the **OFFSET** command.

3. **True or False:** All objects in the drawing can be selected as cutting edges by pressing **<Enter>** at the prompt *Select objects or <select all>:*.

4. **True or False:** The width of a polyline cannot be changed.

5. **True or False:** The **ID Point** command is used to determine the exact distance from one point to another.

List

1. Five commands under the **Modify** panel of the ribbon with the **Home** tab ON.

2. Five options under the **Polyline** command.

3. Five options under the **Offset** command.

4. Five options of the the **Osnap** toolbar.

5. Five options under the **Chamfer** command.

6. Five ways of launching the **Point** command.

7. Five options under the **Polyline Edit** command.

8. Five ways of launching the **Hatch** command.

9. Five commands accessible upon activating a grip.

10. Five tabs in the **Drafting Settings** window.

Questions

1. How does **DIVIDE** differ from **MEASURE**?

2. When should you use **Osnap?**

3. When should you use **LINE** instead of **Polyline**?

4. When should you use **Polyline Edit**?

5. What is the **ARRAY** command used for and what are its options?

Chapter Projects

Project 3-1: *Rectangular Lecture Room Including Furniture* [BASIC]

1. Draw the floor plan of the lecture room as shown in Figure 3-57. Use the dimensions shown in Figure 3-58, or use an architectural scale to measure the floor plan and draw it full scale.

Figure 3-57

Project 3-1: Rectangular lecture room including furniture (scale: 1/4″ = 1′-0″)

NAME
CLASS
DATE

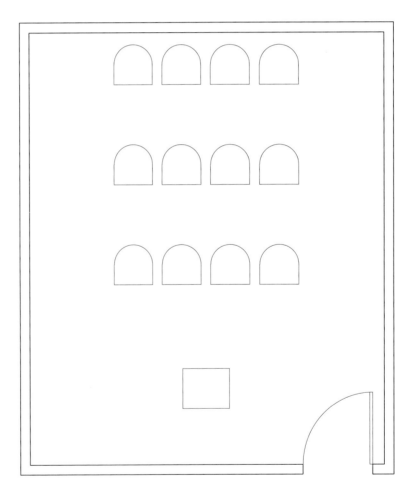

2. Use the **Single Line Text** command to type your name, class number, and date, 6″ high in the upper right corner (Figure 3-57).

3. Print your drawing from the **Model** tab at a scale of **1/4″ = 1′-0″**.

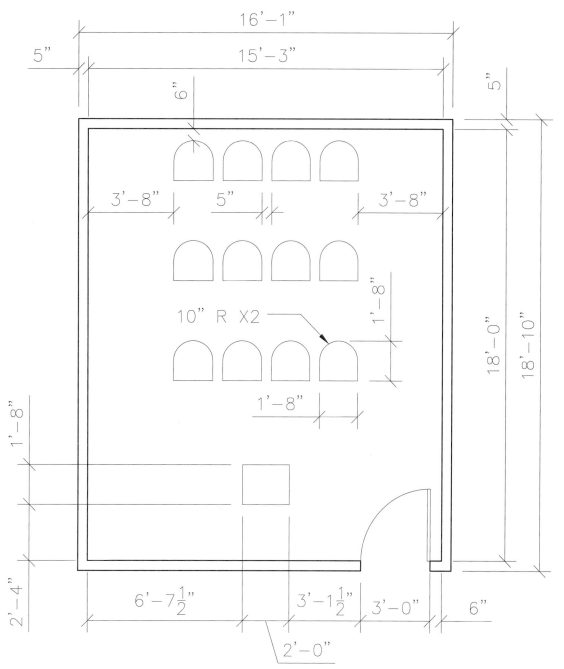

Figure 3-58
Dimensions for Project 3-1 (scale: 1/4″ = 1′-0″)

Project 3-2: *Curved Conference Room Including Furniture* [INTERMEDIATE]

1. Draw the floor plan of the conference room as shown in Figure 3-59. Use the dimensions shown in Figure 3-60, or use an architectural scale to measure the floor plan and draw it full scale. Your drawing will look like Figure 3-59 without the centerline.

Figure 3-59

Project 3-2: Curved conference room including furniture (scale: 1/4″ = 1′-0″)

NAME
CLASS
DATE

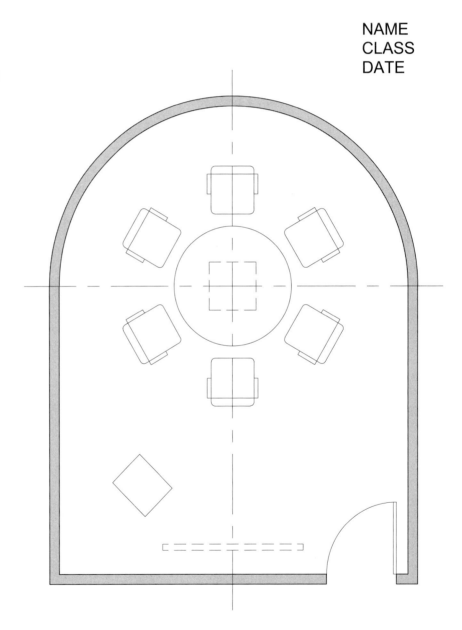

2. Use the **Single Line Text** command to type your name, class number, and date, 6″ high in the upper right corner (Figure 3-59).

3. Print your drawing from the **Model** tab at a scale of **1/4″ = 1′-0″**.

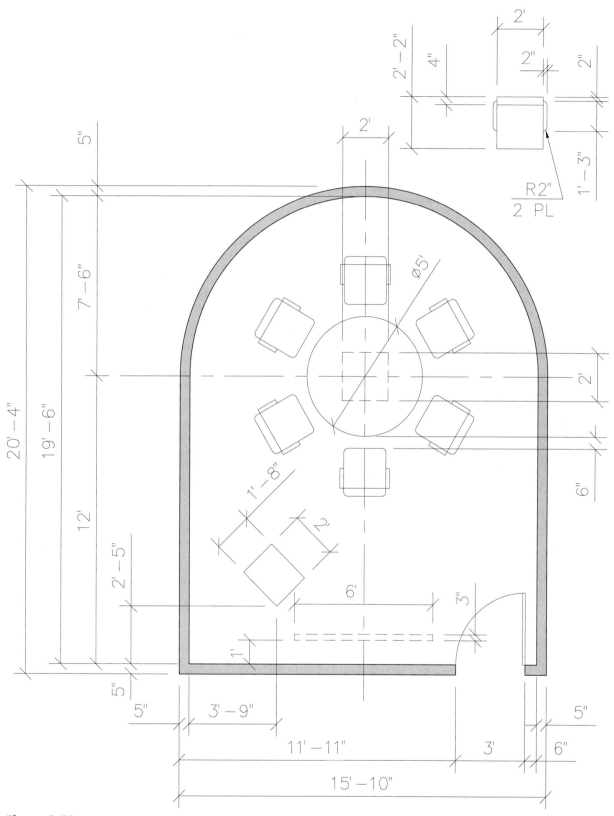

Figure 3-60
Dimensions for Project 3-2 (scale: 1/4″ = 1′-0″)

Project 3-3: *Custom Area Rug* [ADVANCED]

ASSIGNMENT 1

Courtesy of Dr. Stephanie Clemons, Colorado State University, Fort Collins, Colorado

Project Description

Using CAD software, design a custom area rug for a specific client based on four generations of personal family history.

Project Objectives

- Encourage research as a part of the design process.
- Offer exposure to cultural diversity.
- Use CAD as a creative design tool.
- Demonstrate CAD skills.

Process

- Research the past four generations of your family heritage and history.
- Document cultural influences and differences within your family background.
- Research common symbols used for one or two of the countries or cultures.
- Use CAD as a design tool to translate the common symbols and colors found in different arts (e.g., architecture, ceramics, pottery, emblems, shields, textiles, colors) into the design of a custom area rug for a specific client.
- Print out a minimum of 10 different stages of the design process as captured on the computer.
- Use manual and computer skills in conjunction with each other. Save all process drawings.
- Print or plot a final drawing. You may transfer the drawing to other types of paper or materials.
- Select yarn samples. (They must be attached to the front of the final design board.)
- Render (computer or manual) the area rug with colors very similar to yarn samples, and mount or frame the final materials as appropriate. *Extra credit is given for additional color versions of the finished design.*
- Type the following information and attach it to the back of the finished design. Information must include:
  - Yarn content
  - Pile height

- Weaving process
- Scale of design
- Source of inspiration

Deliverables

- Final area-rug design solution
- Documented research of culture/heritage plus design elements in that country (countries)
- Process drawings
- Family history with family tree

ASSIGNMENT 2

Courtesy of Mr. Stephen Huff, High Point University, High Point, North Carolina

Abstract

This project functions as a reinforcement and understanding of beginning-level basic CAD commands through the process of designing a custom area rug for a specific client. Creativity and multiple solutions are encouraged.

Objectives

- To demonstrate understanding of the AutoCAD **Draw** and **Modify** commands in the design and execution of a custom interior design element
- To demonstrate an understanding of printing parameters
- To understand the power of a CAD system when used for repetitious tasks

Criteria

- You will be designing two rugs for this project.
- For rug 1: Use **Draw** and **Modify** commands to design an area rug (1) inspired by a particular historical period style of your choosing or (2) from a specific conceptual design of your choosing. In either case, your rug design must be designed for a specific interior environment and have set design parameters (size, shape/form, etc.).
- For rug 2: Take some aspect of your original design and make a *modular component* in the design for a second rug.
- Determine the size of the area rug and draw it full size. Print it at a scale of 1/2″ = 1′-0″ (minimum). You may select a larger scale if desired.
- Print it on an 8 1/2″ × 11″ or 11″ × 17″ sheet of paper. Do not mix sheet sizes for this project; that is, use the same size sheet for both rug designs.
- Mount your rug designs on foam-core board or mat board.

- Type and mount the following information on the back of the board:

  1. Interior space for which the area rug was designed (room, client)

  2. Scale of the design

  3. Specific historical source of inspiration (elaborate on specific elements and principles of design associated with the historic period/style selected)

  If you used a conceptual drawing, include the drawing on the back of the board.

- Mount color scheme samples (paint chips) on the front of the board. Clearly identify which colors are used in which areas of the rugs (with numbers or letters). Each rug must feature a different color scheme. Do not use the same color palettes for both rugs.

- Render your rugs with **HATCH** commands using various stippling or other fine-line patterns. Do not use solids or other specialty patterns. The hatching should be representational of hue gradations and textures and **not** actual patterns.

- Show all appropriate lineweights when plotting.

- You are encouraged to submit multiple solutions.

- Save your rug design(s).

Commonly Available Rug Sizes

2′ × 3′	6′ × 9′
2′6 × 4′	6′7″ × 9′10″
3′ × 5′	6′ × 8′
3′6′ × 5′	8′ × 10′
4′ × 6′	8′ × 11′
5′ × 6′6″	9′ × 12′

Other Rug Sizes Used

3′ to 10′ circles and squares

2′6″- to 3′-wide by 6′- to 24′-long runners

Runners: 2′ to 7′ wide × 5′ to 30′ long

Wider runners: 4′ to 7′ wide by 10′ to 18′ long

Custom rugs do not have to have straight edges, round shapes, and so forth. Rather, they may be asymmetric and may possess unusual shapes.

Project Credits

The Edwards Fields Competition and Stephanie Clemons, Colorado State University

Examples of Finished Project

Examples of the custom area rug project are shown in Figures 3-61 and 3-62.

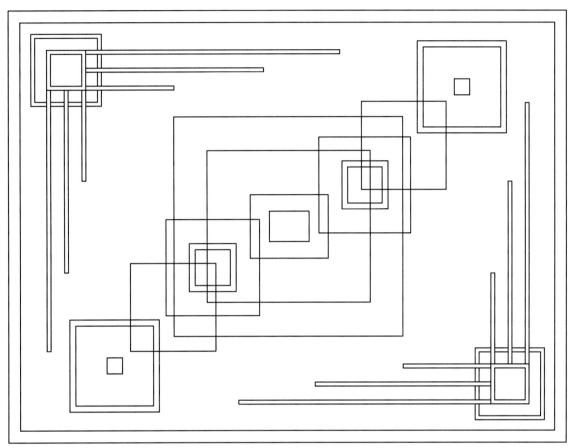

Figure 3-61
Project 3-3, Assignment 1: Custom area rug; example of custom area rug project (scale: 1/2″ = 1′-0″)
(*Courtesy of Laura Cook, High Point University Interior Design Alumna*)

Figure 3-62
Project 3-3, Assignment 2: Custom area rug; example of custom area rug project (scale: 1/2″ = 1′-0″) (*Courtesy of Laura Cook, High Point University Interior Design Alumna*)

Project 3-4: *Video Conference Room Including Furniture* [BASIC]

1. Draw the floor plan of the video conference room as shown in Figure 3-63. Use the dimensions shown in Figure 3-64, or use an architectural scale to measure the floor plan and draw it full scale. Your drawing will look like Figure 3-63 without the centerline.

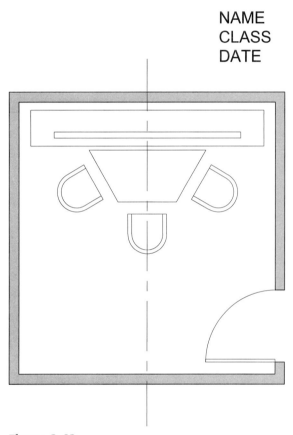

NAME
CLASS
DATE

Figure 3-63
Project 3-4: Video conference room including furniture (scale: 1/4″ = 1′-0″)

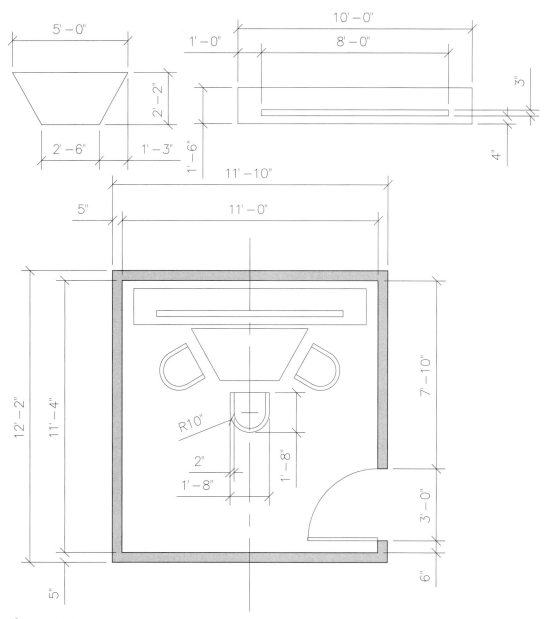

Figure 3-64
Dimensions for Project 3-4 (scale: 1/4″ = 1′-0″)

2. Use the **Single Line Text** command to type your name, class number, and date, 6″ high in the upper right corner (Figure 3-63).

3. Print your drawing from the **Model** tab at a scale of **1/4″ = 1′-0″.**

Project 3-5: *Rectangular Conference Room Including Furniture* [INTERMEDIATE]

1. Draw the floor plan of the conference room as shown in Figure 3-65. Use the dimensions shown in Figure 3-66, or use an architectural scale to measure the floor plan and draw it full scale.

Figure 3-65

Project 3-5: Rectangular conference room including furniture (scale: 1/4″ = 1′-0″)

NAME
CLASS
DATE

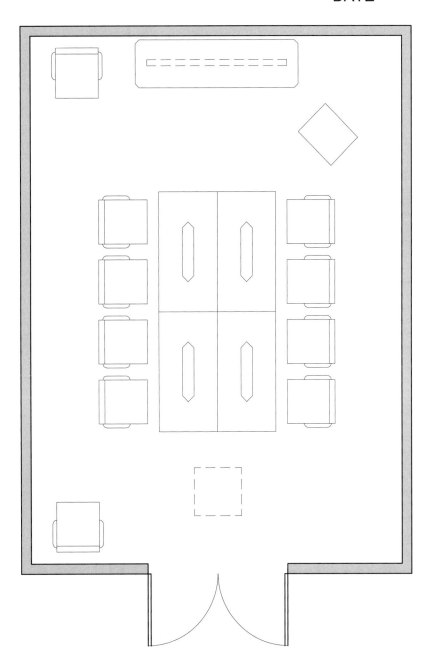

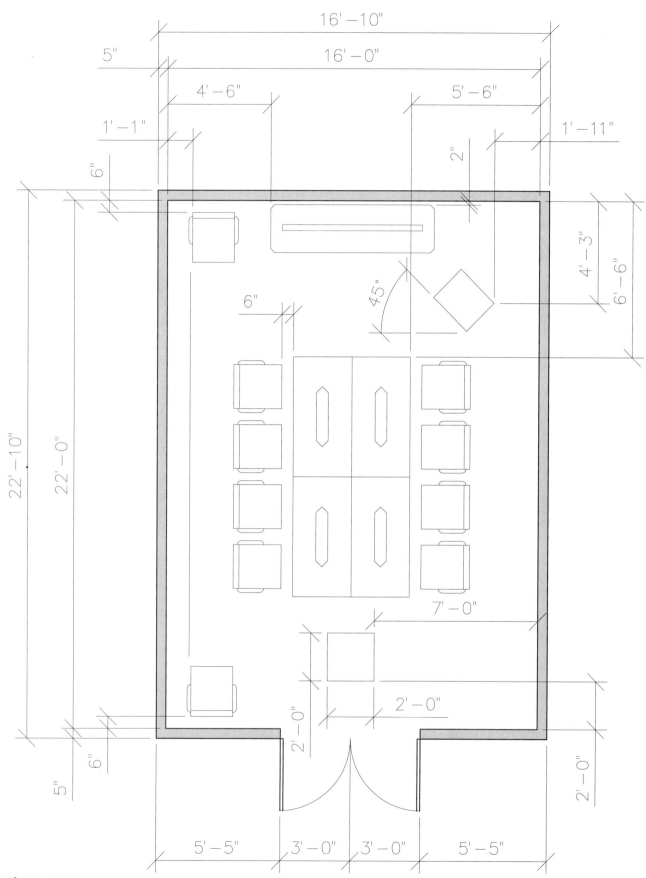

Figure 3-66

Sheet 1 of 2, Dimensions for Project 3-5 (scale: 1/4″ = 1′-0″)

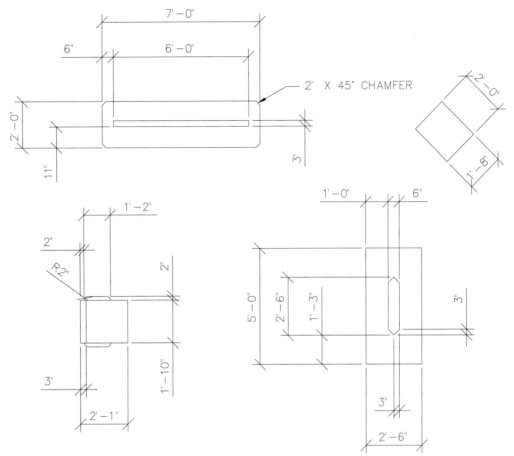

Figure 3-66
(*continued*)

2. Use the **Single Line Text** command to type your name, class number, and date, 6″ high in the upper right corner (Figure 3-65).

3. Print your drawing from the **Model** tab at a scale of **1/4″ = 1′-0″**.

Project 3-6: *Conference Room with Angles Including Furniture* [ADVANCED]

1. Draw the floor plan of the conference room as shown in Figure 3-67. Use the dimensions shown in Figure 3-68, or use an architectural scale to measure the floor plan and draw it full scale.

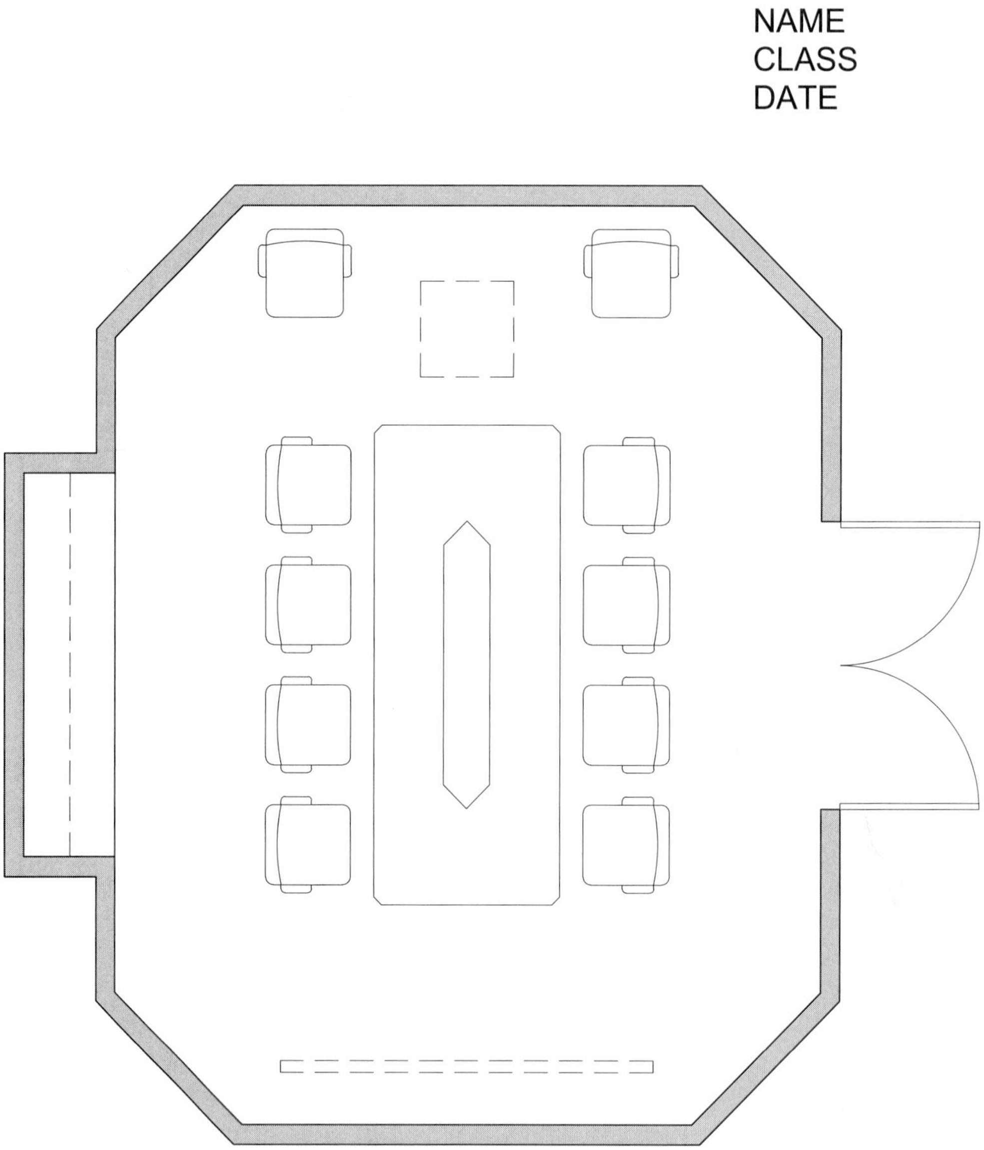

NAME
CLASS
DATE

Figure 3-67
Project 3-6: Conference room with angles including furniture (scale: 1/4″ = 1′-0″)

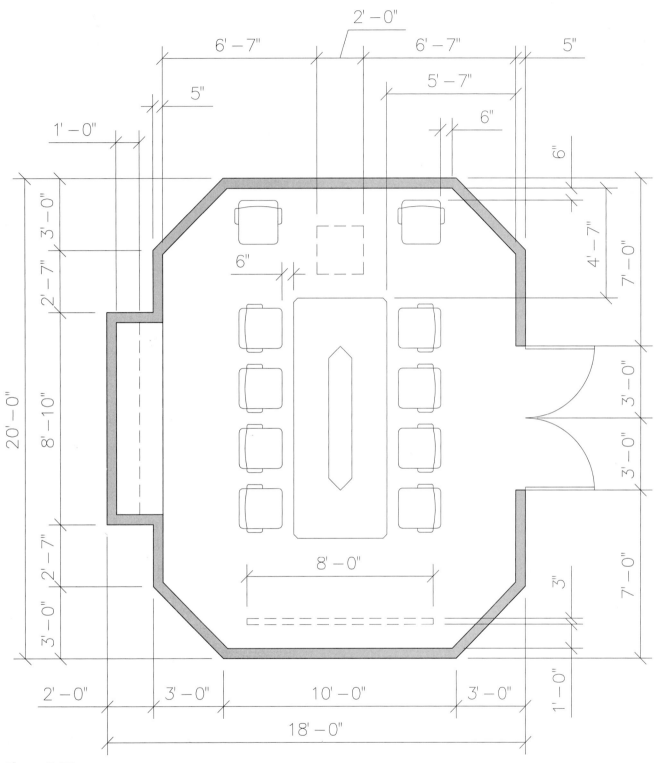

Figure 3-68
Sheet 1 of 2, Dimensions for Project 3-6 (scale: 1/4″ = 1′-0″)

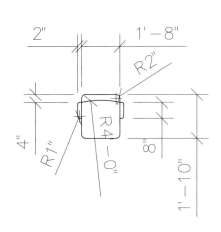

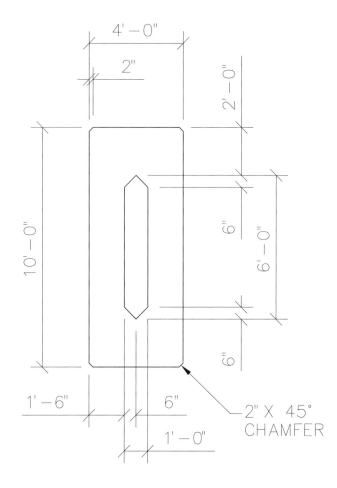

Figure 3-68
(*continued*)

2. Use the **Single Line Text** command to type your name, class number, and date, 6″ high in the upper right corner (Figure 3-67).

3. Print your drawing from the **Model** tab at a scale of **1/4″ = 1′-0″**.

4 chapterfour
Adding Text and Tables to the Drawing

CHAPTER OBJECTIVES

- Define the terms *style* and *font* and describe the function of each.
- Use **Dtext** (single line text) to draw text.
- Use **DDEDIT** to change text contents.
- Use different fonts on the same drawing.
- Place text on several different parts of the drawing with a single command.
- Use the modifiers **Align, Fit, Center, Middle, Right, Top,** and **Style.**
- Use the **Text Style…** setting to create condensed, expanded, rotated, backward, inclined, and upside-down text.

- Use the **Text Style…** setting to change any style on the drawing to a different font.
- Use **Properties** to change text characteristics.
- Use standard codes to draw special characters such as the degree symbol, the diameter symbol, the plus–minus symbol, and underscored and overscored text.
- Use **Mtext** (multiline text) to create paragraph text.
- Spell-check your drawing.
- Use the **Table** command to create door and window schedules.

EXERCISE 4-1
Placing Text on Drawings

To make complete drawings with AutoCAD, you need to know how text is added to the drawings. The following AutoCAD commands, used to place lettering on drawings, are examined in Exercise 4-1.

Text Style…: Used to control the appearance of text

Single Line Text (Dtext): Used to draw text that is not in paragraph form

Multiline Text (Mtext): Used to draw text that is in paragraph form

When you have completed Exercise 4-1, your drawing will look similar to the one in Figure 4-1.

Figure 4-1
Exercise 4-1: Placing text on drawings

**THIS WAS TYPED
WITH THE HEADING STYLE,
AND THE IMPACT FONT,
1/4" HIGH, CENTERED**

THIS WAS TYPED
WITH THE HAND LETTER STYLE
AND THE CITY BLUEPRINT FONT,
3/16" HIGH, CENTERED

STANDARD STYLE, FIT OPTION

OVERSCORE WITH THE OVERSCORE STYLE

OVERSCORE WITH THE STANDARD STYLE

UNDERSCORE WITH THE STANDARD STYLE
STANDARD CODES WITH THE STANDARD STYLE
±1/16"   45°   Ø1/2

ARIAL FONT
WITH THE UPSIDE DOWN STYLE,
UPSIDE DOWN AND BACKWARD

V E R T I C A L   S T Y L E

THIS IS PARAGRAPH OR MULTILINE TEXT TYPED WITH THE SANS SERIF FONT IN *TWO COLUMNS, 1/8" HIGH,* IN AN AREA THAT MEASURES 5-1/2"W X 1"H JUSTIFIED (JUSTIFIED IS ALIGNED ON BOTH SIDES). THE GUTTER SPACE IS BETWEEN THE TWO COLUMNS.

> **TIP**
>
> If you click **New...** and select the **acad.dwt** template, you will be in the same drawing environment as when you simply open the AutoCAD program and begin drawing. AutoCAD uses the acad.dwt template for the drawing settings if no other template is selected.

Step 1. Use your workspace to make the following settings:

1. Use **Save As...** to save the drawing with the name **CH4-EXERCISE1**.
2. Set drawing units: **Architectural**
3. Set drawing limits: **8-1/2,11** (the inch mark is not needed)
4. Set **GRIDDISPLAY: 0**
5. Set grid: **1/4**
6. Set snap: **1/8**
7. Create the following layers:

Layer Name	Color	Linetype	Lineweight
a-anno-text	green	continuous	.006" (.15 mm)
a-area-ttbl	magenta	continuous	.006" (.15 mm)

8. Set layer **a-anno-text** current.

9. Use **Zoom-All** to view the limits of the drawing.

Making Settings for Text Style

It is important to understand the difference between the terms *style name* and *font name* with regard to text:

Style Name

AutoCAD provides in the **Text Style** dialog box (use **ST** for Style to see the **Text Style** dialog box), by default, a style named *Standard.* By default, the Standard style includes the following settings (Figure 4-2):

Font Name:	Arial
Font Style:	Regular
Annotative:	Not checked
Height:	0
Upside down:	Not checked
Backwards:	Not checked
Vertical:	Not checked
Width Factor:	1
Oblique Angle:	0

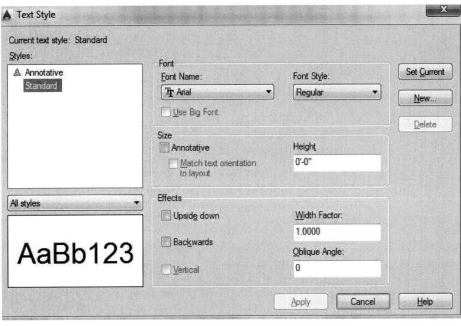

Figure 4-2
The Standard text style default settings

Font Name

This is the name of any ***font*** file. A font determines how text looks by defining its typeface, or graphical design. A font has to be in the AutoCAD program before it can be selected and assigned to a style name. AutoCAD assigns the

Arial font to the Standard style by default. AutoCAD has two types of fonts available, as shown in Figure 4-3:

1 **TrueType fonts:** The standard font type provided by Microsoft Windows. TrueType fonts have the .ttf file name extension. This extension is *not* shown in the **Text Style** dialog box **Font Name** list.

2 **SHX fonts:** AutoCAD's own set of fonts that have the .shx file name extension. This extension *is* shown in the **Text Style** dialog box **Font Name** list.

Figure 4-3
Two types of fonts: .shx and .ttf

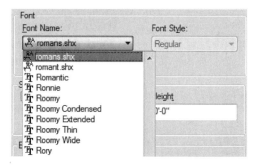

Making a New Text Style

TEXT STYLE	
Ribbon/ Panel	Annotate/ Text
Modify Toolbar:	
Menu Bar:	Format/ Text Style...
Type a Command:	STYLE
Command Alias:	ST

By clicking **New...** in the **Text Style** dialog box (Figure 4-2), you can make new text styles.

1 You can assign any name you choose to the style name. You may use the same name for the style that is used for the font name, or you may use a different name, single number, or letter for the style name.

2 You can assign the settings to the new text style to include **Font Name, Font Style, Annotative, Height, Upside down, Backwards, Vertical, Width Factor,** and **Oblique Angle.**

Step 2. Change the font for the Standard style (Figure 4-4), as described next:

Prompt	Response
Type a command:	**Text Style...** (or type **ST <Enter>**)
The **Text Style** dialog box appears with the **Standard** style current:	Click **TechnicLite** (in the **Font Name:** list)
	Click **Apply**

Any text typed while the Standard style is active will now contain the TechnicLite font. Notice the preview area in the lower left corner that shows you what the font looks like. Notice also that the vertical setting is grayed out, indicating that this font cannot be drawn running up and down.

The other settings should be left as they are. *If you leave the text height set at 0, you will be able to draw different heights of the same style and you will be able to change the height of text if you need to. Leave the text height set to 0 in all cases.* The **Width Factor** allows you to stretch letters so they are wider by making the **Width Factor** greater than 1, and narrower by making the **Width Factor** less than 1. The **Oblique Angle** slants the letters to the right if the angle is positive and to the left if the angle is negative.

Figure 4-4
Select the **TechnicLite** font
for the Standard style

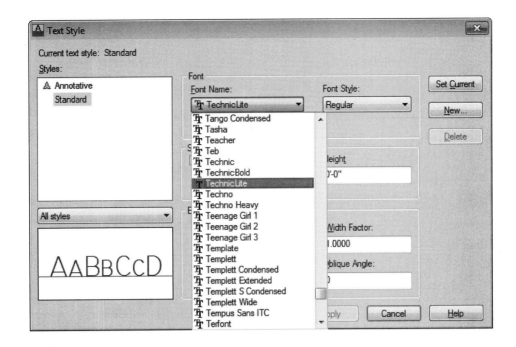

AutoCAD also provides a style named Annotative. This style is used when text is added to a drawing that will be plotted to scale (e.g., 1/4″ = 1′-0′). Any style can be made annotative in the **Text Style** dialog box by clicking the box under **Size** and beside **Annotative** to put a check in the box.

FOR MORE DETAILS

See Chapter 6 for more on annotative text.

Step 3. Make the settings for a new style that will be used on the drawing (Figures 4-5 and 4-6), as described next:

Prompt	Response
The **Text Style** dialog box:	Click **New...** (button on the right)
The **New Text Style** dialog box appears with a **Style Name** that AutoCAD assigns, style1:	Type **HEADING** (to name the style, Figure 4-5)
	Click **OK** (or press **<Enter>**)
The **Text Style** dialog box appears:	Click **romand.shx** (in the **Font Name:** list, Figure 4-6)
	Click **Apply**

Figure 4-5
Name the style, HEADING

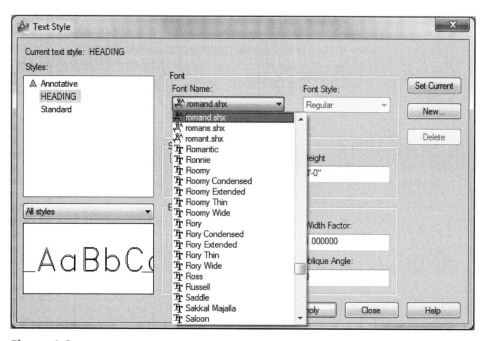

Figure 4-6
Select the romand.shx font for the HEADING style

You now have two styles that have been defined on your drawing, Standard and HEADING.

TIP

To locate a font in the **Font Name:** list, hold your cursor over any font name in the list and type the first few letters of the desired font. You can also scroll through the **Font Name:** list by pressing the up or down arrow key on the keyboard or by using the wheel on your wheel mouse.

Step 4. Make the settings for the following new styles (Figure 4-7):

Style Name	Font Name	Other Settings
HAND LETTER	CityBlueprint	None
OVERSCORE	Arial	None
UPSIDEDOWN	Arial	Place checks in the **Effects** box labeled **Upside down** and the box labeled **Backwards.**
VERTICAL	romand.shx	Place a check in the **Effects** box labeled **Vertical** (Figure 4-7). Remove checks in **Upside down** and **Backwards.**

Step 5. Check the **Styles** list to determine whether your list matches the one shown in Figure 4-8.

Step 6. Click the **HEADING** style name and the **Set Current** button to make it current; close the dialog box.

NOTE

If you make a mistake while making the settings for a new style, go back to the **Text Style** dialog box, highlight the style name, change or fix the settings, and click **Apply.**

Figure 4-7
Make settings for the
VERTICAL style

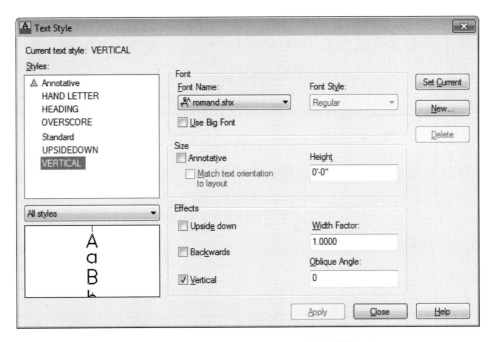

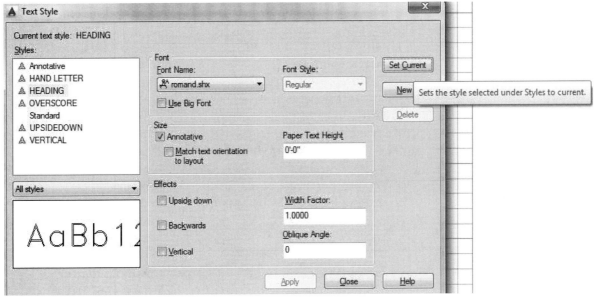

Figure 4-8
Check the **Styles** list and set the HEADING style current

SINGLE-LINE TEXT	
Ribbon/ Panel	Home/ Annotation **A**
Text Toolbar:	**A**
Menu Bar:	Draw/Text/ Single Line Text
Type a Command:	TEXT or DTEXT
Command Alias:	DT

Using the Single Line Text Command to Draw Text

The **Single Line Text** command (also known as **Dtext**) is used to draw text that is not in paragraph form. Although the name of the command might lead you to believe that only a single line can be drawn, such is not the case. To draw one line under another, just press **<Enter>**, and you can draw the next line with the same settings as the first line.

If you are not happy with the location of text, use the **MOVE** command to relocate it.

Step 7. Draw the first two examples at the top of the page using **Single Line Text** (Figure 4-9), as described next:

Prompt	Response
Type a command:	**Single Line Text** (or type **DT** **<Enter>**)
Specify start point of text or [Justify Style]:	Type **C <Enter>** (to center the text)
Specify center point of text:	Type **4-1/4,10 <Enter>** (you are locating the center of the line of text using absolute coordinates, 4-1/4″ to the right and 10″ up)
Specify height <0′-0 3/16″>:	Type **1/4 <Enter>**
Specify rotation angle of text <0>:	**<Enter>**
The **In-Place Text Editor** appears on the screen:	Type **THIS WAS TYPED <Enter>**
	Type **WITH THE HEADING STYLE, <Enter>**
	Type **AND THE ROMAND FONT, <Enter>**
	Type **1/4″ HIGH <Enter>**
	<Enter> (to exit the **Text Editor**)
	<Enter> (repeat **DTEXT**)
Specify start point of text or [Justify Style]:	Type **S <Enter>** (to change styles)
Enter style name or [?] <HEADING>:	Type **HAND LETTER <Enter>**
Specify start point of text or [Justify Style]:	Type **C <Enter>**
Specify center point of text:	Type **4-1/4,8 <Enter>**
Specify height <0′-0 3/16″>:	Type **3/16 <Enter>** (or **<Enter>** to accept a 3/16″ default)
Specify rotation angle of text <0>:	**<Enter>**
The **In-Place Text Editor** appears:	Type **THIS WAS TYPED <Enter>**
	Type **WITH THE HAND LETTER STYLE <Enter>**
	Type **AND THE CITY BLUEPRINT FONT, <Enter>**
	Type **3/16″ HIGH, CENTERED <Enter> <Enter>**

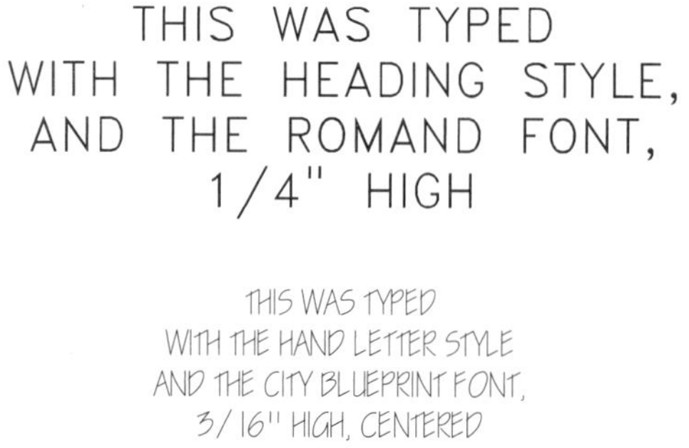

THIS WAS TYPED
WITH THE HEADING STYLE,
AND THE ROMAND FONT,
1/4" HIGH

THIS WAS TYPED
WITH THE HAND LETTER STYLE
AND THE CITY BLUEPRINT FONT,
3/16" HIGH, CENTERED

Figure 4-9
First two examples of **Single Line Text**

THIS WAS TYPED
WITH THE HEADING STYLE,
AND THE ROMAND FONT,
1/4" HIGH

THIS WAS TYPED
WITH THE HAND LETTER STYLE
AND THE CITY BLUEPRINT FONT,
3/16" HIGH, CENTERED

STANDARD STYLE, FIT OPTION

Figure 4-10
Using the **Fit** option of **Single Line Text**

Step 8. Draw the next block of text using the **Fit** option of **Single Line Text** with the Standard style (Figure 4-10), as described next:

Prompt	Response
Type a command:	**Single Line Text** (or type **DT** **<Enter>**)
Specify start point of text or [Justify Style]:	Type **S <Enter>** (to change styles)
Enter style name or [?] <HAND LETTER>:	Type **STANDARD <Enter>**
Specify start point of text or [Justify Style]:	Type **F <Enter>** (for **Fit**)
Specify first endpoint of text baseline:	Type **1-1/2,6 <Enter>**
Specify second endpoint of text baseline:	Type **7,6 <Enter>**
Specify height <0'-0 3/16">:	Type **1/2 <Enter>**
The **In-Place Text Editor** appears:	Type **STANDARD STYLE, FIT OPTION <Enter> <Enter>**

Justify Option

When you activate the **Single Line Text** command, the prompt is *Specify start point of text or [Justify Style]:*. The **Style** option allows you to select a different style (that has already been defined) for the text you are about to draw. *If you type* **J <Enter>**, the prompt then becomes *Enter an option [Align Fit Center Middle Right TL TC TR ML MC MR BL BC BR]:*.

Align: Draws the text between two points that you click. It does not condense or expand the font but instead *adjusts the letter height* so that the text fits between the two points.

Fit: Draws the text between two clicked points as used in the **Align** option, but instead of changing the letter height, **Fit** *condenses or expands the font* to fit between the points.

Center: Draws the text so that the *bottom of the line of lettering* is centered on the clicked point. You may also choose the top or the middle of the line of lettering by typing **TC** or **MC** at the justify prompt.

Middle: Draws the text so that the *middle of the line of lettering* is centered around a clicked point. This is useful when a single line of text must be centered in an area such as a box.

Right: Draws the text so that *each line of text is right justified* (ends at the same right margin). The top or center of the line may also be selected by typing **TR** or **MR** at the justify prompt.

TL TC TR ML MC MR BL BC BR: These are the alignment options: **Top Left, Top Center, Top Right, Middle Left, Middle Center, Middle Right, Bottom Left, Bottom Center, Bottom Right.** They are used with horizontal text.

Step 9. Draw a line of text using the VERTICAL style (Figure 4-11), as described next:

(Remember that you checked **Vertical** in the **Text Style** dialog box for this text style.)

Figure 4-11
Using the **Vertical** option of
Single Line Text

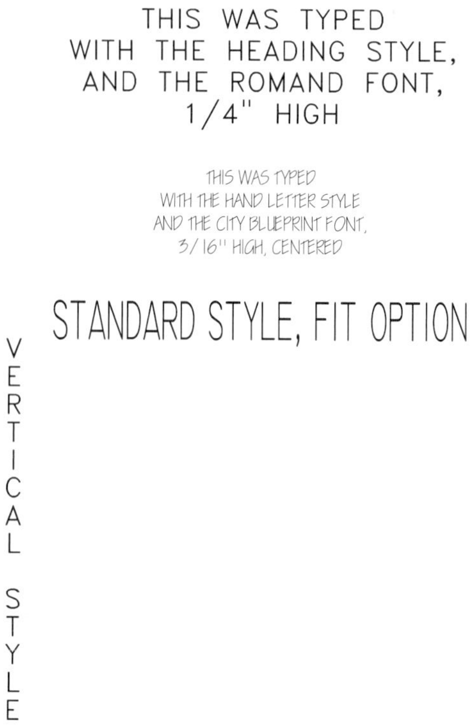

THIS WAS TYPED
WITH THE HEADING STYLE,
AND THE ROMAND FONT,
1/4" HIGH

THIS WAS TYPED
WITH THE HAND LETTER STYLE
AND THE CITY BLUEPRINT FONT,
3/16" HIGH, CENTERED

STANDARD STYLE, FIT OPTION

V
E
R
T
I
C
A
L

S
T
Y
L
E

Prompt	Response
Type a command:	**<Enter>** (repeat **DTEXT**)
Specify start point of text or [Justify Style]:	Type **S <Enter>**
Enter style name or [?] <Standard>:	Type **VERTICAL <Enter>**
Specify start point of text or [Justify Style]:	Type **1,6 <Enter>**
Specify height <0'-0" 3/16">:	Type **1/4 <Enter>**
Specify rotation angle of text <0>:	270 **<Enter>**
The **In-Place Text Editor** appears:	Type **VERTICAL STYLE <Enter>** **<Enter>**

Using Standard Codes to Draw Special Characters

45%%D

45°

Figure 4-12
Degree symbol code

%%C.500

⌀.500

Figure 4-13
Diameter symbol code

%%P.005

±.005

Figure 4-14
Plus–minus symbol code

Figures 4-12 through 4-16 show the use of codes to obtain several commonly used symbols, such as the degree symbol, the diameter symbol, the plus–minus symbol, and underscored and overscored text. The top line of Figure 4-12 shows the code that must be typed to obtain the degree symbol following the number 45. Two percent symbols followed by the letter D produce the degree symbol.

Figure 4-13 illustrates that two percent symbols followed by the letter C produce the diameter symbol.

Figure 4-14 shows the code for the plus–minus symbol.

Figure 4-15 shows the code for underscore: two percent symbols followed by the letter U. Notice that the first line contains only one code. The second line contains two codes: one to start the underline and one to stop it.

Figure 4-16 shows the code for overscored text. The same code sequence applies for starting and stopping the overscore.

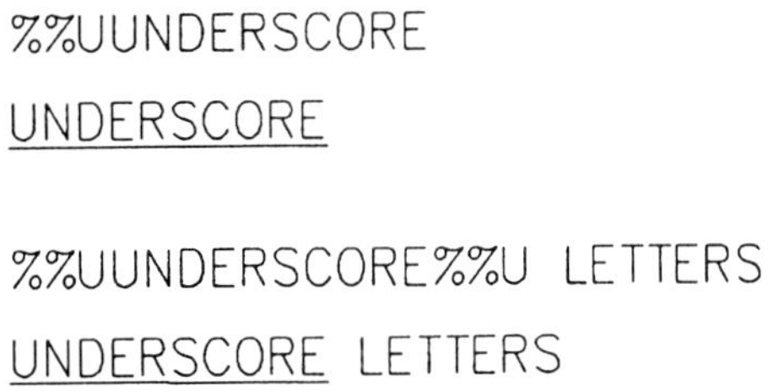

%%UUNDERSCORE
UNDERSCORE

%%OOVERSCORE
OVERSCORE

%%UUNDERSCORE%%U LETTERS
UNDERSCORE LETTERS

Figure 4-15
Underscore code

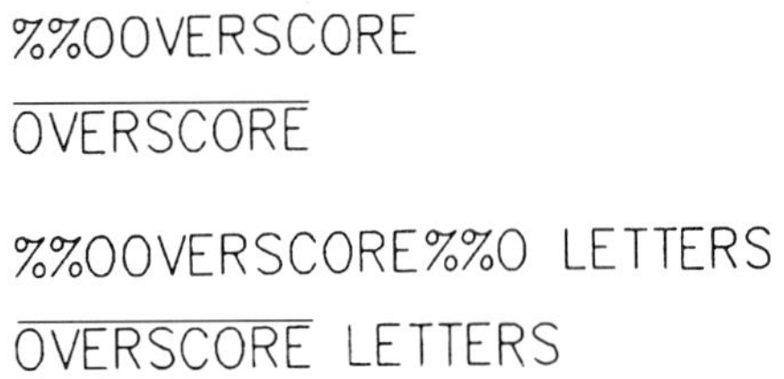

%%OOVERSCORE%%O LETTERS
OVERSCORE LETTERS

Figure 4-16
Overscore code

Step 10. Draw five lines containing special codes for the overscore, under-score, plus–minus, degree, and diameter symbols (Figure 4-17), as described next:

Prompt	Response
Type a command:	**<Enter>** (repeat **DTEXT**)
Specify start point of text or [Justify Style]:	Type **S <Enter>**
Enter style name or [?] <VERTICAL>:	Type **OVERSCORE <Enter>**
Specify start point of text or [Justify Style]:	Type **1-1/2,5 <Enter>**

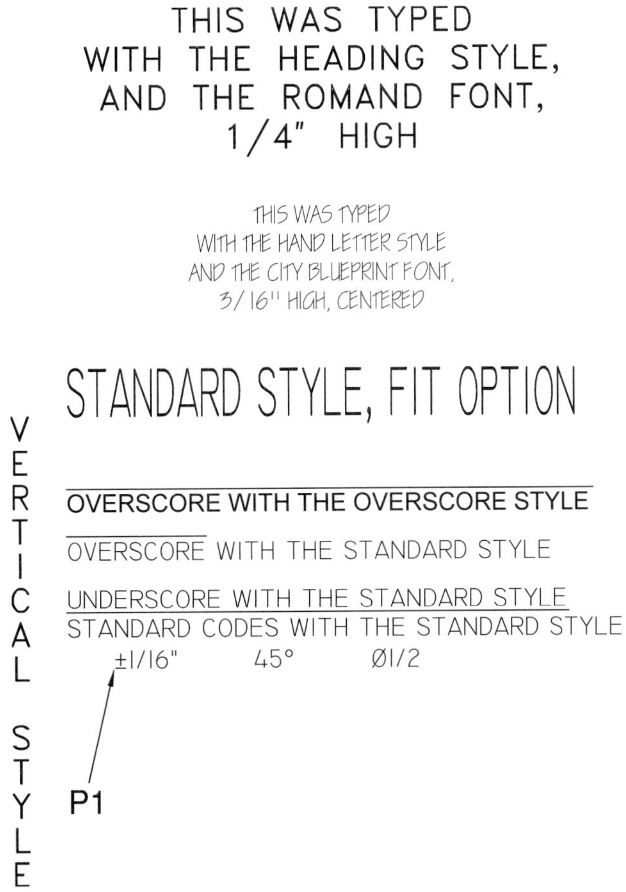

THIS WAS TYPED
WITH THE HEADING STYLE,
AND THE ROMAND FONT,
1/4" HIGH

THIS WAS TYPED
WITH THE HAND LETTER STYLE
AND THE CITY BLUEPRINT FONT,
3/16" HIGH, CENTERED

STANDARD STYLE, FIT OPTION

V
E
R
T
I
C
A
L

S
T
Y
L
E

OVERSCORE WITH THE OVERSCORE STYLE

OVERSCORE WITH THE STANDARD STYLE

UNDERSCORE WITH THE STANDARD STYLE
STANDARD CODES WITH THE STANDARD STYLE
±1/16"   45°   Ø1/2

P1

Figure 4-17
Using **Single Line Text** to draw symbols with standard codes

Prompt	Response
Specify height <0'-0 3/16">:	Type **3/16 <Enter>**
Specify rotation angle of text <0>:	**<Enter>**
The **In-Place Text Editor**	
appears:	Type **%%OOVERSCORE WITH THE OVERSCORE STYLE <Enter> <Enter>**
Type a command:	**<Enter>** (repeat **DTEXT**)
Specify start point of text or [Justify Style]:	Type **S <Enter>**
Enter style name or [?] <OVERSCORE>:	Type **STANDARD <Enter>**
Specify start point of text or [Justify Style]:	Type **1-1/2,4-1/2 <Enter>**
Specify height <0'-0 1/2">:	Type **3/16 <Enter>**
Specify rotation angle of text <0>:	**<Enter>**
The **In-Place Text Editor**	
appears:	Type **%%OOVERSCORE%%O WITH THE STANDARD STYLE <Enter> <Enter>**
Type a command:	**<Enter>** (repeat **DTEXT**)
Specify start point of text or [Justify Style]:	Type **1-1/2,4 <Enter>**
Specify height <0'-0 3/16">:	Type **3/16 <Enter>**
Specify rotation angle of text <0>:	**<Enter>**
The **In-Place Text Editor**	
appears:	Type **%%UUNDERSCORE WITH THE STANDARD STYLE <Enter> <Enter>**
Type a command:	**<Enter>** (repeat **DTEXT**)
Specify start point of text or [Justify Style]:	
The **In-Place Text Editor**	**<Enter>**
appears:	Type **STANDARD CODES WITH THE STANDARD STYLE <Enter> <Enter>**
Type a command:	**<Enter>** (repeat **DTEXT**)
Specify start point of text or [Justify Style]:	Click **P1 <Enter>** (a point in the approximate location as shown in Figure 4-17)
Specify height <0'-0 3/16">:	**<Enter>** (to accept the 3/16" default height)
Specify rotation angle of text <0>:	**<Enter>**
The **In-Place Text Editor**	
appears:	Type **%%P1/16" <Enter> <Enter>**
Type a command:	

Step 11. Use **Single Line Text (DTEXT)** to add the following text (3/16 height) to your drawing, as shown in Figure 4-17:

45° (45 %%D)
(Ø1/2″ (%%C1/2″)

Step 12. Make the style name UPSIDE DOWN current.

> **TIP**
>
> When you are typing using the UPSIDE DOWN style, it does not show as upside down and backward on your screen until you have completed typing the text and pressed the **<Enter>** key twice, once to indicate you do not want a second line of text and once to exit the **DTEXT** command.

Step 13. Use **Single Line Text** to draw the following phrase (3/16 height) upside down and backward with its start point at 7,2-1/2 (Figure 4-18):

UPSIDE DOWN AND BACKWARD <Enter>
WITH THE UPSIDEDOWN STYLE, <Enter>
ARIAL FONT <Enter> <Enter>

Figure 4-18

Draw a phrase upside down and backward with the UPSIDE DOWN style

THIS WAS TYPED
WITH THE HEADING STYLE,
AND THE ROMAND FONT,
1/4" HIGH

THIS WAS TYPED
WITH THE HAND LETTER STYLE
AND THE CITY BLUEPRINT FONT,
3/16" HIGH, CENTERED

STANDARD STYLE, FIT OPTION

V
E
R   OVERSCORE WITH THE OVERSCORE STYLE
T
I   OVERSCORE WITH THE STANDARD STYLE
C
A   UNDERSCORE WITH THE STANDARD STYLE
L   STANDARD CODES WITH THE STANDARD STYLE
         ±1/16"   45°   Ø1/2
S   ARIAL FONT
T   WITH THE UPSIDE DOWN STYLE,
Y   UPSIDE DOWN AND BACKWARD
L
E

Using the Multiline Text Command to Draw Text Paragraphs in Columns

The **Multiline Text** command (also known as **Mtext**) is used to draw text in paragraph form. The command activates the **Text Formatting Editor** and the **Text Editor** tab on the ribbon (Figure 4-19). You can select a defined style, change the text height and case, boldface and italicize some fonts,

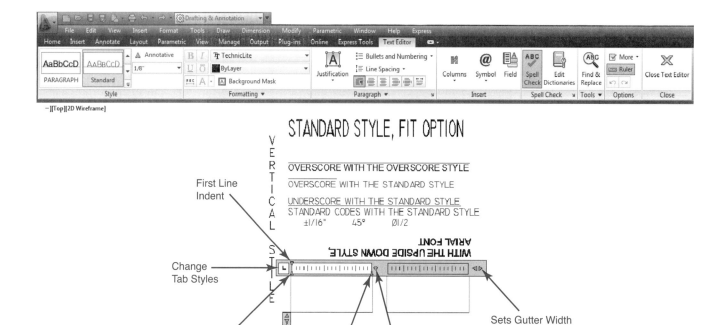

Figure 4-19
Text Formatting Editor with columns and the **Text Editor** tab of the ribbon

sans serif: Any text font that does not contain serifs. Serifs are the small features at the ends of letters and numbers.

select a justification style, specify the width of the paragraph (or columns and the space between columns within the paragraph), search for a word and replace it with another, import text, number lines, insert bullets, and select symbols for use on your drawing. In this exercise, you will create a paragraph in two columns using the **SansSerif** font.

Sans serif is a term that means "without serifs." Serifs are the small features at the ends of letters and numbers, as shown in Figure 4-20.

SANS SERIF LETTERING
(NO SERIFS)

SERIF LETTERING
(WITH SERIFS)

These Are Serifs

Figure 4-20
Serifs

Step 14. Create a new text style and use **Multiline Text** to draw a paragraph in two columns, as described next:

Prompt	Response
Type a command:	Type **ST <Enter>**
The **Text Style** dialog box appears:	Click **New**
The **New Text Style** dialog box appears:	Type **PARAGRAPH** (as the new style name)
	Click **OK**
The **Text Style** dialog box appears:	Change the **Font Name:** to **SansSerif**
	Remove checks from **Annotative, Upside down,** and **Backwards** (if these are checked)
	Click **Set Current**
The current style has been modified.	
Do you want to save your changes?	Click **Yes**
	Click **Close**
Type a command:	**Multiline Text...** (or type **MT <Enter>**)
Specify first corner:	Type **1-1/2, 2 <Enter>**
Specify opposite corner or [Height Justify Linespacing Rotation Style Width Columns]:	Type **H <Enter>**
Specify height <3/16″>:	Type **1/8 <Enter>**
Specify opposite corner or [Height Justify Linespacing Rotation Style Width Columns]:	Type **C <Enter>**
Enter column type [Dynamic Static No columns] <Dynamic>:	Type **S <Enter>**
Specify total width: <1′-6″>:	Type **5-1/2 <Enter>**
Specify number of columns: <2>:	Type **2 <Enter>**
Specify gutter width: <1″>:	Type **1/2 <Enter>**
Specify column height: <2″>:	Type **1 <Enter>**
The **Text Formatting Editor** appears, and the ribbon changes:	Click the **Justify** icon (Figure 4-21) (so the text is flush right and flush left)
	Type the paragraph shown in Figures 4-21 and 4-23. When you type 1/8 and 1/2 in the paragraph, the dialog box shown in Figure 4-22 appears. Remove the check from **Enable Autostacking**; click **OK**
	After the paragraph is typed correctly, click **Close Text Editor** (on the ribbon)

MULTILINE TEXT	
Ribbon/ Panel	Home/ Annotation **A**
Text Toolbar:	**A**
Menu Bar:	Draw/Text/ Multiline Text...
Type a Command:	MTEXT
Command Alias:	T or MT

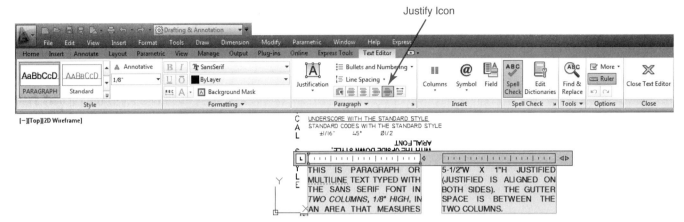

Justify Icon

[−][Top][2D Wireframe]

C
A
L

UNDERSCORE WITH THE STANDARD STYLE
STANDARD CODES WITH THE STANDARD STYLE
±1/16"   45°   Ø1/2

ARIAL FONT

WITH THE UPSIDE DOWN STYLE.

THIS IS PARAGRAPH OR
MULTILINE TEXT TYPED WITH
THE SANS SERIF FONT IN
TWO COLUMNS, 1/8" HIGH, IN
AN AREA THAT MEASURES

5-1/2"W X 1"H JUSTIFIED
(JUSTIFIED IS ALIGNED ON
BOTH SIDES). THE GUTTER
SPACE IS BETWEEN THE
TWO COLUMNS.

Figure 4-21
Multiline text in two columns with the **Justify** icon clicked

Figure 4-22
Do not stack fractions and tolerances

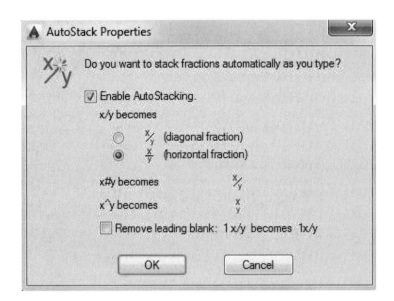

TIP

When the column width and height have been set in the **Text Formatting Editor,** you do not need to press **<Enter>** to go to the next line in the paragraph—this happens automatically as you type.

Changing Text Properties

Sometimes you will need to change the text font, height, or content. AutoCAD has several commands that can be used to do this:

Text Style…: Use this command to change the font of a text style that already exists on your drawing.

DDEDIT: (same as double-click): Use this command if you want to change the text contents only for single line text. This command allows you to select multiline text to change its contents and several of its properties.

Properties: Use this command to change any of the text's characteristics: properties, justification, style, height, rotation angle, the text content, or any of several other properties.

Figure 4-23
Type multiline text in two columns

THIS WAS TYPED
WITH THE HEADING STYLE,
AND THE IMPACT FONT,
1/4" HIGH, CENTERED

THIS WAS TYPED
WITH THE HAND LETTER STYLE
AND THE CITY BLUEPRINT FONT,
3/16" HIGH, CENTERED

STANDARD STYLE, FIT OPTION

OVERSCORE WITH THE OVERSCORE STYLE

OVERSCORE WITH THE STANDARD STYLE

UNDERSCORE WITH THE STANDARD STYLE
STANDARD CODES WITH THE STANDARD STYLE
±1/16"   45°   Ø1/2

UPSIDE DOWN AND BACKWARD
WITH THE UPSIDE DOWN STYLE,
ARIAL FONT

VERTICAL STYLE

THIS IS PARAGRAPH OR MULTILINE TEXT TYPED WITH THE SANS SERIF FONT IN *TWO COLUMNS, 1/8" HIGH,* IN AN AREA THAT MEASURES	5-1/2"W X 1"H JUSTIFIED (JUSTIFIED IS ALIGNED ON BOTH SIDES). THE GUTTER SPACE IS BETWEEN THE TWO COLUMNS.

Step 15. Use the **Text Style...** command to change the font of text typed with the HEADING name from Romand to Impact (Figure 4-24), as described next:

Prompt	Response
Type a command:	**Text Style...** (or type **ST <Enter>**)
The **Text Style** dialog box appears:	Click **HEADING** (in the **Styles:** list)
	Click **Set Current**
	Click **Impact** (from the **Font Name:** list, Figure 4-24)
	Click **Apply**
	Click **Close**

Notice that everything you typed with the HEADING style name is now still in the HEADING style but changed to the Impact font.

Step 16. Use the **DDEDIT** command to change "**AND THE ROMAND FONT**" at the top of the page to "**AND THE IMPACT FONT**" (Figure 4-25), as described next:

Prompt	Response
Type a command:	Double-click **AND THE ROMAND FONT,**
The **In-Place Text Editor** appears:	Click to the right of **ROMAND,** backspace over **ROMAND,** and type **IMPACT <Enter>** (Figure 4-25)
Select an annotation object or [Undo]:	**<Enter>**

DDEDIT	
Text Toolbar:	A⁄
Menu Bar:	Modify/Object Text/Edit
Type a Command:	DDEDIT
Command Alias:	ED

Figure 4-24
Select the Impact font for
the HEADING style

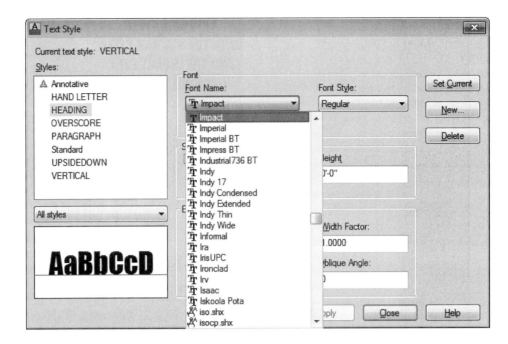

Figure 4-25
Change text using **DDEDIT**
(Edit Text)

THIS WAS TYPED
WITH THE HEADING STYLE,
AND THE IMPACT FONT,
1/4" HIGH

NOTE

Double-click on any text to edit it. If you double-click and nothing happens, go to **Options, Selection** tab, **Selection modes**, and make sure there is a check in the **Noun/verb** selection box.

Step 17. Double-click on the line of text that reads **1/4″ HIGH** and change it to **1/4″ HIGH, CENTERED**

Step 18. Use **DDEDIT** to change the words **TWO COLUMNS, 1/8″ HIGH,** to the italic font (Figure 4-26), as described next:

Prompt	Response
Type a command:	Double-click any point on the multiline text
The **Text Formatting Editor** (Figure 4-26) appears:	Click the left mouse button to the left of the word **TWO,** hold it down, and drag it to the end to the word **HIGH** so that **TWO COLUMNS, 1/8″ HIGH,** is highlighted, then click **I** (for italic) on the ribbon
	Click **Close Text Editor** (on the ribbon)

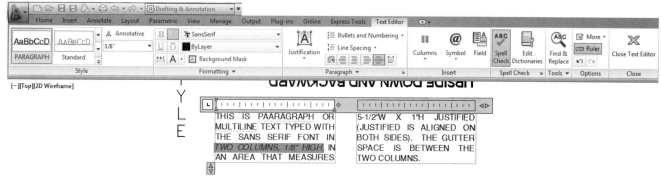

Figure 4-26
Change multiline text to italic

Step 19. Use the **Properties** palette to change the vertical line of text from layer **a-anno-text** to layer **a-area-ttbl** (Figure 4-27), as described next:

Prompt	Response
Type a command:	Click the vertical line of text (VERTICAL STYLE) and right-click
The right-click menu appears:	Click **Properties**
The **Properties** palette appears:	Click **Layer**
	Click **the down arrow** (Figure 4-27)
	Click **a-area-ttbl**
	Click the **X** in the upper left corner to close
	VERTICAL STYLE is now changed to **a-area-ttbl**

Step 20. Use **Single Line Text**, Standard style, 1/8″ high to place your name in the upper left corner and class number in the upper right corner. The start point for your name is 1,10-1/2. Use right-justified text for class number (at the **Dtext** prompt *Specify start point of text or [Justify Style]:* type **R <Enter>.** The right endpoint of text baseline is 7-1/2,10-1/2.

Checking the Spelling

AutoCAD has a spell checker that allows you to check the spelling on your drawing. The **Spelling** command is located on the **Annotate** panel, or type **SP <Enter>** at the command prompt to access it.

Step 21. When you have completed Exercise 4-1, save your work in at least two places.

Step 22. Print your drawing from the **Model** tab at a scale of **1:1.**

When you create Mtext in AutoCAD 2015, it automatically applies bullets or numbering, provided these options are enabled in the **Text Editor** ribbon tab. You can use **Manage** (from the **Menu Bar**) and **Customize User Interface (CUI)** from the **Customization** panel to add the **Text Editor** contextual tab to the ribbon. You can use the **tcount** command to add numbering to existing Mtext objects. For example, the Mtext shown in the left box below becomes that shown in the right box below by using the

PROPERTIES	
Ribbon/ Panel	View/ Palettes
Standard Toolbar:	
Menu Bar:	Modify/ Properties
Type a Command:	PROPERTIES
Command Alias:	PR

CHECK SPELLING	
Ribbon/ Panel	Annotate/ Text
Text Toolbar:	ABC
Menu Bar:	Tools/ Spelling...
Type a Command:	SPELL
Command Alias:	SP

Figure 4-27
Change text to layer
a-area-ttbl

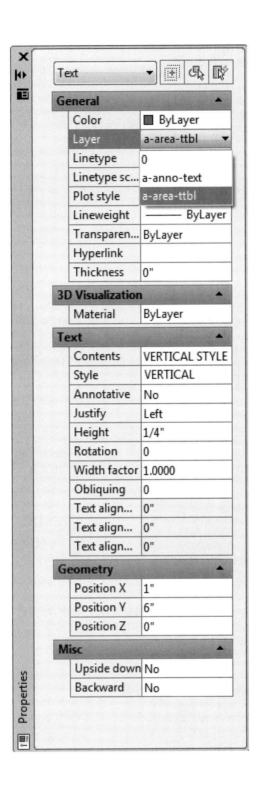

tcount command and with Starting number = 1, increment = 1, added as prefix:

Text sample line one	1 Text sample line one
Text sample line two	2 Text sample line two
Text sample line three	3 Text sample line three
Text sample line four	4 Text sample line four
Text sample line five	5 Text sample line five

> **TIP**
>
> When a drawing has a lot of text and annotations, zooming in and out requires auto regeneration of the drawing. This could be time consuming for a very busy drawing. If **QTEXT (Quick Text)** is turned on, each text and attribute object is displayed as a bounding box around the text object. Turning **QTEXT** mode on reduces the time it takes to regenerate drawings that contain many text objects. Use the **REGEN** command to display the results of QTEXT on existing text, with the **Visual Style** set to **2D Wireframe**.

EXERCISE 4-2
Using the TABLE Command to Create a Door Schedule

The **TABLE** command in AutoCAD 2015 is a tool to create professional-appearing tables such as door schedules, tables for drawing sets, window schedules, and similar items.

When you have completed Exercise 4-2, your drawing will look similar to Figure 4-28. This is a commonly used means of specifying the number and types of doors used in a commercial or residential building.

DOOR SCHEDULE			
MARK	**SIZE**	**QUANTITY**	**REMARKS**
1	2'0" X 6'8"	8	FLUSH DOOR
2	2'6" X 6'8"	2	FLUSH DOOR
3	2'6" X 6'8"	1	EXT FLUSH DOOR
4	3'0" X 7'0"	1	EXT FLUSH DOOR
5	4'0" X 6'8"	3	DOUBLE DOOR
6	3'0" X 6'8"	1	DOUBLE DOOR
7	9'4" X 6'8"	1	SLIDING DOOR

Figure 4-28
Completed door schedule table (Scale: 1″=1″)

Step 1. Use your workspace to make the following settings:

1. Use **Save As...** to save the drawing with the name **CH4-EXERCISE2**.
2. Set drawing units: **Architectural**
3. Set drawing limits: **11,8-1/2**
4. Set **GRIDDISPLAY: 0**
5. Set grid: **1/4″**
6. Set snap: **1/8″**
7. Make a new text style, name it **Title,** use the **Arial Font,** and change the Font Style to **Bold**.

8. Create the following layer:

Layer Name	Color	Linetype	Lineweight
a-anno-schd	green	continuous	.006″ (.15 mm)

9. Set layer **a-anno-schd** current.
10. Use **Zoom-All** to view the limits of the drawing.

Step 2. Use the **TABLE** command to modify the Standard table, as described next:

TABLE	
Ribbon/Panel	Home/Annotation
Draw Toolbar:	
Menu Bar:	Draw/Table...
Type a Command:	TABLE
Command Alias:	TB

Figure 4-29
Insert Table dialog box

Prompt

Type a command:

The **Insert Table** dialog box, Figure 4-29, appears:

Response

Click **Table** (or type **TB <Enter>**)

Click the **Launch the Table Style dialog** icon (the icon next to the **Standard Table style** name)

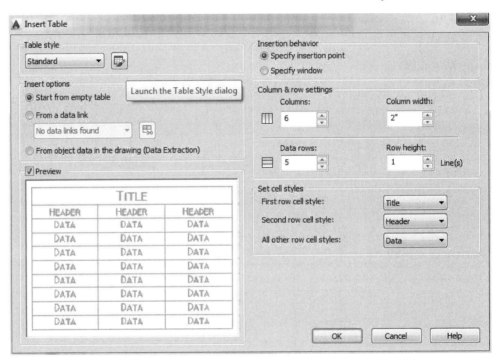

Prompt

The **Table Style** dialog box, Figure 4-30, appears:

The **Modify Table Style: Standard** dialog box (Figure 4-31) appears:

Response

At this point you could specify a new table name, but for now just modify the Standard table.
Click **Modify...**

Three cell styles, **Title, Header,** and **Data**, are provided within the Standard table.
Click **Title** under **Cell styles** [Figure 4-31] to make the following settings:

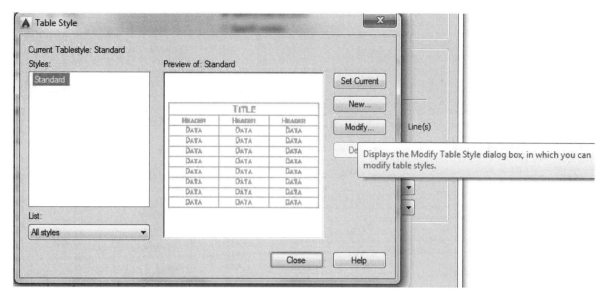

Figure 4-30
Table Style dialog box

Figure 4-31
Modify Table Style:
Standard dialog box

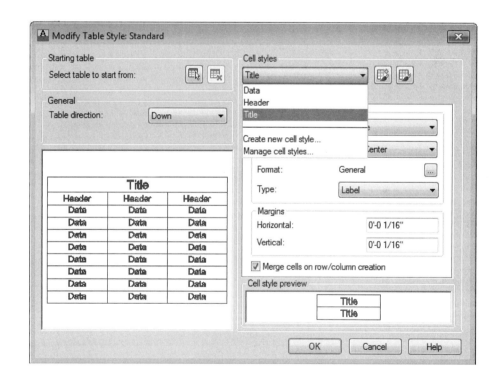

Prompt	Response
	Click the **General tab** (Figure 4-32)
	Click the **Fill color:** list down arrow and **Select Color… 9** (a light gray as the background color for the Title cell) (You have to click **Select Color…** at the bottom of the list to access the **Index Color** tab [Figure 4-32]); click **OK**

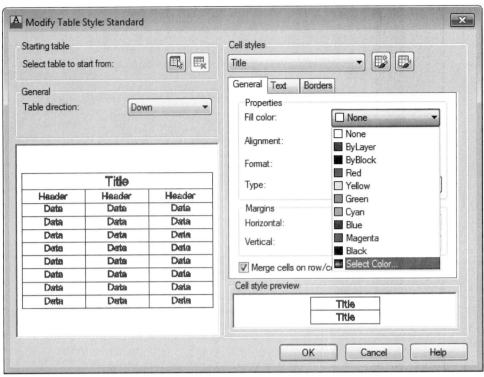

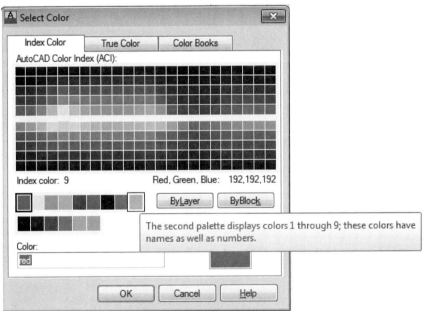

Figure 4-32
Click the **General tab** and **Select Color...** 9

Prompt	Response
	Click the **Text tab** (Figure 4-33)
	Click the **Text style:** list down arrow to set the **Text style: Title** current (Figure 4-33)
	Click **Data** under **Cell styles** (Figure 4-34) to make the following settings:
	Click the **General tab** (Figure 4-34)

Figure 4-33
Click the **Text tab** and set
Text Style: Title current

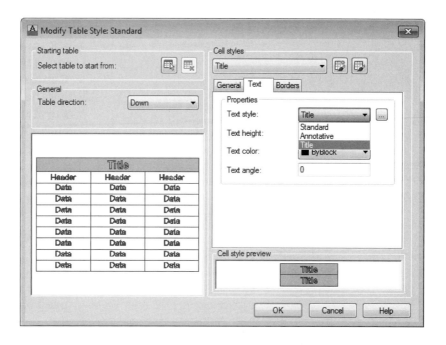

Figure 4-34
Click **Data** under **Cell styles**,
click **Alignment:** list arrow
and set alignment to **Middle
Center**, click **...button** to set
Format: to **Text**

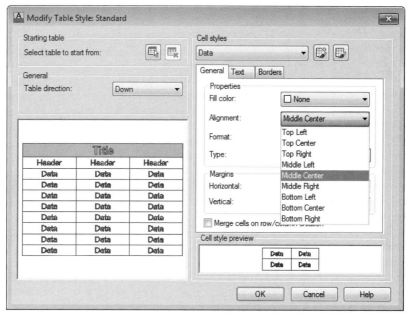

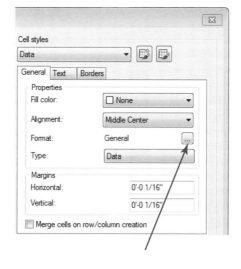

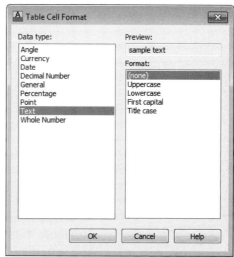

Prompt	Response
	Click the **Alignment:** list down arrow and set the alignment to **Middle Center** (Figure 4-34)
	Click the **... button** to set the **Format:** to **Text** (Figure 4-34); click **OK**
	Click the **Text tab** (Figure 4-35)
	Set **Text height:** to **1/8″** (Figure 4-35)
	Click **OK**
The **Table Style** dialog box appears:	Click **Close**
The **Insert Table** dialog box appears:	Make the settings shown in Figure 4-36: **6** columns (you will need only 4, but specify 6 anyway—you will delete 2 of them); set **Column width** at **2″** (you will change the column widths as you create the table); **5** rows (you will need 7, but specify 5 for now— adding rows is very easy); set **Row height:** at **1** if it is not the default; click **OK**

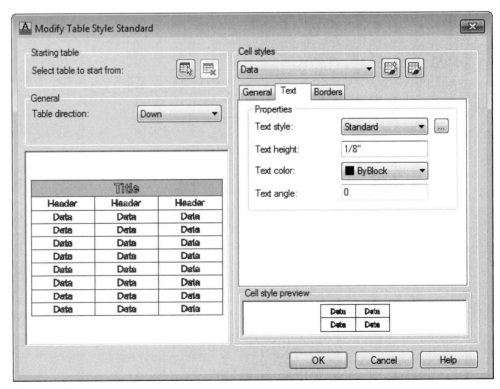

Figure 4-35
Set **Data Text height:** to 1/8″

Figure 4-36
Make settings for columns and rows

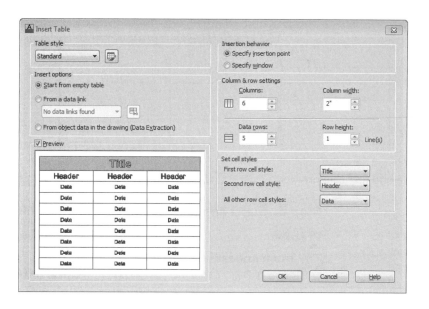

Step 3. Insert the table and type the title, as described next:

Prompt	Response
Specify insertion point:	Click a point to place the table in the approximate center of the page (It will hang outside the drawing limits for now.)
The **Text Formatting** dialog box appears with the cursor flashing in the center of the **Title** area:	Type **DOOR SCHEDULE <Enter>**

Step 4. Create column 1 head and all data in column 1, as described next:

Prompt	Response
The **Text Formatting** dialog box appears with the cursor flashing in the center of the column 1 header area:	Type **MARK <Enter>**
The **Text Formatting** dialog box appears with the cursor flashing in the center of the first data area:	Type **1 <Enter>**
The **Text Formatting** dialog box appears with the cursor flashing in the center of the second data area:	Type **2 <Enter>** **3 <Enter>** through **5** (so the table appears as shown in Figure 4-37. If numbers in the data cells are not in the center, click once on each number, then right-click and click **Alignment— Middle Center**. You can also select all the data cells at once using a crossing window and align them all at once.)

DOOR SCHEDULE					
MARK					
1					
2					
3					
4					
5					

Figure 4-37
Door schedule title and first column

Step 5. Insert and delete rows, as described next:

Prompt	**Response**
The table appears as shown in Figure 4-37:	Click once on the **4** data box, as shown in Figure 4-38
The ribbon changes (Figure 4-38):	Hold down the **<Shift>** key (so you can select two rows at the same time), and click the next row below, release the **<Shift>** key, then click **Insert Below** on the **Ribbon Row panel**
	Click the blank box under item **5** and type **6 <Enter>**, and **7 <Enter>**

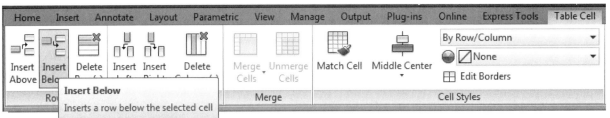

Figure 4-38
Insert two rows below

Step 6. Add the remaining column headers (Figure 4-39), as described next:

Prompt	**Response**
	Double-click the second column head area
The ribbon changes and the cursor flashes in the center of the column 2 header:	Type **SIZE** (do not press **<Enter>**)
	Press the **<Tab>** key

Figure 4-39
Text Editor and the door schedule

	A	B	C	D	E	F
1			DOOR SCHEDULE			
2	MARK	SIZE	QUANTITY	REMARKS		
3	1					
4	2					
5	3					
6	4					
7	5					
8	6					
9	7					

Prompt

The cursor is flashing in the center of the third column header:

The cursor is flashing in the center of the fourth column header:

Response

Type **QUANTITY**
Press the **<Tab>** key

Type **REMARKS**
Click any point in the screen area

Step 7. Delete unneeded columns (Figure 4-40), as described next:

Prompt

Response

Click the two columns to the right of the **REMARKS** column (hold down the **<Shift>** key to select the second column)
With the two blank columns highlighted, click **Delete Column(s)** (Figure 4-40)

Figure 4-40
Delete columns

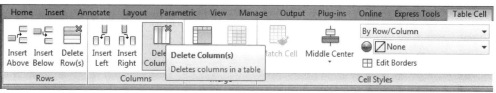

	A	B	C	D	E	F
1			DOOR SCHEDULE			
2	MARK	SIZE	QUANTITY	REMARKS		
3	1					
4	2					
5	3					
6	4					
7	5					
8	6					
9	7					

Step 8. Change the width of the columns to fit the data text (Figure 4-41), as described next:

Prompt

The right-click menu appears:
The **Properties** palette appears:

Response

Click once on the first column header **(MARK)** and right-click
Click **Properties**
Change **Cell width** to **1″** and **Cell height** to **1/2″** (Figure 4-41)

Figure 4-41
Use the **Properties** palette to change cell width and height

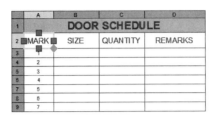

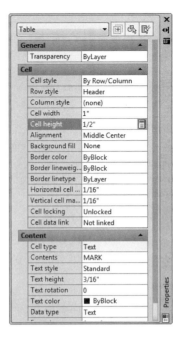

Step 9. Change the width of the remaining columns (Figure 4-42):

Column **2 (SIZE)**—change to **1-1/2"**

Column **3 (QUANTITY)**—change to **1-1/2"**

Column **4 (REMARKS)**—change to **2"**

Close the **Properties** palette.

Figure 4-42
Use the **Properties** palette to change cell width

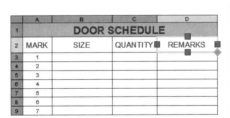

Step 10. Click the first cell under the **SIZE** column header and type **2′0″** × **6′8″** **<Enter>**. Type each remaining door size (Figure 4-43) and press **<Enter>**.

Step 11. Double-click the first cell under the **QUANTITY** column header and type each door quantity (Figure 4-43) and press **<Enter>**.

Step 12. Double-click the first cell under the **REMARKS** column header and type each door description (Figure 4-43) and press **<Enter>**.

Step 13. Align data in the **REMARKS** column middle left (Figures 4-43, 4-44, and 4-45), as described next:

Figure 4-43
Type each door size, quantity, and description; select all data cells in the REMARKS column

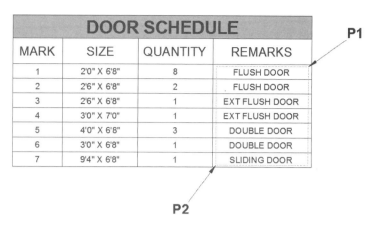

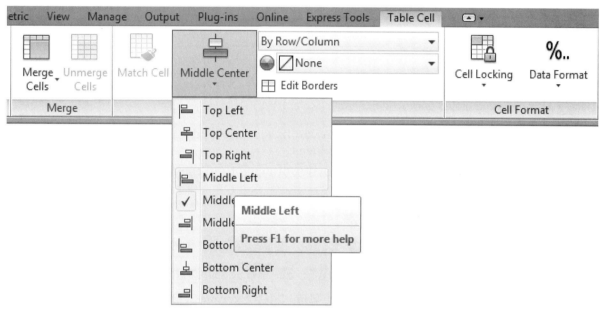

Figure 4-44
Align REMARKS column middle left

Prompt	Response
With no command active:	Click **P1→** (Figure 4-43)
Specify opposite corner:	Click **P2→** (to window the data in the **REMARKS** column)
The ribbon changes:	Click **Alignment—Middle Left** (from the **Cell Styles** panel, Figure 4-44)

Step 14. Type your name **1/8″** high in the upper right corner.

DOOR SCHEDULE

MARK	SIZE	QUANTITY	REMARKS
1	2'0" X 6'8"	8	FLUSH DOOR
2	2'6" X 6'8"	2	FLUSH DOOR
3	2'6" X 6'8"	1	EXT FLUSH DOOR
4	3'0" X 7'0"	1	EXT FLUSH DOOR
5	4'0" X 6'8"	3	DOUBLE DOOR
6	3'0" X 6'8"	1	DOUBLE DOOR
7	9'4" X 6'8"	1	DOUBLE DOOR

Figure 4-45
Completed door schedule table (Scale: 1″=1″)

Step 15. When you have completed Exercise 4-2, save your work in at least two places.

Step 16. Print your drawing from the **Model** tab at a scale of **1:1.**

EXERCISE 4-3
Using the TABLE Command to Create a Window Schedule

When you have completed Exercise 4-3, your drawing will look similar to Figure 4-46. This is a commonly used means of specifying the number and types of windows used in a commercial or residential building.

WINDOW SCHEDULE

MARK	SIZE	HEIGHT	QUANTITY	REMARKS
A	4' 5-1/8"	4' 2-5/8"	1	METAL FRAME
B	3' 1-1/8"	4' 2-5/8"	9	METAL FRAME
C	6'-0"	4' 2-5/8"	1	METAL FRAME
D	5'-0"	4' 2-5/8"	1	METAL FRAME
E	9'-0"	4' 2-5/8"	1	METAL FRAME

Figure 4-46
Completed window schedule table (Scale: 1″=1″)

Step 1. Use the information described in Exercise 4-2 to complete the window schedule shown in Figure 4-46.

Step 2. You may copy **CH4-EXERCISE2**, save it as **CH4-EXERCISE3**, and make changes as needed to make the new table.

Chapter Summary

In this chapter you learned to add text and tables to drawings. In addition, you learned to make window and door schedules and a title block, and to spell-check drawings. Now you have the skills and information necessary to add text to drawings and to make window and door schedules. You also learned to use the **SPELLING** command to make sure there are no misspelled words in your drawings.

Chapter Test Questions

Multiple Choice

Circle the correct answer.

1. The command used in this chapter to place line text (text not in paragraph form) on drawings is:
   a. **Single Line Text (Dtext)**
   b. **TXT**
   c. **Multiline Text (Mtext)**
   d. **DDedit**

2. The command used in this chapter to place paragraph text on drawings is:
   a. **Single Line Text (Dtext)**
   b. **TXT**
   c. **Multiline Text (Mtext)**
   d. **DDedit**

3. Which of the following could be used as a style name?
   a. SIMPLEX
   b. TITLE
   c. NAMES
   d. All these could be used as a style name.

4. Which of the following is a font name?
   a. SIMPLEX
   b. TITLE
   c. NAMES
   d. All these are font names.

5. When you set the text style, which of the following text height settings will allow you to draw different heights of the same text style?
   a. 1/4
   b. 0'-0"
   c. 1
   d. 100

6. Which of the following **Single Line Text** options draws text between two clicked points and adjusts the text height so that it fits between the two points?
   a. **Fit**
   b. **Align**
   c. **Justify**
   d. **Style**

7. Which of the following **Single Line Text** options draws text between two clicked points and condenses or expands the text to fit between the two points but does not change the text height?
   a. **Fit**
   b. **Align**
   c. **Justify**
   d. **Style**

8. The justification letters **MR** stand for:
   a. Middle, Right-justified
   b. Margin, Right-justified
   c. Midpoint, Left-justified
   d. Bottom, Right-justified

9. Which of the following modifiers should be selected if you want the bottom of the line of text to end 1/2″ above and 1/2″ to the left of the lower right corner of the drawing limits?
   a. **TL**
   b. **BR**
   c. **BL**
   d. **TR**

10. Which of the following best describes the text properties that can be modified for the title, header, and data cell styles?
   a. Style
   b. Height
   c. Color and angle
   d. All of the above

Matching

Write the number of the correct answer on the line.

a. **TABLE** _____

b. Middle Center _____

c. **Single Line Text** _____

d. Standard codes _____

e. **DDEDIT** _____

1. The same as double-clicking text
2. A command used to draw text not in paragraph form
3. A command used to make door and window schedules
4. Used to draw commonly used symbols, such as the degree symbol
5. A text alignment description

True or False

Circle the correct answer.

1. **True or False:** You can change from one text style to another from within the **Single Line Text** command.

2. **True or False:** Columns in a table cannot be deleted.

3. **True or False:** The **Properties** command allows you to change text height, contents, properties, justification, and style.

4. **True or False:** The default text style name is Standard, and the default font is Arial.

5. **True or False:** Paragraph text cannot be used in a drawing.

List

1. Five aliases for text placement and editing available in AutoCAD.

2. Five settings for creating a text style.

3. Five text justifications available in AutoCAD upon launching the text command.

4. Five standard codes for special characters such as the degree (°) and percent (%) symbols.

5. Five Unicode control codes for the following special symbols:

    o

    ₵

    ±

    Ø

    ≠

6. Five options of the **Stack Properties** dialog box.
7. Five ways of the **Check Spelling** dialog box.
8. Five options of the **New Table Style** dialog box.
9. Five options of the **Table Cell Format** dialog box.
10. Five steps in editing the contents of a cell of a table.

Questions

1. How can tables be modified to contain several lines of headings?
2. When should you use paragraph text?
3. What is **Single Line Text** used for and what are its options?
4. Name the three cell styles that the standard table style provides.
5. What is the best and most efficient way to modify text?

Chapter Projects

Project 4-1: *Lighting Legend* [BASIC]

1. Draw the lighting legend as shown in Figure 4-47. Measure Figure 4-47 using a ¼″ = 1′-0″ scale and draw it full size.

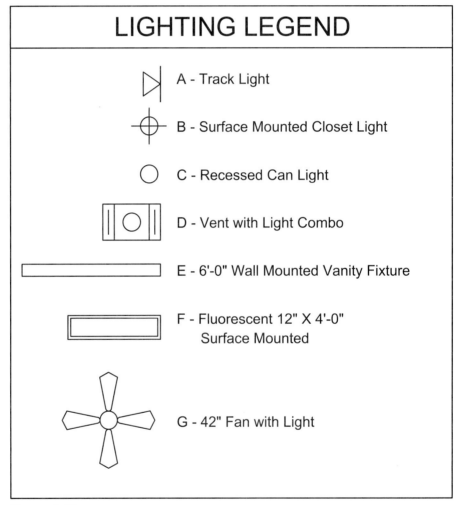

Figure 4-47
Project 4-1: Lighting schedule (Scale: ¼″ = 1′-0″)

2. Type your name 6″ high in the upper right corner.

3. Save the drawing in at least two places and print the drawing to Scale: ¼″=1′-0″.

Project 4-2: *Room Finish Schedule* [INTERMEDIATE]

1. Use the **TABLE** command to draw the room finish schedule as shown in Figure 4-48. Measure Figure 4-48 and draw it full size.

2. Type your name on the drawing.

3. Save the table in at least two places and print the table at a scale of 1:1, landscape orientation, on an 8-1/2″ × 11″ sheet.

ROOM FINISH SCHEDULE - UNITS

Rm. No.	Rm. Name	Base North	Base South	Base East	Base West	Walls North	Walls South	Walls East	Walls West	Ceiling Type	Ceiling Height
101	Living Room	WB	WB	WB	WB	-	-	-	-	GYP	VARIES
102	Kitchen	WB	WB	WB	WB	-	-	-	-	GYP	VARIES
103	Dining Area	WB	WB	WB	WB	-	-	-	-	GYP	VARIES
104	Storage Room	WB	WB	WB	WB	-	-	-	-	GYP	8'-0"
105	Corridor	WB	WB	WB	WB	-	-	-	-	GYP	8'-0"
106	Laundry	WB	WB	WB	WB	-	-	-	-	GYP	8'-0"
107	Master Bedroom	TB	TB	TB	TB	-	-	-	-	GYP	7'-0"
108	Master Bath	TB	TB	TB	TB	-	-	-	-	GYP	8'-0"
109	Bedroom	WB	WB	WB	WB	-	-	-	-	GYP	7'-0"
110	Bath	TB	TB	TB	TB	-	-	-	-	GYP	8'-0"
111	Closet	WB	WB	WB	WB	-	-	-	-	GYP	8'-0"
112	Master Closet	WB	WB	WB	WB	-	-	-	-	GYP	8'-0"
113	Garage	WB	WB	WB	WB	-	-	-	-	GYP	8'-0"
114	Garage Storage	WB	WB	WB	WB	-	-	-	-	GYP	8'-0"
115	Wet Bar	WB	WB	WB	WB	-	-	-	-	GYP	VARIES

Figure 4-48
Project 4-2: Room finish schedule (Scale: 1″ = 1″)

Project 4-3: *Door and Frame Schedule* [ADVANCED]

1. Use the **TABLE** command to draw the door and frame schedule as shown in Figure 4-49. Measure Figure 4-49 and draw it full size.

2. Type your name on the drawing.

3. Save the table in at least two places and print the table at a scale of 1:1, landscape orientation, on an 8-1/2″ × 11″ sheet.

DOOR AND FRAME SCHEDULE

Door Description	Door Type	Door Material	Frame Width	Frame Height	Frame Thickness	Frame Type	Hardware Sets
Entry Door	1	Aluminum Clad Wood	3'-0"	6'-8"	0'-1 3/4"	ACW	To have (3) spring hinge, 1250 4-1/2 X 4-1/2, 652 ,HAG., (1) entrance lock, D53PD RHO, 626 SCH., (1) wall stop,WS407CCV, 630 IVE., (1) dead bolt lock B661P, 626 SCH.,
							(1) sweep 315 CN, 628 PEM, and (1) threshold (per door manufacturer's recommendations).
French Door	2	Aluminum Clad Wood	2'-11"	6'-8"	0'-1 3/4"	ACW	To have (6) spring hinge, 1250 4-1/2 X 4-1/2, 652 ,HAG., (1) entrance lock, D53PD RHO, 626 SCH., (1) wall stop,WS407CCV, 630 IVE., (1) dead bolt lock B661P, 626 SCH.,
							(1) sweep 315 CN, 628 PEM, and (1) threshold (per door manufacturer's recommendations).
Exterior Door	3	Aluminum Clad Wood	2'-0"	6'-8"	0'-1 3/4"	ACW	
Interior Door	4	Hollow Core Wood	2'-8"	6'-8"	0'-1 3/4"	W	To have (3) hinge BB1279 4-1/2 X 4-1/2, 652 HAG., (1) privacy lock D40S RHO, 626 SCH., (1) wall stop WS407CCV, 630 IVE., and (1) weatherstrip 297AV head & jambs, 628PEM.
Interior Door	5	Hollow Core Wood	2'-0"	6'-8"	0'-1 3/4"	W	To have (3) hinge BB1279 4-1/2 X 4-1/2, 652 HAG., (1) privacy lock D40S RHO, 626 SCH., (1) wall stop WS407CCV, 630 IVE., and (1) weatherstrip 297AV head & jambs, 628PEM.
Closet Door	6	Mirror panels	(2) 1'-11 1/2"	6'-8"	0'-1 3/4"	MR	Manufacturer provided
Closet Door	7	Mirror panels	(2) 1'-11 1/2"	6'-8"	0'-1 3/4"	MR	Manufacturer provided
Laundry Door	8	Wood louvered panels	3'-11"	6'-8"	0'-1 3/4"	W	Manufacturer provided
Shower Door	9	Glass	2'-0"	6'-8"	0'-1 3/4"	G	Manufacturer provided
Laundry Door	10	Aluminum Vinyl	(2) 1'-11 1/2"	6'-8"	0'-1 3/4"	AV	Manufacturer provided
Garage Door	12	Aluminum	10'-0"	7'-0"	0'-1 3/4"	A	Manufacturer provided
Hollow Metal Door	11	Hollow Metal	3'-0"	6'-8"	0'-1 3/4"	HM	To have (3) hinge BB1279 4-1/2 X 4-1/2, 652 HAG., (1) storeroom lock D80PD RHO, 626 SCH., (1) threshold 171A X MS&A, 628 PEM, and (1) wall stop WS407CCV, 630 IVE.

NOTES:
ACW - aluminum clad wood   W - wood
MR - Mirror   G - Glass   HM - hollow metal
A - aluminum   AV - aluminum vinyl
General Note: T = tempered glass

Figure 4-49
Project 4-3: Door and frame schedule (Scale: 1"=1")

chapterfive

Advanced Plotting: Using Plot Styles, Paper Space, Multiple Viewports, and PDF Files

CHAPTER OBJECTIVES

- Create a color-dependent plot style.
- Print/plot drawings with one viewport from a layout tab.
- Toggle between **PAPER** space and **MODEL** space while in a layout tab.
- Correctly use the following commands:

Page Setup Manager	**MVIEW**
INSERT-BLOCK	**Properties**
VIEWPORTS (VPORTS)	**Convert Plot Styles**

- Print/plot drawings with multiple viewports from a layout tab.
- Print/plot drawings at various scales on the same sheet.
- Print/plot drawings to a PDF file.

Layer Names, Colors, and Lineweights

Layers, their colors, and lineweights are very significant in plotting and printing. Varying the thickness of different types of lines such as those used to draw walls, doors, text, and furniture can make a drawing much more useful and esthetically pleasing.

The *AIA CAD Layer Guidelines* have been used as a guide for naming the layers used in this book. Different lineweights have been used to provide drawing legibility in the plans: very heavy, heavy, medium, light, and very light. Colors have been selected to be applied consistently to these layers.

Figure 5-1 shows the lineweights. There are two sets of lineweights, one for A- and B-size sheets and one for C- and D-size sheets. Larger lineweights are used on the C- and D-size sheets to accommodate the larger scale of the drawings.

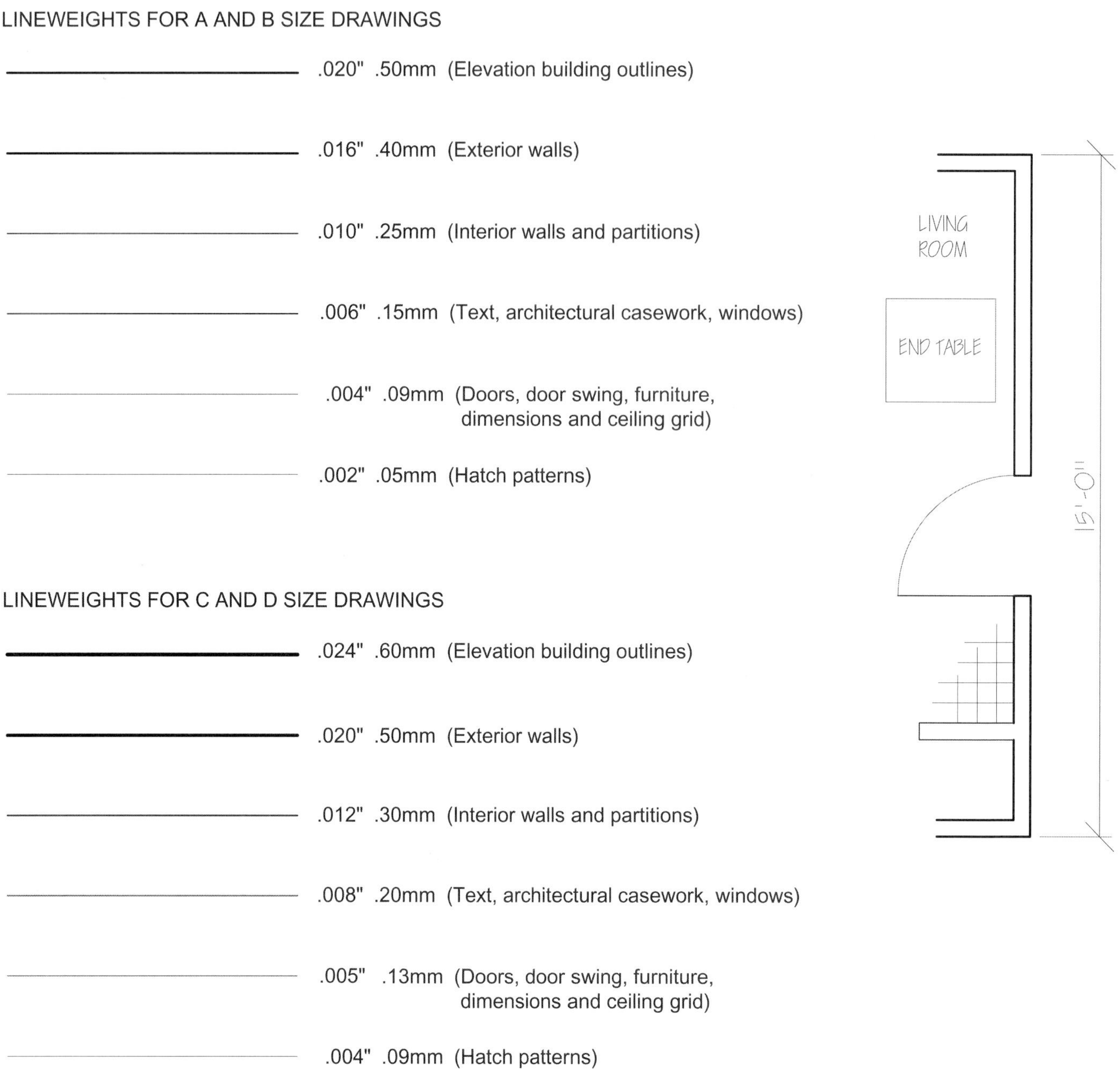

LINEWEIGHTS FOR A AND B SIZE DRAWINGS

———————————— .020" .50mm (Elevation building outlines)

———————————— .016" .40mm (Exterior walls)

———————————— .010" .25mm (Interior walls and partitions)

———————————— .006" .15mm (Text, architectural casework, windows)

———————————— .004" .09mm (Doors, door swing, furniture,
                          dimensions and ceiling grid)

———————————— .002" .05mm (Hatch patterns)

LINEWEIGHTS FOR C AND D SIZE DRAWINGS

———————————— .024" .60mm (Elevation building outlines)

———————————— .020" .50mm (Exterior walls)

———————————— .012" .30mm (Interior walls and partitions)

———————————— .008" .20mm (Text, architectural casework, windows)

———————————— .005" .13mm (Doors, door swing, furniture,
                          dimensions and ceiling grid)

———————————— .004" .09mm (Hatch patterns)

Figure 5-1
Lineweights for A-, B-, C-, and D-size drawings

Figure 5-2 shows the layer names, colors, and lineweights used in this book. This provides a basic outline of layers, colors, and lineweights for architectural plans, which can be adjusted or changed as required for individual needs or preferences.

Plot Styles

plot style: An object property that makes a collection of settings for color, dithering, gray scale, pen assignments, screening, linetype, lineweight, end styles, join styles, and fill styles. Plot styles are used at plot time.

Plot styles allow you to plot the same drawing in different ways. AutoCAD provides some plot styles, or you can create your own. A plot style contains settings that can override an object's color, linetype, and lineweight. There are two types of plot styles: named and color-dependent.

LAYER NAME	DESCRIPTION	COLOR	LINEWEIGHT	
			A & B SIZE	**C & D SIZE**
Architectural				
a-anno-area	area calculation	green	.006" (.15mm)	.008" (.20mm)
a-anno-dims	dimensions	red	.004" (.09mm)	.005" (.13mm)
a-anno-revs	revisions	white	.014" (.35mm)	.016" (.40mm)
a-anno-schd	schedules	green	.006" (.15mm)	.008" (.20mm)
a-anno-text	general text	green	.006" (.15mm)	.008" (.20mm)
a-anno-ttbl	border & title block	magenta	.006" (.15mm)	.008" (.20mm)
a-anno-vprt	viewport boundary	green	.006" (.15mm)	.008" (.20mm)
a-clng-susp	suspended elements	red	.004" (.09mm)	.005" (.13mm)
a-door	doors & door swings	red	.004" (.09mm)	.005" (.13mm)
a-fixt	fixtures	green	.006" (.15mm)	.008" (.20mm)
a-fixt-fauc	faucets	white	.002" (.05mm)	.004" (.09mm)
a-flor-case	casework	green	.006" (.15mm)	.008" (.20mm)
*a-flor-case-spec	specialty items (closet rod)	red	.004" (.09mm)	.005" (.13mm)
*a-flor-case-uppr	upper casework	red	.004" (.09mm)	.005" (.13mm)
*a-flor-whch	wheelchair circle	red	.004" (.09mm)	.005" (.13mm)
a-glaz	glass	green	.006" (.15mm)	.008" (.20mm)
a-wall-extr	exterior building wall	white	.016" (.40mm)	.020" (.50mm)
a-wall-head	door & window headers	blue	.010" (.25mm)	.012" (.30mm)
a-wall-intr	interior building wall	blue	.010" (.25mm)	.012" (.30mm)
a-wall-patt-blck	hatch fill	red	.004" (.09mm)	.005" (.13mm)
a-wall-patt-gray	hatch fill	gray(253)	.004" (.09mm)	.005" (.13mm)
Architectural - Elevations				
a-elev-dims	dimensions	red	.004" (.09mm)	.005" (.13mm)
*a-elev-hdln	hidden lines	red	.004" (.09mm)	.005" (.13mm)
a-elev-lwt1	elevation	blue	.010" (.25mm)	.012" (.30mm)
a-elev-lwt2	elevation	white	.002" (.05mm)	.004" (.09mm)
a-elev-otln	building outlines	white	.020" (.50mm)	.024" (.60mm)
a-elev-patt	hatch patterns	white	.002" (.05mm)	.004" (.09mm)
a-elev-text	text	green	.006" (.15mm)	.008" (.20mm)
Architectural –Sections				
a-sect-dims	dimensions	red	.004" (.09mm)	.005" (.13mm)
a-sect-fixt	fixtures	green	.006" (.15mm)	.008" (.20mm)
*a-sect-hdln	hidden lines	red	.004" (.09mm)	.005" (.13mm)
a-sect-lwt1	section	blue	.010" (.25mm)	.012" (.30mm)
a-sect-lwt2	section	white	.002" (.05mm)	.004" (.09mm)
a-sect-patt	hatch patterns	white	.002" (.05mm)	.004" (.09mm)
a-sect-text	text	green	.006" (.15mm)	.008" (.20mm)
Architectural –Details				
a-detl-dims	dimensions	red	.004" (.09mm)	.005" (.13mm)
a-detl-lwt1	detail	blue	.010" (.25mm)	.012" (.30mm)
a-detl-patt	hatch patterns	white	.002" (.05mm)	.004" (.09mm)
a-detl-text	text	green	.006" (.15mm)	.008" (.20mm)
Electrical				
e-anno-symb-lite	symbols	blue	.010" (.25mm)	.012" (.30mm)
e-anno-symb-powr	symbols	blue	.010" (.25mm)	.012" (.30mm)
e-anno-text-lite	text	green	.006" (.15mm)	.008" (.20mm)
e-anno-text-powr	text	green	.006" (.15mm)	.008" (.20mm)
*e-lite-circ	lighting circuits	white	.016" (.40mm)	.020" (.50mm)
Interiors				
i-anno-text-furn	text	green	.006" (.15mm)	.008" (.20mm)
*i-eqpm-ovhd	equipment: overhead	red	.004" (.09mm)	.005" (.13mm)
i-furn	furnishings	cyan	.004" (.09mm)	.005" (.13mm)

All layers have a continuous linetype, except those with an * beside them. The * denotes a layer with a hidden linetype.

Figure 5-2
Layer names, colors, and linetypes

Named Plot Style (STB)

named plot style: A plot style that is organized by a user-defined name. Named plot styles can be assigned to AutoCAD layers or to individual drawing objects.

Named plot styles are assigned to objects and layers. They are saved as an STB file. Color-dependent plot styles are used by a majority of architects and are used in this book.

Color-Dependent Plot Style (CTB)

color-dependent plot style: A plot style that is organized by the AutoCAD Color Index (ACI) number. Color-dependent plot styles are automatically assigned by the color of the AutoCAD object and can be changed to plot any color specified. Color-dependent plot styles are often made to print all colors black.

With a *color-dependent plot style*, any object that has the same color will be plotted using the same characteristics described in the plot style. For example, the color-dependent plot style can be set for the colors green and blue to be printed black with a lineweight of .006″. The color-dependent plot style can also be set for green and blue to be printed black but with the object lineweight assigned by the layer on which the object was drawn. The plot style allows you to plot with either of the following:

Lineweight assigned to the layer

Lineweight assigned in the plot style

This same method applies to linetype; for example, all blue lines will print with the object linetype assigned to the layer or with the linetype assigned in the plot style.

In Exercise 5-1 you will make your own color-dependent plot style, then plot a drawing using that plot style in Exercises 5-2, 5-3, and 5-4. This plot style will print or plot object colors 1 (red) through 7 (black) as black with the object lineweight assigned by the layer on which the item was drawn.

EXERCISE 5-1
Make a Color-Dependent Plot Style to Change Colors to Plot Black

ADD COLOR-DEPENDENT PLOT STYLE TABLE	
Menu Bar:	Tools/Wizards Add Color-Dependent Plot Styles
Type a Command:	R15PENWIZARD

Step 1. Open drawing **CH3-EXERCISE1**.

Step 2. Add a color-dependent plot style table, as described next:

Prompt	Response
Type a command:	Click **Add Color-Dependent Plot Style Table Wizard** (or type **r15penwizard <Enter>**)
The **Add Color-Dependent Plot Style Table** dialog box (Figure 5-3) appears:	Click **Start from scratch** Click **Next** Type **Your name Color to Black** (in the **File name** box) Click **Next** Click **Plot Style Table Editor...**
The **Plot Style Table Editor** appears (Figure 5-4):	Click **Color 1**, hold down the **<Shift>** key and click **Color 7** so that colors 1 through 7 are selected In the **Properties:** area Click **Black** (in the **Color:** Input) **Use object linetype** and **Use object lineweight** should be active, as shown in Figure 5-4. Click **Save & Close**

Figure 5-3
Add Color-Dependent Plot Style Table wizard

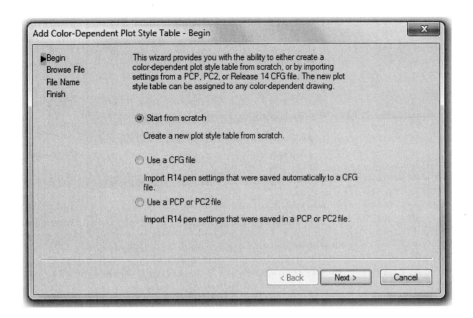

Figure 5-4
Plot Style Table Editor
changing colors 1 through 7
to plot black

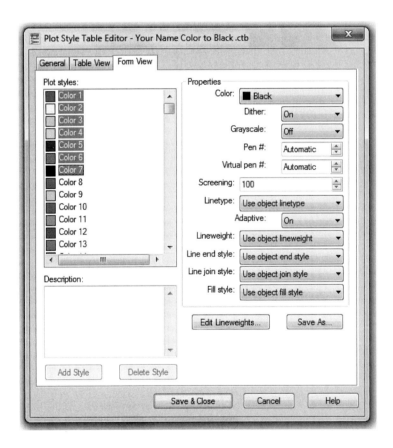

Prompt	Response
The **Add Color-Dependent Plot Style Table-Finish** dialog box appears with **Use this plot style table for the current drawing** checked:	Click **Finish**

Step 3. Use the **Convert Plot Styles** command to make sure your drawings are set to use color-dependent plot styles, as described next:

Prompt	Response
Type a command:	Type **CONVERTPSTYLES <Enter>**
A warning indicating that you are converting your drawing to a different type of plot style appears:	
	Click **Cancel** if the warning shows you are converting the drawing to a named plot style
	Click **OK** if the warning shows you are converting the drawing to a color-dependent plot style

Step 4. Save your drawing. It is now set to use color-dependent plot styles.

EXERCISE 5-2
Plot a Layout with One Viewport

The following is a hands-on, step-by-step exercise to make a hard copy of CH3-EXERCISE1 using a color-dependent plot style. When you have completed Exercise 5-2, your print will look similar to Figure 5-5.

Step 1. Open drawing **CH3-EXERCISE1** so it is displayed on the screen and save it as **CH5-EXERCISE2**.

Step 2. Create the following new layer and set it as the current layer:

Layer Name	Color	Linetype	Lineweight
a-anno-vprt	green	continuous	.006″ (.15 mm)

Figure 5-5
CH5-EXERCISE2 complete

NAME
CLASS
DATE

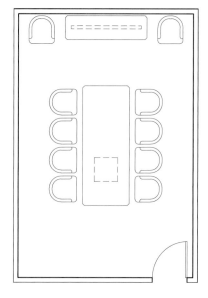

Model, Layout1, and Layout2 Tabs

At the bottom of the drawing window are **Model, Layout1**, and **Layout2** tabs. Model space is the 2D (and also 3D) environment in which you have been working to this point. *Model space* is where your 2D and 3D models (drawings) are created and modified. You can also print from the **Model** tab. A *layout* tab is used to view paper space. *Paper space* shows the actual printed or plotted drawing on a real-size piece of paper.

model space: One of the two primary spaces in which objects are made.

layout: A two-dimensional page setup made in paper space that represents the paper size and what the drawing will look like when it is plotted. Multiple layouts can be created for each drawing.

paper space: One of the two spaces in which objects are made or documented. Paper space is used for making a finished layout for printing or plotting. Often, drawings are restored in paper space in a drawing title block and border.

> **NOTE**
>
> While on the **Layout1 tab**, it may be helpful to turn the grid off. Click the **PAPER** toggle in the status bar to return to **MODEL**, turn the grid off, and click the **MODEL** toggle to return to **PAPER**.

Step 3. Click the **Layout1** tab at the bottom of drawing CH5-EXERCISE2. You are now in paper space. Notice that the toggle on the status bar shows the paper space icon or reads **PAPER**. Clicking it will change it to **MODEL**. Make sure you are in paper space and the toggle reads **PAPER**.

Page Setup Manager

Step 4. Right-click the **Layout1** tab and click **Page Setup Manager...**. The **Page Setup Manager** (Figure 5-6) appears.

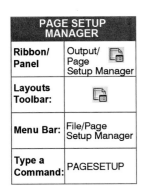

PAGE SETUP MANAGER	
Ribbon/ Panel	Output/ Page Setup Manager
Layouts Toolbar:	
Menu Bar:	File/Page Setup Manager
Type a Command:	PAGESETUP

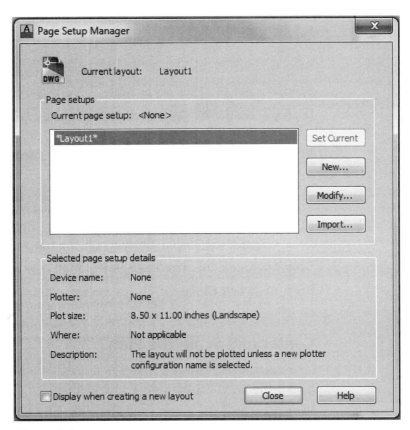

Figure 5-6
Page Setup Manager

Step 5. With **Layout1** in **Page setups** selected, click **Modify...**. The **Page Setup** dialog box for Layout1 appears (Figure 5-7).

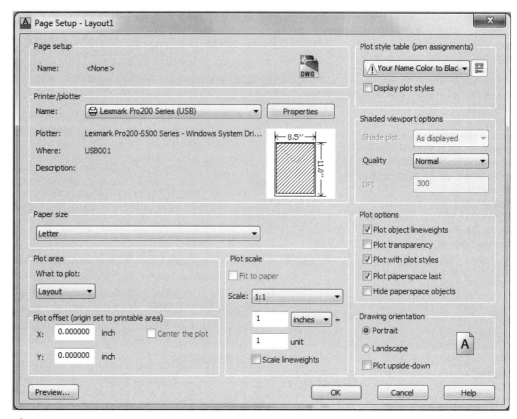

Figure 5-7
Page Setup - Layout1 dialog box

Step 6. Select the printer you will use for a letter-size paper.

Step 7. Set the **Plot style table** to **Your Name Color to Black**.

Step 8. Make the settings shown in Figure 5-7 in the **Page Setup** dialog box.

Step 9. Make sure the **Portrait** drawing orientation is selected and the **Plot scale** is **1:1** (Figure 5-7).

> The **Plot scale** on the **Page Setup - Layout1** is 1:1. The drawing on the **Layout1** tab within the green **viewport boundary line** will be scaled to ¼″ = 1′-0″ using **Properties** in Step 16. You will then plot the scaled viewport on the Layout1.

Step 10. Click **OK**. The **Page Setup Manager** appears.

Step 11. Click **Close**.

Center and Scale the Plan

If you completed Steps 1 and 2 and created a new layer with the color green, the viewport boundary line is green.

Step 12. Click the green viewport boundary line to select it. If your viewport boundary line is not shaped as shown in Figure 5-8, click one of the small squares on each corner (called grips). It becomes red. Reshape the viewport by moving the grip. Be sure **ORTHO** and **OSNAP** are off.

You can reshape, resize, move, erase, and copy the viewport.

Figure 5-8
Select the viewport boundary

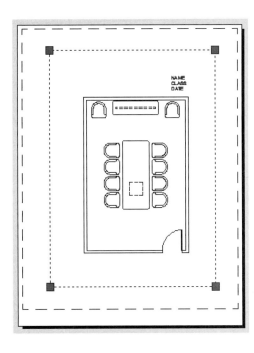

PROPERTIES

Ribbon/ Panel	View/ Palettes
Standard Toolbar:	
Menu Bar:	Modify/ Properties
Type a Command:	PROPERTIES
Command Alias:	PR

NOTE

The viewport boundary line (green line) comes in on the layer that is current. That's why you created a layer named **Viewport** and assigned the green color to it.

Step 13. If your drawing is not centered in the viewport, click **PAPER** in the status bar to return to **MODEL** (model space). Use the **PAN** or **ZOOM** command to center the drawing. Click **MODEL** to return to **PAPER** (paper space) before continuing with the plot setup.

Step 14. Click the green viewport boundary line to select it (Figure 5-8).

Step 15. Click **Properties** from the **Palettes** panel.

Step 16. Click **Standard scale** in the **Properties** palette (Figure 5-9). Click the arrow to the right of **Standard scale** and scroll down to select

Figure 5-9
Set viewport scale to 1/4″ = 1′-0″ and lock the display

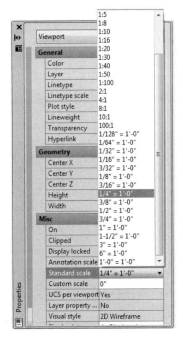

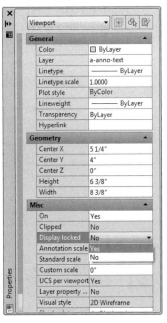

1/4″ = 1′-0″. This scale is applied to the drawing in the paper space viewport. Click **Display locked** (above the scale) and click **Yes** to lock the display scale for this viewport. Close the **Properties** palette.

Step 17. Turn the **a-anno-vprt** layer off so the viewport boundary line will not print.

When the display is locked, you cannot accidentally zoom in or out while in model space and lose the 1/4″ = 1′-0″ scale. If you zoom in or out while in paper space, you do not change the scale because you are zooming in or out on the paper only. When the display is locked, you cannot reposition the drawing. If you need to reposition or change the drawing in any way, you must turn the **Viewport** layer back on, select the viewport boundary line, select **Properties**, and unlock the display to make any changes.

TIP

While in a layout tab you can click the **PAPER** toggle to return to **MODEL**, and the **MODEL** toggle to return to **PAPER**. You can also click the **Model** tab to return to the drawing, make any changes, and then click the **Layout** tab to return to the layout tab and paper space.

Complete the Layout

Step 18. Click **PAPER** to return to model space and erase the existing name, class, and date on the upper right of your drawing. Then, click **MODEL** to return to paper space.

TIP

While in a layout, you can type **MS <Enter>** to return to **MODEL** space or type **PS <Enter>** to return to **PAPER** space.

Step 19. Use a text style with the Arial font, set layer **a-anno-text** current, and add your name, your class, and the date in all capitals, 3/16″ high, to the paper (Figure 5-10).

Figure 5-10
Add your name, class, and the current date 3/16″ high

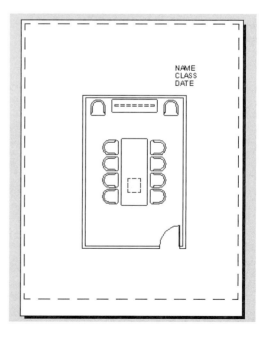

NOTE

When you type your name or anything else 3/16″ high in **PAPER** space, it will be printed 3/16″ high when the layout is printed at a scale of 1:1.

PLOT	
Ribbon/ Panel	Output/Plot 🖨
Quick Access Toolbar:	🖨
Menu Bar:	File/Plot...
Type a Command:	PLOT/PRINT
Command Alias:	<Ctrl>+P

Step 20. While in **PAPER**, change **LTSCALE** as needed to show the **HIDDEN** linetype.

Step 21. Right-click the **Layout1** tab. The right-click menu appears.

Step 22. Click **Rename.** Type **Furniture Plan** for the new layout name. Press **<Enter>**.

Step 23. Right-click the **Furniture Plan** tab. The right-click menu appears.

Step 24. Click **Plot...**. The **Plot** dialog box appears.

Step 25. Click **Preview...**. If the preview is OK, right-click and click **Plot**. If not, exit and correct the problem. The plot proceeds from this point.

Step 26. Save the drawing in at least two places.

EXERCISE 5-3
Plot a Layout with Two Viewports

The following is a step-by-step exercise to make a hard copy of CH3-EXERCISE1 and CH3-EXERCISE2 on one sheet of letter-size paper. When you have completed Exercise 5-3, your print will look similar to Figure 5-11.

Step 1. Open drawing **CH3-EXERCISE1** so it is displayed on the screen and save it as **CH5-EXERCISE3**.

Insert an Entire Drawing into a Current Drawing

INSERT BLOCK	
Ribbon/ Panel	Block/ Insert
Draw Toolbar:	
Menu Bar:	Insert/ Block
Type a Command:	INSERT
Command Alias:	I

The **Insert-Block** command can be used to insert any drawing into the current drawing and will define it as a block in that drawing. Simply use the **Insert-Block** command to insert the drawing. Use the **Browse...** button in the **Insert** dialog box to locate the drawing.

Step 2. Insert **CH3-EXERCISE2** into the current drawing as described next:

Prompt	Response
Type a command:	Type **I <Enter>**
The **Insert** dialog box appears:	Use **Browse** to locate **CH3-EXERCISE2** in your folder and click on it as shown in Figure 5-12
The **Select Drawing File** dialog box:	Click **Open**
The **Insert** dialog box appears:	Click **OK**
Specify Insertion point or [Basepoint Scale X Y Z Rotate]:	Click a point to locate the drawing directly above **CH3-EXERCISE1** (Figure 5-13)

Figure 5-11

CH5-EXERCISE3 complete

NAME
CLASS
DATE

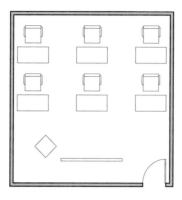

SCALE: 1/8"=1'-0"

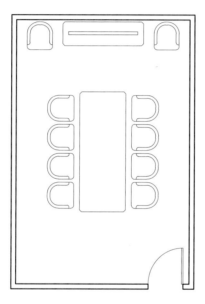

SCALE 3/16"=1'-0"

Figure 5-12

Browse to locate CH3-EXERCISE2

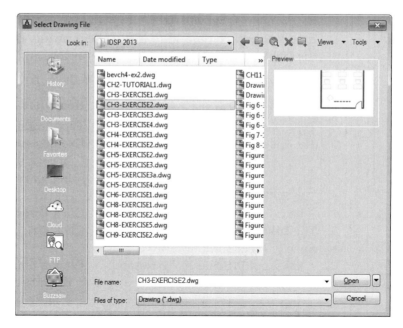

Figure 5-13
INSERT CH3-EXERCISE2
directly above CH3-EXERCISE1

NAME
CLASS
DATE

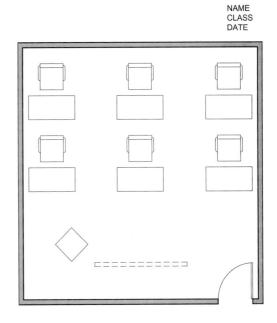

NAME
CLASS
DATE

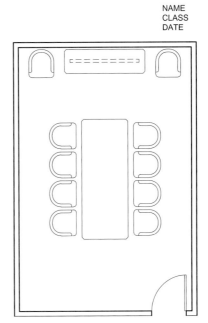

Step 3. The inserted drawing comes in as a single entity. **Explode** the CH3-EXERCISE2 drawing.

FOR MORE DETAILS

For more about the **Insert-Block** command and the advantages of using blocks see Chapter 6.

Step 4. Erase the name, class, and date from both drawings.

Step 5. Make sure the **Model** tab is current. Turn the grid off.

Page Setup Manager

Step 6. Create the following new layer and set it as the current layer:

Layer Name	Color	Linetype	Lineweight
a-anno-vprt	green	continuous	.006″ (.15 mm)

Step 7. Click the **Layout1** tab at the bottom of the drawing.

Step 8. Right-click the **Layout1** tab and click **Page Setup Manager...**. The **Page Setup Manager** appears.

Step 9. Click **Modify...**. The **Page Setup** dialog box for Layout1 appears.

Step 10. Select the printer you will use for a letter-size paper.

Step 11. Set the **Plot style table** to **Your Name Color to Black**.

Step 12. Make the settings shown in Figure 5-14 in the **Page Setup** dialog box.

Step 13. Make sure the **Portrait** drawing orientation is selected and the **Plot scale** is **1:1** (Figure 5-14).

Step 14. Click **OK**. The **Page Setup Manager** appears.

Step 15. Click **Close.**

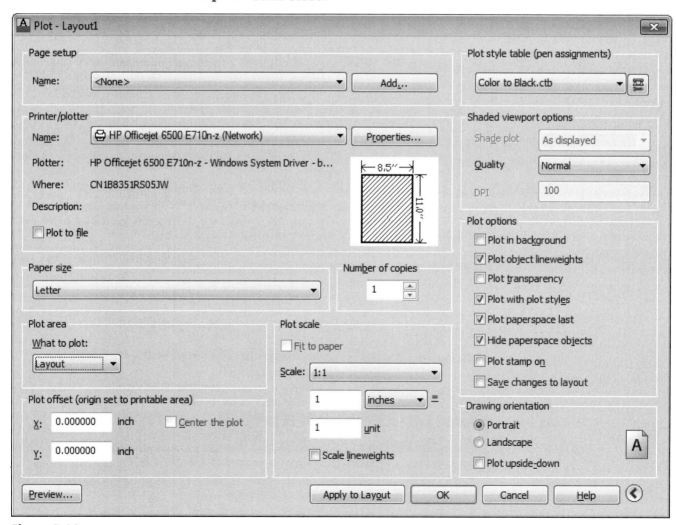

Figure 5-14
Page Setup – Layout1 dialog box

Copy a Viewport

Step 16. If your green viewport boundary line is not shaped as shown in Figure 5-15, use grips to reshape it.

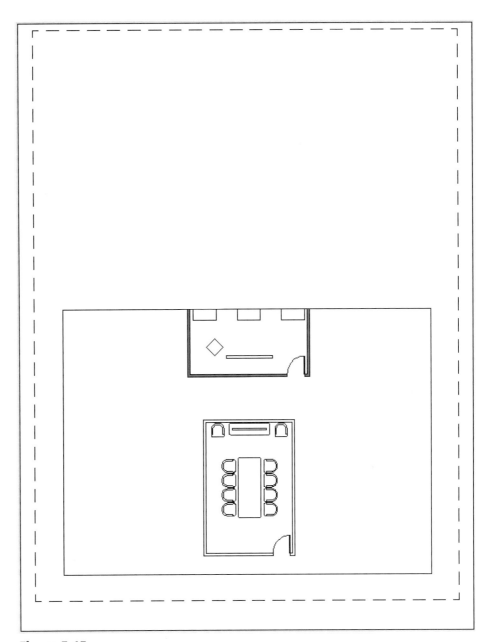

Figure 5-15
Viewport boundary

Step 17. While in **PAPER** space use the **COPY** command to copy the viewport (click on any point on the green viewport boundary line to select it) to the approximate location shown in Figure 5-16.

Center and Scale the Plans

Step 18. Click the **PAPER** toggle to go to **MODEL**, click inside each viewport to select it, and center **CH3-EXERCISE1** in the bottom viewport and **CH3-EXERCISE2** in the top viewport. Return to **PAPER**.

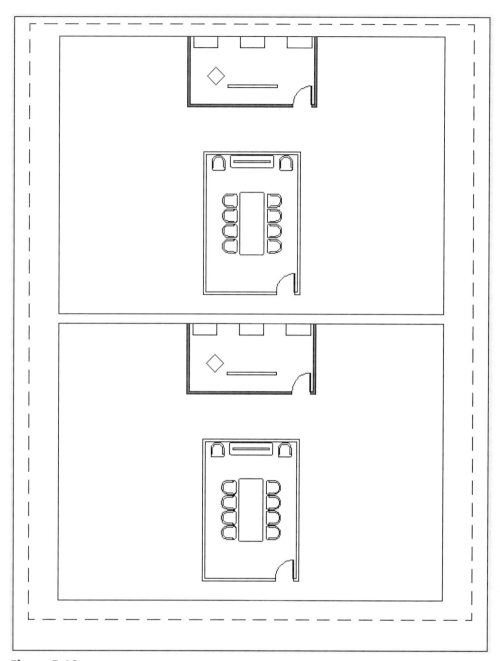

Figure 5-16
Copy the viewport

Step 19. While in **PAPER**, click the green viewport **boundary line** of the bottom viewport to select it and use **Properties** to set the scale of **CH3-EXERCISE1** to **3/16″ = 1′-0″**. While in **PAPER** you can change the size of the viewport boundary. While in **MODEL** you can move the drawing to center it. When the drawing is centered and scaled, be sure to lock the display (Figure 5-17).

TIP
Remember to use **Properties** to unlock the display if you want to change the location of a drawing within a viewport boundary that has a locked display.

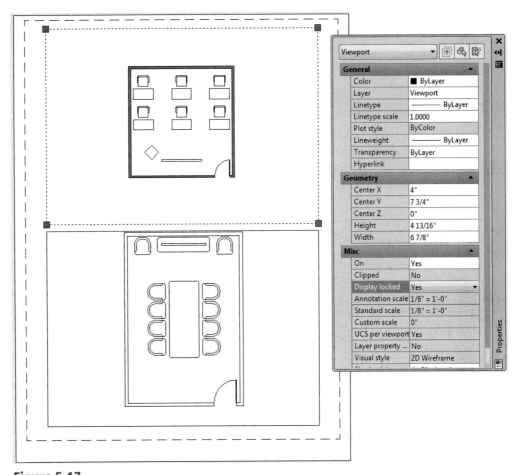

Figure 5-17
Set the scale of the bottom viewport to 3/16″ = 1′-0″. Set the scale of the top viewport to 1/8″ = 1′-0″. Lock the display of both viewports.

Step 20. Set the scale of **CH3-EXERCISE2** in the top viewport to **1/8″= 1′-0″** (Figure 5-17) and lock the display.

Step 21. Turn the **a-anno-vprt** layer off (the outline of the viewports, shown in green) so they will not print.

TIP

If you accidentally use a **ZOOM** command while in **MODEL** space and change the scale of an unlocked display, turn the **Viewport** layer on. Click on the viewport boundary line and then click on **Properties**, input the scale, and lock the display. Zooming while you are in **PAPER** space will not change the scale of the drawing.

Complete the Layout

Step 22. While in **PAPER** use a text style with the Arial font, set layer **a-anno-text** current, and add your name, your class, and the date in all capitals, 3/16″ high, to the paper (Figure 5-18).

Step 23. Type the scale of each viewport 1/8″ high and complete as shown in Figure 5-18.

Step 24. While in **PAPER**, change **LTSCALE** as needed to show the **HIDDEN** linetype.

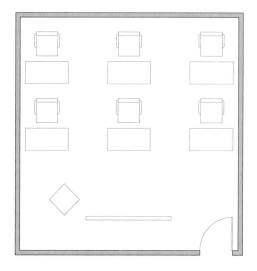

SCALE: 1/8"=1'-0"

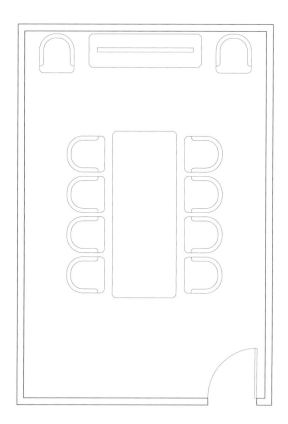

SCALE 3/16"=1'-0"

Figure 5-18
CH5-EXERCISE3 complete

Step 25. Rename Layout1 to **Furniture Plan** for the new layout name.

Step 26. Plot **CH5-EXERCISE3** at a scale of 1:1. The viewport scales are already set.

Step 27. Save the drawing in two places.

EXERCISE 5-4
Plot a Layout with Four Viewports

The following is a step-by-step exercise to make a hard copy of CH3-EXERCISE1, CH3-EXERCISE2, CH3-EXERCISE3, and CH3-EXERCISE4 on one sheet of letter-size paper. When you have completed Exercise 5-4, your print will look similar to Figure 5-19.

NAME
CLASS
DATE

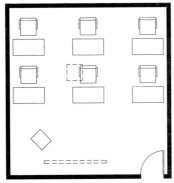

CH3-EXERCISE 2
SCALE: 1/8" = 1'-0"

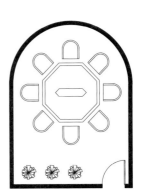

CH3-EXERCISE 3
SCALE: 1/8" = 1'-0"

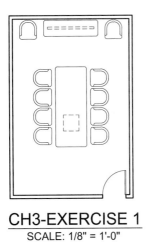

CH3-EXERCISE 1
SCALE: 1/8" = 1'-0"

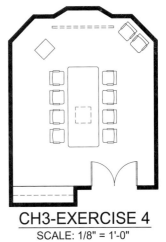

CH3-EXERCISE 4
SCALE: 1/8" = 1'-0"

Figure 5-19
CH5-EXERCISE4 complete

Step 1. Open drawing **CH3-EXERCISE1** so it is displayed on the screen and save it as **CH5-EXERCISE4**.

Step 2. Insert **CH3-EXERCISE2, CH3-EXERCISE3,** and **CH3-EXERCISE4** into the current drawing.

Step 3. Arrange the four drawings as shown in Figure 5-20.

Step 4. The inserted drawings come in as a single entity. **Explode** the inserted drawings.

Step 5. Erase the name, class, and date from all drawings.

Step 6. Make sure the **Model** tab is current. Turn the grid off.

Step 7. Use **Zoom-Extents** to view the extents of the drawing.

Figure 5-20
Arrange the drawings

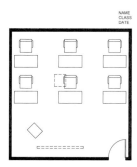

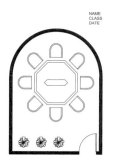

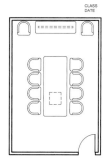

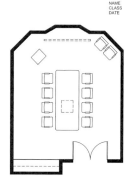

VIEWPORTS	
Ribbon/ Panel	View/ Viewports
Viewports Toolbar:	
Menu Bar:	View/ Viewports/ Named Viewports
Type a Command:	VIEWPORTS
Command Alias:	VPORTS

Viewports (VPORTS)

MODEL space is where your 2D or 3D model (drawing) is created and modified. While in **MODEL** space, you can use the **Viewports** command to divide the display screen into multiple viewports as shown in Figure 5-21. **MODEL** space is limited in that although several viewports may be visible on the display screen, only one viewport can be plotted.

Figure 5-21
The screen is divided into four viewports

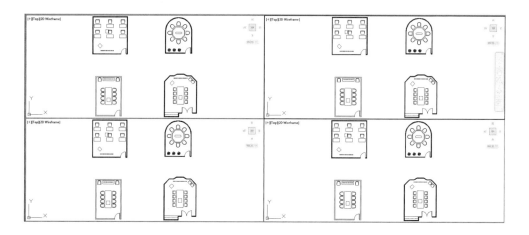

When you click any of the **layout** tabs, your drawing is in **PAPER** space. **PAPER** space shows a piece of paper on which you can arrange a single drawing (viewport) or as many drawings or views (viewports) as you need. In **PAPER** space you can also plot as many viewports as you need.

Step 8. Divide the screen into four viewports as described next:

Prompt	Response
Type a command:	**New Viewports...** (or type **VPORTS** **\<Enter\>**)
The **Viewports** dialog box appears	Click **Four: Equal** on the **New Viewports** tab and name the viewport configuration **VP4** as shown in the **New name:** text box in Figure 5-22
	Click **OK** (the screen is divided into four viewports, Figure 5-21)

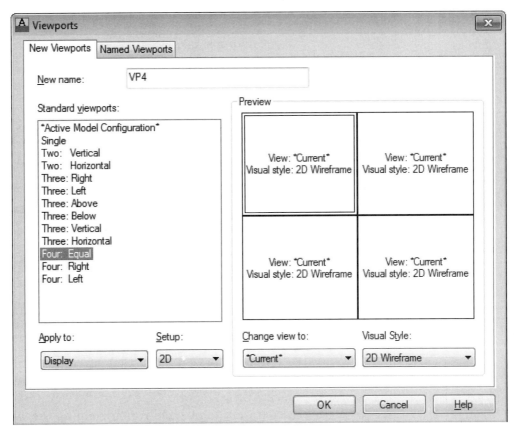

Figure 5-22
Divide the screen into four equal viewports and name the viewport configuration **VP4**

The active viewport, outlined with a solid line, displays the lines of the cursor when the cursor is moved into it. Inactive viewports display an arrow when the cursor is moved into those areas. To make a different viewport active, position the arrow in the desired viewport and click.

The **Viewports** dialog box allows you to name, save, preview, and recall any number of configurations of viewports and change the configuration of the current viewport.

While in **MODEL** space, the model (drawing) is the same in each viewport. If you edit the model in any one viewport, you are doing it in all viewports. You may, however, freeze different layers in each viewport, display a different UCS in each viewport, and zoom in or out in a viewport without affecting other viewport magnifications.

Use MVIEW to Restore the Viewport VP4 into Layout1

Step 9. Create the following new layer and set it as the current layer:

Layer Name	Color	Linetype	Lineweight
a-anno-vprt	green	continuous	.006″ (.15 mm)

Step 10. Click the **Layout1** tab at the bottom of the drawing.

Step 11. Click on the current green viewport boundary line and erase the existing single viewport.

Step 12. Use the **MVIEW** command to restore the saved model space viewport VP4 into Layout1 as described next:

MVIEW	
Type a Command:	MVIEW
Command Alias:	MV

Prompt	Response
Type a command:	Type **MVIEW <Enter>**
Specify corner of viewport or [On Off Fit Shadeplot Lock Object Polygonal Restore Layer 2 3 4] <Fit>:	Type **R <Enter>**
Enter viewport configuration name or [?] <*Active>:	Type **VP4 <Enter>**
Specify first corner or [Fit] <Fit>:	**<Enter>** (to accept **Fit** and the viewport configuration VP4 fills the page, Figure 5-23)

The **MVIEW** command is used in a Layout with **PAPER** current. The **MVIEW** options are as follows:

OFF: A viewport can be copied, stretched, erased, moved, or scaled. The drawing within the viewport cannot be edited while in **PAPER** space. The **OFF** option turns off the view inside the viewport and saves regeneration time while you are editing the viewports. You can turn the views back on when editing is complete.

ON: Turns on the **MODEL** space view (drawing inside the viewport).

Shadeplot: Allows you to choose from among five options: **Wireframe, As displayed, Hidden, Visual styles,** and **Rendered**. These options are used in 3D.

Lock: Allows you to lock the scale of a viewport so it does not change when you zoom in or out.

Object: Allows you to create a new viewport by selecting an existing object such as a circle.

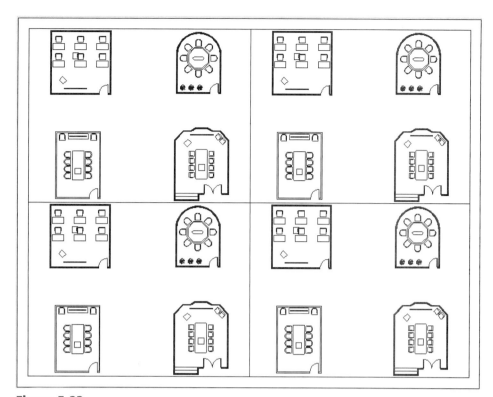

Figure 5-23
The viewport configuration fills the page

Polygonal: Allows you to draw an irregular-shaped viewport using polyline lines and arcs.

Fit: Creates a single viewport to fill current paper space limits. Other viewports can be erased before or after the **Fit** option is used.

Layer: Allows you to remove viewport property overrides.

2,3,4: Creates two, three, or four viewports in a specified area or to fit the current paper space limits.

Restore: Restores saved model space viewports (saved with the Viewports command) into **PAPER** space.

Specify Corner of Viewport: Creates a new viewport defined by picking two corners or by typing the X and Y coordinates of the lower left and upper right corners.

Page Setup Manager

Step 13. Right-click the **Layout1** tab and click **Page Setup Manager....** The **Page Setup Manager** appears.

Step 14. Click **Modify....** The **Page Setup** dialog box for Layout1 appears.

Step 15. Select the printer you will use for a letter-size paper.

Step 16. Set the **Plot style table** to **Your Name Color to Black**.

Step 17. Make the settings shown in Figure 5-24 in the **Page Setup** dialog box.

Step 18. Make sure the **Landscape** drawing orientation is selected and the **Plot scale** is **1:1** (Figure 5-24).

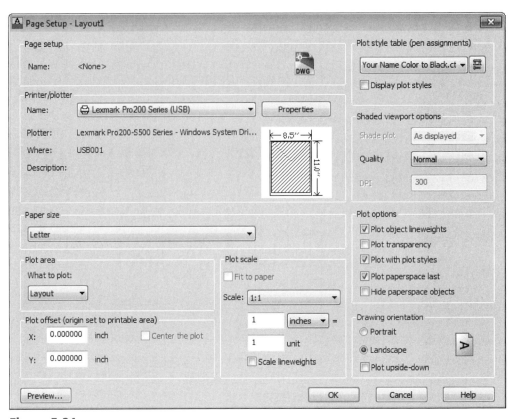

Figure 5-24
Page Setup - Layout1 dialog box

> **Step 19.** Click **OK**. The **Page Setup Manager** appears.
>
> **Step 20.** Click **Close**.

Center and Scale the Plans

> **Step 21.** Click the **PAPER** toggle to go to **MODEL** and click inside each viewport to select it. Center **CH3-EXERCISE1** in the bottom left viewport, **CH3-EXERCISE2** in the top left viewport, **CH3-EXERCISE3** in the top right viewport, and **CH3-EXERCISE4** in the bottom right viewport as shown in Figure 5-25. Return to **PAPER**.
>
> **Step 22.** While in **PAPER**, click the green viewport **boundary line** of all the viewports to select them and use **Properties** to set the scale of all viewports to **1/8″** = **1′-0″** (Figure 5-25). While in **MODEL** you can move the drawing to center it. When the drawing is centered and scaled, be sure to lock the display.
>
> **Step 23.** Turn the **a-anno-vprt** layer off (the outline of the viewports, shown in green) so they will not print.

Complete the Layout

> **Step 24.** While in **PAPER** use a text style with the Arial font, set layer **a-anno-text** current, and add your name, your class, and the date in all capitals, 3/16″ high, to the paper (Figure 5-25).
>
> **Step 25.** Type the name of each viewport 3/16″ high, type the scale of each viewport 1/8″ high, and complete as shown in Figure 5-25.

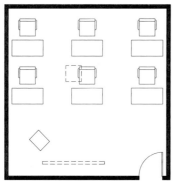

CH3-EXERCISE 2
SCALE: 1/8" = 1'-0"

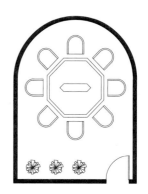

NAME
CLASS
DATE

CH3-EXERCISE 3
SCALE: 1/8" = 1'-0"

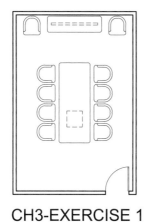

CH3-EXERCISE 1
SCALE: 1/8" = 1'-0"

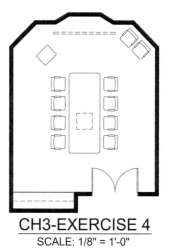

CH3-EXERCISE 4
SCALE: 1/8" = 1'-0"

Figure 5-25
CH5-EXERCISE4 complete

Step 26. While in **PAPER**, change **LTSCALE** as needed to show the **HIDDEN** linetype.

Step 27. Plot **CH5-EXERCISE4** at a scale of 1:1. The viewport scales are already set.

Step 28. Save the drawing in two places.

FOR MORE DETAILS

See Chapter 12 for information about freezing and thawing layers within different viewports.

EXERCISE 5-5
Make PDF Files That Can Be Attached to E-mails and Opened without the AutoCAD Program

PDF (portable document format) files: Files of drawings that are made using the **Plot** dialog box. These files can be opened and read without the use of the AutoCAD program.

Often, it is necessary to send files to clients who do not have the AutoCAD program. ***PDF (portable document format) files*** can be used to show drawings without sending .dwg files. The following exercise shows you how to do that.

PLOT	
Ribbon/ Panel	Output/Plot 🖶
Quick Access Toolbar:	🖶
Menu Bar:	File/Plot...
Type a Command:	PLOT/PRINT
Command Alias:	<Ctrl>+P

Step 1. Open drawing **CH5-EXERCISE3** on the **Layout1** tab so it is displayed on the screen.

Step 2. Make a PDF file from the **CH5-EXERCISE3** drawing, as described next:

Prompt	Response
Type a command:	Click **PLOT**
The **Plot - Layout1** dialog box appears.	In the **Printer/plotter Name:** box, click **DWG To PDF.pc3** as shown in Figure 5-26
	Check other parts of the **Plot** dialog box to be sure all settings are as shown in Figure 5-26
	Click **OK**
The **Browse for Plot File** box appears:	Locate the folder and drive where you want to save the file and change the name to **CH5-EXERCISE5** as shown in Figure 5-27
	Click **Save**
The PDF image appears:	If the image is complete, close the program. If not, redo the plot making any necessary changes such as plotting extents on a larger sheet of paper

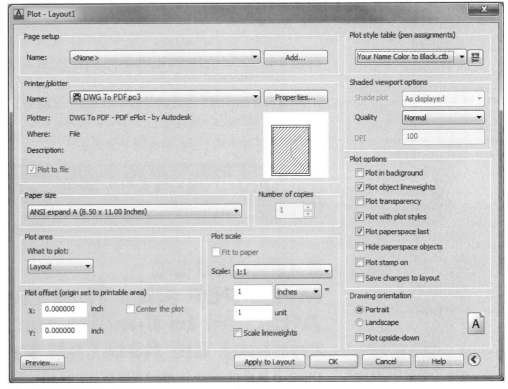

Figure 5-26
Plot - Layout1 dialog box

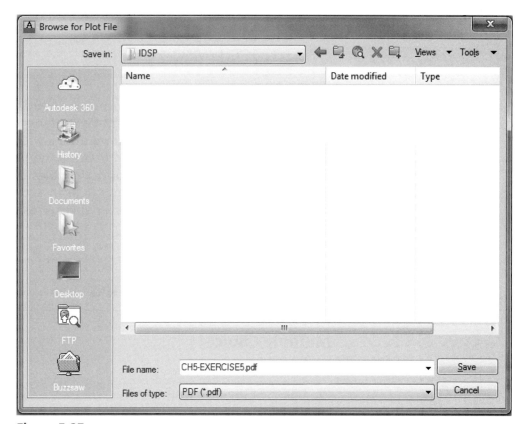

Figure 5-27
Locate the folder to save the PDF file and change the name to CH5-EXERCISE5

> **TIP**
> Use Windows Explorer to view a PDF file.

That's it. You now have a PDF file of your drawing that can be sent to anyone, and others can view it whether or not they have AutoCAD.

Chapter Summary

This chapter provided you the information necessary to make a color-dependent plot style, make different layout tabs for your drawings, print or plot drawings with multiple viewports from layout tabs, and print and plot drawings. In addition, you learned to print and plot drawings at various scales on the same sheet and to print drawings to a PDF file. Now you have the skills and information necessary to print and plot drawings in a variety of ways on any of the standard paper sheet sizes or to a PDF file that can be viewed without AutoCAD.

Chapter Test Questions

Multiple Choice

Circle the correct answer.

1. Which of the following contains the **Plot...** command?
   a. **Utilities** panel
   b. **Annotate** panel
   c. **Quick Access** toolbar
   d. **Clipboard** panel

2. Properties that can be set in a plot style table are:
   a. Color
   b. Linetype
   c. Lineweight
   d. All of the above

3. When a viewport is restored into a layout (**PAPER** space), what color is the viewport boundary line?
   a. The color of the furniture layer
   b. The color of the current layer
   c. The color of the text layer
   d. None of the above

4. Which tab in the **Viewports** dialog box must be current for you to name the new viewport?
   a. **New Viewports**
   b. **New Name Viewports**
   c. **Standard Viewports**
   d. **Named Viewports**

5. Which of the following is **not** an option for the **MVIEW** command?
   a. **Polygonal**
   b. **OFF**
   c. **Select**
   d. **Layer**

6. Which of the following is a configuration option in the **Viewports** dialog box?
   a. **Two: Vertical**
   b. **Four: Below**
   c. **Five: Horizontal**
   d. **Two: Above**

7. Which of the following **MVIEW** options allows you to draw an irregular-shaped viewport?
   a. **Layer**
   b. **Circle**
   c. **Fit**
   d. **Polygonal**

8. When you click a viewport boundary in **PAPER** space, what command allows you to set the scale of the viewport?

   a. **Scale**

   b. **Properties**

   c. **Viewport**

   d. **Insert**

9. When you are using the **Plot...** command to plot a layout tab that has a single viewport that is already scaled to $1/2'' = 1'\text{-}0''$, in the **Plot** dialog box use a **Plot scale** of:

   a. **1:1**

   b. **1:2**

   c. **1:48**

   d. **Fit to paper**

10. Which of the following is **not** one of the three tabs at the bottom of the drawing window (when **Model** and **Layout** tabs are displayed)?

   a. **Model**

   b. **Layout1**

   c. **Layout2**

   d. **Model2**

Matching

Write the number of the correct answer on the line.

a. Plot style _____

b. Layout tab _____

c. PDF files _____

d. Drawing orientation _____

e. Viewports _____

1. An area in **PAPER** space containing views of a drawing

2. Color-dependent

3. Used to view **PAPER** space

4. A drawing that can be viewed without AutoCAD

5. Landscape

True or False

Circle the correct answer.

1. **True or False:** Named and color-dependent are the two different types of plot styles.

2. **True or False:** You can reshape, resize, move, erase, and copy a viewport.

3. **True or False:** While working on a layout tab you can only work in **PAPER** space.

4. **True or False:** A color-dependent plot style can be made to allow you to plot with the lineweights that are assigned to the layers in the drawing.

5. **True or False:** A color-dependent plot style can be made to allow you to plot all colors in the drawing as black.

List

1. Five ways of accessing **Page Setup Manager** in paper space.

2. Five options from the **Page Setup** window once you select **Modify** from **Page Setup Manager**.

3. Five ways of accessing the **Plot/print** command.

4. Five ways of inserting an entire drawing into the current drawing.

5. Five standard drawing sheet sizes based on U.S. customary system.

6. Five operations that can be performed on a PAPER space viewport.

7. Five options from the **Plot Style Table Editor**.

8. Five MODEL space viewport configurations.

9. Five shortcuts for space switching (**MODEL/PAPER**) and the related system parameters.

10. Five options from the **Viewports** dialog box in MODEL space.

Questions

1. How does a named plot style differ from a color-dependent plot style?

2. In Exercise 5-4, with four drawings, why is the layout plotted at a scale of 1:1?

3. Why would you want to have a drawing with multiple viewports?

4. Why would you want to plot drawings at different scales on the same sheet?

5. What are PDF files used for and how can they be done quickly and efficiently?

Chapter Projects

Project 5-1: *Make a PDF File (Using Project 3-1)* [BASIC]

1. Open Project 3-1.

2. Use the procedure described in Exercise 5-5 to make a PDF file of Project 3-1.

Project 5-2: *Plot a Single Viewport to Scale and a Color-Dependent Plot Style (Using Project 3-2)* [INTERMEDIATE]

1. Open Project 3-2.

2. Use the procedure described in Exercise 5-2 (with one viewport) to plot Project 3-2.

Project 5-3: *Plot Two Viewports at Two Different Scales and a Color-Dependent Plot Style (Using Projects 3-1 and 3-2)* [ADVANCED]

1. Open Project 3-1 and insert Project 3-2.

2. Use the procedure described in Exercise 5-3 (with two viewports) to plot Projects 3-1 and 3-2.

6

chaptersix

Drawing the Floor Plan: Walls, Doors, and Windows

CHAPTER OBJECTIVES

- Correctly use the following commands and settings:

		Lineweight	Multiline Style
Annotative Text	**Edit Multiline**	LIST	OSNAP
AutoCAD Design Center	**EXTEND**	**Make Object's Layer**	**PROPERTIES**
Autodesk Seek	**HATCH**	**Current**	**RECTANGLE**
Block-Make	**Insert-Block**	**Match Properties**	**RECTANGULAR ARRAY**
COLOR	**Linetype**	**Multiline**	**WBLOCK**

The Tenant Space Project

Exercise 6-1 contains step-by-step instructions for using **Multiline** (a command that allows up to 16 lines to be drawn at a time) to draw the exterior and interior walls of a tenant space. The exercise also contains step-by-step instructions for inserting windows and doors into the plan.

Chapters 7, 8, 9, and 11 provide step-by-step instructions to complete the tenant space project started in this chapter. Each chapter will use the building plan drawn in this chapter to complete a part of the project as described next.

Chapter 7: The tenant space is dimensioned and the square footage calculated.

Chapter 8: Elevations, sections, and details are drawn.

Chapter 9: Furniture is drawn, attributes are assigned (furniture specifications), and the furniture is added to the plan.

Chapter 11: The reflected ceiling plan and voice/data/power plan are drawn.

EXERCISE 6-1
Tenant Space Floor Plan

When you have completed Exercise 6-1, the tenant space floor plan, your drawing will look similar to Figure 6-1.

NAME
CLASS
DATE

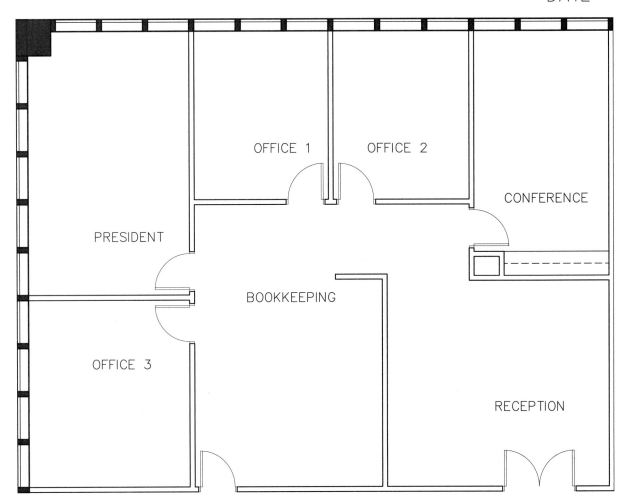

TENANT SPACE FLOOR PLAN
SCALE: 1/8" = 1'-0"

Figure 6-1
Exercise 6-1: Tenant space floor plan (scale: 1/8" = 1'-0")

Step 1. Use your workspace to make the following settings:

1. Use **Save As...** to save the drawing with the name **CH6-EXERCISE1**.
2. Set drawing units: **Architectural**
3. Set precision: **1/32"**
4. Set drawing limits: **75',65'**
5. Set **GRIDDISPLAY: 0**
6. Set grid: **12"**

7. Set snap: **6″**
8. Create the following layers. Be sure to type and enter a comma after each layer name. The cursor will move to the next line so you can type the next layer name:

Layer Name	Color	Linetype	Lineweight
a-anno-text	green	continuous	.006″ (.15 mm)
a-door	red	continuous	.004″ (.09 mm)
a-flor-case	green	continuous	.006″ (.15 mm)
a-flor-case-uppr	green	hidden	.006″ (.15 mm)
a-glaz	green	continuous	.006″ (.15 mm)
a-wall-extr	white	continuous	.016″ (.40 mm)
a-wall-intr	blue	continuous	.010″ (.25 mm)
a-wall-patt-blck	red	continuous	.004″ (.09 mm)

9. Set layer **a-wall-extr** current.
10. Use **Zoom-All** to view the limits of the drawing.

> **NOTE**
>
> If you cannot see the entire name of the layer, right-click on one of the titles such as **Name, Color,** or **Linetype,** and a right-click menu will appear. Click **Maximize all columns** in the right-click menu to be able to see the entire layer name you have typed.

RECTANGLE

RECTANGLE	
Ribbon/ Panel	Home/Draw
Draw Toolbar:	
Menu Bar:	Draw/ Rectangle
Type a Command:	RECTANGLE
Command Alias:	REC

The following part of Exercise 6-1 uses the **RECTANGLE** and **HATCH** commands to draw the window mullions and the 3′-square corner column located in the northwest corner of the tenant space.

Step 2. Use the **RECTANGLE** command to draw the 3′-square corner column (Figure 6-2), as described next:

Prompt

Type a command:
Specify first corner point or
   [Chamfer Elevation Fillet
   Thickness Width]:
Specify other corner point or
   [Area Dimensions Rotation]:

Response

RECTANGLE (or type **REC <Enter>**)

Type **17′,51′ <Enter>**

Type **@3′,-3′ <Enter>** (be sure to
   include the minus)

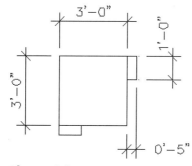

Figure 6-2
Use the **RECTANGLE** and **Solid Hatch** commands to draw the corner column and two mullions

Step 3. Zoom in close around the column and use the **RECTANGLE** command to draw the two separate mullions (5″ × 12″) that are on the east and south sides of the column just drawn, as shown in Figure 6-2. Use snap and relative coordinates (click the top right corner for the first point, then **@5,−12** for the other corner points) to draw the mullion much like you just drew the corner column. Remember, with relative coordinates, enter the *X*-axis value first, then a comma, then the *Y*-axis value.

Step 4. Set layer **a-wall-patt-blck** current.

HATCH

HATCH	
Ribbon/ Panel	Home/Draw
Draw Toolbar:	
Menu Bar:	Draw/ Hatch...
Type a Command:	HATCH
Command Alias:	H

Step 5. Use the **HATCH** command to make the corner column solid (Figure 6-2), as described next:

Prompt	Response
Type a command:	**HATCH** (or type **H <Enter>**)
Pick internal point or [Select objects seTtings]:	Type **T <Enter>**
The **Hatch and Gradient** dialog box appears:	Select **SOLID** at the top of the **Pattern** list and click **Add: Pick points**
Pick internal point or [Select objects seTtings]:	Click any point inside the square
Pick internal point or [Select objects seTtings]:	**<Enter>**
The area is hatched.	

Step 6. Use the **HATCH** command to make the mullions solid. Hatch one mullion, then exit the **HATCH** command before hatching the second mullion so you can array them separately.

ARRAY

RECTANGULAR ARRAY	
Ribbon/ Panel	Home/Modify Array
Modify Toolbar:	
Menu Bar:	Modify/Array/ Rectangular
Type a Command:	ARRAY
Command Alias:	AR

The **Rectangular** option of **ARRAY** allows you to make copies of an object in a rectangular pattern. The array is made up of horizontal rows and vertical columns.

You specify the direction and spacing of rows and columns:

When a positive number is specified for the distance between rows, the array is drawn up. When a negative number is specified, the array is drawn down.

When a positive number is specified for the distance between columns, the array is drawn to the right. When a negative number is specified, the array is drawn to the left.

Step 7. Use the **ARRAY** command to finish drawing the mullions on the north exterior wall (Figure 6-3), as described next:

Prompt	Response
Type a command:	**Rectangular Array** (or Type **ARRAYRECT<Enter>**)

Prompt	Response
Select objects:	Click a crossing window to select the mullion rectangle and hatch pattern on the east side of the column**<Enter>**
Type = Rectangular Associative = Yes Select grip to edit array or [Associative Base point COUnt Spacing COLumns Rows Levels eXit]<eXit>:	Type **S<Enter>**
Specify the distance between columns or [Unit cell] <7 1/2">:	Type **4'<Enter>**
Specify the distance between rows <1'-6">:	Type **1<Enter>**

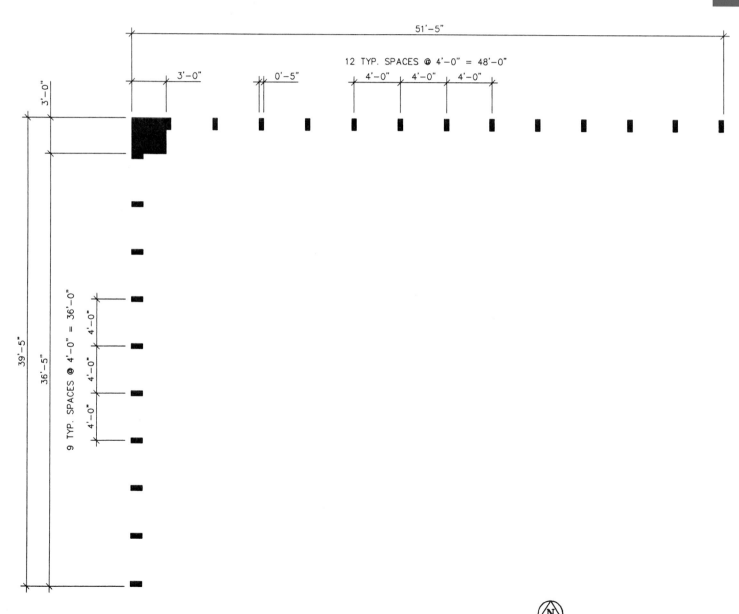

Figure 6-3
Use the **ARRAY** command to finish drawing the mullions

Prompt	Response
Select grip to edit array or [Associative Base point COUnt Spacing COLumns Rows Levels eXit]<eXit>:	Type **COU<Enter>**
Enter the number of columns or [Expression] <4>:	Type **13<Enter>**
Enter the number of rows or [Expression] <3>:	Type **1<Enter>**
Select grip to edit array or [Associative Base point COUnt Spacing COLumns Rows Levels eXit]<eXit>:	**<Enter>**

Step 8. Use the **ARRAY** command to draw the remaining mullions on the west exterior wall, as shown in Figure 6-3. Specify **1** for the distance between columns, **–4′** for the distance between rows, **1** for the number of columns, and **10** for the number of rows.

Step 9. Next, you will draw the walls using **Multiline**. It is helpful if the column and mullions are not solid. Set **FILL** off (or FILLMODE to 0) and regenerate the drawing (type in REGEN and <Enter>) so that the columns and mullions are not solid.

Step 10. Zoom to extents and use the **Distance** command (type **DI <Enter>**) with **OSNAP** to verify that all your measurements are correct.

Step 11. Set layer **a-wall-extr** current.

Multiline Style

With the column and mullions now completed, you are ready to use **Multiline** to draw the walls. The **Multiline Style** dialog box allows you to make the settings necessary to draw up to 16 lines at the same time with the **Multiline** command. You can specify color and linetype for any of the 16 lines and end caps for each multiline. You can specify the walls as solid (background fill) or not. You must add the name of the multiline style to the list of current styles before you can draw with it.

Next, you will use **Multiline Style** to create a multiline style named THREE for the north exterior wall of the tenant space. You will make settings to have one line at 0, one at 9″, and one at 12″ (the 3″ glass line is offset 3″ from the outside line of the 12″ wall).

Step 12. Use **Multiline Style...** to make the settings for a new style named THREE (Figures 6-4 and 6-5), as described next:

MULTILINE STYLE	
Menu Bar	Format/ Multiline Style...
Type a Command:	MLSTYLE

Prompt	Response
Type a command:	**Multiline Style...** (or type **MLSTYLE <Enter>**)
The **Multiline Style** dialog box appears with **Standard** highlighted:	Click **New...**
The **Create New Multiline Style** dialog box appears:	Type **THREE** in the **New Style Name** box
	Click **Continue**

Figure 6-4
WALLS style THREE and elements with offsets of 0″, 9″, and 12″

Figure 6-5
Multiline style named THREE

Prompt	Response
The **New Multiline Style: THREE** dialog box appears:	Type **WALLS** in the **Description:** box
	Highlight **0.500** in the **Offset:** input box (below the **Add** and **Delete** buttons) and type **9**
	Click **Add**
	Highlight **0.000** in the **Offset:** input box and type **12**
	Click **Add**
	Do you have a scroll bar in the **Elements** list box that indicates more lines? If so, scroll down to look. If you have a –0.5 offset, click **–0.5** in the list and click **Delete** to delete an unnecessary offset.

You should now have a 12, a 9, and 0 in the **Elements** list, as shown in Figure 6-4, and nothing else—no scroll bar to the right indicating more lines. You could now assign colors and linetypes to the lines. If you do not assign colors or linetypes, the lines will assume the color and linetype of the layer on which the multilines are drawn. Leave colors and linetypes assigned BYLAYER.

Prompt	Response
	Click **OK**
The **Multiline Style** dialog box appears with **THREE** highlighted (Figure 6-5)	Click **Set Current** Click **OK**

Multiline

The **Multiline** prompt is *Specify start point or [Justification Scale STyle]:*. The *Multiline* command uses the current multiline style to draw up to 16 lines at the same time with or without end caps.

Style: You can set any style current that has been defined with the **Multiline Style** command if it is not already current (type **ST <Enter>** to the **Multiline** prompt, then type the style name **<Enter>** and begin drawing).

Justification: This option allows you to select top, zero, or bottom lines to begin drawing multilines. The default is **Top**. In this case **Zero** and **Bottom** are the same because there are no negative offsets. If you have a positive 3 offset, a 0, and a negative 3 offset, your three lines will be drawn from the middle line with justification set to zero.

Scale: This option allows you to set the scale at which lines will be drawn. If your multiline style has a 10 offset, a 6 offset, and a 0, and you set the scale at .5, the lines will be drawn 5″ and 3″ apart. The same style with a scale of 2 draws lines 20″ and 12″ apart.

> **NOTE**
> You cannot have spaces in the style name, but spaces are OK in the description.

multiline: A method of drawing as many as 16 lines at the same time with or without end caps.

MULTILINE	
Menu Bar	Draw/ Multiline
Type a Command:	MULTILINE
Command Alias:	ML

Step 13. Use **Multiline** to draw the north exterior wall of the tenant space (Figure 6-6), as described next:

Prompt	Response
Type a command:	**Multiline** (or type **ML <Enter>**)
Current settings: Justification = Top, Scale = 1.00, Style = THREE	
Specify start point or [Justification Scale STyle]: of	**Osnap-Intersection** **P1→** (Figure 6-6)
Specify next point:	Turn **ORTHO** on. Move your mouse to the right and type **48′ <Enter>**
Specify next point or [Undo]:	**<Enter>**

Step 14. Create a new multiline style with the name **THREE-WEST; Start With THREE; Description: WALLS**; and offsets of **0, 3,** and **12**. Just change the 9 to 3. Set this style current (Figure 6-7).

Step 15. Use **Multiline** with a justification of **Bottom** to draw the west wall of the tenant space with the THREE-WEST multiline style. Use **Osnap-Intersection** and click **P2→** (Figure 6-6) to start the multiline and make the line **36′** long (subtract 2′5″ from the dimension on the right side of Figure 6-6 to account for the 3′-square corner column and the 5″ mullion).

Step 16. Next, draw the interior walls. Keep layer **a-wall-extr** current. The layer on which the interior walls are drawn will be changed to **a-wall-intr** in this exercise with the **PROPERTIES** command.

Step 17. Create a new multiline style with the name **TWO; Start With** the **STANDARD** style; **Description: INTERIOR WALLS**; and offsets of **0** and **5** (Figure 6-8). Set this style current.

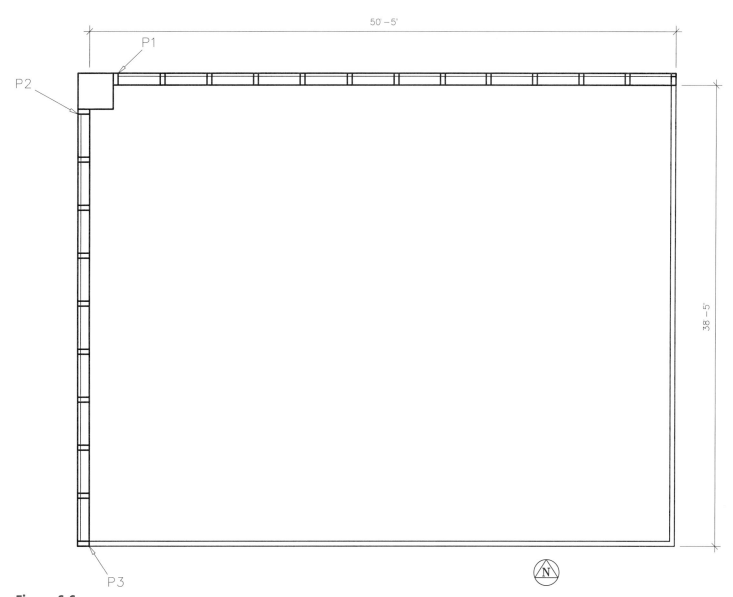

Figure 6-6
Use **Multiline** to draw exterior walls with the multiline styles THREE, THREE-WEST, and TWO

Figure 6-7
Make a new multiline style named THREE-WEST

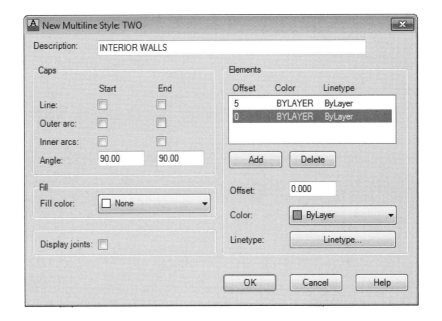

Figure 6-8
Make a new multiline style named TWO

Step 18. Use **Multiline** with a justification of **Bottom** to draw the south and east walls of the tenant space. Use **Osnap-Intersection** and click **P3→** (Figure 6-6). Make the line to the right **50′5″** and the line up **38′5″**.

Step 19. Use **Multiline** with the multiline style **TWO** to draw **5″**-wide horizontal and vertical interior walls inside the tenant space (Figure 6-9), as described next:

Prompt	Response
Type a command:	**Multiline** (or type **ML <Enter>**)
Current settings: Justification = Bottom, Scale = 1.00, Style = TWO	
Specify start point or [Justification Scale STyle]:	**Osnap-Intersection**
of	Click **P1→** (Figure 6-9)

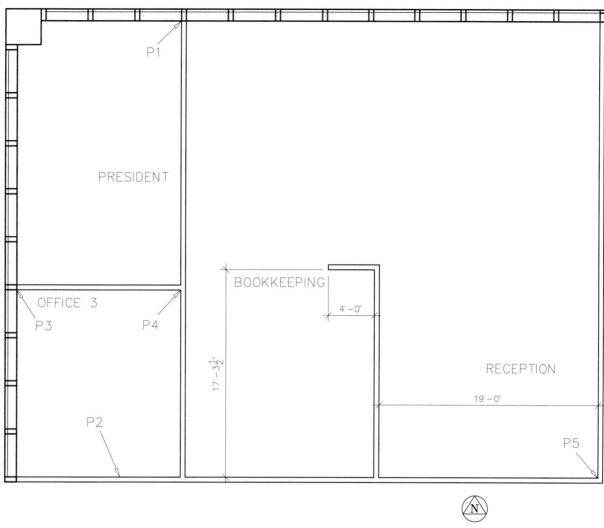

Figure 6-9
Use **Multiline** to draw interior walls

Prompt	Response
Specify next point:	**Osnap-Perpendicular** (turn **SNAP** off as needed)
to	**P2→**
Specify next point or [Undo]:	**<Enter>** (the intersection will be edited later)
Type a command:	**<Enter> (repeat MLINE)**
Current settings: Justification = Bottom, Scale = 1.00, Style = TWO:	
Specify start point or [Justification Scale STyle]:	**Osnap-Intersection**
of	**P3→**
Specify next point:	**Osnap-Perpendicular**
to	**P4→**
Specify next point or [Undo]:	**<Enter>** (the intersection will be edited later)

Step 20. Create a new multiline style that uses the settings of the TWO style but adds an end cap at the end of the line. Then use **Multiline** and

From to draw the wall that separates the reception and book-keeping areas (Figures 6-9 and 6-10), as described next:

Prompt	Response
Type a command:	**Multiline Style...**
The **Multiline Style** dialog box appears:	Click **TWO** and click **New...**
The **Create New Multiline Style** dialog box appears:	Type **TWO-CAP-END** in the **New Style Name** box; click **Continue**
The **New Multiline Style: TWO-CAP-END** dialog box appears:	In the **Caps** area click **End** in the **Line:** row so a check appears in it, as shown in Figure 6-10
	Click **OK**
The **Multiline Styles dialog box** appears with **TWO-CAP-END** highlighted:	Click **Set Current;** click **OK**
Type a command:	Type **ML <Enter>**
Current settings: Justification = Bottom, Scale = 1.00 Style = TWO-CAP-END	
Specify start point or [Justification Scale STyle]:	**From** (or type **FRO <Enter>**)
Base point:	**Osnap-Endpoint**
of	**P5→** (Figure 6-9)
<Offset>:	Type **@19'<180 <Enter>**
Specify next point:	Turn **ORTHO** on; move your mouse up and type **17'8-1/2 <Enter>**
Specify next point or [Undo]:	Move your mouse to the left and type **4'5 <Enter>**
Specify next point or [Close/Undo]:	**<Enter>** (the intersection will be edited next)

Figure 6-10
Add an end cap to the interior walls

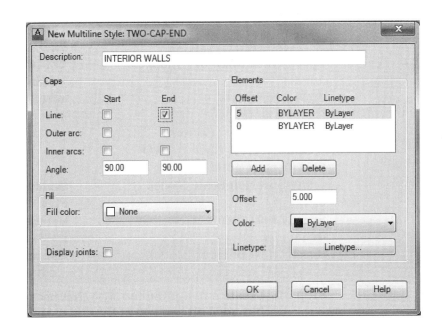

Look at the **Fill color:** area in Figure 6-10. When a color is selected from the list, the walls are drawn with a solid fill and can be filled with any color.

Edit Multiline

The **Edit Multiline** command allows you to change the intersections of multilines in a variety of ways, as shown in Figure 6-11. Just click the change you want, and then click the two multilines whose intersection you want to change.

Figure 6-11
Edit multiline tools

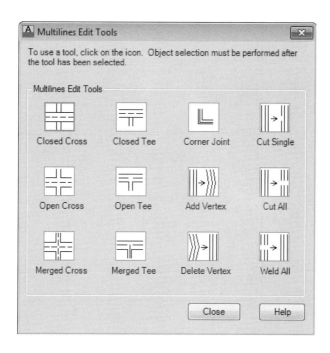

EDIT MULTILINE	
Menu Bar	Modify/ Object/ Multiline...
Type a Command:	MLEDIT or Double-Click a Multiline

Step 21. Use **Edit Multiline** to trim the intersections of the multilines forming the interior walls to an open tee (Figures 6-11 and 6-12), as described next:

Prompt	Response
Type a command:	Click **Modify**, then **Object**, then **Multiline** (or type **MLEDIT <Enter>** or double-click any multiline)
The **Multilines Edit Tools** dialog box appears (Figure 6-11):	Click **Open Tee**
Select first mline:	Click **P1→**, the vertical wall separating the reception and bookkeeping areas (Figure 6-12)
Select second mline:	Click **P2→**, the south horizontal wall
Select first mline (or Undo):	Click **P3→**, the interior vertical wall of office 3
Select second mline:	Click **P2→**, the south horizontal wall
Select first mline (or Undo):	Click **P4→**, the interior horizontal wall of the president's office
Select second mline:	Click **P3→**, the interior vertical wall of office 3
Select first mline (or Undo):	**<Enter>**

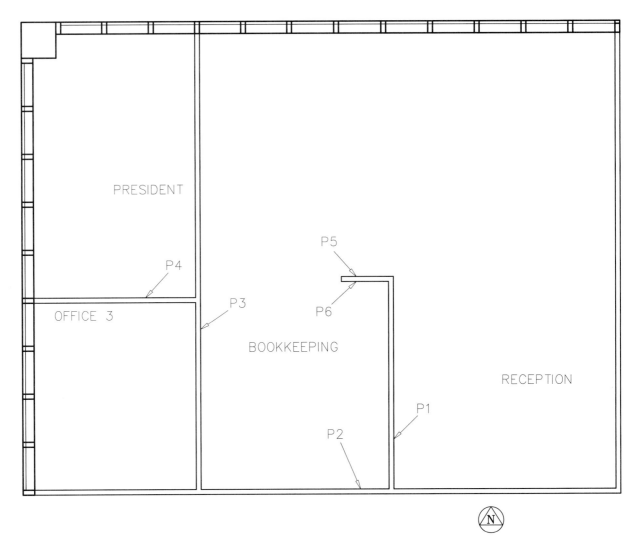

Figure 6-12
Using the **EXTEND** command

EXTEND	
Ribbon/ Panel	Home/ Modify ‒‒/
Modify Toolbar:	‒‒/
Menu Bar:	Modify/Extend
Type a Command:	EXTEND
Command Alias:	EX

EXTEND

The **EXTEND** command allows you to lengthen an existing multiline or line segment to meet a specified boundary edge. As an example, Figure 6-12 shows the multiline **P3** selected as the boundary edge; press **<Enter>**, then click **P5** as the multiline to extend. The multiline junction **EXTEND** options are **Closed, Open,** and **Merged**. **Closed** does not trim the line at the wall intersection. **Open** and **Merged** do trim the line.

You can also **EXPLODE** the multiline (not recommended as the MLEDIT tools work only on multilines). When the multiline is exploded it becomes separate line segments. You can then use the **EXTEND** command to lengthen existing lines. Figure 6-12 shows the line selected as **P3** for the boundary edge and **P5** and **P6** as the lines to extend. You would then have to erase the end cap.

properties: All the attributes of an object such as color, layer, linetype, linetype scale, lineweight, and thickness.

PROPERTIES

The *Properties* palette (Figure 6-13) allows you to change any property that can be changed.

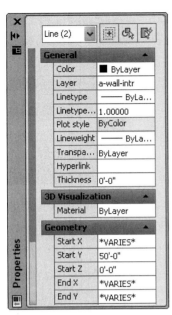

Figure 6-13
Properties palette

PROPERTIES	
Ribbon/ Panel	View/ Palettes
Standard Toolbar:	
Menu Bar:	Modify/ Properties
Type a Command:	PROPERTIES
Command Alias:	PR

LIST	
Ribbon/ Panel	Home/ Properties
Inquiry Toolbar:	
Menu Bar:	Tools/Inquiry/ List
Type a Command:	LIST
Command Alias:	LI

Step 22. Use the **PROPERTIES** command to change the layer of the interior walls from the **a-wall-extr** layer to the **a-wall-intr** layer, as described next:

Prompt	Response
Type a command:	**Properties**
The **Properties** palette appears:	Use a crossing window to select all the interior walls including the east and south interior walls.
The **Properties** palette lists all the interior wall properties:	Click **Layer...** Click the down arrow Click **a-wall-intr** Close the dialog box and press **<Esc>**

To change a property using the **Properties** palette, select the object and then either enter a new value or select a new value from a list. You can leave the **Properties** palette open, and you can also right-click in the **Properties** palette to dock it.

Step 23. Explode the outside wall line of the exterior north and west walls of the tenant space.

Step 24. Use the **PROPERTIES** command to change the layer property of the glass line (the middle line on the north and west walls) from the **a-wall-extr** layer to the **a-glaz** layer.

> **TIP**
> When the **QP (Quick Properties)** toggle is **ON** in the status bar, the quick properties palette is displayed when you click on an object. The quick properties palette can be used to view and change an object's layer as well as other properties of the object.

LIST

After you have changed the property of an entity and would like to confirm the change, or if you need additional information about an entity, using the **LIST** command is very helpful. Depending on the type of entity selected, the **LIST** command provides a screen display of the data stored for the entity.

Step 25. Use the **LIST** command to examine the data stored for one of the glass lines, as described next.

Prompt	Response
Type a command:	**List** (or type **LI <Enter>**)
Select objects:	Click only one of the glass lines **<Enter>**
Information appears:	Press **<F2>** (to exit the command)

COLOR

To access the **Select Color** dialog box (Figure 6-14), click **Select Colors...** on the **Properties** panel (or type **COL <Enter>**).

Set Color ByLayer: We have discussed and used color by assigning color to a layer, thus controlling the color **ByLayer**. The object is drawn with a layer current and inherits the color assigned to the layer.

Figure 6-14
Select Color dialog box

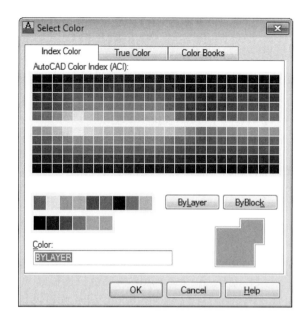

COLOR	
Ribbon/ Panel	Home/ Properties Select Colors...
Properties Toolbar:	Select Colors...
Menu Bar:	Format/ Color...
Type a Command:	COLOR
Command Alias:	COL

The **Select Color** dialog box sets the color for drawing. When **ByLayer** is selected, the objects are drawn with the color of the layer on which they are drawn.

Set Color Individually: The color property of objects can also be set individually. When a color, such as red, is selected in the **Select Color** dialog box, the objects subsequently drawn are red. The objects will be red regardless of the layer that is current when they are drawn.

To keep your drawing simple, when a new color is needed, create a layer and assign the new color to that layer.

Set Color ByBlock: Library parts that are blocks can be drawn on the **0** layer, which is the same as setting the color, lineweight, and linetype properties to **ByBlock**. The reason for this is explained in the following examples.

EXAMPLE 1

A door (library part) is drawn on a layer named **DOOR** that is assigned the color red, and a wblock is made of the door. The door block is inserted into a new project. Because the block was originally drawn on a layer named **DOOR** (color red), the layer name is dragged into the new drawing layer listing, and the door will be red, regardless of the layer current in the new drawing.

EXAMPLE 2

A door (library part) is drawn on the **0** layer, a wblock is made of the door, and the door wblock is inserted into a new project. Because the block was originally drawn on the **0** layer, the door is generated on the drawing's current layer and inherits all properties of that layer.

Before drawing any entity that will be used as a block, you need to decide how it will be used in future drawings; that will determine how color, lineweight, and linetype are assigned.

Linetype

When the **Linetype** command is selected from the **Format** menu, the **Linetype Manager** dialog box appears. Like the **Color** command, the linetype property can be set to **ByLayer**, individually, or **ByBlock**.

NOTE

You can set the color, linetype, and lineweight of an object individually. Make sure you do not do that. Create a new layer and assign the new color, linetype, or lineweight to the layer.

Lineweight

When **Lineweight...** is selected from the **Format** menu, the **Lineweight Settings** dialog box (Figure 6-15) is displayed. Like the **Color** and **Linetype** commands, the lineweight property can be set to **ByLayer**, individually, or **ByBlock**. Click **LWT** on the status bar to display lineweight properties.

Figure 6-15
Lineweight Settings dialog box

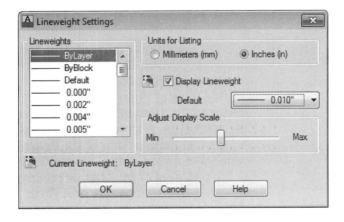

MAKE OBJECT'S LAYER CURRENT	
Ribbon/ Panel	Home/ Layers
Layer Toolbar:	
Menu Bar:	Format/Layer Tools/Make Object's Layer Current
Type a Command:	LAYMCUR

Make Object's Layer Current

This is another useful command on the **Layers** panel. When you activate this command and pick any object, the layer that object is on becomes current.

MATCHPROP	
Ribbon/ Panel	Home/ Clipboard
Standard Toolbar:	
Menu Bar:	Modify/ Match Properties
Type a Command:	MATCHPROP or PAINTER

Match Properties

When you select the **Match Properties** command from the **Modify** menu, or type and enter **MATCHPROP** at the command prompt, the prompt is *Select source object:*. At that prompt you can select the object whose properties you want to copy, and a paintbrush is attached to the cursor. The prompt changes to *Select destination object(s) or [Settings]:* and you can then select the object to which you want to copy the properties.

When you type and enter the **Settings** option to the **Match Properties** prompt, the **Property Settings** dialog box is displayed (Figure 6-16). Properties that can be copied are shown in Figure 6-16. By default, all properties are selected and show a check in the box beside the property name. Remove the check if you do not want a property copied.

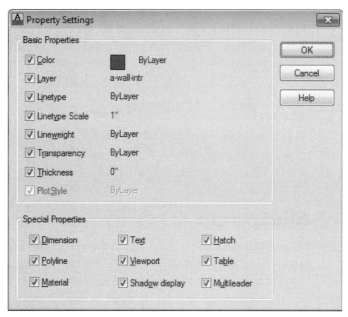

Figure 6-16
Property Settings dialog box

Step 26. Set layer **a-wall-intr** current. Use **Multiline** with the correct multiline style current to finish drawing the interior walls of the tenant space. Use the dimensions shown in Figure 6-17. Use MLEDIT tools of Figure 6-11 as much as possible to finish the interior walls. However, the **Modify** commands (**Extend, Trim, Edit Multiline**, and so on) can be used to fix the multiline. To prepare for the insertion of the doors, the interior walls are to be opened a distance of 3′4″ for single and 6′4″ for double doors. Use the 'Cut All' tool of MLEDIT or the Trim command to complete this using the dimensions provide in Figure 6-21.

Step 27. Set **FILL** on (or FILLMODE to 1) and regenerate the drawing.

Step 28. Use the dimensions shown in Figure 6-18 to draw the two door types—single door and double door—that will be defined as blocks and inserted into the tenant space. Draw the lines representing the doors, door frames, and the arcs showing the door swings on the **a-door** layer. Pick any open space on your drawing and draw each door full size. In the following part of this exercise the **BLOCK** and **WBLOCK** commands are used to define the doors as blocks.

Block-Make

The **Block-Make** command allows you to define any part of a current drawing as a block. Copies of the block can be inserted only into that drawing. Copies of a block defined with the **Block-Make** command cannot be used in any other drawing without using the AutoCAD **DesignCenter** (described in Chapter 10).

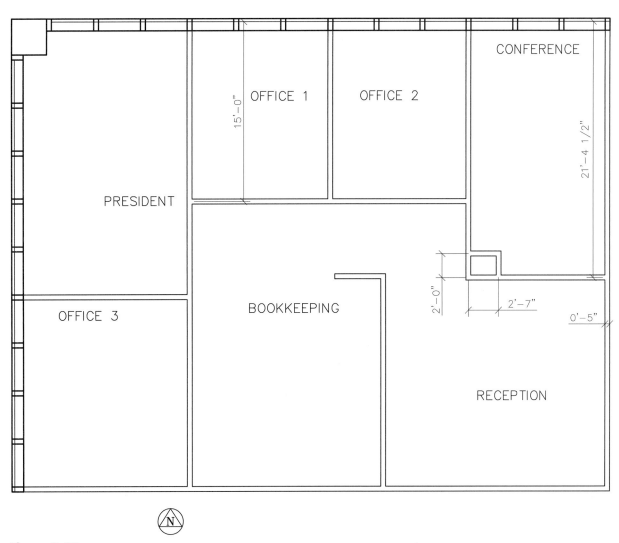

Figure 6-17
Use **Multiline** to finish drawing the interior walls

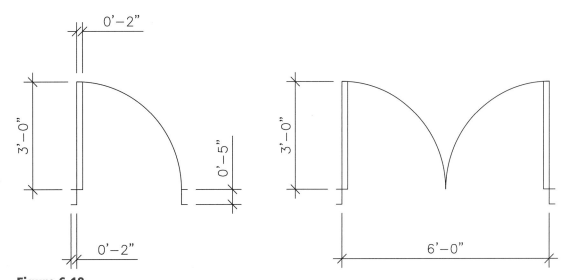

Figure 6-18
Two door types that will be defined as blocks and inserted into the tenant space

BLOCK-MAKE	
Ribbon/ Panel	Home/Block ⊡ Create
Draw Toolbar:	⊡ Create
Menu Bar:	Draw/Block/ Make...
Type a Command:	BLOCK
Command Alias:	B

Step 29. Use the **Block-Make** command to define the single-door drawing as a block named **DOOR** stored in the current drawing (Figure 6-19), as described next:

Prompt	Response
Type a command:	**Block-Make...** (or type **B <Enter>**)
The **Block Definition** dialog box appears:	Type **DOOR** in the **Name:** input box Click the **Delete** option button under **Objects** Click the **Pick point** button
Specify insertion base point: of:	**Osnap-Endpoint** **P1→** (Figure 6-19)
The **Block Definition** dialog box appears:	Click the **Select objects** button
Select objects:	Click a point to locate the first corner of a selection window
Specify opposite corner:	Window only the single-door drawing
Select objects:	**<Enter>**
The **Block Definition** dialog box appears:	Make all settings as shown in Figure 6-19; click **OK**

The single-door symbol is gone and is now defined as a block within your drawing.

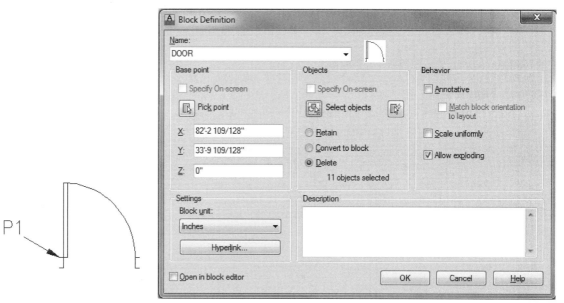

Figure 6-19
Make a block of the door; name it **DOOR**

The three option buttons in the **Objects** area of the **Block Definition** dialog box specify what happens to the selected object (in this instance, the door) after you create the block:

Retain: After the block is created, the door symbol will remain in the drawing but will not be a block.

Convert to block: After the block is created, the door symbol will remain in the drawing and will be a block.

Delete: After the block is created, the door symbol will be deleted.

The four check boxes in the **Behavior** area of the **Block Definition** dialog box (Figure 6-19) specify the following:

Annotative: Annotative blocks can be used for inserting objects such as elevation reference symbols that contain a circle (balloon) and numbers. When the annotative balloon and number block are inserted into a drawing, the sizes change according to the annotation scale. They are always the same size when plotted, regardless of the scale of the plotted drawing, if the annotation scale is the same as the plot scale. In this chapter we do not annotate the blocks because the tenant space is drawn full scale, and we want the door plotted sizes to change depending on the plotted scale.

Match block orientation to layout: When **Annotative** is checked, this specifies that the orientation of the block in paper space viewports matches the orientation of the layout.

Scale uniformly: When checked, the block is uniformly scaled in X, Y, and Z planes—**do not check this box**.

Allow exploding: When checked, the block can be exploded.

A block name can be 1 to 255 characters long. It may include only letters, numbers, and three special characters—$ (dollar sign), - (hyphen), and _ (underscore).

The **Insert** command is used later in this exercise to insert copies of the DOOR block into your drawing. *The Specify insertion base point:* is the point on the inserted block to which the crosshairs attach. It allows you to position copies of the block exactly into the drawing. It is also the point around which the block can be rotated when it is inserted.

Step 30. Use the **Block-Make** command to view a listing of the block just created, as described next.

Prompt	Response
Type a command:	**Block-Make...** (or type **B <Enter>**)
The **Block Definition** dialog box appears:	Click the down arrow below **Name:**
The block name appears:	Click **<Cancel>**

When you want to build a library of parts defined as blocks that can be inserted into any drawing, use the **WBLOCK** command, described next.

Wblocks

The **WBLOCK** command allows you to define any part of a drawing or an entire drawing as a block. Blocks created with the **WBLOCK** command can be stored on any disk, drive, or network. Copies of the blocks can then be inserted into any drawing. These wblocks become drawing files with a .dwg extension, just like any other AutoCAD drawing.

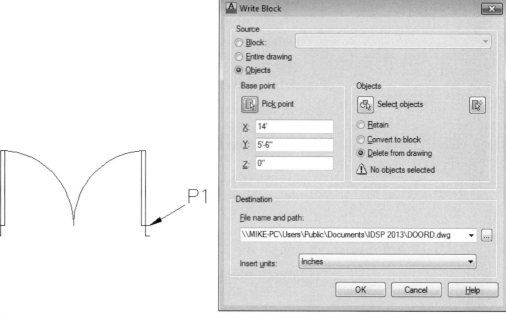

Figure 6-20
Write Block dialog box for DOORD drawing

Step 31. Create a new folder named **Blocks** in which to store your wblocks.

Step 32. Use **WBLOCK** to save the double-door drawing as a block on your hard drive or on a network (Figure 6-20), as described next:

WRITE BLOCK	
Type a Command:	WBLOCK
Command Alias:	W

Prompt	Response
Type a command:	Type **W <Enter>**
The **Write Block** dialog box appears:	Type **DOORD** (to replace the "new block" name in the **File name and path:** input box)
	Click the **...** button (to the right of **File name and path:**); this will allow you to browse for files or folders and select the path to where you want to save
The **Browse for Drawing File** dialog box appears:	Click the down arrow in the **Save in:** input box to select the drive and folder where you want to save the double-door drawing
	Click **Save**
The **Write Block** dialog box appears:	Click the **Delete from drawing** button
	Click the **Pick point** button
Specify insertion base point:	**Osnap-Endpoint**
of	**P1→** (Figure 6-20)
The **Write Block** dialog box appears:	Click the **Select objects** button
Select objects:	Window the entire double-door drawing
Select objects:	**<Enter>**
The **Write Block** dialog box appears:	Click **OK**

The double-door drawing disappears and is saved as a wblock.

The double-door drawing is now saved as a drawing file with a .dwg file extension. Copies of the DOORD drawing can be recalled and inserted into any other drawing. It is obvious that building a library of parts that can be inserted into any drawing saves time.

The three option buttons in the **Source** area of the **Write Block** dialog box specify what you are defining as a wblock:

Block: This helps define a block that is stored in a current drawing as a wblock.

Entire drawing: Not only parts of a drawing but also an entire drawing can be defined as a block. Use 0,0,0 as the base point when defining an entire drawing as a block.

Objects: Allows you to select an object to define as a block.

Step 33. Use the **WBLOCK** command to write the **DOOR** block stored in your current drawing to a disk and folder of your choice.

Step 34. In the following part of this exercise the doors will be inserted into the tenant space. Before the doors are inserted, openings for all doors must be added to the drawing. Each single door is 3′4″ wide, including the 2″ frame, so each opening for a single door is 3′4″ wide. As shown in Figure 6-21, the dimension from the corner of

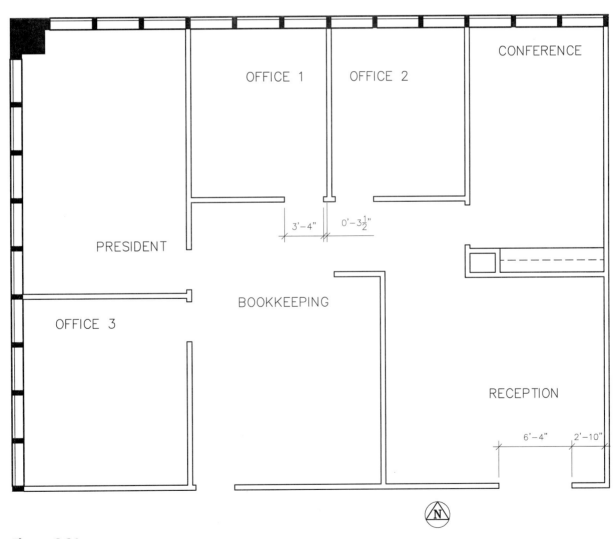

Figure 6-21
Use the dimensions shown to draw the openings for all doors

each room to the outside edge of the single door frame is 3-1/2″. The dimensions shown in Figure 6-21 for the door to office 1 apply to all single-door openings.

Use the dimensions shown in Figure 6-21 to draw the openings for the six single doors (layer **a-wall-intr**) and for the double-entry door (layer **a-wall-intr**). A helpful hint: Use **From** or **ID** with the **LINE** command to draw the first door opening line, and **OFFSET** for the second door opening line. Then, use **TRIM** to complete the opening.

Insert-Block

The **Insert-Block** command allows you to insert the defined blocks into your drawing. It may be used to insert a block defined with either the **Block-Make** command or the **WBLOCK** command.

The **Insert** mode found in the **Osnap** menu allows you to snap to the insertion point of text or a block entity.

The following part of the exercise uses the **Insert** command to insert the DOOR block into the tenant space. Don't forget to zoom in on the area of the drawing on which you are working. Remember also that the insertion point of the DOOR block is the upper left corner of the door frame.

Step 35. Use the **Insert** command to insert the block named DOOR into office 2 (Figures 6-22 and 6-23), as described next:

INSERT BLOCK	
Ribbon/ Panel	Block/ Insert
Draw Toolbar:	
Menu Bar:	Insert/ Block
Type a Command:	INSERT
Command Alias:	I

Prompt

Type a command:
The **Insert** dialog box appears (Figure 6-22):

Specify insertion point or
   [Basepoint Scale Rotate]:
of

Response

Insert-Block... (or type **I <Enter>**)

Click **DOOR** (in the **Name:** input box) (be sure there is a check in the **Specify On-screen** box under **Insertion point**; make all settings as shown in Figure 6-22
Click **OK**

Osnap-Intersection
P1→ (Figure 6-23)

Figure 6-22
Insert dialog box

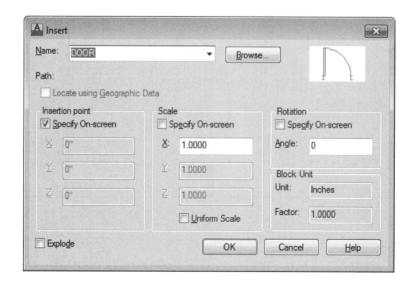

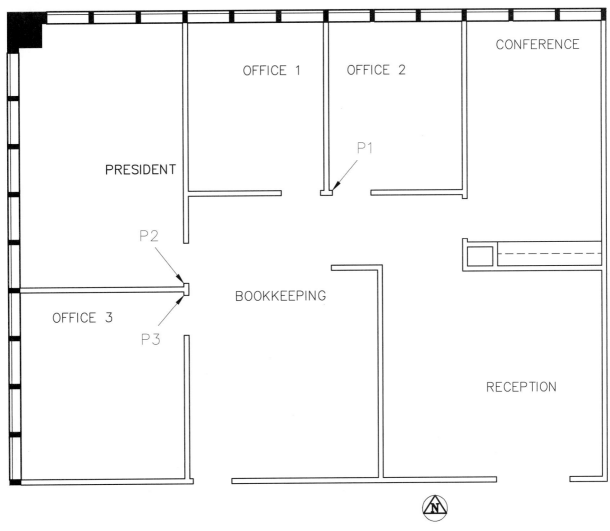

Figure 6-23
Use the **Insert-Block** command to insert the block named DOOR

Step 36. Use the **Insert-Block** command to insert the block named DOOR into the president's office (Figure 6-23), as described next:

Prompt	Response
Type a command:	**Insert-Block...** (or type **I <Enter>**)
The **Insert** dialog box appears with **DOOR** in the **Name:** input box:	Type **90** (in the **Rotation Angle:** input box)
	Click **OK**
Specify insertion point or [Basepoint Scale Rotate]:	**Osnap-Intersection**
of	**P2→**

When a copy of a block is inserted into the drawing, it is inserted as a single object. Before the **TRIM** command can be used or a copy of a block can be edited, the block must be exploded. When a block is exploded, it returns to separate objects.

If you want a block to be inserted already exploded, check the **Explode** box in the lower left corner of the **Insert** dialog box.

Insertion Point

The *Insertion point:* of the incoming block is the point where the insertion base point specified when the door was defined as a block will be placed. In the preceding exercises, **Osnap-Intersection** was used to position copies of the block exactly into the drawing. You can also use the **ID** command or **From** (on the **Osnap** menu) when inserting a block. Use the **ID** command to identify a point on the drawing, and then initiate the **Insert-Block** command after the point has been located. You can then enter the *Insertion point:* of the block by using relative or polar coordinates to specify a distance from the established point location.

X Scale Factor, Y Scale Factor

The X and Y scale factors provide flexibility in how the copy of the block will appear when it is inserted. The default X and Y scale factor is 1. A scale factor of 1 inserts the block as it was originally drawn.

New scale factors can be typed and entered in response to the prompts. AutoCAD multiplies all X and Y dimensions of the block by the X and Y scale factors entered. By default, the Y scale factor equals the X scale factor, but a different Y scale factor can be entered separately. This is helpful when you are inserting a window block into a wall with windows of varying lengths. The block can be inserted, the X scale factor can be increased or decreased by the desired amount, and the Y scale factor can remain stable by being entered as 1.

Negative X or Y scale factors can be entered to insert mirror images of the block. When the X scale factor is negative, the Y scale factor remains positive. When the Y scale factor is negative, the X scale factor remains positive. Either a negative X or Y scale factor will work in the following example, but negative X will be used.

Step 37. Use the **Insert-Block** command and a negative X scale factor, and rotate the angle of the block to insert the block named **DOOR** into office 3 (Figure 6-23), as described next:

Prompt	Response
Type a command:	**Insert-Block...**
The **Insert** dialog box appears with **DOOR** in the **Name:** input box:	**Uncheck** the **Uniform Scale** box (if checked)
	Type **–1** (in the **X Scale** input box); type **90** (in the **Rotation Angle:** input box)
	Click **OK**
Specify insertion point or [Basepoint Scale X Y Z Rotate]:	**Osnap-Intersection**
of	**P3→** (Figure 6-23)

Step 38. Use the **Insert-Block** command to complete the insertion of all doors in the tenant space. Use **Browse...** to locate the wblock **DOORD** (double door) for the reception area (Figure 6-24).

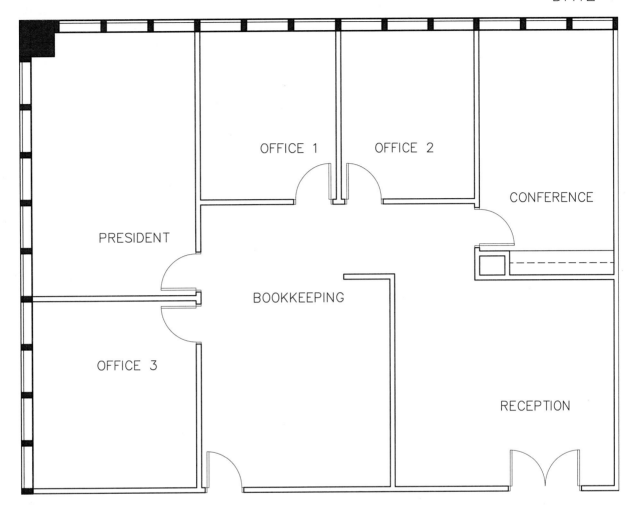

TENANT SPACE FLOOR PLAN
SCALE: 1/8" = 1'-0"

Figure 6-24
Exercise 6-1: Tenant space floor plan (scale: 1/8" = 1'-0")

Step 39. Set layer **a-flor-case** current. Draw a line to show the conference room base cabinets, 24" deep. Set layer **a-flor-case-uppr** current. Draw a line to show the upper cabinets, 12" deep. Set **LTSCALE** to show the **HIDDEN** line of the upper cabinets (Figure 6-24).

Step 40. Set layer **a-anno-text** current.

Step 41. In the **Text Style** dialog box, change the text style **Standard** to the **simplex** font and set the **Standard Style** current.

Annotative Text

When the tenant space floor plan is drawn full scale, the text on the full-scale screen drawing must be large so it can be seen on the screen. For example, if you want text to be 1/8" high on the paper drawing that is printed at $1/8'' = 1'\text{-}0''$, the text will be $12''$ high on the full-scale drawing on the screen (a scale factor of 96).

Annotation scale controls how the text and other annotative objects appear on the drawing. When you make the text ***annotative*** and set the annotation scale of the drawing in the lower right corner of the status bar, AutoCAD automatically does the arithmetic for you and controls how the text looks on your screen. When adding the text, you have to enter only the height of the text you want in the plotted drawing (paper height), and Auto-CAD calculates the height of the text on the full-scale screen drawing using the annotation scale setting.

Step 42. In the **Text Style** dialog box, select the box beside **Annotative** under **Size** to make sure the annotative property is set to on for the **Standard Style** (Figure 6-25).

Figure 6-25
Text Style dialog box with **simplex** font and **Annotative** selected

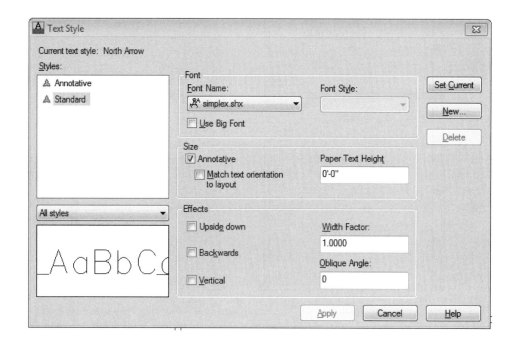

Step 43. Set the drawing annotation scale to **1/8″ = 1′-0″** (located in the lower right area on the AutoCAD screen (Figure 6-26).

Step 44. Use **Dtext**, height **3/32″** to type the identifying name in each room. Use the approximate locations shown in Figure 6-24; the names can be moved as needed when furniture is inserted into the drawing.

Step 45. Use **Dtext**, height **1/8″** to type your name, class, and date in the upper right area, as shown in Figure 6-24.

Step 46. Use **Dtext**, height **1/8″** to type the underlined text TENANT SPACE FLOOR PLAN.

Step 47. Use **Dtext**, height **3/32″** to type the drawing scale.

Step 48. Draw the North arrow similar to the North arrow on Figure 6-24. Use a **2′-2″**–diameter circle. Make a new text style named **North Arrow**, Romant font, not annotative, and set it current. Use **Dtext** to make an **8″-high** letter **N** in the circle.

Figure 6-26
Set annotation scale to
1/8″ = 1′-0″

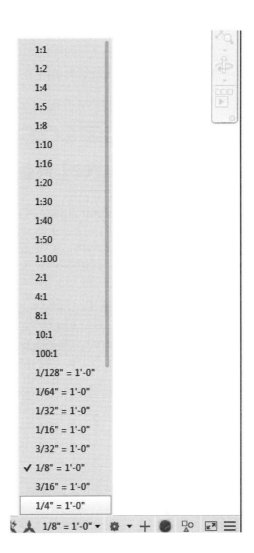

1:1
1:2
1:4
1:5
1:8
1:10
1:16
1:20
1:30
1:40
1:50
1:100
2:1
4:1
8:1
10:1
100:1
1/128" = 1'-0"
1/64" = 1'-0"
1/32" = 1'-0"
1/16" = 1'-0"
3/32" = 1'-0"
✓ 1/8" = 1'-0"
3/16" = 1'-0"
1/4" = 1'-0"

Inserting Entire Drawings as Blocks

The **Insert-Block** command can be used to insert into the current drawing any drawing that has not been defined as a block and to define it as a block within that drawing. Simply use the **Insert-Block** command to insert the drawing. Use the **Browse...** button in the **Insert** dialog box to locate the drawing.

Advantages of Using Blocks

The use of blocks in drawings has many advantages that can save you time.

1 A library of drawing parts allows an often-used part to be drawn once instead of many times.

2 Blocks can be combined with customized menus to create a complete applications environment around AutoCAD that provides the building and furnishings parts that are used daily.

3 Once a block is defined and inserted into the drawing, all references to that block can be updated by redefining the block.

4 Because AutoCAD treats a block as a single object, less disk space is used for each insertion of a block.

Step 49. When you have completed Exercise 6-1, save your work in at least two places.

Step 50. Print the tenant space floor plan at a scale of **1/8″ = 1′-0″**.

EXERCISE 6-2
Hotel Room 1 Floor Plan

In Exercise 6-2, you will draw a hotel room floor plan. The AutoCAD **DesignCenter** is used to insert existing fixtures such as a tub, toilet, sink, and faucet into the floor plan. Lineweights are used to make the drawing more attractive, and a solid hatch pattern with a gray color is used to make the walls solid. When you have completed Exercise 6-2, your drawing will look similar to Figure 6-27 without dimensions.

Step 1. Use your workspace to make the following settings:

1. Use **Save As...** to save the drawing with the name **CH6-EXERCISE2.**
2. Set drawing units: **Architectural**
3. Set drawing limits: **40′,40′**
4. Set **GRIDDISPLAY: 0**
5. Set grid: **12″**
6. Set snap: **6″**
7. Create the following layers:

Layer Name	Description	Color	Linetype	Lineweight
a-anno-text	text	green	continuous	.006″ (.15 mm)
a-door	doors and door swings	red	continuous	.004″ (.09 mm)
a-fixt	bathroom fixtures	green	continuous	.006″ (.15 mm)
a-fixt-fauc	sink faucet	white	continuous	.002″ (.05 mm)
a-flor-case	closet shelf	green	continuous	.006″ (.15 mm)
a-flor-case-spec	closet rod	red	hidden	.004″ (.09 mm)
a-flor-whch	wheelchair circle	red	hidden	.004″ (.09 mm)
a-glaz	glass	green	continuous	.006″ (.15 mm)
a-wall-extr	exterior building wall	white	continuous	.016″ (.40 mm)
a-wall-intr	interior building wall	blue	continuous	.010″ (.25 mm)
a-wall-patt-gray	hatch fill	gray (253)	continuous	.004″ (.09 mm)

8. Set layer **a-wall-intr** current.

Step 2. Use the correct layers and the dimensions shown in Figure 6-27 to draw the exterior and interior walls, window glass, doors, closet shelf, and closet rod of the hotel room. Your drawing will look similar to Figure 6-28 when Step 2 is completed.

Step 3. Set layer **a-wall-patt-gray** current and use the **HATCH** command to shade the walls of the hotel room as shown in Figure 6-27.

Step 4. Set layer **a-fixt** current.

NOTE:
ALL WALLS ARE 7" WIDE EXCEPT FOR THE 12"OUTSIDE
WINDOW WALL

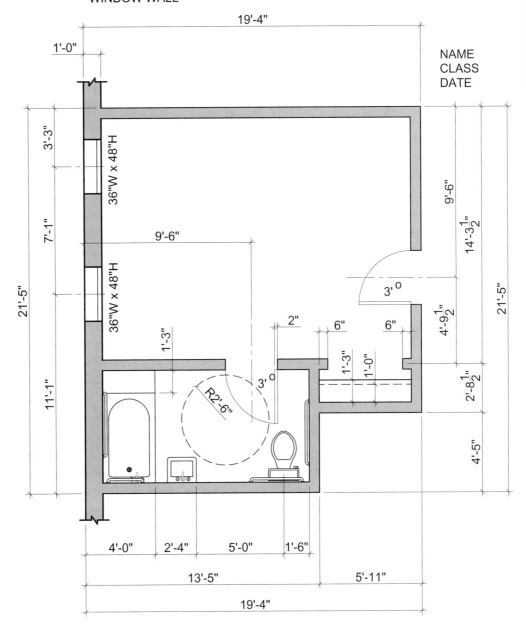

HOTEL ROOM 1 FLOOR PLAN
SCALE: 3/16" = 1'-0"

Figure 6-27
Exercise 6-2: Hotel room 1 floor plan (scale: 3/16″ = 1′-0″)

AutoCAD DesignCenter

Step 5. Open the AutoCAD **DesignCenter** and locate the **2D Architectural House Designer** blocks drawing (Figure 6-29), as described next:

Prompt	Response
Type a command:	**DesignCenter** (or type **DC <Enter>**)

Figure 6-28

Draw exterior and interior walls, doors, closet shelf, and rod

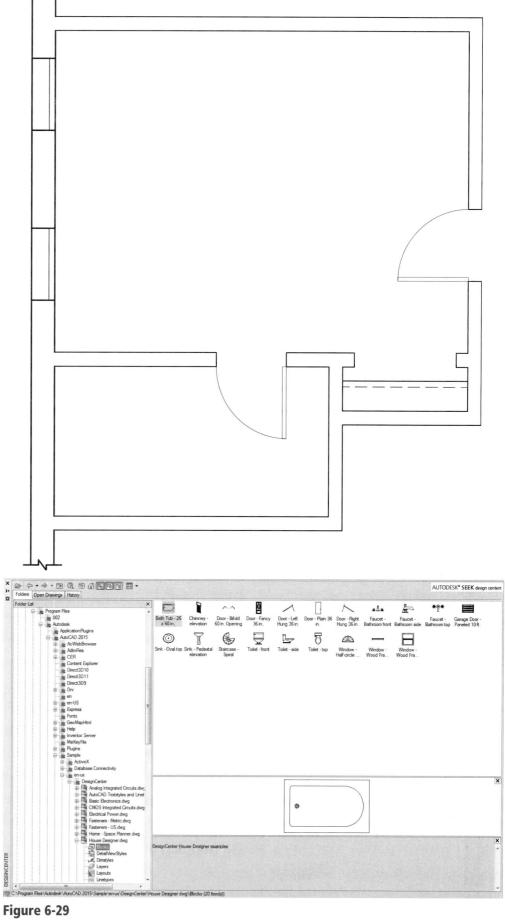

Figure 6-29

Select the **Bath Tub - 26 × 60 in.** from the **DesignCenter**

DESIGN CENTER	
Ribbon/ Panel	View/Palettes
Standard Toolbar:	
Menu Bar:	Tools/Palettes/ Design Center
Type a Command:	ADCENTER
Command Alias:	DC

Prompt

The **DesignCenter** appears:

The **DesignCenter** shows the blocks and other items in the **House Designer.dwg** (Figure 6-29). Your **DesignCenter** may appear different, depending on what is selected in the **Views** icon or **Tree View** toggle at the top of the **DesignCenter**.
All the predefined blocks for the drawing appear.

Response

Look at the bottom of Figure 6-29. Use the same or similar path to locate the **DesignCenter** folder
Click **HouseDesigner.dwg**

Double-click **Blocks**

Click **Bath Tub - 26 x 60 in.** (hold down the click button and drag and drop the bathtub into the drawing) (*Note:* The bathtub size is 36″ × 60.″)

Step 6. Rotate the tub and use **Osnap-Intersection** to locate the tub (Figure 6-30). Add a line to show the tub seat (Figure 6-31).

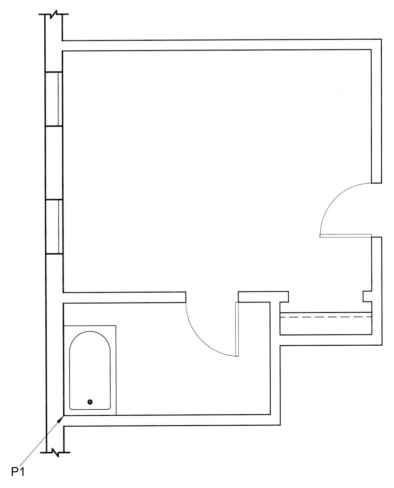

P1

Figure 6-30
Insert the bathtub

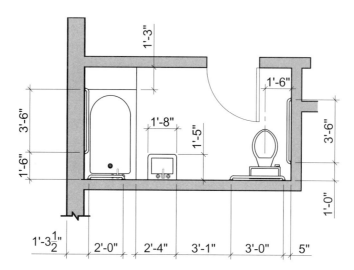

Figure 6-31
Bathroom dimensions for Exercise 6-2: Hotel room 1 floor plan (scale: 3/16″ = 1′-0″)

Step 7. Insert the toilet in the location shown 2″ from the south wall (Figure 6-31). Locate the toilet symbol in the **DesignCenter, House Designer.dwg, Blocks, Toilet - top**.

Step 8. Draw the sink using the dimensions shown in Figure 6-32.

Step 9. Set layer **a-fixt-fauc** current and insert the top view of the faucet in the locations shown (Figure 6-31) in the bathtub and sink. You will have to insert it on the **a-fixt-fauc** layer because the faucet is so detailed the lines will flow together unless they are very thin. Locate the faucet symbol in the **DesignCenter, House Designer.dwg, Blocks, Faucet - Bathroom top**.

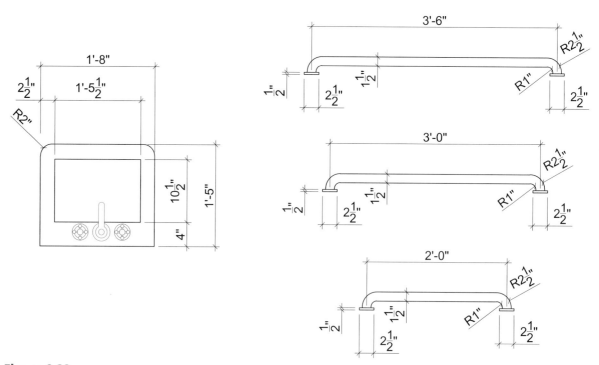

Figure 6-32
Sink and grab bar dimensions

Step 10. Draw the grab bars on the **a-fixt** layer, using the dimensions shown in Figures 6-31 and 6-32, or set layer **a-fixt** current and use the **Autodesk Seek design content** to locate the grab bars, as described next (Figure 6-33):

Prompt	Response
Type a command:	Type **DC <Enter>**
The **DesignCenter** appears:	Click the **Autodesk Seek design content button** (in the upper right corner)
The **Autodesk Seek** online source for product specifications and design files appears:	Click **AutoCAD (2D)** (for file type in the **Search** input area)
	Type **grab bars** in the Search input area **to the right of AutoCAD (2D)**
	Click the **Search** button
The product specification files appear:	Scroll down to the **Library AutoCAD Architecture** image area, locate a grab bar (24″, 36″, and 42″ grab bars are available), and click the **DWG** icon
The selected grab bar specification appears:	Check the file **check box** (Figure 6-33) and with **Download Selected to Local** click the **Download Selected to Local** button to save the file in your drive and folder

Step 11. Download the 24″, 36″, and 42″ grab bars to your drive and folder.

Step 12. Use the **INSERT** command to insert the grab bars into your drawing (Figure 6-31).

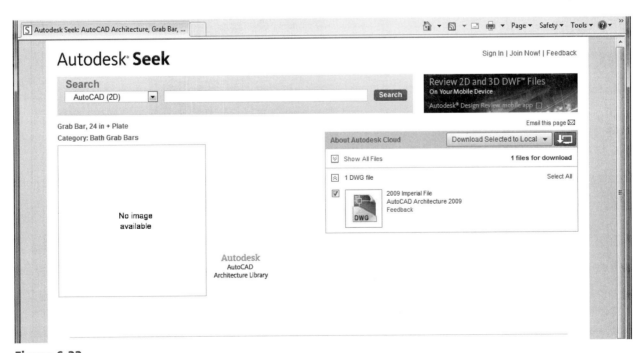

Figure 6-33
Autodesk Seek online

Step 13. Trim the toilet, sink, faucet, and tub seat lines that show through the grab bars. You will have to explode the blocks before you can trim. When the blocks are exploded, they will return to the **0** layer. Window the exploded blocks and put them back on the green **a-fixt** layer so they will plot with the correct lineweight.

Step 14. Set layer **a-flor-whch** current and draw the 60″-diameter wheelchair turning space (Figure 6-27).

Step 15. Set layer **a-anno-text** current.

Step 16. Set the drawing annotation scale to **1/4″ = 1′-0″** (located in the lower right area on the AutoCAD screen).

Step 17. Change the text style **Standard** to the **CityBlueprint** font.

Step 18. In the **Text Style** dialog box, select the box beside **Annotative** under **Size** to make sure the annotative property is on.

Step 19. Use **Dtext**, height **1/8″** to type your name, class, and date in the upper right area (Figure 6-27).

Step 20. Use **Dtext**, height **3/16″** to type the underlined text HOTEL ROOM 1 FLOOR PLAN.

Step 21. Use **Dtext**, height **1/8″** to type the drawing scale.

Step 22. When you have completed Exercise 6-2, save your work in at least two places.

Step 23. Print the hotel room 1 floor plan at a scale of **1/4″ = 1′-0″**.

Chapter Summary

This chapter provided you the information necessary to set up and draw floor plans. In addition you learned to create and insert blocks and to use the **DesignCenter**. You also learned how to use annotative text, **Multiline, HATCH, ARRAY, RECTANGLE**, and other commands relating to floor plans. Now you have the skills and information necessary to produce floor plans that can be used in interior design.

Chapter Test Questions

Multiple Choice

Circle the correct answer.

1. What is the maximum number of lines you can draw at the same time with **Multiline?**

   a. 2   c. 12

   b. 4   d. 16

2. Which of the following **Multiline** justification options can be used to draw a three-line multiline that has a 3 offset, a 0, and a −3 offset, using the middle line?

   a. Top   c. Zero

   b. Right   d. Left

3. When you have created a new multiline style, what must you pick in the **Multiline Style** dialog box to set the new style current?

   a. **Set Current**   c. **Save...**

   b. **Load**   d. **Add**

4. Which of the following must be selected first when using the **EXTEND** command?

   a. The correct layer

   b. The correct color

   c. Object to extend

   d. Boundary edge

5. Which of the following may not be changed with the **PROPERTIES** command?

   a. Color   c. Layer

   b. Linetype   d. Drawing name

6. Which of the following commands tells you the layer a line is on and its length?

   a. **Status**   c. **DIST**

   b. **LIST**   d. **Area**

7. If a block is inserted with a check in the **Explode box** option of the **Insert** dialog box, which of the following is true?

a. The block must be exploded before it can be edited.

b. Each element of the block is a separate object.

c. AutoCAD will not accept the block name.

d. The block comes in smaller than originally drawn.

8. The **WBLOCK** command does which of the following?

a. Creates a drawing file on any disk, drive, or network

b. Creates a drawing on the hard drive only

c. Creates blocks of parts of the current drawing only

d. Uses only named blocks on the current drawing

9. Which scale factor can be used to create a mirror image of a block with the **Insert-Block** command?

a. Negative X, Negative Y

b. Positive X, Positive Y

c. Negative X, Positive Y

d. Mirrored images cannot be created with the **Insert-Block** command.

10. Which of the following commands attaches a paintbrush to the cursor so you can copy properties from one object to another?

a. **Match Properties**

b. **Copy Prop**

c. **Make Object's Layer Current**

d. **PROPERTIES**

Matching

Write the number of the correct answer on the line.

a. **ARRAY** _____

b. **EXTEND** _____

c. **Multiline Edit** _____

d. **Multiline** _____

e. **LIST** _____

1. A command that allows you to draw up to 16 lines at a time

2. A command that allows objects to be copied in rows and columns

3. A command that tells you what line a layer is on and its length

4. A command that can be used to modify a multi-line without exploding it

5. A command that allows you to change the length of a line so it touches a boundary edge

True or False

Circle the correct answer.

1. **True or False:** When a block is created using the **Block-Make** command and the **Retain Objects** box is selected, the objects selected remain on the screen.

2. **True or False: Multiline Edit** can be used on exploded multilines.

3. **True or False:** One advantage of using blocks is that you have to draw the object only once.

4. **True or False:** If you want your annotative text to be 1/8″ high on a drawing printed at a scale of 1/8″ = 1′-0″, your text will measure 8″ high when you are drawing full scale.

5. **True or False:** The boundary edge must be picked first before lines can be extended.

List

1. Five ways of accessing the **RECTANGLE** command.

2. Five parameters needed to construct a **Rectangular Array**.

3. Five parameters to specify under **Element** when you define a new **Multiline Style**.

4. Five tools of the **Multilines Edit Tools** dialog box.

5. Five ways of accessing the **LIST** command.

6. Five entity properties **MatchProp** can match between the source and destination objects.

7. Five ways of accessing the **Block-Make** command.

8. Five parameters to specify when inserting a block into a drawing.

9. Five ways of accessing AutoCAD's Design Center.

10. Five advantages of using blocks.

Questions

1. In what situations would you use the **Multiline** command?

2. For what purpose would you want to use the **ARRAY** command?

3. How can objects drawn on the same layer be a different color?

4. What can the **LIST** command tell you about an object?

5. How can the **HATCH** command be used in drawing a floor plan?

Chapter Projects

Project 6-1: *Hotel Room 2 Floor Plan* [BASIC]

1. Draw the floor plan of hotel room 2 as shown in Figure 6-34. Use the dimensions shown or use an architectural scale to measure the floor plan and draw it full scale. Your drawing should look similar to Figure 6-34 without dimensions.

2. Plot or print the drawing to scale.

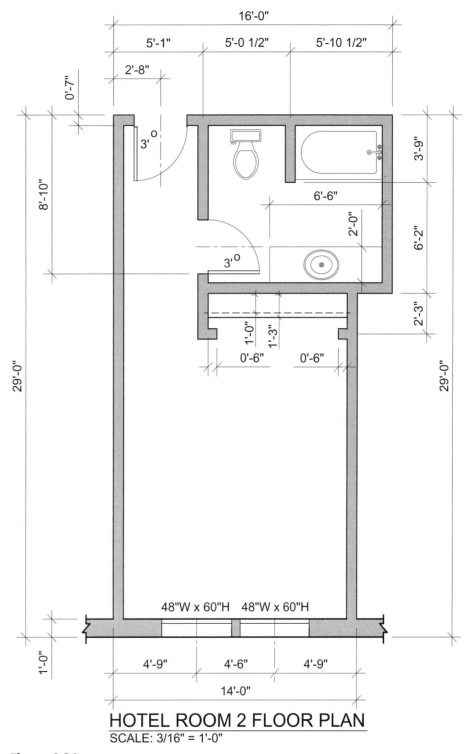

HOTEL ROOM 2 FLOOR PLAN
SCALE: 3/16" = 1'-0"

Figure 6-34
Project 6-1: Hotel room 2 floor plan (scale: 3/16″ = 1′-0″)

Project 6-2: *Wheelchair-Accessible Commercial Restroom Floor Plan* [INTERMEDIATE]

1. Draw the floor plan of the commercial restroom shown in Figure 6-35. Use the dimensions shown in Figure 6-35 (Sheets 1 and 2), or use an architectural scale to measure the floor plan and draw it full scale. Your drawing should look similar to Figure 6-35 (Sheet 1) without dimensions.

2. Plot or print the drawing to scale.

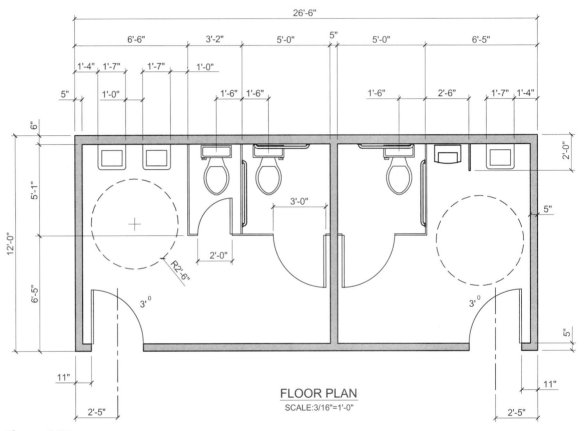

FLOOR PLAN
SCALE:3/16"=1'-0"

Figure 6-35
Sheet 1 of 2, Project 6-2: Wheelchair-accessible commercial restroom floor plan (scale: 3/16″ = 1'-0″)

Figure 6-35
Sheet 2 of 2, Project 6-2: Wheelchair-accessible commercial restroom floor plan grab bar detail (scale: 3/16″ = 1'-0″)

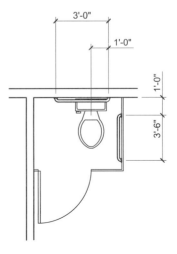

Project 6-3: *Bank Floor Plan* [ADVANCED]

1. Draw the bank floor plan as shown in Figure 6-36 (Sheets 1 and 2). Use the dimensions shown, or use an architectural scale to measure the floor plan and draw it full scale. Your drawing should look similar to Figure 6-36 (Sheet 1) without dimensions.

2. Plot or print the drawing to scale.

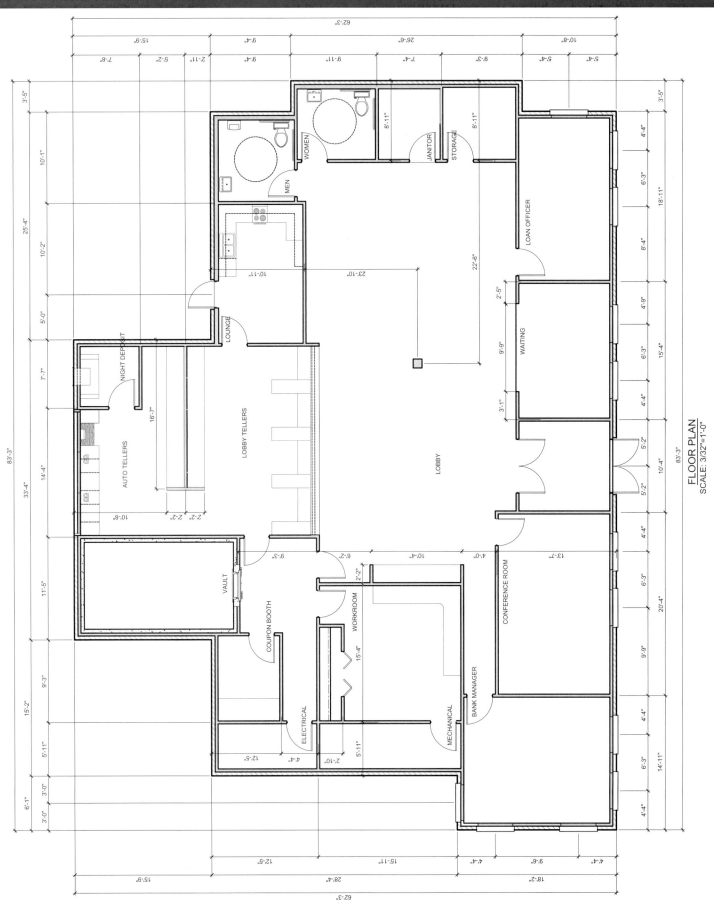

Figure 6-36

Sheet 1 of 2, Project 6-3: Bank floor plan (scale: 3/32″ = 1′-0″)

(Courtesy of Benjamin Puente, Jr.)

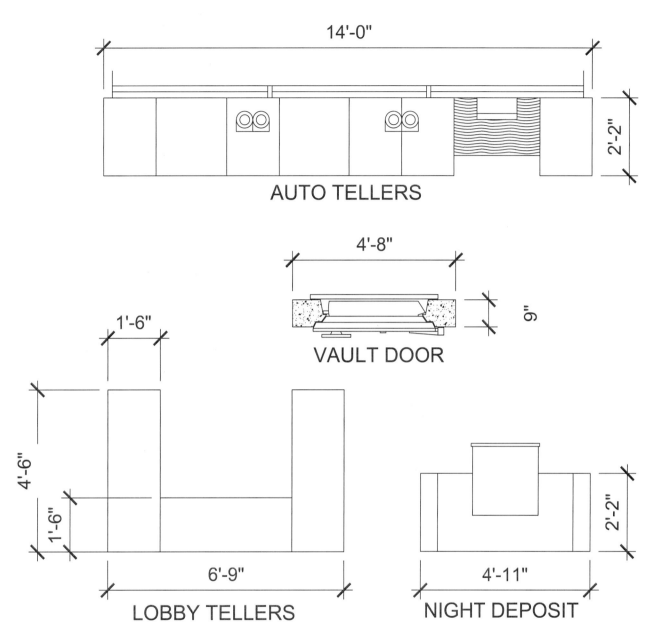

Figure 6-36
Sheet 2 of 2, Project 6-3: Bank floor plan detail (scale: 3/8″ = 1′-0″)
(Courtesy of Benjamin Puente, Jr.)

Project 6-4: *Log Cabin Floor Plan*
[INTERMEDIATE]

1. Draw the floor plan of the log cabin shown in Figure 6-37. Use the dimensions shown in Figure 6-38 (Sheets 1 and 2), or use an architectural scale to measure the floor plan or fireplace detail and draw it full scale. Your drawing should look similar to Figure 6-38 (Sheet 2) without dimensions.

2. Plot or print the drawing to scale.

Figure 6-37
Log cabin—Huntsman
(Courtesy of Tech Art)

Figure 6-38
Sheet 1 of 2, Project 6-4: Log cabin floor plan, fireplace dimensions (scale: 3/8″ = 1′-0″)
(Courtesy of Tech Art)

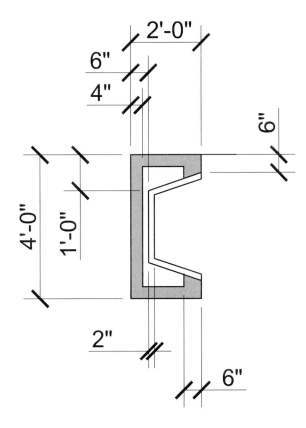

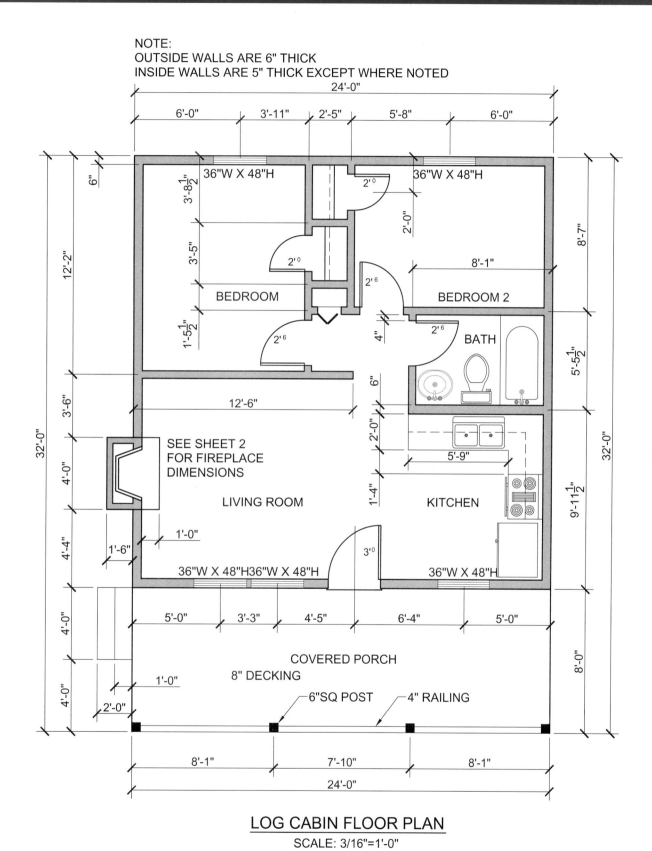

NOTE:
OUTSIDE WALLS ARE 6" THICK
INSIDE WALLS ARE 5" THICK EXCEPT WHERE NOTED

LOG CABIN FLOOR PLAN
SCALE: 3/16"=1'-0"

Figure 6-38
Sheet 2 of 2, Project 6-4: Log cabin floor plan (scale: 3/16″ = 1'-0″)

Project 6-5: *House 1 Floor Plan* [ADVANCED]

1. Draw the floor plan of house 1 as shown in Figure 6-39 (Sheets 1 and 2). Use the dimensions shown or use an architectural scale to measure the floor plan and draw it full scale. Your drawing should look similar to Figure 6-39 (Sheet 1) without dimensions.

2. Plot or print the drawing to scale.

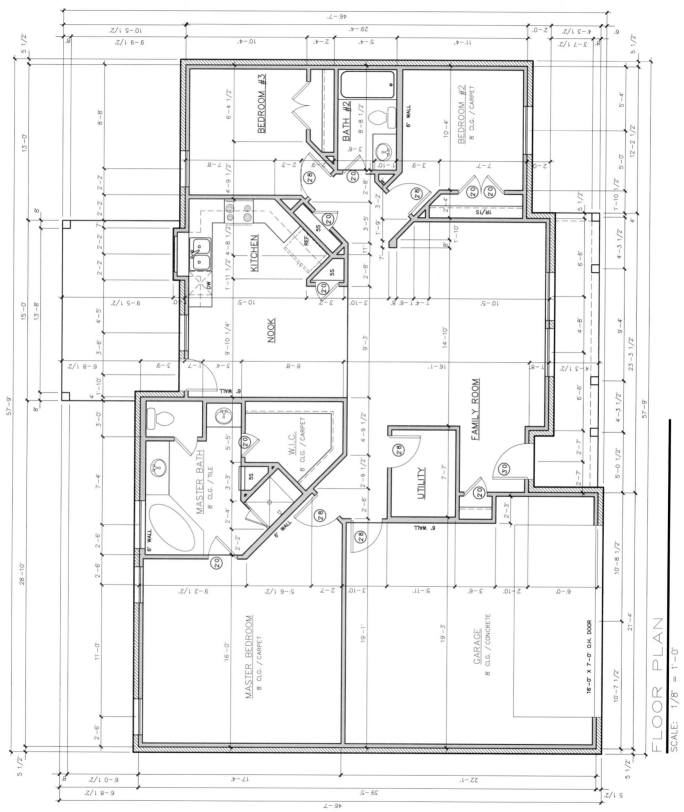

Figure 6-39
Sheet 1 of 2, Project 6-5: House 1 floor plan (scale: 1/8″ = 1′-0″)
(Courtesy of Paul Flournoy with Center Line Design and Drafting)

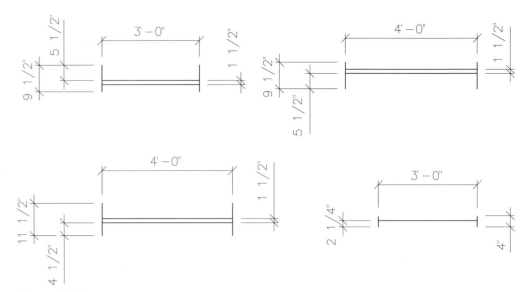

Figure 6-39
Sheet 2 of 2, House 1 window dimensions

Project 6-6: *House 2 Floor Plan* [ADVANCED]

1. Draw the floor plan of house 2 as shown in Figure 6-40 (Sheets 1 and 2). Use the dimensions shown or use an architectural scale to measure the floor plan and draw it full scale. Your drawing should look similar to Figure 6-40 (Sheet 1) without dimensions.

2. Plot or print the drawing to scale.

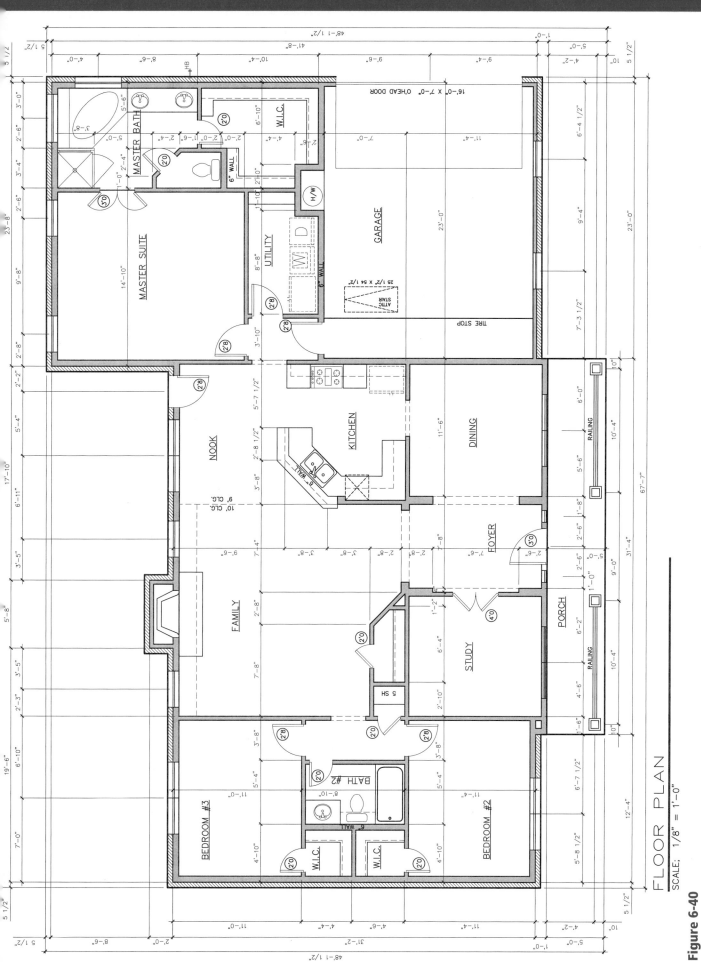

FLOOR PLAN

SCALE; 1/8" = 1'-0"

Figure 6-40

Sheet 1 of 2, Project 6-6: House 2 floor plan (scale: 1/8" = 1'-0")

(Courtesy of Paul Flournoy with Center Line Design and Drafting)

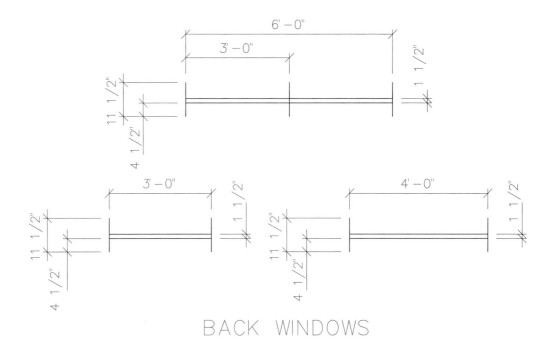

BACK WINDOWS

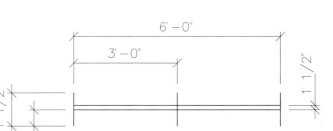

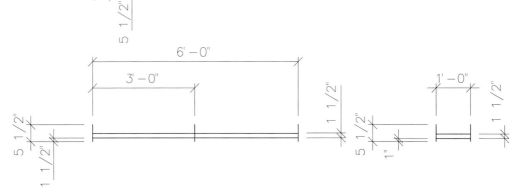

FRONT WINDOWS

GARAGE

Figure 6-40
Sheet 2 of 2, House 2 window dimensions

7 chapterseven

Dimensioning and Area Calculations

CHAPTER OBJECTIVES

- Understand the function of dimensioning variables.
- Set dimensioning variables.
- Save and restore dimensioning styles.
- Correctly use the following commands and settings:

Aligned Dimensioning	Baseline Dimensioning	
Align Text	CAL	
AREA	Continue Dimensioning	

DIMASSOC
DIMBREAK
DIMDLE
DIMEDIT
Dimension Edit
Dimension Style
DIMSCALE
DIMSPACE
DIMTXT

Grips
Linear Dimensioning
MATCHPROP
Oblique
Override
QDIM
REVCLOUD
STATUS
Update

Eight Basic Types of Dimensions

Eight basic types of dimensions can be automatically created using AutoCAD. They are linear, aligned, arc length, ordinate, radius, jogged, diameter, and angular. They are listed in the **Dimension** menu of the menu bar and are shown on the **Annotate** tab of the ribbon. Each dimension type shown in Figure 7-1 can be activated by selecting one of the following:

Linear: For dimensioning the length of horizontal, vertical, and angled lines

Aligned: For showing the length of features that are drawn at an angle

Arc Length: For dimensioning the length of an arc

Ordinate: To display the X or Y coordinate of a feature

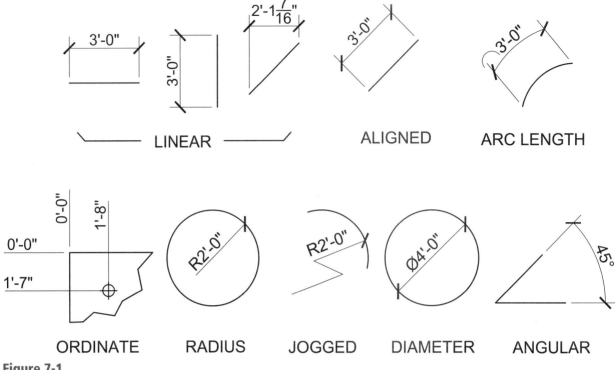

Figure 7-1
Basic types of dimensions

Radius: To create radius dimensioning for arcs and circles

Jogged: To create jogged radius dimensioning for arcs and circles

Diameter: To create diameter dimensioning for arcs and circles

Angular: For dimensioning angles

Additionally, leaders and center marks can be drawn by selecting **Multileader** or **Center Mark**.

The appearance of these eight basic types of dimensions, leaders, and center marks when they are drawn and plotted is controlled by settings called *dimensioning variables.*

Dimensioning Variables

dimensioning variables: A set of numeric values, text strings, and settings that control dimensioning features.

Dimensioning variables are settings that determine what your dimensions look like on your drawing. For instance, as shown in Figure 7-2, setting the dimensioning variables determines the size of a tick mark, how far the dimension line extends beyond the tick, how far the extension line extends beyond the dimension line, and so on.

A list of dimensioning variables and a brief description of each variable appears when **STATUS** is typed at the *Dim:* prompt (type **DIM <Enter>**, type **STATUS <Enter>**, press **<F2>** to return to the graphics screen). Figure 7-3 shows the list of dimensioning variables and the default setting for each as they appear when **STATUS** is typed at the *Dim:* prompt and architectural units have been set. Some users of AutoCAD prefer to use the **STATUS** list to set dimensioning variables. Others like to use the **Dimension Style Manager** dialog box.

Figure 7-2
Dimension terms and
variables

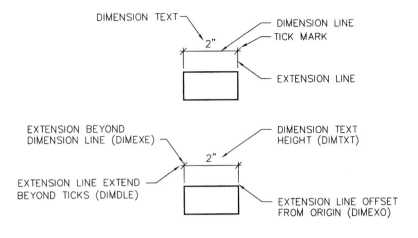

DIMASO	Off	Create dimension objects	DIMLIM	Off	Generate dimension limits
DIMSTYLE	Standard	Current dimension style (read-only)	DIMLTEX1	BYBLOCK	Linetype extension line 1
DIMADEC	0	Angular decimal places	DIMLTEX2	BYBLOCK	Linetype extension line 2
DIMALT	Off	Alternate units selected	DIMLTYPE	BYBLOCK	Dimension linetype
DIMALTD	2	Alternate unit decimal places	DIMLUNIT	2	Linear unit format
DIMALTF	25.40000	Alternate unit scale factor	DIMLWD	-2	Dimension line-leader lineweight
DIMALTMZF	8'-4"	Alternate sub-zero factor for metric dimensions	DIMLWE	-2	Extension line lineweight
DIMALTMZS		Alternate sub-zero suffix for metric dimensions	DIMMZF	8'-4"	Sub-zero factor for metric dimensions
DIMALTRND	0"	Alternate units rounding value	DIMMZS		Sub-zero suffix for metric dimensions
DIMALTTD	2	Alternate tolerance decimal places	DIMPOST		Prefix and suffix for dimension text
DIMALTTZ	0	Alternate tolerance zero suppression	DIMRND	0"	Rounding value
			DIMSAH	Off	Separate arrow blocks
DIMALTU	2	Alternate units	DIMSCALE	1.00000	Overall scale factor
DIMALTZ	0	Alternate unit zero suppression	DIMSD1	Off	Suppress the first dimension line
DIMAPOST		Prefix and suffix for alternate text	DIMSD2	Off	Suppress the second dimension line
DIMARCSYM	0	Arc length symbol	DIMSE1	Off	Suppress the first extension line
DIMASZ	3/16"	Arrow size	DIMSE2	Off	Suppress the second extension line
DIMATFIT	3	Arrow and text fit	DIMSOXD	Off	Suppress outside dimension lines
DIMAUNIT	0	Angular unit format	DIMTAD	0	Place text above the dimension line
DIMAZIN	0	Angular zero suppression	DIMTDEC	4	Tolerance decimal places
DIMBLK	ClosedFilled	Arrow block name	DIMTFAC	1.00000	Tolerance text height scaling factor
DIMBLK1	ClosedFilled	First arrow block name	DIMTFILL	0	Text background enabled
DIMBLK2	ClosedFilled	Second arrow block name	DIMTFILLCLR	BYBLOCK	Text background color
DIMCEN	3/32"	Center mark size	DIMTIH	On	Text inside extensions is horizontal
DIMCLRD	BYBLOCK	Dimension line and leader color			
DIMCLRE	BYBLOCK	Extension line color	DIMTIX	Off	Place text inside extensions
DIMCLRT	BYBLOCK	Dimension text color	DIMTM	0"	Minus tolerance
DIMDEC	4	Decimal places	DIMTMOVE	0	Text movement
DIMDLE	0"	Dimension line extension	DIMTOFL	Off	Force line inside extension lines
DIMDLI	3/8"	Dimension line spacing	DIMTOH	On	Text outside horizontal
DIMDSEP	.	Decimal separator	DIMTOL	Off	Tolerance dimensioning
DIMEXE	3/16"	Extension above dimension line	DIMTOLJ	1	Tolerance vertical justification
DIMEXO	1/16	Extension line origin offset	DIMTP	0"	Plus tolerance
DIMFRAC	0	Fraction format	DIMTSZ	0"	Tick size
DIMFXL	1"	Fixed Extension Line	DIMTVP	0.00000	Text vertical position
DIMFXLON	Off	Enable Fixed Extension Line	DIMTXSTY	Standard	Text style
DIMGAP	3/32"	Gap from dimension line to text	DIMTXT	3/16"	Text height
DIMJOGANG	45	Radius dimension jog angle	DIMTXTDIRECTION	Off	Dimension text direction
DIMJUST	0	Justification of text on dim line	DIMTZIN	0	Tolerance zero suppression
DIMLDRBLK		Leader block name	DIMUPT	Off	User positioned text
DIMLFAC	1.00000	Linear unit scale factor	DIMZIN	0	Zero suppression

Figure 7-3
Dimensioning variables

The **Dimension Style Manager** dialog box (Figure 7-4) allows you to set the dimensioning variables using a dialog box. It allows you to name the dimension style and change dimension variables using tabs on the dialog box. While dimensioning a drawing you may want some of the dimensions to have different variable settings from the rest of the dimensions. Two or

Figure 7-4
Dimension Style Manager

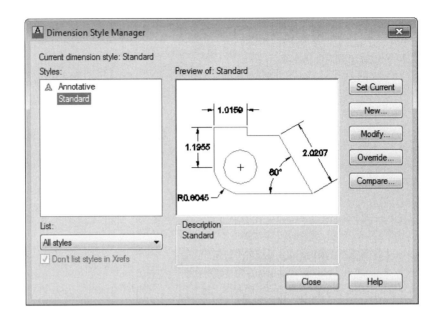

more distinct styles of dimensioning can be used in the same drawing. Each style (and the variable settings for that style) may be saved separately and recalled when needed.

EXERCISE 7-1
Dimensioning the Tenant Space Floor Plan Using Linear Dimensions

Exercise 7-1 provides instructions for setting the dimensioning variables for the tenant space floor plan drawn in Exercise 6-1, saving the dimensioning variables, and dimensioning the exterior and interior of the tenant space floor plan using linear dimensions. When you have completed Exercise 7-1, your drawing will look similar to Figure 7-5.

> **NOTE**
>
> In **EXERCISE 12-1** and **EXERCISE 12-2** you will freeze layers to make a presentation that displays the dimensioned floor plan, furniture plan, reflected ceiling plan, and the voice/data/power plan. This will work only if you have saved **CH6-EXERCISE1**, **CH7-EXERCISE1**, **CH9-EXERCISE1**, and **CH11-EXERCISE1** as a single drawing.

Step 1. Begin drawing CH7-EXERCISE1 by opening existing drawing **CH6-EXERCISE1** and saving it as **CH7-EXERCISE1** on the hard drive or network drive, as described next:

Prompt	Response
Type a command:	Click **Open...**
The **Select File** dialog box appears:	Locate **CH6-EXERCISE1**
	Double-click **CH6-EXERCISE1**
CH6-EXERCISE1 is opened.	
Type a command:	**Save As...**

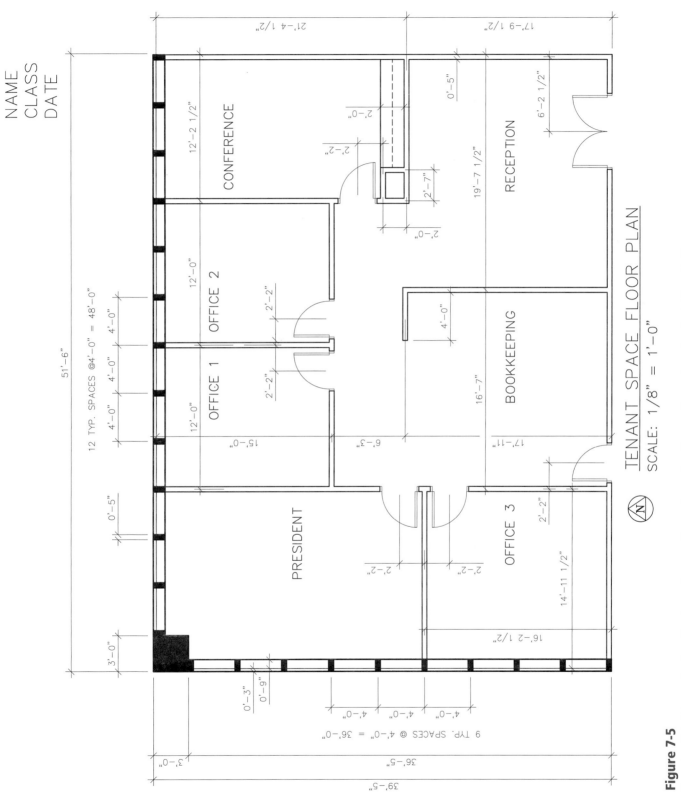

NAME
CLASS
DATE

TENANT SPACE FLOOR PLAN
SCALE: 1/8" = 1'-0"

Figure 7-5
Exercise 7-1: Dimensioning the tenant space floor plan using linear dimensions (scale: 1/8" = 1'-0")

Prompt	Response
The **Save Drawing As...**	
dialog box is displayed:	Type **CH7-EXERCISE1** (replace **CH6-EXERCISE1** in the **File Name:** input box)
	Click the correct drive and folder
	Click **Save**

You are now working on the hard drive or network with a drawing named CH7-EXERCISE1.

Step 2. Verify that **UNITS** is set to **Architectural**, as described next:

Prompt	Response
Type a command:	Type **UN <Enter>**
The **Drawing Units** dialog	
box appears:	Select **Architectural** in the **Type:** input box
	Select **0′-0 1/32″** in the **Precision:** input box
	Click **OK**

> **NOTE**
> Be sure to select **32** as the denominator of the smallest fraction to display when setting drawing units so that the dimensioning variable settings will display the same fraction if they are set in 32nds.

There are two different ways to set the dimensioning variables: by using the *Dim:* prompt or by using the **Dimension Style Manager** dialog box. The following describes the two ways to set dimensioning variables.

Set the Dimensioning Variables Using the *Dim:* Prompt

Step 3. Use **STATUS** to view the current status of all the dimensioning variables and change the setting for **DIMDLE**, as described next:

Prompt	Response
Type a command:	Type **DIM <Enter>**
Dim:	Type **STATUS <Enter>**
The dimension variables	
appear on the screen:	Scroll to see how the variables are currently set.
Dim:	Type **DLE <Enter>** (dimension line extension)
Enter new value for dimension	
variable <default>:	Type **1/16 <Enter>**
Dim:	Press **<F2>**
	Press **<Esc>**

> **NOTE**
> When the *Dim:* prompt is current, you can type the dimensioning variable name without the **DIM** prefix (example: **DLE**). When the command prompt is current, you must type the **DIM** prefix (example: **DIMDLE**).

Set the Dimensioning Variables Using the Dimension Style Manager Dialog Box

The **Dimension Style Manager** (type D and <Enter>) dialog box (Figure 7-6) allows you to change dimension variables using tabs on the dialog box. The default dimension style is **Standard**. Notice that there is a *style override* to the **Standard** dimension style. The override was created when you just typed a new setting for **DIMDLE**, using the command line. You can also create an override using the dialog box (see the **Override...** button). A dimension style override changes a dimensioning system variable without changing the current dimension style. All dimensions created in the style include the override until you delete the override, save the override to a new style, or set another style current.

Figure 7-6
Dimension Style Manager showing a style override

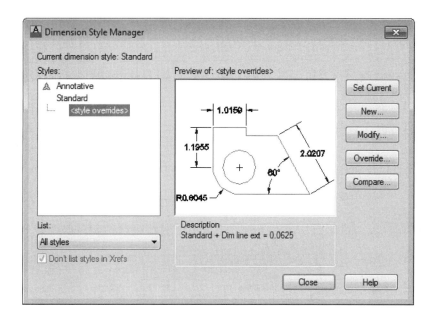

You can use the **Modify...** button to modify the existing **Standard** style, or you can name a new style and make that style current when you begin dimensioning. In this exercise you will create a new style that has several dimensioning variables that are different from the **Standard** style.

Step 4. Use the **Dimension Style Manager** to create a new style (Figures 7-6 through 7-12), as described next:

DIMENSION STYLE	
Ribbon/ Panel	Home/ Annotation
Dimension Toolbar:	
Menu Bar:	Dimension/ Dimension Style...
Type a Command:	DIMSTYLE
Command Alias:	DDIM

Prompt	Response
Type a command:	**Dimension Style...** (or type **DDIM** <Enter>)
The **Dimension Style Manager** dialog box (Figure 7-6) appears:	Click **New...**
The **Create New Dimension Style** dialog box (Figure 7-7) appears:	Type **STYLE1** in the **New Style Name:** input box Click **Start With: Standard** (Figure 7-7) Click **Continue** (or press **<Enter>**)

Figure 7-7
Create New Dimension Style dialog box

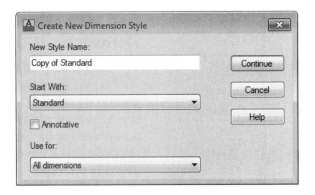

Prompt	Response
The **New Dimension Style** dialog box appears:	Click **the Primary Units tab** (Figure 7-8) (setting the **Primary Units** first will allow you to view how dimensions will appear as you set other variables)
The **Primary Units** tab is shown:	Select **Architectural** in the **Unit format:** input box
	Select **0'-0 1/2"** in the **Precision:** input box
	Set all other variables for this tab as shown in Figure 7-8
	Click **the Symbols and Arrows tab** (Figure 7-9)

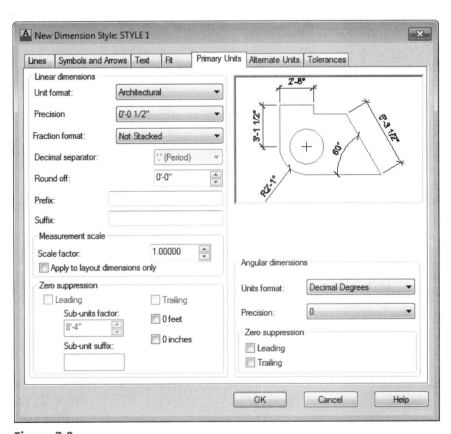

Figure 7-8
Primary Units tab of the **New Dimension Style** dialog box

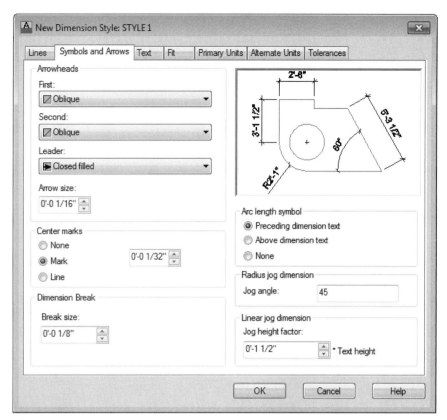

Figure 7-9
Symbols and Arrows tab

> **TIP**
> It is sometimes quicker to type a value in the text box instead of using the up and down arrows.

Prompt	Response
The **Symbols and Arrows** tab is shown:	Click **Oblique** in the **Arrowheads: First:** list
	Select **1/16″** in the **Arrow size:** list
	Select **1/32″** in the **Center marks: Mark** size list
	Set all other variables for this tab as shown in Figure 7-9
	Click the **Lines** tab (Figure 7-10)
The **Lines** tab is shown:	Click an arrow so that **1/16″** appears in the **Extend beyond dim lines:** box in the **Extension lines** area
	Click an arrow so that **1/16″** appears in the **Extend beyond ticks:** box in the **Dimension lines** area
	Set all other variables for this tab as shown in Figure 7-10
	Click the **Text** tab

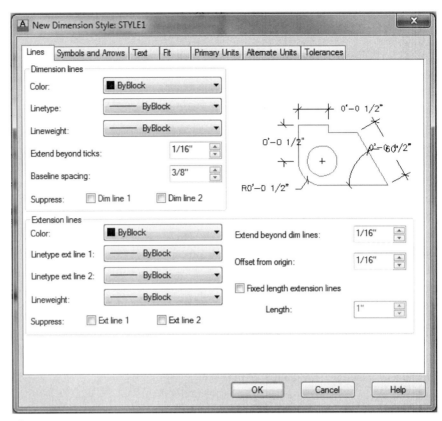

Figure 7-10
Lines tab

Prompt	Response
The **Text** tab is shown:	Click **1/16″** in the **Text height:** box (Figure 7-11)
	Click **Above** in the **Vertical:** box of the **Text placement** area (this places dimension text above the dimension line)
	Click **0'-0 1/32″** in the **Offset from dim line:** box in the **Text Placement** area
	Click the **Aligned with dimension line** option button in the **Text alignment** area
	Click the three dots (ellipsis) to the right of the **Standard Text style:** input box
The **Text Style** dialog box appears:	Check to make sure the **Standard** text style with the **simplex.shx** font is set current
	Set all other variables for this tab as shown in Figure 7-11
	Click the **Fit** tab

NOTE

If you want a thicker tick, select **Architectural tick** in the **Arrowheads: First:** list on the **Symbols and Arrows** tab.

Figure 7-11
Text tab and **Text Style**
dialog box

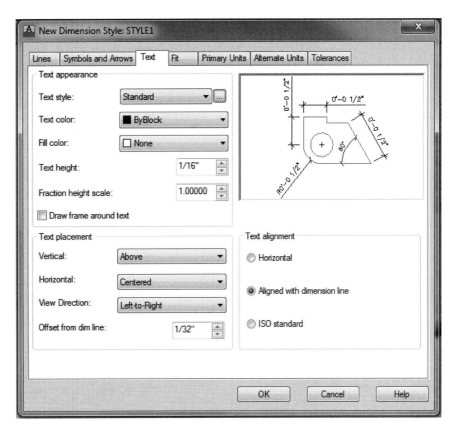

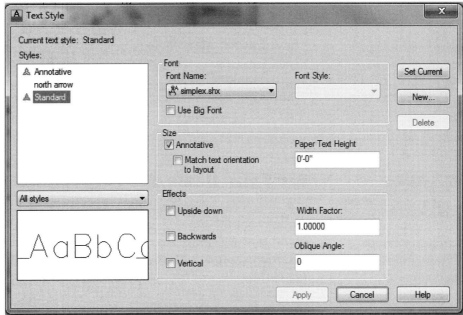

Prompt	Response
The **Fit** tab is shown:	Click the **Either text or arrows (best fit)** option button in the **Fit options** area (Figure 7-12)
	Click the box next to **Annotative** so a check mark is in the box.
	Set all variables for this tab as shown in Figure 7-12
	Click **OK**

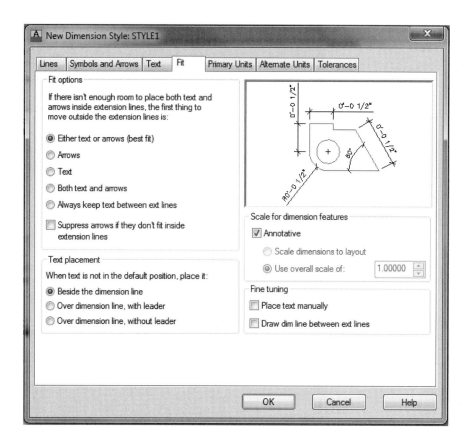

Figure 7-12
Fit tab

Prompt	Response
The **AutoCAD Alert** dialog box appears:	Click **OK**
The **Dimension Style Manager** appears with **STYLE1** highlighted:	Click **Set Current** (to set **STYLE1** current) Click **Close**

Fit Tab—Scale for Dimension Features

The preceding section set dimensioning variables that govern the sizes, distances, and spacing of dimensioning elements. It is important to understand how the value that is entered for a variable that governs a size, distance, or spacing of a dimensioning element relates to your drawing as it appears on the screen and when the drawing is plotted. This is controlled by the following settings as shown on the **Fit** tab in Figure 7-12.

Use Overall Scale of: (DIMSCALE)

This setting is also referred to as the *overall scale factor* and the variable **DIMSCALE**. When a drawing such as the tenant space or a large house is drawn full scale, the dimensions that are added to the drawing must also be large. For example, if you want the text of the dimensions to be 1/16″ high when plotted at a scale of 1/8″ = 1′-0″, the text of the dimensions that you add while dimensioning full scale will be 6″ high. **DIMSCALE** is the variable that controls the overall scale factor, or how the dimensioning parts appear on the screen display while you are drawing full scale and how they appear when plotted. For example, if you decide that the dimensioning text (**DIMTXT**) will be 1/16″ high when a drawing is plotted, enter 1/16″ for the text height value (**DIMTXT**). If you plan to plot the drawing at 1/8″ = 1′-0″, set the overall scale factor (**DIMSCALE**) to **96** (1/8″ = 12″, 1 = 96). While you are drawing full scale the text height will be 1/16″ = 96″, or 6″ high on the screen. When the drawing is plotted at 1/8″ = 1′–0″, the entire drawing including the dimensioning text is reduced by a scale factor of 96 (6″ ÷ 96 = 1/16″). If you type **STATUS** at the *Dim:* prompt, you will see this setting as **DIMSCALE** in the dimensioning variable list, as shown in Figure 7-13.

DIMASO	Off	Create dimension objects		DIMLIM	Off	Generate dimension limits
DIMSTYLE	Style1	Current dimension style (read-only)		DIMLTEX1	BYBLOCK	Linetype extension line 1
DIMADEC	0	Angular decimal places		DIMLTEX2	BYBLOCK	Linetype extension line 2
DIMALT	Off	Alternate units selected		DIMLTYPE	BYBLOCK	Dimension linetype
DIMALTD	2	Alternate unit decimal places		DIMLUNIT	4	Linear unit format
DIMALTF	25.40000	Alternate unit scale factor		DIMLWD	-2	Dimension line-leader lineweight
DIMALTMZF	8′-4″	Alternate sub-zero factor for metric dimensions		DIMLWE	-2	Extension line lineweight
DIMALTMZS		Alternate sub-zero suffix for metric dimensions		DIMMZF	8′-4″	Sub-zero factor for metric dimensions
DIMALTRND	0″	Alternate units rounding value		DIMMZS		Sub-zero suffix for metric dimensions
DIMALTTD	2	Alternate tolerance decimal places		DIMPOST		Prefix and suffix for dimension text
DIMALTTZ	0	Alternate tolerance zero suppression		DIMRND	0″	Rounding value
DIMALTU	2	Alternate units		DIMSAH	Off	Separate arrow blocks
DIMALTZ	0	Alternate unit zero suppression		DIMSCALE	96.00000	Overall scale factor
DIMAPOST		Prefix and suffix for alternate text		DIMSD1	Off	Suppress the first dimension line
DIMARCSYM	0	Arc length symbol		DIMSD2	Off	Suppress the second dimension line
DIMASZ	1/16″	Arrow size		DIMSE1	Off	Suppress the first extension line
DIMATFIT	3	Arrow and text fit		DIMSE2	Off	Suppress the second extension line
DIMAUNIT	0	Angular unit format		DIMSOXD	Off	Suppress outside dimension lines
DIMAZIN	0	Angular zero suppression		DIMTAD	1	Place text above the dimension line
DIMBLK	Oblique	Arrow block name		DIMTDEC	1	Tolerance decimal places
DIMBLK1	ClosedFilled	First arrow block name		DIMTFAC	1.00000	Tolerance text height scaling factor
DIMBLK2	ClosedFilled	Second arrow block name		DIMTFILL	0	Text background enabled
DIMCEN	0″	Center mark size		DIMTFILLCLR	BYBLOCK	Text background color
DIMCLRD	BYBLOCK	Dimension line and leader color		DIMTIH	Off	Text inside extensions is horizontal
DIMCLRE	BYBLOCK	Extension line color		DIMTIX	Off	Place text inside extensions
DIMCLRT	BYBLOCK	Dimension text color		DIMTM	0″	Minus tolerance
DIMDEC	1	Decimal places		DIMTMOVE	0	Text movement
DIMDLE	1/16″	Dimension line extension		DIMTOFL	Off	Force line inside extension lines
DIMDLI	3/8″	Dimension line spacing		DIMTOH	Off	Text outside horizontal
DIMDSEP	.	Decimal separator		DIMTOL	Off	Tolerance dimensioning
DIMEXE	1/16″	Extension above dimension line		DIMTOLJ	1	Tolerance vertical justification
DIMEXO	1/16	Extension line origin offset		DIMTP	0″	Plus tolerance
DIMFRAC	2	Fraction format		DIMTSZ	0″	Tick size
DIMFXL	1″	Fixed Extension Line		DIMTVP	0.00000	Text vertical position
DIMFXLON	Off	Enable Fixed Extension Line		DIMTXSTY	Standard	Text style
DIMGAP	1/32″	Gap from dimension line to text		DIMTXT	1/16″	Text height
DIMJOGANG	45	Radius dimension jog angle		DIMTXTDIRECTION	Off	Dimension text direction
DIMJUST	0	Justification of text on dim line		DIMTZIN	0	Tolerance zero suppression
DIMLDRBLK	ClosedFilled	Leader block name		DIMUPT	Off	User positioned text
DIMLFAC	1.00000	Linear unit scale factor		DIMZIN	1	Zero suppression

Figure 7-13
Dimensioning variables with **DIMSCALE** set to **96**

The overall scale factor (**DIMSCALE**) for a drawing that is plotted at 1/4″ = 12″ is 48 (1/4 = 12, 1 = 48). For a plotting ratio of 1/2″ = 12″, the overall scale factor (**DIMSCALE**) is 24 (1/2 = 12, 1 = 24).

Annotative

When the tenant space floor plan is drawn full scale, the dimensions on the full-scale screen drawing must be large so they can be seen on the screen. For example, if you want the dimension text to be 1/8″ high on the paper drawing that is printed at $1/8'' = 1'\text{-}0''$, the dimension text will be $12''$ high on the full-scale drawing on the screen (a scale factor of 96).

Annotation scale controls how the dimensions and other ***annotative*** objects appear on the drawing. When you make the dimension style annotative and set the annotation scale of the drawing in the lower right corner of the status bar, AutoCAD automatically does the arithmetic for you and controls how the dimensions look on your screen. When adding the dimensions, AutoCAD calculates the size of the dimension variables on the full-scale screen drawing using the annotation scale setting.

> **TIP**
>
> Start a drawing, set the dimensioning variables, and save the drawing as a template for future dimensioning projects.

Step 5. Create the following new layer and set it as the current layer:

Layer Name	Color	Linetype	Lineweight
a-anno-dims	Red	continuous	.004" (.09 mm)

Step 6. Make sure the **Annotation Scale** is set to $1/8'' = 1'\text{-}0''$.

Linear and Continue Dimensioning

Step 7. Using **Linear**, dimension the column and one mullion on the north exterior wall of the tenant space floor plan (Figure 7-14), as described next:

Figure 7-14
Linear dimensioning

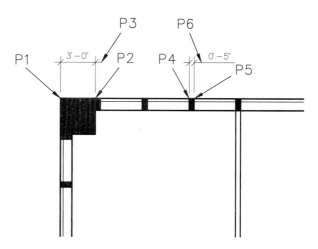

LINEAR	
Ribbon/ Panel	Home/ Annotation
Dimension Toolbar:	
Menu Bar:	Dimension/ Linear
Type a Command:	DIMLINEAR
Command Alias:	DIMLIN

Prompt

Type a command:

Specify first extension line origin or <select object>:

Specify second extension line origin:

Specify dimension line location or [Mtext Text Angle Horizontal Vertical Rotated]:

Response

Linear (or type **HOR <Enter>** at the *Dim:* prompt)

P1→ (with **SNAP** on)

P2→

P3→ (on snap, three grid marks up, with 12" grid)

Prompt	Response
Type a command:	**<Enter>** (repeat **Linear**)
Specify first extension line origin or <select object>:	**Osnap-Intersection**
of	**P4→**
Specify second extension line origin:	**Osnap-Intersection**
of	**P5→**
Specify dimension line location or [Mtext Text Angle Horizontal Vertical Rotated]:	**P6→** (on snap, three grid marks up)

In the **Linear** command, after the second extension line origin is selected, the prompt reads: *Specify dimension line location or [Mtext Text Angle Horizontal Vertical Rotated]:*.

Before you pick a dimension line location, you may type the first letter of any of the options in the brackets and press **<Enter>** to activate it. These options are as follows:

Mtext: To activate the **Multiline Text** command for dimensions requiring more than one line of text.

Text: To replace the default text with a single line of text. To suppress the text entirely, press the space bar.

Angle: To rotate the text of the dimension to a specific angle.

Horizontal: To specify that you want a horizontal dimension; this is normally not necessary.

Vertical: To specify that you want a vertical dimension; this is normally not necessary.

Rotated: To specify that you want to rotate the entire dimension.

Step 8. Using **Linear** and **Continue**, dimension horizontally (center to center) the distance between four mullions on the north exterior wall of the tenant space (Figure 7-15), as described next. (Before continuing, zoom in or pan over to the four mullions to be dimensioned.)

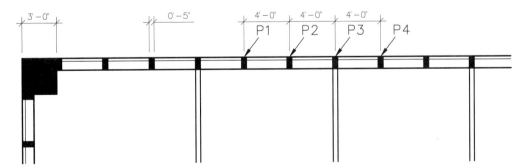

Figure 7-15
Linear dimensioning with the **Continue** command to draw horizontal dimensions

Prompt	Response
Type a command:	**Linear** (from the **Dimensions** panel)
Specify first extension line origin or <select object>:	**Osnap-Midpoint**
of	**P1→**

CONTINUE	
Ribbon/ Panel	Annotate/ Dimensions ╟╫╢
Dimension Toolbar:	╟╫╢
Menu Bar:	Dimension/ Continue
Type a Command:	DIMCONTINUE
Command Alias:	DIMCONT

Prompt	Response
Specify second extension line origin: of	**Osnap-Midpoint** **P2→**
Specify dimension line location or [Mtext Text Angle Horizontal Vertical Rotated]:	Click a point on snap, three grid marks up, to align with previous dimensions
Type a command:	**Continue** (from the **Dimension** menu)
Specify a second extension line origin or [Undo Select]<Select>: of	**Osnap-Midpoint** **P3→**
Specify a second extension line origin or [Undo Select]<Select>: of	**Osnap-Midpoint** **P4→**
Specify a second extension origin or [Undo Select]<Select>:	**<Enter>**
Select continued dimension:	**<Enter>** (to complete the command)

NOTE

You may change the dimension string at the prompt *Specify dimension line location by typing T <Enter>*, then typing new dimensions from the keyboard and pressing **<Enter>**.

Step 9. Using **Linear** and **Continue**, dimension vertically (center to center) the distance between four mullions on the west exterior wall of the tenant space (Figure 7-16), as described next. (Before continuing, zoom in on the four mullions to be dimensioned.)

Prompt	Response
Type a command:	**Linear** (or type **VER <Enter>** at the *Dim:* prompt)
Specify first extension line origin or <select object>: of	**Osnap-Midpoint** Click the first mullion (dimension south to north)
Specify second extension line origin: of	**Osnap-Midpoint** Pick the second mullion
Specify dimension line location or [Mtext Text Angle Horizontal Vertical Rotated]:	Pick a point on snap, three grid marks to the left, similar to previous dimension line locations
Type a command:	**Continue** (on the **Dimensions** panel)
Specify a second extension line origin or [Undo Select]<Select>: of	**Osnap-Midpoint** Pick the third mullion
Specify a second extension line origin or [Undo Select]<Select>: of	**Osnap-Midpoint** Pick the fourth mullion
Specify a second extension line origin or [Undo Select]<Select>:	**<Enter>**
Select continued dimension:	**<Enter>**

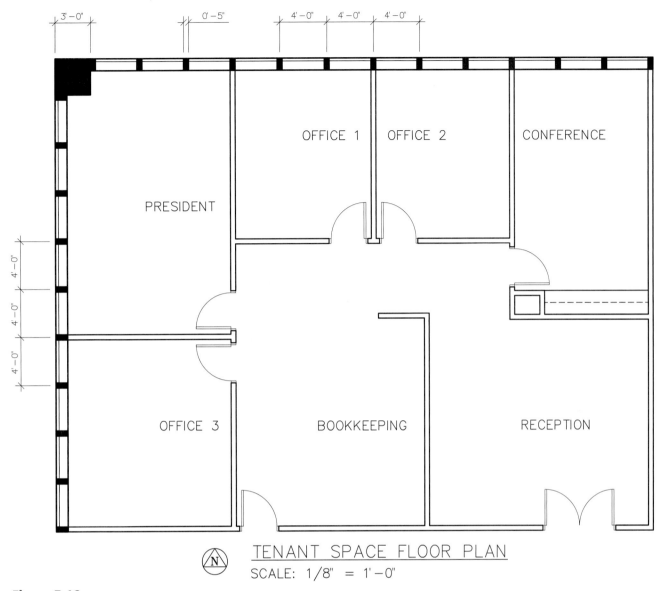

Figure 7-16
Linear dimensioning with the **Continue** command to draw vertical dimensions (scale: 1/8″ = 1′-0″)

> **TIP**
> Use **OSNAP** commands to select extension line origins. Set a running **Osnap** mode.

ALIGNED

Figure 7-17
Dimensioning with the **Aligned** command

Aligned Dimensioning

When you use **Aligned** you can select the first and second extension line origin points of a line that is at an angle, and the dimension line will run parallel to the origin points. Figure 7-17 shows an example of aligned dimensioning.

Baseline Dimensioning

With linear dimensioning, after the first segment of a line is dimensioned, picking the **Baseline** command in the **Dimensions** panel automatically continues the next linear dimension from the baseline (first extension line) of the first linear dimension. The new dimension line is offset to avoid drawing on top of the previous dimension. The **DIMDLI** variable controls the size of the offset. Figure 7-18 shows linear dimensioning with the **Baseline** command.

Figure 7-18
Linear dimensioning with the **Baseline** command

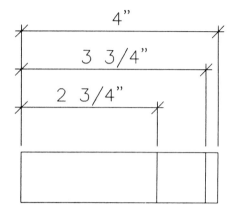

> **TIP**
>
> When erasing construction lines, avoid selecting definition points; otherwise, the dimension associated with that point will be erased.

Step 10. Use **DTEXT**, centered, to add the text **12 TYP. SPACES @ 4'-0″ = 48'-0″** to the plan (Figure 7-19). Place it two grid marks (on a 12″ grid) above the dimension line of the mullions dimension. Set the text height to **1/16″** (text is annotative).

> **NOTE**
>
> When stacking dimension lines, locate the first dimension line farther from the object being dimensioned than subsequent dimension lines are from each other. For example, locate the first dimension line three grid marks from the object and the second dimension line two grid marks from the first dimension line.

ALIGNED	
Ribbon/ Panel	Home/ Annotation
Dimension Toolbar:	
Menu Bar:	Dimension/ Aligned
Type a Command:	DIMALIGNED
Command Alias:	DIMALI

Step 11. Use **Linear** to dimension the overall north exterior wall of the tenant space. You may snap to the tick (intersection) of a previous dimension (Figure 7-19).

Step 12. Use **DTEXT**, centered, to add the text **9 TYP. SPACES @ 4'-0″ = 36'-0″** to the plan (Figure 7-19). Place it two grid marks (on a 12″ grid) above the dimension line of the mullions dimension. Set the text height to **1/16″**.

Step 13. Use **Linear** to dimension from the southwest corner of the tenant space to the southern corner of the column. Use **Continue** to continue the dimension to the outside northwest corner of the building (Figure 7-19).

Step 14. Use **Linear** to dimension the overall west exterior wall of the tenant space (Figure 7-19).

Step 15. Set a running **Osnap** mode of **Nearest**.

Step 16. Dimension from the middle of the west wall of Office 2 to the center of the door in Office 2. Use the **<Shift>** key and right-click to get the **Osnap** menu and pick **Mid Between 2 Points** to complete the dimension (Figure 7-19), as described next:

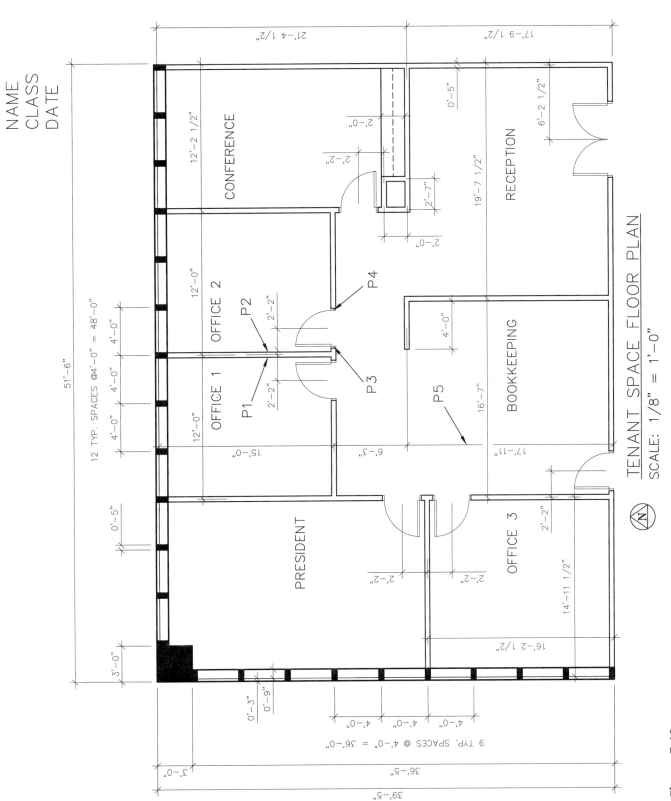

NAME
CLASS
DATE

TENANT SPACE FLOOR PLAN
SCALE: 1/8" = 1'-0"

CONFERENCE

OFFICE 2

OFFICE 1

PRESIDENT

RECEPTION

BOOKKEEPING

OFFICE 3

P1
P2
P3
P4
P5

21'-4 1/2"
17'-9 1/2"
51'-6"
12 TYP. SPACES @4'-0" = 48'-0"
12'-2 1/2"
12'-0"
12'-0"
0'-5"
0'-5"
2'-0"
2'-2"
2'-7"
2'-0"
19'-7 1/2"
6'-2 1/2"
4'-0"
16'-7"
17'-11"
6'-3"
15'-0"
2'-2"
2'-2"
2'-2"
2'-2"
14'-11 1/2"
16'-2 1/2"
4'-0"
4'-0"
4'-0"
4'-0"
4'-0"
4'-0"
3'-0"
0'-3"
0'-9"
9 TYP. SPACES @ 4'-0" = 36'-0"
36'-5"
3'-0"
39'-5"

N

Figure 7-19
Exercise 7-1 complete (scale: 1/8" = 1'-0")

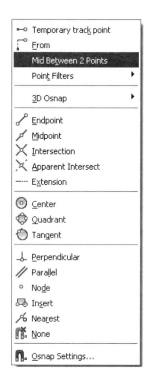

Figure 7-20
Mid Between 2 Points

Prompt	Response
Type a command:	**Linear**
Specify first extension line origin or <select object>:	**<Shift>** + right-click Click **Mid Between 2 Points** (Figure 7-20)
Specify first extension line origin or <select object>: _m2p First point of mid:	Click **P1→** (left side of wall symbol)
Second point of mid:	Click **P2→** (right side of wall symbol)
Specify second extension line origin:	**<Shift>** + right-click Click **Mid Between 2 Points**
Specify second extension line origin: _m2p First point of mid:	Click **P3→** (left side of door opening)
Second point of mid:	Click **P4→** (right side of second wall)

Specify dimension line location
   or [Mtext Text Angle Horizontal
   Vertical Rotated]:
	Pick a point to locate the dimension

Step 17. Complete the dimensioning using the **Linear** dimension commands and the appropriate **Osnap** modifiers. When you are dimensioning from left to right, any outside dimension line and text will be placed to the right. Dimensioning from right to left draws any outside dimension line and text to the left.

Dimension Break

DIMENSION BREAK	
Ribbon/ Panel	Annotate/ Dimensions
Dimension Toolbar:	
Menu Bar:	Dimension/ Dimension Break
Type a Command:	DIMBREAK

Step 18. Add a dimension break in the vertical dimension line in the book-keeping area that crosses over another dimension line, as described next (Figure 7-19):

Prompt	Response
Type a command:	Type **DIMBREAK <Enter>**
Select dimension to add/ remove break or [Multiple]:	**P5→** (Figure 7-19)
Select object to break dimension or [Auto Manual Remove]<Auto>:	**<Enter>**
1 object modified	
The break is added	

A break can be added to a dimension line, extension line, or to a multileader (described in Chapter 8).

   Multiple: Allows you to select more than one dimension line that you want to break

   Manual: Allows you to pick the first and second break point for the break

   Remove: Allows you to select the dimension and remove the break from that dimension

Adjust Space

ADJUST SPACE	
Ribbon/ Panel	Annotate/ Dimensions
Dimension Toolbar:	
Menu Bar:	Dimension/ Dimension Space
Type a Command:	DIMSPACE

Adjust Space (DIMSPACE) is used to make the spacing between parallel dimension lines equal. This command asks you to select a base dimension—the dimension you do not want to move. The command then asks you to select dimensions that are parallel to the base dimension and that you want to space equally. After you have selected the dimensions, press **<Enter>**. You can then enter a distance (for example, 24″), or you can press **<Enter>** and the dimensions will be automatically spaced—the automatic space is twice the height of the dimension text.

If you have a series of dimensions that you want to align, enter a **0** for the spacing value, and they will align.

Step 19. Move your name, class, and date outside any dimension lines, if needed.

Step 20. When you have completed Exercise 7-1, save your work in at least two places.

Step 21. Print Exercise 7-1 at a scale of **1/8″ = 1′-0″**.

EXERCISE 7-2
Revisions and Modifying Dimensions

DIMASSOC System Variable

This setting is not one of the dimensioning variables and is not stored in a dimension style, but it does affect how dimensions behave in relation to the object being dimensioned. It has three states:

0   **DIMASSOC** is off. This setting creates exploded dimensions. Each part of the dimension (arrowheads, lines, text) is a separate object.

1   **DIMASSOC** is on. This setting creates dimensions that are single objects but are not associated with the object being dimensioned. When the dimension is created, definition points are formed (at the ends of extension lines, for example). If these points are moved, as with the **Stretch** command, the dimension changes, but it is not directly associated with the object being dimensioned.

2   **DIMASSOC** is on. This setting creates **associative dimension** objects. The dimensions are single objects, and one or more of the definition points on the dimension are linked to association points on the object. When the association point on the object moves, the dimension location, orientation, and text value of the dimension change. For example: Check **DIMASSOC** to make sure the setting is **2** (type **DIMASSOC** **<Enter>**. If the value is not 2, type **2 <Enter>**). Draw a 2′ diameter circle and dimension it using the **Diameter** dimensioning command. With no command active, click any point on the circle so that grips appear at the quadrants of the circle. Click any grip to make it hot, and move the grip. The dimension changes as the size of the circle changes.

The **AM toggle (Annotation Monitor)** in the drawing tools area of the status bar keeps track of associated dimensions. When the **AM toggle** is **ON**, dimensions that are disassociated will have a badge beside them. When you pick or right-click the badge, a menu appears with commands that allow you to reassociate or delete the dimension. When the **AM toggle** is **ON**, a red cross shows up in the tray area of the status bar.

Exercise 7-2 describes commands that can be used to modify dimensions and how to make a revision cloud. When you have completed Exercise 7-2, your drawing will look similar to Figure 7-21.

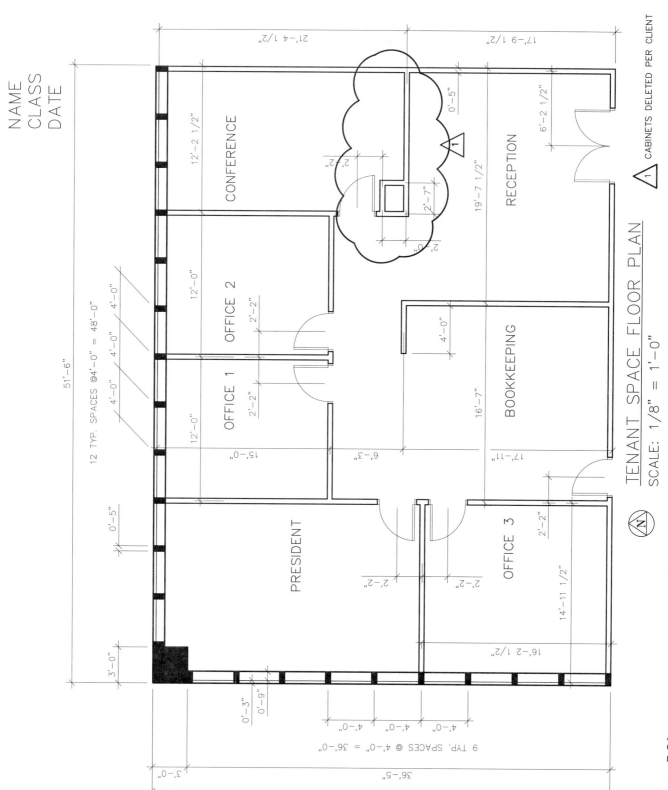

NAME
CLASS
DATE

TENANT SPACE FLOOR PLAN
SCALE: 1/8" = 1'-0"

CABINETS DELETED PER CLIENT

Figure 7-21

Exercise 7-2 complete (scale: 1/8" = 1'-0")

Step 1. Open drawing **CH7-EXERCISE1** and save it as **CH7-EXERCISE2** to the hard drive or network drive.

Associative Dimension Commands

When the **DIMASSOC** variable is on, each dimension that is drawn is created as a block. That means that the extension lines, dimension lines, ticks or arrows, text, and all other parts of the dimensions are entered as a single object. When **DIMASSOC** is on and set to **2**, the dimensions drawn are called *associative dimensions*. When **DIMASSOC** is off, the extension lines, dimension lines, and all other parts of the dimension are drawn as separate entities.

Four dimension commands—**Oblique, Align Text, Override**, and **Update**—can be used only if **DIMASSOC** was on while you drew the dimensions. The following sections describe these commands.

Oblique

OBLIQUE	
Ribbon/ Panel	Annotate/ Dimensions
Dimension Toolbar:	
Menu Bar:	Dimension/ Oblique
Type a Command:	DIMEDIT
Command Alias:	DIMED

Step 2. Create an oblique angle for the extension lines of the four mullions on the north exterior wall of the tenant space (Figure 7-22), as described next:

Prompt	Response
Type a command:	**Oblique** (or type **OB <Enter>** at the *Dim:* prompt)
Select objects:	Pick the extension lines of the mullion dimensions on the north exterior wall until they are all highlighted
Select objects:	**<Enter>**
Enter obliquing angle (press **<Enter>** for none):	Type **45 <Enter>**
The extension lines of the mullion dimensions appear as shown in Figure 7-22.	

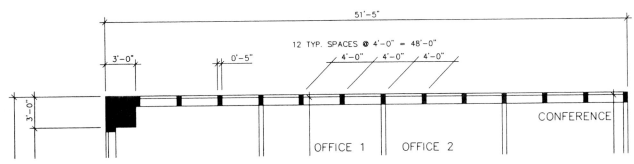

Figure 7-22
Using the **Oblique** command

Align Text-Home-Angle-Left-Center-Right

Step 3. Change the placement of the text for the overall dimension on the west exterior wall of the tenant space to flush right, and return it to the center position, as described next.

ALIGN TEXT	
Dimension Toolbar:	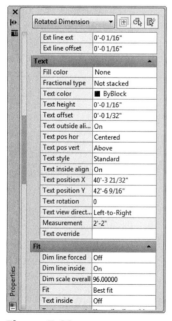
Menu Bar:	Dimension/ Align Text
Type a Command:	DIMTEDIT
Command Alias:	DIMTED

Prompt	Response
Type a command:	**Right Justify**
Select dimension:	Pick the dimension text **39'-5"**
The text moves to the right side of the dimension line (if the dimension line was drawn bottom to top, the dimension moves to the bottom).	
Type a command:	**Center Justify**
Select dimension:	Pick the same dimension **<Enter>**
The text moves back to the center of the dimension line.	

The **Left** option left justifies the text along the dimension line. The **Angle** option allows you either to type a new text angle (and press **<Enter>**) or to pick two points to show AutoCAD the new text angle. The **Home** option returns the dimension text to its home position.

Override

OVERRIDE	
Menu Bar:	Dimension/ Override
Type a Command:	DIMOVERRIDE
Command Alias:	DIMOVER

The **Override** command is helpful when you are in the middle of dimensioning a project or have completed dimensioning a project and decide that one or more of the dimension variables in a named style need to be changed. The **Override** command can be used to change one or more dimension variables for selected dimensions but does not affect the current dimension style.

Update

UPDATE	
Ribbon/ Panel	Annotate/ Dimensions
Dimension Toolbar:	
Menu Bar:	Dimension/ Update
Type a Command:	-DIMSTYLE/ Apply

Update differs from **Override** in that it updates dimensions using the current settings of the dimension style. For example, if you decide that a dimension variable needs to be changed in a dimension style, change the variable. You may click the **Save** button in the **Dimension Styles** dialog box to save the changed variable to the dimension style. If you do not save the changed variable, AutoCAD prompts you with an **ALERT** dialog box, *Save changes to current style?*, when you change dimension styles. Use **Update** to include the new variable settings in all or part of the dimensions within the drawing.

Defpoints Layer

When **DIMASSOC** is on, a special layer named **Defpoints** also is created. Definition points for dimensions are drawn on the **Defpoints** layer. They are small points on the drawing that are not plotted but are used to create the dimension. When the dimension is updated or edited, the definition points are redefined. Note: Elements on Defpoints layer are not displayed on the final print.

PROPERTIES

The **PROPERTIES** command can be used to change the properties of any dimension, as shown in Figure 7-23. Begin by selecting the dimension to be modified, then click **Properties** from the **Modify** panel on the ribbon, or right-click and click **Properties**. The **Properties** palette appears. Clicking the arrows to the right of the **Property** group displays a list of those items

Figure 7-23
Use the **Properties** palette to change dimension text

that can be changed. To change dimension text, click **Text override** (below **Measurement**) and type the new text in the box to the right.

Match Properties

MATCHPROP	
Ribbon/ Panel	Home/ Clipboard
Standard Toolbar:	
Menu Bar:	Modify/ Match Properties
Type a Command:	MATCHPROP or PAINTER

When the **Match Properties** command is selected, or **MATCHPROP** is typed and entered at the command prompt, the prompt is *Select source object:*. At that prompt you can select the dimension whose properties you want to copy, and a paintbrush is attached to the cursor. The prompt changes to *Select destination object(s) or [Settings]:*, and you can then select the dimension to which you want to copy the properties.

When you type and enter the **Settings** option at the **Match Properties:** prompt, the **Property Settings** dialog box is displayed. Properties that can be copied are shown in the **Property Settings** dialog box. By default, all properties are selected and show a check in the box beside the property name. You can copy some or all of the properties of a dimension. If you do not want a property copied, suppress that property in the **Property Settings** dialog box.

Grips

Grips are small, solid-filled squares that appear on an object when you click on the object. Grips are particularly useful in modifying the placement of dimension text and the location of extension and dimension lines.

Step 4. Practice using grips, as described next:

Prompt	**Response**
Type a command:	Click the **14′-11 1/2″** dimension in office 3
Five squares appear on the dimension: one at the end of each extension line, one at the center of each tick, and one in the center of the dimension text:	Click the grip in the center of the dimension text
The grip changes color (becomes hot): Specify stretch point or [Base point Copy Undo eXit]:	With **SNAP** and **ORTHO** on, move your mouse up and click a point two grid marks up
The dimension is stretched up two grid marks:	Click the same grip to make it hot, move your mouse to the right, and click a point two grid marks to the right

> **TIP**
> To use multiple grips and to keep the shape of the dimension or any object with which you are using grips, hold down the **<Shift>** key before selecting the grips to make them hot.

Prompt	Response
The dimension text moves two grid marks to the right:	Click the grip at the origin of the first extension line to make it hot, and move your mouse up two grid marks
The origin of the first extension line moves up two grid marks:	Click the grip in the center of the dimension text to make it hot, and press the space bar one time
The prompt changes to Specify move point or [Base point Copy Undo eXit]:	Move your cursor two grid marks down and click a point
The entire dimension moves down two grid marks:	Press **\<Esc\>**
The grips disappear:	Type **U \<Enter\>**, and continue pressing **\<Enter\>** until the dimension is returned to its original state

To use grips, select a grip to act as the base point. Then, select one of the **Grip** modes—**Stretch, Move, Rotate, Scale**, or **Mirror**. You can cycle through these modes by pressing **\<Enter\>** or the space bar, or right-click to see all the modes and options.

Revision Cloud

REVISION CLOUD	
Ribbon/ Panel	Home/Draw
Draw Toolbar:	
Menu Bar:	Draw/ Revision Cloud
Type a Command:	REVCLOUD

Any change on a plan is submitted with a change order. A revision cloud is used to identify any area of a plan that has been changed. The cloud is coordinated with a note in the title block that gives a brief description of the change.

Step 5. Create the following new layer and set it as the current layer:

Layer Name	Color	Linetype	Lineweight
a-anno-revs	white	Continuous	.014" (.35 mm)

Step 6. Erase the two lines that represent the cabinets in the conference room.

Step 7. Draw a revision cloud to identify the area on the plan that has been changed (Figure 7-24), as described next:

Prompt	Response
Type a command:	**Revision Cloud** or type **REVCLOUD \<Enter\>**
Minimum arc length: 0'-0" Maximum arc length: 0'-0 1/2" Style: Normal Specify start point or [Arc length Object Style] \<Object\>:	Type **A\<Enter\>**
Specify minimum length of arc \<0'- 0 1/2"\>:	Type **4' \<Enter\>**

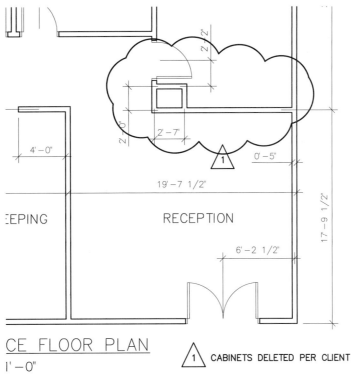

Figure 7-24
Draw a revision cloud to identify an area that has
been changed

Prompt	Response
Specify maximum length of arc <4'-0">:	**<Enter>**
Specify start point or [Arc length Object Style] <Object>:	Hold down the click button
Guide crosshairs along cloud path...	Guide your cursor along the cloud path until the cloud is finished
Revision cloud finished.	

> **Arc Length:** Allows you to specify the minimum and maximum arc length in the revision cloud.
>
> **Object:** Allows you to select an object to convert to a revision cloud. You can convert a circle, ellipse, polyline, or spline to a revision cloud.
>
> **Style:** Allows you to select a style named **Calligraphy**, which gives the appearance of a revision cloud drawn with a pen.

Step 8. Use grips to move any dimensions that are hidden by the cloud or to edit individual arcs in the revision cloud.

Step 9. Set layer **a-anno-text** current and add the 2'-2" triangle, revision number, and revision note to the plan (Figure 7-24).

Step 10. When you have completed Exercise 7-2, save your work in at least two places.

Step 11. Print Exercise 7-2 at a scale of **1/8″ = 1'-0″**.

EXERCISE 7-3
Tenant Space Total Square Footage

Exercise 7-3 provides step-by-step instructions for using the **AREA** command to compute the total square footage of the tenant space floor plan. It also provides instructions for using the **CAL** (calculator) command. When you have completed Exercise 7-3, your drawing will look similar to Figure 7-25.

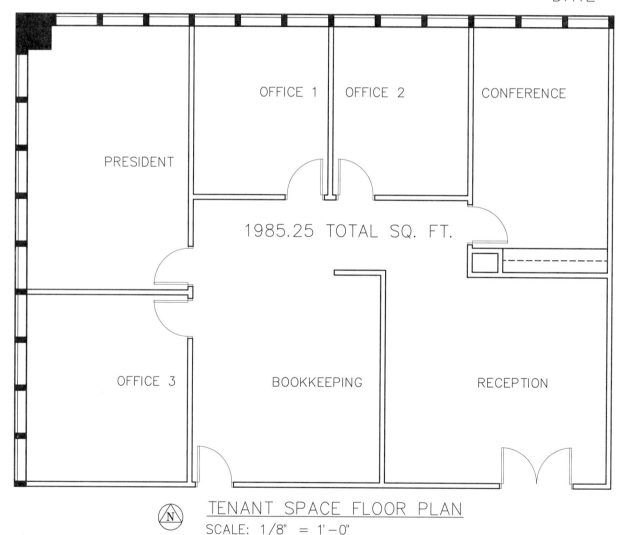

NAME
CLASS
DATE

OFFICE 1   OFFICE 2   CONFERENCE

PRESIDENT

1985.25 TOTAL SQ. FT.

OFFICE 3   BOOKKEEPING   RECEPTION

TENANT SPACE FLOOR PLAN
SCALE: 1/8" = 1'-0"

Figure 7-25
Exercise 7-3: Tenant space total square footage

Step 1. Open drawing **CH7-EXERCISE1** and save it as **CH7-EXERCISE3** to the hard drive.

Area

In order for the total square footage of any space to be computed, the exact area that is to be included must be identified. In the tenant space, the face of the exterior building glass on the north and west walls is used as the building's exterior measuring points, and the center of the south and east walls is used as the interior measuring points.

Step 2. Freeze layers **a-anno-dims** and **Defpoints**.

Step 3. Create the following new layer and set it as the current layer:

Layer Name	Color	Linetype	Lineweight
a-anno-area	green	Continuous	.006" (.15 mm)

Step 4. Type **FILL <Enter>**, then **OFF <Enter>** so that the column and mullions are not solid. Regenerate the drawing (type **RE <Enter>**).

Step 5. To be able to select the defining points of the exact area, as described above, use the **LINE** command to draw separate lines in each corner of the tenant space to which you can snap using **Osnap-Intersection** and **Osnap-Midpoint**. Each corner with the added lines is shown in Figure 7-26.

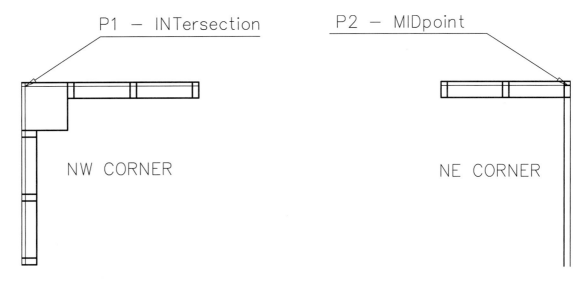

Figure 7-26
Defining points of the exact area included in the total square footage of the tenant space

AREA	
Measurement Tools Toolbar	
Pull-down Menu:	Tools/ Inquiry/ Area
Command Line:	AREA

Step 6. Compute the total square footage of the tenant space (Figure 7-26), as described next:

Prompt	Response
Type a command:	**Area** (or type **AREA <Enter>**)
Specify first corner point or [Object Add area Subtract area]: <Object>:	**Osnap-Intersection** Zoom a window around the northwest corner
of	**P1→** (Figure 7-26) Zoom a window around the northeast corner
Specify next point or [Arc Length Undo]:	**Osnap-Midpoint**
of	**P2→** Zoom a window around the southeast corner
Specify next point or [Arc Length Undo]:	**Osnap-Midpoint**
of	**P3→** Zoom a window around the southwest corner
Specify next point or [Arc Length Undo Total] <Total>:	**Osnap-Midpoint**
of	**P4→**
Specify next corner point or [Arc Length Undo Total]<Total>:	**<Enter>**
Area = 285876.25 square in. (1985.2517 square ft), Perimeter = 179'-10"	
Type a command:	Use the **DTEXT** command **1/8"** high (annotative text) to write the number of total square feet on the drawing (Figure 7-25)

Add: When **Add** is picked, the **AREA** command is placed in an add mode. **Add** must be picked before the first space (of all the spaces to be added together) is specified. When the first space is specified, the area information is displayed. When the second space is specified, its individual area information is displayed along with the total area information of the two spaces together. Each subsequent space specified is displayed as an individual area total and is added to the running total.

Subtract: When **Subtract** is picked, each subsequent space specified is displayed as an individual area total and is subtracted from the running total.

Object: Allows you to compute the area of a selected circle, ellipse, polygon, solid, or closed polyline. For a circle, the area and circumference are displayed. When a wide, closed polyline is picked, the area defined by the center line of the polyline is displayed (the polyline width is ignored). **Object** is the fastest way to find the area of a closed polyline.

Step 7. Turn **FILL** on.

Step 8. Regenerate the drawing (type **RE <Enter>**).

Cal

AutoCAD provides a handy calculator that functions much like many hand-held calculators. The following uses the add and divide features of the calculator. You may want to try other features on your own.

Use **CAL** to add three figures: $+=$ add
$-=$ subtract
$\times=$ multiply
$/=$ divide

TIP

CAL can be used within any command, such as **LINE** or **MOVE**, to specify a point. This avoids having to add and subtract dimensions beforehand. You must add an apostrophe before the **CAL** (**'CAL**) to use it within a command.

Prompt	**Response**
Type a command:	Type **CAL <Enter>**
>>Expression:	Type: **2′6 + 6′2 + 4′1 <Enter>**
12′-9″	

QUICKCALC

AutoCAD also has a calculator that can be used for scientific calculations, unit conversion, and basic calculations.

Step 9. When you have completed Exercise 7-3, save your work in at least two places.

Step 10. Print Exercise 7-3 at a scale of **1/8″ = 1′-0″**.

Chapter Summary

This chapter provided you the information necessary to dimension floor plans. In addition you learned to set dimensioning variables, edit dimensions, update dimensions, make revisions, and calculate total square footage using the **AREA** command. Now you have the skills and information necessary to produce dimensioned floor plans that can be used in interior design.

Chapter Test Questions

Multiple Choice

Circle the correct answer.

1. A complete list of current dimensioning variables and settings is displayed when which of the following is typed at the *Dim:* prompt?
   a. **LINEAR**   c. **STATUS**
   b. **DIMSTYLE**   d. **UPDATE**

2. Which of the following dimensioning variables controls the height of text used in the dimension?
   a. **DIMSTYLE**   c. **DIMTIX**
   b. **DIMASZ**   d. **DIMTXT**

3. Which tab on the **New Dimension Style** dialog box would you use to change a tick to a closed, filled arrowhead?
   a. **Lines**   c. **Fit**
   b. **Symbols and Arrows**   d. **Primary Units**

4. Which tab on the **New Dimension Style** dialog box would you use to change the appearance of the dimension text from one text style to another?
   a. **Lines**   c. **Text**
   b. **Fit**   d. **Primary Units**

5. Which tab on the **New Dimension Style** dialog box would you use to change the overall scale factor from 96 to 48?
   a. **Symbols and Arrows**   c. **Text**
   b. **Primary Units**   d. **Fit**

6. Which tab on the **New Dimension Style** dialog box would you use to set the distance that the dimension line extends beyond the tick?
   a. **Lines**   c. **Text**
   b. **Symbols and Arrows**   d. **Fit**

7. Which tab on the **New Dimension Style** dialog box would you use to make a setting to always display the dimension text horizontally on the page?
   a. **Lines**   c. **Text**
   b. **Fit**   d. **Primary Units**

8. If a full-size drawing is to be plotted at a plotting ratio of 1/8″ = 12″, the **DIMSCALE** value should be set to:

    a. 1   c. 12

    b. 48   d. 96

9. A Defpoints layer is created when a dimension is drawn with which of the following variables set to on?

    a. **DIMSTYLE**   c. **DIMTAD**

    b. **DIMTOH**   d. **DIMASSOC**

10. To find the area of a closed polyline most quickly, which of the **AREA** command options should be used?

    a. **Object**   c. **Subtract**

    b. **Poly**   d. **First point**

Matching

Write the number of the correct answer on the line.

a. **AREA** _____

b. **Revision Cloud** _____

c. Definition point _____

d. Defpoints _____

e. Grips _____

1. When this is erased, the associated dimension will be erased also
2. A command that calculates the total square footage of a room
3. Squares that appear on a dimension when it is clicked with no command active
4. A layer that is created when **DIMASSOC** is on
5. A command that allows you to draw a feature that shows a change has been made on the drawing

True or False

Circle the correct answer.

1. **True or False:** The seven tabs in the **New Dimension Style** dialog box are **Lines, Symbols and Arrows, Text, Fit, Primary Units, Alternate Units**, and **Tolerances**.

2. **True or False:** Ordinate dimensioning is used to show the length of features that are drawn at an angle.

3. **True or False:** The two styles available in the **Revision Cloud** command are **Normal** and **Calligraphy**.

4. **True or False:** The five **Grip** modes you can cycle through are **Stretch, Copy, Rotate, Move**, and **Mirror**.

5. **True or False: Units** must be set to **Architectural** and **Precision** must be set to 1/32″ for dimensioning variables to be displayed in 32nds of an inch.

List

1. Five types of dimensions.

2. Five dimension variables and their functions from **Dimension Style Manager**.

3. Five components of a dimension.

4. Five ways of accessing **Dimension Style Manager**.

5. Five dimension commands available when **DIMASSOC** is ON while the dimension is placed.

6. Five ways of accessing the **Linear** dimension command.

7. Five commands under the ribbon's **Home** tab/**Utilities** panel/**Measure**.

8. Five options under the **AREA** (**MeasureGeom**) command.

9. Five **Unit Conversion** parameters of the **QUICKCALC** command.

10. Five ways of accessing the **Oblique** dimension command.

Questions

1. In what situations would you use the **AREA** command?

2. For what purpose would you use annotative dimensions?

3. Which dimensioning variables will you most likely change from the default setting?

4. How many ways are there to edit dimensions?

5. Name and describe the eight types of dimensions.

Chapter Projects

Project 7-1: *Hotel Room 2 Dimensioned Floor Plan* [BASIC]

1. Set dimensioning variables for the hotel room floor plan.

2. Create a new layer for dimensions, and dimension the hotel room floor plan (Figure 7-27).

3. Locate the first row of dimensions farther from the drawing (e.g., 2′) than the first row of dimensions is from the second row of dimensions (e.g., 1′6″). Consistently space each row of dimensions on all four sides of the drawing.

4. Plot or print the drawing to scale.

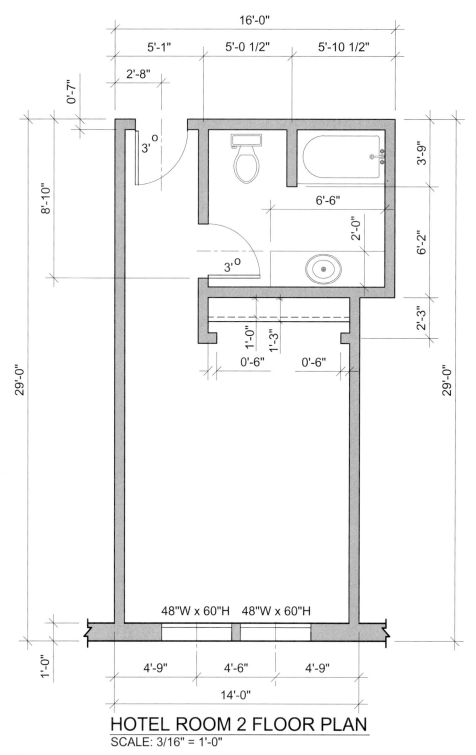

HOTEL ROOM 2 FLOOR PLAN
SCALE: 3/16" = 1'-0"

Figure 7-27
Project 7-1: Hotel room 2 dimensioned floor plan (scale: 3/16″ = 1′-0″)

Project 7-2: *Wheelchair-Accessible Commercial Restroom Dimensioned Floor Plan* [INTERMEDIATE]

1. Set dimensioning variables for the commercial restroom floor plan.

2. Create a new layer for dimensions, and dimension the commercial restroom floor plan (Figure 7-28).

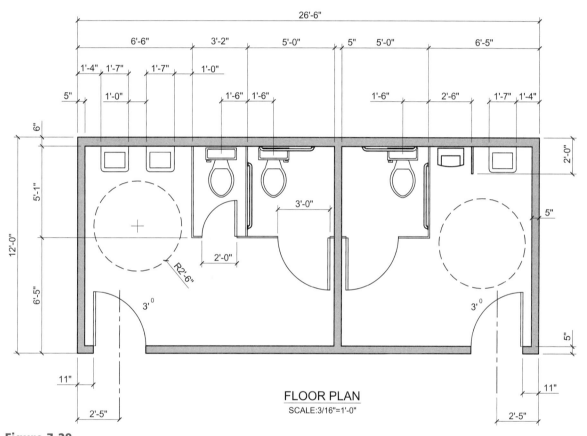

Figure 7-28

Project 7-2: Wheelchair-accessible commercial restroom dimensioned floor plan (scale: 3/16″ = 1′-0″)

3. Locate the first row of dimensions farther from the drawing (e.g., 2′) than the first row of dimensions is from the second row of dimensions (e.g., 1′6″). Consistently space each row of dimensions on all four sides of the drawing.

4. Plot or print the drawing to scale.

Project 7-3: *Bank Dimensioned Floor Plan* [ADVANCED]

1. Set dimensioning variables for the bank plan.

2. Create a new layer for dimensions, and dimension the bank floor plan (Figure 7-29).

3. Locate the first row of dimensions farther from the drawing (e.g., 2′) than the first row of dimensions is from the second row of dimensions (e.g., 1′6″). Consistently space each row of dimensions on all four sides of the drawing.

4. Plot or print the drawing to scale.

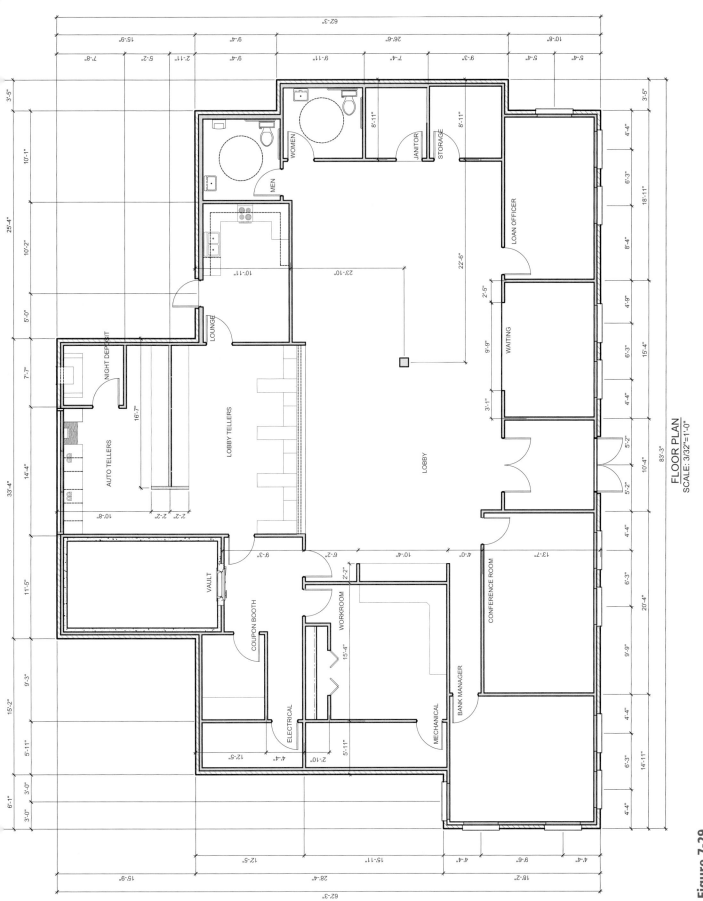

Figure 7-29

Project 7-3: Bank dimensioned floor plan (scale: 3/32" = 1'-0")

FLOOR PLAN
SCALE: 3/32"=1'-0"

Project 7-4: *Log Cabin Dimensioned Floor Plan* [INTERMEDIATE]

1. Set dimensioning variables for the log cabin floor plan.

2. Create a new layer for dimensions, and dimension the log cabin floor plan (Figure 7-30).

3. Locate the first row of dimensions farther from the drawing (e.g., 2′) than the first row of dimensions is from the second row of dimensions (e.g., 1′6″). Consistently space each row of dimensions on all four sides of the drawing.

4. Plot or print the drawing to scale.

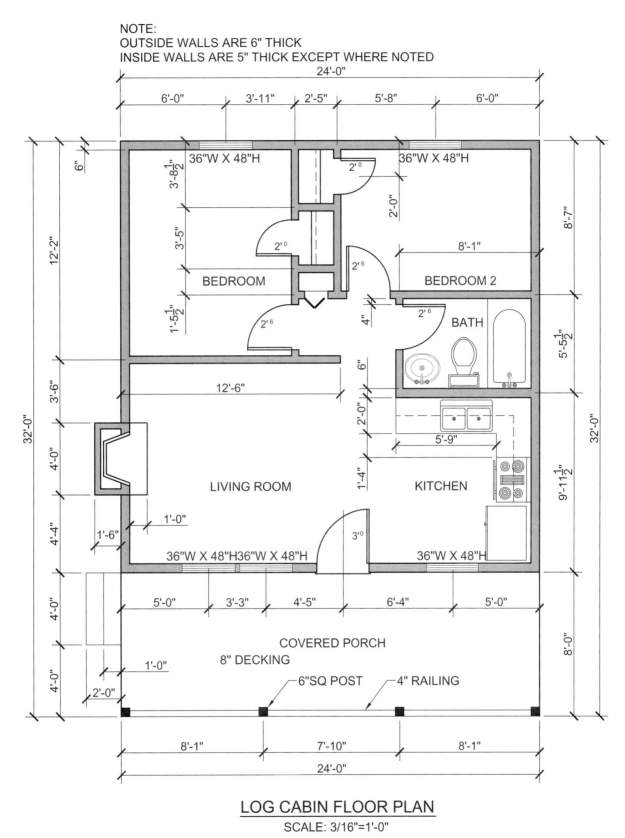

LOG CABIN FLOOR PLAN

SCALE: 3/16"=1'-0"

Figure 7-30

Project 7-4: Log cabin dimensioned floor plan (scale: 3/16″ = 1′-0″)

Project 7-5: *House 1 Dimensioned Floor Plan* [ADVANCED]

1. Set dimensioning variables for the house 1 floor plan.

2. Create a new layer for dimensions, and dimension the house 1 floor plan (Figure 7-31).

3. Locate the first row of dimensions farther from the drawing (e.g., 2′) than the first row of dimensions is from the second row of dimensions (e.g., 1′6″). Consistently space each row of dimensions on all four sides of the drawing.

4. Plot or print the drawing to scale.

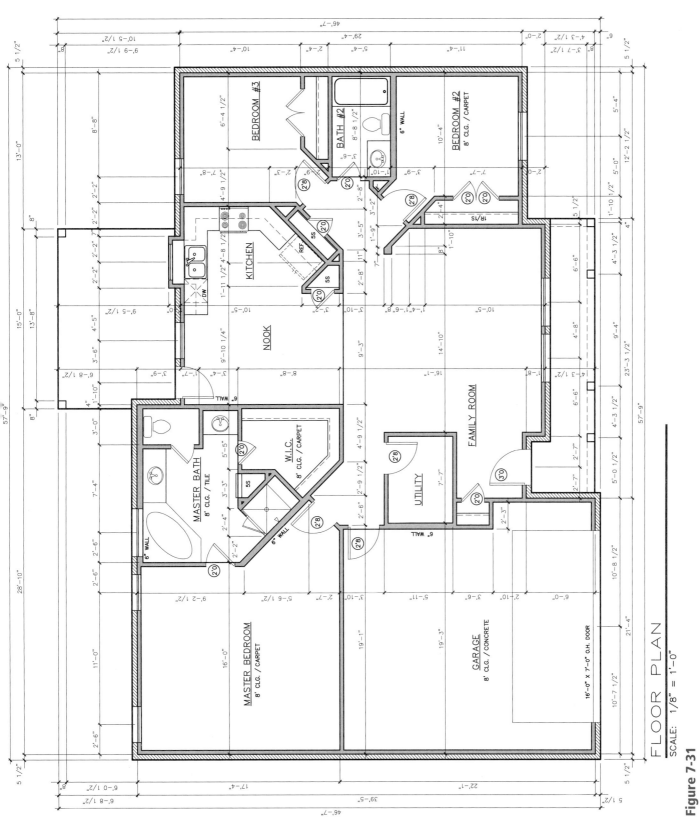

FLOOR PLAN

SCALE: 1/8" = 1'-0"

Figure 7-31

Project 7-5: House 1 dimensioned floor plan (scale: 1/8" = 1'-0")

(Courtesy of Paul Flournoy with Center Line Design and Drafting)

Project 7-6: *House 2 Dimensioned Floor Plan* [ADVANCED]

1. Set dimensioning variables for the house 2 floor plan.

2. Create a new layer for dimensions, and dimension the house 2 floor plan (Figure 7-32).

3. Locate the first row of dimensions farther from the drawing (e.g., 2′) than the first row of dimensions is from the second row of dimensions (e.g., 1′6″).

4. Plot or print the drawing to scale.

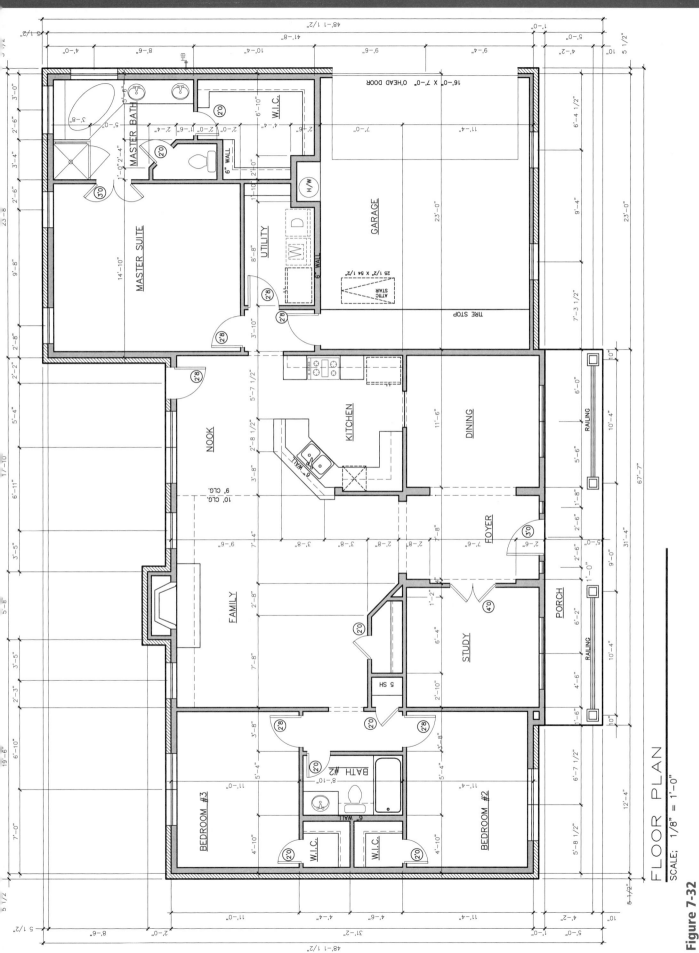

FLOOR PLAN

SCALE; 1/8" = 1'-0"

Figure 7-32

Project 7-6: House 2 dimensioned floor plan (scale: 1/8" = 1'-0")

(Courtesy of Paul Flournoy with Center Line Design and Drafting)

8 chaptereight
Drawing Elevations, Sections, and Details

CHAPTER OBJECTIVES

- Correctly use the following commands and settings:

Edit Hatch	MIRROR	Multileader Style	STRETCH
HATCH	Multileader	OTRACK	UCS
		Point Filters	UCS Icon

Introduction

The AutoCAD program makes it possible to produce clear, accurate, and impressive drawings of elevations, sections, and details. Many of the commands you have already learned are used in this chapter, along with some new commands.

EXERCISE 8-1
Tenant Space: Elevation of Conference Room Cabinets

In Exercise 8-1, an elevation of the south wall of the tenant space conference room is drawn. The south wall of the tenant space conference room has built-in cabinets that include a refrigerator and a sink. When you have completed Exercise 8-1, your drawing will look similar to Figure 8-1.

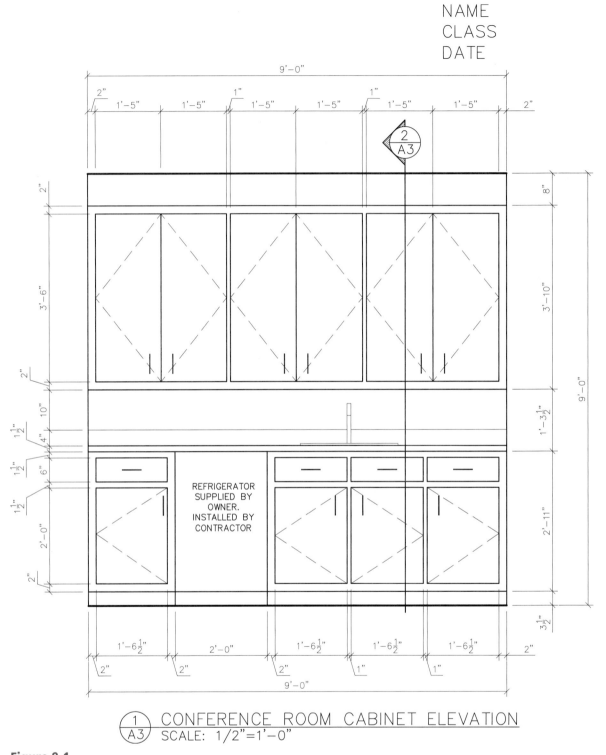

CONFERENCE ROOM CABINET ELEVATION
SCALE: 1/2"=1'-0"

REFRIGERATOR
SUPPLIED BY
OWNER.
INSTALLED BY
CONTRACTOR

Figure 8-1
Exercise 8-1: Tenant space, elevation of conference room cabinets (scale: 1/2′ = 1′-0″)

Step 1. Use your workspace to make the following settings:

1. Use **Save As...** to save the drawing on the hard drive with the name **CH8-EXERCISE1**.
2. Set drawing units: **Architectural**
3. Set drawing limits: **25′,24′**

4. Set **GRIDDISPLAY**: **0**
5. Set grid: **12″**
6. Set snap: **6″**
7. Create the following layers:

Layer Name	Color	Linetype	Lineweight
a-elev-dims	red	continuous	.004″ (.09 mm)
a-elev-hdln	red	hidden	.004″ (.09 mm)
a-elev-lwt1	blue	continuous	.010″ (.25 mm)
a-elev-lwt2	white	continuous	.002″ (.05 mm)
a-elev-otln	white	continuous	.016″ (.40 mm)
a-elev-patt	white	continuous	.002″ (.05 mm)
a-elev-text	green	continuous	.006″ (.15 mm)

8. Set layer **a-elev-lwt1** current.
9. Use **Zoom-All** to view the limits of the drawing.

UCS

UCS	
Ribbon/ Panel	View/ Coordinates
UCS Toolbar:	
Menu Bar:	Tools/ New UCS
Shortcut Menu	Right Click The UCSICON
Type a Command:	UCS

While you were drawing with AutoCAD in previous chapters the UCS icon was located in the lower left corner of your drawings. A coordinate system is simply the X, Y, and Z coordinates used in your drawings. For 2D drawings, only the X and Y coordinates are meaningful. The Z coordinate is used for a three-dimensional model.

Notice that the 2D UCS icon (Figure 8-2) has a W on it. The W stands for *world coordinate system.* This is the AutoCAD fixed coordinate system, which is common to all AutoCAD drawings. Your version of AutoCAD uses the 3D icon by default, showing only *X*- and *Y*-axes, so the W is not visible.

Figure 8-2
2D model space, 3D model space, and paper space UCS icons

2D Model Space Icon

3D Model Space Icon

Paper Space Icon

user coordinate system: A user-defined variation of the world coordinate system. Variations in the coordinate system range from moving the default drawing origin (0,0,0) to another location to changing orientations for the *X*-, *Y*-, and *Z*-axes. It is possible to rotate the world coordinate system on any axis to make a UCS with a different two-dimensional XY plane.

The **UCS** command is used to set up a new ***user coordinate system***. When **UCS** is typed from the command prompt, the prompt is *Specify origin of UCS or [Face NAmed OBject Previous View World X Y Z ZAxis] <World>:*. The Z coordinate is described and used extensively in the chapters that cover 3D modeling. The UCS command options that apply to two dimensions are listed next.

Specify origin of UCS: Allows you to create a new UCS by selecting a new origin and a new *X*-axis. If you select a single point, the origin of the current UCS moves without changing the orientation of the *X*- and *Y*-axes.

NAmed: When this option is entered, the prompt *Enter an option [Restore Save Delete?]* appears. It allows you to restore, save, delete, and list named user coordinate systems.

OBject: Allows you to define a new UCS by pointing to a drawing object such as an arc, point, circle, or line.

Previous: Makes the previous UCS current.

World: The AutoCAD fixed coordinate system, which is common to all AutoCAD drawings. In most cases you will want to return to the world coordinate system before plotting any drawing.

Step 2. Use the **UCS** command to change the origin of the current UCS, as described next:

Prompt	Response
Type a command:	Type **UCS <Enter>**
Specify origin of UCS or 　[Face NAmed OBject Previous 　　View World X Y Z ZAxis] <World>	Type: **8′,12′ <Enter>**
Specify point on X-axis or <Accept>:	**<Enter>**

> **NOTE**
>
> You can change the UCS so you can move 0,0 to any point on your drawing to make it more convenient to locate points.

The origin for the current user coordinate system is now 8′ in the X direction and 12′ in the Y direction. The UCS icon may not have moved from where 0,0 was originally located. The **UCS Icon** command, described next, is used to control the orientation and visibility of the UCS icon.

UCS Icon

There are two model space UCS icons that you can choose to use: one for 2D drawings and one for 3D drawings. The default is the 3D icon, which you will probably use for both 2D and 3D. The **UCS Icon** command is used to control the visibility and orientation of the UCS icon (Figure 8-2). The UCS icon appears as lines (most often located in the lower left corner of an AutoCAD drawing) that show the orientation of the *X*-, *Y*-, and *Z*-axes of the current UCS. It appears as a triangle in paper space. The **UCS Icon** command options are *ON OFF All Noorigin ORigin Properties:*. The **UCS Icon** command options follow.

ON: Allows you to turn on the UCS icon if it is not visible.

OFF: Allows you to turn off the UCS icon when it gets in the way. This has nothing to do with the UCS location—only the visibility of the UCS icon.

All: Allows you to apply changes to the UCS icon in all active viewports. (The **Viewports** command, which allows you to create multiple viewports, is described in Chapter 12.)

Noorigin: When **Noorigin** is current, the UCS icon is displayed at the lower left corner of the screen.

ORigin: Forces the UCS icon to be displayed at the origin of the current UCS. For example, when **USC Icon - Origin** is clicked, the new UCS that you just created will appear in its correct position. If the origin of the UCS is off the screen, the icon is still displayed in the lower left corner of the screen.

Properties: When **Properties** is selected, the **UCS Icon** dialog box appears (Figure 8-3). This box allows you to select the 2D or 3D model space icon and to change the size and color of model space and paper space (**Layout** tab) icons.

NOTE

The **Coordinates** panel is hidden in the **Ribbon View** tab by default. Right-click on the **View** tab to show the **Coordinates** panel.

Figure 8-3
UCS Icon dialog box

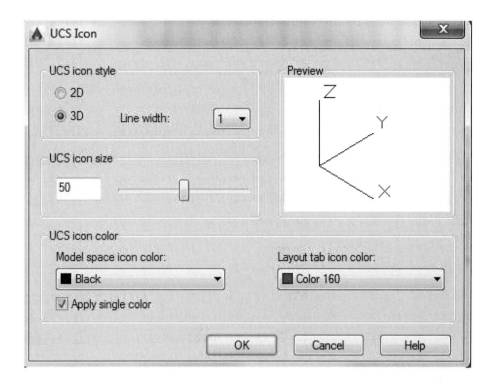

FOR MORE DETAILS

See Chapters 14 and 15 for more on **UCS** and **UCSICON**.

Step 3. If the UCS icon did not move, use the **UCS Icon** command to force the UCS icon to be displayed at the origin of the new, current UCS, as described next:

UCSICON	
Ribbon/ Panel	🖳 UCSICON View/ Coordinates
Menu Bar:	🖳 UCSICON View/ Display
Right Click UCSICON	Click UCSICON Settings/ Properties...
Type a Command:	UCSICON

Prompt

Type a command:
Enter an option [ON OFF All Noorigin ORigin Selectable Properties] <ON>:

Response

Type **UCSICON <Enter>**

Type **OR <Enter>** (the UCS icon moves to the 8′,12′ coordinate location)

Draw the Upper Cabinets

Step 4. Using absolute coordinates, draw a rectangle forming the **first upper cabinet door**. Start the drawing at **2, 2** (two inches above and two inches to the right of the new UCS), Figure 8-4, as described next:

Figure 8-4

Draw the lines forming the first upper cabinet door

Prompt	Response
Type a command:	**Rectangle** (or type **REC <Enter>**)
Specify first corner point or [Chamfer Elevation Fillet Thickness Width]:	Type **2,2 <Enter>**
Specify other corner point or [Area Dimensions Rotation]:	Type **19,44 <Enter>**

Step 5. Use **Polyline** to draw the door hardware using absolute coordinates (Figure 8-4), as described next:

Prompt	Response
Type a command:	**Polyline** (or type **PL <Enter>**)
Specify start point:	Type **16,4 <Enter>**
Specify next point or [Arc Halfwidth Length Undo Width]:	Type **W <Enter>**
Specify starting width <0′-0″>:	Type **1/4 <Enter>**
Specify ending width <0′-0 1/4″>:	**<Enter>**
Specify next point or [Arc Halfwidth Length Undo Width]:	Type **16,9 <Enter>**
Specify next point or [Arc Close Halfwidth Length Undo Width]:	**<Enter>**

Step 6. Set layer **a-elev-hdln** current and draw the dashed lines of the door using absolute coordinates (Figure 8-4), as described next:

Prompt	Response
Type a command:	**Line** (or type **L <Enter>**)
Specify first point:	Type **19,3′8 <Enter>**
Specify next point or [Undo]:	Type **2,23 <Enter>**
Specify next point or [Undo]:	Type **19,2 <Enter>**
Specify next point or [Close Undo]:	**<Enter>**

Step 7. Change the linetype scale of the Hidden linetype to make it appear as dashes, change the linetype to **Hidden2**, or both. A large linetype scale such as 12 is needed. (Type **LTSCALE <Enter>**, then type **12 <Enter>**.)

Mirror

MIRROR	
Ribbon/ Panel	Home/ Modify ◢◣
Modify Toolbar:	◢◣
Menu Bar:	Modify/Mirror
Type a Command:	MIRROR
Command Alias:	MI

The **MIRROR** command allows you to mirror about an axis any entity or group of entities. The axis can be at any angle.

Step 8. Draw the **second upper cabinet door**, using the **MIRROR** command to copy the cabinet door just drawn (Figure 8-5), as described next:

Prompt	Response
Type a command:	**Mirror** (or type **MI <Enter>**)
Select objects:	**P1→**
Specify opposite corner:	**P2→**
Select objects:	**<Enter>**
Specify first point of mirror line:	**P3→** (with **ORTHO** and **OSNAP-INTERSECTION** on)
Specify second point of mirror line:	**P4→**
Erase source objects? [Yes No] <N>:	**<Enter>** (to complete command)

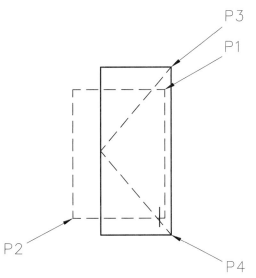

Figure 8-5
Use the **MIRROR** command to copy the
cabinet door

> **NOTE**
>
> If you want to mirror a part of a drawing containing text but do not want the text to be a
> mirror image, change the **MIRRTEXT** system variable setting to **0**. This allows you to mirror
> the part and leave the text "right reading." When **MIRRTEXT** is set to **1**, the text is given a
> mirror image. To change this setting, type **MIRRTEXT <Enter>**, then type **0 <Enter>**.

Step 9. Set layer **a-elev-lwt1** current. Using relative coordinates, draw a
rectangle forming the outside of the upper cabinet. Start the rectangle at the **0,0** location of the new UCS (Figure 8-6), as described
next:

Prompt	Response
Type a command:	**Rectangle** (or type **REC <Enter>**)
Specify first corner point or [Chamfer Elevation Fillet Thickness Width]:	Type **0,0 <Enter>**
Specify other corner point or [Area Dimensions Rotation]:	Type **@9',3'10 <Enter>**

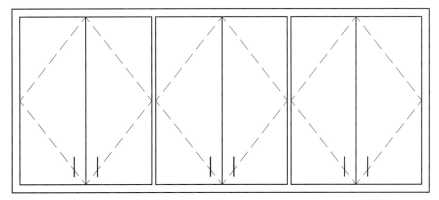

Figure 8-6
Draw the upper cabinets

Step 10. Copy the first two **upper cabinet doors** 2'11" and 5'10" to the right (Figure 8-6) as described next:

Prompt	Response
Type a command:	**Copy** (or type **CP <Enter>**)
Select objects:	Use a window to select the first two upper cabinet doors
Select objects:	**<Enter>**
Specify base point or [Displacement mOde] <Displacement>:	Click any point
Specify second point or [Array] <use first point as displacement>:	With **ORTHO** on, move your mouse to the right and type **2'11 <Enter>**
Specify second point or [Array Exit Undo] <Exit>:	Move the mouse to the right and type **5'10 <Enter>**
Specify second point or [Exit Undo] <Exit>:	**<Enter>**

Draw the Lower Cabinets

Step 11. Use the **MIRROR** command to draw the **first lower cabinet door** (Figure 8-7), as described next:

Figure 8-7
Use the **MIRROR** command to draw the first lower cabinet door

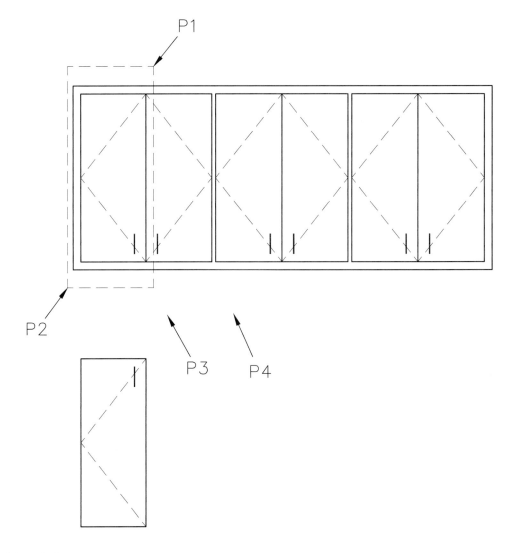

Prompt	Response
Type a command:	**Mirror** (or type **MI <Enter>**)
Select objects:	**P2→** (left to right)
Specify opposite corner:	**P1→**
Select objects:	**<Enter>**
Specify first point of mirror line:	**P3→** (with **ORTHO** and **SNAP** on; the lower cabinets will be moved to the accurate location later)
Specify second point of mirror line:	**P4→**
Erase source objects? [Yes No] <N>:	**<Enter>** (the lower cabinet is now too high and too narrow)

Stretch

STRETCH	
Ribbon/Panel	Home/Modify
Modify Toolbar:	
Menu Bar:	Modify/Stretch
Type a Command:	STRETCH
Command Alias:	S

The **STRETCH** command can be used to stretch entities to make them longer or shorter. It can also be used to move entities that have other lines attached to them without removing the attached lines (described later in this exercise). **STRETCH** requires you to use a crossing window to select objects. As with many other **Modify** commands, you may select objects initially, then remove or add objects to the selection set before you perform the stretch function.

Step 12. Use the **STRETCH** command to change the height of the **first lower cabinet door** just drawn (Figure 8-8), as described next:

Figure 8-8
Use the **STRETCH** command to change the height of the first lower cabinet door

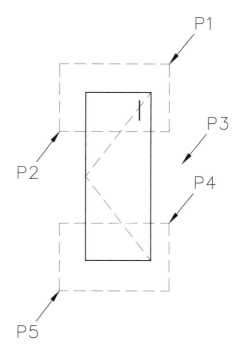

Prompt	Response
Type a command:	**Stretch** (or type **S <Enter>**)
Select objects to stretch by crossing-window or crossing-polygon... Select objects:	**P1→**
Specify opposite corner:	**P2→**
Select objects:	**<Enter>**

Prompt	Response
Specify base point or [Displacement] <Displacement>:	**P3→** (any point)
Specify second point or <use first point as displacement>:	Type **@9<270 <Enter>** (or with **ORTHO** on move your mouse down and type **9 <Enter>**) (the upper door height, 3′6″, minus the lower door height, 2′, divided by 2; take half off the top of the door and half off the bottom)
Type a command:	**Stretch** (or press **<Enter>**)
Select objects to stretch by crossing-window or crossing-polygon... Select objects:	**P4→**
Specify opposite corner:	**P5→**
Select objects:	**<Enter>**
Specify base point or [Displacement] <Displacement>:	**P3→** (any point)
Specify second point or <use first point as displacement>:	Type **@9<90 <Enter>** (or move your mouse up and type **9 <Enter>**). The lower cabinet door should now be 18″ shorter than the upper cabinet door from which it was mirrored (3′6″ minus 18″ equals 2′, the cabinet door height)

Step 13. Use the **STRETCH** command to change the width of the **first lower cabinet door** (Figure 8-9), as described next:

Figure 8-9
Use the **STRETCH** command to change the width of the cabinet door

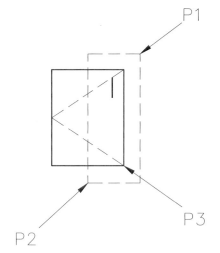

Prompt	Response
Type a command:	**Stretch**
Select objects to stretch by crossing-window or crossing-polygon... Select objects:	**P1→**
Specify opposite corner:	**P2→**
Select objects:	**<Enter>**

Prompt	Response
Specify base point or [Displacement] <Displacement>:	**P3→** (any point)
Specify second point or <use first point as displacement>:	Type **@1-1/2<0 <Enter>** (or move the mouse to the right and type **1-1/2 <Enter>**) (the upper door width, 1′5″, plus 1-1/2″, equals the lower door width, 1′6-1/2″)

Step 14. Save the current UCS used to draw the upper cabinets, as described next:

Prompt	Response
Type a command:	Type **UCS <Enter>**
Specify origin of UCS or [Face NAmed OBject Previous View World X Y Z ZAxis] <World>:	Type **S <Enter>**
Enter name to save current UCS or [?]:	Type **UPPER <Enter>**

Step 15. Create a new UCS origin for drawing the lower cabinets by **moving the existing UCS origin** –4′2-1/2″ in the Y direction, as described next.

Prompt	Response
Type a command:	**<Enter>** (repeat **UCS**)
Specify origin of UCS or [Face NAmed OBject Previous View World X Y Z ZAxis] <World>:	Type **O <Enter>**
Specify new origin point <0,0,0>:	Type **0,-4′2-1/2 <Enter>** (be sure to include the minus)

Step 16. Move the **lower cabinet door** to a point 2″ above and 2″ to the right of the origin of the current UCS (Figure 8-10), as described next:

Figure 8-10
Move the lower cabinet door to a point 2″ above and 2″ to the right of the origin of the current UCS

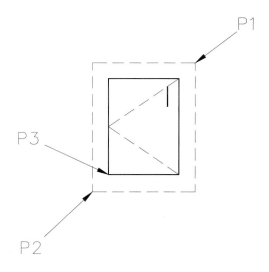

Prompt	Response
Type a command:	**Move** (or type **M <Enter>**)
Select objects:	**P1→** (Figure 8-10)

Prompt	Response
Specify opposite corner:	**P2→**
Select objects:	**<Enter>**
Specify base point or [Displacement] <Displacement>:	**Osnap-Intersection**
of	**P3→**
Specify second point or <use firstpoint as displacement>:	Type **2,2 <Enter>**

Step 17. Using relative coordinates, draw a rectangle forming the drawer above the lower cabinet door (Figure 8-11), as described next:

Prompt	Response
Type a command:	**Rectangle** (or type **REC <Enter>**)
Specify first corner point or [Chamfer Elevation Fillet Thickness Width]:	Type **FRO <Enter> Osnap-Intersection**
Base point:	Click the upper left corner of the lower cabinet door.
<Offset>:	Type **@1-1/2<90 <Enter>**
Specify other corner point or [Area Dimensions Rotation]:	Type **@1′6-1/2,6 <Enter>**

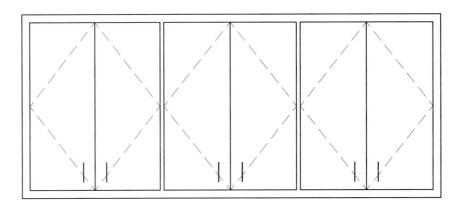

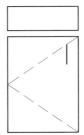

Figure 8-11
Draw the drawer

Step 18. Copy the door handle from the handle midpoint to the midpoint of the bottom line of the drawer, rotate it 90°, and move it up 3″ as shown in Figure 8-12.

Figure 8-12
Copy the door handle,
rotate it, and move it

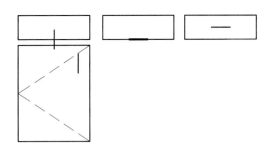

Step 19. Explode the upper cabinet outer rectangle. Offset the bottom line of the rectangle several times and change two lines to other layers (Figure 8-13) as described next:

Offset the bottom line of the rectangle down **10″** and change it to the **a-elev-lwt2** layer.
Offset the bottom line of the rectangle down **14″**.
Offset that line down **1-1/2″**.
Offset that line down **2′11″**.
Offset that line down **3-1/2″** and change the offset line to the **a-elev-otln** layer.

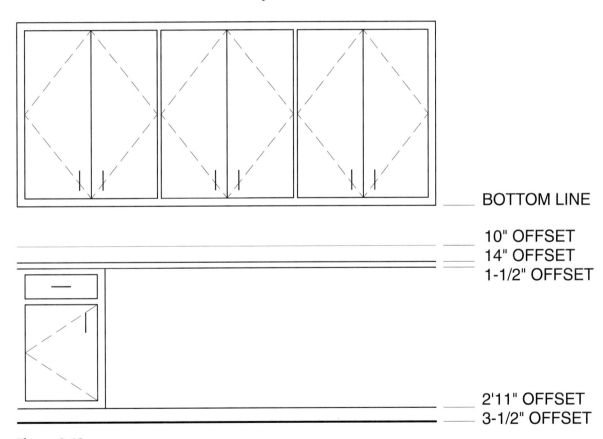

BOTTOM LINE

10" OFFSET
14" OFFSET
1-1/2" OFFSET

2'11" OFFSET
3-1/2" OFFSET

Figure 8-13
EXPLODE the cabinet rectangle and offset the bottom line

Step 20. Use zero radius **Fillet** to extend lines on both sides of the cabinets as described next:

Prompt	Response
Type a command:	**Fillet** (or type **F <Enter>**)
Select first object or [Undo Polyline Radius Trim Multiple]:	Type **M <Enter>**

Prompt	Response
Select first object or [Undo Polyline Radius Trim Multiple]:	Click **P1**→ (Figure 8-14)
Select second object or shift-select to apply corner or [Radius]:	Click **P2**→
Select first object or [Undo Polyline Radius Trim Multiple]:	Click **P3**→
Select second object or shift-select to apply corner or [Radius]:	Click **P4**→
Select first object or [Undo Polyline Radius Trim Multiple]:	**<Enter>**

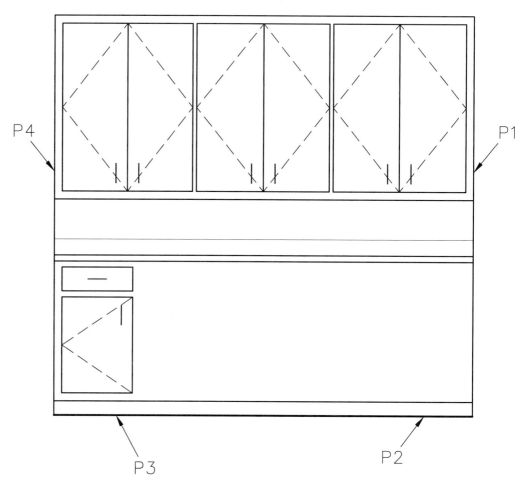

Figure 8-14
Use the **FILLET** command to extend lines on both sides

Step 21. Use the **MIRROR** command to draw the door and drawer on the right side of the lower cabinet (Figure 8-15).

Step 22. Use the **COPY** command to copy the door and drawer on the left 3′10-1/2″ to the right (Figure 8-16).

Step 23. Use the **COPY** command to copy the door and drawer on the far right 1′7-1/2″ to the left.

Figure 8-15
Use the **MIRROR** command to draw the door and drawer on the far right

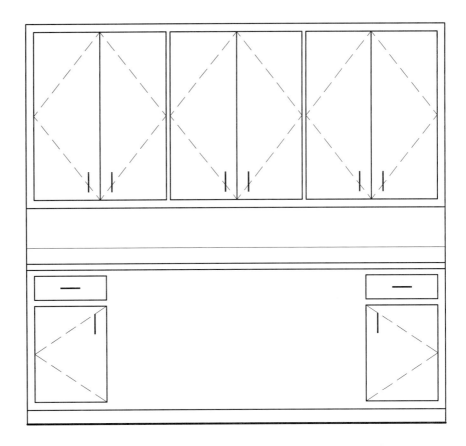

Figure 8-16
COPY drawers and doors; **OFFSET** and **TRIM** lines to form the refrigerator

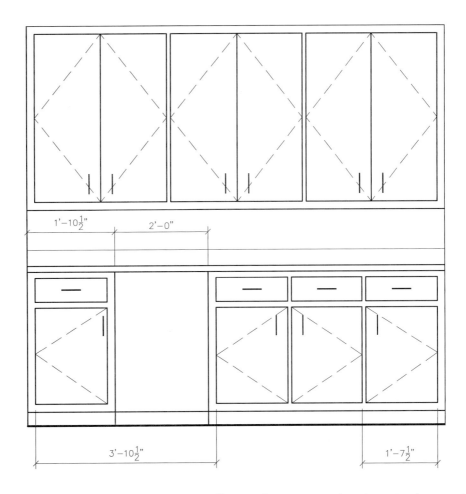

Step 24. Offset the cabinet line on the far left, 1'10-1/2" to the right. Offset that line 2'0" to the right to form the refrigerator. Trim lines as needed (Figure 8-16).

Step 25. Set layer **a-elev-lwt2** current. Draw the sink in the approximate location shown in Figure 8-17 (the **STRETCH** command will be used later to move the sink to the correct location), as described next:

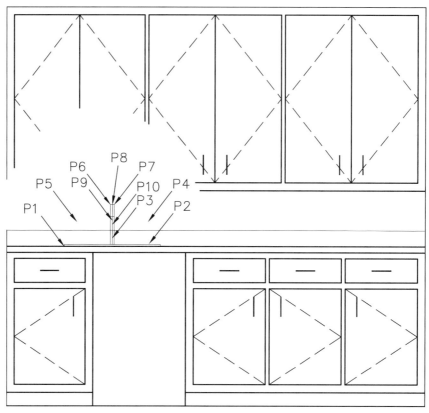

Figure 8-17
Draw the sink in the approximate location shown

Prompt	Response
Type a command:	**Line** (or type **L <Enter>**)
Specify first point:	**P1→ (Osnap-Nearest)**
Specify next point or [Undo]:	Type **@1/2<90 <Enter>**
Specify next point or [Undo]:	Type **@25<0 <Enter>**
Specify next point or [Close Undo]:	Type **@1/2<270 <Enter>**
Specify next point or [Close Undo]:	**<Enter>**
Type a command:	**<Enter>** (repeat **LINE**)
Specify first point:	**Osnap-Midpoint**
of	**P2→**
Specify next point or [Undo]:	Type **@10<90 <Enter>**
Specify next point or [Undo]:	**<Enter>**
Type a command:	**Offset** (or type **O <Enter>**)
Specify offset distance or [Through Erase Layer] <default>:	Type **1/2 <Enter>**
Select object to offset or [Exit Undo] <Exit>:	**P3→** (the line just drawn)

Prompt	Response
Specify point on side to offset or [Exit Multiple Undo] <Exit>:	**P4→** (to the right)
Select object to offset or [Exit Undo] <Exit>:	**P3→**
Specify point on side to offset or [Exit Multiple Undo] <Exit>:	**P5→** (to the left)
Select object to offset or [Exit Undo] <Exit>:	**<Enter>**
Type a command:	**Line**
Specify first point:	**Osnap-Endpoint**
of	**P6→**
Specify next point or [Undo]:	**Osnap-Endpoint**
of	**P7→**
Specify next point or [Undo]:	**<Enter>** (to complete the command)
Type a command:	**Offset**
Specify offset distance or [Through Erase Layer] <0′-1/2″>:	Type **3** **<Enter>**
Select object to offset or [Exit Undo] <Exit>:	**P8→**
Specify point on side to offset or [Exit Multiple Undo] <Exit>:	**P10→**
Select object to offset or [Exit Undo] <Exit>:	**<Enter>**
Type a command:	**Erase** (or type **E <Enter>**)
Select objects:	**P9→** (the center vertical line)
Select objects:	**<Enter>**

Step 26. Trim out the line of the backsplash where it crosses the faucet.

Step 27. You can use the **STRETCH** command to move entities that have other lines attached to them without removing the attached lines. Use **STRETCH** to move the sink to its correct location (Figure 8-18), as described next:

Prompt	Response
Type a command:	**Stretch** (or type **S <Enter>**)
Select objects to stretch by crossing-window or crossing-polygon... Select objects:	**P2→**
Specify opposite corner:	**P1→**
Select objects:	**<Enter>**
Specify base point or [Displacement], Displacement:	**Osnap-Midpoint**
of	**P3→**
Specify second point or <use first point as displacement>:	**P4→** (with **ORTHO** on, pick a point directly above the space between the two center doors, Figures 8-18 and 8-19)

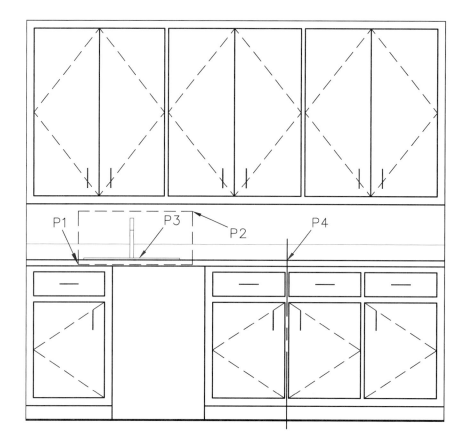

Figure 8-18
Use the **STRETCH** command to move the sink to its correct location

Complete the Drawing

Step 28. Use the **OFFSET** and **EXTEND** commands to draw the ceiling line above the cabinets (Figure 8-19). Change the ceiling line to the **a-elev-otln** layer.

Step 29. Use the **UCS** command to save the current UCS, and name it **LOWER**. Set the UCS to **World**.

Step 30. Set the drawing annotation scale to **1/2″ = 1′-0″**.

Step 31. Set layer **a-elev-text** current.

Step 32. Change the text style to **Standard** with the **simplex** font.

Step 33. In the **Text Style** dialog box, select the box beside **Annotative** under **Size** to make sure the annotative property is set to on.

Step 34. Use **DTEXT**, height **1/16″** to place the note on the refrigerator.

Step 35. Use **DTEXT**, height **1/8″** to type your name, class, and the current date in the upper right area.

Step 36. Use **DTEXT**, height **1/8″** to type the underlined text **CONFERENCE ROOM CABINET ELEVATION**.

Step 37. Add the elevation and section symbols to the elevation drawing, as shown in Figure 8-19. Use a **4″** radius circle and **3/32″** high text.

Step 38. Use **DTEXT**, height **3/32″** to type the drawing scale.

Step 39. Set layer **a-elev-dims** current.

Step 40. Set the dimensioning variables.

Step 41. Add the dimensions as shown in Figure 8-19.

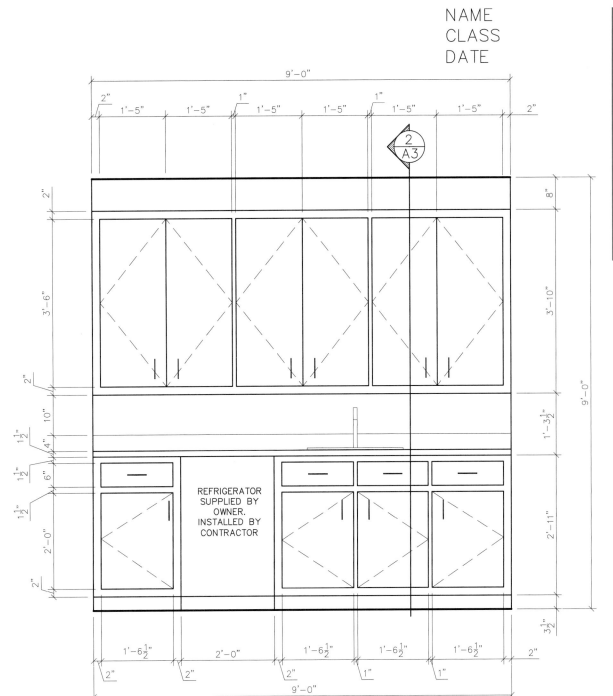

CONFERENCE ROOM CABINET ELEVATION
SCALE: 1/2"=1'-0"

Figure 8-19
Complete the elevation drawing (scale: 1/2″ = 1′-0″)

Step 42. When you have completed Exercise 8-1, save your work in at least two places.

Step 43. Print Exercise 8-1 at a scale of **1/2″ = 1′-0″**.

Step 44. Add the elevation symbol, as shown in Figure 8-20, to your tenant space floor plan drawing. Use a **1′**-radius circle and **1/16″**-high text (annotative).

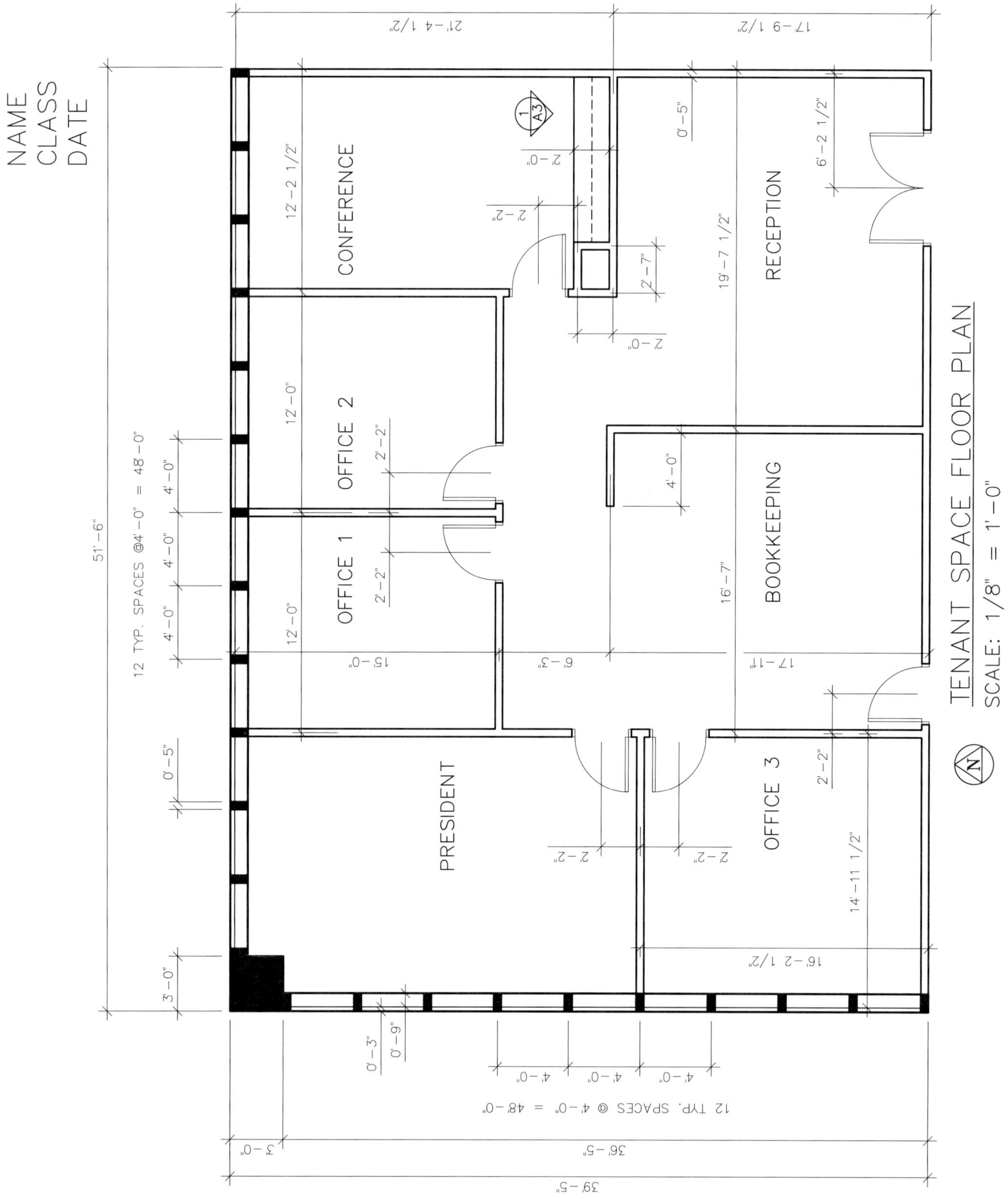

Figure 8-20
Tenant space floor plan with elevation symbol (scale: 1/8" = 1'-0")

EXERCISE 8-2
The Multileader Command

multileader: A leader with multiple leader lines. These leaders can be customized to show index numbers inside circles, hexagons, and other polygons.

The *Multileader* command can be used in a variety of ways. With **Multileader** you can draw a leader arrowhead first, tail first, or content first. You can align the text or balloons after you have drawn them. You can gather balloons so you have several balloons on the same leader, and you can add or delete leaders. In Exercise 8-2, all these options are used.

Step 1. Use your workspace to make the following settings:

1. Set drawing units: **Architectural**
2. Set drawing limits: **8-1/2,11**
3. Set **GRIDDISPLAY: 0**
4. Set grid: **1/2″**
5. Set snap: **1/8″**
6. Create the following layers:

Layer Name	Color	Linetype	Lineweight
Circles	magenta	continuous	.010″ (.25 mm)
Leaders	red	continuous	.004″ (.09 mm)

7. Set the **Circles** layer current.
8. Use the **Standard** text style with the Arial font.
9. Make sure **ATTDIA** is set to **0**.
10. Save the drawing as **CH8-EXERCISE2**.

Circles to Be Used with Multileaders

Step 2. Draw all the 1/4″-radius circles shown in Figure 8-21 in the approximate locations shown. Space the circles 1″ apart so you have space for the leaders. Draw the concentric circles as shown in the lower left. Radii for the concentric circles are 1/4″, 3/8″, 1/2″, and 5/8″.

Step 3. Set the **Leaders** layer current.

Multileader Style

Step 4. Open the **Multileader Style** dialog box and make the settings for the Standard style as described next:

MULTILEADER STYLE	
Ribbon/ Panel	Home/ Annotation
Multileader Toolbar:	
Type a Command:	MLEADER STYLE
Command Alias:	MLS

Prompt	Response
Type a command:	**Multileader Style** (or type **MLS <Enter>**)
The **Multileader Style Manager** appears with the Standard style current:	Click **Modify...**
The **Modify Multileader Style: Standard** dialog box appears:	Click the **Content** tab. Make the settings shown in Figure 8-22 if they are not there already: Multileader type: **Mtext** Text height: **3/16**

Figure 8-21
Draw 1/4″-radius circles and 1/4″-, 3/8″-, 1/2″-, and 5/8″-radius concentric circles

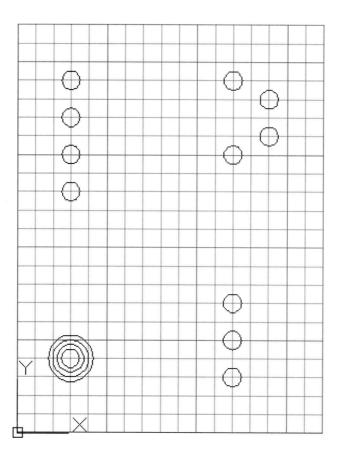

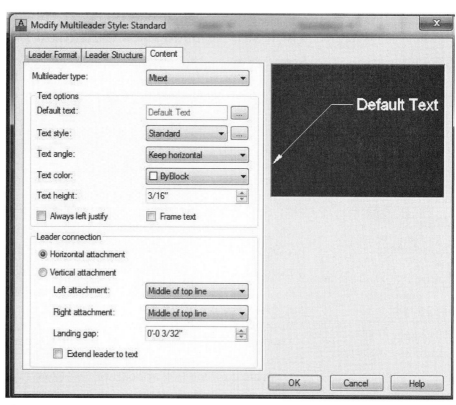

Figure 8-22
Modify Multileader Style: Standard dialog box, **Content** tab

Prompt	Response
	Left attachment: **Middle of top line**
	Right attachment: **Middle of top line**
	Landing gap: **3/32** (The landing is the horizontal line of the leader, and the landing gap is the distance between the landing and the text.)
	Click the **Leader Structure** tab (Figure 8-23) and make the following settings:
	Landing distance: **3/8″**
	Scale: **1**
	Click the **Leader Format** tab (Figure 8-24), and make the following settings:
	Type: **Straight**
	Arrowhead Symbol: **Closed filled**
	Arrowhead Size: **3/16″**
	Click **OK**
The **Multileader Style Manager** with the **Standard** style highlighted appears:	Click **Set Current**
	Click **Close**

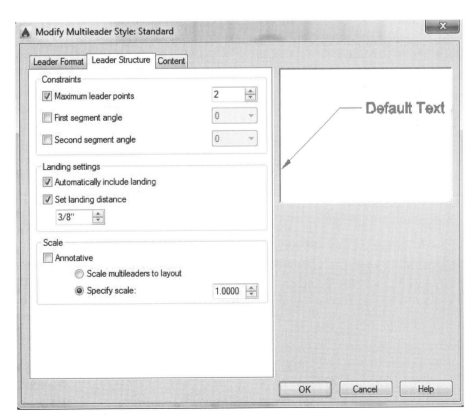

Figure 8-23
Modify Multileader Style: Standard dialog box, **Leader Structure** tab

Figure 8-24
Modify Multileader Style:
Standard dialog box, **Leader**
Format tab

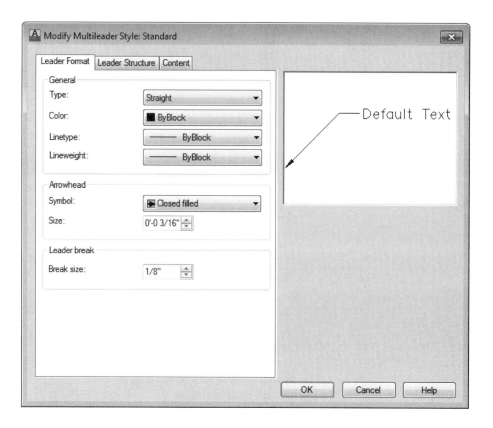

MULTILEADER	
Ribbon/ Panel	Home/ Annotation
Multileader Toolbar:	
Menu Bar:	Dimension/ Multileader
Type a Command:	MLEADER

Multileader

Step 5. Draw four multileaders using the **Standard** multileader style. Draw two leaders arrowhead first, one leader landing first, and one leader content first, as described next:

Prompt	Response
Type a command:	**Multileader** (or type **MLEADER** **<Enter>**)
Specify leader arrowhead location or [leader Landing first Content first Options] <Options>:	**Osnap-Nearest** (The arrow should touch the outside of the circle but point toward the center of the circle.)
to	**P1→**(Figure 8-25)
Specify leader landing location:	**P2→**
The **Multiline Text Editor** appears:	Type **CIRCLE1** Click **Close Text Editor** (on the ribbon)
Type a command:	**<Enter>**
Specify leader arrowhead location or [leader Landing first Content first Options] <Options>:	**Osnap-Nearest**
to	**P3→** (Figure 8-25)
Specify leader landing location:	**P4→**
The **Multiline Text Editor** appears:	Type **CIRCLE2** Click **Close Text Editor**
Type a command:	**<Enter>**

Figure 8-25
Draw two leaders arrowhead
first with the **Standard** multileader style

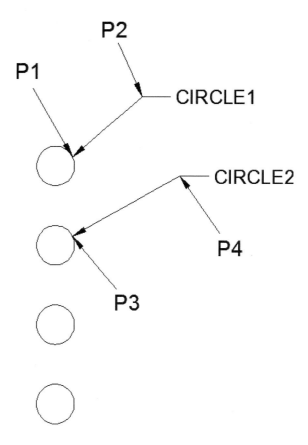

Prompt	Response
Specify leader arrowhead location or [leader Landing first Content first Options] <Options>:	Type **L <Enter>** (to select **Landing** first)
Specify leader landing location or [leader arrowHead first Content first Options] <Content first>:	**P2→** (Figure 8-26)

Figure 8-26
Draw one leader landing first
(P1, P2), draw another leader
content first (P3, P4, P5)

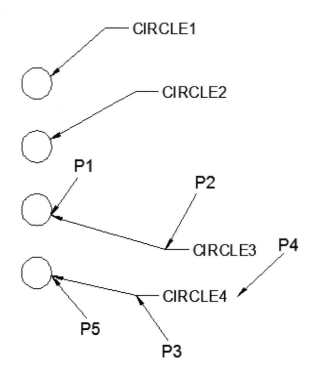

Prompt	Response
Specify leader arrowhead location:	**P1→ (Osnap-Nearest)**
The **Multiline Text Editor** appears:	Type **CIRCLE3**
	Click **Close Text Editor**
Type a command:	**<Enter>**
Specify leader landing location or [leader arrowHead first Content first Options] <Options>:	Type **C <Enter>**
Specify first corner of text or [leader arrowHead first leader Landing first Options] <Options>:	**P3→**
Specify opposite corner:	**P4→**
The **Multiline Text Editor** appears:	Type **CIRCLE4**
	Click **Close Text Editor**
Specify leader arrowhead location:	**P5→ (Osnap-Nearest)**

Multileader Align

Step 6. Align the leaders so all the text starts at the same distance from the left, as described next:

MULTILEADER ALIGN	
Ribbon/ Panel	Home/ Annotation
Multileader Toolbar:	
Type a Command:	MLEADER ALIGN
Command Alias:	MLA

Prompt	Response
Type a command:	**Align Multileaders** (or type **MLA <Enter>**)
Select multileaders:	Use a window to select all four leaders (The window can include the circles also.)
Specify opposite corner: 4 found	
Select multileaders:	**<Enter>**
Current mode: Use current spacing Select multileader to align to or [Options]:	Click the top leader (CIRCLE1)
Specify direction:	With **ORTHO** on, click a point below the bottom leader (CIRCLE4)

The leaders are aligned (Figure 8-27).

Change Multileader Style

Step 7. Set a multileader style so the text appears inside a circle, as described next:

Prompt	Response
Type a command:	**Multileader Style** (or type **MLS <Enter>**)
The **Multileader Style Manager** appears:	Click **New...**
The **Create New Multileader Style** dialog box appears:	Type **BALLOON** in the **New style name**: text box (Figure 8-28)
	Click **Continue**
The **Modify Multileader Style**: **BALLOON** dialog box appears:	Click the **Content** tab
	Click **Block** in the **Multileader type**: list
	Click **Circle** in the **Source block**: list (Figure 8-29)

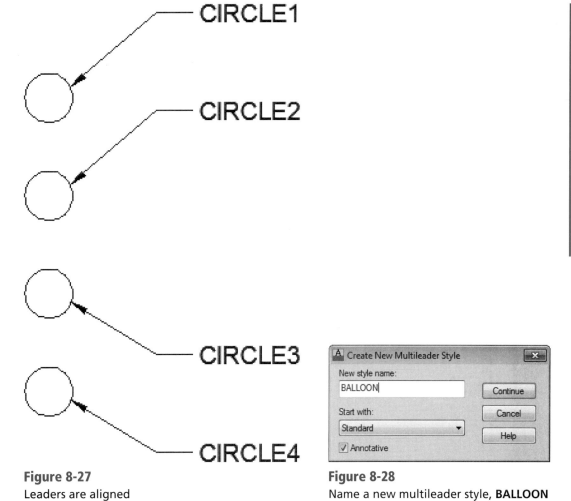

Figure 8-27
Leaders are aligned

Figure 8-28
Name a new multileader style, **BALLOON**

Figure 8-29
Select **Block** for **Multileader type, Circle** for the **Source block**, and **2** for the **Scale**

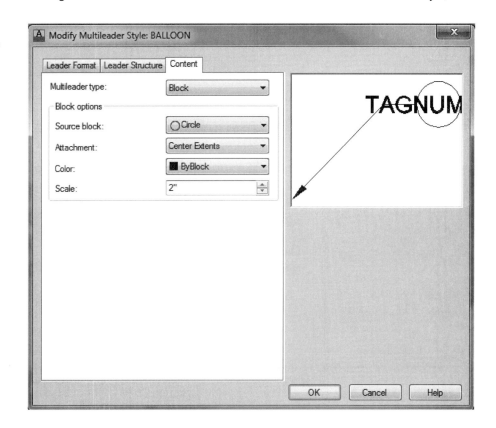

Prompt	Response
	Type **2** in the **Scale:** text box
	Click the **Leader Structure** tab
	Click the **Specify scale**: option button
	Type **1** in the **Specify scale**: text box
	(Figure 8-30)

Figure 8-30
Modify Multileader Style:
BALLOON dialog box,
Leader Structure, and
Leader Format tabs

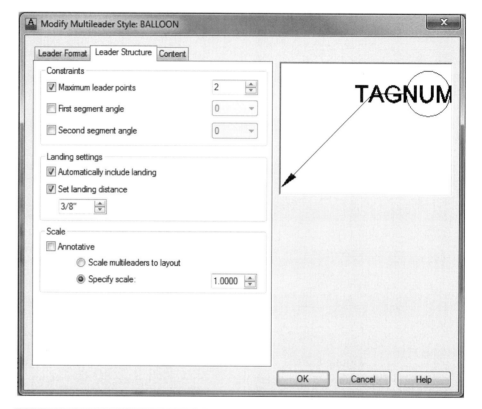

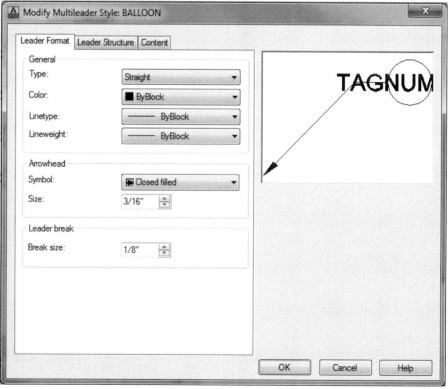

Prompt	Response
	Click the **Leader Format** tab and change the arrowhead size to **3/16** (Figure 8-30)
	Click **OK**
The **Multileader Style Manager** appears with the BALLOON Style highlighted:	Click **Set Current**
	Click **Close**

Step 8. Draw four multileaders using the BALLOON multileader style. Draw all four with the content first (Figure 8-31), as described next:

Figure 8-31
Collected content attached to one leader

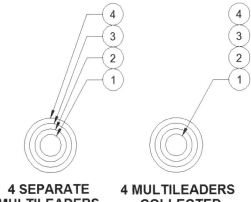

**4 SEPARATE
MULTILEADERS**

**4 MULTILEADERS
COLLECTED**

Prompt	Response
Type a command:	**Multileader** (or type **MLEADER <Enter>**)
Specify insertion point for block or [leader arrowHead first leader Landing first Options] <Options>:	A circle appears on your cursor **Click a snap point on the drawing** to locate the center point of the circle, containing the number 1 (Figure 8-31)
Enter attribute values Enter tag number <TAGNUMBER>: Specify leader arrowhead location: to	Type **1 <Enter>** **Osnap-Nearest** Click a point on the 1/4″-radius circle (the arrow should touch the outside of the circle but point toward the center of the circle)
Type a command: Specify insertion point for block or [leader arrowHead first leader Landing first Options] <Options>:	**<Enter>**
	Click a snap point to locate the center point of the circle containing the number 2 (Figure 8-31)

Prompt	Response
Enter attribute values	
Enter tag number <TAGNUMBER>:	Type **2 <Enter>**
Specify leader arrowhead location:	**Osnap-Nearest**
to	Click a point on the 3/8″-radius circle (pointing toward the center is not important on the circles containing the numbers 2, 3, and 4)
Type a command:	**<Enter>**
Specify insertion point for block or [leader arrowHead first leader Landing first Options] <Options>:	Click the center point of the circle containing the number 3 (Figure 8-31)
Enter attribute values	
Enter tag number <TAGNUMBER>:	Type **3 <Enter>**
Specify leader arrowhead location:	**Osnap-Nearest**
to	Click a point on the 1/2″-radius circle
Type a command:	**<Enter>**
Specify insertion point for block or [leader arrowHead first leader Landing first Options] <Options>:	Click the center point of the circle containing the number 4 (Figure 8-31)
Enter attribute values	
Enter tag number <TAGNUMBER>:	Type: **4 <Enter>**
Specify leader arrowhead location: <Osnap on>	**Osnap-Nearest**
to	Click a point on the 5/8″-radius circle
Type a command:	**<Enter>**

Multileader Collect

Step 9. Collect the four leaders so all the balloons are attached to one leader, as described next (Figure 8-31):

MULTILEADER COLLECT	
Ribbon/ Panel	Home/ Annotation
Multileader Toolbar:	
Type a Command:	MLEADER COLLECT
Command Alias:	MLC

Prompt	Response
Type a command:	Collect multileaders (or type **MLC <Enter>**)
Select multileaders:	Select all four leaders
Select multileaders:	**<Enter>**
Specify collected multileader location or [Vertical Horizontal Wrap] <Horizontal>:	Type **V <Enter>**
Specify collected multileader location or [Vertical Horizontal Wrap] <Vertical>:	Move your mouse so you can see one leader attached to the number 1 balloon. Click a point to locate the balloons as shown in Figure 8-31

Step 10. Set a running **Osnap-Nearest**.

Multileader Add

Step 11. Draw a multileader and add three leaders to it, as described next, Figures 8-32 and 8-33:

	MULTILEADER ADD
Ribbon/ Panel	Home/ Annotation
Multileader Toolbar:	
Type a Command:	AIMLEADER EDITADD

Prompt	**Response**
Type a command:	**Multileader** (or type **MLEADER <Enter>**)
Specify insertion point for block or [leader arrowHead first leader Landing first Options] <Options>:	A circle appears on your cursor. **Click a snap point** on the drawing to locate the center point of the circle containing the number 5 (Figure 8-32)
Enter attribute values Enter tag number <TAGNUMBER>:	Type **5 <Enter>**
Specify leader arrowhead location:	Click a point on the top circle, **Osnap-Nearest** (Figure 8-32)
Type a command:	**Add Leader** (or Type **AIMLEADEREDITADD<Enter>**)
Select a multileader: 1 found Specify leader arrowhead location or [Remove leaders]:	Click the multileader you just drew Click a point on the next circle, **Osnap-Nearest** (Figure 8-33)
Specify leader arrowhead location or [Remove leaders]:	Click a point on the next circle, **Osnap-Nearest**
Specify leader arrowhead location or [Remove leaders]:	Click a point on the last circle, **Osnap-Nearest <Enter>**

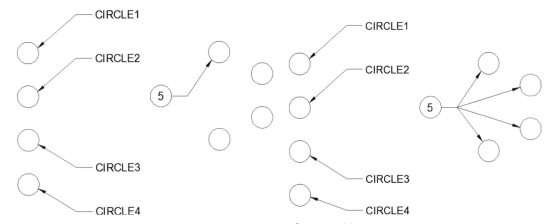

Figure 8-32
Draw the multileader for the number 5

Figure 8-33
Draw one leader and add three more

Step 12. Make a new multileader style with the following settings:

1. Name it **HEX** (start with a copy of **BALLOON**).
2. Change the **Source block:** to a **Hexagon**.
3. Set the **HEX** style current.

Step 13. Draw one leader with a **6** in the hexagon and add two leaders to it as shown in Figure 8-34.

Figure 8-34
Exercise 8-2 Complete

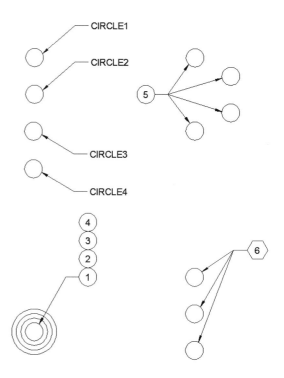

Step 14. Save your drawing in two places.

Step 15. Print the drawing at a scale of **1:1**.

EXERCISE 8-3
Tenant Space: Section of Conference Room Cabinets with Hatching

In Exercise 8-3, a sectional view of the built-in cabinets on the south wall of the tenant space conference room is drawn. The sectional view of the south wall of the cabinets (Figure 8-35) shows many construction details that elevation and plan views cannot. Sectional views are imaginary cuts through an area. Hatched lines are used to show where the imaginary saw used to make these imaginary cuts touches the cut objects.

This crosshatching is done in AutoCAD by drawing hatch patterns. Exercise 8-3 will describe the **HATCH** command, used to draw hatch patterns.

When you have completed Exercise 8-3, your drawing will look similar to Figure 8-35.

Step 1. Begin drawing **CH8-EXERCISE3** on the hard drive or network drive by opening existing drawing **CH8-EXERCISE1** and saving it to the hard drive or network drive with the name **CH8-EXERCISE3**. You can use all the settings and text created for Exercise 8-1.

Step 2. Reset drawing limits, grid, and snap as needed.

Step 3. Create the following layers by renaming the existing layers and adding the **a-sect-fixt** layer.

Layer Name	Description	Color	Linetype	Lineweight
a-sect-dims	dimensions, dimension notes	red	continuous	.004" (.09 mm)
a-sect-fixt	sink	green	continuous	.006" (.15 mm)
a-sect-hdln	sink hidden lines	red	hidden	.004" (.09 mm)
a-sect-lwt1	section lines except for those under lwt2	blue	continuous	.010" (.25 mm)
a-sect-lwt2	recessed standards, ¼" upper & lower cabinet plywood backing	white	continuous	.002" (.05 mm)
a-sect-patt	hatch patterns	white	continuous	.002" (.05 mm)
a-sect-text	text	green	continuous	.006" (.15 mm)

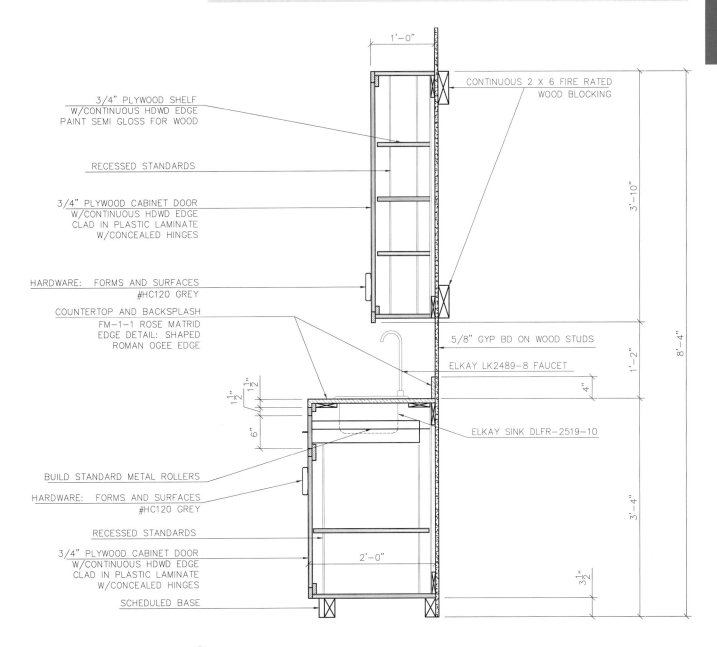

CONFERENCE ROOM CABINET SECTION
2 / A3   SCALE: 3/4"=1'-0"

Figure 8-35

Exercise 8-3: Tenant space, section of conference room cabinets with hatching (scale: 3/4" = 1'-0")

Step 4. After looking closely at Figure 8-36, you may want to keep some of the conference room elevation drawing parts. Use **Erase** to eliminate the remainder of the drawing.

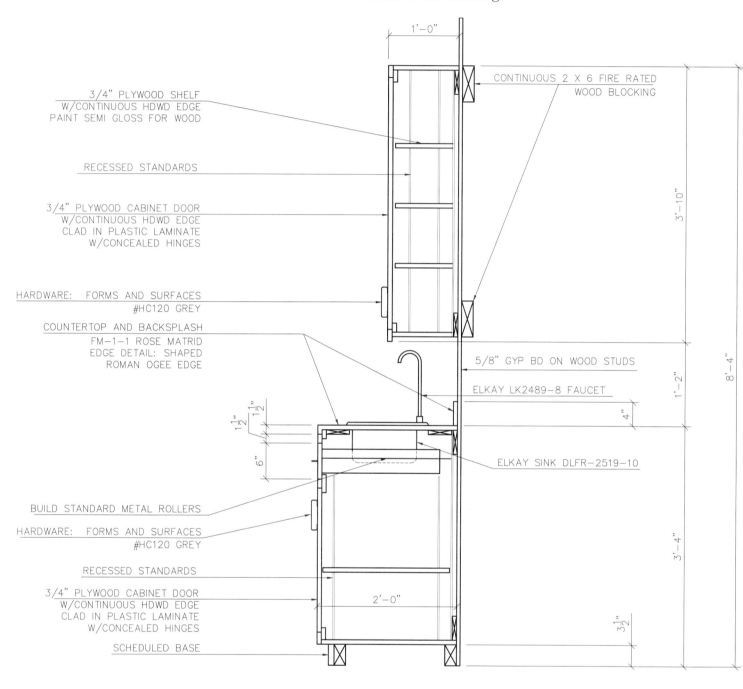

3/4" PLYWOOD SHELF
W/CONTINUOUS HDWD EDGE
PAINT SEMI GLOSS FOR WOOD

RECESSED STANDARDS

3/4" PLYWOOD CABINET DOOR
W/CONTINUOUS HDWD EDGE
CLAD IN PLASTIC LAMINATE
W/CONCEALED HINGES

HARDWARE: FORMS AND SURFACES
#HC120 GREY

COUNTERTOP AND BACKSPLASH
FM-1-1 ROSE MATRID
EDGE DETAIL: SHAPED
ROMAN OGEE EDGE

BUILD STANDARD METAL ROLLERS

HARDWARE: FORMS AND SURFACES
#HC120 GREY

RECESSED STANDARDS

3/4" PLYWOOD CABINET DOOR
W/CONTINUOUS HDWD EDGE
CLAD IN PLASTIC LAMINATE
W/CONCEALED HINGES

SCHEDULED BASE

CONTINUOUS 2 X 6 FIRE RATED
WOOD BLOCKING

5/8" GYP BD ON WOOD STUDS

ELKAY LK2489-8 FAUCET

ELKAY SINK DLFR-2519-10

2 / A3 CONFERENCE ROOM CABINET SECTION
SCALE: 3/4"=1'-0"

Figure 8-36
Exercise 8-3: Tenant space, section of conference room cabinets before hatching (scale: 3/4″ = 1'-0″)

Step 5. Change the underlined text to read CONFERENCE ROOM CABINET SECTION, change the top number in the balloon, and change the drawing scale to read as shown in Figure 8-36.

Step 6. Set the drawing annotation scale to ¾″ = **1'-0″**.

Step 7. Use the correct layers and the dimensions shown in Figure 8-36 to draw the sectional view of the south wall of the tenant space conference room cabinets *before using the* **HATCH** *command*. Draw the section full size (measure features with an architectural scale of ¾″ = 1′ to find the correct size). Include the text and the dimensions. Your drawing will look similar to Figure 8-36 when it is completed prior to adding hatch patterns.

Step 8. When the cabinet section is complete with text and dimensions, freeze the **a-sect-dims** layer so it will not interfere with drawing the hatch patterns.

Prepare to Use the Hatch Command with the Add: Select Objects Boundary Option

When using the **HATCH** command there are two options for selecting the **boundary** of the area you will hatch; those two options are **Add: Pick points** and **Add: Select objects**. The **Add: Select objects** option requires additional preparation.

The most important aspect of using the **HATCH** command *when you use* **Select Objects** *to create the boundary* is to define clearly the boundary of the area to be hatched. If the boundary of the hatching area is not clearly defined, some of the hatch pattern may go outside the boundary area, or the boundary area may not be completely filled.

Before you use the **HATCH** command in this manner, all areas to which hatching will be added must be prepared so that none of their boundary lines extend beyond the area to be hatched. When the views on which you will draw hatching have already been drawn, it is often necessary to use the **BREAK** command to break the boundary lines into line segments that clearly define the hatch boundaries.

Step 9. Use the **BREAK** command to help clearly define the right edge of the horizontal plywood top of the upper cabinets (Figure 8-37), as described next:

Prompt	Response
Type a command:	**Break** (or type **BR <Enter>**)
Select object:	**P1→** (to select the vertical line)
Specify second break point or [First point]:	Type **F <Enter>**
Specify first break point:	**P2→** (use **Osnap-Intersection**)
Specify second break point:	Type **@ <Enter>** (places the second point exactly at the same place as the first point, and no gap is broken out of the line)
Type a command:	**<Enter>** (repeat **BREAK**)
Select object:	**P3→** (to select the vertical line)
Specify second break point or [First point]:	Type **F <Enter>**
Specify first break point:	**P4→** (use **Osnap-Intersection**)
Specify second break point:	Type **@ <Enter>**

You have just used the **BREAK** command with the @ option to break the vertical line so that it is a separate line segment that clearly defines the right edge of the plywood top area.

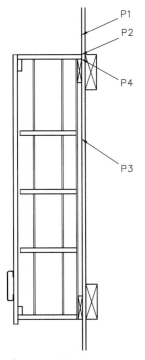

Figure 8-37
Use the **BREAK** command to define clearly the right edge of the horizontal top area of the upper cabinets

Step 10. Use the **BREAK** command to define the bottom left edge of the plywood top boundary. Break the vertical line at the intersection of the bottom of the left edge (Figure 8-38).

Step 11. When the boundary of the plywood top is clearly defined, the top, bottom, right, and left lines of the top are separate line segments that do not extend beyond the boundary of the plywood top. To check the boundary, pick and highlight each line segment. Use the **BREAK** command on the top horizontal line of the plywood top, if needed (Figure 8-38).

Step 12. Use the **BREAK** command to prepare the three plywood shelves and the plywood bottom of the upper cabinet boundaries for hatching (Figure 8-38).

Step 13. The **HATCH** command will also not work properly if the two lines of an intersection do not meet, that is, if there is any small gap. If you need to check the intersections of the left side of the plywood shelves to make sure they intersect properly, do this before continuing with the **HATCH** command.

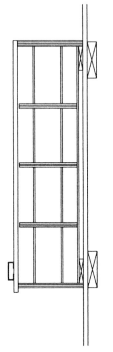

Figure 8-38
Upper cabinets with hatch patterns drawn

Use the Hatch Command with the Add: Select Objects Boundary Option

Step 14. Set layer **a-sect-patt** current.

Step 15. Use the **HATCH** command with the **Add: Select objects** boundary option to draw a uniform horizontal-line hatch pattern on the plywood top of the upper cabinets (Figure 8-39), as described next:

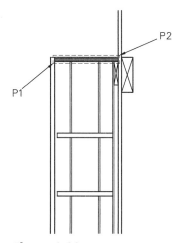

Figure 8-39
Use the **Hatch** command with the **Select Objects <Boundary>** option to draw a uniform horizontal-line hatch pattern on the plywood top of the upper cabinets

Prompt	Response
Type a command:	**Hatch** (or type **H <Enter>**,
Pick internal point or [Select objects seTtings]:	**T <Enter>**)

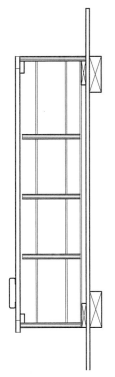

Figure 8-40
Draw a hatch pattern on the three plywood shelves and the plywood bottom of the upper cabinet

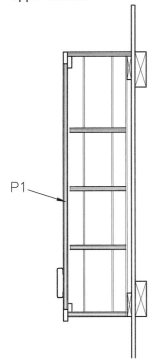

Figure 8-41
Use the **HATCH** command with the **Pick points** boundary option to draw a uniform vertical-line hatch pattern on the upper cabinet door

Prompt	Response
The **Hatch and Gradient** dialog box appears:	Click **User-defined** in the **Type**: area of **Type and pattern**: Angle: **0** Spacing: **1/4″** Click **Add: Select objects**
Select objects or [picK internal point setTings]:	(Figure 8-39) Click **P1→**
Specify opposite corner:	Click **P2→**
Select objects or [picK internal point seTtings]:	
(A preview of your hatching appears):	**<Enter>** (if the correct hatch pattern was previewed; if not, click **<Esc>** and fix the problem)

NOTE

Although the **Pick points** method of creating hatch boundaries is often much easier, you must know how to use **Select objects** as well. There are instances when **Pick points** just does not work.

The plywood top of the upper cabinet is now hatched.

Step 16. Use the same hatching procedure to draw a hatch pattern on the three plywood shelves and the plywood bottom of the upper cabinet, as shown in Figure 8-40.

TIP

Turn off or freeze the text and dimension layers if they interfere with hatching.

Use the Hatch Command with the Add: Pick Points Boundary Option

When you use the **Add: Pick points** boundary option to create a boundary for the hatch pattern, AutoCAD allows you to pick any point inside the area, and the boundary is automatically created. You do not have to prepare the boundary of the area as you did with the **Select objects** boundary option, but you have to make sure there are no gaps in the boundary.

Step 17. Use the **HATCH** command with the **Pick points** boundary option to draw a uniform vertical-line hatch pattern on the upper cabinet door (Figure 8-41), as described next:

Prompt	Response
Type a command:	**Hatch** (or type **H <Enter>**
Pick internal point or [Select objects seTtings]:	Type **T**
The **Hatch and Gradient** dialog box appears:	Click **User-defined** in the **Type**: area of **Type and pattern**: Angle: **90** Spacing: **1/4″** Click **Add: Pick points**

Prompt	Response
Pick internal point or [Select objects seTtings]:	Click **P1** → (inside the door symbol)
Pick internal point or [Select objects seTtings]:	
(A preview of your hatching appears):	**<Enter>** (if the correct hatch pattern was previewed; if not, click **<Esc>** and fix the problem)

> **TIP**
> You may have to draw a line across the top of the 5/8″ gypsum board to create the hatch pattern on the gypsum board.

Step 18. Use the **HATCH** command with the **Pick points** boundary option to draw the AR-SAND hatch pattern on the 5/8″ gypsum board (Figures 8-42, 8-43, and 8-44), as described next:

Prompt	Response
Type a command:	**Hatch**
Pick internal point or [select objects seTtings]:	Type **T<Enter>**
The **Hatch and Gradient** dialog box appears:	Click **Predefined** (in the **Type:** area)
	Click **...** (to the right of the **Pattern:** list box)
The **Hatch Pattern Palette** appears:	Click the **Other Predefined** tab
	Click **AR-SAND** (Figure 8-42)
	Click **OK**

Figure 8-42
Select AR-SAND

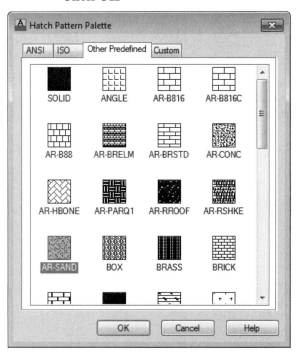

> **NOTE**
> When **Associative** is checked in the **Hatch and Gradient** dialog box, pick any point on the hatch pattern to erase it.

Prompt	Response
The **Hatch and Gradient dialog** box appears (Figure 8-43):	Click **0** (in the **Angle** box) Type **3/8″** (in the **Scale:** box) Click **Add: Pick points**
Pick internal point or [Select objects seTtings]:	Click any point inside the lines defining the 5/8″ gypsum board boundary (Figure 8-44)
Pick internal point or [Select objects seTtings]:	**<Enter>**

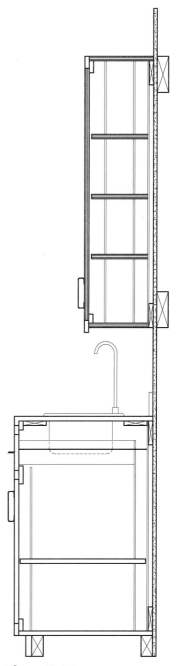

Figure 8-43
Specify scale for AR-SAND

Figure 8-44
Use the **HATCH** command to draw the AR-SAND hatch pattern on the 5/8″ gypsum board

The 5/8″ gypsum board is now hatched. (If you get an error message, try 1/2″ for scale in the **Scale:** box or draw a line across the top of the gypsum board.)

HATCH	
Ribbon/ Panel	Home/Draw
Draw Toolbar:	
Menu Bar:	Draw/ Hatch...
Type a Command:	HATCH
Command Alias:	H

Hatch; Hatch and Gradient Dialog Box; Hatch Tab

Type and Pattern

When the **HATCH** command is activated (type **H <Enter>**, then **T <Enter>**) the **Hatch and Gradient** dialog box with the **Hatch** tab selected appears (Figure 8-45). As listed in the **Type and pattern**: list box, the pattern types can be as follows:

> **NOTE**
>
> When you type **H <Enter>**, the **Hatch Creation** panel appears on the ribbon with most of the same features as the **Hatch and Gradient** dialog box. You may use either of these to define a hatch pattern.

Figure 8-45
Hatch and Gradient dialog box, **Hatch** tab

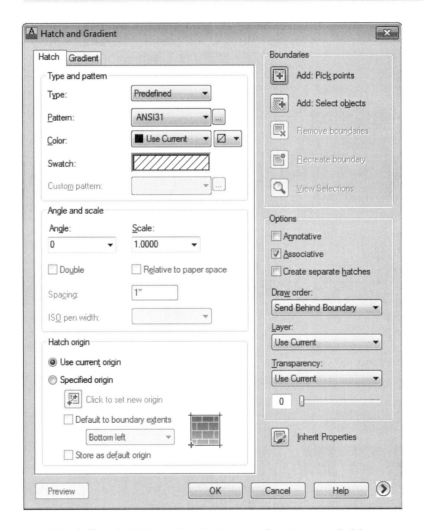

Predefined: Makes the **Pattern...** button available.

User-defined: Defines a pattern of lines using the current linetype.

Custom: Specifies a pattern from the ACAD.pat file or any other PAT file.

To view the predefined hatch pattern options, click the ellipsis (...) to the right of the **Pattern**: list box. The **Hatch Pattern Palette** appears (Figure 8-46). Other parts of the **Hatch and Gradient** dialog box are as follows:

Pattern: Specifies a predefined pattern name.

Color: Allows you to use the current color or to choose another color for the hatch.

Background color: The area to the right of the **Color** box allows you to specify a background color for a hatch. The default color is none.

Custom pattern: This list box shows a custom pattern name. This option is available when **Custom** is selected in the **Type**: area.

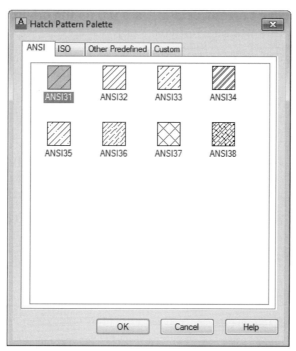

Figure 8-46
Hatch Pattern Palette

Angle and Scale

Angle: Allows you to specify an angle for the hatch pattern relative to the *X*-axis of the current UCS.

Scale: This allows you to enlarge or shrink the hatch pattern to fit the drawing. It is not available if you have selected **User-defined** in the **Type**: list box.

Double: When you check this box, the area is hatched with a second set of lines at 90° to the first hatch pattern (available when **User-defined** pattern type is selected).

Relative to paper space: Scales the pattern relative to paper space so you can scale the hatch pattern to fit the scale of your paper space layout.

Spacing: Allows you to specify the space between lines on a user-defined hatch pattern.

ISO pen width: If you select one of the 14 ISO (International Organization for Standardization) patterns at the bottom of the list of hatch patterns and on the **ISO** tab of the **Hatch Pattern Palette**, this option scales the pattern based on the selected pen width. Each of these pattern names begins with ISO.

Hatch Origin

Controls where the hatch pattern originates. Some hatch patterns, such as brick, stone, and those used as shingles, need to start from a particular point on the drawing. By default, all hatch origins are the same as the current UCS origin.

Use current origin: Uses 0,0 as the origin by default. In most cases this will be what you want.

Specified origin: Specifies a new hatch origin. When you click this option, the following options become available.

Click to set new origin: When you click this box, you are then prompted to pick a point on the drawing as the origin for the hatch pattern.

Default to boundary extents: This option allows you to select a new origin based on the rectangular extents of the hatch. Choices include each of the four corners of the extents and its center.

Store as default origin: This option sets your specified origin as the default.

Preview button: Allows you to preview the hatch pattern before you apply it to a drawing.

Boundaries

Add: Pick points: Allows you to pick points inside a boundary to specify the area to be hatched.

Add: Select objects: Allows you to select the outside edges of the boundary to specify the area to be hatched.

Remove boundaries: Allows you to remove from the boundary set objects defined as islands by the **Pick Points** option. You cannot remove the outer boundary.

Recreate boundary: Allows you to create a polyline or a region around the hatch pattern.

View Selections: Displays the currently defined boundary set. This option is not available when no selection or boundary has been made.

Options

Annotative: You can make the hatch annotative by selecting the box beside **Annotative** under **Options** in the dialog box. To add the annotative hatch to your drawing, first, set the desired annotation scale for your drawing. Second, hatch the object (using type, pattern, angle, and scale) so you can see that the hatch is the correct size and appearance. If you change the plotting scale of your drawing, you can change the size of the hatch pattern by changing the annotation scale, located in the lower right corner of the status bar.

Associative: When a check appears in this button, the hatch pattern is a single object and stretches when the area that has been hatched is stretched.

Create separate hatches: When this button is clicked so that a check appears in it, you can create two or more separate hatch areas by using the **HATCH** command only once. You can erase those areas individually.

Draw order: The **Draw order:** list allows you to place hatch patterns on top of or beneath existing lines to make the drawing more legible.

Layer: Allows you to use the current layer for the hatch or to choose any other predefined layer.

Transparency: Allows you to use the current transparency setting for the hatch or to choose another setting.

Inherit Properties: Allows you to pick an existing hatch pattern to use on another area. The pattern picked must be associative (attached to and defined by its boundary).

More Options

When the **More Options** arrow in the lower right corner is clicked, the following options (Figure 8-47) appear.

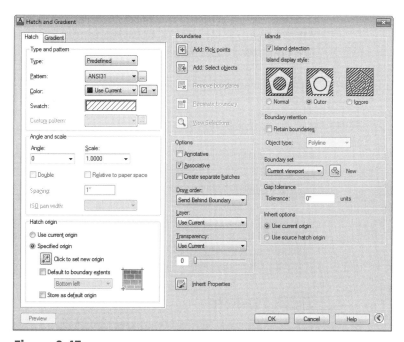

Figure 8-47
Hatch and Gradient dialog box, more options

Islands

The following **Island display style** options are shown in Figure 8-47:

Normal: When clicked (and a selection set is composed of areas inside other areas), alternating areas are hatched, as shown in the **Island display style**: area.

Outer: When clicked (and a selection set is composed of areas inside other areas), only the outer area is hatched, as shown in the **Island display style**: area.

Ignore: When clicked (and a selection set is composed of areas inside other areas), all areas are hatched, as shown in the **Island display style**: area.

Boundary Retention

Retain boundaries: Specifies whether the boundary objects will remain in your drawing after hatching is completed.

Object type: Allows you to select either a polyline or a region if you choose to retain the boundary.

Boundary Set

List box: This box allows you to select a boundary set from the current viewport or an existing boundary set.

New: When clicked, the dialog box temporarily closes and you are prompted to select objects to create the boundary set. AutoCAD includes only objects that can be hatched when it constructs the new boundary set. AutoCAD discards any existing boundary set and replaces it with the new boundary set. If you don't select any objects that can be hatched, AutoCAD retains any current set.

Gap Tolerance

Allows a gap tolerance of between 0 and 5000 units to hatch areas that are not completely enclosed.

Inherit Options

Allows you to choose either the current hatch origin or the origin of the inherited hatch for the new hatch pattern.

> **NOTE**
>
> The **Gradient** tab (Figure 8-48) is discussed fully in Chapter 13.

> **NOTE**
>
> When you double-click on a hatch pattern, **Hatch Editor** appears on the ribbon. The **Hatch Editor** has most of the features of the **Hatch Edit** dialog box.

Edit Hatch

Select **Edit Hatch...** or type **HE <Enter>** and click on a hatch pattern to access the **Hatch Edit** dialog box (Figure 8-49). You can edit the pattern, angle, scale, origin, and draw order of the hatch pattern.

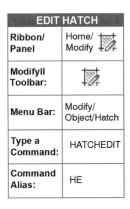

EDIT HATCH	
Ribbon/ Panel	Home/ Modify
ModifyII Toolbar:	
Menu Bar:	Modify/ Object/Hatch
Type a Command:	HATCHEDIT
Command Alias:	HE

Figure 8-48
Gradient tab

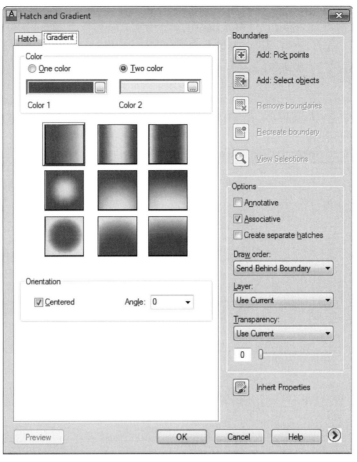

Figure 8-49
Hatch Edit dialog box

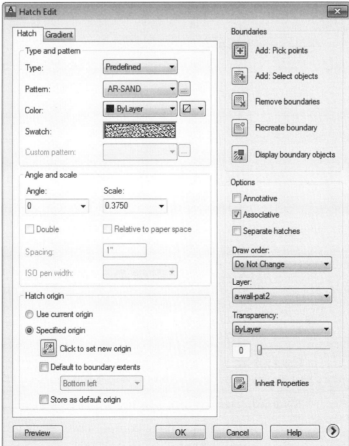

If you have an associative hatch pattern on a drawing that has one or two lines extending outside the hatch area, explode the hatch pattern. You may then trim the lines, because they are individual lines.

Step 19. Using the patterns described in Figure 8-50, draw hatch patterns by using the **Pick points** option on the lower cabinets and the end views of wood in the upper cabinets.

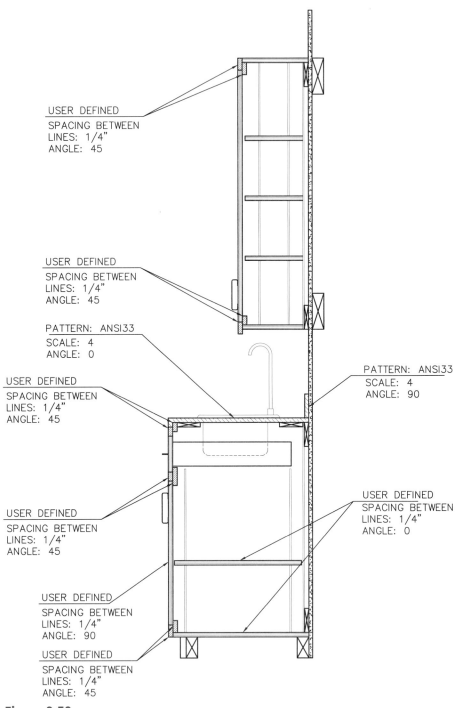

Figure 8-50
Draw the hatch patterns on the upper and lower cabinets as shown

Step 20. Thaw frozen layers.

Step 21. When you have completed Exercise 8-3 (Figure 8-51), save your work in at least two places.

Step 22. Print Exercise 8-3 at a scale of **3/4″ = 1′-0″**.

Step 23. Add the section symbol as shown in Figure 8-52 to your <u>TENANT SPACE FLOOR PLAN</u> drawing. Use a **1′**-radius circle and **1/16″**-high text (annotative). You may need to move two dimensions as shown and add a layer for the cutting plane line below the symbol. Use **PHANTOM 2** linetype and **.004″** lineweight, color **red**.

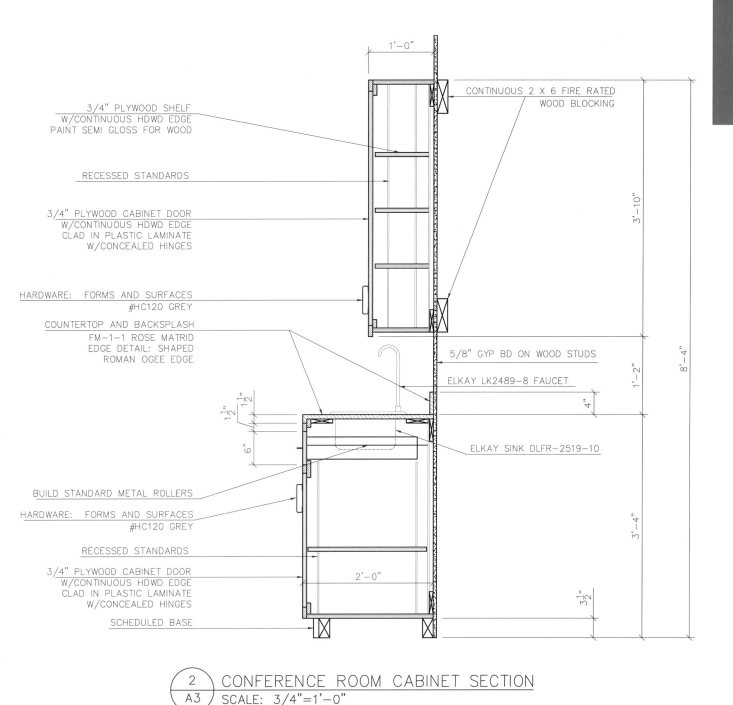

Figure 8-51
Exercise 8-3: Completed section drawing (scale: 3/4″ = 1′-0″)

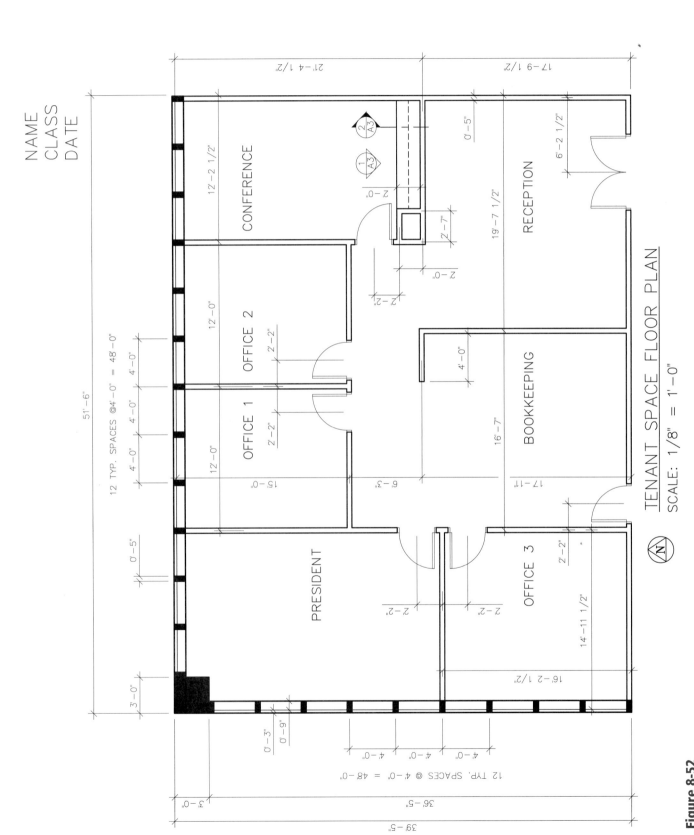

Figure 8-52
Tenant space floor plan with elevation and section symbols (scale: 1/8″ = 1′-0″)

EXERCISE 8-4
Detail of Door Jamb with Hatching

In Exercise 8-4, a detail of a door jamb is drawn. When you have completed Exercise 8-4, your drawing will look similar to Figure 8-53.

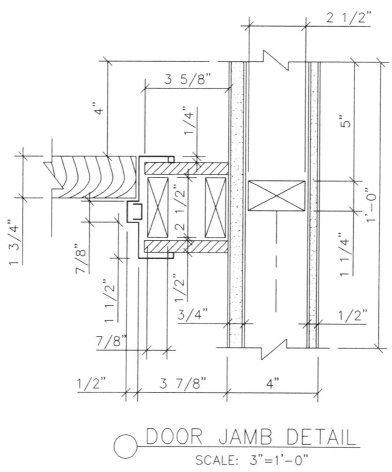

Figure 8-53
Exercise 8-4: Detail of a door jamb with crosshatching (scale: 3″ = 1′-0″)

Step 1. Use your workspace to make the following settings:

1. Use **Save As...** to save the drawing on the hard drive with the name **CH8-EXERCISE4**.
2. Set drawing units, limits, grid, and snap.
3. Create the following layers:

Layer Name	Color	Linetype	Lineweight
a-detl-lwt1	blue	continuous	.010″ (.25 mm)
a-detl-dims	red	continuous	.004″ (.09 mm)
a-detl-patt	white	continuous	.002″ (.05 mm)
a-detl-text	green	continuous	.006″ (.15 mm)

4. Set layer **a-detl-lwt1** current.

Step 2. Using the dimensions shown in Figure 8-53, draw all the door jamb components. Drawing some of the components separately and copying or moving them into place will be helpful. Measure any dimensions not shown with a scale of **3″ = 1′-0″**.

Step 3. Set layer **a-detl-patt** current, and draw the hatch patterns as described in Figure 8-54. Use a spline and array it to draw the curved wood grain pattern.

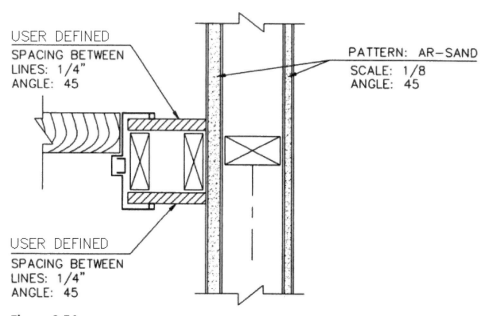

Figure 8-54
Exercise 8-4: Hatch patterns

Step 4. Set layer **a-detl-dims** current, set the dimensioning variables, and draw the dimensions as shown in Figure 8-53.

Step 5. Set layer **a-detl-text** current, and add the name of the detail as shown in Figure 8-53. Add your name, class, and current date in the upper right.

Step 6. Save the drawing in two places.

Step 7. Print the drawing at a scale of **3″ = 1′-0″**.

EXERCISE 8-5
Use Point Filters and OTRACK to Make an Orthographic Drawing of a Conference Table

point filters: A method of entering a point by which the X, Y, and Z coordinates are given in separate stages. Any one of the three coordinates can be first, second, or third.

OTRACK: A setting that allows you to specify points by hovering your pointing device over osnap points.

In Exercise 8-5, the AutoCAD features called *point filters* and *OTRACK* are used. These features are helpful when you are making 2D drawings showing the top, front, and side views of an object. All the features in these views must line up with the same features in the adjacent view. When you have completed Exercise 8-5, your drawing will look similar to Figure 8-55.

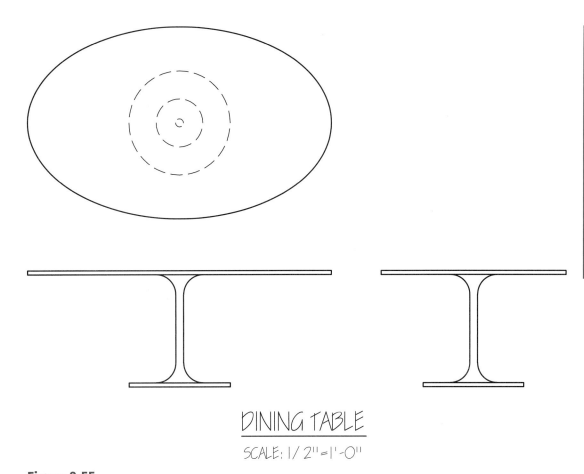

DINING TABLE

SCALE: 1/2"=1'-0"

Figure 8-55

Exercise 8-5: Use point filters and **OTRACK** to draw three views of a dining table (scale: 1/2″ = 1′-0″)

Step 1. Use your workspace to make the following settings:

1. Set drawing units: **Architectural**
2. Set drawing limits: **16′,14′**
3. Set **GRIDDISPLAY: 0**
4. Set grid: **2″**
5. Set snap: **1″**
6. Create the following layers:

Layer Name	Color	Linetype	Lineweight
Layer1	blue	continuous	.010″ (.25 mm)
Layer2	red	hidden	.004″ (.09 mm)
Layer3	green	continuous	.006″ (.15 mm)

7. Set **Layer2** current.
8. Set **LTSCALE: 16**.
9. Save the drawing as **CH8-EXERCISE5**.

Step 2. Draw the base and column of the table (hidden line), as shown in the top view (Figure 8-56), as described next:

Prompt	Response
Type a command:	**Circle-Center, Diameter** (not **Radius**)
Specify center point for circle or [3P 2P Ttr (tan tan radius)]:	Type **4′,9′<Enter>**

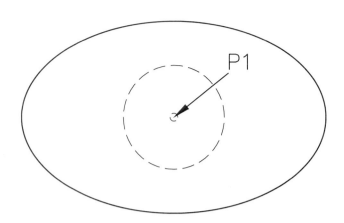

Figure 8-56
Draw the top view of the
base, column, and top of
the table

P1

Prompt	Response
Specify diameter of circle <default>:	Type **2'2 <Enter>**
Type a command:	**Circle-Center, Diameter** (not **Radius**)
Specify center point for circle or [3P 2P Ttr (tan tan radius)]:	Type **4',9'** (the same center as the first circle)
Specify diameter of circle <default>:	Type **2 <Enter>**

Step 3. Set **Layer1** current.

Step 4. Draw the elliptical top of the table (continuous linetype), as shown in the top view (Figure 8-56), as described next:

	ELLIPSE
Ribbon/ Panel	Home/Draw
Draw Toolbar:	Ellipse
Menu Bar:	Draw/Ellipse
Type a Command:	ELLIPSE
Command Alias:	EL

Prompt	Response
Type a command:	**Ellipse-Center**
Specify center of ellipse:	**Osnap-Center**
of	**P1→**
Specify endpoint of axis:	With **ORTHO** on, move your mouse up and type **2' <Enter>**
Specify distance to other axis or [Rotation]:	Type **39 <Enter>**

Point Filters

Step 5. Use point filters to draw the front view of the top of this elliptical table (Figure 8-57), as described next:

Figure 8-57
Draw the front view of the
top of the table using point
filters

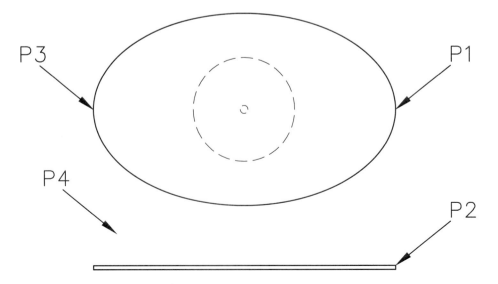

P3

P1

P4

P2

Prompt	Response
Type a command:	**Line**
Specify first point:	Type **.X <Enter>**
of	**Osnap-Quadrant**
of	**P1→** (Figure 8-57)
(need YZ):	**P2→** (with **SNAP** on, pick a point in the approximate location shown in Figure 8-57)
Specify next point or [Undo]:	Type **.X <Enter>**
of	**Osnap-Quadrant**
of	**P3→**
(need YZ):	**P4→** (with **ORTHO** on, pick any point to identify the Y component of the point; **ORTHO** makes the Y component of the new point the same as the Y component of the previous point)
Specify next point or [Close Undo]:	With **ORTHO** on, move your mouse straight down, and type **1 <Enter>**
Specify next point or [Close Undo]:	Type **.X <Enter>**
of	**Osnap-Endpoint**
of	(Figure 8-57) **P2→**
(need YZ):	With **ORTHO** on, move your mouse to the right, and pick any point
Specify next point or [Close Undo]:	Type **C <Enter>**

OTRACK

Step 6. Set running **Osnap** modes of **Endpoint, Quadrant,** and **Intersection** and turn **OSNAP** and **OTRACK** on.

Step 7. Use **OTRACK** and **Offset** to draw the front view of the column (Figure 8-58), as described next:

Prompt	Response
Type a command:	**Line**
Specify first point:	Move your mouse to the right quadrant shown as **P1→** (Figure 8-58) but do not click

Figure 8-58
Use **OTRACK** to draw the front view of the column

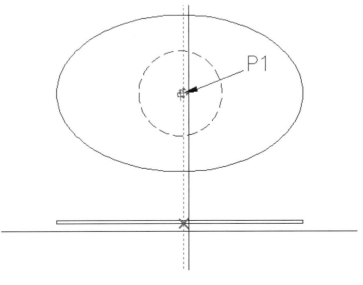

Prompt	Response
	Hold it until the quadrant symbol appears, then move your mouse straight down until the dotted line shows the intersection symbol on the bottom line of the tabletop as shown, then click the intersection point (Figure 8-58)
Specify next point or [Undo]:	With **ORTHO** on, move your mouse straight down and type **27 <Enter>**
Specify next point or [Undo]:	**<Enter>**
Type a command:	**Offset** (or type **O <Enter>**)
Specify offset distance or [Through Erase Layer] <Through>:	Type **2 <Enter>**
Select object to offset or [Exit Undo] <Exit>:	Click **P1**→ (Figure 8-59)
Specify point on side to offset or [Exit Multiple Undo] <Exit>:	Click **P2**→ (any point to the left of the 27″ line)
Select object to offset or [Exit Undo] <Exit>:	**<Enter>**

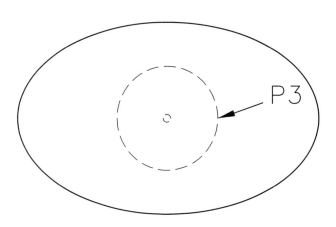

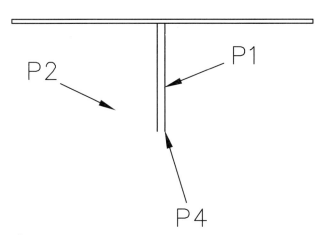

Figure 8-59
Use **OTRACK** to draw the front view of the base

Step 8. Use **OTRACK** to draw the front view of the base (Figure 8-59), as described next:

Prompt	Response
Type a command:	**Line**
Specify first point:	Move your mouse to the quadrant shown as **P3→** (Figure 8-59) but do not click
	Hold it until the quadrant symbol appears, then move your mouse to **P4→** (do not click) (the dotted line shows the endpoint symbol), then move your mouse back to the vertical dotted tracking line and click
Specify next point or [Undo]:	With **ORTHO** on, move your mouse straight down and type **1 <Enter>**
Specify next point or [Undo]:	With **ORTHO** on, move your mouse to the left and type **26 <Enter>**
Specify next point or [Close Undo]:	With **ORTHO** on, move your mouse straight up, and type **1 <Enter>**
Specify next point or [Close Undo]:	Type **C <Enter>**

Step 9. Use **OTRACK** to draw the right-side view of the table with the **LINE** and **COPY** commands (Figure 8-60). Be sure to get depth dimensions from the top view.

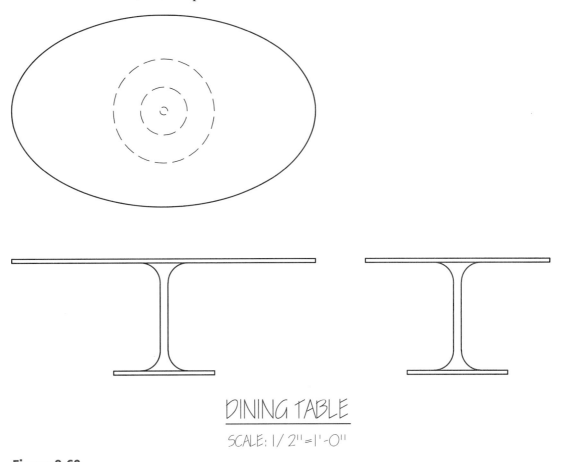

DINING TABLE

SCALE: 1/2"=1'-0"

Figure 8-60
Draw the right-side view using **COPY, LINE,** and **OTRACK**. Complete front and right-side views with a 5" no trim radius and the **TRIM** command

Step 10. Use a **5″**-radius fillet (no trim) and trim to complete front and right-side views.

Step 11. Set **Layer3** current. Label the drawing as shown in Figure 8-55. Add your name, class, and current date in the upper right.

Step 12. Save your drawing in two places.

Step 13. Print the drawing at a scale of **1/2″ = 1′-0″**.

Chapter Summary

This chapter provided you the information necessary to set up and draw interior elevations, sections, and details. The **UCS** and **UCS Icon** commands were used extensively in drawing the elevations. In addition, the **Multileader** command was explored in detail, and point filters and **OTRACK** were used to draw 2D views. Now you have the skills and information necessary to produce elevations, sections, and drawing details that can be used in interior design sales pieces, information sheets, contract documents, and other similar types of documents.

Chapter Test Questions

Multiple Choice

Circle the correct answer.

1. The **W** on the **2D UCS** icon indicates which of the following?
   a. face
   b. view
   c. world
   d. object

Figure 3-61

2. Which of the following angles produces the user-defined pattern shown in Figure 8-61?
   a. 45
   b. 90
   c. 0
   d. 135

3. Which of the following angles produces the user-defined pattern shown in Figure 8-62?
   a. 45
   b. 90
   c. 0
   d. 135

Figure 3-62

4. Which of the following commands can be used to correct a hatch pattern that extends outside a hatch boundary, after it has been exploded?
   a. **ARRAY**
   b. **COPY**
   c. **MOVE**
   d. **TRIM**

5. When the **Noorigin** option of the **UCS Icon** is selected, where is the **UCS Icon** displayed?
   a. The lower left corner of the screen.
   b. It is turned off.
   c. It moves to the new UCS origin.
   d. It rotates.

6. Which of the following tabs is used to set the landing distance of a **multileader**?
   a. Leader Format
   b. Leader Structure
   c. Content
   d. Attachment

7. The **Multileader Collect** command can be used to:

    a. Align leaders
            c. Change a circle to a hexagon

    b. Add leaders
            d. Attach multiple balloons to one leader

8. Which setting allows an image to be mirrored without mirroring the text?

    a. **MIRRTEXT = 1**
            c. **MIRRTEXT = 3**

    b. **MIRRTEXT = 0**
            d. **DTEXT-STYLE = 0**

9. The **STRETCH** command is best used for:

    a. Stretching an object in one direction

    b. Moving an object along attached lines

    c. Shrinking an object on one direction

    d. All of the above

10. Which of the following is an option in the **Boundaries** area of the **Hatch and Gradient** dialog box?

    a. Find boundaries
            c. Remove boundaries

    b. Subtract boundaries
            d. Define boundaries

Matching

Write the number of the correct answer on the line.

a. **UCS** _____

b. **STRETCH** _____

c. **Hatch Editor** _____

d. **HPGAPTOL** _____

e. **Point Filters** _____

1. Appears on the ribbon when you double-click on a hatch pattern.

2. A command used to move entities without removing attached lines

3. A setting that allows a small space in the hatch boundary

4. A method of entering a point by which the X and Y coordinates are given separately

5. A command that is used to move coordinates 0,0 to another point on the drawing

True or False

Circle the correct answer.

1. **True or False:** The **Coordinates** panel is hidden in the **View** tab of the ribbon by default.

2. **True or False:** A **multileader** can be drawn with content first only.

3. **True or False:** You must clearly define the boundary of the area to be hatched when you use the **Add: Select Objects** option of the **Hatch** command.

4. **True or False: Origin** is the name of the **UCS Icon** command option that forces the UCS icon to be displayed at the 0,0 point of the current UCS.

5. **True or False:** Picking any point on an associative 35-line hatch pattern with the **ERASE** command and then pressing **<Enter>** will erase it.

List

1. Five ways of accessing the **UCS** command.

2. Five commands of the **Modify** panel under the **Draw Ribbon** tab.

3. Five options of the **Lengthen** command.

4. Five options of the **Osnap** menu that begin with *M* or *N*.

5. Five options available once the **UCS** command is launched.

6. Five ways of accessing the **Multileader Style** dialog box.

7. Five ways of accessing the **Multileader** command.

8. Five options of the **Multileader Style Manager/Modify** dialog box.

9. Five options under the **Multileader** command.

10. Five options of the **Hatch and Gradient** dialog box.

Questions

1. What is a user coordinate system and how is it used?

2. What are predefined hatch patterns and how are they used?

3. How are point filters and **OTRACK** similar?

4. When would you use multileaders?

5. How were the **STRETCH** and **MIRROR** commands used in this chapter, and how could you use them in the future?

Chapter Projects

Project 8-1: *Detail Drawing of a Bar Rail* [BASIC]

1. Draw the bar rail detail shown in Figure 8-63. Measure the drawing with an architectural 1/2 scale and draw it full size (1:1) using AutoCAD.

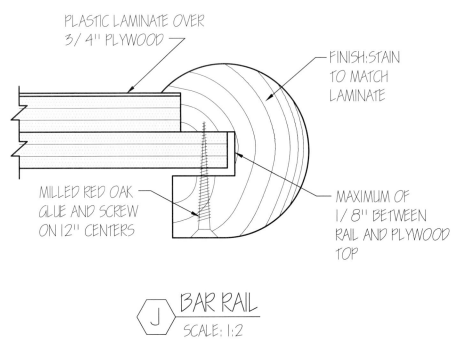

Figure 8-63
Project 8-1: Bar rail detail

2. Set your own drawing limits, grid, and snap. Create your own layers with varying lineweights as needed.

3. Label the drawing as shown in Figure 8-63 in the City Blueprint font. Add your name, class, and the current date in the upper right.

4. Save the drawing in two places and print the drawing at a scale of 1:2.

Project 8-2: *Wheelchair-Accessible Commercial Restrooms Elevation* [INTERMEDIATE]

Figure 8-64 shows the floor plan of the commercial restrooms with the elevations indicated. The line of text at the bottom of Figure 8-65 shows where the **House Designer** drawing is located in the AutoCAD **DesignCenter**. The front view of the toilets, urinals, sinks, grab bars, faucets, and toilet paper holders are blocks contained within this drawing and in **Autodesk Seek** design content online. Just double-click on any of these blocks to activate the **INSERT** command and insert these blocks into your elevation drawing as needed. You may need to modify the sink, and you will have to draw the mirror and paper towel holder.

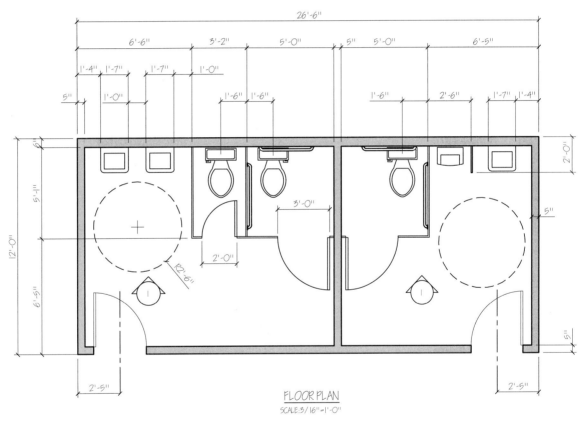

FLOOR PLAN
SCALE:3/16"=1'-0"

Figure 8-64
Project 8-2: Floor plan of the wheelchair-accessible commercial restrooms (scale: 3/16″ = 1′-0″)

Figure 8-65
Project 8-2: **House Designer**
blocks in the **DesignCenter**

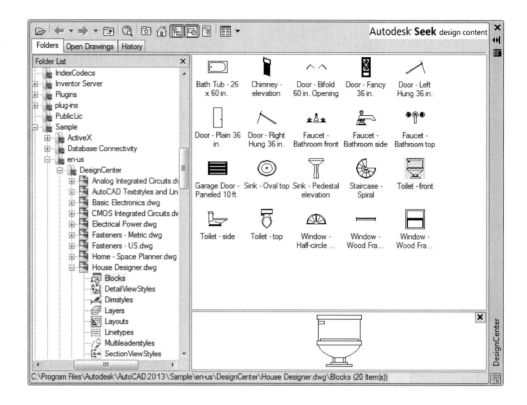

Draw elevation 1 of the commercial wheelchair-accessible restrooms as shown in Figure 8-66. Use the dimensions shown or use an architectural scale of 3/16″ = 1′0″ to measure elevation 1, and draw it full scale without dimensions. Use lineweights to make the drawing more attractive and a solid hatch pattern with a gray color to make the walls solid. Use the same gray color for the layer on which you draw the ceramic tile. When you have completed Project 8-2, your drawing will look similar to Figure 8-66. You may locate drawings of the sinks and urinal that are a little different from those shown on this drawing. If so, use them. Just be sure they are located correctly. Add dimensions as required. Save the drawing in two places and print the drawing to scale.

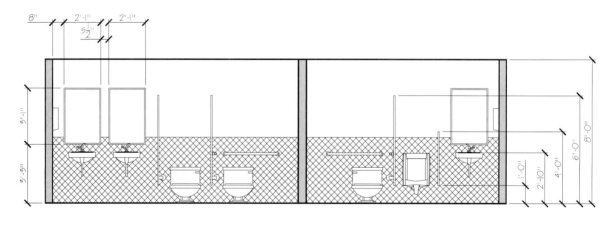

ELEVATION OF COMMERCIAL WHEELCHAIR ACCESSIBLE RESTROOMS
SCALE: 3/16″=1′-0″

Figure 8-66
Project 8-2: Wheelchair-accessible commercial restrooms elevation (scale: 3/16″ = 1′-0″)

Project 8-3: *Drawing a Mirror and Sections of a Mirror from a Sketch* [ADVANCED]

1. Use the dimensions shown to draw the mirror in Figure 8-67 using AutoCAD.

Figure 8-67
Project 8-3: Mirror

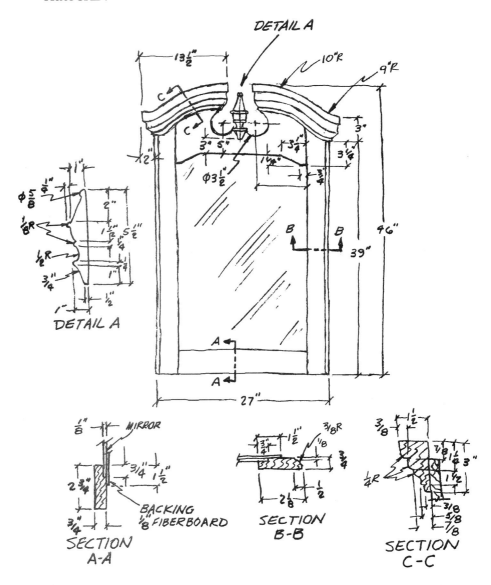

2. Set your own drawing limits, grid, and snap. Create your own layers as needed.

3. Do not place dimensions on this drawing, but do show the cutting plane lines and label them as shown.

4. Do not draw Detail A. This information is shown so you can draw that part.

5. Draw and label sections A-A, B-B, and C-C in the approximate locations shown on the sketch. Use the ANSI31 hatch pattern for the sectional views, or draw splines and array them to show wood. Do not show dimensions.

6. Save the drawing in two places and print the drawing to scale.

Project 8-4, Part 1: *Log Cabin Kitchen Elevation 1* [BASIC]

Figure 8-68 shows the floor plan of the log cabin kitchen with two elevations indicated. The line of text at the bottom of Figure 8-69 shows where the **Kitchen** drawing is located in the AutoCAD **DesignCenter**. The front view of the dishwasher, faucet, range-oven, and refrigerator are blocks contained within this drawing. Just double-click on any of these blocks to activate the **INSERT** command, and insert these blocks into your elevation drawing as needed.

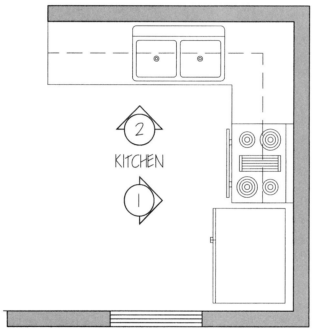

Figure 8-68
Project 8-4: Plan view of the log cabin kitchen

Draw elevation 1 of the log cabin kitchen as shown in Figure 8-70. Use the dimensions shown or use an architectural scale of 1/2″ = 1′0″ to measure elevation 1, and draw it full scale with dimensions. Use lineweights to make the drawing more attractive and a solid hatch pattern with a gray color to make the walls solid.

When you have completed Project 8-4, Part 1, your drawing will look similar to Figure 8-70 with dimensions. Save the drawing in two places and print the drawing to scale.

Project 8-4, Part 2: *Log Cabin Kitchen Elevation 2* [BASIC]

Figure 8-68 shows the floor plan of the log cabin kitchen with arrows indicating the line of sight for two elevations of this room. The line of text at the bottom of Figure 8-69 shows where the **Kitchen** drawing is located in the AutoCAD **DesignCenter**. The front view of the dishwasher, faucet, range-oven, and refrigerator are blocks contained within this drawing. Just double-click on any of these blocks to activate the **INSERT** command, and insert these blocks into your elevation drawing as needed.

Figure 8-69

Project 8-4: **DesignCenter** with the **Kitchen** drawing blocks displayed

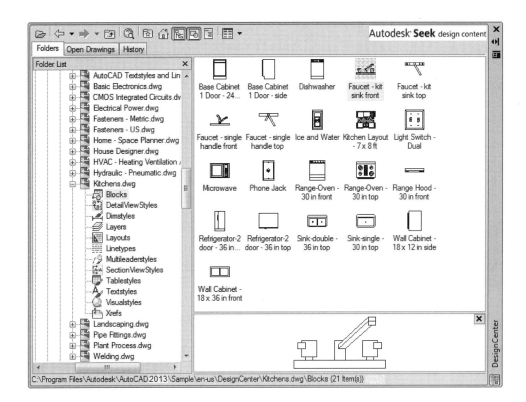

Draw elevation 2 of the log cabin kitchen as shown in Figure 8-71. Use the dimensions shown or use an architectural scale of 1/2″ = 1′0″ to measure elevation 2, and draw it full scale with dimensions. Use lineweights to make the drawing more attractive and a solid hatch pattern with a gray color to make the walls solid.

When you have completed Project 8-4, Part 2, your drawing will look similar to Figure 8-71 with dimensions. Save the drawing in two places and print the drawing to scale.

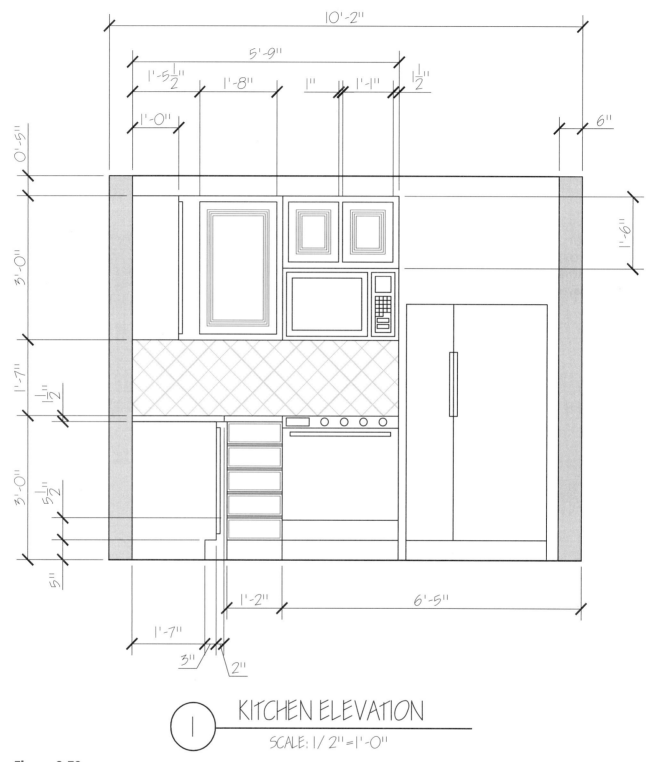

KITCHEN ELEVATION

SCALE: 1/2"=1'-0"

Figure 8-70
Project 8-4, Part 1: Log cabin kitchen elevation 1 (scale: 1/2" = 1'–0")

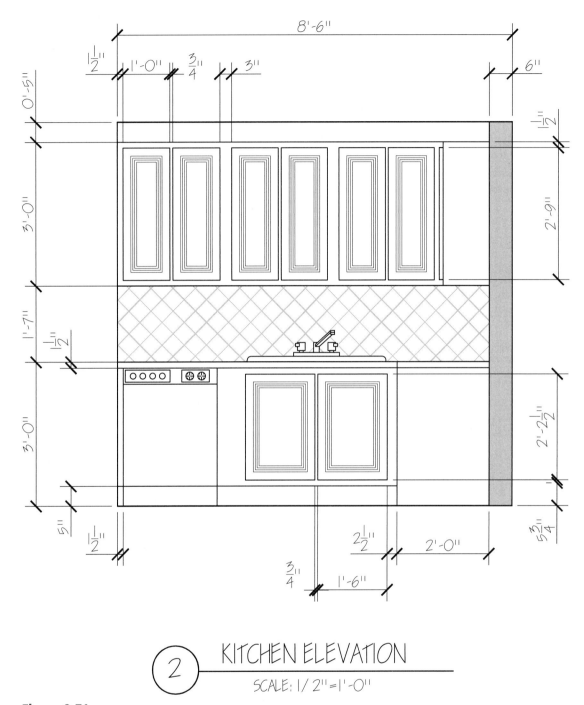

KITCHEN ELEVATION

$\overline{2}$

SCALE: 1/2"=1'-0"

Figure 8-71
Project 8-4, Part 2: Log cabin kitchen elevation 2 (scale: 1/2" = 1'–0")

Project 8-5: *Family Room, House 1 Elevation*
[ADVANCED]

Project 8-5 is an elevation of the family room, house 1, Figure 8-72, Sheet 1. When you have completed Project 8-5, your drawing will look like that figure with dimensions added.

Measure the features in the elevation using the scale indicated and draw them full scale.

Use the dimensions in Figure 8-72, Sheet 2 for some of the details. Add dimensions to the elevation as required. Save the drawing in two places and plot or print the drawing to scale.

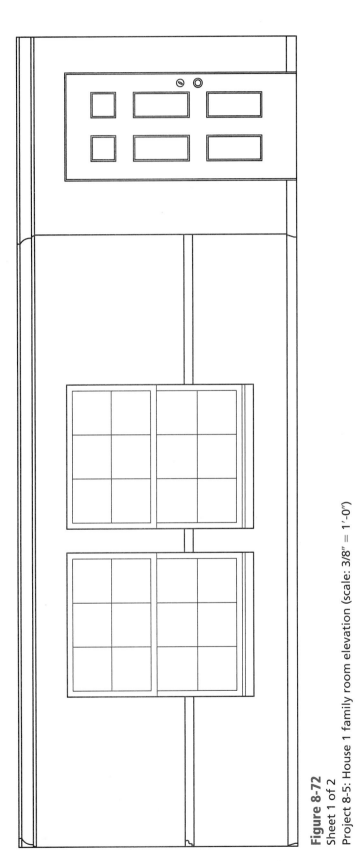

Figure 8-72
Sheet 1 of 2
Project 8-5: House 1 family room elevation (scale: 3/8" = 1'-0")

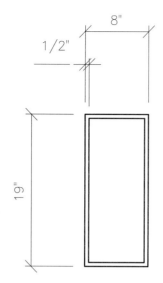

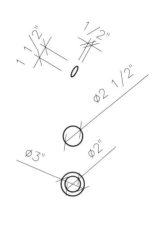

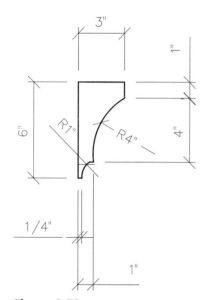

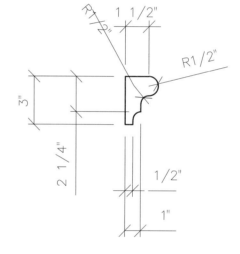

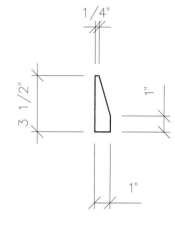

Figure 8-72
Sheet 2 of 2
Dimensions for Project 8-5

Drawing the Furniture Installation Plan, Adding Specifications, and Extracting Data

CHAPTER OBJECTIVES

- Correctly use the following commands and settings:

ATTDIA system variable	**Data Extraction**	**Modify Attribute Global (-ATTEDIT)**	**Synchronize Attributes (ATTSYNC)**
Attribute Display (ATTDISP)	**Define Attributes (ATTDEF)**	**Modify Attribute Single (EATTEDIT)**	**Write Block (WBLOCK)**
Block Attribute Manager (BATTMAN)	**Edit Text (DDEDIT)**	**Properties**	
	Insert	**Quick Properties**	

Introduction

This chapter describes the AutoCAD commands that allow specifications to be added to furnishings and how the specifications are extracted from the drawing. These commands are especially important because they reduce the amount of time it takes to count large amounts of like furniture pieces (with specifications) from the plan. There are many software programs available that can be used with AutoCAD to save even more time. These programs provide furniture symbols already drawn and programs that extract specification information in a form that suits your individual needs. Although you may ultimately combine one of these programs with the AutoCAD program, learning the commands included in this chapter will help you to understand how they interact with AutoCAD.

EXERCISE 9-1
Tenant Space Furniture Installation Plan with Furniture Specifications

When you have completed Exercise 9-1, your drawing will look similar to Figure 9-1.

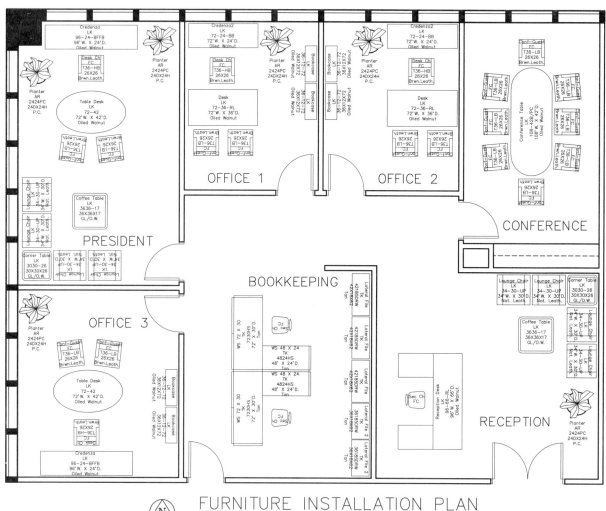

FURNITURE INSTALLATION PLAN
SCALE: 1/8" = 1'-0"

Figure 9-1
Exercise 9-1: Tenant space furniture installation plan with furniture specifications (scale: 1/8" = 1'-0")

> **NOTE**
>
> In **EXERCISE 12-1** and **EXERCISE 12-2** you will freeze layers to make a presentation that displays the dimensioned floor plan, furniture plan, reflected ceiling plan, and voice/data/power plan. This will work only if you have saved **CH6-EXERCISE1**, **CH7-EXERCISE1**, **CH9-EXERCISE1**, and **CH11-EXERCISE1** as a single drawing.

Step 1. Use your workspace to make the following settings:

1. Begin drawing **CH9-EXERCISE1** on the hard drive or network drive by opening existing drawing **CH7-EXERCISE1** and saving it as **CH9-EXERCISE1**.
2. Set **Layer0** current.
3. Freeze layers **a-anno-dims**, **Defpoints**, and **a-anno-area**.

Draw the Furniture Symbols

> **NOTE**
>
> Remember, the furniture and the attributes that are added to the furniture are drawn on **Layer0**, so they assume the characteristics of the layer on which they are inserted.

Step 2. The furniture symbols must be drawn in plan view as shown in Figure 9-2 before you add specifications. Reference the tenant space reception furniture symbols as shown in Figures 9-3, 9-4, 9-5, and 9-6 to draw each piece full scale on your drawing. Pick any open space on your drawing to draw the furniture. Draw each symbol on **Layer0**. Blocks will be made of each symbol, so it does not matter where the furniture is drawn on the plan.

Define Attributes... (ATTDEF)

DEFINE ATTRIBUTES	
Ribbon/ Panel	Insert/ Block Definition
Menu Bar:	Draw/Block/ Define Attributes...
Type a Command:	ATTDEF
Command Alias:	ATT

attribute: An attribute is a label that attaches data to a block. It consists of a tag and a value.

The **Define Attributes...** command allows you to add attributes (furniture specifications) to the furniture symbols drawn in plan view. After the attributes are added, a block is made of the symbol. When the block is inserted into a drawing, the specifications appear on the drawing if they have been defined as visible (attributes can be visible or invisible). You can then extract the attribute information from the drawing using the **Data Extraction...** dialog box.

As shown in Figures 9-3, 9-4, 9-5, and 9-6, each piece of furniture in the tenant space has five *attributes*. An attribute is made up of two parts: the *tag* and the *value*. The tag is used to name the attribute but does not appear on the inserted drawing. It does appear on the drawing while attributes are being defined and before it is made into a block. The tag is used when the attribute information is extracted from the drawing. The attribute tag may contain any characters, but no spaces, and it is automatically converted to uppercase.

The value is the actual specification, such as Reception Desk, LK, 96-66-RL, 96″W × 66″D, and Oiled Walnut. The attribute value may contain any characters, and it may also have spaces. The value appears on the drawing after it is inserted as a block. It appears exactly as it was entered.

There are seven optional modes for the value of **ATTDEF**; these are set at the beginning of the attribute definition:

Invisible: This value is not displayed on the screen when the block is inserted. You may want to use the **Invisible** mode for pricing, or you may want to make some attributes invisible so that the drawing does not become cluttered.

Constant: This value is fixed and cannot be changed. For example, if the same chair is used throughout a project but the fabric varies, then

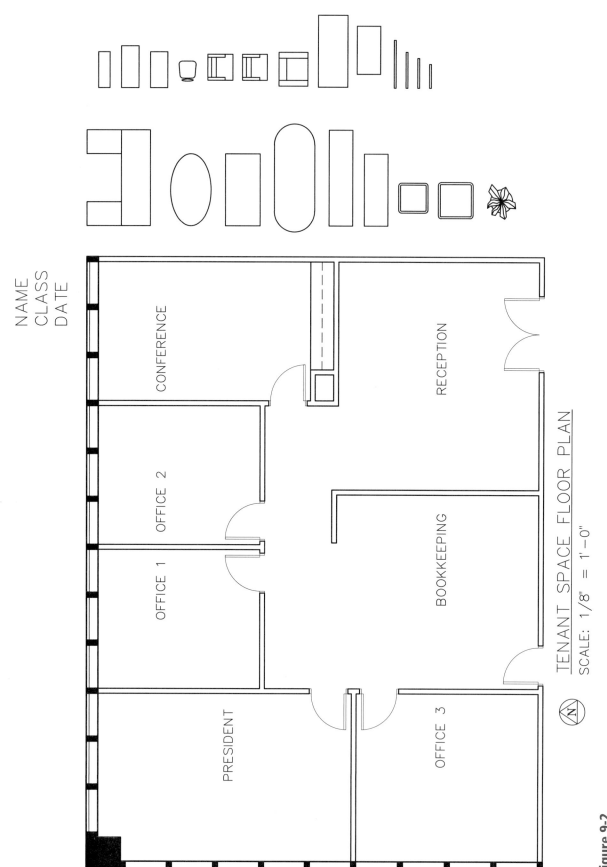

NAME
CLASS
DATE

CONFERENCE

OFFICE 2

OFFICE 1

PRESIDENT

RECEPTION

BOOKKEEPING

OFFICE 3

TENANT SPACE FLOOR PLAN
SCALE: 1/8" = 1'-0"

Ⓝ

Figure 9-2
Draw furniture symbols outside (or inside) the tenant space floor plan (scale: 1/8" = 1'-0")

MAKE SURE YOU DRAW THE FURNITURE AND THE ATTRIBUTES ON THE 0 LAYER

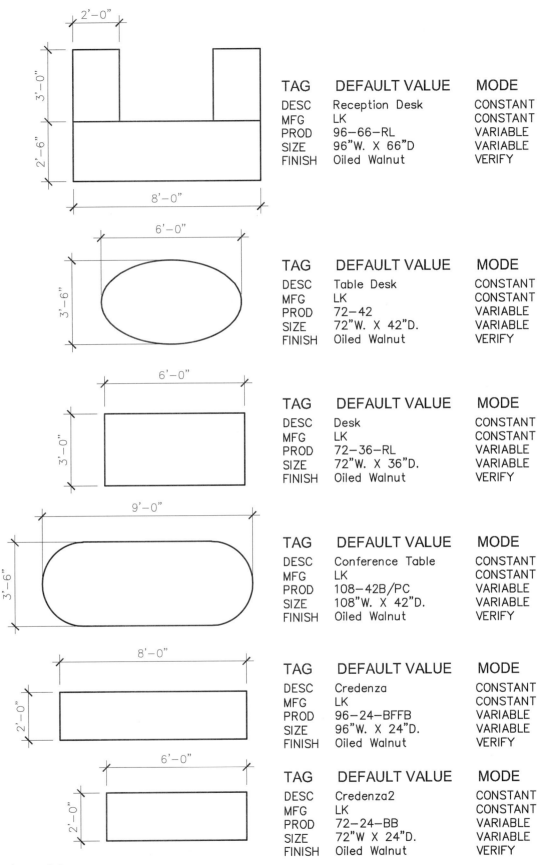

TAG	DEFAULT VALUE	MODE
DESC	Reception Desk	CONSTANT
MFG	LK	CONSTANT
PROD	96—66—RL	VARIABLE
SIZE	96"W. X 66"D	VARIABLE
FINISH	Oiled Walnut	VERIFY

TAG	DEFAULT VALUE	MODE
DESC	Table Desk	CONSTANT
MFG	LK	CONSTANT
PROD	72—42	VARIABLE
SIZE	72"W. X 42"D.	VARIABLE
FINISH	Oiled Walnut	VERIFY

TAG	DEFAULT VALUE	MODE
DESC	Desk	CONSTANT
MFG	LK	CONSTANT
PROD	72—36—RL	VARIABLE
SIZE	72"W. X 36"D.	VARIABLE
FINISH	Oiled Walnut	VERIFY

TAG	DEFAULT VALUE	MODE
DESC	Conference Table	CONSTANT
MFG	LK	CONSTANT
PROD	108—42B/PC	VARIABLE
SIZE	108"W. X 42"D.	VARIABLE
FINISH	Oiled Walnut	VERIFY

TAG	DEFAULT VALUE	MODE
DESC	Credenza	CONSTANT
MFG	LK	CONSTANT
PROD	96—24—BFFB	VARIABLE
SIZE	96"W. X 24"D.	VARIABLE
FINISH	Oiled Walnut	VERIFY

TAG	DEFAULT VALUE	MODE
DESC	Credenza2	CONSTANT
MFG	LK	CONSTANT
PROD	72—24—BB	VARIABLE
SIZE	72"W X 24"D.	VARIABLE
FINISH	Oiled Walnut	VERIFY

Figure 9-3
Tenant space furniture symbols with specifications (scale: 1/4″ = 1′-0″)

MAKE SURE YOU DRAW THE FURNITURE
AND THE ATTRIBUTES ON THE 0 LAYER

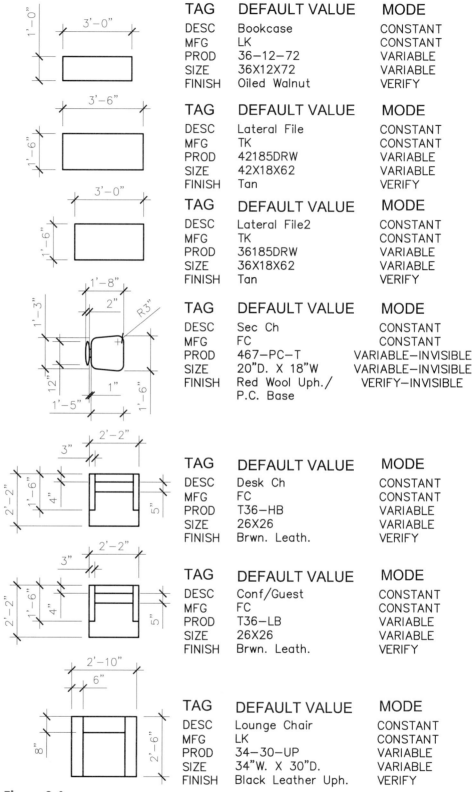

TAG	DEFAULT VALUE	MODE
DESC	Bookcase	CONSTANT
MFG	LK	CONSTANT
PROD	36—12—72	VARIABLE
SIZE	36X12X72	VARIABLE
FINISH	Oiled Walnut	VERIFY

TAG	DEFAULT VALUE	MODE
DESC	Lateral File	CONSTANT
MFG	TK	CONSTANT
PROD	42185DRW	VARIABLE
SIZE	42X18X62	VARIABLE
FINISH	Tan	VERIFY

TAG	DEFAULT VALUE	MODE
DESC	Lateral File2	CONSTANT
MFG	TK	CONSTANT
PROD	36185DRW	VARIABLE
SIZE	36X18X62	VARIABLE
FINISH	Tan	VERIFY

TAG	DEFAULT VALUE	MODE
DESC	Sec Ch	CONSTANT
MFG	FC	CONSTANT
PROD	467—PC—T	VARIABLE—INVISIBLE
SIZE	20"D. X 18"W	VARIABLE—INVISIBLE
FINISH	Red Wool Uph./ P.C. Base	VERIFY—INVISIBLE

TAG	DEFAULT VALUE	MODE
DESC	Desk Ch	CONSTANT
MFG	FC	CONSTANT
PROD	T36—HB	VARIABLE
SIZE	26X26	VARIABLE
FINISH	Brwn. Leath.	VERIFY

TAG	DEFAULT VALUE	MODE
DESC	Conf/Guest	CONSTANT
MFG	FC	CONSTANT
PROD	T36—LB	VARIABLE
SIZE	26X26	VARIABLE
FINISH	Brwn. Leath.	VERIFY

TAG	DEFAULT VALUE	MODE
DESC	Lounge Chair	CONSTANT
MFG	LK	CONSTANT
PROD	34—30—UP	VARIABLE
SIZE	34"W. X 30"D.	VARIABLE
FINISH	Black Leather Uph.	VERIFY

Figure 9-4
Tenant space furniture symbols with specifications (scale: 1/4″ = 1′-0″)

MAKE SURE YOU DRAW THE FURNITURE
AND THE ATTRIBUTES ON THE 0 LAYER

TAG	DEFAULT VALUE	MODE
DESC	Panel 48	CONSTANT–INVISIBLE
MFG	TK	CONSTANT–INVISIBLE
PROD	T4812TS	VARIABLE–INVISIBLE
SIZE	48" X 2" 62"H	VARIABLE–INVISIBLE
FINISH	Rose Fabric	VERIFY–INVISIBLE

TAG	DEFAULT VALUE	MODE
DESC	Panel 36	CONSTANT–INVISIBLE
MFG	TK	CONSTANT–INVISIBLE
PROD	T3612TS	VARIABLE–INVISIBLE
SIZE	48" X 2" 62"H	VARIABLE–INVISIBLE
FINISH	Rose Fabric	VERIFY–INVISIBLE

TAG	DEFAULT VALUE	MODE
DESC	Panel 30	CONSTANT–INVISIBLE
MFG	TK	CONSTANT–INVISIBLE
PROD	T3012TS	VARIABLE–INVISIBLE
SIZE	48" X 2" 62"H	VARIABLE–INVISIBLE
FINISH	Rose Fabric	VERIFY–INVISIBLE

TAG	DEFAULT VALUE	MODE
DESC	Panel 24	CONSTANT–INVISIBLE
MFG	TK	CONSTANT–INVISIBLE
PROD	T2412TS	VARIABLE–INVISIBLE
SIZE	24" X 2" 62"H	VARIABLE–INVISIBLE
FINISH	Rose Fabric	VERIFY–INVISIBLE

TAG	DEFAULT VALUE	MODE
DESC	WS 72 X 30	CONSTANT
MFG	TK	CONSTANT
PROD	7230HS	VARIABLE
SIZE	72" X 30"D.	VARIABLE
FINISH	Tan.	VERIFY

TAG	DEFAULT VALUE	MODE
DESC	WS 48 X 24	CONSTANT
MFG	TK	CONSTANT
PROD	4824HS	VARIABLE
SIZE	48" X 24"D.	VARIABLE
FINISH	Tan.	VERIFY

Figure 9-5

Tenant space furniture symbols with specifications (scale: 1/4″ = 1′-0″)

the furniture manufacturer value of the chair will be constant, but the finish value will vary. A constant value cannot be edited.

Verify: This mode allows the value to be variable and allows you to check (verify) the value you have entered. Changes in the value may be entered as needed when the block is inserted.

Preset: This mode allows the value to be variable. It is similar to **Constant**, but unlike a constant value, the preset value can be changed.

Variable: If none of the above modes is selected, the value is variable. The **Variable** mode allows the value to be changed.

Figure 9-6
Tenant space furniture symbols with specifications (scale: 1/4″ = 1'-0″)

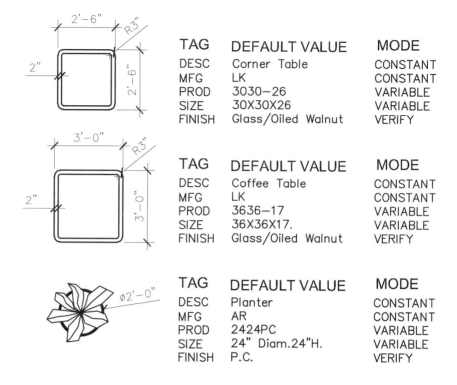

MAKE SURE YOU DRAW THE FURNITURE AND THE ATTRIBUTES ON THE 0 LAYER

TAG	DEFAULT VALUE	MODE
DESC	Corner Table	CONSTANT
MFG	LK	CONSTANT
PROD	3030-26	VARIABLE
SIZE	30X30X26	VARIABLE
FINISH	Glass/Oiled Walnut	VERIFY

TAG	DEFAULT VALUE	MODE
DESC	Coffee Table	CONSTANT
MFG	LK	CONSTANT
PROD	3636-17	VARIABLE
SIZE	36X36X17.	VARIABLE
FINISH	Glass/Oiled Walnut	VERIFY

TAG	DEFAULT VALUE	MODE
DESC	Planter	CONSTANT
MFG	AR	CONSTANT
PROD	2424PC	VARIABLE
SIZE	24" Diam.24"H.	VARIABLE
FINISH	P.C.	VERIFY

Lock Position: This option locks the attribute location inside the block. This is useful when dynamic blocks are used.

Multiple Lines: This option allows the attribute value to contain multiple lines of text. When this option is selected, you can specify a boundary width for the attribute.

Step 3. Keep **Layer0** current.

Step 4. Create a new text style named **Attribute** with the simplex font. Do not make it annotative. Set it current.

Step 5. Zoom in on the reception desk.

Constant Attribute

Step 6. Use **Define Attributes...** to define the attributes of the reception desk. Make the first two attributes of the reception desk constant (Figure 9-7), as described next:

Prompt	Response
Type a command:	**Define Attributes...** (or type **ATT <Enter>**)
The **Attribute Definition** dialog box Appears (Figure 9-7):	Click **Constant** (so a check appears in that **Mode** check box)
The **Prompt:** text box is grayed (if the attribute is constant, there can be no prompt).	Type **DESC** in the **Tag:** box

Figure 9-7
Use **Define Attributes...** to define the first constant attribute

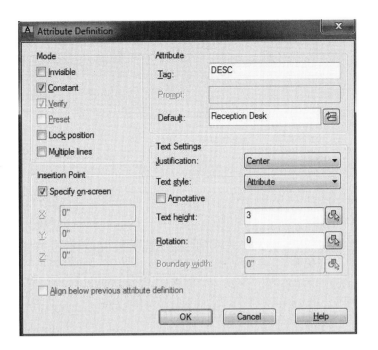

Prompt	Response
	Type **Reception Desk** in the **Default:** (value) box
	Click the down arrow in the **Justification** box and click **Center**
	Text style: **Attribute**
	Type **3** in the **Text height:** box

All other parts of the dialog box should be as shown in Figure 9-7.

> **Annotative:** An attribute can be annotative. The annotative attribute is always the same size when plotted, regardless of the scale of the plotted drawing, if the annotation scale is the same as the plot scale. In this chapter we do not annotate the attributes because the furniture is drawn full scale, and we want the plotted attribute size to change depending on the plotted scale.

Prompt	Response
	Click **OK**
Specify start point:	**P1→** (Figure 9-8)
The first attribute is complete; the attribute tag appears on the drawing.	
Type a command:	**<Enter>** (repeat **ATTDEF**)

Figure 9-8
Specify the start point of the first attribute

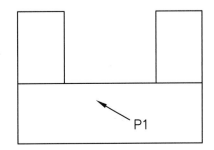

Prompt	Response
The **Attribute Definition** dialog box appears:	**Constant** is checked already; if not, click **Constant** (so a check appears in that **Mode** check box)
The **Prompt:** text box is grayed (if the attribute is constant, there can be no prompt).	Type **MFG** in the **Tag:** box Type **LK** in the **Default:** (value) box Click **Align below previous attribute definition** (so a check appears in that **Mode** check box)

All other parts of the dialog box should be as shown in Figure 9-9. Notice that the **Insertion Point** and **Text Settings** areas are grayed when **Align below previous attribute definition** is checked.

Prompt	Response
	Click **OK**
The second attribute is complete; the attribute tag appears on the drawing.	

Figure 9-9
Define the second **Constant** attribute

Variable Attribute

Step 7. Make the third and fourth attributes variable and the fifth one verify as described next.

Prompt	Response
Type a command:	**<Enter>** (repeat **ATTDEF**)
The **Attribute Definition** dialog box appears:	Clear all the checks in the **Mode** area (the third attribute is variable)
The **Prompt:** text box is no longer grayed (this attribute is variable, so a prompt is needed).	Type **PROD** in the **Tag:** box

Prompt	Response
	Type **Enter product number** in the **Prompt:** box
	Type **96-66-RL** in the **Default:** (value) box
	Click **Align below previous attribute definition** (so a check appears in that **Mode** check box)

The dialog box should be as shown in Figure 9-10.

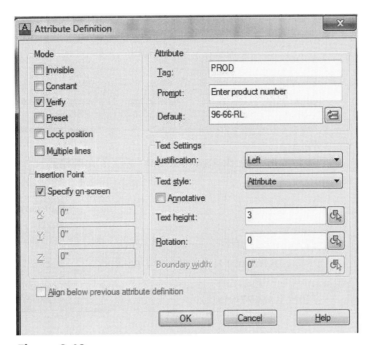

Figure 9-10
Define the third attribute and make it **Variable**

Prompt	Response
	Click **OK**
The third attribute is complete; the attribute tag appears on the drawing.	
Type a command:	**<Enter>** (repeat **ATTDEF**)
The **Attribute Definition** dialog box appears:	
This attribute also is variable, so there should be no checks in the **Mode** boxes.	
	Type **SIZE** in the **Tag:** box
	Type **Enter size** in the **Prompt:** box
	Type **96″ W × 66″ D** in the **Default:** (value) box
	Click **Align below previous attribute definition** (so a check appears in that **Mode** check box)

The dialog box should be as shown in Figure 9-11.

Figure 9-11
Define the fourth attribute and make it **Variable**

Prompt	Response
	Click **OK**
The fourth attribute is complete; the attribute tag appears on the drawing.	
Type a command:	**<Enter>** (repeat **ATTDEF**)

Verify Attribute

Prompt	Response
The **Attribute Definition** dialog box appears: This attribute also is variable and should be one that is verified (so you have two chances to make sure it is correct).	Click **Verify** in the **Mode** check box. Type **FINISH** in the **Tag:** box Type **Enter finish** in the **Prompt:** box Type **Oiled Walnut** in the **Default:** (value) box Click **Align below previous attribute definition** (so a check appears in that **Mode** check box)

The dialog box should be as shown in Figure 9-12.

Prompt	Response
	Click **OK**
The fifth attribute is complete; that attribute tag appears on the drawing.	

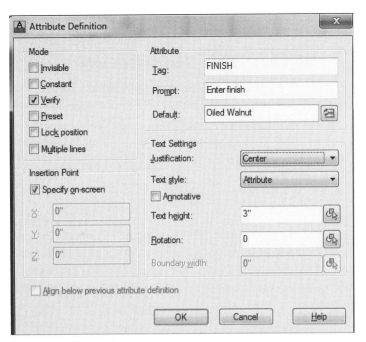

Figure 9-12
Define the fifth attribute and make it a **Verify** one

When you have completed defining the five attributes, your drawing of the reception desk will look similar to the desk in Figure 9-13.

Figure 9-13
Reception desk with attribute tags

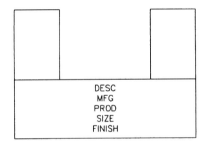

> **NOTE**
>
> If you are not happy with the location of the attribute tags, use the **MOVE** command to relocate them before using the **BLOCK** command.

EDIT TEXT	
Text Toolbar:	
Menu Bar:	Modify/Object Text/Edit
Type a Command:	DDEDIT
Command Alias:	ED

Edit Text (DDEDIT)

Did you make a mistake while typing the attribute tag, attribute prompt, or default attribute value? The **Edit Text** command allows you to use the **Edit Attribute Definition** dialog box (Figure 9-14) to correct any typing mistakes you may have made while defining the attributes. Type **ED <Enter>**, then click the tag to activate the **Edit Attribute Definition** dialog box. The **Edit Text** prompt is *Select an annotation object or [Undo]:*. When you pick a tag, the **Edit Attribute Definition** dialog box appears and allows you to change the attribute tag, prompt, or default value for a variable, verify, or

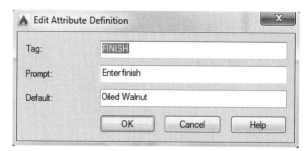

Figure 9-14
Edit Attribute Definition dialog box

preset attribute. The tag and the default (actually the value) can be changed for a constant attribute; adding a prompt for an attribute defined as constant does not change the attribute mode, and the prompt does not appear.

QP (Quick Properties)

When the **QP (Quick Properties)** toggle is **ON** in the status bar, the **Quick Properties** palette is displayed when you click on an attribute tag. The **Quick Properties** palette is similar to Edit Text and can also be used to view and change an attribute tag's color, layer, text style, and height (Figure 9-15).

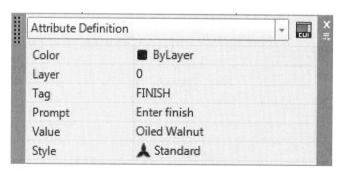

Figure 9-15
Quick Properties palette

Properties

The **Properties** palette (Figure 9-16) allows you to change any property that can be changed.

WBLOCK the Furniture with Attributes Symbol

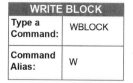

WRITE BLOCK	
Type a Command:	WBLOCK
Command Alias:	W

Step 8. Use the **Write Block** command (Figure 9-17) to save the reception desk as a wblock (a drawing). Save the reception desk to the folder of your choice. Name the wblock **Reception Desk**. Use the insertion base point as shown in Figure 9-18. Orient the desk as shown in Figure 9-18.

Figure 9-16
Properties palette

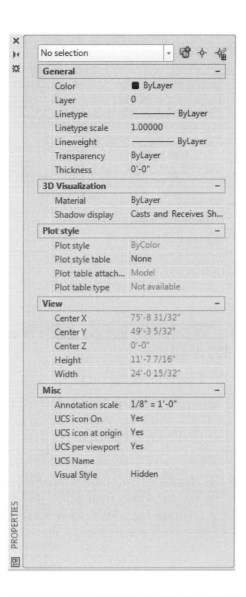

Figure 9-17
Write Block dialog box

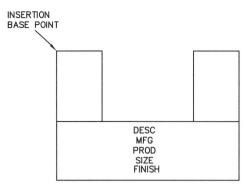

INSERTION
BASE POINT

DESC
MFG
PROD
SIZE
FINISH

Figure 9-18
Save the reception desk as a wblock (a drawing) to the folder named **Blocks**

INSERT BLOCK	
Ribbon/ Panel	Block/ Insert
Draw Toolbar:	
Menu Bar:	Insert/ Block
Type a Command:	INSERT
Command Alias:	I

Insert the Wblock with Attributes into the Drawing

Step 9. Set the **i-furn** layer current.

Step 10. Type **ATTDIA <Enter>** and set **ATTDIA** to **1**. With **ATTDIA** set to **1**, the **Edit Attributes** dialog box is used for the attributes. When **ATTDIA** is set to **0**, the command prompts are used.

Step 11. Use the **INSERT** command to insert the Reception Desk wblock into the tenant space floor plan. Use **From** (on the **Osnap** menu) to help position the block, as described next:

Prompt	Response
Type a command:	**INSERT** (or type **I <Enter>**)
The **Insert** dialog box appears:	Click **Browse...**
The **Select Drawing File** dialog box appears:	Locate and click the **Reception Desk** file
	Click **Open**
The **Insert** dialog box appears with **Reception Desk** in the **Name:** box:	Place a check mark in the two **Specify On-screen** boxes for **Insertion point** and **Rotation** (Figure 9-19). Click **OK**
Specify insertion point or [Basepoint Scale X Y Z Rotate]:	Type **FRO <enter>**
Base point:	**Osnap-Endpoint**
of	**P1→** (Figure 9-20)
<Offset>:	Type **@24,30 <Enter>**
Specify rotation angle <0>:	Type **90 <Enter>**
The **Edit Attributes** dialog box appears (Figure 9-21):	Change anything that needs to be changed—then click **OK**

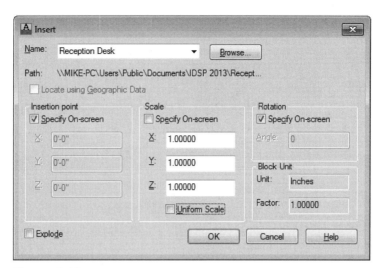

Figure 9-19
Insert dialog box

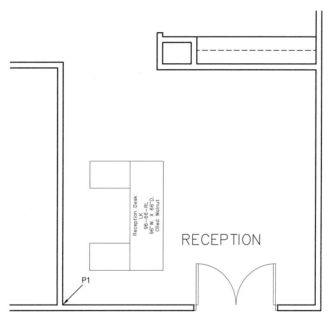

Reception Desk
LK
96-66-RL
96"W. X. 66"D.
Oiled Walnut

P1

RECEPTION

Figure 9-20
Use the **INSERT** command to insert the reception desk block into the tenant space floor plan

Complete the Tenant Space Furniture Installation Plan

Step 12. Keep **Layer0** current.

Step 13. Use **Define Attributes...** to define the five attributes for each of the remaining furniture symbol drawings. Refer to Figures 9-3, 9-4, 9-5, and 9-6 to determine the attribute tag, default value, and mode for each symbol. Use the same text settings for all attributes, as shown in Figures 9-7, 9-9, 9-10, 9-11, and 9-12.

Figure 9-21
Edit Attributes dialog box

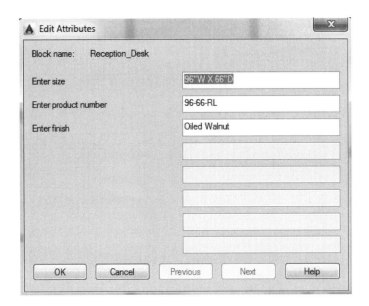

Step 14. Use the **Write Block** command to wblock each of the furniture symbol drawings into a folder using the **DESC VALUE** as the wblock drawing name. Select an insertion base point that is helpful in positioning the block when you insert it into the drawing. Refer to Figures 9-3, 9-4, 9-5, and 9-6, for example:

DESC VALUE	WBLOCK NAME
Reception Desk	Reception Desk
Table Desk	Table Desk

Step 15. Use the **INSERT** command to insert the remaining furniture symbols into the tenant space furniture installation plan (Figure 9-22). Locate the furniture approximately as shown. Once a block is inserted, it can be copied or moved to a different location.

Some of the values that appeared on the corner table are too long; they go outside the table symbol. These will be fixed next.

Edit Attribute, Single...

The **Edit Attribute, Single...** command uses the **Enhanced Attribute Editor** dialog box (Figure 9-23) to edit **Variable, Verify**, and **Preset Attributes** values of each inserted block one at a time. Attributes defined with the **Constant** mode cannot be edited.

Step 16. Use the **Edit Attribute, Single...** command to edit the values on the inserted corner table, as described next:

Prompt	Response
Type a command:	**Edit Attribute...** (or type **EATTEDIT** **<Enter>**)
Select a block:	Pick any place on the corner table

EDIT ATTRIBUTES SINGLE	
Ribbon/ Panel	Insert/Block/ Edit Attribute
ModifyII Toolbar:	
Menu Bar:	Modify/Object/ Attribute/ Single
Type a Command:	EATTEDIT

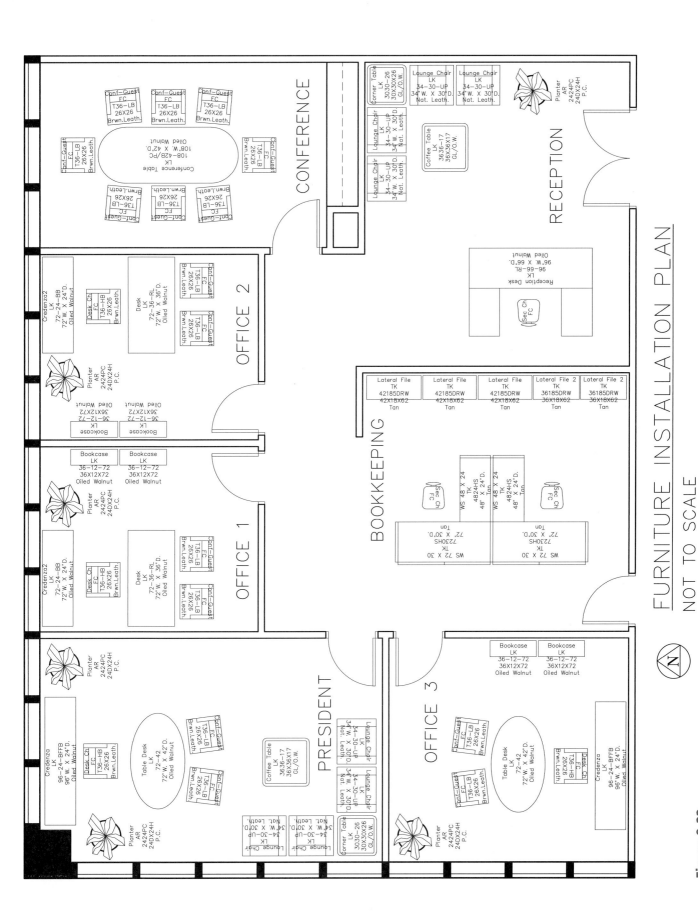

FURNITURE INSTALLATION PLAN
NOT TO SCALE

Figure 9-22
Tenant space furniture installation plan

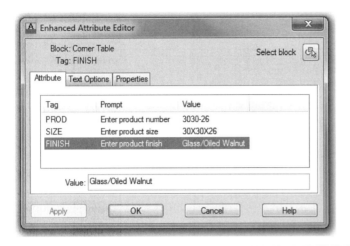

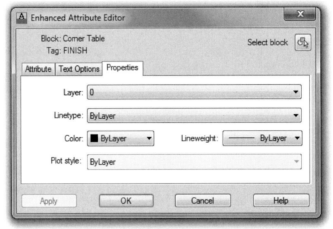

Figure 9-23
Enhanced Attribute Editor dialog box

Prompt	Response
The **Enhanced Attribute Editor** dialog box appears (Figure 9-23):	Use the dialog box to change the **FINISH** value to **GL/O.W.** Highlight the attribute, then change the value in the **Value:** text box
	Click **Apply**
	Click **OK**

The values that appear on the corner table now fit within the table symbol (Figure 9-24).

Edit Attribute, Global

The **Edit Attribute, Global** command uses prompts to edit inserted attribute values. Constant values cannot be edited.

The **Edit Attribute, Global** prompts allow you to narrow the value selection by entering a specific block name, tag specification, and value specification.

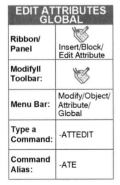

EDIT ATTRIBUTES GLOBAL	
Ribbon/ Panel	Insert/Block/ Edit Attribute
ModifyII Toolbar:	
Menu Bar:	Modify/Object/ Attribute/ Global
Type a Command:	-ATTEDIT
Command Alias:	-ATE

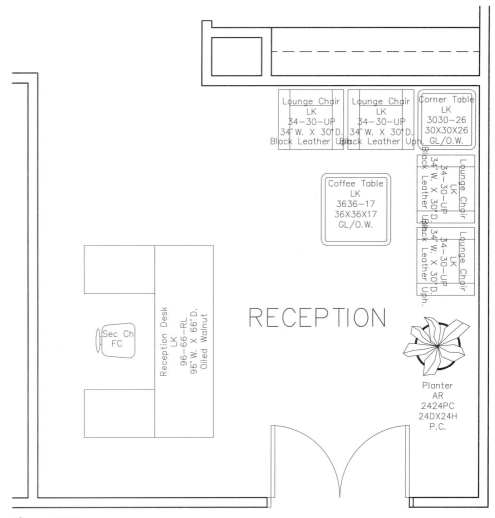

Figure 9-24
Tenant space reception area (scale: 1/4″ = 1′-0″)

Only visible attributes can be edited when you respond with **Yes** to the prompt *Edit attributes one at a time?*. If you respond with **No** to the prompt, visible and invisible attribute value text strings can be edited.

Let's use the **Edit Attribute, Global** command to edit a value on the eight lounge chairs all at once.

Step 17. Use the **Edit Attributes** command to edit the text string of the FINISH value on all the lounge chairs at once, as described next:

Prompt	Response
Type a command:	**Edit Attributes** (or type **-ATTEDIT** **<Enter>**) (be sure to include the dash)
Edit attributes one at a time? [Yes No] <Y>	Type **N <Enter>**
Edit only attributes visible on screen? [Yes No] <Y>	**<Enter>**
Enter block name specification <*>:	Type **Lounge Chair <Enter>**
Enter attribute tag specification <*>:	Type **FINISH <Enter>**
Enter attribute value specification <*>:	Type **Black Leather Uph. <Enter>**

Prompt	Response
Select Attributes:	Click the Black Leather Uph. attribute on all four chairs in the reception area and the four lounge chairs in the president's office **<Enter>**

8 attributes selected.

Enter string to change:	Type **Black Leather Uph. <Enter>**
Enter new string:	Type **Nat. Leath. <Enter>**

Type and enter the block name, tag, and value exactly. You may also enter **No** in response to the prompt *Edit only attributes visible on screen?* and you may also change invisible attribute values.

> **TIP**
>
> When the **QP (Quick Properties)** toggle is **ON** in the status bar, the **Quick Properties** palette is displayed when you click on an inserted block's attribute value. The **Quick Properties** palette can be used to view and change an inserted block's Values, Layer, Name, and Rotation, individually or globally. The **Properties** palette allows you to change any property that can be changed.

Attribute Display (ATTDISP)

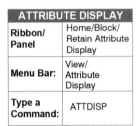

ATTRIBUTE DISPLAY	
Ribbon/ Panel	Home/Block/ Retain Attribute Display
Menu Bar:	View/ Attribute Display
Type a Command:	ATTDISP

The **Attribute Display** (**ATTDISP**) command allows you to turn on the invisible attributes of the secretarial chair. The prompt is *Enter attribute visibility setting [Normal ON OFF] <Normal>:*.

ON: Pick **ON** to make the invisible attributes appear. Try this, and you will be able to see the invisible attributes of the secretarial chair.

OFF: Pick **OFF** to make all the attributes on the drawing invisible. Try this, and you will see that all the attributes are not visible.

Normal: Pick **Normal** to make visible attributes defined as **Visible** and to make invisible attributes defined as **Invisible**. Set **Normal** as the default.

Redefining an Inserted Block with Attributes Using the BLOCK Command

As described in Chapter 6, you can redefine a block using the **BLOCK** command. When a block that has attributes assigned is redefined using the **BLOCK** command, previous insertions of the block are affected as follows:

1 Old constant attributes are lost and are replaced by new constant attributes, if any.

2 Variable attributes remain unchanged, even if the new block definition does not include those attributes.

3 New variable attributes are not added.

Future insertions of the block will use the new attributes. The previous insertions of the block must be erased and inserted again to use the new attributes.

BLOCK ATTRIBUTE MANAGER	
Ribbon/ Panel	Home/Block/ Attribute, Block Attribute Manager...
Ribbon/ Panel	Insert/Block Definition/ Attribute, Block Attribute Manager...
Toolbar:	Modify II/ Block Attribute Manager...
Type a Command:	BATTMAN

Block Attribute Manager (BATTMAN)

The **Block Attribute Manager** allows you to locate blocks in the drawing and edit attributes within those blocks in the current drawing. You can also remove attributes from blocks and change the order in which you are prompted for attribute values when inserting a block (Figure 9-25).

Figure 9-25
Block Attribute Manager

Synchronize Attributes (ATTSYNC)

SYNCHRONIZE ATTRIBUTES	
Ribbon/ Panel	Home/Block/ Synchronize Attributes
Ribbon/ Panel	Insert/Block Definition/ Synchronize Attributes
Toolbar:	Modify II/ Synchronize Attributes
Type a Command:	ATTSYNC

When a block has been redefined (for example, the shape and attributes) using the **BLOCK** or **BEDIT** command, the redefined symbol or shape changes in all existing instances of the redefined block. The attributes do not change. The **Synchronize Attributes** command allows you to select each block whose attributes you want to update to the current redefined attributes.

Step 18. Change the underlined title text to read as shown in Figure 9-26.

Step 19. When you have completed Exercise 9-1, save your work in at least two places.

Step 20. Print Exercise 9-1 to scale.

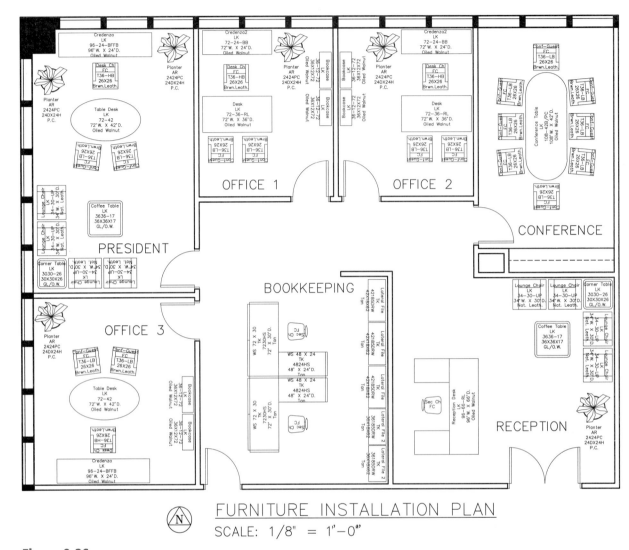

FURNITURE INSTALLATION PLAN

SCALE: 1/8" = 1'-0"

Figure 9-26

Tenant space furniture installation plan with furniture specifications (scale: 1/8" = 1'-0")

EXERCISE 9-2
Extracting Attributes from the Tenant Space Furniture Installation Plan

When you have completed Exercise 9-2, your drawing will look similar to Figure 9-27.

Step 1. Begin drawing **CH9-EXERCISE2** on the hard drive or network drive by opening the existing drawing **CH9-EXERCISE1** and saving it as **CH9-EXERCISE2**.

Step 2. Set layer **a-anno-text** current.

Figure 9-27
Exercise 9-2 complete

Chapter 9

FURNITURE TOTALS

Count	Name	DESC	FINISH	MFG	PROD	SIZE
1	Panel 48	Panel 48	Rose Fabric	TK	T4812TS	48" X 2" X 62" H.
1	Reception Desk	Reception Desk	Oiled Walnut	LK	96-66-RL	96"W. X 66"D.
1	Conference Table	Conference Table	Oiled Walnut	LK	108-42B/PC	108"W. X 42"D.
2	Corner Table	Corner Table	GL/O.W.	LK	3030-26	30X30X26
2	Coffee Table	Coffee Table	GL/O.W.	LK	3636-17	36X36X17
2	WS 72 X 30	WS 72 X 30	Tan	TK	7230HS	72" X 30"D.
2	Panel 24	Panel 24	Rose Fabric	TK	T2412TS	24" X 2" X 62" H.
2	WS 48 X 24	WS 48 X 24	Tan	TK	4824HS	48" X 24"D.
2	Desk	Desk	Oiled Walnut	LK	72-36-RL	72"W. X 36"D.
2	Table Desk	Table Desk	Oiled Walnut	LK	72-42	72"W. X 42"D.
2	Credenza	Credenza	Oiled Walnut	LK	96-24-BFFB	96"W. X 24"D.
2	Lateral File 2	Lateral File 2	Tan	TK	36185DRW	36X18X62
2	Credenza2	Credenza2	Oiled Walnut	LK	72-24-BB	72"W. X 24"D.
3	Panel 30	Panel 30	Rose Fabric	TK	T3012TS	30" X 2" X 62" H.
3	Lateral File	Lateral File	Tan	TK	42185DRW	42X18X62
3	Sec Ch	Sec Ch	Red Wool Uph./P.C. Base	FC	467-PC-T	20"D X 18"W
4	Panel 36	Panel 36	Rose Fabric	TK	T3612TS	36" X 2" X 62" H.
4	Desk Ch	Desk Ch	Brwn.Leath.	FC	T36-HB	26X26
6	Planter	Planter	P.C.	AR	2424PC	24DX24H
6	Bookcase	Bookcase	Oiled Walnut	LK	36-12-72	36X12X72
8	Lounge Chair	Lounge Chair	Nat. Leath.	LK	34-30-UP	34"W. X 30"D.
16	Conf-Guest	Conf-Guest	Brwn.Leath.	FC	T36-LB	26X26

Step 3. Prepare the drawing to accept the extracted attributes in a tabular form as follows:

1. Make a new layout using the **Create Layout** wizard (on the **Insert** menu or key-in **LayoutWizard** and **<ENTER>**):

Begin:	Name it **Furniture Totals**
Printer:	Select a printer
Paper Size:	**Letter (8.5″ × 11″)**
Orientation:	**Landscape**
Title Block:	**None**
Define Viewports:	**Single**
Viewport Scale:	**1:1**
Pick Location:	Click **Next>**
Finish:	Click **Finish**

2. Erase the viewport border created on the new layout so this layout will contain nothing but the table with the extracted attributes (Figure 9-27).
3. Make sure the **Furniture Totals** layout tab is selected, to continue.

Data Extraction...

The **Data Extraction** wizard can be used to produce a parts list or bill of materials directly from a drawing that contains blocks with attributes. The drawing you made in this chapter is an excellent example of this type of drawing. With the **Data Extraction** wizard, you can extract existing attributes and create a table as described in this exercise.

Step 4. Extract attributes from this drawing using the **Data Extraction...** command and create a table on the blank **Furniture Totals** layout, as described next:

EXTRACT DATA	
Ribbon/ Panel	Insert/ Linking & Extraction
ModifyII Toolbar:	
Menu Bar:	Tools/Data Extraction...
Type a Command:	DATA EXTRACTION
Command Alias:	DX

Prompt	**Response**
Type a command:	**Data Extraction...** or (Type **DX <Enter>**)
The **Data Extraction** wizard (Figure 9-28) appears:	With the **Create a new data extraction** button selected, click **Next**

Figure 9-28
Data Extraction Wizard -
Begin (Page 1 of 8)

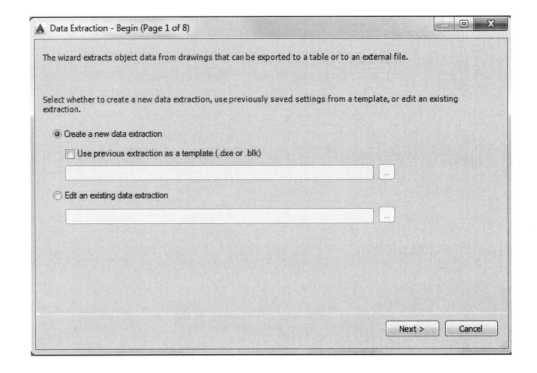

Prompt	Response
The **Save Data Extraction As** dialog box appears:	Select the folder where your drawings are stored, and name the file **FURNITURE TOTALS**
	Click **Save**
The **Data Extraction - Define Data Source (Page 2 of 8)** appears:	
	Click **Next**
Select Objects (Page 3 of 8) appears:	Make sure checks are in **Display blocks with attributes only** and **Display objects currently in-use only**. Have the **Display blocks only** radio button on (Figure 9-29).
	Click **Next>**
Select Properties (Page 4 of 8) appears:	Place a check mark only in **Attribute** (Figure 9-30)
	Click **Next**
Refine Data (Page 5 of 8) appears:	Right-click on the column name for any blank columns if there are any and click **Hide Column** (Figure 9-31)
	Click **Next**
Choose Output (Page 6 of 8) appears:	Place a check mark in **Insert data extraction table into drawing**
	Click **Next**
Table Style (Page 7 of 8) appears:	Type **FURNITURE TOTALS** in the **Enter a title for your table**: box (Figure 9-32)

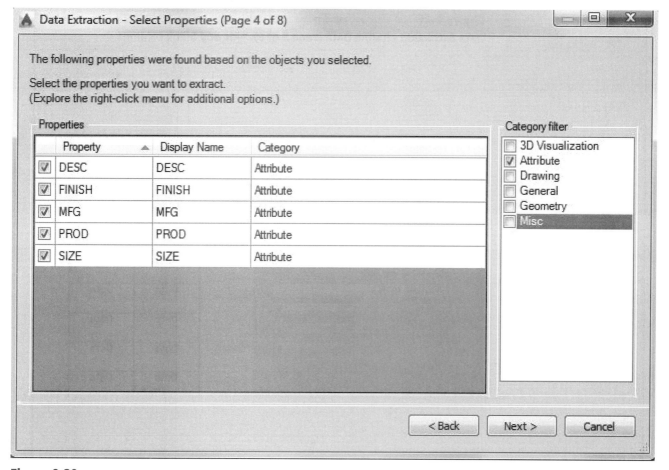

Figure 9-29
Data Extraction - Select Objects (Page 3 of 8)

Figure 9-30
Data Extraction - Select Properties (Page 4 of 8)

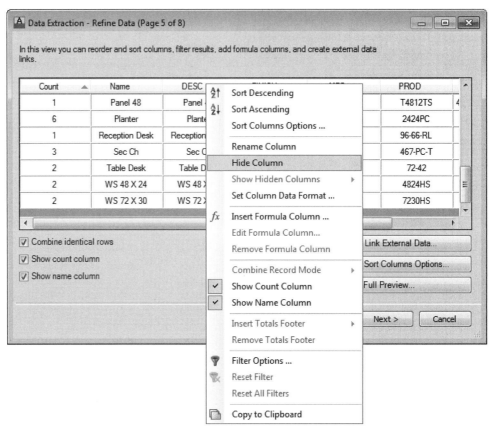

Figure 9-31
Data Extraction - Refine Data (Page 5 of 8), hide any blank columns

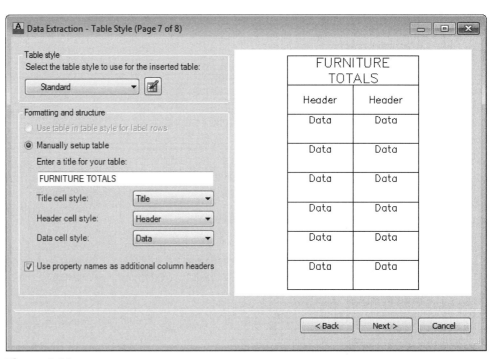

Figure 9-32
Data Extraction - Table Style (Page 7 of 8), name the table **FURNITURE TOTALS**

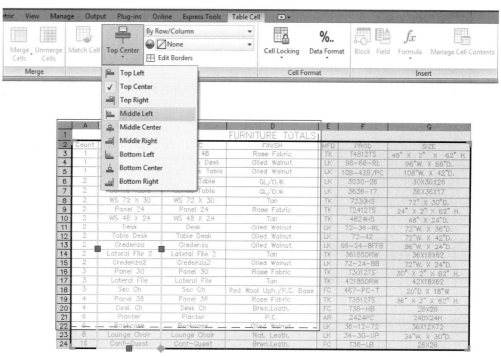

Prompt	Response
	Click **Next**
Finish (Page 8 of 8) appears:	Click **Finish**
Specify insertion point:	Click **a point** to locate the table

Step 5. Align DESC, FINISH, Name, PROD, and SIZE columns middle left (Figure 9-33), as described next:

Prompt	Response
Type a command:	Click the open area to the right in the first cell under the **Name** column to start a crossing window and move your mouse to the left and down so your crossing window selects all cells in the **Name** column but DOES NOT CROSS THE BOTTOM LINE OF THE TABLE
	Select **Middle Left** (Figure 9-33) on the ribbon **Table Cell** tab, **Cell Styles** panel

Figure 9-33
Align columns middle left

Step 6. Align the DESC, FINISH, PROD, and SIZE columns middle left.

Step 7. Use the **Reference** option of the **SCALE** command to scale the long side (the horizontal side) of the table to **10″**.

Step 8. Move the table if necessary so it is centered in the viewport.

Step 9. When you have completed Exercise 9-2, add your name, class, and current date to the drawing and save your work in at least two places.

Step 10. Print the Furniture Totals layout at a scale of **1:1** on an **11″ × 8-1/2″** sheet.

 **chapternine**

Chapter Summary

This chapter provided you the information necessary to set up and draw furniture installation plans. In addition, you learned to assign attributes and extract data from furniture installation plans. Now you have the skills and information necessary to produce furniture installation plans that can be used in interior design. You also are able to extract data that can be used to count and specify furniture.

Chapter Test Questions

Multiple Choice

Circle the correct answer.

1. In which of the following parts of an attribute definition may spaces **not** be used?
   a. Value
   b. Default value
   c. Prompt
   d. Tag

2. Which of the following parts of an attribute appears on the inserted furniture symbol when the attribute mode is not **Invisible**?
   a. Tag
   b. Prompt
   c. Value
   d. Block name

3. To use the **Edit Attributes** dialog box to change or accept default values of attributes when inserting wblocks, which of the following system variables must be set to 1?
   a. **ATTREQ**
   b. **ATTDIA**
   c. **ATTMODE**
   d. **AUPREC**

4. Which of the following commands can be used to make invisible all the visible attributes on the drawing?
   a. **WATTEDIT**
   b. **ATTEXT**
   c. **ATTEDIT**
   d. **ATTDISP**

5. Which of the following commands can be used to edit variable, verify, and preset attribute values of an inserted block using a dialog box?
   a. **ATTEXT**
   b. **ATTDEF**
   c. **EATTEDIT**
   d. **ATTDISP**

Matching

Write the number of the correct answer on the line.

a. **Data Extraction** _____

b. **Define Attributes...** _____

1. A command that allows you to assign attributes to a furniture symbol

2. A command that can be used to produce a parts list or bill of materials

c. **WBLOCK** _____

d. **ATTDISP** _____

e. Value _____

3. A command that is used to save a part of a drawing with defined attributes

4. A part of an attribute that appears on an inserted block

5. A command that makes all attributes appear visible

True or False

Circle the correct answer.

1. **True or False:** AutoCAD can automatically align an attribute definition below one that was defined with the previous **Define Attributes... (ATTDEF)** command.

2. **True or False:** The **Edit Attribute, Single... (EATTEDIT)** command uses the **Enhanced Attribute** dialog box to edit variable, verify, and preset attribute values of one inserted block at a time.

3. **True or False:** The existing variable attributes on a drawing become constant when a block with attributes is redefined.

4. **True or False:** The **Synchronize Attributes (ATTSYNC)** command does **not** allow you to select each redefined block whose attributes you want to update to the current redefined attributes.

5. **True or False:** The **Properties** palette is used to extract attributes from a drawing.

List

1. Five ways of accessing a block's **Define Attributes...** command.
2. Five **Mode** options in **Attribute Definition** dialog box.
3. Five **Attribute** fields in **Attribute Definition** dialog box.
4. Five ways of accessing a block's **Edit Attributes** command.
5. Five options of the **Attribute Definition** dialog box when the **Quick Properties** toggle in **ON**.
6. Five ways of accessing the **Insert Block** command.
7. Five command line key-ins that begin with "ATT".
8. Five ways of accessing the **Block Attribute Manager (BATTMAN)**.
9. Five ways of accessing the **Data Extraction** command.
10. Five reasons why blocks with attributes and **Data Extraction** from a drawing are desirable.

Questions

1. What are attributes and when should they be used?
2. How can blocks with attributes be used to make a furniture installation plan?
3. What are the uses of the **Data Extraction** command?
4. How can tables made with the **Data Extraction** command be aligned and otherwise edited?
5. What are the modes that an attribute can have and how are they used?

Chapter Projects

Project 9-1: *Hotel Room 2 Furniture Plan* [BASIC]

1. Begin CH9-P1 on the hard drive or network drive by opening the existing hotel room 2 floor plan (Project 7-1) and saving it as **CH9-P1**. Your final drawing will look similar to Figure 9-34.

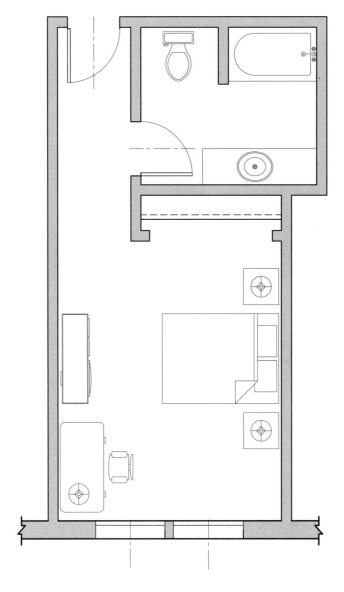

FURNITURE PLAN
SCALE: 3/16" = 1'-0"

Figure 9-34
Project 9-1: Hotel room 2 furniture plan (scale: 3/16″ = 1'-0″)

2. Set the **i-furn** layer current and turn off any layers that are not needed.

3. Select furniture from the **DesignCenter**. Place the furniture in the approximate locations shown in Figure 9-34. You will find all this furniture in the **Home - Space Planner** drawing. Use a 3/16″ = 1′-0″ architectural scale to measure any furniture you do not find, and draw it full scale.

4. Save the drawing in two places and plot or print the drawing to scale.

Project 9-2: *Hotel Room 1 Furniture Plan* [BASIC]

1. Begin CH9-P2 on the hard drive or network drive by opening the existing hotel room 1 floor plan (Exercise 6-2) and saving it as **CH9-P2**. Your final drawing will look similar to Figure 9-35.

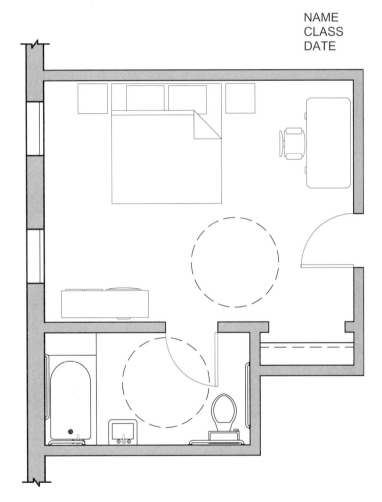

NAME
CLASS
DATE

FURNITURE PLAN
SCALE: 3/16" = 1'-0"

Figure 9-35
Project 9-2: Hotel room 1 furniture plan (scale: 1/4″ = 1′-0″)

2. Set the **i-furn** layer current and turn off any layers that are not needed.

3. Select furniture from the **DesignCenter**. Place the furniture in the approximate locations shown in Figure 9-35. You will find all this furniture in the **Home - Space Planner** drawing.

4. Save the drawing in two places and plot or print the drawing to scale.

Project 9-3: *Bank Furniture Plan* [ADVANCED]

1. Begin CH9-P3 by opening the existing bank floor plan (Project 7-3) and saving it as **CH9-P3**.

2. Create a new layer for furniture and set it current. Turn off any layers that are not needed.

3. Your final drawing will look similar to Figure 9-36, Sheet 1. Select furniture from the **DesignCenter**. Place the furniture in the approximate locations shown in Figure 9-36, Sheet 1. You will find this furniture in the **Home - Space Planner** drawing and **Autodesk Seek**. Use a 3/32″ = 1′-0″ architectural scale to measure any furniture you do not find, and draw it full scale.

4. Measure the two areas shown on Figure 9-36, Sheet 2, with a 1/4″ = 1′-0″ architectural scale, and draw them full size in the approximate location shown on Sheet 1.

5. Save the drawing in two places and plot or print the drawing to scale.

Figure 9-36

Sheet 1 of 2, Project 9-3: Bank furniture plan (scale: 3/32" = 1'-0")

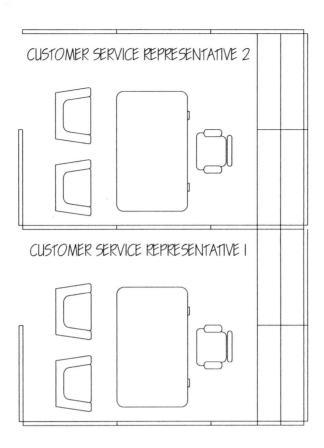

CUSTOMER SERVICE REPRESENTATIVE 2

CUSTOMER SERVICE REPRESENTATIVE 1

Project 9-4: *Log Cabin Furniture Plan* [INTERMEDIATE]

1. Begin CH9-P4 by opening the existing log cabin floor plan (Project 7-4) and saving it as **CH9-P4**. Your final drawing will look similar to Figure 9-37.

Figure 9-37

Project 9-4: Log cabin furniture plan (scale: 3/16″ = 1′-0″)

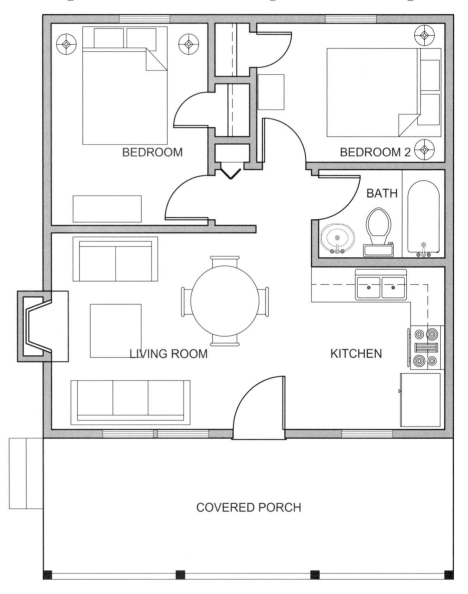

FURNITURE PLAN

SCALE: 3/16"=1'-0"

2. Set the **i-furn** layer current and turn off any layers that are not needed.

3. Select furniture from the **DesignCenter**. Place the furniture in the approximate locations shown in Figure 9-37. You will find this furniture in the **Home - Space Planner** drawing. Use a 3/16″ = 1′-0″ architectural scale to measure any furniture you do not find and draw it full scale.

4. Save the drawing in two places and plot or print the drawing to scale.

Project 9-5: *House 1 Furniture Plan* [ADVANCED]

1. Begin CH9-P5 by opening the existing house 1 floor plan (Project 7-5) and saving it as **CH9-P5**.

2. Create a new layer for furniture and set it current. Turn off any layers that are not needed.

3. Your final drawing will look similar to Figure 9-38.

   You will find most of the furniture in the **Home - Space Planner** drawing in the **DesignCenter**.

   You will find the single bed (Bedroom #2) in **Autodesk Seek**. Because it is 3D you will have to select the top view using the ViewCube, or just use a 1/8″ = 1′-0″ architectural scale to measure the bed and draw it full scale.

   You will have to draw the lamp tables. Use a 1/8″ = 1′-0″ architectural scale to measure them, and draw them full scale.

4. Save the drawing in two places and plot or print the drawing to scale.

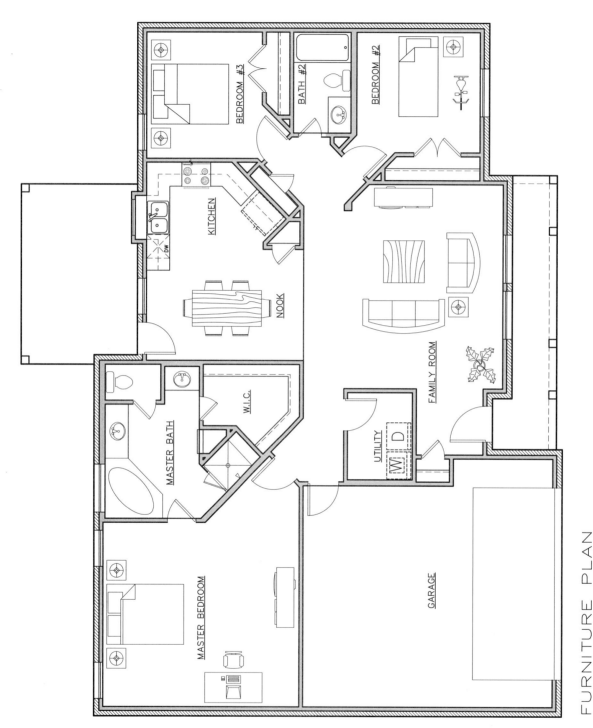

FURNITURE PLAN

SCALE: 1/8" = 1'-0"

Figure 9-38

Project 9-5: House 1 furniture plan (scale: 1/8" = 1'-0")

Project 9-6: *House 2 Furniture Plan* [ADVANCED]

1. Begin CH9-P6 by opening the existing house 2 floor plan (Project 7-6) and saving it as **CH9-P6**.

2. Create a new layer for furniture and set it current. Turn off any layers that are not needed.

3. Your final drawing will look similar to Figure 9-39.

   You will find most of the furniture in the **Home - Space Planner** drawing in the **DesignCenter**.

   You will find some of it in **Autodesk Seek**. If it is 3D, you will have to select the top view using the ViewCube, or just use a 1/8″ = 1′-0″ architectural scale to measure this furniture and draw it full scale.

   You will have to draw a few items: lamp tables, chest of drawers, and the large chairs in the study. Use a 1/8″ = 1′-0″ architectural scale to measure this furniture and draw it full scale.

4. Save the drawing in two places and plot or print the drawing to scale.

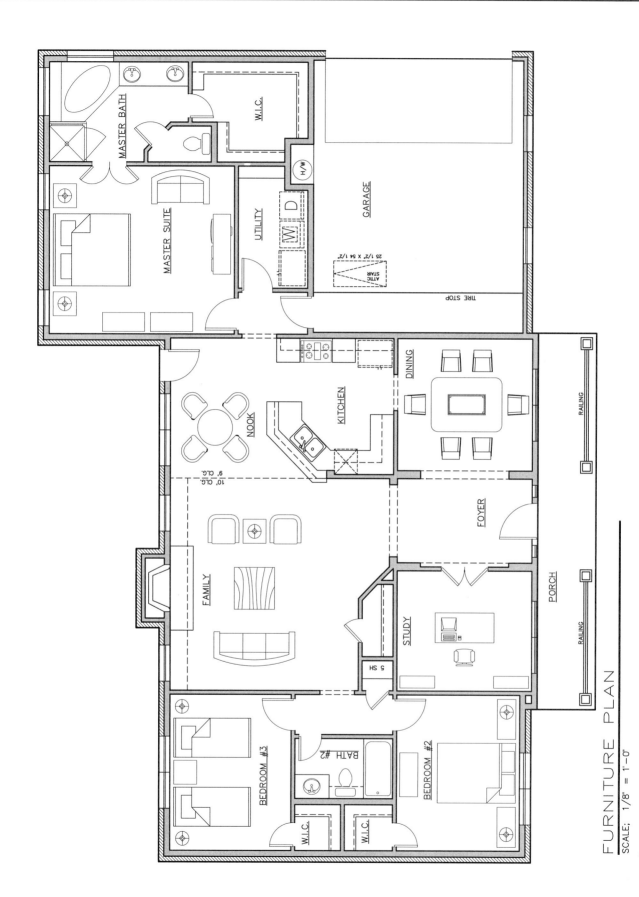

FURNITURE PLAN

SCALE; 1/8" = 1'-0"

Figure 9-39
Project 9-6: House 2 furniture plan (scale: 1/8" = 1'-0")

10 chapterten

DesignCenter, Autodesk Seek, Dynamic Blocks, and External References

CHAPTER OBJECTIVES

- Correctly use the following commands and settings:

Attach External Reference (XATTACH)	**Block Editor (BE)** **DesignCenter (DC)**	**(External Bind) XBIND** **External Reference (XREF)**
		Set Base Point (BASE)

Introduction

In this chapter, you will use the AutoCAD **DesignCenter** to copy layers and blocks (furniture) from one drawing to another. You will also make blocks that perform actions dynamically. Finally, you will use external reference commands that allow you to attach drawings to other drawings so that they appear in the primary drawing without inserting them.

EXERCISE 10-1
Reception Area Furniture Installation Plan Using the DesignCenter

When you have completed Exercise 10-1, your drawing will look similar to Figure 10-3 without dimensions.

Step 1. Use your workspace to make the following settings:

1. Use **Save As...** to save the drawing with the name **CH10-EXERCISE1.**
2. Set drawing units: **Architectural**
3. Set drawing limits: **44′,34′**
4. Set **GRIDDISPLAY: 0**
5. Set grid: **12″**
6. Set snap: **6″**

The DesignCenter

DesignCenter: A dialog box that allows you to use existing blocks that AutoCAD has provided. Drag and drop blocks, layers, linetypes, lineweights, text and dimension styles, and external references from any existing drawing. Search for drawings and other files.

The *DesignCenter* allows you to do the following:

- Use existing blocks arranged in categories that AutoCAD has provided.
- Use blocks, layers, linetypes, text and dimension styles, and external references from any existing drawing using the drag-and-drop technique.
- Examine drawings and blocks as either drawing names or pictures.
- Search for drawings and other files.

Step 2. Open the **DesignCenter** and examine it, as described next:

DESIGN CENTER	
Ribbon/Panel	View/Palettes
Standard Toolbar:	
Menu Bar:	Tools/Palettes/Design Center
Type a Command:	ADCENTER
Command Alias:	DC

Prompt	Response
Type a command:	**DesignCenter** (or type **DC <Enter>**)
The **DesignCenter** appears:	Look at the bottom of Figure 10-1. Use the same or similar path to locate the **Design Center** folder
	Click **Home - Space Planner.dwg**
The **DesignCenter** shows the blocks and other items in the **Home - Space Planner.dwg** (Figure 10-1). Your **DesignCenter** may appear different, depending on what is selected in the **Views** icon or **Tree View Toggle** at the top of the **DesignCenter.**	
	Double-click **Blocks**
All the predefined blocks for the drawing appear.	

You can now click on any of these drawings, hold down the left mouse button, drag the drawing into the current drawing, and drop it. However, do not do that for this exercise. You will use layers and blocks from CH9-EXERCISE1 to complete CH10-EXERCISE1. Let's look at the parts of the **DesignCenter**.

DesignCenter Tabs

The tabs at the top of the **DesignCenter** allow you to access all the following options of the **DesignCenter**:

Folders Tab: Clicking this tab shows you the folders existing on the hard drive of your computer.

Open Drawings Tab: Shows you the drawing that is currently open.

History Tab: Shows you a list of the most recently opened drawings.

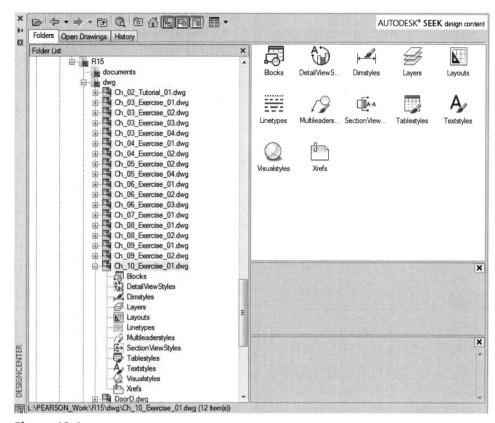

Figure 10-1
The **DesignCenter Home - Space Planner** drawing

DesignCenter Buttons

Now, examine the buttons above the tabs. They are listed next, starting from the first one on the left. Click the **Folders** tab to display all the icons.

> **Load:** Allows you to load drawings and other items that you want to use in your current drawing.
>
> **Back:** Returns you to the previous screen.
>
> **Forward:** Sends you forward from a screen obtained from clicking back.
>
> **Up:** Sends you to the next higher folder structure.
>
> **Search:** Allows you to search for and locate data you need.
>
> **Favorites:** Shows what you have in the **Favorites** folder. You can save your most-often-used items here.
>
> **Home:** Returns you to the default starting folder.
>
> **Tree View Toggle:** Displays and hides the tree view. The tree view shows the structure of the files and folders in the form of a chart, the area on the left.
>
> **Preview:** Allows you to look at a preview of any selected item. If there is no preview image saved with the selected item, the **Preview** area will be empty.
>
> **Description:** Shows a text description of any selected item.
>
> **Views:** Provide you with different display formats for the selected items.

You can select a view from the **View** list or choose the **View** button again to cycle through display formats.

Large Icons: Shows the names of loaded items with large icons.

Small Icons: Shows the names of loaded items with small icons.

List: Shows a list of loaded items.

Details: Places a name for each item in an alphabetical list.

Autodesk Seek Design Content: Gives you access to thousands of blocks from manufacturers.

Step 3. Use the **DesignCenter** to load **i-furn, a-door,** and **a-wall-intr** layers from **CH9-EXERCISE1** into the new drawing, as described next:

Prompt	Response
Type a command:	Click **Load**
	Click locate drawing **CH9-EXERCISE1** and double-click **CH9-EXERCISE1**
	Double-click **Layers** (on the left)
The display (Figure 10-2) appears:	Click layer **a-door,** hold down the pick button, drag it into the current drawing (to the right of the **Design-Center**), and release the pick button
	Repeat the previous for layers **i-furn** and **a-wall-intr**
	Close the **DesignCenter**

Figure 10-2
Layers in CH9-EXERCISE1

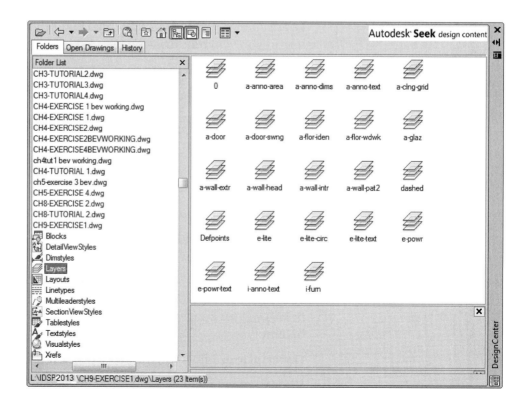

Step 4. Set layer **a-wall-intr** current.

Step 5. Use **Polyline** to draw the outside walls of the reception area using the dimensions from Figure 10-3. Set an offset of 5″ for the wall thickness.

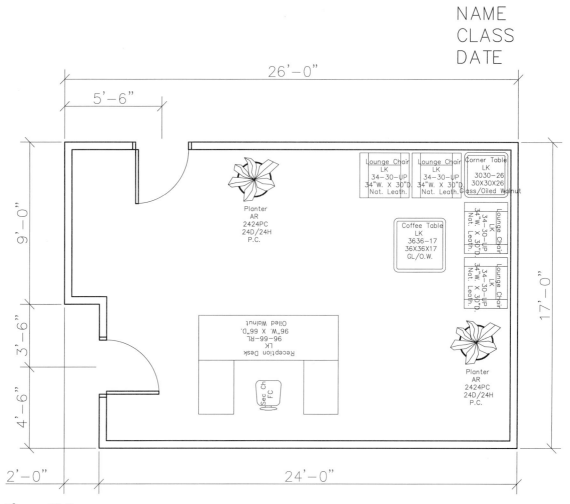

Figure 10-3
Dimensions for Exercise 10-1 (scale: 3/16″ = 1′-0″)

Step 6. Set layer **a-door** current.

Step 7. Open the **DesignCenter** and click **Blocks** under **CH9-EXERCISE1,** find the block named **DOOR,** and drag and drop it into the current drawing.

Step 8. Use the **MIRROR** and **ROTATE** commands if necessary to correctly position the door.

Step 9. Place doors in the correct locations using the dimensions from Figure 10-3.

Step 10. Use the **TRIM** command to trim the walls from the door openings.

Step 11. Set layer **i-furn** current.

Step 12. Click **Blocks** under **CH9-EXERCISE1,** find the blocks named **Planter, Corner Table, Coffee Table, Reception Desk, Sec Ch,**

and **Lounge Chair,** and drag and drop them into the current drawing.

Step 13. Place furniture in the approximate locations shown in Figure 10-3.

Step 14. When you have completed Exercise 10-1, add your name, class, and the current date to the drawing in the upper right and save your work in at least two places.

Step 15. Print Exercise 10-1 to scale.

EXERCISE 10-2

Training Room Furniture Installation Plan Using the DesignCenter, Autodesk Seek, and Dynamic Blocks

When you have completed Exercise 10-2 your drawing will look similar to Figure 10-4.

Step 1. Use your workspace to make the following settings:

1. Open drawing **CH3-EXERCISE2** and save it to the hard drive with the name **CH10-EXERCISE2**.
2. Erase all furniture and the door so that only the walls remain.
3. Set layer **a-door** current.

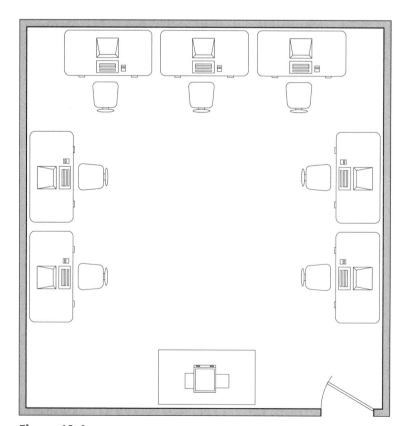

Figure 10-4
Exercise 10-2: Training room

DesignCenter

Step 2. Use a block from the **DesignCenter - House Designer** drawing to draw a new door, as described next:

Prompt	**Response**
Type a command:	**DesignCenter** (or type **DC <Enter>**)
The **DesignCenter** appears	Look at the bottom of Figure 10-5. Use the same or similar path to locate the **DesignCenter** folder. Click **House Designer.dwg**
The available items in the **House Designer** drawing appear:	Double-click **Blocks** and click **Large Icons** in the **Views** list, as shown in Figure 10-6.
	Click **Tree View Toggle** to remove the tree view.
	Click on the **Door - Right Hung 36 in.** icon and continue to hold down the left mouse button (Figure 10-7). Drag the door off the **DesignCenter** and use **Osnap-Endpoint** to place it as shown in Figure 10-8.

Step 3. Set the **i-furn layer** current.

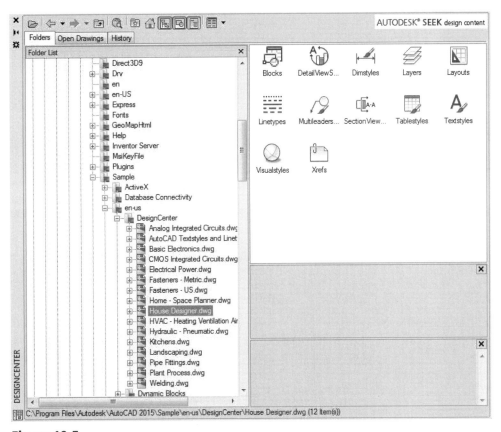

Figure 10-5
Locate **House Designer** blocks

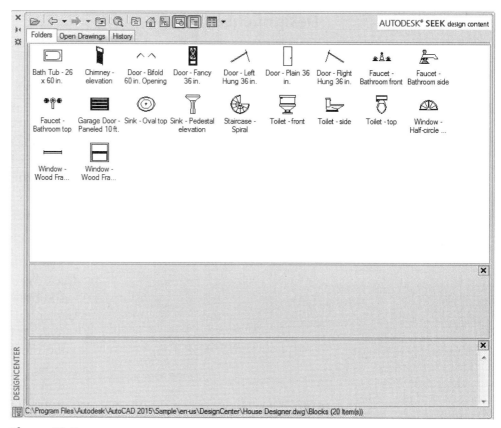

Figure 10-6
Click **Blocks** and **Large Icons** in the **Views** list. Click **Tree View Toggle**

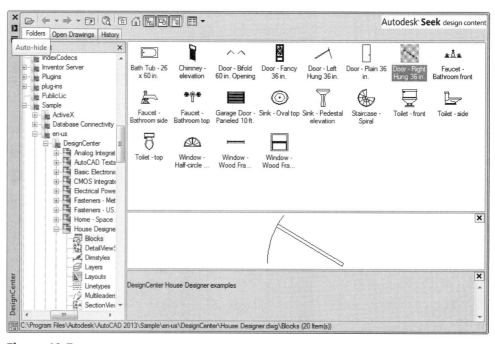

Figure 10-7
Click the **Door - Right Hung 36 in.** Hold down the pick button and drag the door off the **DesignCenter**

Figure 10-8
Use **Osnap-Endpoint** to place the door in the
opening

Step 4. Drag and drop blocks from the **Home - Space Planner** drawing to
create furniture in the training room, as described next:

Prompt	Response
Type a command:	Click **Tree View Toggle** to return to tree view
The left side of the **DesignCenter** opens up again:	Double-click **Home - Space Planner .dwg** (Figure 10-9)

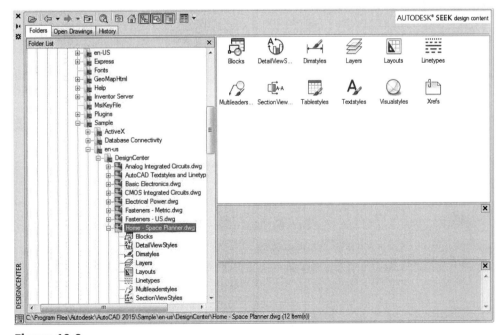

Figure 10-9
Open **Home - Space Planner** drawing

Prompt	Response
The available items in the **Home - Space Planner.dwg** appear:	Double-click **Blocks**
	Click on the **Desk - 30 × 60 in.** icon and continue to hold down the left mouse button as you drag the **Desk** off the **DesignCenter** and place it on the drawing

> **TIP**
>
> To minimize the **DesignCenter**, click on the **Auto-hide** button (the two triangles below the **X**) in the upper left corner.

Step 5. Drag and drop the following blocks from the **Home - Space Planner** drawing (Figure 10-10):

1. **Computer Terminal**
2. **Table - Rectangular Woodgrain 60 × 30 in.**

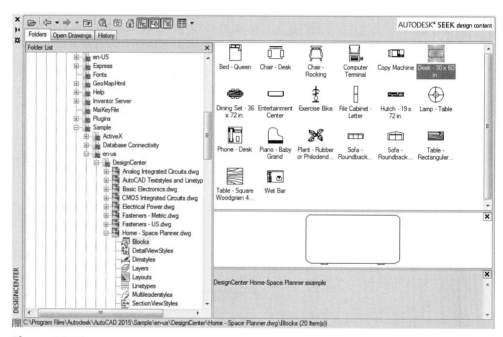

Figure 10-10
Home - Space Planner drawing blocks

Step 6. Move the **Computer Terminal** on top of the **Desk - 30 × 60 in.** (Figure 10-11).

Step 7. Explode the **Table - Rectangular Woodgrain 60 × 30 in.** and erase the woodgrain so you can see the items you are going to place on top of it. Return the exploded table to the **i-furn** layer.

Step 8. Place the woodgrain table in the drawing. Copy and rotate the desk and computer terminal, so your drawing looks like Figure 10-11.

Figure 10-11

Desk, computer, and rectangular woodgrain table with woodgrain erased

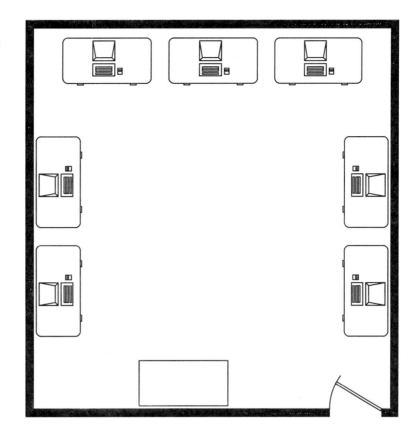

Autodesk Seek

Step 9. Locate a copier in **DesignCenter Autodesk Seek,** download it, and insert it on top of the woodgrain table, as described next:

Prompt	Response
Type a command:	Move your mouse back to the **DesignCenter** palette
The **DesignCenter** opens up again:	Click the **Autodesk Seek design content** button (Figure 10-12)
The **Autodesk Seek** online source for product specifications and design files appears:	Click **AutoCAD (2D)** for file type in the **Search** input area, Figure 10-12. Type **copier** in the **Search** input area. Click the **Search** button.
The product specification files appear:	Scroll down to the **Library AutoCAD Architecture** image area, locate the **Copier - Collator**, and click the **DWG** icon.
The selected **Copier - Collator** specification appears:	Check the file **check box** and with **Download Selected to Local** click the **Download Selected to Local** button to save the file in your drive and folder.

Step 10. Download the **Copier - Collator** to your drive and folder.

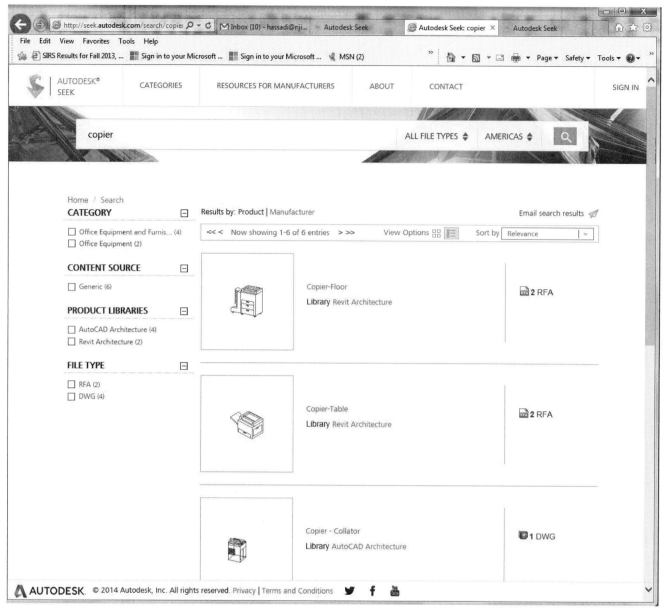

Figure 10-12
Autodesk Seek - 2D copier-collator

> **Step 11.** Use the **INSERT** command to insert the **Copier - Collator** into your drawing.
>
> **Step 12.** Locate the **Copier - Collator** on top of the woodgrain table as shown in Figure 10-4.

Use Block Editor to Make Dynamic Blocks

dynamic block: The user-defined collection of drawing objects that can be changed without exploding the block.

You can move part of an inserted ***dynamic block*** within the dynamic block (such as a chair within a chair-and-desk combination) without exploding the block. A dynamic inserted block can be changed without exploding it. A standard inserted block must be exploded before it can be changed. You can also change the size of the dynamic block as you work. For example, if the desk is needed in a variety of sizes, you can define it as a dynamic block that has a parameter (a feature) that allows the width, depth, or both to be changed without exploding the block or redefining it.

BLOCK EDITOR	
Ribbon/ Panel	Home/ Block/ Edit
Menu Bar:	Tools/ Block Editor
Command Alias:	BE

The **Block Editor** is used to create dynamic blocks. The **Block Editor** allows you to add the elements that make a block dynamic. You can create a block from scratch, or you can add dynamic features to an existing block.

In the following part of this exercise you will redefine the existing woodgrain table as a dynamic block that can change size. You will add dynamic blocks of desk chairs that can be visible or invisible. You will also redefine the existing right-hung 36-in. door as a dynamic block that can flip from one side of the wall to the other. Start with the woodgrain table.

> **TIP**
> While in the **Block Editor** you can zoom in and out.

Step 13. Use the **Block Editor** to add a linear parameter to the woodgrain table (so the length can be easily changed) as described next:

Prompt	Response
Type a command:	**Block Editor** (or type **BE <Enter>**)
The **Edit Block Definition** dialog box appears:	Click **Table - Rectangular Woodgrain 60 × 30 in.** (Figure 10-13)
	Click **OK**
The table appears with woodgrain (you are still in the **Block Editor**)	Erase the woodgrain
	Click the **Parameters** tab of the **Block Authoring Palettes**
	Click **Linear**
Specify start point or [Name Label Chain Description Base Palette Value set]:	Click **Osnap-Endpoint**, the upper left corner of the table
Specify endpoint:	Click **Osnap-Endpoint**, the upper right corner of the table

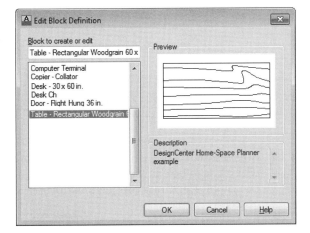

Figure 10-13
Click **Table - Rectangular Woodgrain 60 × 30 in.** in the list of blocks

Prompt	Response
Specify label location:	Click to place the label (**Distance1**) as shown in Figure 10-14
	Click the **Actions** tab of the **Block Authoring Palettes**
	Click **Stretch**
Select parameter:	Click **Distance1** (on the top of the table).
Specify parameter point to associate with action or enter [sTart point Second point] \<Start\>:	Click the arrow on the upper right corner of the table
Specify first corner of stretch frame or [CPolygon]:	Click **P1→** (Figure 10-15)
Specify opposite corner:	Click **P2→** (Figure 10-15)
Specify objects to stretch:	Click **P3→**
Select objects:	Click **P4→**
Select objects:	Click **P5→**
Select objects:	**\<Enter\>**

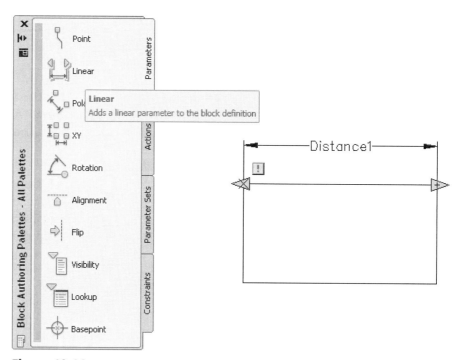

Figure 10-14
Add a linear parameter to the table length

Step 14. Add a lookup parameter and a lookup action that will appear when the block is inserted (so you can just click a number and the block becomes longer or shorter) as described next:

Prompt	Response
	Click the **Parameters** tab of the **Block Authoring Palettes**
	Click **Lookup**

Figure 10-15
Add the stretch action to
the linear parameter

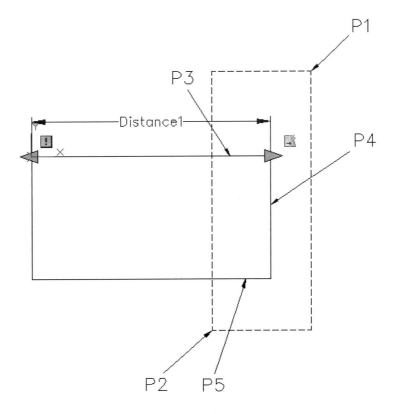

Prompt

Specify parameter location or
  [Name Label Description Palette]:

Select parameter:

The **Property Lookup Table**
  appears:
The **Add Parameter Properties**
  dialog box appears with **Linear**
  selected and **Add input
  properties** checked

Response

Click a point close to the table above
  it (Figure 10-16)
Click the **Actions** tab of the **Block
  Authoring Palettes**
Click **Lookup**
Click the **Lookup1** parameter you
  just made

Click **Add Properties**...

Click **OK**

Figure 10-16
Locating parameters and
actions

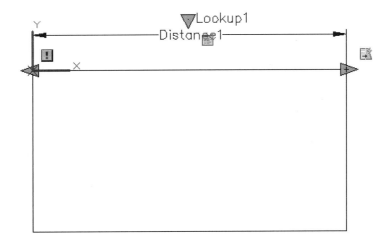

Prompt	Response
The **Property Lookup Table** appears:	Type the properties shown in Figure 10-17; be sure both columns are identical, then press **\<Enter\>**
	Click **Audit** (if both columns are identical, you will get the message that no errors were found)
	Click **Close**
	Click **OK** (to exit the **Property Lookup Table**)
	Click **Save Block As** (or type **BSAVEAS \<Enter\>**)
The **Save Block As** dialog box appears:	In the **Block Name** box, type **Table 5'-5'6-6'**
	Click **OK**

SAVE BLOCK AS	
Ribbon/ Panel	Block Editor/ Open Save/ Save Block As
Type a Command:	BSAVEAS

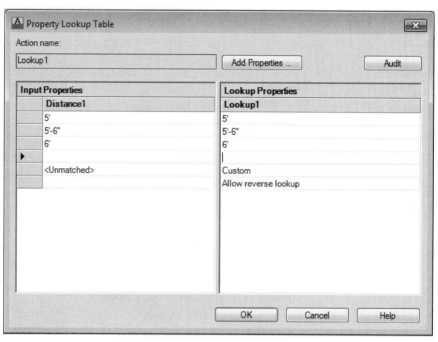

Figure 10-17
Lookup properties for **Lookup1** action

Step 15. Close the **Block Editor** and insert your dynamic block as described next:

CLOSE BLOCK EDITOR	
Ribbon/ Panel	Block Editor/ Close Block Editor
Shortcut in Block Editor	Right-Click/ Close Block Editor
Type a Command:	BCLOSE

Prompt	Response
The **Block Editor** is open.	Type **BC \<Enter\>** or **Close Block Editor**
The current drawing appears:	**Erase** the copier table (do not erase the copier)
Type a command:	Type **I \<Enter\>**
The **Insert** dialog box appears:	Select: **Table 5'-5'6-6'**
	Click **OK**

Prompt	Response
Specify insertion point or [Basepoint Scale X Y Z Rotate]:	Click a point to replace the copier table you just erased **<Enter>**
	Click any point on a line of the inserted table
	Click the **Lookup** symbol, Figure 10-18 (to see the three sizes)

Figure 10-18
Insert the dynamic block
and click the **Lookup** symbol

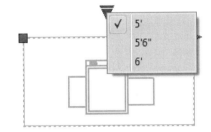

Step 16. You can now click on any of the three numbers, and the block changes length. Change the length to **5′6″**.

Step 17. Press the **<Esc>** key to get rid of the block parameters.

Step 18. Add a linear parameter to make the depth of the copier table dynamic so you have 2′-6″ and 3′ table depths, as described next:

Prompt	Response
Type a command:	**Block Editor** (or type **BE <Enter>**)
The **Edit Block Definition** dialog box appears:	Click **Table 5′-5′6-6′**
	Click **OK**
The table appears:	Click the **Parameters** tab of the **Block Authoring Palettes**
	Click **Linear**
Specify start point or [Name Label Chain Description Base Palette Value set]:	Click **Osnap-Endpoint,** the lower right corner of the table
Specify endpoint:	Click **Osnap-Endpoint,** the upper right corner of the table
Specify label location:	Click to place the label (**Distance2**) on the right side of the table (Figure 10-19)

Figure 10-19
Add the stretch and lookup
actions to the linear
parameter distance 2

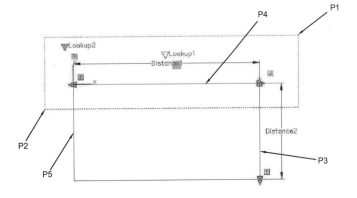

Prompt	Response
	Click the **Actions** tab of the **Block Authoring Palettes**
	Click **Stretch**
Select parameter:	Click **Distance2** (on the right side of the table)
Specify parameter point to associate with action or enter [sTartpoint Second point] <Start>:	Click the arrow on the upper right corner of the table
Specify first corner of stretch frame or [CPolygon]:	Click **P1→** (Figure 10-19)
Specify opposite corner:	Click **P2→** (Figure 10-19)
Specify objects to stretch:	Click **P3→**
Select objects: 1 found	Click **P4→**
Select objects: 1 found, 2 total	Click **P5→**
Select objects: 1 found, 3 total	**<Enter>**

Step 19. Add a lookup parameter and a lookup action that will appear when the block is inserted (so you can just click a number, and the block becomes more or less deep), as described next:

Prompt	Response
	Click the **Parameters** tab of the **Block Authoring Palettes**
	Click **Lookup**
Specify parameter location or [Name Label Description Palette]:	Click a point above and to the left of the table (Figure 10-19)
	Click the **Actions** tab of the **Block Authoring Palettes**
	Click **Lookup**
Select parameter:	Click the **Lookup2** parameter you just made
The **Property Lookup Table** appears:	Click **Add Properties...**
The **Add Parameter Properties** dialog box appears with **Linear** selected and **Add input properties** checked	Click **Linear1**
	Click **OK**
The **Property Lookup Table** appears:	Type the properties shown in Figure 10-20; be sure both columns are identical and click **<Enter>**
	Click **Audit** (if both columns are identical, you will get the message that no errors were found)
	Click **Close**
	Click **OK** (to exit the **Property Lookup Table**)
	Click **Save Block As** (or type **BSAVEAS <Enter>**)

Figure 10-20
Lookup properties for **Lookup3** action

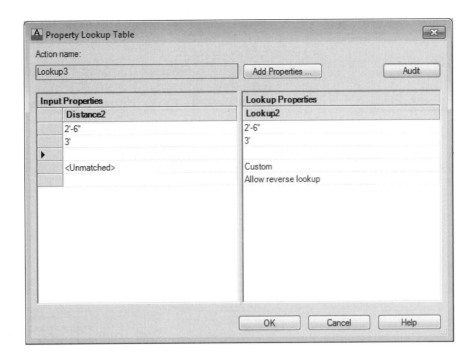

Prompt	Response
The **Save Block As** dialog box appears:	Click **Table 5′-5′6-6′** (so it appears in the **Block Name** area)
	Click **OK**
The AutoCAD warning appears: Block name: is already defined as a block. What do you want to do?	Click **Redefine block**
The AutoCAD warning appears: Block—Save parameter changes?	Click **Save the changes**

Step 20. On your own, close the **Block Editor**, erase the previous **Table 5′-5′6-6′** block, and insert the new dynamic block.

Step 21. Click any point on the inserted copier table and click the **Lookup** symbol showing depth.

Step 22. You can now click on any of the two numbers, and the block changes depth. Change the length to 5′6″ and the depth to 3′. The table is now 5′6″ × 3′ (Figure 10-21).

Figure 10-21
Lookup symbols for depth and length

Step 23. Press the **<Esc>** key to get rid of the block parameters.

Step 24. Make the **Sec Ch** and **Desk Ch** blocks dynamic so you can make one or the other invisible by clicking on it, as described next:

1. Open the **DesignCenter** (type **DC <Enter>**). Use the **Folders** tab to open your drawing **CH9-EXERCISE1**.
2. Locate the two blocks **Sec Ch** and **Desk Ch** and insert both of them into the current drawing, **CH10-EXERCISE2**.

3. Explode both drawings and erase the attribute tags.
4. Rotate the chairs so they both face the same direction (Figure 10-22).
5. Make a block of the **Desk Ch** drawing with the name **chair1**.
6. Make a block of the **Sec Ch** drawing with the name **chair2**.
7. Open the **Block Editor**, select **chair1** (Figure 10-23), and click **OK**.

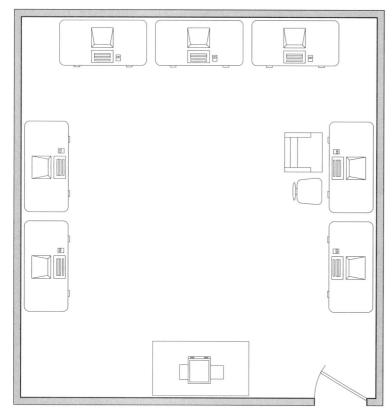

Figure 10-22
Insert **Desk Ch** and **Sec Ch** blocks, explode them, and erase the attribute tags

Figure 10-23
Select **chair1** to edit

8. Click the **Parameters** tab of the **Block Authoring Palettes**, click the **Visibility** parameter, and place the parameter below the chair (Figure 10-24). (Below the chair will make it easy to find after the block is inserted again.)
9. Click **Visibility States** on the **Visibility** panel on the ribbon.
10. Click **New** (Figure 10-25) and click **Hide all existing objects in new state**. Click **OK** (to exit the **New Visibility State** dialog box).
11. Click **OK** (to exit the **Visibility States** dialog box—you are still in the **Block Editor**).
12. Click **Save Block As** and save and redefine the dynamic block as **chair1**. Close the **Block Editor**.
13. **Erase** the existing chair1 block if not deleted.
14. Insert chair1 in the approximate location shown in front of a desk (Figure 10-26). Click on **chair1** and test your **Visibility** parameter, **VisibilityState0**, and **VisibilityState1**. Chair1 should be visible for State0 and invisible for State1.
15. Repeat items 7 through 13 for chair2.

Figure 10-24
Select the **Visibility** parameter and locate it as shown

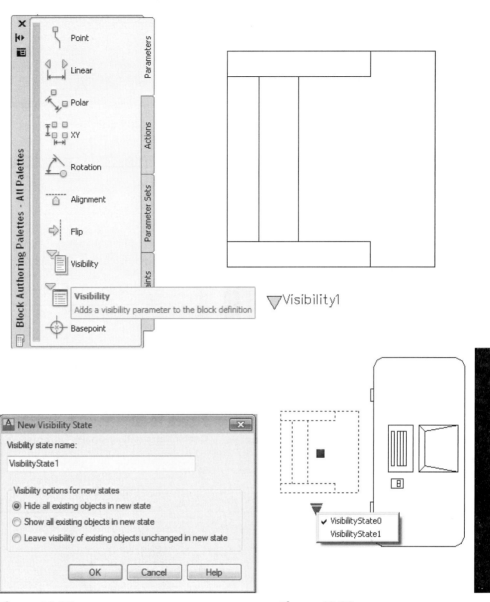

Figure 10-25
Make a **Visibility State** that shows chair1

Figure 10-26
Chair1 inserted with two visibility states—visible and invisible

16. **Insert chair2** so it is positioned as shown in Figure 10-27.
17. Copy **chair1** and **chair2** so each desk has the two chairs.
18. Select all chair1s and use the **Properties** command to change the **Visibility State** to 1 (invisible) as shown in Figure 10-28.
19. Make all chair2s visible as shown in Figure 10-28.

> **NOTE**
>
> To make an invisible block visible again, open the **Block Editor** and erase the existing visibility parameter on the block. You can then save and redefine the block with no parameter or you can add a new visibility parameter and save and redefine the block.

Step 25. Make the door a dynamic block so it will open in or out, as described next:

1. Open the **Block Editor,** select **Door - Right Hung 36 in.,** and click **OK.**

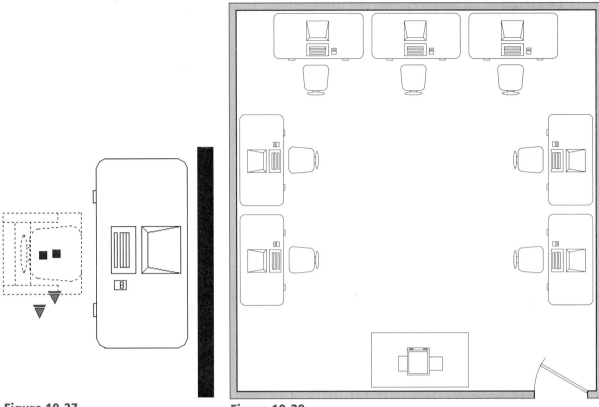

Figure 10-27
Both chairs with visibility parameters

Figure 10-28
Both chairs with visibility parameters

Figure 10-29
Add the flip parameter and
flip action to the door

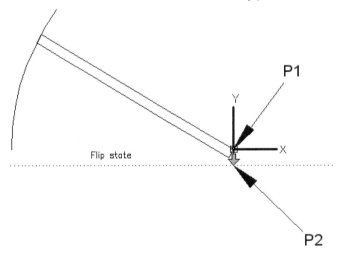

2. Draw a line from **P1→** (Figure 10-29) **2-1/2″** straight down. (This line goes to the middle of the wall, so the flip action will flip the door to either side of the room.)
3. Click the **Parameters** tab of the **Block Authoring Palettes**; click the **Flip** parameter.
4. Click **P2→** (Figure 10-29, the lower end of the 2-1/2″ line) as the base point of the reflection line. With **ORTHO** on, click any point to the left of the base point as the endpoint of the reflection line.
5. Locate the label (Figure 10-29).
6. Click the **Actions** tab of the **Block Authoring Palettes**, click **Flip action**, click the **Flip state** parameter, and then select the entire door and press **<Enter>.**
7. Save the dynamic block as **Door - Right Hung 36 in.** to redefine the block and close the **Block Editor.**

8. Click any point on the door so the flip action is available, flip the door so you see that it works, then leave it as shown in Figure 10-28.

Step 26. When you have completed Exercise 10-2, add your name, class, and current date to the drawing in the upper right and save your work in at least two places.

Step 27. Print Exercise 10-2 to scale.

EXERCISE 10-3
Attach an External Reference to an Office Plan

XATTACH (Attach External Reference)

Before you start the **XATTACH** command, your primary drawing must be open. When you activate the **XATTACH** command, the **Select Reference File** dialog box opens and allows you to select the drawing that you want to attach. When you select and open a drawing to be attached as an *external reference* to your primary drawing, the **External Reference** dialog box opens. The **External Reference** dialog box allows you to specify whether the xref will be an attachment or an overlay.

> **external reference (xref):** A drawing file that is inserted into another drawing. External references have the advantage that the primary drawing always contains the most recent version of the external reference.

Attachment: An attached xref that is then attached to another drawing becomes a nested xref with all its features fully recognized.

Overlay: An overlay is ignored when the drawing on which it is overlaid is then attached as an xref to another drawing.

The **XATTACH** command allows you to attach an external reference (xref) (drawing) to a primary drawing. For each drawing, the data are stored in their own separate file. Any changes made to the external reference drawing are reflected in the primary drawing each time the primary drawing is loaded into the **Drawing Editor.**

There are three distinct advantages to using external references:

1 The primary drawing always contains the most recent version of the external reference.

2 There are no conflicts in layer names and other similar features (called *named objects*), such as linetypes, text styles, and block definitions. AutoCAD automatically inserts the drawing name of the xref and a slash (/) in front of the external reference layer name or other object name. For example, if the primary drawing and the external reference (named **CHAIR**) have a layer named **Symbol,** then the current drawing layer retains the name **Symbol,** and the external reference layer in the current drawing becomes **CHAIR/symbol.**

3 Drawing files are often much smaller.

External references are used, for example, for drawing a large furniture plan containing several different levels of office types, such as assistant, associate, manager, vice president, and president. Each office typical (furniture configuration used in the office) is attached to the current drawing as an external reference. When changes are made to the external reference drawing of the manager's office (as a result of furniture substitution, for example), the change is reflected in each instance of a manager's office in the primary large furniture plan when it is loaded into the **Drawing Editor.**

External Reference (XREF)

When you activate the **XREF** command, the **External Reference** palette appears. After an external reference has been attached to your drawing, you can right-click on the external reference drawing name to select from the following options:

EXTERNAL REFERENCE	
Ribbon/ Panel	Insert/Reference External Reference
Reference Toolbar:	External Reference
Type a Command:	XREF

Attach...: Allows you to attach any drawing as an external reference to the current drawing. There is no limit to the number of external references that you can attach to your drawing. This is the same command as **XATTACH.**

Detach: Lets you remove unneeded external references from your drawing.

Reload: Allows you to update the current drawing with an external reference that has been changed since you began the current drawing. You do not have to exit the current drawing to update it with an external reference that you or someone else changed while in the current drawing.

Unload: Temporarily clears the external reference from the current drawing until the drawing is reloaded.

Bind...: The **Insert** option in the **Bind** dialog box creates a block of the external reference in the current drawing and erases any reference to it as an external reference. The **Bind** option binds the selected xref to the drawing and renames layers in a manner similar to that of the attached xref. This is the same command as **XBIND.**

XBIND

EXTERNAL BIND	
Menu Bar: Toolbar:	Modify/Object External Reference/ Bind...
Type a Command:	XBIND

The **XBIND** (**External Bind**) command allows you to bind a selected subset of an external reference's dependent symbols to the current drawing. For example, if you did not want to create a block of the entire external reference but wanted permanently to add only a dimension style of the external reference to the drawing, you could use **XBIND.**

Features of External References

Following is a list of external reference features:

1 An external reference cannot be exploded.

2 An external reference can be changed into a block with the **Bind...** option and then exploded. The advantage of using the external reference is then lost. The **Bind** option would be used if you wanted to send a client a disk or file containing only the current drawing without including external references.

3 External references can be nested. That means that a current drawing containing external references can itself be used as an external reference on another current drawing. There is no limit to the number of drawings you can nest like this.

4 An xref icon appears in the lower right corner of the screen when xrefs are attached to a drawing.

Step 1. Draw the floor plan shown in Figure 10-30 and save it as **CH10-EXERCISE3.**

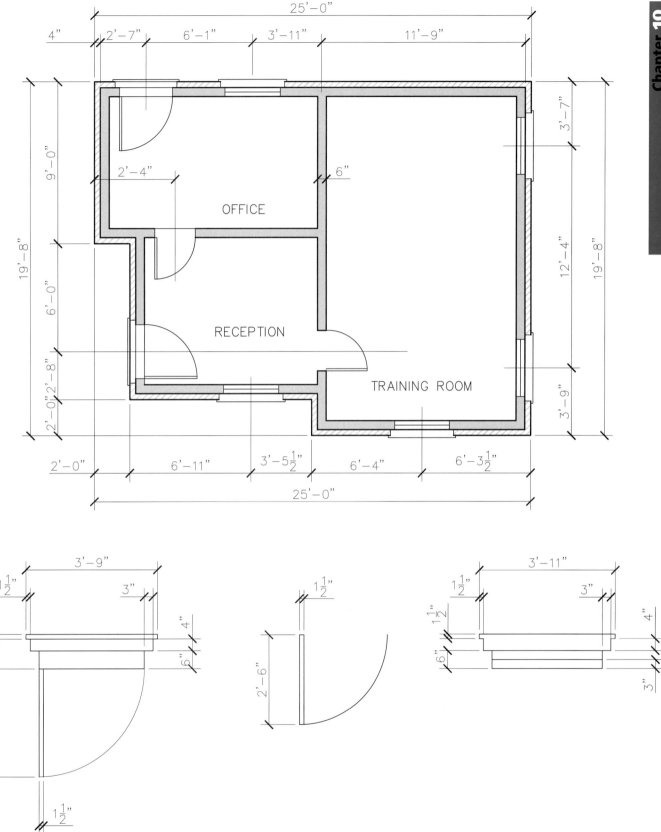

Figure 10-30
Exercise 10-3: Floor plan dimensions (scale: 3/16″ = 1′-0″). Door and window detail dimensions (scale: 3/8″ = 1′-0″)

Step 2. Start a new drawing and draw the typical workstation shown in Figure 10-31. Estimate any dimension not shown.

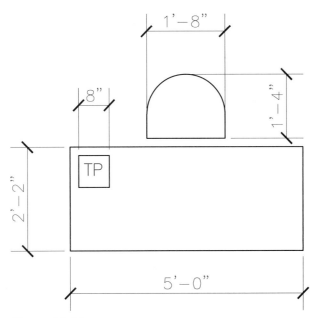

Figure 10-31
Exercise 10-3: Typical workstation dimensions

SET BASE POINT	
Ribbon/ Panel	Insert/ Block Definition/ Set Base Point
Menu Bar:	Draw/ Block/Base
Type a Command:	BASE

Step 3. Use the **Set Base Point** command (or type **BASE**) to select the midpoint on the arc of the chair as the insertion point for the workstation.

Step 4. Save the typical workstation drawing as **WS10-1** in the same folder with **CH10-EXERCISE3.** Exit the drawing.

Step 5. Open the floor plan drawing **CH10-EXERCISE3.**

Step 6. Attach the workstation to the floor plan drawing, as described next:

ATTACH EXTERNAL REFERENCE	
Ribbon/ Panel	Insert/ Reference/ Attach
Menu Bar:	Insert/DWG Reference...
Toolbar:	Reference/ Attach Xref
Type a Command:	XATTACH

Prompt	Response
Type a command:	**XATTACH**
The **Select Reference File** dialog box (Figure 10-32) appears:	Locate drawing **WS10-1** and click on it
	Click **Open**
The **Attach External Reference** dialog box (Figure 10-33) appears:	Click **OK**
Specify insertion point or [Scale X Y Z Rotate PScale PX PY PZ PRotate]:	Click **P1→** (Figure 10-34)

That's all there is to attaching an external reference to another drawing.

Step 7. Copy the external reference to four other locations on the floor plan as shown in Figure 10-35 (the exact location is not important).

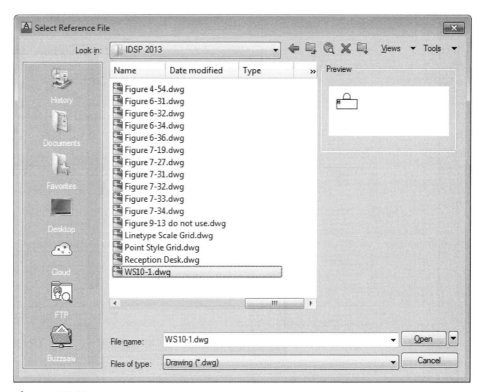

Figure 10-32
Locate drawing **WS10-1** and select it

Step 8. Save your drawing (**CH10-EXERCISE3**) to the same folder or disk as **WS10-1.** Exit the drawing.

You have been informed that all the workstations must now have a computer.

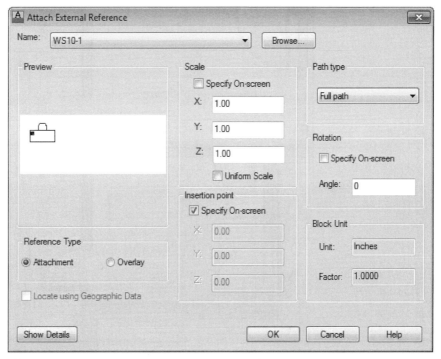

Figure 10-33
Attach External Reference dialog box with **WS10-1** selected

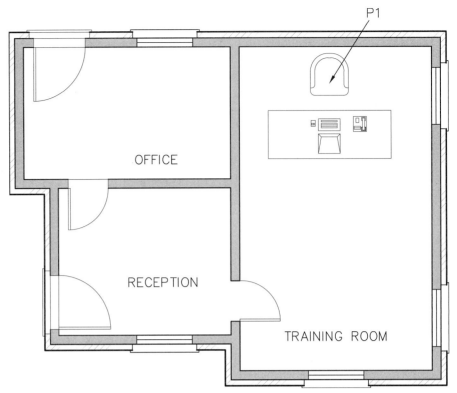

Figure 10-34
Insert the external reference

Step 9. Open drawing **WS10-1** and draw a computer approximately the size shown in Figure 10-36 and label it. Save the new workstation drawing in the same place from which it came.

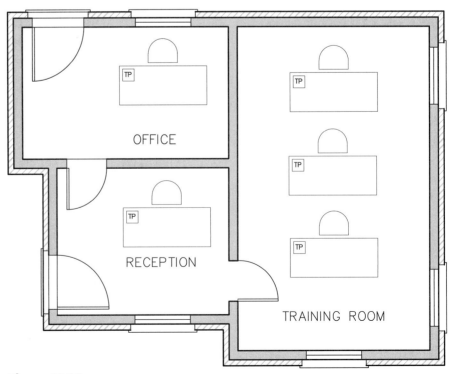

Figure 10-35
Copy the external reference to four other locations

Figure 10-36
The new workstation

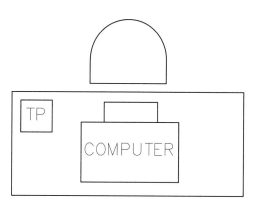

Step 10. Open drawing **CH10-EXERCISE3.** It should appear as shown in Figure 10-37.

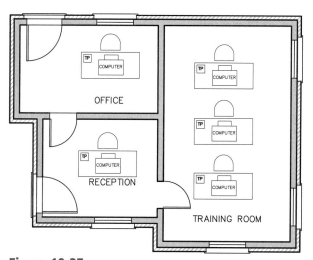

Figure 10-37
The office floor plan with new workstations

Step 11. Add your name, class, and current date to the drawing in the upper right and save **CH10-EXERCISE3** in the same folder or disk from which it came.

Step 12. Print the drawing to scale.

Chapter Summary

This chapter described the AutoCAD **DesignCenter, Autodesk Seek,** dynamic blocks, and external references. It showed you how to use the **DesignCenter** to take blocks, layers, linetypes, and text and dimension styles from any existing drawing using drag and drop and place them in the current drawing. It also showed you how to make external references and dynamic blocks. You will now be able to use these commands to make drawings quickly and efficiently.

Chapter Test Questions

Multiple Choice

Circle the correct answer.

1. The **History** tab on the **DesignCenter** allows you to do which of the following?
   a. Look at a preview of a selected item
   b. Return to the previous screen
   c. Display a list of the most recently opened drawings
   d. Search for data using the **Search** command

2. Which of the following opens the **Block Editor**?
   a. **BOPEN**   c. **BLOCKE**
   b. **BE**   d. **BED**

3. Which of the following closes the **Block Editor**?
   a. **BCL**   c. **BC**
   b. **CLOSE**   d. **EDCL**

4. Which of the following **External Reference** options allows you to make a block of an external reference in the current drawing?
   a. **Reload**   c. **Attach...**
   b. **Bind**   d. **Detach**

5. How many external references can be nested on a primary drawing?
   a. 1   c. 32
   b. 16   d. Unlimited

Matching

Write the number of the correct answer on the line.

a. External reference _____   1. An inserted file that can have varying size parameters attached

b. Dynamic block _____   2. A primary drawing always contains the most recent version of this inserted file

c. **DesignCenter** _____

d. **Autodesk Seek** _____

e. **Block Authoring Palettes** _____

3. Can be used to copy blocks from one drawing to another

4. Used for adding parameters to dynamic blocks

5. An online source for product and design files

True or False

1. **True or False:** The **DesignCenter** allows you to drag and drop blocks, layers, linetypes, and text and dimension styles from an existing drawing into the current drawing.

2. **True or False:** You cannot add dynamic features to an existing block.

3. **True or False:** Dynamic block parameters and actions can be added to a block using the **Block Editor**.

4. **True or False:** Unneeded external references cannot be removed from a drawing.

5. **True or False:** Only two visibility options are available in the **New Visibility State** dialog box.

List

1. Five ways of accessing the **DesignCenter**.

2. Five buttons above the tabs in the **DesignCenter**.

3. Five types of items available from the **DesignCenter/Home Designer** list.

4. Five ways of accessing **AutoDesk Seek**.

5. Five options from **Block Authoring Palettes/Adding a lookup parameter**.

6. Five ways of accessing the **XREF** command.

7. Five ways of accessing **Attach Ext Ref**.

8. Five **XREF** command options that do not make a block of the XREF in your current drawing.

9. Five features of XREFs.

10. Five block-related commands.

Questions

1. What is the **DesignCenter** used for?

2. How can dynamic blocks be used effectively?

3. What are the uses of parameters and their actions?

4. How can external references be used to keep the same office configurations consistent?

5. How can you locate items in **Autodesk Seek** that you need for your drawings?

Chapter Projects

Project 10-1: *Dynamic Block (Table and Chair) with Stretch and Move Actions* [BASIC]

1. Draw the table with the phone and the computer as shown in Figure 10-38. The phone and the computer terminal are found in the **Design-Center** in the **Home - Space Planner** drawing. The table measures 6′ × 2′-8″.

2. Copy the chair from one of the drawings you completed in Chapter 3.

   Place the chair at the midpoint of the table in the X direction and 6″ up.

3. Block the entire drawing with the name **table with chair.**

4. Access the **Block Editor** (type **BE <Enter>**) and add a linear parameter and a lookup parameter to the table.

5. Add a stretch action and a lookup action to the table as shown in Figure 10-39, similar to those in Exercise 10-2. The lengths of the table should be 8′ and 10′.

6. Add a point parameter and a lookup parameter to the chair.

7. Add a move action and a lookup action to the chair as shown in Figure 10-40. The chair should move 1′ and 2′.

8. Save the block and exit the **Block Editor.**

9. Insert the table with chair block and test it. Move the chair 1′ using the lookup action when you stretch the table to 8′ with its lookup action. Move the chair 2′ when you stretch the table 10′.

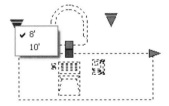

Figure 10-39

The stretch and lookup actions

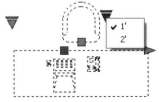

Figure 10-40

The move and lookup actions

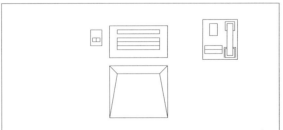

Figure 10-38

The table with chair block

Project 10-2: *Dynamic Block (Bed)* [BASIC]

1. Insert the Bed-queen as shown in Figure 10-41 and explode it. (You will find it in the **DesignCenter** in the **Home - Space Planner** drawing.)

2. Block the entire drawing with the name **bed**.

3. Access the **Block Editor** (type **BE <Enter>**) and add two linear parameters and two lookup parameters to the bed.

4. Add two stretch actions and two lookup actions to the bed as shown in Figure 10-42 similar to those in Exercise 10-2. The lengths of the bed should be 75″ and 80″. The widths of the bed should be 54″, 60″, and 76″.

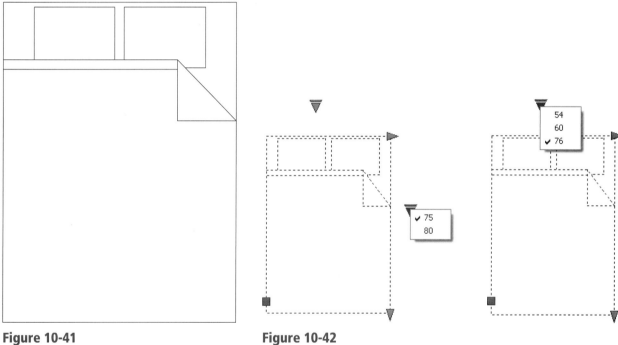

Figure 10-41
The bed block

Figure 10-42
Two stretch and two lookup actions

5. Save the block and exit the **Block Editor**.

6. Insert the bed block and test it. You should have a dynamic block that gives you three standard bed sizes:

   Full size is 54″ × 75″
   Queen size is 60″ × 80″
   King size is 76″ × 80″

Project 10-3: *Condo Floor Plan with External References* [ADVANCED]

1. Draw full size the floor plan of the condo as shown in Figure 10-43. Use an 1/8″ architect's scale to measure any features that do not have dimensions. The scale is 1/8″ = 1'-0″.

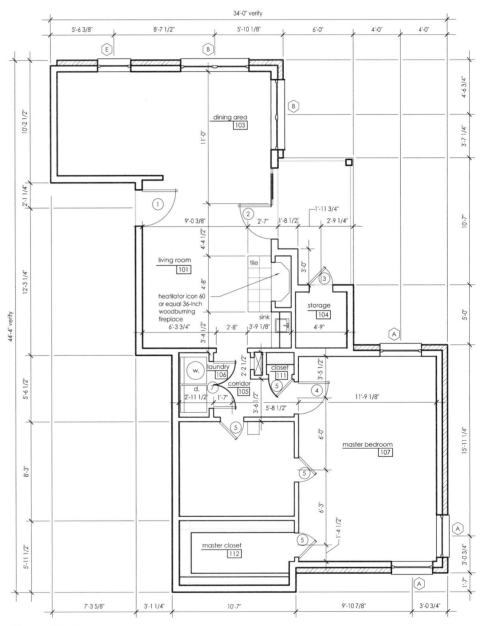

Figure 10-43
Condo floor plan (scale: 1/8″ = 1'-0″)

2. Draw full size the original xref kitchen as shown in Figure 10-44. The scale of this figure is 1/4″ = 1'-0″.

Figure 10-44
Original xref kitchen (scale: 1/4″ = 1′-0″)

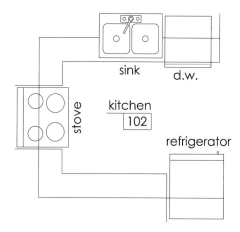

3. Attach the original xref kitchen to the condo floor plan as shown in Figure 10-45 and close the condo drawing.

Figure 10-45
Condo floor plan with original xrefs attached (scale: 1/8″ = 1′-0″)

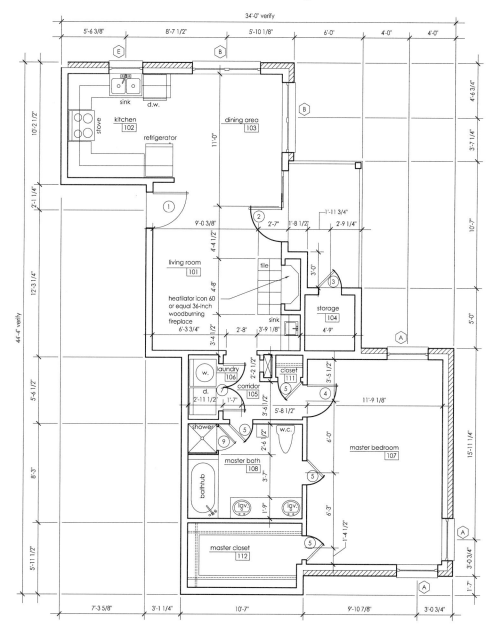

4. Make changes to the original xref kitchen as shown in Figure 10-46. The scale of this figure is 1/4″ = 1′-0″. You will find the new sink, stove, and refrigerator in the **Kitchen** drawing in the **DesignCenter**.

5. Draw full size the original xref bathroom as shown in Figure 10-47. The scale of this figure is 1/4″ = 1′-0″.

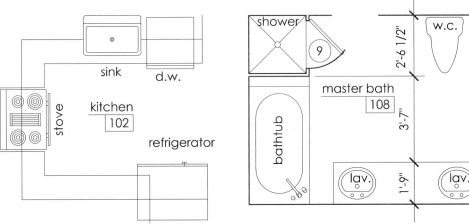

Figure 10-46
Revised xref kitchen (scale: 1/4″ = 1′-0″)

Figure 10-47
Original xref bathroom (scale: 1/4″ = 1′-0″)

6. Attach the original xref bathroom to the condo floor plan as shown in Figure 10-45 and close the condo drawing.

7. Make changes to the original xref bathroom as shown in Figure 10-48. The scale of this figure is 1/4″ = 1′-0″. You will find the new toilet, tub, and sinks in the **House Designer** drawing in the **DesignCenter**.

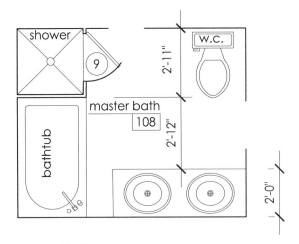

Figure 10-48
Revised xref bathroom (scale: 1/4″ = 1′-0″)

8. Open the condo floor plan. Your drawing should appear as shown in Figure 10-49. You may need to reload the xrefs.

9. Save the drawing in at least two places and print the drawing to scale.

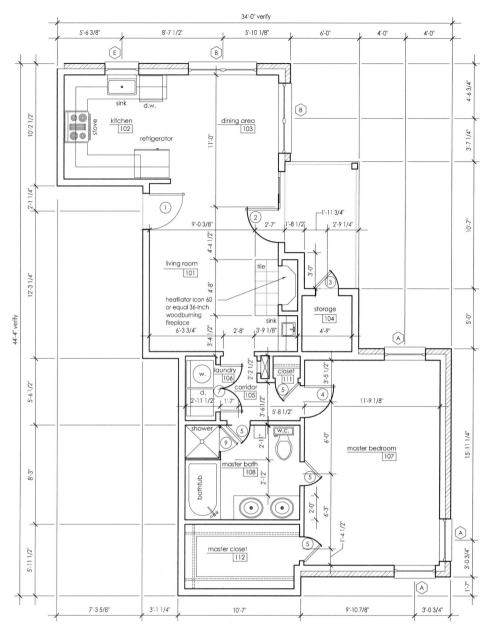

Figure 10-49
Condo floor plan with revised xrefs attached (scale: 1/8″ = 1′-0″)

Project 10-4: *Log Cabin Floor Plan with External References* [INTERMEDIATE]

1. Draw full size the floor plan of the log cabin (or use the one you drew previously) as shown in Figure 10-50. Use a 3/16″ architect's scale to measure any features that do not have dimensions. The scale is 3/16″ = 1′-0″.

2. Draw full size the original xref bedroom 1 as shown in Figure 10-51. The scale of this figure is 1/4″ = 1′-0″. You will find the bed and lamps in the **Home - Space Planner** drawing in the **DesignCenter**. Measure and draw the rectangle as shown.

3. Attach the original xref bedroom 1 to the log cabin floor plan as shown in Figure 10-52 and close the log cabin drawing.

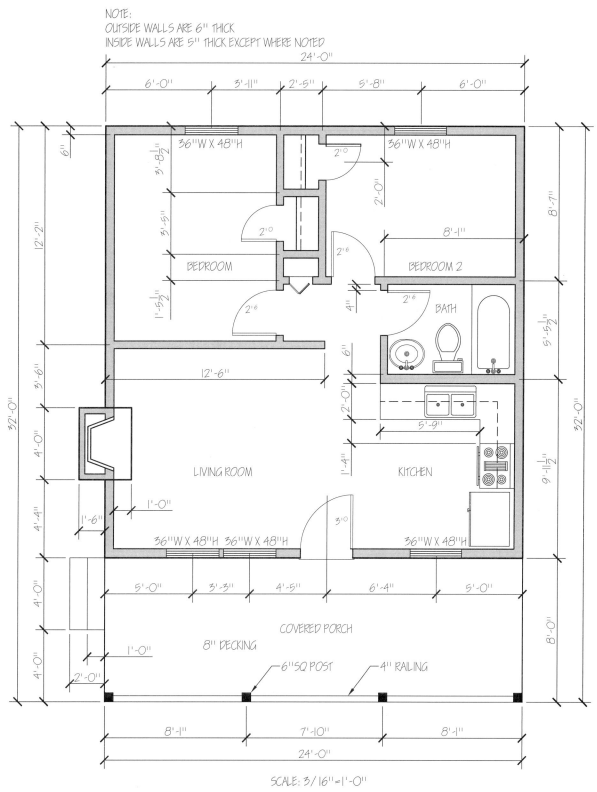

NOTE:
OUTSIDE WALLS ARE 6" THICK
INSIDE WALLS ARE 5" THICK EXCEPT WHERE NOTED

24'-0"

6'-0"   3'-11"   2'-5"   5'-8"   6'-0"

6"

36"W X 48"H   2'0   36"W X 48"H

3'-8 1/2"

2'-0"

8'-7"

3'-5"   2'0

BEDROOM   2'6   8'-1"   BEDROOM 2

1'-5 1/2"   2'6   4"   2'6   BATH

5'-5 1/2"

12'-2"

32'-0"

3'-6"

12'-6"   6"

2'-0"   5'-9"

4'-0"

1'-4"   9'-11 1/2"

LIVING ROOM   KITCHEN

32'-0"

4'-4"

1'-6"   1'-0"

3'0

36"W X 48"H 36"W X 48"H   36"W X 48"H

5'-0"   3'-3"   4'-5"   6'-4"   5'-0"

4'-0"

COVERED PORCH
8" DECKING

8'-0"

1'-0"

2'-0"   6"SQ POST   4" RAILING

4'-0"

8'-1"   7'-10"   8'-1"

24'-0"

SCALE: 3/16"=1'-0"

Figure 10-50
Log cabin floor plan (scale: 3/16" = 1'-0")

Figure 10-51
Original xref bedroom 1
(scale: 1/4″ = 1′-0″)

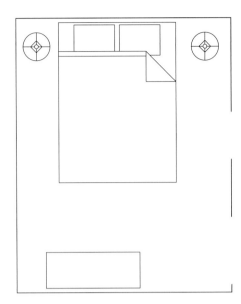

Figure 10-52
Log cabin floor plan with
original xrefs

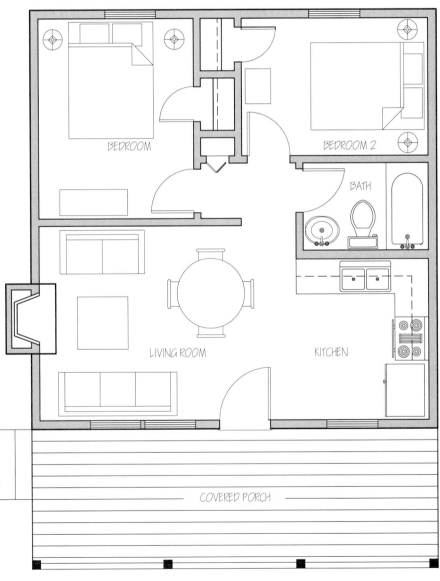

BEDROOM

BEDROOM 2

BATH

LIVING ROOM

KITCHEN

COVERED PORCH

SCALE: 3/16″=1′-0″

4. Make changes to the original xref bedroom 1 as shown in Figure 10-53. The scale of this figure is $1/4'' = 1'-0''$. You will find the entertainment center in the **Home - Space Planner** drawing in the **DesignCenter**.

5. Draw full size the original xref bedroom 2 as shown in Figure 10-54. The scale of this figure is $1/4'' = 1'-0''$. Use a $1/4''$ architect's scale to measure and draw the rectangle on the west wall.

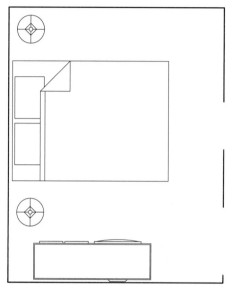

Figure 10-53
Revised xref bedroom 1 (scale: 1/4" = 1'-0")

Figure 10-54
Original xref bedroom 2 (scale: 1/4" = 1'-0")

6. Attach the original xref bedroom 2 to the log cabin floor plan (Figure 10-52) and close the log cabin drawing.

7. Make changes to the original xref bedroom 2 as shown in Figure 10-55. The scale of this figure is $1/4'' = 1'-0''$. Use a $1/4''$ architect's scale to measure and draw the rectangle on the west wall.

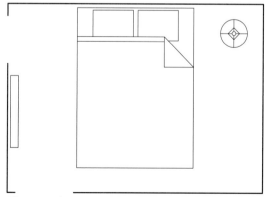

Figure 10-55
Revised xref bedroom 2 (scale: 1/4" = 1'-0")

8. Draw full size the original xref living room as shown in Figure 10-56. The scale of this figure is $1/4'' = 1'-0''$. Use a $1/4''$ architect's scale to measure and draw the rectangle and the dining room set. You will find the sofas in the **Home - Space Planner** drawing in the **DesignCenter**.

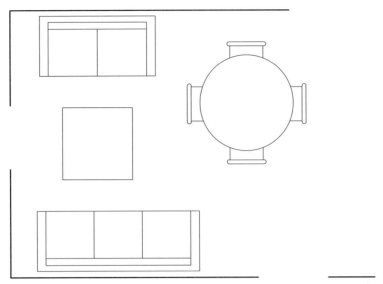

Figure 10-56
Original xref living room (scale: 1/4″ = 1′-0″)

9. Attach the original xref living room to the log cabin floor plan (Figure 10-52) and close the log cabin drawing.

10. Make changes to the original xref living room as shown in Figure 10-57. The scale of this figure is 1/4″ = 1′-0″. Use a 1/4″ architect's scale to measure and draw the rectangle. You will find the remaining furniture in the **Home - Space Planner** drawing in the **DesignCenter**.

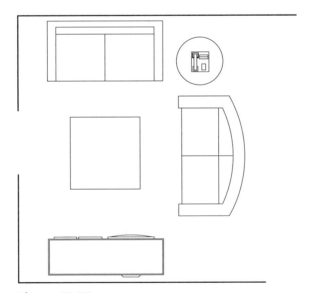

Figure 10-57
Revised xref living room (scale: 1/4″ = 1′-0″)

11. Open the log cabin floor plan. Your drawing should appear as shown in Figure 10-58.

12. Save the drawing in at least two places and print the drawing to scale.

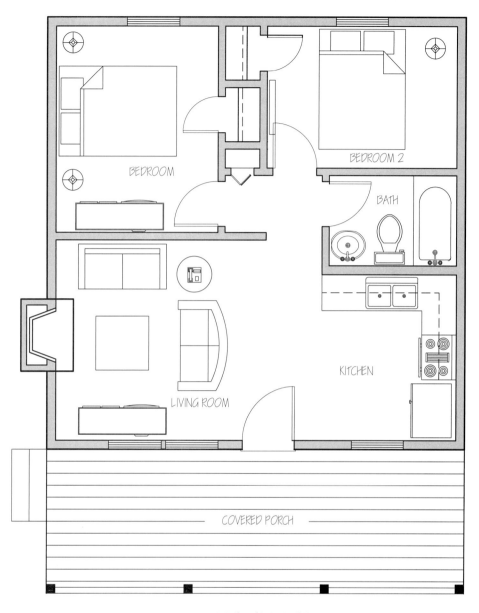

BEDROOM

BEDROOM 2

BATH

LIVING ROOM

KITCHEN

COVERED PORCH

SCALE: 3/16"=1'-0"

Figure 10-58
Log cabin floor plan with revised xrefs (scale: 3/16″ = 1′-0″)

Project 10-5: *House 1 Floor Plan with External References* [ADVANCED]

1. Draw full size (without dimensions) the floor plan of house 1 (or use the one you drew previously) as shown in Figure 10-59. Use an 1/8″ architect's scale to measure any features that do not have dimensions. The scale is 1/8″ = 1′-0″.

2. Draw full size the original xref master bedroom as shown in Figure 10-60. The scale of this figure is 1/4″ = 1′-0″. You will find most of the furniture and the computer in the **Home - Space Planner** drawing in the **DesignCenter**. Measure and draw the square lamp table and desk as shown.

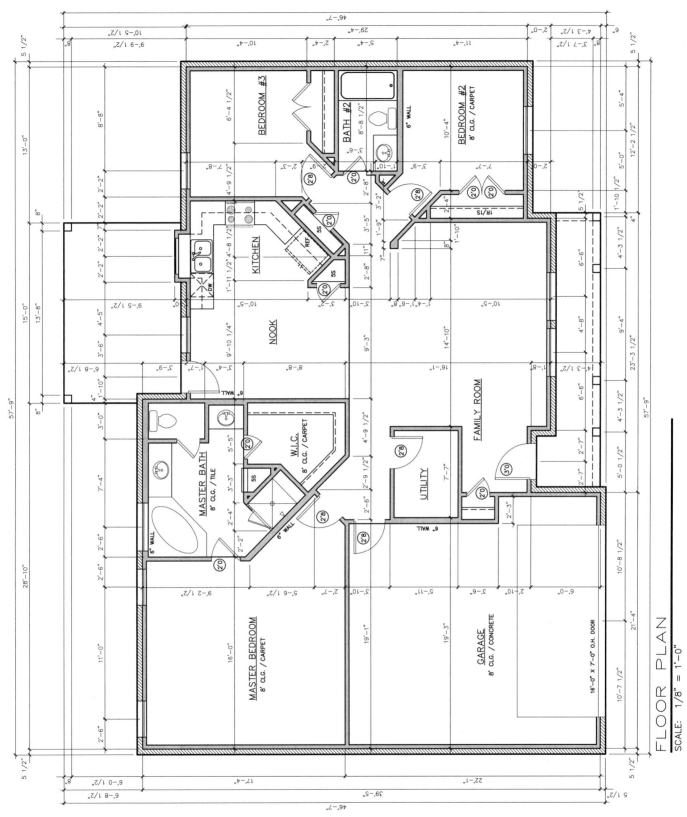

Figure 10-59
House 1 floor plan (scale: 1/8″ = 1′-0″)

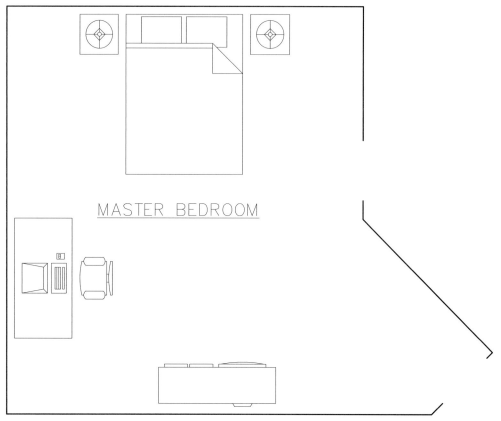

Figure 10-60
Original xref master bedroom (scale: 1/4″ = 1′-0″)

3. Attach the original xref master bedroom to the house 1 floor plan as shown in Figure 10-61 and close the house 1 floor plan.

4. Make changes to the original master bedroom as shown in Figure 10-62. The scale of this figure is 1/4″ = 1′-0″. You will find most of the furniture in the **Home - Space Planner** drawing and in **Autodesk Seek** in the **DesignCenter**. Measure and draw the chests of drawers as shown.

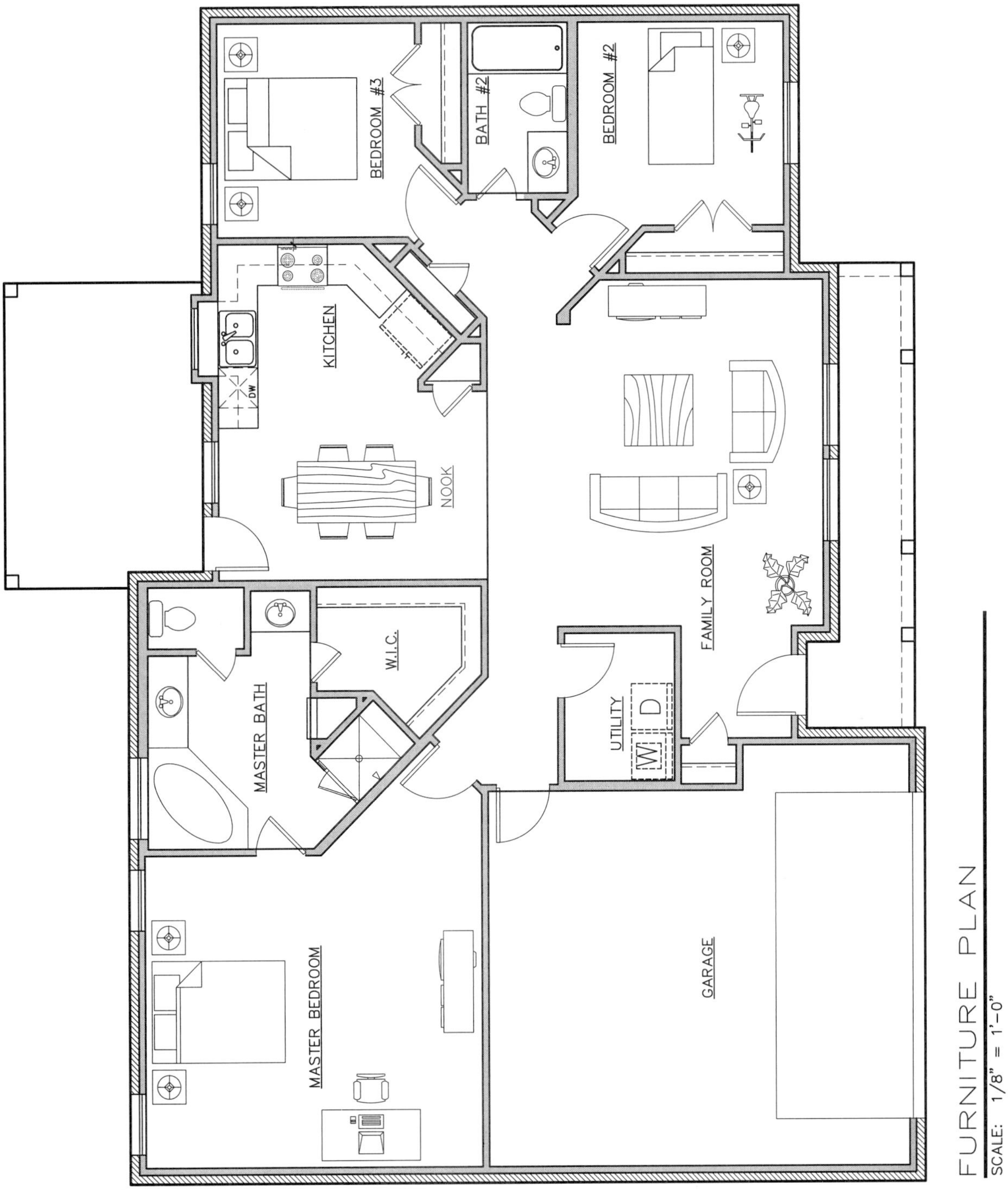
BEDROOM #3
BATH #2
BEDROOM #2
KITCHEN
DW
NOOK
FAMILY ROOM
W.I.C.
MASTER BATH
UTILITY
W
D
MASTER BEDROOM
GARAGE
FURNITURE PLAN
SCALE: 1/8" = 1'–0"

Figure 10-61
House 1 floor plan with original xrefs (scale: 1/8" = 1'-0")

Figure 10-62
Revised xref master bed-
room (scale: 1/4″ = 1′-0″)

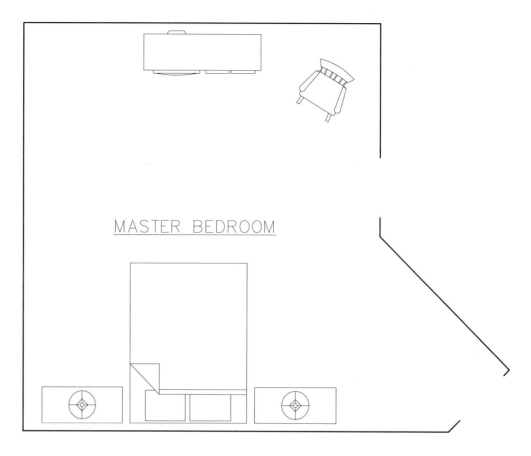

MASTER BEDROOM

5. Draw full size the original xref bedroom 2 as shown in Figure 10-63. The scale of this figure is 1/4″ = 1′-0″. You will find most of the furniture in the **Home - Space Planner** drawing and in **Autodesk Seek** in the **DesignCenter.** Use a 1/4″ architect's scale to measure and draw the square lamp table.

6. Attach the original xref bedroom 2 to the house 1 floor plan (Figure 10-61) and close the house 1 floor plan.

Figure 10-63
Original xref bedroom 2
(scale: 1/4″ = 1′-0″)

BEDROOM #2

7. Make changes to the original xref bedroom 2 as shown in Figure 10-64. The scale of this figure is 1/4″ = 1′-0″. Use a 1/4″ architect's scale to measure and draw the rectangle on the south wall.

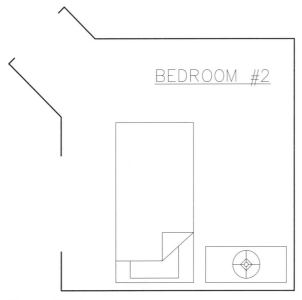

Figure 10-64
Revised xref bedroom 2 (scale: 1/4″ = 1′-0″)

8. Draw full size the original xref bedroom 3 as shown in Figure 10-65. The scale of this figure is 1/4″ = 1′-0″. You will find the furniture in the **Home - Space Planner** drawing in the **DesignCenter**. Use a 1/4″ architect's scale to measure and draw the square lamp table.

9. Attach the original xref bedroom 3 to the house 1 floor plan (Figure 10-61) and close the house 1 floor plan.

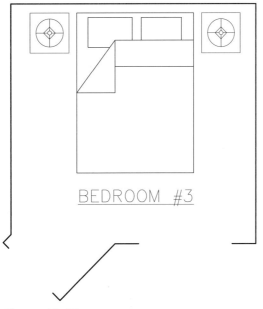

Figure 10-65
Original xref bedroom 3 (scale: 1/4″ = 1′-0″)

10. Make changes to the original xref bedroom 3 as shown in Figure 10-66. The scale of this figure is 1/4″ = 1′-0″. Use a 1/4″ architect's scale to measure and draw the square lamp table. You will find the lamp, bed, and bicycle in the **Home - Space Planner** drawing and in **Autodesk Seek** in the **DesignCenter**.

Figure 10-66
Revised xref bedroom 3
(scale: 1/4″ = 1′-0″)

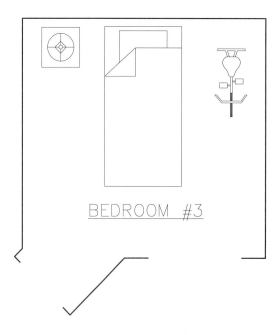

11. Draw full size the original xref family room as shown in Figure 10-67. The scale of this figure is 1/4″ = 1′-0″. Use a 1/4″ architect's scale to measure and draw the square lamp table. You will find the sofas and other items in the **Home - Space Planner** drawing in the **DesignCenter**.

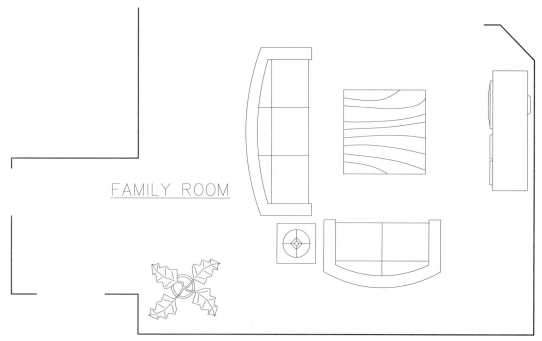

Figure 10-67
Original xref family room (scale: 1/4″ = 1′-0″)

12. Attach the original xref family room to the house 1 floor plan (Figure 10-61) and close the house 1 floor plan.

13. Make changes to the original xref living room as shown in Figure 10-68. The scale of this figure is 1/4″ = 1′-0″. Use a 1/4″ architect's scale to measure and draw the square lamp table. You will find the remaining furniture in the **Home - Space Planner** drawing in the **DesignCenter**.

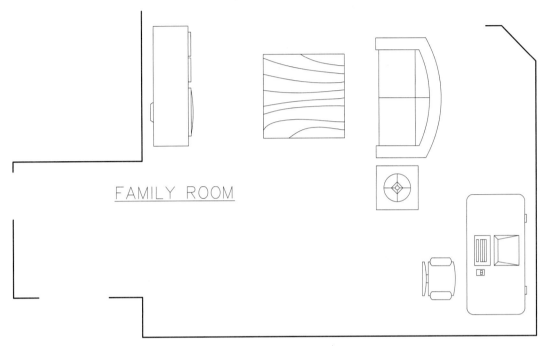

FAMILY ROOM

Figure 10-68
Revised xref family room (scale: 1/4″ = 1′-0″)

14. Open the house 1 floor plan. Your drawing should appear as shown in Figure 10-69.

15. Save the drawing in at least two places and print the drawing to scale.

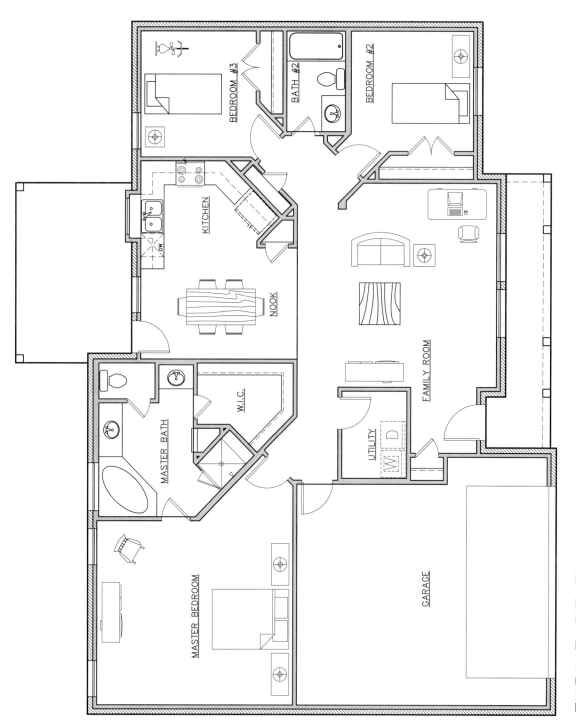

FURNITURE PLAN

SCALE: 1/8" = 1'-0"

Figure 10-69
House 1 floor plan with revised xrefs (scale: 1/8" = 1'-0")

11 chaptereleven

Drawing the Reflected Ceiling Plan and Voice/Data/Power Plan

CHAPTER OBJECTIVES

- Draw a reflected ceiling plan.
- Draw a voice/data/power plan.

- Draw a power/communication/lighting plan

Introduction

Previously learned commands are used to draw the tenant space reflected ceiling plan in Exercise 11-1, Part 1, and the tenant space voice/data/power plan in Exercise 11-1, Part 2. Helpful guidelines for drawing Exercise 11-1, Parts 1 and 2, are provided.

The **reflected ceiling plan** shows all the lighting symbols and other items such as exit signs that attach to the ceiling in their correct locations in the space. The plan also shows all the switching symbols needed to turn the lights on and off.

The voice/data/power plan shows symbols for telephones (voice), computers (data), and electrical outlets (power).

reflected ceiling plan: A drawing showing all the lighting symbols and other items such as exit signs that attach to the ceiling in their correct locations in the space. The plan also shows all the switching symbols needed to turn the lights on and off.

lighting legend: A collection of symbols and text that identify lights and other lighting items such as switches.

EXERCISE 11-1
Part 1, Tenant Space Lighting Legend and Reflected Ceiling Plan

In Exercise 11-1, Part 1, you will make a wblock of each lighting symbol and then insert each symbol into the tenant space reflected ceiling plan. When you have completed Exercise 11-1, Part 1, your reflected ceiling plan drawing will look similar to Figure 11-1.

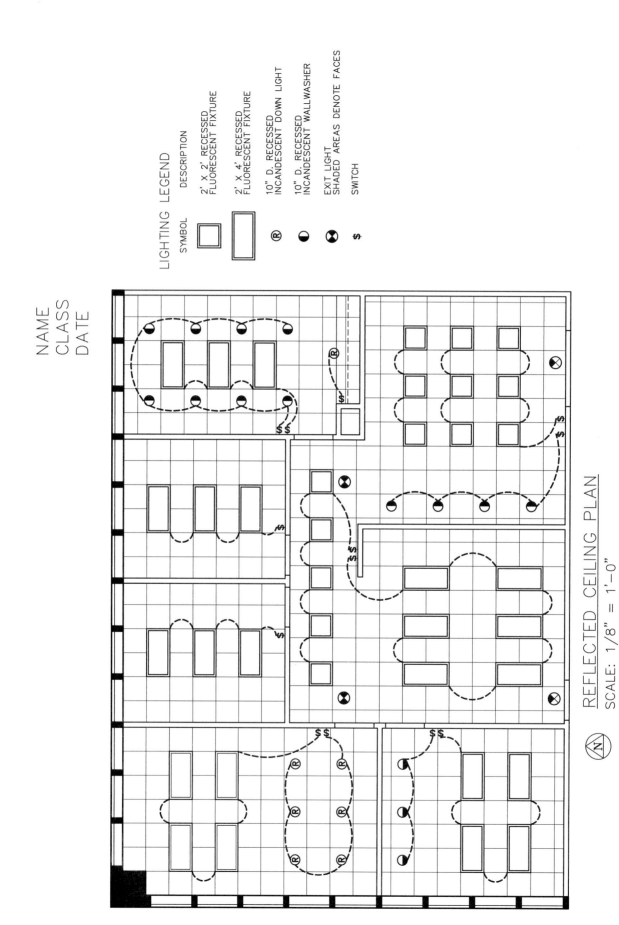

LIGHTING LEGEND

SYMBOL	DESCRIPTION
□	2' x 2' RECESSED FLUORESCENT FIXTURE
▭	2' x 4' RECESSED FLUORESCENT FIXTURE
®	10" D. RECESSED INCANDESCENT DOWN LIGHT
◗	10" D. RECESSED INCANDESCENT WALLWASHER
⊗	EXIT LIGHT SHADED AREAS DENOTE FACES
$	SWITCH

REFLECTED CEILING PLAN

SCALE: 1/8" = 1'-0"

Figure 11-1

Exercise 11-1: Part 1, Tenant space reflected ceiling plan (scale: **1/8" = 1'-0"**)

Step 1. Create the following new layers:

Layer Name	Color	Linetype	Lineweight
a-clng-susp	red	continuous	.004″ (.09 mm)
e-anno-symb-lite	blue	continuous	.010″ (.25 mm)
e-anno-symb-powr	blue	continuous	.010″ (.25 mm)
e-anno-text-lite	green	continuous	.006″ (.15 mm)
e-anno-text-powr	green	continuous	.006″ (.15 mm)
e-lite-circ	white	hidden	.016″ (.40 mm)

Tenant Space Lighting Legend Symbols

Step 2. Draw each lighting symbol, as shown in Figure 11-2, on the **e-anno-symb-lite** layer, full size. Wblock each symbol to a new folder named **Lighting Symbols**. Identify a logical insertion point, such as a corner of a rectangle or center of a circle.

Figure 11-2
Exercise 11-1: Part 1, Tenant space lighting legend (scale: 1/4″ = 1′-0″)

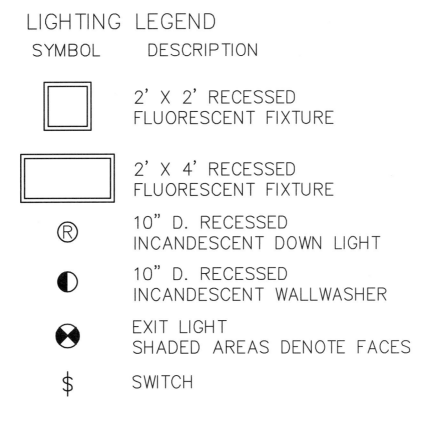

Tenant Space Reflected Ceiling Plan

NOTE

In **EXERCISE 12-1** and **EXERCISE 12-2** you will freeze layers to make a presentation that displays the dimensioned floor plan, furniture plan, reflected ceiling plan, and voice/data/power plan. This will work only if you have saved **CH6-EXERCISE1**, **CH7-EXERCISE1**, **CH9-EXERCISE1**, and **CH11-EXERCISE1** as a single drawing.

Step 3. Begin drawing **CH11-EXERCISE1-REFLECTED CEILING** on the hard drive or network drive by opening the existing drawing

CH9-EXERCISE1 and saving it as **CH11-EXERCISE1-REFLECTED CEILING**.

Step 4. Freeze all the layers that are not needed to draw the reflected ceiling plan.

Step 5. Set layer **a-wall-head** current. Draw lines across the door openings as shown in Figure 11-1.

Step 6. Set layer **a-clng-susp** current and draw the 2′ × 2′ separate balanced ceiling grid in each area as shown in Figure 11-1.

Step 7. Insert the lighting legend symbols, full scale, into the location shown on the tenant space reflected ceiling plan in Figure 11-1.

Step 8. Set layer **e-anno-text-lite** current.

Step 9. Add the text to the lighting legend as shown in Figure 11-1, and make it annotative. The words LIGHTING LEGEND are 3/32″ high text; the remaining text is all 1/16″ high.

Step 10. Prepare the ceiling grid for insertion of the 2′ × 4′ recessed fixture symbols by using the **ERASE** command to erase the ceiling grid lines that will cross the centers of the symbols.

Use the **COPY** command and an **Osnap** modifier to copy the lighting symbols from the legend and place them on the plan as shown in Figure 11-1.

The wallwasher, 2′ × 4′ fixture, and switch symbols appear on the reflected ceiling plan in several different orientations. Copy each symbol and rotate the individual symbols into the various positions, then use **COPY** to draw the additional like symbols in the correct locations on the plan.

Step 11. Set layer **e-lite-circ** current. Use the **ARC** command to draw the symbol for the circuitry. Adjust **LTSCALE** as needed so lines appear as dashed.

Step 12. Change the title text to read as shown in Figure 11-1.

Step 13. When you have completed Exercise 11-1, Part 1, save your work in at least two places.

Step 14. Plot or print Exercise 11-1, Part 1, to scale.

EXERCISE 11-1
Part 2, Tenant Space Voice/Data/ Power Legend and Plan

In Exercise 11-1, Part 2, you will make a wblock of each voice, data, and power symbol and then insert each symbol into the tenant space voice/ data/power plan. When you have completed Exercise 11-1, Part 2, your voice/data/power plan drawing will look similar to Figure 11-3.

Tenant Space Voice/Data/Power Legend Symbols

Step 1. Draw each voice, data, and power symbol, as shown in Figure 11-4, on the **e-anno-symb-power** layer, full size. Wblock each symbol to a

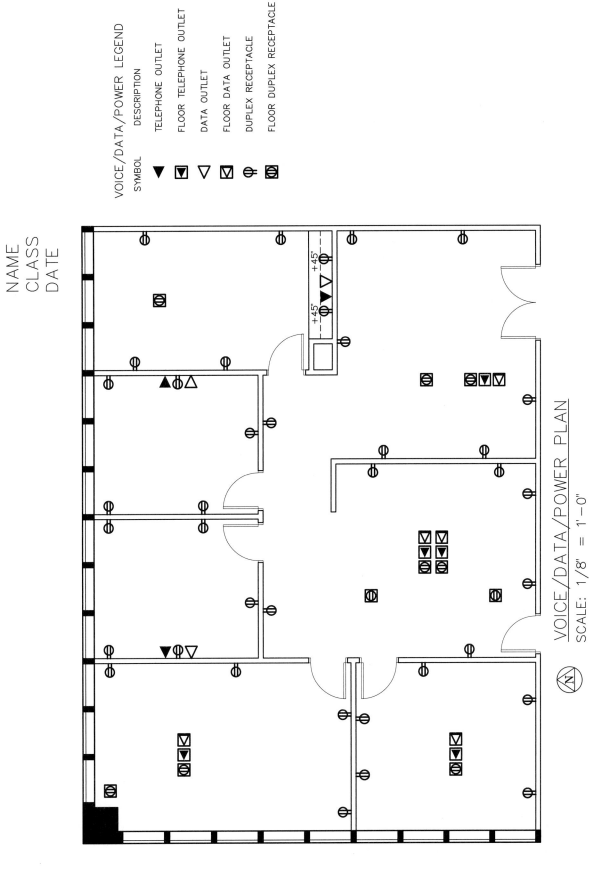

NAME
CLASS
DATE

VOICE/DATA/POWER LEGEND

SYMBOL	DESCRIPTION
▼	TELEPHONE OUTLET
▼ (boxed)	FLOOR TELEPHONE OUTLET
▽	DATA OUTLET
▽ (boxed)	FLOOR DATA OUTLET
⊖	DUPLEX RECEPTACLE
⊖ (boxed)	FLOOR DUPLEX RECEPTACLE

VOICE/DATA/POWER PLAN
SCALE: 1/8" = 1'-0"

Figure 11-3
Exercise 11-1: Part 2, Tenant space voice/data/power plan (scale: 1/8" = 1'-0")

VOICE/DATA/POWER LEGEND

SYMBOL   DESCRIPTION

◀   TELEPHONE OUTLET

◧   FLOOR TELEPHONE OUTLET

◁   DATA OUTLET

◲   FLOOR DATA OUTLET

⌽   DUPLEX RECEPTACLE

⊕   FLOOR DUPLEX RECEPTACLE

new folder named **Voice Data Power Symbols**. Identify a logical insertion point, such as the tip of a triangle or center of a circle.

voice/data/power plan: A drawing showing all symbols for telephones (voice), computers (data), and electrical outlets (power), and the locations of all these items.

Tenant Space Voice/Data/Power Plan

Step 2. Begin drawing **CH11-EXERCISE1-VOICE-DATA-POWER** on the hard drive or network drive by opening the existing drawing **CH11-EXERCISE1-REFLECTED CEILING** and saving it as **CH11-EXERCISE1-VOICE-DATA-POWER**.

Step 3. Freeze all layers that are not required to draw the voice/data/power plan. Thaw any layers that are required, as shown in Figure 11-3.

Step 4. Insert the voice/data/power legend symbols, full scale, in the location shown on the tenant space voice/data/power plan in Figure 11-3.

Step 5. Set layer **e-anno-text-powr** current.

Step 6. Add the text to the voice/data/power legend as shown in Figure 11-4, and make it annotative. The words VOICE/DATA/POWER LEGEND are 3/32″ high text; the remaining text is all 1/16″ high.

Step 7. Thaw the **i-furn** layer. Use the furniture to help you locate the voice/data/power symbols.

Step 8. Use the **COPY** command and an **Osnap** modifier to copy the symbols from the legend and place them on the plan as shown in Figure 11-3.

The duplex receptacle symbol appears on the plan in several different orientations. Copy the symbol and use **ROTATE** to obtain the rotated positions as shown on the plan. Use the **COPY** command to draw like rotated symbols in the correct locations on the plan.

It is helpful to use **Osnap-Mid Between 2 Points** and pick the two endpoints of the two lines in the duplex receptacle. Use this point to locate the duplex receptacle along the walls when using the **COPY** command. Use **Osnap-Center** to help locate the floor receptacle symbol.

Step 9. Freeze the **i-furn** layer.

Step 10. Change the title text to read as shown in Figure 11-3.

Step 11. When you have completed Exercise 11-1, Part 2, save your work in at least two places.

Step 12. Plot or print Exercise 11-1, Part 2, to scale.

Chapter Summary

This chapter provided you the information necessary to set up and draw reflected ceiling plans and voice/data/power plans. In drawing these plans you have enhanced your skills in using commands and settings such as **WBLOCK, Annotation Scale, Linetype Scale, Lineweight, COPY, BLOCK, INSERT, MOVE, TEXT, SCALE, Polyline, Polyline Edit**, and other commands. Now you have the skills and information necessary to produce reflected ceiling plans, voice/data/power plans, and power/communication/lighting plans.

Chapter Test Questions

Multiple Choice

Circle the correct answer.

1. Which of the following plans would most likely contain a symbol for a duplex receptacle?

   a. Reflected ceiling plan   c. Circuitry plan

   b. Voice/data/power plan   d. None of the above

2. Which of the following plans would most likely contain a symbol for a fluorescent fixture?

   a. Reflected ceiling plan   c. Circuitry plan

   b. Voice/data/power plan   d. None of the above

3. Which of the following plans would most likely contain a symbol for a telephone outlet?

   a. Reflected ceiling plan   c. Circuitry plan

   b. Voice/data/power plan   d. None of the above

4. Which of the following would most likely contain a symbol for an exhaust fan?

   a. Reflected ceiling plan   c. Circuitry plan

   b. Voice/data/power plan   d. None of the above

5. Which of the following linetypes was used to show circuitry?

   a. Continuous   c. Hidden

   b. Center   d. Dash-Dot

Matching

Write the number of the correct answer on the line.

a. Voice/data/power plan _____

b. Reflected ceiling plan _____

c. Circuitry _____

1. A plan that shows all the lights in an office

2. A plan that shows all the telephone outlets in an office

3. An Osnap mode

d. Mid Between 2 Points _____

e. **INSERT** _____

4. A command that is used to add a block from a symbol library to a drawing

5. A hidden line, arc, or polyline used to show which switch connects to which light

True or False

Circle the correct answer.

1. **True or False:** A reflected ceiling plan contains all the symbols needed for power.

2. **True or False:** A voice/data/power plan contains all the symbols needed for power.

3. **True or False:** Drawing symbols on the correct layer is not really necessary.

4. **True or False:** The width of a polyline can be changed.

5. **True or False:** The appearance of a hidden linetype can be changed with the **LTSCALE** command.

List

1. Five parameters that control a polar array.

2. Five plot area selection options in Plot window.

3. Five essential steps in making a Wblock.

4. Five options of the **Polyline** command.

5. Five options of the **Lengthen** command.

6. Five options of the **Zoom** command.

7. Five options of the navigation bar.

8. Five ways of accessing the plot command.

9. Five line/Mline commands.

10. Five parameters that control a rectangular array.

Questions

1. How does a reflected ceiling plan differ from a voice/data/power plan?

2. Why is it necessary to have both reflected ceiling plans and voice/data/power plans?

Chapter Projects

Project 11-1: *Hotel Room 2 Power/Communication/Lighting Legend and Plan* [BASIC]

1. Draw the hotel room power/communication/lighting symbols as shown in Figure 11-5. Do not redraw any symbols you have already drawn and wblocked to a folder. Use an architect's scale to measure the symbols and draw them full scale.

POWER/COMMUNICATION/LIGHTING LEGEND

SYMBOL	DESCRIPTION
⊖	DUPLEX RECEPTACLE
⊖ GFIC	DUPLEX RECEPTACLE WITH GROUND FAULT INTERRUPTER CIRCUIT
◀	TELEPHONE OUTLET
◁	DATA OUTLET
TV	CABLE TV OUTLET
S/A	SMOKE ALARM – WIRE DIRECT W/BATTERY BACK–UP
⊕	CEILING MOUNTED LIGHT FIXTURE
⊕+	WALL MOUNTED LIGHT FIXTURE
EX	EXHAUST FAN/LIGHT COMBINATION
$	SWITCH

Figure 11-5
Project 11-1: Hotel room 2 power/communication/lighting legend (scale: 1/4″ = 1′-0″)

2. Complete the hotel room power/communication/lighting plan as shown in Figure 11-6.

3. Plot or print the drawing to scale.

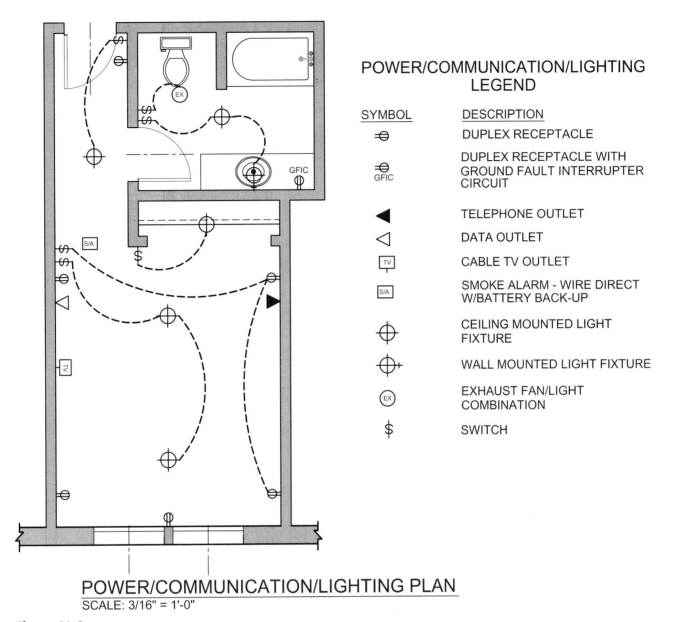

POWER/COMMUNICATION/LIGHTING LEGEND

SYMBOL	DESCRIPTION
⊖	DUPLEX RECEPTACLE
⊖ GFIC	DUPLEX RECEPTACLE WITH GROUND FAULT INTERRUPTER CIRCUIT
◀	TELEPHONE OUTLET
◁	DATA OUTLET
TV	CABLE TV OUTLET
S/A	SMOKE ALARM - WIRE DIRECT W/BATTERY BACK-UP
⊕	CEILING MOUNTED LIGHT FIXTURE
⊕⊢	WALL MOUNTED LIGHT FIXTURE
EX	EXHAUST FAN/LIGHT COMBINATION
$	SWITCH

POWER/COMMUNICATION/LIGHTING PLAN
SCALE: 3/16" = 1'-0"

Figure 11-6
Project 11-1: Hotel room 2 power/communication/lighting plan (scale: 3/16″ = 1′-0″)

Project 11-2: *Wheelchair-Accessible Commercial Restroom Lighting Legend and Plan* [INTERMEDIATE]

1. Draw the wheelchair-accessible commercial restroom lighting symbols as shown in Figure 11-7. Do not redraw any symbols you have already drawn and wblocked to a folder. Use an architect's scale to measure the symbols and draw them full scale.

Figure 11-7
Project 11-2: Wheelchair-accessible commercial restroom lighting legend (scale: 3/16″ = 1′-0″)

LIGHTING LEGEND

SYMBOL	DESCRIPTION
Ⓡ	RECESSED LIGHT FIXTURE
$	SWITCH
⌐	EMERGENCY LIGHT WALL MOUNTED

2. Complete the wheelchair-accessible commercial restroom lighting plan as shown in Figure 11-8.

3. Plot or print the drawing to scale.

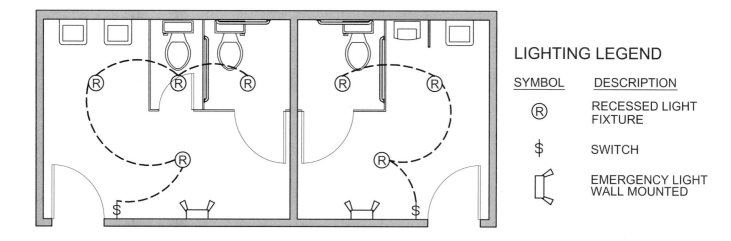

LIGHTING PLAN
SCALE:3/16"=1'-0"

LIGHTING LEGEND

SYMBOL	DESCRIPTION
Ⓡ	RECESSED LIGHT FIXTURE
$	SWITCH
⌐	EMERGENCY LIGHT WALL MOUNTED

Figure 11-8
Project 11-2: Wheelchair-accessible commercial restroom lighting plan (scale: 3/16″ = 1′-0″)

Project 11-3, Part 1: *Bank Lighting Legend and Reflected Ceiling Plan* [ADVANCED]

1. Draw the bank lighting symbols as shown in Figure 11-9. Do not redraw any symbols you have already drawn and wblocked to a folder. Use an architect's scale to measure the symbols and draw them full scale.

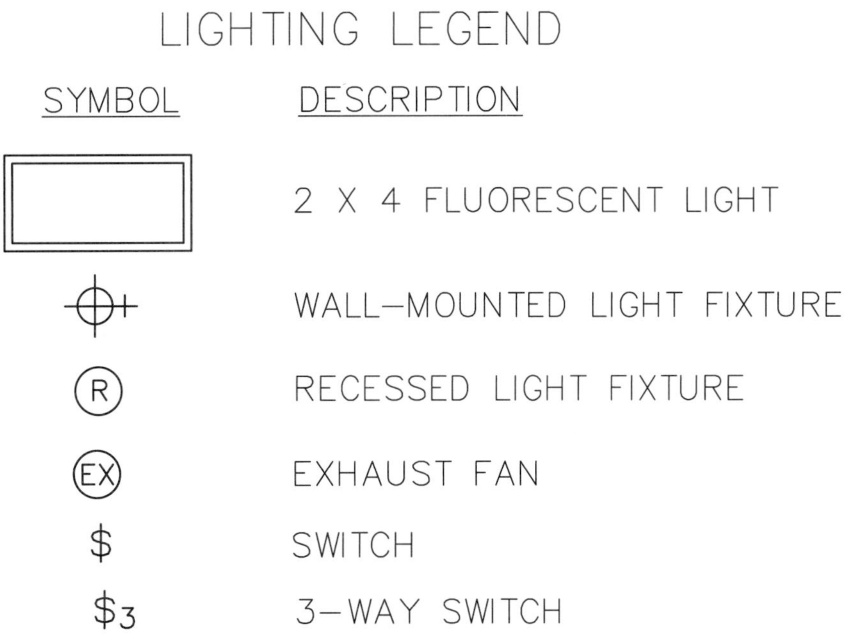

Figure 11-9
Project 11-3, Part 1: Bank lighting legend (scale: 1/4″ = 1′-0″)

LIGHTING LEGEND

SYMBOL	DESCRIPTION
[rectangle]	2 X 4 FLUORESCENT LIGHT
⊕	WALL—MOUNTED LIGHT FIXTURE
Ⓡ	RECESSED LIGHT FIXTURE
ⒺⓍ	EXHAUST FAN
$	SWITCH
$3	3—WAY SWITCH

2. Complete the bank reflected ceiling plan as shown in Figure 11-10.

3. Plot or print the drawing to scale.

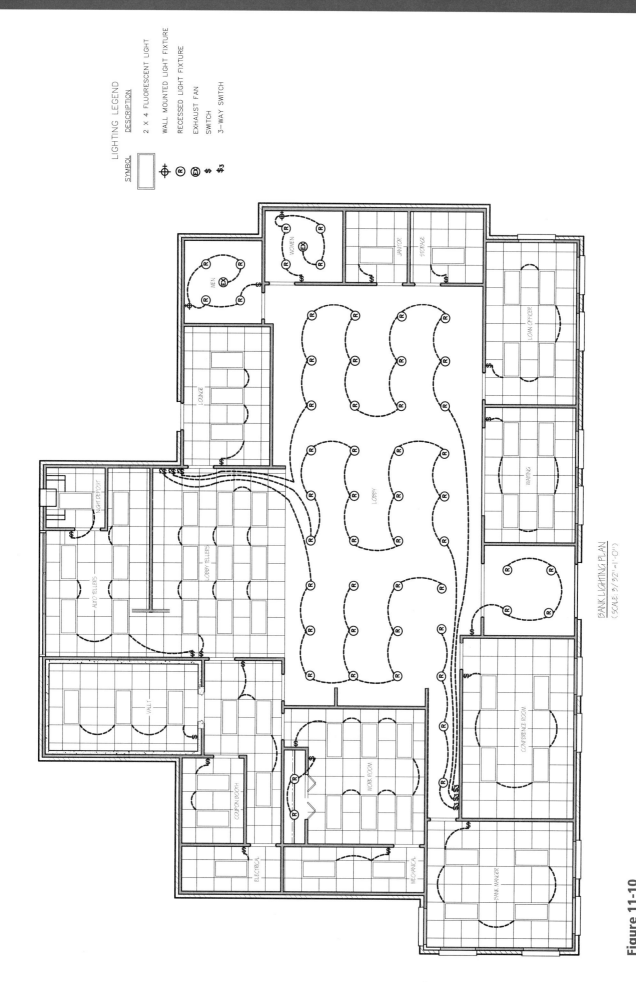

Figure 11-10

Project 11-3, Part 1: Bank reflected ceiling plan (scale: 3/32″ = 1′-0″)

Project 11-3, Part 2: *Bank Voice/Data/Power Legend and Plan* [ADVANCED]

1. Draw the bank voice/data/power symbols as shown in Figure 11-11. Do not redraw any symbols you have already drawn and wblocked to a folder. Use an architect's scale to measure the symbols and draw them full scale.

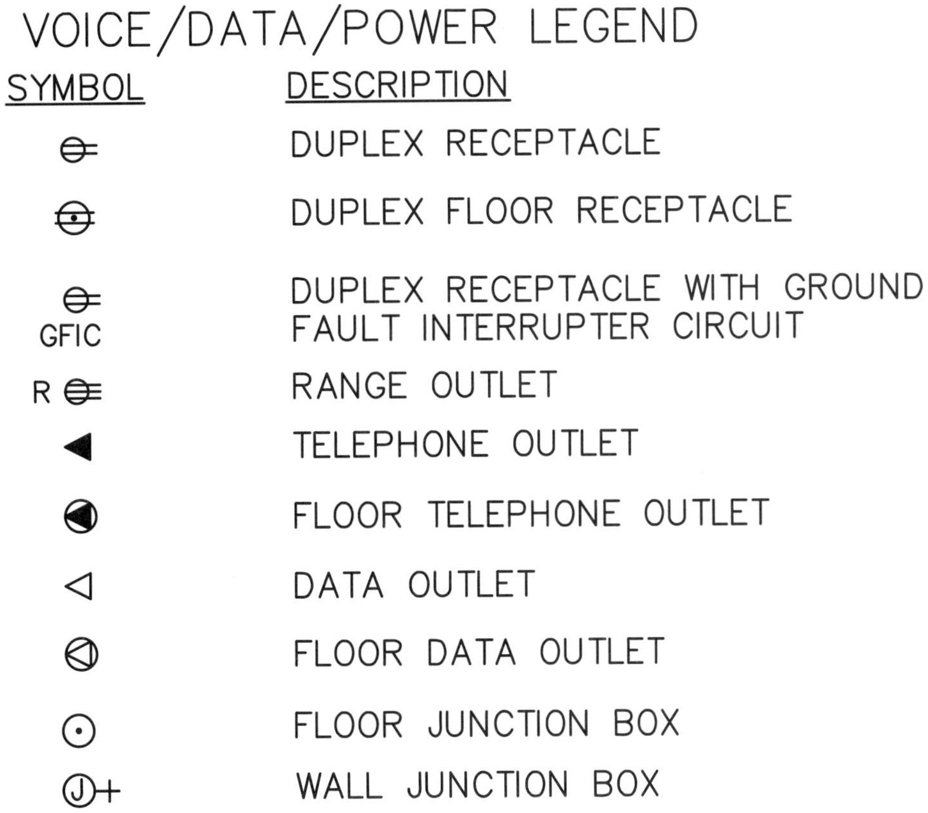

Figure 11-11
Project 11-3, Part 2: Bank voice/data/power legend (scale: 1/4″ = 1′-0″)

VOICE/DATA/POWER LEGEND

SYMBOL	DESCRIPTION
⊖	DUPLEX RECEPTACLE
⊕	DUPLEX FLOOR RECEPTACLE
⊖ GFIC	DUPLEX RECEPTACLE WITH GROUND FAULT INTERRUPTER CIRCUIT
R ⊖	RANGE OUTLET
◀	TELEPHONE OUTLET
◉	FLOOR TELEPHONE OUTLET
◁	DATA OUTLET
◁	FLOOR DATA OUTLET
⊙	FLOOR JUNCTION BOX
Ⓙ+	WALL JUNCTION BOX

2. Complete the bank voice/data/power plan as shown in Figure 11-12.

3. Plot or print the drawing to scale.

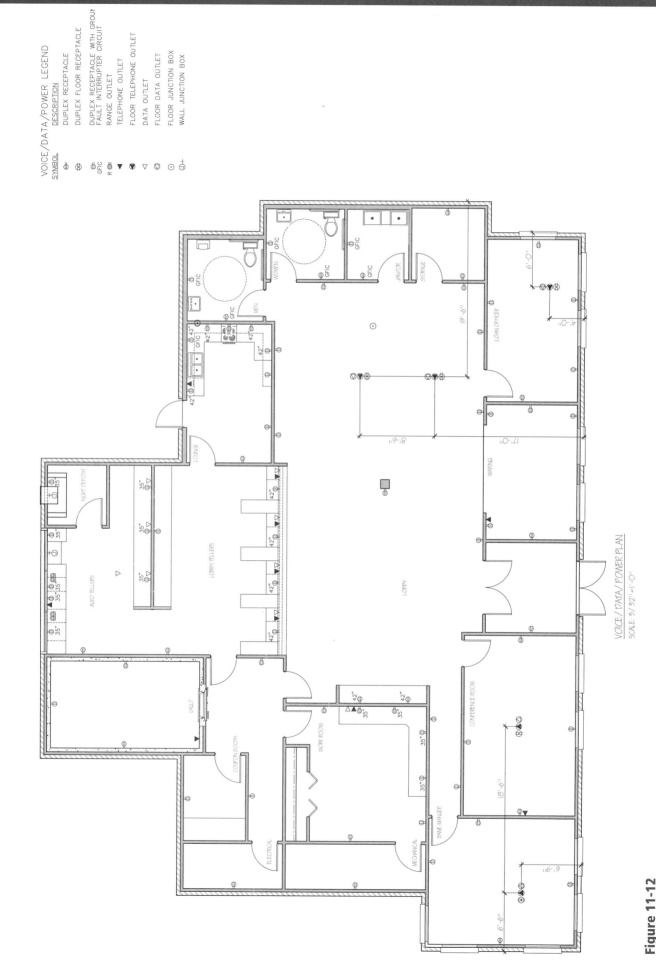

Project 11-4, Part 1: *Log Cabin Lighting Legend and Plan* [INTERMEDIATE]

1. Draw the log cabin lighting symbols as shown in Figure 11-13. Do not redraw any symbols you have already drawn and wblocked to a folder. Use an architect's scale to measure the symbols and draw them full scale.

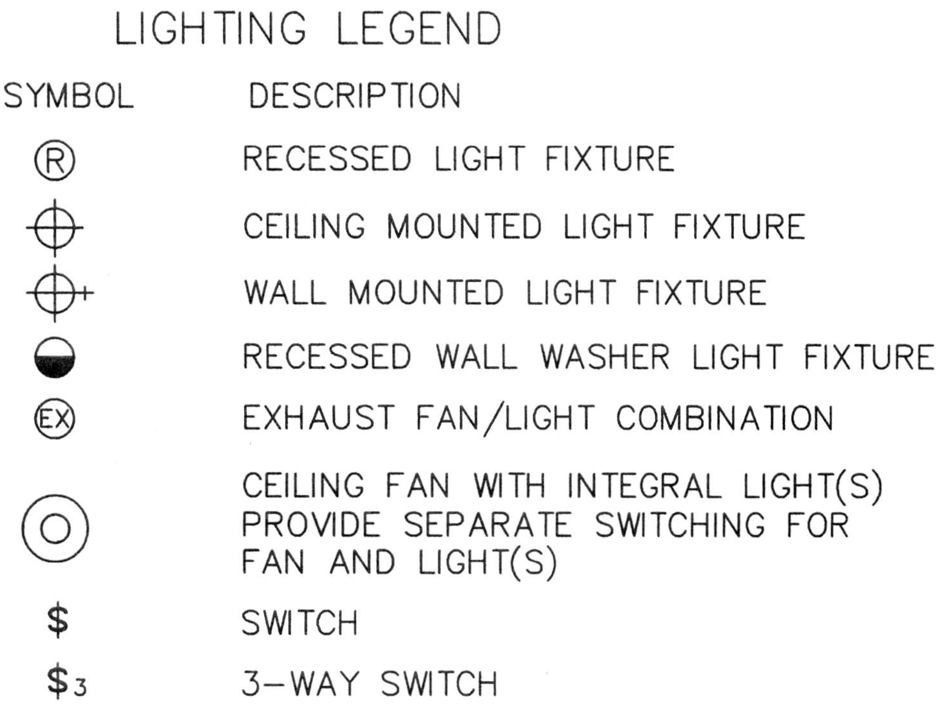

Figure 11-13
Project 11-4, Part 1: Log cabin lighting legend (scale: 1/4″ = 1′-0″)

LIGHTING LEGEND

SYMBOL	DESCRIPTION
Ⓡ	RECESSED LIGHT FIXTURE
⊕	CEILING MOUNTED LIGHT FIXTURE
⊕⁺	WALL MOUNTED LIGHT FIXTURE
⬤	RECESSED WALL WASHER LIGHT FIXTURE
(EX)	EXHAUST FAN/LIGHT COMBINATION
(O)	CEILING FAN WITH INTEGRAL LIGHT(S) PROVIDE SEPARATE SWITCHING FOR FAN AND LIGHT(S)
$	SWITCH
$₃	3—WAY SWITCH

2. Complete the log cabin lighting plan as shown in Figure 11-14.

3. Plot or print the drawing to scale.

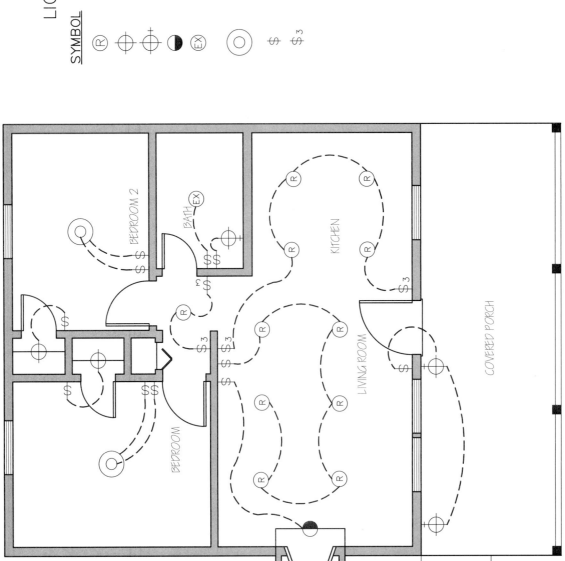

LIGHTING LEGEND

SYMBOL   DESCRIPTION

(R)   RECESSED LIGHT FIXTURE

⊕   CEILING MOUNTED LIGHT FIXTURE

⊕   WALL MOUNTED LIGHT FIXTURE

◗   RECESSED WALL WASHER LIGHT FIXTURE

(EX)   EXHAUST FAN/LIGHT COMBINATION

(◯)   CEILING FAN WITH INTEGRAL LIGHT(S)
PROVIDE SEPARATE SWITCHING FOR
FAN AND LIGHT(S)

$ SWITCH

$₃   3—WAY SWITCH

LIGHTING PLAN
SCALE: 3/16" = 1'-0"

Figure 11-14
Project 11-4, Part 1: Log cabin lighting plan (scale: 3/16" = 1'-0")

Project 11-4, Part 2: *Log Cabin Power/ Communication Legend and Plan*
[INTERMEDIATE]

1. Draw the log cabin power and communication symbols as shown in Figure 11-15. Do not redraw any symbols you have already drawn and wblocked to a folder. Use an architect's scale to measure the symbols and draw them full scale.

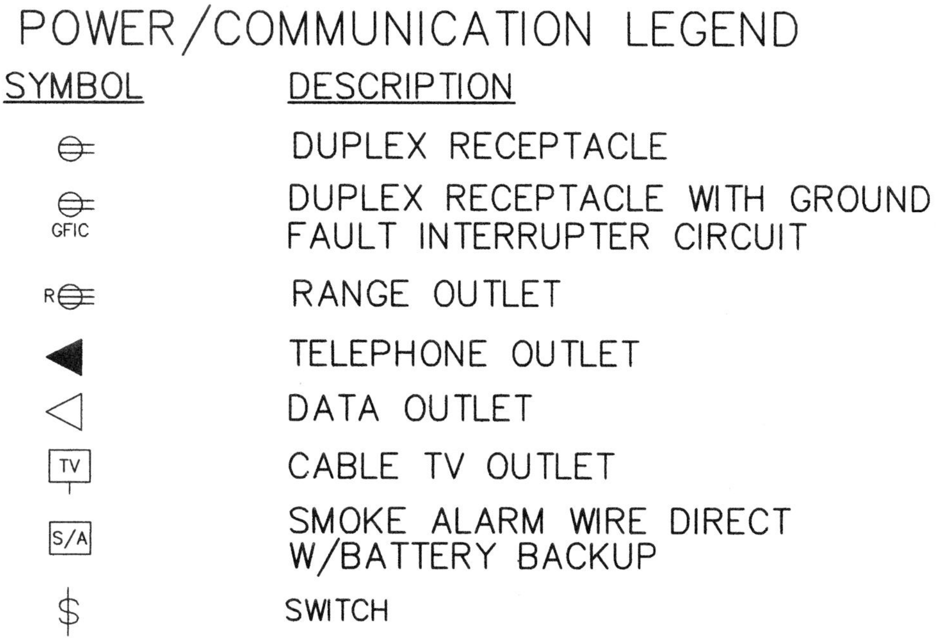

Figure 11-15
Project 11-4, Part 2: Log cabin power/communication legend (scale: 1/4″ = 1′-0″)

POWER/COMMUNICATION LEGEND

SYMBOL	DESCRIPTION
⊖	DUPLEX RECEPTACLE
⊖ GFIC	DUPLEX RECEPTACLE WITH GROUND FAULT INTERRUPTER CIRCUIT
R⊖	RANGE OUTLET
◀	TELEPHONE OUTLET
◁	DATA OUTLET
TV	CABLE TV OUTLET
S/A	SMOKE ALARM WIRE DIRECT W/BATTERY BACKUP
$	SWITCH

2. Complete the log cabin power/communication plan as shown in Figure 11-16. The 45″ notation on three of the receptacles shows the distance from the floor to the receptacle.

3. Plot or print the drawing to scale.

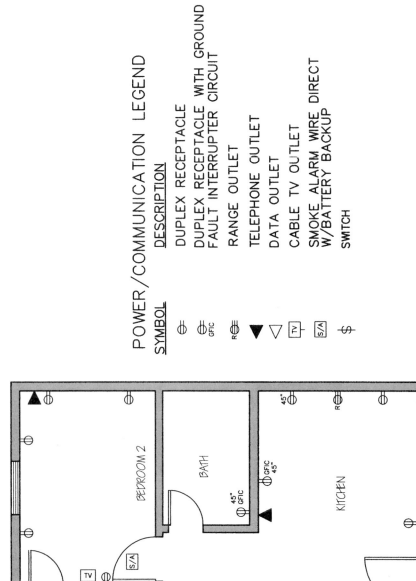

POWER/COMMUNICATION LEGEND

SYMBOL	DESCRIPTION
	DUPLEX RECEPTACLE
GFIC	DUPLEX RECEPTACLE WITH GROUND FAULT INTERRUPTER CIRCUIT
R	RANGE OUTLET
▼	TELEPHONE OUTLET
▽	DATA OUTLET
TV	CABLE TV OUTLET
S/A	SMOKE ALARM WIRE DIRECT W/BATTERY BACKUP
S	SWITCH

POWER/ COMMUNICATION PLAN

SCALE: 3/16" = 1'-0"

Figure 11-16
Project 11-4, Part 2: Log cabin power/communication plan (scale: 3/16″ = 1′-0″)

Project 11-5: *House 1 Power/ Communication/ Lighting Plan* [ADVANCED]

1. Draw the house 1 power/communication/lighting symbols as shown in Figure 11-17. Do not redraw any symbols you have already drawn and wblocked to a folder. Use an 1/8″ architect's scale to measure the symbols and draw them full scale.

2. Complete the house 1 power/communication/lighting plan as shown in Figure 11-17.

3. Save the drawing in two places and plot or print the drawing to scale.

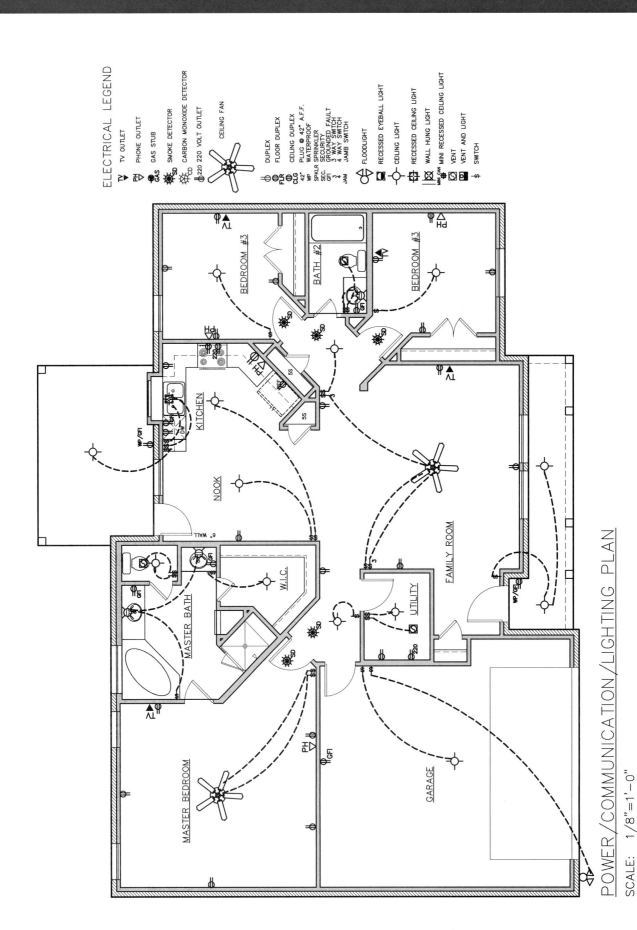

POWER/COMMUNICATION/LIGHTING PLAN

SCALE: 1/8" = 1'-0"

Figure 11-17

Project 11-5: House 1 power/communication/lighting plan (scale: 1/8" = 1'-0")

Project 11-6: *House 2 Power/Communication/Lighting Plan* [ADVANCED]

1. Draw the house 2 power/communication/lighting symbols as shown in Figure 11-18. Do not redraw any symbols you have already drawn and wblocked to a folder. Use an 1/8″ architect's scale to measure the symbols and draw them full scale.

2. Complete the house 2 power/communication/lighting plan as shown in Figure 11-18.

3. Save the drawing in two places and plot or print the drawing to scale.

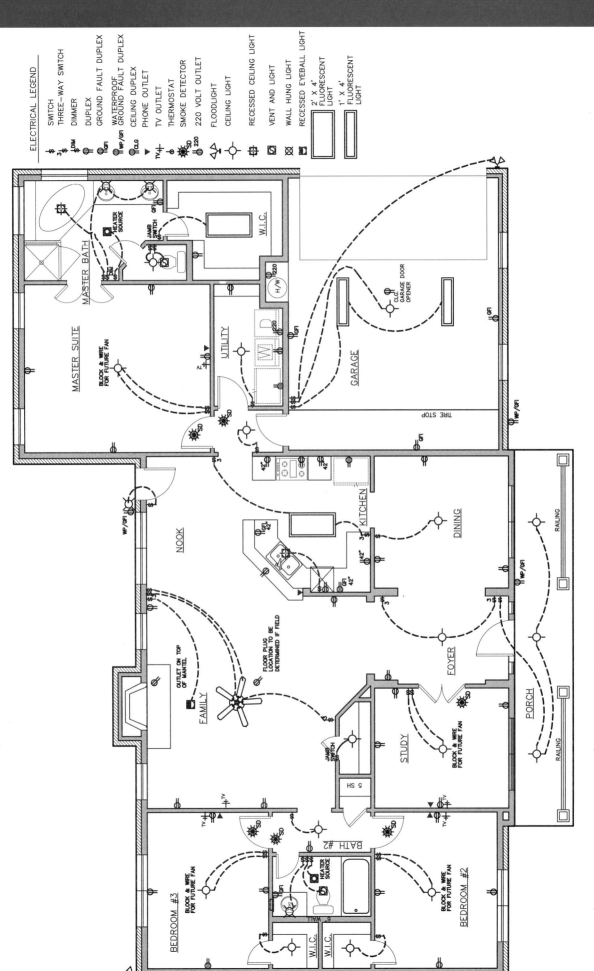

ELECTRICAL LEGEND

Symbol	Description
$	SWITCH
$_3	THREE-WAY SWITCH
$^{DIM}	DIMMER
⊕	DUPLEX
⊕_{GFI}	GROUND FAULT DUPLEX
⊕_{WP/GFI}	WATERPROOF GROUND FAULT DUPLEX
⊕_{CLG}	CEILING DUPLEX
▶	PHONE OUTLET
TV⊣	TV OUTLET
⊖	THERMOSTAT
SD	SMOKE DETECTOR
⊕_{220}	220 VOLT OUTLET
	FLOODLIGHT
⊙	CEILING LIGHT
⊞	RECESSED CEILING LIGHT
⊠	VENT AND LIGHT
⊠	WALL HUNG LIGHT
⊠	RECESSED EYEBALL LIGHT
▭	2' x 4' FLUORESCENT LIGHT
▯	1' x 4' FLUORESCENT LIGHT

POWER/COMMUNICATION/LIGHTING PLAN

SCALE: 1/8" = 1'-0"

Figure 11-18

Project 11-6: House 2 power/communication/lighting plan (scale: 1/8" = 1'-0")

12 chapter twelve

Creating Presentations with Layouts and Making a Sheet Set

CHAPTER OBJECTIVES

- Make new layout tabs and rename them.
- Scale and lock viewports.
- Use the **Layer Properties Manager VP Freeze** column to freeze layers in different viewports.
- Correctly use the following commands and settings:

Create Layout Wizard	**Page Setup Manager**
Layer Properties Manager	**Paper Space**
Model Space	**Properties**
MVSETUP	**Quick View Layouts**
New Sheet Set	**Sheet Set Manager**

EXERCISE 12-1

Make a Printed Presentation of the Tenant Space Project by Combining Multiple Plans on One Sheet of Paper

When you have completed Exercise 12-1, your drawing will look similar to Figure 12-1. **Exercise 12-1** and **Exercise 12-2** will work only if you have saved **CH6-EXERCISE1, CH7-EXERCISE1, CH9-EXERCISE1,** and **CH11-EXERCISE1** as a single drawing. In both exercises, you will freeze layers to make a presentation that displays the dimensioned floor plan, furniture plan, reflected ceiling plan, and voice/data/power plan.

Figure 12-1
Exercise 12-1 complete

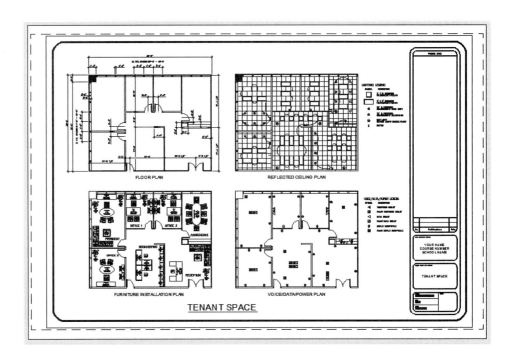

Step 1. Open existing drawing **CH11-EXERCISE1-VOICE-DATA-POWER**; save it as **CH12-EXERCISE1**.

Step 2. **Erase** the north arrow, title text, scale, your name, class, and date.

Step 3. Use **Zoom-All** to view the entire drawing.

Step 4. Turn the **Grid OFF**.

Step 5. Create the following new layer and set it as the current layer:

Layer Name	Color	Linetype	Lineweight
a-anno-ttbl	magenta	continuous	.008″ (.20 mm) (for a D-size drawing)

Use Create Layout Wizard to Set Up Four Viewports on a Single Sheet

Step 6. Use the **Create Layout** wizard to create a presentation of the Tenant Space Project consisting of four viewports and an architectural title block, as described next:

Prompt	Response
Type a command:	Click **Create Layout Wizard**
The **Create Layout-Begin** wizard appears with the name **Layout 3**	Type **Tenant Space Project**
	Click **Next**
The **Printer** option appears:	Click **DWF6 ePlot.pc3** (or a plotter that plots ARCH D size [36.00 × 24.00 inches])
	Click **Next**
The **Paper Size** option appears:	Click **ARCH D (36.00 × 24.00 inches)** in the **Paper Size** list
	Click **Next**

viewports: Windows in either model space or paper space. Two types of viewports are available in AutoCAD, tiled and nontiled. Tiled viewports are those that exist in model space with **TILEMODE** on. Nontiled viewports exist in either model space or paper space with **TILEMODE** off.

CREATE LAYOUT WIZARD	
Menu Bar:	Insert/Layout/ Create Layout Wizard
Type a Command:	LAYOUT WIZARD

Prompt	Response
The **Orientation** option appears:	Click **Landscape**
	Click **Next**
The **Title Block** option appears:	Click **Architectural Title Block.dwg**
	Click **Next**
The **Define Viewports** option appears:	Click **Array** in the **Viewport setup** list (Figure 12-2)
	Click **3/16″ = 1′-0″** in the **Viewport scale:** input box
	Type **2** in the **Rows:** input box
	Type **2** in the **Columns:** input box
	Type **0.1** in the **Spacing between rows:** input box
	Type **0.1** in the **Spacing between columns:** input box
	Click **Next**
The **Pick Location** option appears:	Click **Select location:**
Specify first corner:	Type **2,2 <Enter>**
Specify opposite corner:	Type **28,22 <Enter>**
The **Finish** option appears:	Click **Finish**
	You are now in **PAPER** space

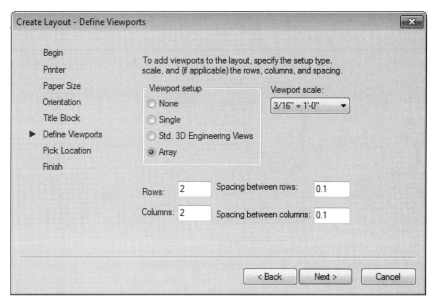

Figure 12-2
Create Layout – Define Viewports

Complete the Title Block

The **hidden line border** in the **Tenant Space Project Layout tab** shows the **plottable area** of your plotter, as shown in Figure 12-3. If the title block is too large and extends outside the plottable area, you can either explode and edit the size of the title block or use the **SCALE** command to reduce the title block size.

Step 7. While in **PAPER** space reduce the size of the title block to fit within the plottable area, Figure 12-4.

Figure 12-3
Hidden line border shows
the plottable area of your
plotter

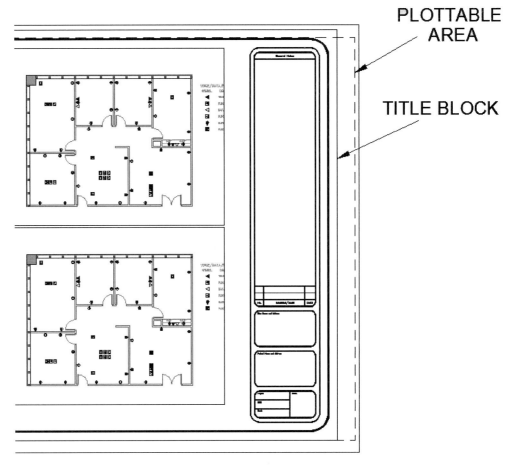

PLOTTABLE
AREA

TITLE BLOCK

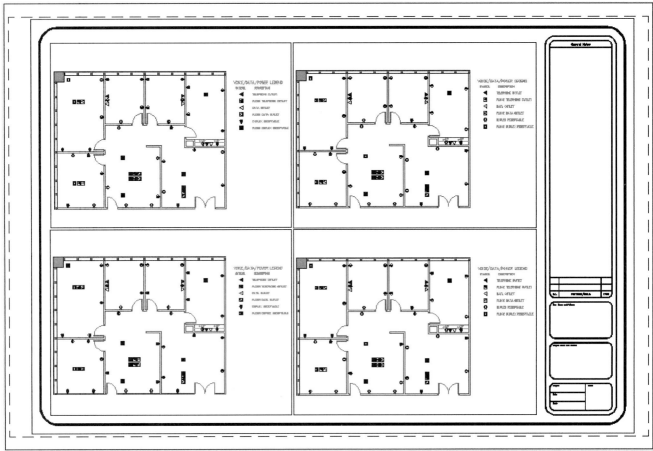

Figure 12-4
Reduce the title block to fit within the plottable area and center viewports inside the title block

Step 8. While in **PAPER** space use the **MOVE** command to center the four viewports in the title block, Figure 12-4. Click the edge of any viewport boundary to move it, or select all four viewports by using a crossing window.

Step 9. While in **PAPER** space click the viewport boundary edge and use **GRIPS** to make any of the four viewport boundaries larger or smaller, as needed (Figure 12-5).

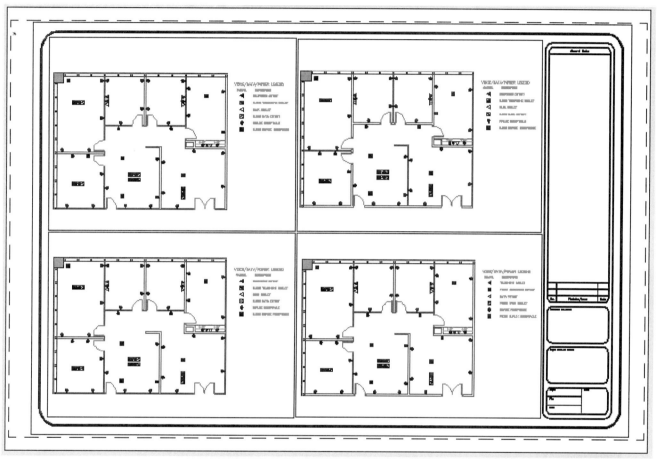

Figure 12-5
Make viewports larger or smaller using **Grips** and use **Pan** to center drawings within viewports

Step 10. While in **MODEL** space use the **PAN** command to center the drawings within the four viewports (Figure 12-5).

Step 11. While in **PAPER** space make a new text style (not annotative), set the **a-anno-text** layer current, and complete the title block as described next (Figure 12-6):

YOUR NAME *(3/16″ high, Arial font, Center justification)*

COURSE NUMBER *(3/16″ high, Arial font, Center justification)*

SCHOOL NAME *(3/16″ high, Arial font, Center justification)*

TENANT SPACE *(3/16″ high, Arial font, Center justification)*

CH12-EXERCISE1 *(1/8″ high, Arial font, Left justification)*

DATE *(1/8″ high, Arial font, Left justification)*

3/16″ = 1′-0″ *(1/8″ high, Arial font, Left justification)*

Figure 12-6
Complete the title block

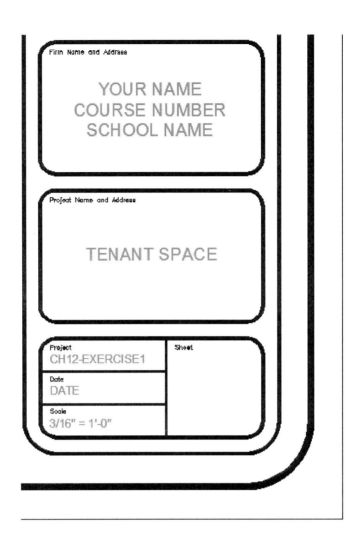

Firm Name and Address

YOUR NAME
COURSE NUMBER
SCHOOL NAME

Project Name and Address

TENANT SPACE

Project
CH12-EXERCISE1

Sheet

Date
DATE

Scale
3/16" = 1'-0"

Use Layer Properties Manager to Freeze Viewport Layers

Step 12. While in **MODEL** space use the **Layer Properties Manager** to thaw all frozen layers and to turn all layers on. When all layers are thawed and turned on, they will all be visible in all viewports, and you will be able to create a unique drawing in each viewport by turning individual layers off.

Step 13. While in **MODEL** space use the **Layer Properties Manager** to freeze layers in the upper left viewport so only the dimensioned floor plan is visible as described next (Figures 12-7 and 12-8):

Figure 12-7
Use the **Layer Properties Manager** to freeze layers using the **VP Freeze** column

Plot	New VP Freeze	VP Freeze

Figure 12-8
Freeze the required layers in all viewports

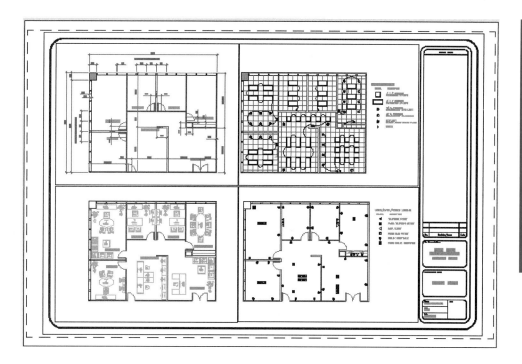

Prompt	Response
Type a command:	Click the upper left viewport to make it active; type **LA <Enter>**
The **Layer Properties Manager** appears:	In the **VP Freeze** column, click the **Freeze/Thaw** symbol to freeze all layers not used to view the dimensioned floor plan in the upper left viewport (Figure 12-7).

TIP

Position the **viewport** and the **Layer Properties Manager** palette on your display screen so you can watch both. When you freeze a layer, you can see it go away in the floor plan.

Step 14. Click the **lower left viewport** to make it active. Use the **Layer Properties Manager** to freeze layers in the lower left viewport so only the **Furniture Installation Plan** is visible (Figure 12-8).

Step 15. Click the **upper right viewport** to make it active. Use the **Layer Properties Manager** to freeze layers in the upper right viewport so only the **Reflected Ceiling Plan** is visible (Figure 12-8).

Step 16. Click the **lower right viewport** to make it active. Use the **Layer Properties Manager** to freeze layers in the lower right viewport so only the **Voice/Data/Power Plan** is visible (Figure 12-8).

TIP

There will be occasions when you will want to select or deselect all layers at the same time. To do that, position the cursor in an open area in the dialog box and press the right mouse button, then click **Select All** or **Clear All**.

Scale and Center the Plans

Step 17. While in **PAPER** space click the boundary line of all viewports, click **Properties,** and set a standard scale of **3/16″ = 1′-0″** in all four viewports, as shown in Figure 12-9.

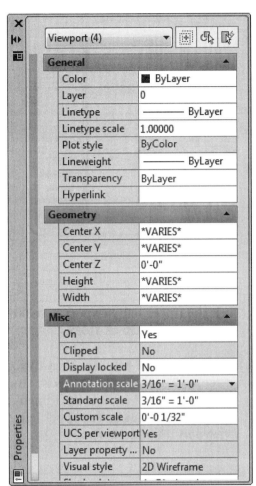

Figure 12-9
Use **Properties** to set a scale of 3/16″ = 1′-0″ in all viewports

Step 18. While in **MODEL** space use **PAN** to center images in each viewport. Do not zoom in or out while in **MODEL** space. If you do zoom in or out while in **MODEL** space, you will have to reset the scale of the drawing. You will lock the display in Step 21.

Use MVSETUP to Align the Plans

The **MVSETUP** command can be used to align the model space views horizontally and vertically within each viewport.

Step 19. While in **MODEL** space use the **MVSETUP** command to align the plans in the viewports as described next (Figure 12-10):

Prompt	Response
Type a command:	Type **MVSETUP <Enter>**
Enter an option [Align Create Scale viewports Options Title block Undo]:	Type **A <Enter>**

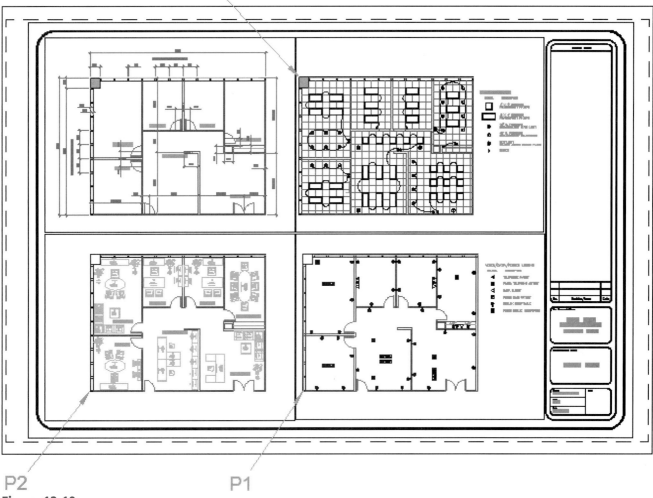

P3

P2   P1

Figure 12-10
Use **MVSETUP** to align viewports horizontally and vertically

Prompt	Response
Enter an option [Angled Horizontal Vertical Alignment Rotate view Undo]:	Type **H <Enter>**
	Click the lower right viewport to make it active
	Osnap-Intersection
of	**P1→** (Figure 12-10)
Specify point in viewport to be panned:	Click the lower left viewport to make it active
	Osnap-Intersection
of	**P2→** (Figure 12-10)
Enter an option [Angled Horizontal Vertical Alignment Rotate view Undo]:	Type **V <Enter>**
	Click the upper right viewport to make it active
	Osnap-Intersection
of	**P3→** (Figure 12-10)
Specify point in viewport to be panned:	Click the lower right viewport to make it active

Prompt	Response
	Osnap-Intersection
of	P1→ (Figure 12-10)

Step 20. Align, horizontally and vertically, any remaining **MODEL** space views that need to be aligned.

Step 21. While in **PAPER** space, use the **Properties** command to lock the display of all four viewports.

Step 22. Create the following new layer and turn it **OFF**:

Layer Name	Color	Linetype	Lineweight
a-anno-vprt	green	continuous	.006″ (.15 mm)

Step 23. While in **PAPER** space change the outside edges of the four viewports to the **a-anno-vprt** layer. The outside edges of the viewports will no longer be visible and will not print.

Complete the Presentation

Step 24. While in **PAPER** space with the **a-anno-text** layer current, label the views using **Dtext** with the Arial font, ¼″ high, as shown in Figure 12-11.

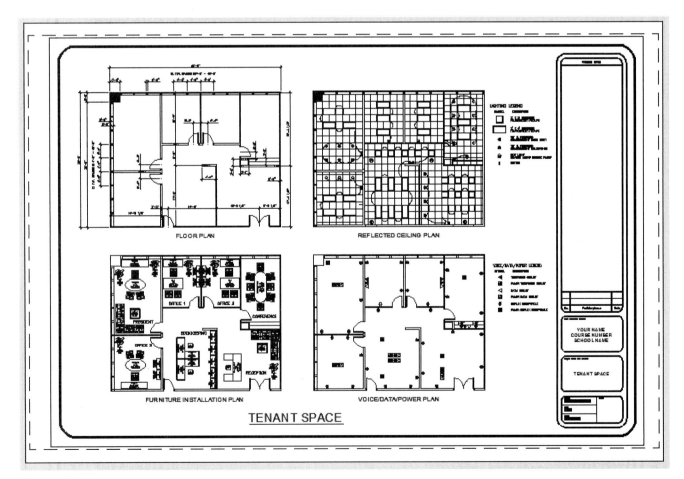

Figure 12-11
Exercise 12-1 complete

Step 25. Use the same font, ½″ high to label the entire drawing **TENANT SPACE**.

Step 26. Make a color-dependent plot style set for all colors to plot black. Set it current.

Step 27. When you have completed Exercise 12-1, save your work in at least two places.

Step 28. **Plot** Exercise 12-1. Verify the information in the **Tenant Space Project layout** tab, **Page Setup Manager**, and plot the layout at a scale of 1:1.

EXERCISE 12-2
Making a Four-Sheet Presentation of the Tenant Space Project Using a Sheet Set

When you have completed Exercise 12-2, your drawings will look similar to the four separate sheets shown in Figure 12-12 A–D.

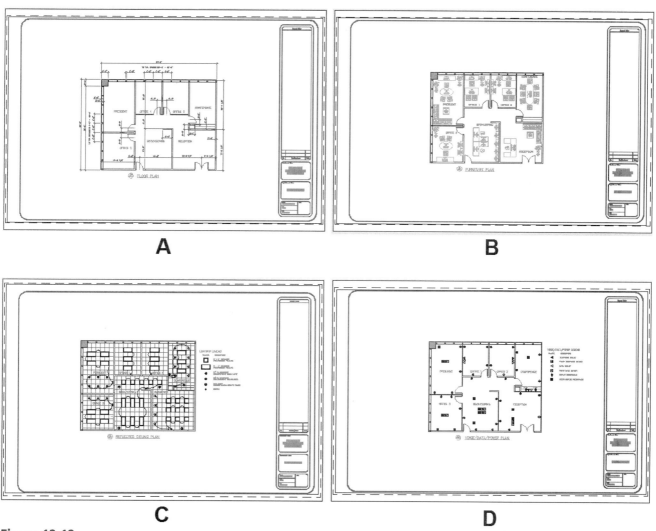

A

B

C

D

Figure 12-12
Exercise 12-2 complete

Step 1. Open existing drawing **CH11-EXERCISE1-VOICE-DATA-POWER**; save it as **CH12-EXERCISE2**.

Step 2. **Erase** your name, class, and date.

Step 3. Use **Zoom-All** to view the entire drawing.

Step 4. Turn the **Grid OFF**.

Step 5. While in the **MODEL** tab, use the **Layer Properties Manager** to thaw all frozen layers and to turn all layers on. When all layers are thawed and turned on, they will all be visible in all viewports, and you will be able to create a unique drawing in each layout viewport by freezing individual layers.

Step 6. Change the layer lineweights to the **D-size sheet** lineweights as described in Chapter 5.

Step 7. Create the following new layer and set it as the current layer:

Layer Name	Color	Linetype	Lineweight
a-anno-vprt	green	continuous	.006″ (.15 mm)

Make New Layout Tabs and Rename the New Layout Tabs

Step 8. Use the right-click menu to **Rename** Layout1, **Floor Plan**, Figure 12-13.

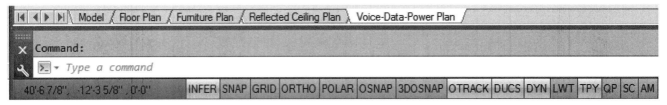

Figure 12-13
Rename layout tabs

Step 9. Use the right-click menu to **Rename** Layout 2, **Furniture Plan**, Figure 12-13.

Step 10. Use the right-click menu to make two **New layout** tabs.

Step 11. Use the right-click menu to **Rename** the two **New layout** tabs **Reflected Ceiling Plan** and **Voice-Data-Power Plan**, Figure 12-13.

Prepare the Layout Tabs for Plotting Drawings

Step 12. Click on the **Floor Plan** layout tab.

MVIEW	
Type a Command:	MVIEW
Command Alias:	MV

TIP

You can erase an existing viewport. You can use **MVIEW** to **Restore the Active Viewport** if you find the viewport is missing from a layout tab. Use the **MVIEW, Fit** option to **Restore the Active Viewport**. You can always use the layout tab right-click menu to **Delete** a layout tab and click **New layout** to make a new layout tab to start afresh if needed.

Step 13. Right-click the **Floor Plan** tab and click **Page Setup Manager...**. The **Page Setup Manager** appears with **Floor Plan** highlighted in the **Current page setup** list.

Step 14. Click **Modify...**. The **Page Setup – Floor Plan** dialog box appears.

Step 15. Click **DWF6 ePlot.pc3** or the plotter you will use for **ARCH D (36.00 × 24.00 Inches)** paper.

Step 16. Make the settings shown for the **Page Setup – Floor Plan** dialog box as shown in Figure 12-14. Click **OK** and click **Close**.

Figure 12-14
Settings for **Page Setup - Floor Plan**

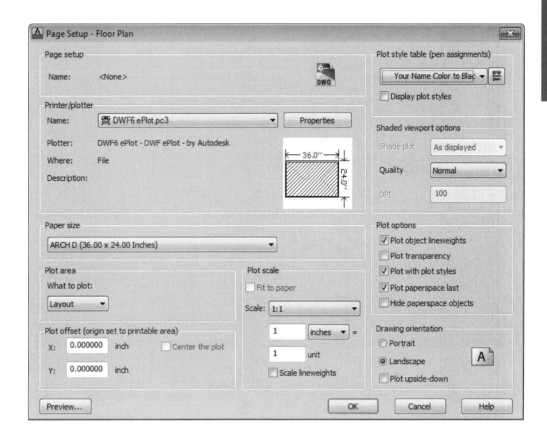

Step 17. While in **PAPER** space click the **viewport boundary line** and use **grips** to make the viewport size similar to Figure 12-15.

Step 18. While in **MODEL** space use the **PAN** and **Zoom** commands to center the drawing within the viewport, Figure 12-15.

Step 19. While in **MODEL** space use the **Layer Properties Manager, VP Freeze** to freeze layers in the **current Viewport only** so only the dimensioned Floor Plan is visible as shown in Figure 12-15.

Step 20. **Erase** the Scale text, keep the North arrow, and center the title **FLOOR PLAN**.

Step 21. While in **PAPER** space click the boundary line of the viewport, click **Properties,** and set a standard scale of **1/4″ = 1′-0″** in the viewport, as shown in Figure 12-15, and lock the display.

Step 22. While in **PAPER** space set the **LTSCALE** as needed to see the dashed linetype.

Step 23. Repeat Step 12 through Step 22 for the **Furniture Plan, Reflected Ceiling Plan**, and **Voice-Data-Power Plan** layout tabs.

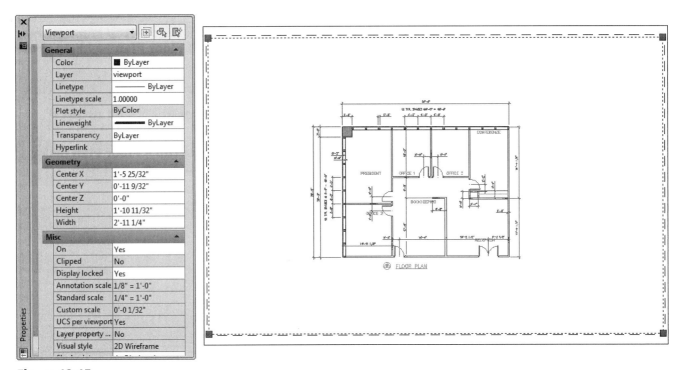

Figure 12-15
Center the floor plan, freeze required layers, set a scale of ¼″ = 1′0″, and lock the display

Use MVSETUP to Insert a Title Block

The **MVSETUP** command can be used to insert a title block into the **Floor Plan** layout tab.

Step 24. Create the following new layer and set it as the current layer:

Layer Name	Color	Linetype	Lineweight
a-anno-ttbl	magenta	continuous	.008″ (.20 mm) (for a D-size drawing)

Step 25. While in **PAPER** space use the **MVSETUP** command to insert an architectural title block as described next (Figure 12-16):

Prompt	Response
Type a command:	Type **MVSETUP <Enter>**
Enter an option [Align Create Scale viewports Options Title block Undo]:	Type **T <Enter>**
Enter title block option [Delete objects Origin Undo Insert] <Insert>:	**<Enter>** (to accept Insert)
Enter number of title block to load or [Add Delete Redisplay]:	Type **12 <Enter>**
Create a drawing named arching. dwg? <Y>:	Type **N <Enter>**

The **hidden line border** in the **Layout tab** shows the **plottable area** of your plotter, as shown in Figure 12-16. If the title block is too large and extends outside the plottable area, you can either explode and edit the size of the title block or use the **SCALE** command to reduce the title block size.

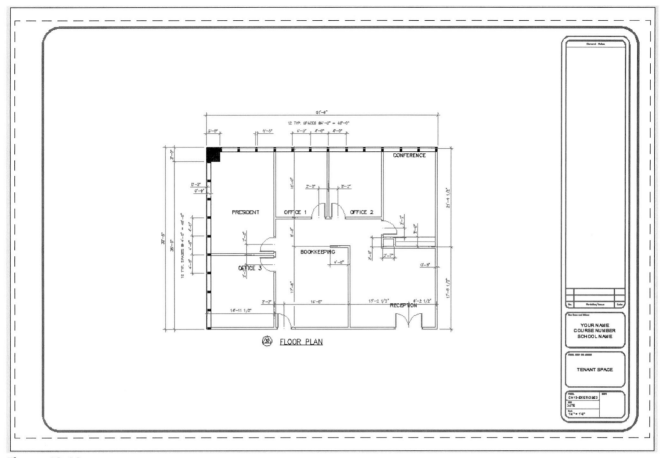

Figure 12-16
Insert the architectural title block, scale it if needed, and complete the title block

Step 26. While in **PAPER** space reduce the size of title block to fit within the plottable area and erase the four lines around the outside of the title block (Figure 12-16).

Step 27. While in **PAPER** space make a new text style, set the **a-anno-text** layer current, and complete the title block as described next (Figure 12-16):

YOUR NAME *(3/16″ high, Arial font, Center justification)*
COURSE NUMBER *(3/16″ high, Arial font, Center justification)*
SCHOOL NAME *(3/16″ high, Arial font, Center justification)*
TENANT SPACE *(3/16″ high, Arial font, Center justification)*
CH12-EXERCISE2 *(1/8″ high, Arial font, Left justification)*
DATE *(1/8″ high, Arial font, Left justification)*
1/4″ = 1′-0″ *(1/8″ high, Arial font, Left justification)*

Step 28. While in **PAPER** space make sure the outside edges of the viewport are on the **a-anno-vprt** layer and turn the **a-anno-vprt** layer **OFF**. The outside edges of the viewport will no longer be visible and will not print (Figure 12-16).

Step 29. While in **PAPER** space **WBLOCK** the title block you just completed and **INSERT** it into the **Furniture Plan**, **Reflected Ceiling Plan**, and **Voice-Data-Power Plan** layout tabs to complete each layout tab.

Quick View Tools

The **Quick View Layouts** tool in the status bar allows you to preview and switch between the current drawing and its layouts. The **Quick View Drawings** tool in the status bar allows you to preview and switch between open drawings and their layouts.

Step 30. Click **Quick View Layouts** to display the **Model** tab and all four layout tabs (Figure 12-17).

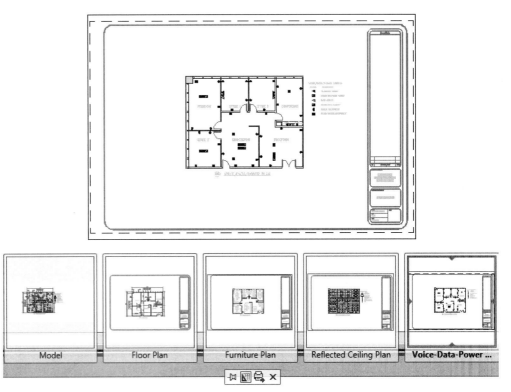

Figure 12-17
Use **Quick View Layouts** to display the Model tab and all four layout tabs

When you click **Quick View Layouts**, the model space and paper space layouts in the current drawing are displayed as thumbnail images (Figure 12-17). If you click an image of a layout, it becomes the current layout. You can also click the **Plot** or **Publish** icon on the image to plot or publish each individual layout.

New Sheet Set and Sheet Set Manager

The **New Sheet Set** command is used to organize layouts into one set when you have several different drawings that you want to package together. Save all of the drawings into a separate folder and use the **New Sheet Set** command to organize the layouts of each drawing into a single sheet set. The sheet set is named and saved as a .dst file type within the **New Sheet Set** command. The **Sheet Set Manager** is used to open sheet sets. You can plot, publish, eTransmit, and ZIP sheet sets.

Step 31. Make a new folder labeled **Tenant Space Sheet Set** in the drive in which you want to save. Save drawing **CH12-EXERCISE2**

in the new folder. Be sure to save the drawing instead of copying the drawing so AutoCAD recognizes the completed layout tabs.

Step 32. Make a new sheet set with the name **TENANT SPACE PROJECT**, as described next:

NEW SHEET SET	
Application Menu/New	
Menu Bar:	File
Type a Command:	NEWSHEETSET
Command Alias:	NEWSHE

Prompt	Response
Type a command:	New Sheet Set... (or type **NEWSHEETSET <Enter>**)
The **Create Sheet Set – Begin** tab appears:	Click **Existing drawings** Click **Next**
The **Create Sheet Set – Sheet Set Details** tab appears:	Type **TENANT SPACE PROJECT** in the **Name of new sheet set**: input box (Figure 12-18).
Click **the ellipsis (...) button** to the right of **Store sheet set data file (.dst) here:**	Click the **Tenant Space Sheet Set** folder Click **Open** Click **Next**
The **Create Sheet Set – Choose Layouts** tab appears:	Click **Browse**
The **Browse for Folder** dialog box appears:	Click the **Tenant Space Sheet Set** folder Click **OK**
The layouts in the drawings in that folder appear as shown in Figure 12-19.	Click **Next**

Figure 12-18
Create Sheet Set – Sheet Set Details tab

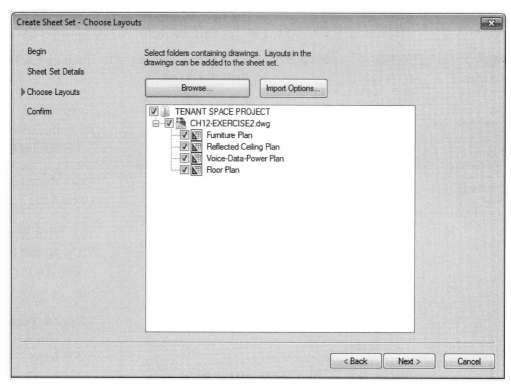

Figure 12-19
Create Sheet Set – Choose Layouts tab

Prompt	Response
The **Create Sheet Set – Confirm** tab appears (Figure 12-20):	Click **Finish**
The **Sheet Set Manager** palette appears with the sheet list.	

Figure 12-20
Create Sheet Set – Confirm tab

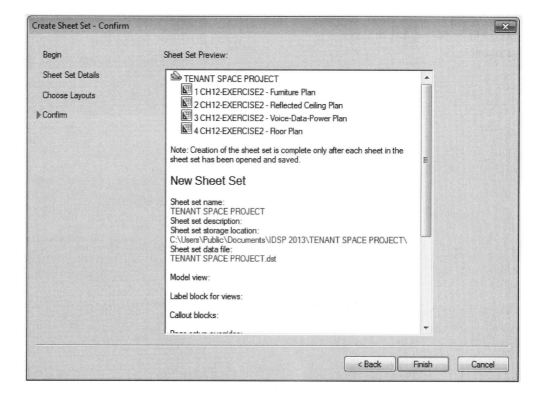

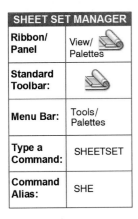

SHEET SET MANAGER	
Ribbon/ Panel	View/ Palettes
Standard Toolbar:	
Menu Bar:	Tools/ Palettes
Type a Command:	SHEETSET
Command Alias:	SHE

Step 33. Hold your mouse over any sheet that needs to be renumbered or renamed and use the right-click menu **Rename and Renumber...** command to correct any numbers or names, so your sheets appear as shown on the right in Figure 12-21.

Step 34. If you need to rearrange the order of the sheets, click on the sheet name, hold down the mouse button as you move your mouse so a black line appears, and release the click button.

Step 35. With the **Sheet Set Manager** open, test your sheet set by double-clicking on each sheet in the drawing set.

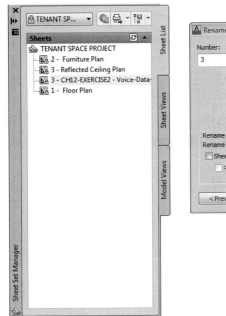

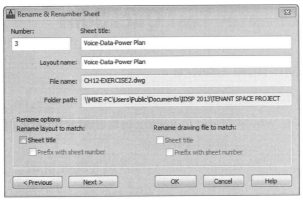

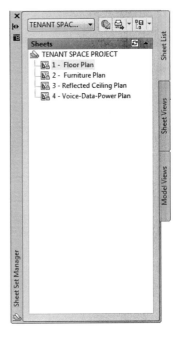

Figure 12-21
Rename and renumber sheets. Correct order is on the right

Step 36. When you have completed Exercise 12-2, save your work in at least two places.

Step 37. **Plot** Exercise 12-2. Plot each layout at a scale of 1:1.

Chapter Summary

This chapter provided you the information necessary to make presentations with layouts and how to make a sheet set. In addition you learned to make layouts with different layers frozen on each layout, to use model space and paper space, and to use the following commands: **Create Layout Wizard, MVSETUP,** and **Quick View Layouts**. Now you have the skills and information necessary to make presentations that can be used in interior design and architecture.

Chapter Test Questions

Multiple Choice

Circle the correct answer.

1. Which of the following is a characteristic of paper space?

    a. Models are created.

    b. Dimensions are added to a floor plan.

    c. A title block is added.

    d. Attributes are assigned to furniture.

2. What command is used to insert an architectural title block around a paper space layout?

    a. **MVIEW**   c. **MVSETUP**

    b. **VPORTS**   d. **Properties**

3. The **Create Layout Wizard** command does ***not*** do which of the following?

    a. Turn viewports on and off

    b. Scale viewports

    c. Allow you to name the layout

    d. Allow you to specify the corners of a viewport's location

4. What does the hidden line border in a paper space layout represent?

    a. A viewport boundary

    b. The plottable area

    c. A hidden layer

    d. A title block

5. What command can be used to replace a missing viewport in a layout tab?

    a. **MVSETUP**   c. **RESTORE**

    b. **MVIEW**   d. **MODIFY**

6. What command can be used to center drawings in while in model space?

    a. **PAN**   c. **MVIEW**

    b. **RESTORE**   d. **Properties**

7. What command can be used to set a standard scale of 1/4″ - 1′ in paper space viewports?
   a. **Paper Space**
   c. **Properties**
   b. **Model Space**
   d. **Tilemode**

8. Which of the following can be used to align objects in adjacent viewports accurately in model space?
   a. **MVIEW**
   c. **VPORTS**
   b. **MOVE**
   d. **MVSETUP**

9. Which of the following commands is used to open a sheet set after it has been made?
   a. **MVSETUP**
   b. **Properties**
   c. **Sheet Set Manager**
   d. **Create Layout Wizard**

10. Which of the following settings in the **Properties** palette is used to lock the scale of a viewport?
    a. **Display Locked**
    c. **Clipped**
    b. **UCS per viewport**
    d. **ON or OFF**

Matching

Write the number of the correct answer on the line.

a. **Sheet Set**_____

b. **Quick View Layouts**_____

c. **VP Freeze**_____

d. **Model Space**_____

e. **Paper Space**_____

1. The space where a title block is placed around a floor plan
2. The space where a floor plan is made
3. A command used to organize multiple layouts into a single package
4. A command used to display multiple layouts as thumbnail images
5. A column in the **Layer Properties Manager** palette

True or False

Circle the correct answer.

1. **True or False:** A viewport boundary cannot be enlarged.

2. **True or False:** Model space may be active when you are working with paper space viewports.

3. **True or False:** A viewport boundary can be moved to a layer that is turned OFF so it will not print.

4. **True or False:** The **MVSETUP** command cannot be used to align objects in adjacent viewports.

5. **True or False:** Sheets in a sheet set can be renamed and renumbered.

List

1. Five ways of accessing the **Layers Properties Manager**.
2. Five options from the **Layers Properties Manager** window.
3. Five wild-card characters in the **Search** box of the **Layers Properties Manager**.
4. Five file extensions of the pen settings file in Plot window.
5. Five prompts for the **MVSETUP** command in model space.
6. Five steps to rotate a **Layout View** using **MVSETUP**.
7. Five options of the **Layout** command.
8. Five layout-related commands.
9. Five view configurations available once the **VPORTS** command is executed.
10. Five view configurations available once the **MVIEW** command is executed.

Questions

1. Why are sheet sets used?
2. When would you use several viewports on a single sheet for a presentation?
3. Why does AutoCAD have model space and paper space?
4. How can you use **Quick View Layouts**?
5. How can you use the **Properties** command while making layouts?

Project 12-1: *Hotel Room 2 Presentation Sheet* [BASIC]

1. Open the hotel room 2 power/communication/lighting plan and follow the steps listed for CH12-EXERCISE1.

2. Complete the hotel room 2 presentation sheet as shown in Figure 12-22.

3. Save the drawing in two places and plot or print the drawing to scale.

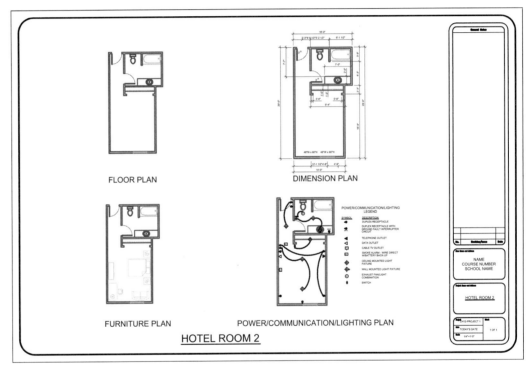

Figure 12-22
Project 12-1: Hotel room 2 presentation sheet

Project 12-2: *Bank Sheet Set* [ADVANCED]

1. Open the bank reflected ceiling plan and follow the steps listed for CH12-EXERCISE2.

2. Complete the bank layouts (Sheet 1, Sheet 2, Sheet 3, and Sheet 4) as shown in Figure 12-23.

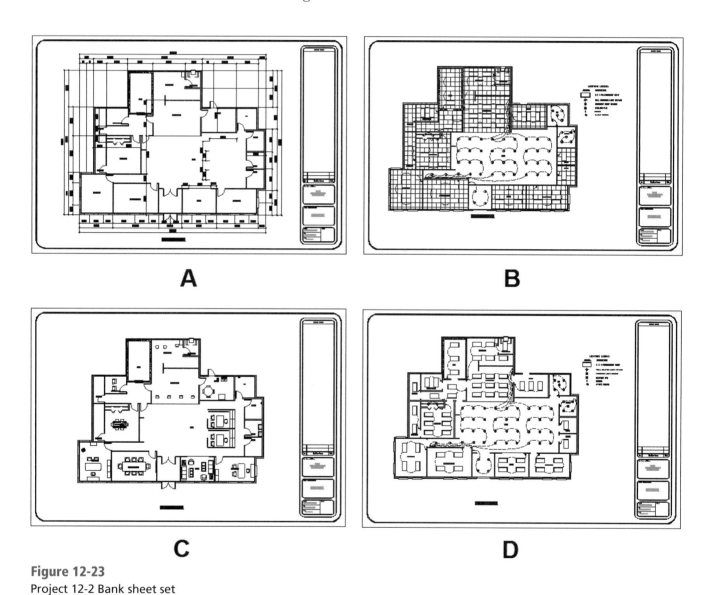

Figure 12-23
Project 12-2 Bank sheet set

3. Make a sheet set for the bank layouts as described.

4. Save the drawing in two places and plot or print the drawing to scale.

Project 12-3: *Log Cabin Sheet Set* [INTERMEDIATE]

1. Open the log cabin power/communication plan and follow the steps listed for CH12-EXERCISE2.

2. Complete the log cabin layouts (Sheet 1, Sheet 2, Sheet 3, and Sheet 4) as shown in Figure 12-24.

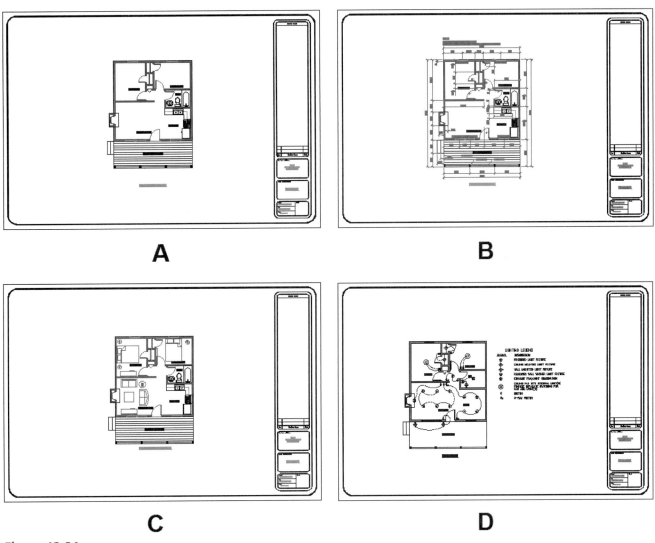

A

B

C

D

Figure 12-24
Project 12-3: Log cabin sheet set

3. Make a sheet set for the log cabin layouts as described.

4. Save the drawing in two places and plot or print the drawing to scale.

Project 12-4: *House 1 Sheet Set* [ADVANCED]

1. Open the house 1 power/communication/lighting plan and follow the steps listed for CH12-EXERCISE2.

2. Complete the house 1 layouts (Sheet 1, Sheet 2, Sheet 3, and Sheet 4) as shown in Figure 12-25.

A

B

C

D

Figure 12-25
Project 12-4: House 1 sheet set

3. Make a sheet set for the house 1 layouts as described.

4. Save the drawing in two places and plot or print the drawing to scale.

Project 12-5: *House 2 Sheet Set* [ADVANCED]

1. Open the house 2 power/communication/lighting plan and follow the steps listed for CH12-EXERCISE2.

2. Complete the house 2 layouts (Sheet 1, Sheet 2, Sheet 3, and Sheet 4) as shown in Figure 12-26.

A

B

C

D

Figure 12-26
Project 12-5: House 2 sheet set

3. Make a sheet set for the house 2 layouts as described.

4. Save the drawing in two places and plot or print the drawing to scale.

chapter thirteen

Isometric Drawing and Gradient Hatch Rendering

CHAPTER OBJECTIVES

- Make isometric drawings to scale from 2D drawings.
- Correctly use the following commands and settings:

  ELLIPSE-Isocircle
  SNAP-Style Iso

- Use the **<Ctrl>+E** or **<F5>** key to change from one isoplane to another.
- Use gradient hatch patterns to render isometric drawings.

Axonometric Drawing

axonometric: Forms of 2D drawing that represent 3D objects. The three axonometric drawing forms are isometric, dimetric, and trimetric.

The forms of **axonometric** drawing are isometric, dimetric, and trimetric, as shown in Figure 13-1. The trimetric form has the most pleasing appearance because each of the three axes uses a different scale. Dimetric uses the same scale on two axes, and isometric uses the same scale on all three axes. Isometric drawing is the axonometric drawing form covered in this book.

Isometric Drawing

isometric: A 2D drawing method that is used to give the appearance of three dimensions.

Isometric drawing is commonly used to show how objects appear in three dimensions. This drawing method is a two-dimensional one that is used to give the appearance of three dimensions. It is not a 3D modeling form such as those covered in later chapters. In 3D modeling you actually create 3D objects that can be viewed from any angle and can be placed into a perspective mode.

You can make isometric drawings quickly and easily using AutoCAD software. Once the proper grid and snap settings are made, the drawing

Figure 13-1
Axonometric drawing forms

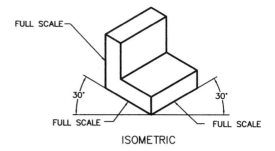

ISOMETRIC

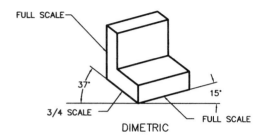

DIMETRIC

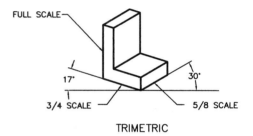

TRIMETRIC

itself proceeds with little difficulty. The three isometric axes are 30° right, 30° left, and vertical.

EXERCISE 13-1
Fundamentals of Isometric Drawing

Seven isometric shapes are drawn in this exercise to acquaint you with the fundamentals of making isometric drawings using AutoCAD. We will begin with a simple isometric box so that you can become familiar with drawing lines on an isometric axis. All seven of these shapes are drawn on the same sheet and plotted on one 8-1/2″ × 11″ sheet. When you have completed Exercise 13-1, your drawing will look similar to Figure 13-2.

Step 1. Use your workspace to make the following settings:

1. Use **Save As...** to save the drawing with the name **CH13-EXERCISE1**.
2. Set drawing units: **Architectural**
3. Set drawing limits: **11′, 8′6″** (be sure to use the foot symbol)
4. Set snap for an isometric grid, as described next:

Prompt	Response
Type a command:	Type **SN <Enter>**
Specify snap spacing or [ON OFF Aspect Legacy Style Type] <0″-0 1/2″>:	Type **S <Enter>**

Figure 13-2

Exercise 13-1 complete

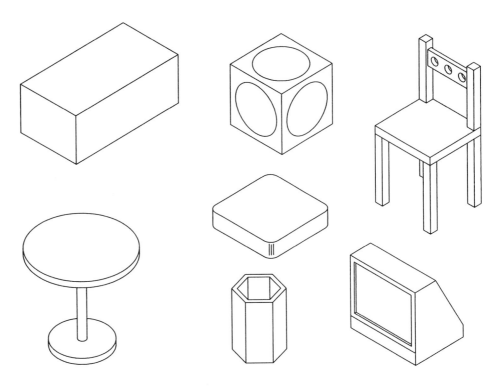

Prompt	Response
Enter snap grid style [Standard Isometric] <S>:	Type **I** **<Enter>** (I for isometric)
Specify vertical spacing <0″-6″>:	Type **1** **<Enter>** (if 1″ is not the default)

When you want to exit the isometric grid, type **SN <Enter>** and then type **S <Enter>**, then type **S <Enter>** again to select the standard grid. Keep the isometric grid for this exercise.

Isometric Drawing (<ISODRAFT>) button on the Status Bar allows easy switching between the standard and isometric styles, as well as switching between isometric planes.

    5. Set **GRIDDISPLAY: 0**
    6. Set grid: **3″**
    7. Create the following layer:

Layer Name	Color	Linetype	Lineweight
Layer1	blue	continuous	.0070″ (.18 mm)

    8. Set **Layer1** current.
    9. Use **Zoom-All**.
   10. Use the **Drafting Settings** dialog box to display the dot grid in 2D model space.

The **Drafting Settings** dialog box is accessed by right-clicking on **SNAP** or **GRID** on the status bar, then clicking **Settings...** (Figure 13-3).

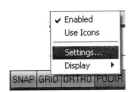

Figure 13-3

Accessing the **Drafting Settings** dialog box

Drafting Settings Dialog Box

When the isometric 1″ snap and 3″ grid are set, **GRIDDISPLAY** is set to **0**, and dot grid is set, the **Drafting Settings** dialog box will appear as shown in Figure 13-4. Grid and snap settings can also be made using the **Drafting Settings** dialog box.

Figure 13-4
Drafting Settings dialog box

Shape 1: Drawing the Isometric Rectangle

Drawing shape 1 (Figure 13-5) helps you become familiar with drawing lines using isometric polar coordinates.

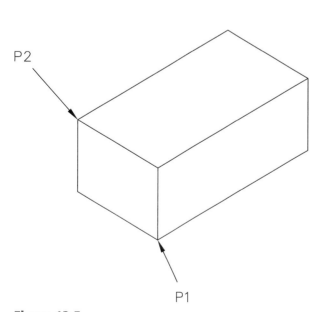

POLAR COORDINATES
FOR ISOMETRIC DRAWING

Figure 13-5
Shape 1: Drawing the isometric rectangle

Step 2. Draw the right face of an isometric rectangular box measuring 12″ × 16″ × 30″ using isometric polar coordinates, as described next:

Prompt	Response
Type a command:	**Line** (or type **L <Enter>**)
Specify first point:	**P1→** (Figure 13-5) (absolute coordinates 1′7-1/16, 4′11″—this is an isometric snap point)
Specify next point or [Undo]:	Type **@30<30 <Enter>**
Specify next point or [Undo]:	Type **@12<90 <Enter>**
Specify next point or [Close Undo]:	Type **@30<210 <Enter>**
Specify next point or [Close Undo]:	Type **C <Enter>**

Step 3. Draw the left face of the isometric rectangular box, as described next:

Prompt	Response
Type a command:	**<Enter>** (repeat **LINE**)
Specify first point:	**P1→** (Figure 13-5) **(Osnap-Endpoint)**
Specify next point or [Undo]:	Type **@16<150 <Enter>**
Specify next point or [Undo]:	Type **@12<90 <Enter>**
Specify next point or [Close Undo]:	Type **@16<330 <Enter>**
Specify next point or [Close Undo]:	**<Enter>**

Step 4. Draw the top of the isometric rectangular box, as described next:

Prompt	Response
Type a command:	**<Enter>** (repeat **LINE**)
Specify first point:	**P2→**
Specify next point or [Undo]:	Type **@30<30 <Enter>**
Specify next point or [Undo]:	Type **@16<–30 <Enter>**
Specify next point or [Close Undo]:	**<Enter>**

Shape 2: Drawing Isometric Ellipses

When using polar coordinates to draw lines in isometric, you can ignore isoplanes. Isoplanes are isometric faces—top, right, and left. Pressing **<Ctrl>+E** toggles your drawing to the correct isoplane—top, right, or left. The function key **<F5>** also can be used to toggle to the correct isoplane.

Shape 2 (Figure 13-6) has a circle in each of the isometric planes of a cube. When drawn in isometric, circles appear as ellipses. You must use the isoplanes when drawing isometric circles using the **ELLIPSE** command. The following part of the exercise starts by drawing a 15″ isometric cube.

Figure 13-6
Shape 2: Drawing an isometric cube with an ellipse in each isoplane

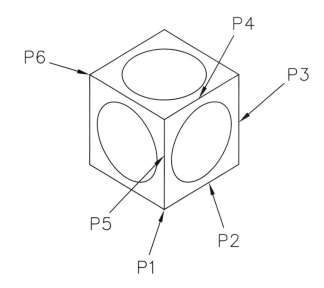

ISOPLANE TOGGLE	
Function Key:	<F5> Edit
Keyboard Combo:	<Ctrl>+E

Step 5. Draw the right face of a 15″ isometric cube using direct distance entry, as described next:

Prompt	Response
Type a command:	Toggle to the right isoplane (press <F5> until <Isoplane Right> appears) and click **Line** (or type **L** <Enter>)
Specify first point:	**P1→** (absolute coordinates 6′3/4″,5′3″)
Specify next point or [Undo]:	With **ORTHO** on, move your mouse upward 30° to the right, and type **15** <Enter>
Specify next point or [Undo]:	Move the mouse straight up, and type **15** <Enter>
Specify next point or [Close Undo]:	Move the mouse downward **210°** to the left, and type **15** <Enter>
Specify next point or [Close Undo]:	Type **C** <Enter>

Step 6. Use the **MIRROR** command to draw the left face of the isometric cube, as described next:

Prompt	Response
Type a command:	**Mirror** (or type **MI** <Enter>)
Select objects:	**P2→, P3→, P4→** <Enter> (Figure 13-6)
Specify first point of mirror line:	**P1→** (be sure **ORTHO** is on) (**Osnap-Endpoint**)
Specify second point of mirror line:	**P5→** (press <F5> to be sure you are in either the right or left isoplane)
Erase source objects? [Yes No]<N>:	**<Enter>**

Step 7. Complete the top face of the isometric cube, as described next:

Prompt	Response
Type a command:	Toggle to the top isoplane and click **Line** (or type **L** <Enter>)
Specify first point:	**P6→** (**Osnap-Endpoint**)
Specify next point or [Undo]:	Move the mouse upward **30°** to the right, and type **15** <Enter>
Specify next point or [Undo]:	Move the mouse downward **330°** to the right, and type **15** <Enter>
Specify next point or [Close Undo]:	**<Enter>**

NOTE

If you do not have the isometric snap style active, the **ELLIPSE** command will not prompt you with **Isocircle** as one of the options for the command.

NOTE

Select **Ellipse-Axis, End** if you select from the ribbon. Neither **Ellipse-Center** nor **Ellipse-Arc** allows you to draw an isometric ellipse.

Step 8. Draw an isometric ellipse (6″ radius) that represents a circle in the left isoplane, as described next:

ELLIPSE	
Ribbon/Panel	Home/Draw
Draw Toolbar:	Ellipse
Menu Bar:	Draw/Ellipse
Type a Command:	ELLIPSE
Command Alias:	EL

Prompt	Response
Type a command:	**Ellipse Axis, End** (or type **EL <Enter>**)
Specify axis endpoint of ellipse or [Arc Center Isocircle]:	Type **I <Enter>**
Specify center of isocircle:	**Osnap-Mid Between 2 Points**
First point of mid:	**P1→**
Second point of mid:	**P6→**
Specify radius of isocircle or [Diameter]:	Press the **<F5>** function key until the command line reads **<Isoplane Left>**, then type **6 <Enter>**

When you type and enter **D** in response to the prompt *Specify radius of Isocircle or Diameter:*, you can enter the diameter of the circle. The default is radius.

Step 9. Follow a similar procedure to draw ellipses in the right and top isoplanes. Be sure to specify **Isocircle** after you have selected the **ELLIPSE** command, and be sure you are in the correct isoplane before you draw the ellipse. Use **<F5>** to toggle to the correct isoplane.

When you have completed this part of the exercise, you have the essentials of isometric drawing. Now you are going to apply these essentials to a more complex shape.

TIP

After you become familiar with isometric angles and toggling to isoplanes, use direct distance entry with **ORTHO** on to draw lines. Just move your mouse in the isometric direction and type the number that tells AutoCAD how far you want to go. You may choose to watch the dynamic display of distance and polar angles and simply pick the desired point.

Shape 3: Drawing a Chair with Ellipses That Show the Thickness of a Material

Step 10. Draw the right side of the front chair leg, as described next:

Prompt	Response
Type a command:	Toggle to the right isoplane and click **Line** (or type **L <Enter>**) (be sure **ORTHO** is on)
Specify first point:	**P1→** (Figure 13-7) (pick a point in the approximate location [**9'-7/8",4'11"**] shown in Figure 13-2)
Specify next point or [Undo]:	With **ORTHO** on, move your mouse straight down **270°** and type **1'5 <Enter>**
Specify next point or [Undo]:	Move your mouse upward **30°** to the right and type **2 <Enter>**
Specify next point or [Close Undo]:	Move your mouse straight up **90°** and type **1'5 <Enter>**
Specify next point or [Close Undo]:	**<Enter>**

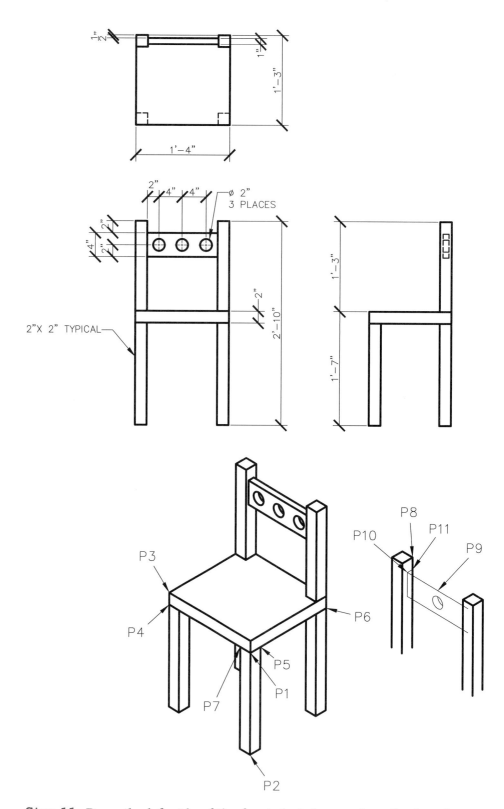

Figure 13-7
Shape 3: Drawing a chair with ellipses that show the thickness of a material

Step 11. Draw the left side of the front chair leg, as described next:

Prompt	Response
Type a command:	Toggle to the left isoplane and click **Line** (or type **L <Enter>**)
Specify first point:	**P2→ (Osnap-Endpoint)** (Figure 13-7)
Specify next point or [Undo]:	Move your mouse upward **150°** to the left, and type **2 <Enter>**

Prompt	Response
Specify next point or [Undo]:	Move your mouse straight up **90°** and type **1′5 <Enter>**
Specify next point or [Close Undo]:	**<Enter>**

Step 12. Draw the chair seat, as described next:

Prompt	Response
Type a command:	**Line** (or type **L <Enter>**)
Specify first point:	**P1→ (Osnap-Endpoint)** (Figure 13-7)
Specify next point or [Undo]:	Move your mouse **150°** upward to the left and type **1′4 <Enter>**
Specify next point or [Undo]:	Move your mouse straight up and type **2 <Enter>**
Specify next point or [Close Undo]:	Move your mouse **330°** downward to the right and type **1′4 <Enter>**
Specify next point or [Close Undo]:	Type **C <Enter>**
Type a command:	**<Enter>** (to begin the **LINE** command)
Specify first point:	**P1→ (Osnap-Endpoint)**
Specify next point or [Undo]:	Toggle to the right isoplane and with **ORTHO** on, move your mouse **30°** upward to the right and type **1′3 <Enter>**
Specify next point or [Undo]:	Move your mouse straight up and type **2 <Enter>**
Specify next point or [Close Undo]:	Move your mouse **210°** downward to the left and type **1′3 <Enter>**
Specify next point or [Close Undo]:	**<Enter>** (to end the **LINE** command)
Type a command:	**<Enter>** (to begin the **LINE** command)
Specify first point:	**P3→ (Osnap-Intersection)**
Specify next point or [Undo]:	Toggle to the top isoplane and with **ORTHO** on, move your mouse **30°** upward to the right and type **1′3 <Enter>**
Specify next point or [Close Undo]:	Move your mouse **330°** downward to the right and type **1′4 <Enter>**
Specify next point or [Close Undo]:	**<Enter>**

Step 13. Copy the front leg to the other three positions.

1. Using the **COPY** command, select the lines of the front leg. Use **P5→ (Osnap-Endpoint)** (Figure 13-7) as the base point and **P6→ (Osnap-Intersection)** as the second point of displacement.
2. Using the **COPY** command, select both legs on the right side. Use **P7→ (Osnap-Endpoint)** (Figure 13-7) as the base point and **P4→ (Osnap-Intersection)** as the second point of displacement.
3. Use the **TRIM** and **ERASE** commands to delete any unnecessary lines.

Step 14. Use the **LINE** command to draw one of the upright posts, and use the **COPY** command to copy it to the other position. Follow the dimensions shown in Figure 13-7.

Step 15. Draw the 1″ × 4″ × 12″ piece containing the three holes, as described next:

Prompt	Response
Type a command:	**Line** (or type **L <Enter>**)
Specify first point:	Type **FRO <Enter>**
Base point:	Click **P8→** (**Osnap-Intersection**) (Figure 13-7)
<Offset>:	Type **@2<–90 <Enter>**
Specify next point or [Undo]:	Type **@1<210 <Enter>**
Specify next point or [Undo]:	Type **@12<-30 <Enter>**
Specify next point or [Close Undo]:	**<Enter>**
Type a command:	Toggle to the left isoplane, and with **ORTHO** off, **Ellipse Axis, End** (or type **EL <Enter>**)
Specify axis endpoint of ellipse or [Arc Center Isocircle]:	Type **I <Enter>**
Specify center of isocircle:	Type **FRO <Enter>**
Base point:	Click **P9→** (**Osnap-Midpoint**)
<Offset>:	Type **@2<–90 <Enter>**
Specify radius of isocircle or [Diameter]:	Type **1 <Enter>**
Type a command:	**COPY** (or type **CP <Enter>**)
Select objects:	Click the ellipse just drawn
Select objects:	**<Enter>**
Specify base point or [Displacement mOde] <Displacement>:	Click **P10→** (**Osnap-Endpoint**)
Specify second point or <use first point as displacement>:	Click **P11→** (**Osnap-Endpoint**)
Specify second point or [Exit Undo] <Exit>:	**<Enter>**

Step 16. Trim the copied ellipse so that only the part within the first ellipse remains.

Step 17. Copy the hole described by the ellipses **4″ 330°** downward to the right and **4″ 150°** upward to the left.

Step 18. Draw a **4″** line straight down from **P10→ (Endpoint)** and a **12″** line **330°** downward to the right from the end of the 4″ line.

Step 19. Draw a **12″** line **330°** downward to the right from **P11→** (Endpoint).

Step 20. Use the **MOVE** command to move the 1″ × 4″ × 12″ piece and three holes **210°** downward to the left **1/2″**.

Step 21. Use **TRIM, EXTEND** and draw a line on the back to complete the drawing.

Shape 4: Drawing a Shape That Has a Series of Isometric Ellipses Located on the Same Centerline

Shape 4 (Figure 13-8), similar to a round table, will help you become familiar with drawing a shape that has a series of ellipses located on the same centerline. Five ellipses must be drawn. The centers of two of them, the extreme top and bottom ellipses, can be located by using endpoints of the centerline.

The following part of the exercise begins by drawing a centerline through the entire height of the object.

Figure 13-8

Shape 4: Drawing a shape that has a series of isometric ellipses located on the same centerline

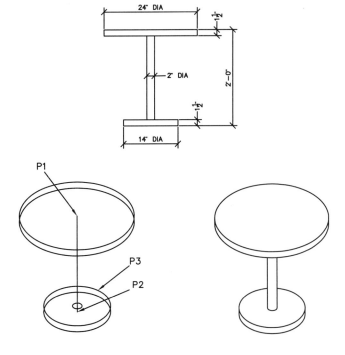

Step 22. Begin to draw a shape containing several ellipses of different sizes located on the same centerline by drawing the centerline, as described next:

Prompt	Response
Type a command:	**Line** (or type **L <Enter>**)
Specify first point:	**P1→** (1'11-7/16,1'4-1/2)
Specify next point or [Undo]:	With **ORTHO** on, move your mouse straight up and type **24 <Enter>**
Specify next point or [Undo]:	**<Enter>**

Step 23. Draw five ellipses:

1. Toggle to the top isoplane and use **Endpoint** to locate the center of the uppermost isometric ellipse on the endpoint of the vertical line. Draw it with a diameter of **24″**.

> **NOTE**
>
> Although **Osnap-Nearest** can be used to end an isometric line on another line, the position is not exact. A more exact method is to draw the line beyond where it should end and trim it to the correct length.

2. Draw a second **24″-diameter** isometric ellipse by copying the 24″ ellipse **1-1/2″** straight down.
3. Draw the **14″-diameter** ellipse using the bottom endpoint, **P2→**, of the vertical line as its center. Copy the 14″-diameter ellipse **1-1/2″** straight up.
4. Draw the **2″-diameter** ellipse at the center of the copied 14″-diameter ellipse using **Osnap-Center, P3→**, to locate its center.

Step 24. To draw the 2″ column, toggle to the right or left isoplane (the top isoplane does not allow you to draw vertical lines using a mouse if **ORTHO** is on). Turn **ORTHO (<F8>)** on. Draw a vertical line from the quadrant of one side of the 2″-diameter ellipse to just above the first 24″-diameter ellipse. Draw a similar line to form the other side of the column.

Step 25. With **ORTHO (<F8>)** on and toggled to the right or left isoplane, draw vertical lines from the quadrants of the ellipse segments to connect each side of the top and bottom ellipses, as shown in Figure 13-9.

Figure 13-9
Shape 4: Drawing tangents to the ellipses

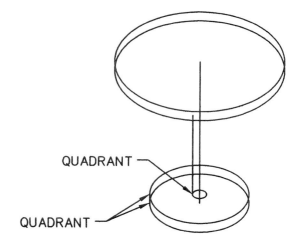

Step 26. Use **TRIM** and **ERASE** to remove unneeded lines. The drawing is complete as shown in the lower right corner of Figure 13-8.

Shape 5: Isometric Detail with Rounded Corners

The fifth drawing (Figure 13-10) in this exercise is a shape that has rounded corners. Rounded corners are common in many items. In 2D drawing, the **FILLET** command allows you to obtain the rounded corners quickly and easily. This is not so in isometric. Drawing shape 5 will help you become familiar with how rounded corners must be constructed with isometric ellipses.

Figure 13-10
Shape 5: Isometric detail with rounded corners

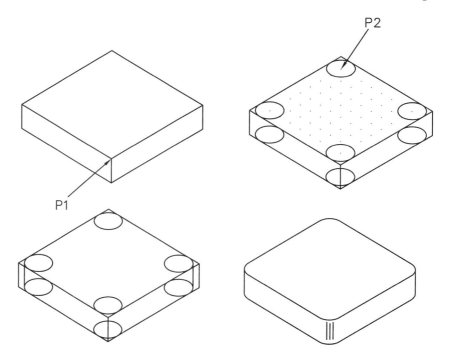

Step 27. Turn **ORTHO** and **SNAP** on, and toggle to the top isoplane. Draw an **18″ × 18″** square shape in the top isoplane (Figure 13-10), as described next:

Prompt	Response
Type a command:	**Line** (or type **L <Enter>**)
LINE Specify first point:	**P1→** (on a grid mark) (**5′11,3′3**)
Specify next point or [Undo]: <Isoplane Top> <Ortho on>	Move your mouse upward **30°** to the right and type **18 <Enter>**
Specify next point or [Undo]:	Move your mouse upward **30°** to the left and type **18 <Enter>**
Specify next point or [Close Undo]:	Move your mouse downward **30°** to the left and type **18 <Enter>**
Specify next point or [Close Undo]:	Type **C <Enter>**

Step 28. Copy the 18″ × 18″ square **4″** down as described below:

1. Copy the front two edges of the square to form the bottom of the shape. Copy using **@4<270** (4″ is the depth) as the polar coordinates for the second point of displacement.
2. Draw lines connecting the top and bottom edges. (These lines are for reference only. You may skip this step if you choose.)

Step 29. Draw a **2″-radius** ellipse in the top isoplane, as described next:

Prompt	Response
Type a command:	**Ellipse** (or type **EL <Enter>**) (toggle to the top isoplane)
Specify axis endpoint of ellipse or [Arc Center Isocircle]:	Type **I <Enter>**
Specify center of isocircle:	**P2→** (count **2″** in both the **330** and **210** directions from the corner to locate the center of the ellipse. Make sure **SNAP** is on.)
Specify radius of isocircle or [Diameter]:	Type **2 <Enter>**

Step 30. Copy the ellipse just drawn to the other four top corners, locating them in a similar manner.

Step 31. Copy the front three ellipses **4″** in the **270** direction to form corners in the bottom plane. Make sure **SNAP** is on.

Step 32. Draw lines connecting the two outside ellipses using **Osnap-Quadrant**.

Step 33. Use the **TRIM** and **ERASE** commands to remove the extra lines.

Step 34. Add highlights on the front corner to complete the drawing.

Shape 6: A TV Shape with an Angled Back

While drawing in isometric, you will often need to draw angles. To do that you will need to locate both ends of the angle and connect them. You will not be able to draw any angle otherwise, such as the 62° angle in Figure 13-11.

Figure 13-11

Shape 6: A TV shape with an angled back

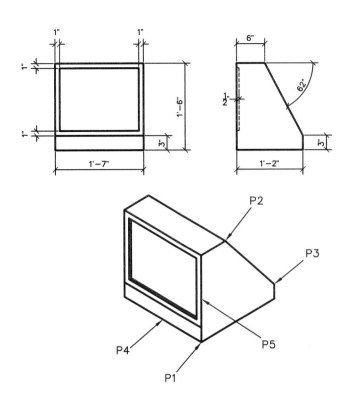

Step 35. Draw the right side of Figure 13-11, as described next:

Prompt	Response
Type a command:	**Line** (or type **L <Enter>**)
Specify first point:	**P1→ (8'9-5/8",9")**
Specify next point or [Undo]:	Toggle to the right isoplane and with **ORTHO** on, move your mouse **30°** upward to the right and type **1'2 <Enter>**
Specify next point or [Undo]:	Move your mouse straight up and type **3 <Enter>**
Specify next point or [Close Undo]:	**<Enter>**
Type a command:	**<Enter>** (to get the **LINE** command back)
Specify first point:	**P1→** (again) **(Endpoint)**
Specify next point or [Undo]:	Move your mouse straight up and type **1'6 <Enter>**
Specify next point or [Close Undo]:	Move your mouse **30°** upward to the right and type **6 <Enter>**
Specify next point or [Undo]:	**P3→ (Endpoint)**
Specify next point or [Close Undo]:	**<Enter>**

Step 36. Draw the left side and top of Figure 13-11, as described next:

Prompt	Response
Type a command:	**Line** (or type **L <Enter>**)
Specify first point:	Click **P1→** (Figure 13-11)
Specify next point or [Undo]:	Toggle to the left isoplane and with **ORTHO** on, move your mouse **150°** upward to the left, and type **1'7 <Enter>**

Prompt	Response
Specify next point or [Undo]:	Move your mouse straight up and type **1'6 <Enter>**
Specify next point or [Close Undo]:	Toggle to the top isoplane and move your mouse **30°** upward to the right and type **6 <Enter>**
Specify next point or [Close Undo]:	Click **P2→**
Specify next point or [Close Undo]:	**<Enter>**
Type a command:	**COPY** (or type **CP <Enter>**)
Select objects:	Click **P4→**
Select objects:	**<Enter>**
Specify base point or [Displacement mOde] <Displacement>:	Click **any point**
Specify second point or <use first point as displacement>:	Toggle to the left isoplane and move your mouse straight up and type **3 <Enter>**
Specify second point or [Exit Undo] <Exit>:	Move your mouse straight up and type **4 <Enter>**
Specify second point or [Exit Undo] <Exit>:	Move your mouse straight up and type **1'5 <Enter>**
Specify second point or [Exit Undo] <Exit>:	Move your mouse straight up and type **1'6 <Enter>**
Specify second point or [Exit Undo] <Exit>:	**<Enter>**
Type a command:	**<Enter>** (to repeat the **COPY** command)
Select objects:	Click **P5→**
Select objects:	**<Enter>**
Specify base point or [Displacement mOde] <Displacement>:	Click **any point**
Specify second point or <use first point as displacement>:	Move your mouse **150°** upward to the left and type **1 <Enter>**
Specify second point or [Exit Undo] <Exit>:	Move your mouse **150°** upward to the left and type **1'6 <Enter>**
Specify second point or [Exit Undo] <Exit>:	**<Enter>**

Step 37. Use the **TRIM** command to trim unnecessary lines.

Step 38. Use the **COPY** command to draw the two lines forming the inside edge of the TV screen. Copy them **1/2", 30°** upward to the right.

Step 39. Draw a line at the intersection of those copied lines.

Step 40. Use the **TRIM** command to trim unnecessary lines. The drawing is complete.

Shape 7: Isometric Detail: A Hexagonal-Shaped Vase

The final shape in this exercise combines several features (Figure 13-12).

Figure 13-12

Shape 7: Isometric detail: A
hexagonal-shaped vase

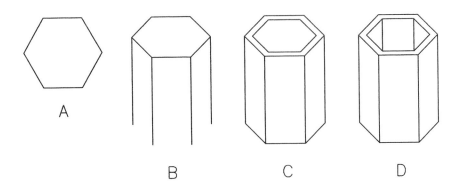

A

B

C

D

Step 41. Draw the hexagonal shape of the vase (Figure 13-12A), as
described next:

POLYGON	
Ribbon/ Panel	Home/ Draw
Draw Toolbar:	
Menu Bar:	Draw/ Polygon
Type a Command:	POLYGON
Command Alias:	POL

Prompt

Type a command:
Enter number of sides <4>:
Specify center of polygon or [Edge]:

Enter an option [Inscribed in circle
   Circumscribed about circle] <1>:
Specify radius of circle:

Response

Polygon (or type **POL <Enter>**)
Type **6 <Enter>**
Click a point on a grid mark in the
   approximate location shown in
   Figure 13-2 (with **SNAP** on)

Type **C <Enter>**
Type **6 <Enter>**

Now you have a hexagon that cannot be used in isometric drawing. To use it,
you must block the hexagon and then insert it with different X and Y values.
Be sure to toggle to the top isoplane when you insert the hexagonal block.

Step 42. Block and insert the hexagon (Figure 13-12B), as described next:

Prompt

Type a command:
The **Block Definition** dialog box
   appears:

Specify insertion base point:
The **Block Definition** dialog box
   appears:
Select objects:
Select objects:
The **Block Definition** dialog box
   appears:
The hexagon disappears:
Type a command:
The **Insert** dialog box appears:

Response

Block (or type **B <Enter>**)

Type **HEX** in the **Name:** input box;
   make sure **Delete** is selected
Click **Pick point**
Click the center of the hexagon

Click **Select objects**
Click any point on the hexagon
<Enter>

Click **OK**

Insert-Block... (or type **I <Enter>**)
Click the down arrow in the **Name:**
   input box
Click **HEX** (if it is not already in the
   Name: input box)
Click the checks in **Uniform Scale**
   and **Rotation - Specify On-
   screen** to remove them.
Do **NOT** remove the check in **Specify
   On-screen**

Prompt	Response
	Change **Y**: in the **Scale area** to **.58** (this is a very close approximation to the isometric scale factor)
	Click **OK**
Specify insertion point or [Basepoint Scale X Y X Rotate]:	Pick the location of the isometric hexagon as shown in Figure 13-2 (**SNAP** on) (**5′7-9/16″, 2′-4″**)

Step 43. Draw **1′-3″** vertical lines from each of the visible corners of the hexagon in the **270** direction (Figure 13-12B). (You can draw one line, then copy it three times.)

Step 44. Using **Osnap-Endpoint**, draw lines to form the bottom of the hexagon (Figure 13-12C).

Step 45. Copy the HEX block and pick the same point for the base point and second point of displacement so that the copied HEX lies directly on top of the first HEX.

Step 46. Use the **Scale** command to scale the copied HEX to a **.8** scale factor. Be sure to click the center of the HEX block as the base point.

Step 47. Draw vertical lines on the inside of the vase, as shown in Figure 13-12D.

Step 48. When you have completed Exercise 13-1, save your work in at least two places.

Step 49. Plot or print the drawing on an **8-1/2″ × 11″** sheet of paper; use **Fit to paper**.

EXERCISE 13-2
Tenant Space Reception Desk in Isometric

The tenant space reception desk is drawn in isometric in Exercise 13-2. When you have completed Exercise 13-2, your drawing will look similar to Figure 13-13.

Step 1. Use your workspace to make the following settings:

1. Use **Save As...** to save the drawing on the hard drive with the name **CH13-EXERCISE2**.
2. Set drawing units: **Architectural**
3. Set drawing limits: **15′,15′**
4. Set snap: **Style-Isometric-1″**
5. Set **GRIDDISPLAY: 0**
6. Set grid: **4′**
7. Create the following layer:

Layer Name	Color	Linetype	Lineweight
Layer1	green	continuous	Default

8. Set **Layer1** current.

9. Use **Zoom-All**.

Figure 13-13
Exercise 13-2: Tenant space
reception desk in isometric

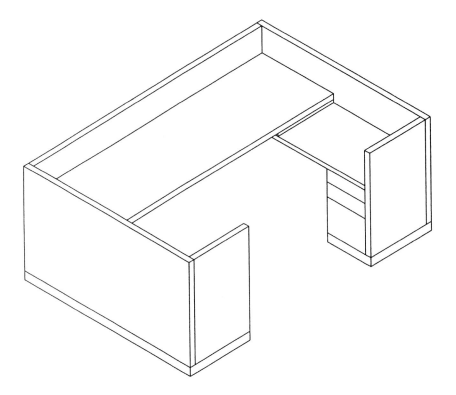

This exercise is a series of straight lines, all of which are on the isometric axes. Follow the step-by-step procedure described next so that you get some ideas about what you can and cannot do when using the isometric drawing method. To draw an isometric view of the reception desk (Figure 13-13), use the dimensions shown in Figure 13-15.

Figure 13-14
Drawing the top edge of
the panels

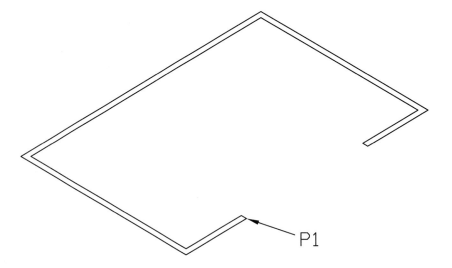

> **TIP**
> You can also use direct distance entry to specify distances when you copy if you toggle to the correct isoplane.

Step 2. Set **SNAP** and **ORTHO** on. Toggle to the top isometric plane. Draw the top edge of the panels (Figure 13-14), as described next:

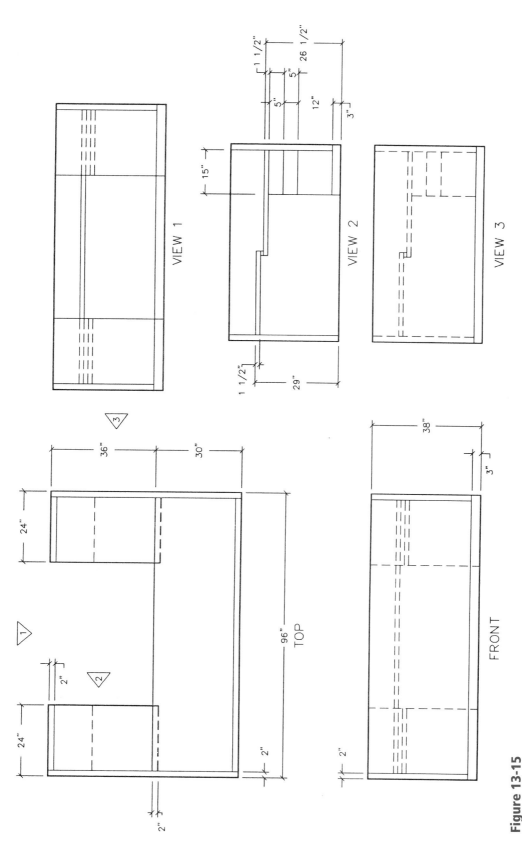

Figure 13-15
Dimensions of the tenant space reception desk (scale: 3/8" = 1'-0")

Prompt	Response
Type a command:	**Line** (or type **L <Enter>**)
Specify first point:	**P1→** (Figure 13-14) (absolute coordinates **8′1,7′4**)
Specify next point or [Undo]:	Type **@24<210 <Enter>** (or move the mouse downward **30°** to the left and type **24 <Enter>**)
Specify next point or [Undo]:	Type **@66<150 <Enter>**
Specify next point or [Close Undo]:	Type **@96<30 <Enter>**
Specify next point or [Close Undo]:	Type **@66<-30 <Enter>**
Specify next point or [Close Undo]:	Type **@24<210 <Enter>**
Specify next point or [Close Undo]:	Type **@2<150 <Enter>**
Specify next point or [Close Undo]:	Type **@22<30 <Enter>**
Specify next point or [Close Undo]:	Type **@62<150 <Enter>**
Specify next point or [Close Undo]:	Type **@92<210 <Enter>**
Specify next point or [Close Undo]:	Type **@62<330 <Enter>**
Specify next point or [Close Undo]:	Type **@22<30 <Enter>**
Specify next point or [Close Undo]:	Type **C <Enter>**

Step 3. Use the **EXTEND** command to extend the inside lines of the panels to form the separate panels (Figure 13-16), as described next:

EXTEND	
Ribbon/ Panel	Home/ Modify ---/
Modify Toolbar:	---/
Menu Bar:	Modify/Extend
Type a Command:	EXTEND
Command Alias:	EX

Prompt	Response
Type a command:	**Extend** (or type **EX <Enter>**)
Select objects or <select all>:	**<Enter>** (enter **Select all objects as boundary edges**)
Select object to extend or shift-select to trim or [Fence Crossing Project Edge Undo]:	**P3→, P4→, P5→, P6→ <Enter>**

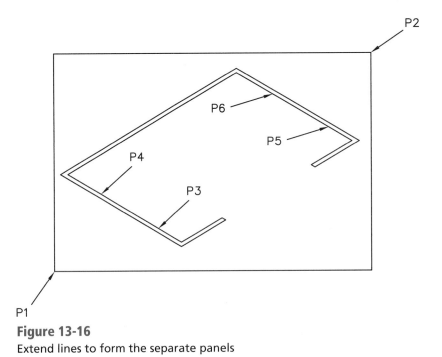

Figure 13-16
Extend lines to form the separate panels

Step 4. Copy the top edges of the panels to form the lower kickplate surfaces (Figure 13-17), as described next:

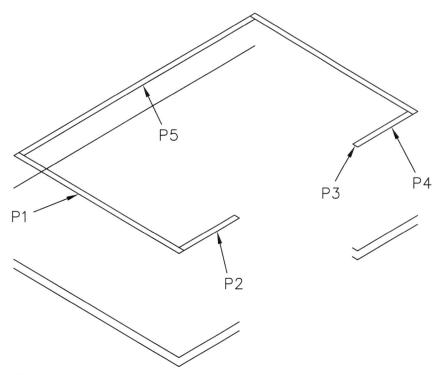

Figure 13-17
Copy the top edges to form the lower kickplate surfaces and the edge of the main work surface

Prompt	Response
Type a command:	**Copy** (or type **CP <Enter>**)
Select objects:	**P1→,P2→,P3→,P4→**
Select objects:	**<Enter>**
Specify base point or [Displacement mOde] <Displacement>:	**P1→** (any point is OK)
Specify second point or <use first point as displacement>:	Type **@35<270 <Enter>**
Specify second point or [Exit Undo] <Exit>:	Type **@38<270 <Enter>**
Specify second point or [Exit Undo] <Exit>:	**<Enter>**

Step 5. Repeat the **COPY** command to draw the edge of the main work surface against the inside of the panel (Figure 13-17), as described next:

Prompt	Response
Type a command:	**<Enter>**
Select objects:	**P5→**
Select objects:	**<Enter>**
Specify base point or [Displacement mOde] <Displacement>:	**P5→** (any point is OK)
Specify second point or <use first point as displacement>:	Type **@9<270 <Enter>**

Step 6. Set a running **Osnap** mode of **Endpoint** and draw vertical lines connecting top and bottom outside lines and the inside corner above the work surface (Figure 13-18).

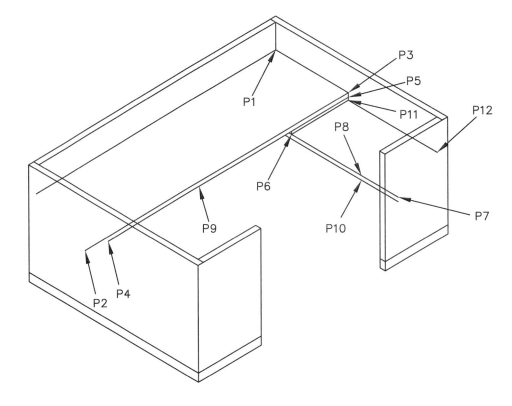

Figure 13-18
Draw the vertical lines connecting top and bottom edges; draw the work surfaces

Step 7 Draw the work surfaces (Figure 13-18), as described next:

Prompt	Response
Type a command:	**Line** (or type **L <Enter>**)
Specify first point:	**Osnap-Endpoint, P1→**
Specify next point or [Undo]:	Type **@28<330 <Enter>**
Specify next point or [Undo]:	**P2→** (with **ORTHO** on and the top isoplane active, move your mouse downward **30°** to the left and pick any point beyond the inside of the left partition; you can trim these later)
Specify next point or [Close Undo]:	**<Enter>**
Type a command:	**<Enter>** (repeat **LINE**)
Specify first point:	**Osnap-Endpoint, P3→**
Specify next point or [Undo]:	Type **@1-1/2<270 <Enter>**
Specify next point or [Undo]:	**P4→** (pick another point outside the left partition)
Specify next point or [Close Undo]:	**<Enter>**
Type a command:	**<Enter>** (repeat **LINE**)
Specify first point:	**Osnap-Endpoint, P5→**
Specify next point or [Undo]:	Type **@1<270 <Enter>**
Specify next point or [Undo]:	Type **@22<210 <Enter>**
Specify next point or [Close Undo]:	Type **@1<90 <Enter>**
Specify next point or [Close Undo]:	**<Enter>**
Type a command:	**<Enter>** (repeat **LINE**)
Specify first point:	**Osnap-Endpoint, P6→** (Figure 13-18)
Specify next point or [Undo]:	**P7→** (move the mouse downward **30°** to the right and pick a point outside the right rear panel)

Prompt	Response
Specify next point or [Undo]:	**<Enter>**
Type a command:	**<Enter>** (repeat **LINE**)
Specify first point:	**Osnap-Endpoint, P11→**
Specify next point or [Undo]:	**P12→** (pick a point outside the right rear panel) **<Enter>**
Type a command:	**Copy** (or type **CP <Enter>**)
Select objects:	**P8→**
Select objects:	**<Enter>**
Specify base point or [Displacement mOde] <Displacement>:	**P8→** (any point)
Specify second point or <use first point as displacement>:	Type **@1-1/2<270 <Enter>**
Type a command:	**Extend** (or type **EX <Enter>**)
Select objects or <select all>:	**P9→ <Enter>**
Select object to extend or [Fence Crossing Project Edge Undo]:	**P8→, P10→ <Enter>**

Step 8 Trim lines that extend outside the panels (Figure 13-19), as described next:

Prompt	Response
Type a command:	**Trim** (or type **TR <Enter>**)
Select objects or <select all>:	**P1→, P2→, P3→ <Enter>**
Select object to trim or shift-select to extend or [Fence Crossing Project Edge eRase Undo]:	**P4→, P5→, P6→, P7→, P8→, P9→ <Enter>**

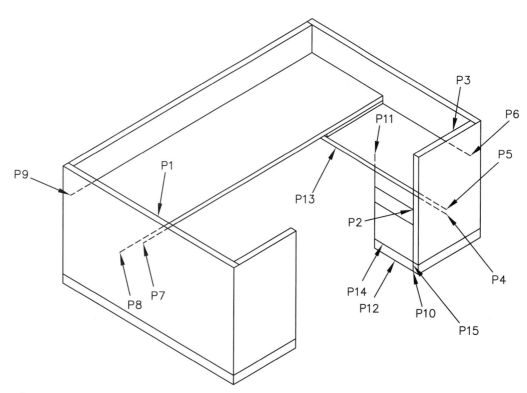

Figure 13-19
Trim lines and draw the drawer pedestal

Chapter 13 | Isometric Drawing and Gradient Hatch Rendering **591**

Step 9 Draw the drawer pedestal (Figure 13-19), as described next:

Prompt	Response
Type a command:	**Line** (or type **L <Enter>**)
Specify first point:	**Osnap-Endpoint, P10→**
Specify next point or [Undo]:	Toggle to the left isoplane and type **@15<150 <Enter>**
Specify next point or [Undo]:	**P11→** (with **ORTHO** on, pick a point above the bottom edge of the desktop)
Specify next point or [Close Undo]:	**<Enter>**
Type a command:	**Copy** (or type **CP <Enter>**)
Select objects:	**P12→** (Figure 13-19)
Select objects:	**<Enter>**
Specify base point or [Displacement mOde] <Displacement>:	**P12→** (any point)
Specify second point or <use first point as displacement>:	Type **@3<90 <Enter>**
Specify second point or [Exit Undo] <Exit>:	Type **@15<90 <Enter>**
Specify second point or [Exit Undo] <Exit>:	Type **@20<90 <Enter>**
Specify second point or [Exit Undo] <Exit>:	**<Enter>**

Step 10 Trim the extra lines, as described next:

Prompt	Response
Type a command:	**Trim** (or type **TR <Enter>**)
Select objects or <select all>:	**P13→, P14→ <Enter>**
Select object to trim or shift-select to extend or [Fence Crossing Project Edge eRase Undo]:	**P15→, P11→ <Enter>**

Step 11 When you have completed Exercise 13-2, save your work in at least two places.

Step 12 Click **Layout1**, click the viewport boundary, right-click, and use the **Properties** menu to set a standard scale of **1/2″ = 1′**. Plot or print the drawing on an **8-1/2″ × 11″** sheet of paper.

Dimensioning in Isometric

You can resolve the problem of placing dimensions on an isometric drawing by buying a third-party software dimensioning package designed specifically for isometric. Other methods, such as using the **Aligned** option in dimensioning and using an inclined font with the style setting, solve only part of the problem. Arrowheads must be constructed and individually inserted for each isoplane. If you spend a little time blocking the arrowheads and customizing your menu, you can speed up the process significantly.

Gradient Hatch

gradient hatch: A method of rendering 2D drawings that is similar to air-brush rendering.

Gradient (the tab on the **Hatch and Gradient** dialog box) can be used to render 2D drawings such as the isometric drawings in this chapter (Figure 13-20). The appearance of these renderings is very similar to air-brush

Figure 13-20
Exercise 13-3 complete

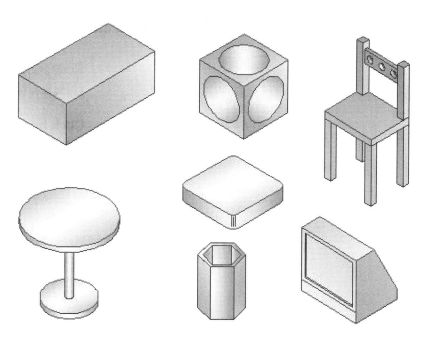

renderings. The three means you can use to change the pattern appearance are as follows:

1 Select one of the nine pattern buttons.

2 Check **Centered** (or uncheck **Centered**).

3 Change the angle of the pattern.

In addition, you can select a color and vary its shade.
In general, follow these guidelines:

1 When selecting a gradient pattern, place it on left and right isoplanes at a 60° angle to a horizontal line. Top isoplanes can vary from a horizontal pattern (90° of rotation) to 30°.

2 Use the center pattern on the top row to shade holes. This pattern should be at a 0° angle in the top isoplane, 120° in the left isoplane, and 60° in the right isoplane. The **Centered** button should be unchecked so that the pattern shows a darker area on one side of the hole than on the other side.

3 Do not be too concerned about where the light is coming from. Consider that there are varying sources of light. Just try to keep light areas next to dark ones and do not be afraid to experiment with any of the nine patterns. Some figures will be challenging and will require several tries before the rendering looks right.

4 Use the **Draw order:** option to **Send to back** all your gradient patterns so that the lines of the drawing show in front of the gradient patterns.

EXERCISE 13-3
Using Gradient Patterns to Render the Shapes of Exercise 13-1

Step 1. Open drawing **CH13-EXERCISE1**.

Step 2. Save the drawing as **CH13-EXERCISE3**.

HATCH	
Ribbon/ Panel	Home/Draw
Draw Toolbar:	
Menu Bar:	Draw/ Hatch...
Type a Command:	HATCH
Command Alias:	H

Step 3. Open the **Hatch and Gradient** dialog box and select a color, as described next:

Prompt	Response
Type a command:	**Hatch...** (or type **H <Enter>**)
The **Hatch Creation** panel is displayed on the ribbon:	Click the arrow in the lower right of the **Options** panel
The **Hatch and Gradient** dialog box appears:	With the **Gradient** tab selected, click the ellipsis (**...**) to the right of the one color swatch
The **Select Color** dialog box (Figure 13-21) appears:	Click the **Index Color** tab
	Click a color (for now, number **42**)
	Click **OK**

Figure 13-21
Select a color for gradient hatch

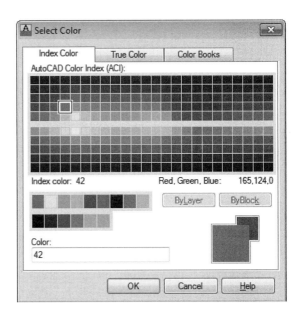

Step 4. Hatch the top plane of shape 1 (Figure 13-22), as described next:

Prompt	Response
The **Hatch and Gradient** dialog box appears:	Click the first pattern from the left on the top row to select it
	Uncheck the **Centered** box
	Change the **Angle** to **300**
	Click **Send to back** (in the **Draw order**: list) so the lines are visible
	Click **Add: Pick points**
Pick internal point or [Select objects seTtings]:	Click any point inside the top plane of shape 1
Pick internal point or [Select objects seTtings]:	Type **T <Enter>**
The **Hatch and Gradient** dialog box appears:	Click **Preview**

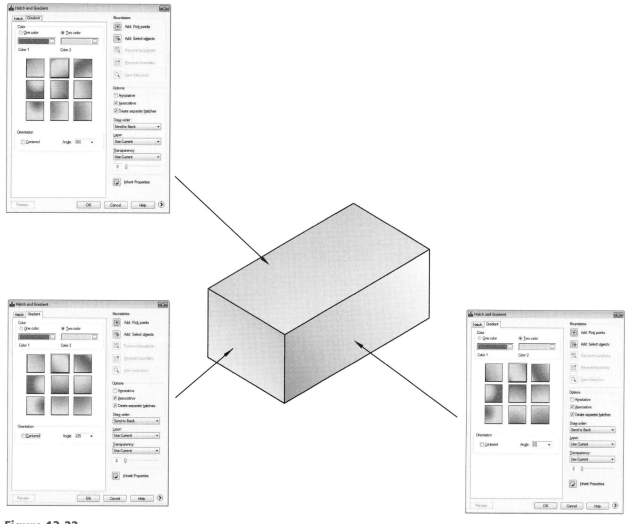

Figure 13-22
Apply gradient hatch patterns to shape 1

Prompt	Response
Pick or press Esc to return to dialog or <Right-click to accept hatch>:	Right-click (if the pattern looks right) **<Enter>** or press **<Esc>** and fix the dialog box
Type a command:	**<Enter>** (repeat **HATCH**) and Type **T<Enter>**

Step 5. Hatch the left plane of shape 1 (Figure 13-22), as described next:

Prompt	Response
The **Hatch and Gradient** dialog box appears:	Click the first pattern from the left on the top row to select it.
	Uncheck the **Centered** box
	Change the **Angle** to **225**
	Click **Send to back**
	Click **Add: Pick points**
Pick internal point or [Select objects seTtings]:	Click any point inside the left plane of shape 1

Prompt	Response
Pick internal point or [Select objects seTtings]:	Type **T <Enter>**
The **Hatch and Gradient** dialog box appears:	Click **Preview**
Pick or press Esc to return to dialog or <Right-click to accept hatch>:	Right-click (if the pattern looks right) **<Enter>** or press **<Esc>** and fix the dialog box
Type a command:	**<Enter>** (repeat **HATCH**) and Type **T<Enter>**

Step 6. Hatch the right plane of shape 1 (Figure 13-22), as described next:

Prompt	Response
The **Hatch and Gradient** dialog box appears:	Click the first pattern from the left on the top row to select it Uncheck the **Centered** box Change the **Angle** to **30** Click **Send to back** Click **Add: Pick points**
Pick internal point or [Select objects seTtings]:	Click any point inside the right plane of shape 1
Pick internal point or [Select objects seTtings]:	Type **T <Enter>**
The **Hatch and Gradient** dialog box appears:	Click **Preview**
Pick or press Esc to return to dialog or <Right-click to accept hatch>:	Right-click (if the pattern looks right) **<Enter>** or press **<Esc>** and fix the dialog box

Step 7. Hatch the top planes of shape 4 (Figure 13-23), as described next:

Prompt	Response
Type a command:	**<Enter>** and click the arrow in the lower right of the **Options** panel

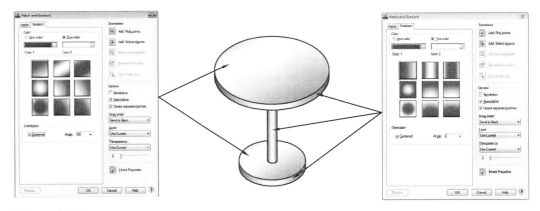

Figure 13-23
Gradient hatch patterns for shape 4

Prompt	Response
The **Hatch and Gradient** dialog box appears:	Click the second pattern from the left on the top row to select it
	Check the **Centered** box
	Change the **Angle** to **300**
	Click **Send to back**
	Click **Add: Pick points**
Pick internal point or [Select objects seTtings]:	Click any point inside the top plane of shape 4, then click any point inside the top plane of the base, as shown in Figure 13-23
Pick internal point or [Select objects seTtings]:	Type **T <Enter>**
The **Hatch and Gradient** dialog box appears:	Click **Preview**
Pick or press **<Esc>** to return to dialog or <Right-click to accept hatch>:	Right-click (if the pattern looks right) **<Enter>** or press **<Esc>** and fix the dialog box

Step 8. Hatch the cylindrical planes of shape 4 (Figure 13-23), as described next:

Prompt	Response
Type a command:	**<Enter>** and click the arrow in the lower right of the **Options** panel
The **Hatch and Gradient** dialog box appears:	Click the second pattern from the left on the top row to select it
	Check the **Centered** box
	Change the **Angle** to **0**
	Click **Send to back**
	Click **Add: Pick points**
Pick internal point or [Select objects seTtings]:	Click any point inside the top edge of the tabletop (Figure 13-23)
Pick internal point or [Select objects seTtings]:	Type **T <Enter>**
The **Hatch and Gradient** dialog box appears:	Click **Preview**
Pick or press Esc to return to dialog or <Right-click to accept hatch>:	Right-click (if the pattern looks right) **<Enter>** or press **<Esc>** and fix the dialog box

Step 9. Use the same settings in the **Hatch and Gradient** dialog box to apply patterns to the post and the base edge. You will have to do each one separately because the areas to be hatched are much different in size. (You can also check **Create separate hatches** in the **Gradient** tab.)

Step 10. Use the **Inherit Properties** option to hatch shape 5 (Figure 13-24), as described next.

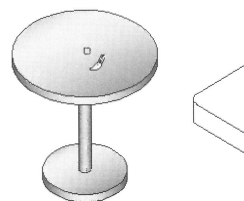

Figure 13-24
Use **Inherit Properties** to hatch shape 5—select **Associative Hatch Object**

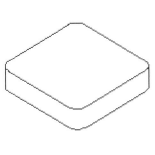

Figure 13-25
Select internal point

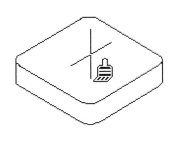

Prompt	Response
Type a command:	**H<Enter>** Click the arrow in the lower right of the **Options** panel
The **Hatch and Gradient** dialog box appears:	Click **Inherit Properties**
Select hatch object:	Click the top surface of shape 4 (Figure 13-24)
Pick internal point or [Select objects seTtings]:	Click the top surface of shape 5 (Figure 13-25)
Pick internal point or [Select objects seTtings]:	Type **T <Enter>** Click **Send to back** Click **OK <Enter>**
Type a command:	**<Enter>** (repeat **HATCH**); click the arrow in the lower right corner of the **Options** panel
The **Hatch and Gradient** dialog box appears:	Click **Inherit Properties**
Select hatch object:	Click the post pattern of shape 4
Pick internal point or [Select objects seTtings]:	Click the unshaded surface of shape 5
Pick internal point or [Select objects seTtings]:	Type **T <Enter>** Click **OK**

Step 11. Use the gradient hatch patterns shown in Figure 13-26 to hatch five of the areas of shape 3. Use **Inherit Properties** to select hatch patterns from shapes 1 and 5 to complete shape 3.

Step 12. Use **Inherit Properties** and any other patterns you need to shade the remaining shapes so your final drawing looks similar to Figure 13-20.

Step 13. Experiment with the **Wipeout** command on the **Draw** menu to create highlights in areas where no hatch pattern should appear. **Wipeout** completely covers any image hiding any part

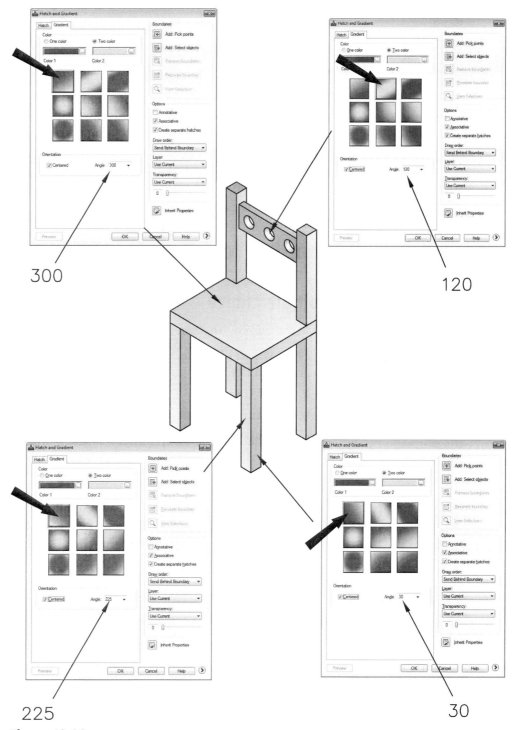

Figure 13-26
Gradient hatch patterns for shape 3

or all of it. You will find uses for **Wipeout** in several types of illustrating.

Step 14. Put your name in the lower right corner and plot the drawing at a scale of **1″ = 1′**. Be sure the **Shade plot**: input box shows: **As Displayed**.

Chapter Summary

This chapter provided you the information necessary to set up and draw isometric drawings. In addition, shading of these drawings was demonstrated, and the exercises drawn in isometric were rendered using gradient hatch patterns. Now you have the skills and information necessary to produce isometric drawings that can be used in interior design sales pieces, information sheets, contract documents, and other similar types of documents.

Chapter Test Questions

Multiple Choice

Circle the correct answer.

1. From which of the following dialog boxes are the isometric snap and grid obtained?
   a. **Layer Control...**
   b. **Drafting Settings...**
   c. **Grid On/Off**
   d. **UCS Control**

2. From which of the **Snap** options is the isometric snap obtained?
   a. **ON**
   b. **OFF**
   c. **Rotate**
   d. **Style**

3. Which isoplane was used to draw the ellipse shown in Figure 13-27?
   a. Top
   b. Left
   c. Right
   d. It was not drawn on an isoplane.

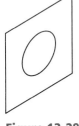

Figure 13-27

4. From which of the **Ellipse** prompts is the isometric ellipse obtained?
   a. **<Axis endpoint 1>**
   b. **Center**
   c. **Isocircle**
   d. **Rotation**

5. Which of the following is **not** one of the normal isometric axes?
   a. 30
   b. 60
   c. 90
   d. 210

6. Which isoplane was used to draw the ellipse shown in Figure 13-28?
   a. Top
   b. Left
   c. Right
   d. It was not drawn on an isoplane.

7. Which tab on the **Hatch and Gradient** dialog box allows you to apply patterns shown in Figure 13-22?
   a. **Gradient**
   b. **Advanced**
   c. **Hatch**
   d. There is no such tab.

8. Which key(s) toggle from one isoplane to another?
   a. **<F5>**
   b. **<F9>**
   c. **<Ctrl>+C**
   d. **<F7>**

Figure 13-28

Figure 13-29

9. Which of the following is the same as −30°?
   a. 60°   c. 210°
   b. 150°   d. 330°

10. Which isoplane was used to draw the ellipse shown in Figure 13-29?
    a. Top   c. Right
    b. Left   d. It was not drawn on an isoplane.

Matching

Write the number of the correct answer on the line.

a. **Draw order** _____

b. Top, right, left _____

c. A 2D drawing method giving the appearance of three dimensions _____

d. Direct distance entry _____

e. 3D objects that can be viewed from any angle _____

1. Isometric drawing
2. 3D models
3. Isometric isoplanes

4. A means of making lines appear more prominent than gradient patterns
5. A means of drawing lines in isometric with **ORTHO** on

True or False

Circle the correct answer.

1. **True or False:** The function key **<F7>** may be used to turn the isometric grid on and off.

2. **True or False:** The syntax **@5.25″<30** draws a line 5.25″ long at an angle upward to the right.

3. **True or False:** The top isoplane will **not** allow vertical lines to be drawn with a mouse when **ORTHO** is on.

4. **True or False:** The **Draw order:** option **Send to back** cannot be used to make lines appear more prominent than a gradient hatch pattern.

5. **True or False:** To draw a line at an angle that is **not** on an isometric axis, locate both ends of the line first, then draw the line.

List

1. Five options of the **Snap** command.

2. Five steps in drawing isometric circles.

3. Five steps for dimensioning in isometric drawings.

4. Five ways of accessing the **Hatch** command.

5. Five **Hatch Settings** parameters.

6. Five **Properties/Options** from the **Hatch/Gradient** window.

7. Five predefined **Hatch Patterns** representing materials.

8. Five **Gradient Settings** parameters.

9. Five isometric angles.

10. Five ways of setting up for an isometric drawing.

Questions

1. What is isometric drawing and how is it used?

2. What is the quickest and best method for drawing isometric lines?

3. Why are isometric ellipses used to draw holes and cylinders?

4. Why must angles in isometric be drawn by locating the ends of the angle instead of drawing a line at a specific angle?

5. How can gradient hatching be used to render shapes other than isometric shapes?

Chapter Projects

Project 13-1: *Using Gradient Patterns to Render the Reception Desk of Exercise 13-2* [BASIC]

1. Open **CH13-EXERCISE2** and use gradient hatch patterns to shade this drawing so it looks similar to Figure 13-30. When you have completed the hatching, put your name in the lower right corner and plot this drawing at a scale of **1/2″ = 1′-0″**. Be sure the **Shade plot:** input box shows: **As Displayed**.

2. Save your drawing in at least two places with the name **CH13-P1**.

Figure 13-30
Project 13-1 completed

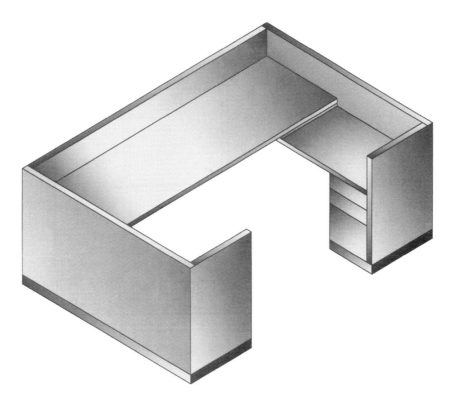

Project 13-2: *Tenant Space Reception Seating Area Isometric* [INTERMEDIATE]

1. Make an isometric drawing, full size, of the chairs, coffee table, and corner table to show the entire reception room seating area. Use the dimensions shown in Figure 13-31.

Figure 13-31

Project 13-2: Tenant space reception seating dimensions (scale: 3/8″ = 1′-0″)

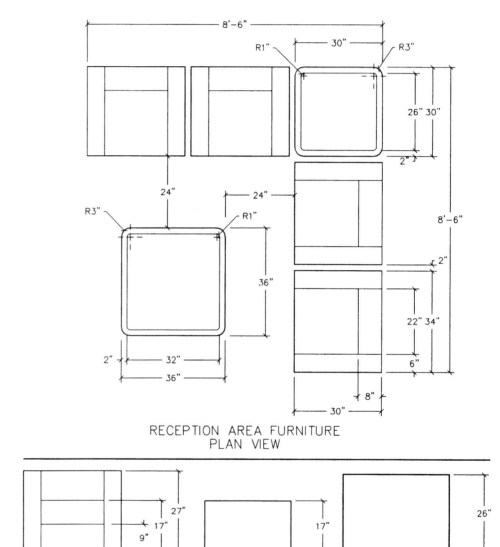

RECEPTION AREA FURNITURE
PLAN VIEW

CHAIR   COFFEE TABLE   CORNER TABLE
RECEPTION AREA FURNITURE ELEVATIONS

2. Click **Layout1**, click the viewport boundary, and use **Properties** from the **Modify** menu to set a standard scale of **1/2″ = 1′**. Plot or print the drawing on an **8-1/2″ × 11″** sheet of paper.

3. Save your drawing in at least two places with the name **CH13-P2.**

Project 13-3: *Tenant Space Conference Chair in Isometric* [ADVANCED]

1. Make an isometric drawing, full size, of the conference room chair. Use the dimensions shown in Figure 13-32.

Figure 13-32

Project 13-3: Tenant space conference chair dimensions (scale: 3/8″ = 1′-0″)

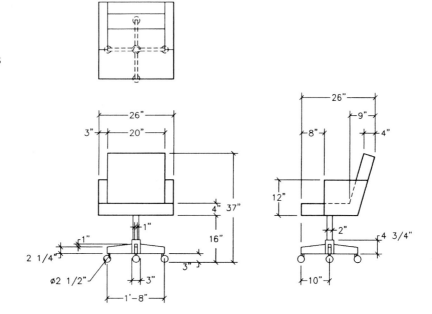

2. Click **Layout 1**, click the viewport boundary, and use **Properties** from the **Modify** menu to set a standard scale of **1/2″ = 1′**. Plot or print the drawing on an **8-1/2″ × 11″** sheet of paper.

3. Save your drawing in at least two places with the name **CH13-P3.**

Project 13-4: *Log Cabin Kitchen Isometric Cutaway Drawing* [ADVANCED]

Project 13-4 is an isometric cutaway drawing of the log cabin kitchen (Figure 13-33). When you have completed Project 13-4, your drawing will look similar to Figure 13-33, but your drawing will be in color.

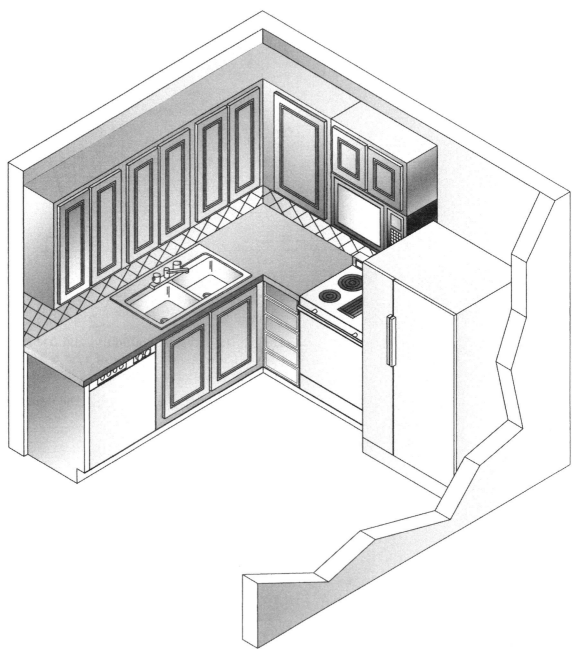

Figure 13-33
Project 13-4: Log cabin kitchen cutaway (scale: 3/8″ = 1′-0″)

1. Use the dimensions from Figures 13-35 and 13-36 and, if necessary, measure some of the features in the isometric drawings (Figures 13-33 and 13-34) using the scales indicated.

Figure 13-34
Project 13-4: Log cabin kitchen sink
(scale: 1″ = 1′-0″)

2. Use different colors in the gradient hatch box (click the ellipsis **(...)** in the **Color** area) to apply gradient hatch patterns to each of the areas such as wood, appliances, and sink. You may also want to try using one of the new predefined hatch patterns with a colored background on some of these areas.

3. The backsplash is a combination of two hatch patterns, a gradient pattern (send to back) and a double, user-defined 60° angle with 4″ spacing on the left side and a double, user-defined 120° angle with 4″ spacing on the right side.

4. You can also insert the appliances from the **DesignCenter** to get measurements of many of the details.

5. Plot the drawing at a scale of **3/8″ = 1′-0″** centered vertically on an **8-1/2″ × 11″** sheet.

6. Save your drawing in at least two spaces with the name **CH13-P4**.

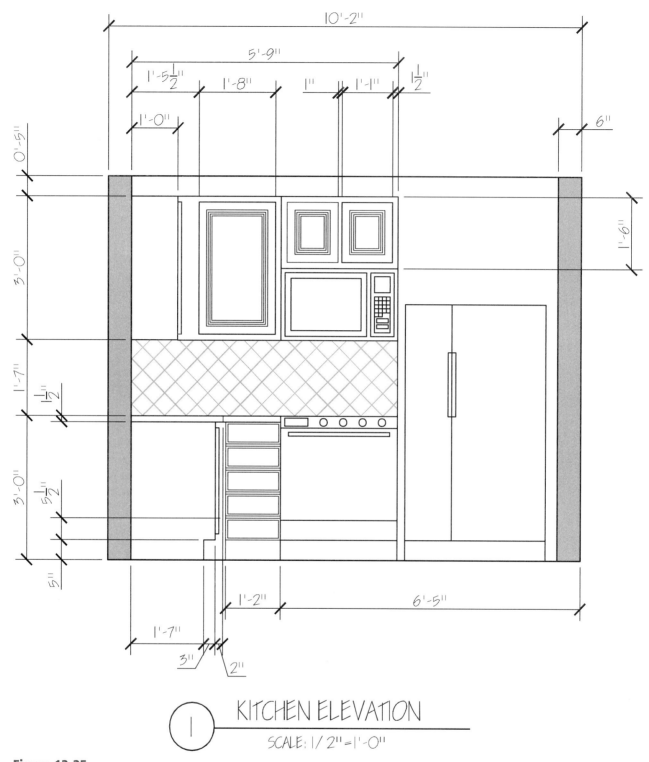

Figure 13-35
Project 13-4: Kitchen elevation 1 (scale: 1/2″ = 1′-0″)

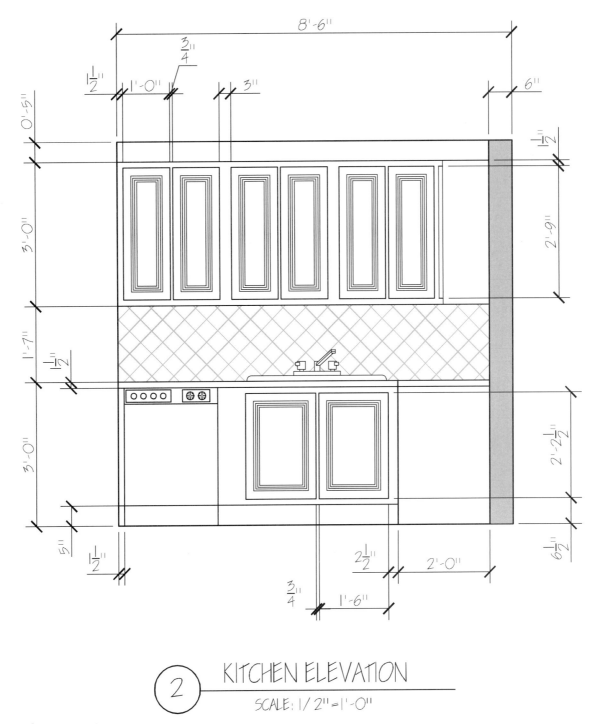

Figure 13-36

Project 13-4: Kitchen elevation 2 (scale: 1/2″ = 1′-0″)

Project 13-5: *Family Room, House 1 Cutaway* [ADVANCED]

Figure 13-37, Sheet 1, is an isometric cutaway drawing of the family room, house 1, Figure 13-37, Sheet 2. When you have completed Project 13-5, your drawing will look like Figure 13-37, Sheet 1.

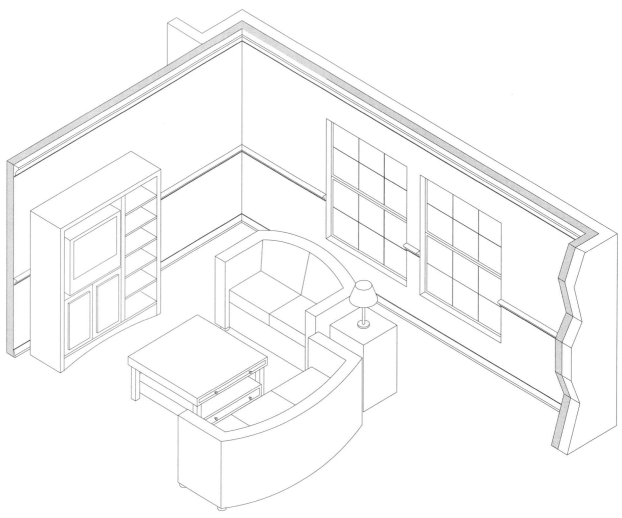

Figure 13-37
Sheet 1 of 2: Family room house 1 cutaway (scale: 1/4″ = 1′-0″)

Figure 13-37

Sheet 2 of 2: Family room house 1 floor plan with furniture (scale: 1/4″ = 1′-0″)

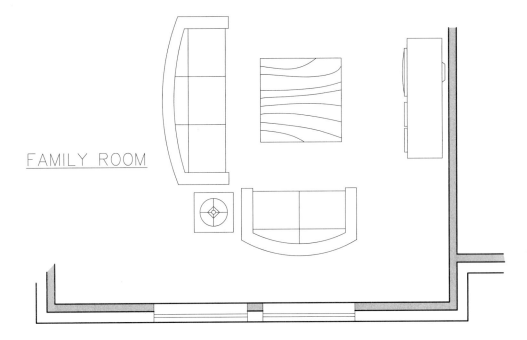

FAMILY ROOM

1. Measure the features in the isometric and the floor plan with furniture using the scale indicated and draw them full scale.

2. Your final drawing will look similar to Figure 13-37, Sheet 1.

3. Save the drawing in two places and plot or print the drawing to scale.

chapter fourteen

Solid Modeling

CHAPTER OBJECTIVES

- Use the 3D workspace to create solids.
- Draw the following primitive solids: box, sphere, wedge, cone, cylinder, torus, pyramid, helix, polysolid, and planar surface.
- Make settings to display solids smoothly.
- Use SteeringWheels and ViewCube to change views of a model.
- Draw extruded solids.
- Draw revolved solids.
- Rotate solids about the *X*-, *Y*-, or *Z*-axis.

- Form chamfers and fillets on solid edges. Join two or more solids.
- Subtract one or more solids from another solid.
- Use the **SOLIDEDIT** command to change existing solids.
- Form a solid model from the common volume of two intersecting solids.
- Obtain perspective views of complex solid models.
- Use **Orbit** and **RENDER** to render solids and print the rendered model.

Introduction

AutoCAD provides four means of creating 3D models: basic 3D using elevation and thickness, surface modeling, solid modeling, and mesh modeling. Basic 3D has very limited uses. Basic 3D and mesh modeling are not covered in this book. Solid modeling creates solids that are much more useful and easier to modify than basic 3D. A solid may be a single object called a *primitive*, or it may be a combination of objects called a *composite*. Mesh modeling is used to create solids that have flowing freeform shapes.

Solids Commands Used to Create Basic Shapes

A primitive solid is a single solid shape that has had nothing added to or subtracted from it. There are 10 solid primitives (box, sphere, wedge, helix, planar surface, polysolid, cone, cylinder, torus, and pyramid) that are the basic shapes often used in solid modeling. They are drawn by using 10 commands:

BOX	**POLYSOLID**
CONE	**PYRAMID**
CYLINDER	**SPHERE**
HELIX	**TORUS**
Planar Surface (PLANESURF)	**WEDGE**

The **POLYSOLID** command may also be used to convert lines, arcs, and polylines into a wall with width and height.

AutoCAD also allows you to form solids by extruding (adding height), sweeping (extruding along a path), lofting (selecting cross-sectional areas), and revolving (rotating about an axis) 2D drawing entities such as polylines, circles, ellipses, rectangles, polygons, and donuts. The commands that extrude, sweep, loft, and revolve drawing entities to form solids are:

EXTRUDE	**SWEEP**
REVOLVE	**LOFT**

Solids Commands Used to Create Composite Solids

Composite solids are formed by joining primitive solids, other solids, or a combination of the two. These combinations may also be added to or subtracted from other solids to form the composite model needed. The following commands used to create composite solids are described in this chapter:

UNION: Allows you to join several solids to form a single solid.

INTERSECT: Allows you to create composite solids from the intersection of two or more solids. **INTERSECT** creates a new solid by calculating the common volume of two or more existing solids.

SUBTRACT: Allows you to subtract solids from other solids.

INTERFERE: Does the same thing as **INTERSECT** except it retains the original objects.

Solids Commands Used to Edit Solids

SLICE: Used to create a new solid by cutting the existing solid into two pieces and removing or retaining either or both pieces.

SECTION: Used to create the cross-sectional area of a solid. That area may then be hatched using the **HATCH** command with any pattern you choose. Be sure the section is parallel with the current UCS when you hatch the area.

THICKEN: Used to make a surface thicker.

SOLIDEDIT

With **SOLIDEDIT**, you can change solid objects by extruding, moving, rotating, offsetting, tapering, copying, coloring, separating, shelling, cleaning, checking, or deleting features such as holes, surfaces, and edges.

Controlling UCS in Three Dimensions

Understanding and controlling the UCS is extremely important in creating 3D models. The UCS is the *location and orientation* of the origin of the X-, Y-, and Z-axes. If you are going to draw parts of a 3D model on a slanted surface, you can create a slanted UCS. If you are going to draw a 3D object, such as the handles on the drawer pedestal, you can locate your UCS so that it is flush with the front plane of the pedestal. You can then make an extrusion from that construction plane and easily create the handles in the correct location.

The UCS command options **Origin, OBject, Previous, Restore, Save, Delete, World**, and **?** were described in Chapter 8. The options described in this chapter are **Move, Origin, 3point, OBject, View**, and **X Y Z**.

Dynamic UCS

You can draw on any face of a 3D solid without changing the UCS orientation with one of the UCS options by activating **DUCS** on the status bar. The UCS then changes automatically when your cursor is over a face of an object, and dynamic UCS is on.

Commands for Viewing Solids

3D Views Menu Options

Viewpoint Presets: The **Viewpoint Presets** dialog box (Figure 14-1) appears when **vp <Enter>** is typed.

From X Axis: Chart: Specifies the viewing angle from the X-axis. The button allows you to type the angle; the chart above it allows you to specify a new angle by clicking the inner region on the circle. The chart, consisting of a square with a circle in it, may be thought of as a viewpoint looking down on the top of an object:

270	Places your view directly in front of the object.
315	Places your view to the right and in front of the object.
0	Places your view on the right side of the object.
45	Places your view to the right and behind the object.
90	Places your view directly behind the object.
135	Places your view to the left and behind the object.
180	Places your view on the left side of the object.
225	Places your view to the left and in front of the object.

From XY Plane: Chart: Specifies the viewing angle from the XY plane. The button allows you to type the angle, and the chart above it allows you to specify a new angle by clicking the inner region on the half circle.

Figure 14-1
Navigation tools

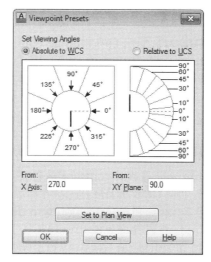

Viewpoint Presets

Steering Wheel

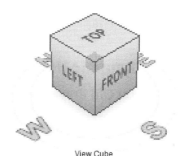

View Cube

Consisting of two semicircles, the chart allows you to specify whether the viewpoint is to be above or below the object:

0	Places your view directly perpendicular to the chosen angle. For example, a view of 270 on the left chart and 0 on the right chart places the viewpoint directly in front of the object.
10 to 60	Places your view above the object.
90	Places your view perpendicular to the top view of the chosen angle.
–10 to –60	Places your view below the object.
–90	Places your view perpendicular to the bottom view of the chosen angle.

Set to Plan View: Sets the viewing angles to plan view (270,90) relative to the selected UCS.

Now, let's look at other **3D Views** menu options:

Plan View: Allows you to select the plan view of the current UCS, the World UCS, or a saved and named UCS.

SW Isometric: Gives you an isometric view from the front, to the left, above.

SE Isometric: Gives you an isometric view from the front, to the right, above.

NE Isometric: Gives you an isometric view from the back, to the right, above.

NW Isometric: Gives you an isometric view from the back, to the left, above.

3DFLY: Changes your view of a 3D model so that it is as if you were flying through the model.

ORBIT: Allows you to control the viewing of a 3D model using an orbit.

3DWALK: Changes your view of a 3D model so that it is as if you were walking through the model.

SteeringWheels

SteeringWheels, Figure 14-1, are icons that are divided into sections. Each section on the SteeringWheel is a tool that allows you to pan, zoom, or show the motion of the current view of a model.

SteeringWheels can save you time because they combine several of the common navigation tools so they all appear on the wheel. There are several different wheels that can be used. You can change the size, transparency, and other settings for each of the wheels.

ViewCube

The *ViewCube*, Figure 14-1, is another 3D viewing tool that can be used to switch from one view of the model to another.

When the ViewCube is displayed, it appears in one of the corners of the drawing area over the model and displays the current viewpoint of the model. When you hold your mouse over the ViewCube, you can switch to one of the preset views, click on the cube, and move your mouse to rotate the model, or return to the **Home** view of the model.

Other Commands That Can Be Used to Edit Solids

3D Move: Moves solids easily.

3D Array: Used to create 3D arrays of objects.

3D Rotate: Used to rotate solids about the *X*-, *Y*-, or *Z*-axis.

3D Mirror: Used to create mirror images of solids about a plane specified by three points.

Fillet: Used to create fillets and rounds. Specify the radius for the fillet and then click the edge or edges to be filleted.

Chamfer: Used to create chamfers. Specify the distances for the chamfer and then click the edge or edges to be chamfered.

Align: Used to move a solid so that a selected plane on the first solid is aligned with a selected plane on a second solid.

Explode: Used to explode a solid into regions or planes. (*Example*: An exploded solid box becomes six regions: four sides, a top, and a bottom.) Use care with **Explode**. When you explode a solid, you destroy it as a solid shape.

Interference Checking: Alerts you if your camera is about to bump into something.

Orbit: A command that allows you to obtain a three-dimensional view in the active viewport.

SteeringWheels: Icons that are divided into sections. Each section on the SteeringWheel is a tool that allows you to pan, zoom, or show the motion of the current view of the model.

ViewCube: A 3D viewing tool that can be used to switch from one view of a model to another.

Settings That Control How the Solid Is Displayed

FACETRES: Used to make shaded solids and those with hidden lines removed appear smoother. Values range from 0.01 to 10.0. The default value is 0.5. Higher values take longer to regenerate but look better. Four is a good compromise. If you change this value, you can update the solid to the new value by using the **Shade** or **HIDE** command again.

ISOLINES: Sets the number of lines on rounded surfaces of solids. Values range from 0 to 2047. The default value is 4. Twenty is a good middle ground. If you change this value, you can update the solid to the new value by regenerating the drawing.

EXERCISE 14-1
Part 1, Drawing Primitive Solids

Exercise 14-1, Parts 1 through 6, provides step-by-step instructions for using the solid commands just described. On completion of this chapter and mastery of the commands included in the chapter, you will have a sound foundation for learning solid modeling.

When you have completed Exercise 14-1, Parts 1 through 6, your drawing will look similar to Figure 14-2.

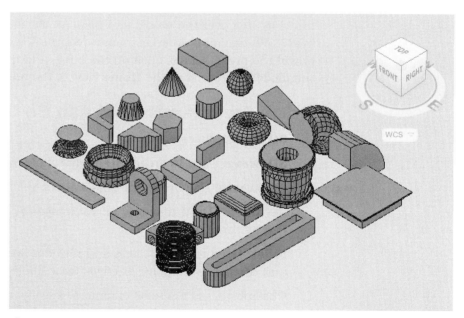

Figure 14-2
Exercise 14-1 complete

Step 1. Make a new workspace for all your 3D drawings as described next:

1. Click **3D Modeling** (Figure 14-3) on the **Workspace Switching** button (in the lower right of the screen). Close the palettes on the right to give yourself more room.
2. Right-click the **SNAP** icon and click **Use Icons** so icons are not used (words are used instead of icons) (Figure 14-4).

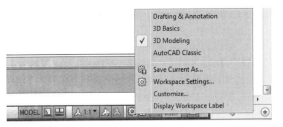

Figure 14-3
3D Modeling workspace

Figure 14-4
Use icons

    3. Right-click the **MODEL** icon and click **Display Layout and Model Tabs** (Figure 14-5).
    4. Click **3D Modeling-Save Current As…** (Figure 14-6) and type **YOUR NAME-3D** (in the **Name:** box), then click **Save**.

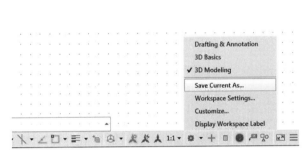

Figure 14-5
Display Layout and Model Tabs

Figure 14-6
Save the workspace

Step 2. Use your new 3D workspace to make the following settings:

    1. Use **Save As…** to save the drawing on the hard drive with the name **CH14-EXERCISE1**.
    2. Set drawing units: **Architectural**
    3. Set drawing limits: **11,8-1/2**
    4. Set **GRIDDISPLAY: 0**
    5. Set grid: **1/2**
    6. Set snap: **1/16**
    7. Create the following layers:

Layer Name	Color	Linetype	Lineweight
3d-m	magenta	continuous	default
3d-r	red	continuous	default
3d-g	green	continuous	default

    8. Set layer **3d-m** current.
    9. Use the **VPORTS** command to make two vertical viewports. Use **Zoom-All** in both viewports to start, then zoom in closer so your

view is similar to the figures shown. Either viewport may be active as you draw. You will need to use **Zoom-All** occasionally in both viewports to see the entire drawing.

10. Click **SE Isometric** from **3D Views** (Figure 14-7) on the **View** menu to set a viewpoint for the right viewport.
11. Set **FACETRES** to **4** (type **FACETRES <Enter>**)
12. Set **ISOLINES** to **20** (type **ISOLINES <Enter>**)

Figure 14-7
SE Isometric

Box

Step 3. Draw a solid box, **1 1/4″ × 3/4″ × 1/2″** height (Figure 14-8), as described next:

	BOX	
Ribbon / Modeling Panel	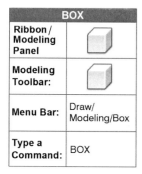	
Modeling Toolbar:		
Menu Bar:	Draw/ Modeling/Box	
Type a Command:	BOX	

Prompt	Response
Type a command:	**Box** (or type **BOX <Enter>**)
Specify first corner or [Center]<0,0,0>:	Type **1/2,7-1/2 <Enter>**
Specify other corner or [Cube Length]:	Type **@1-1/4,3/4 <Enter>**
Specify height or [2Point]:	Type **1/2 <Enter>**

Figure 14-8
Draw a solid box

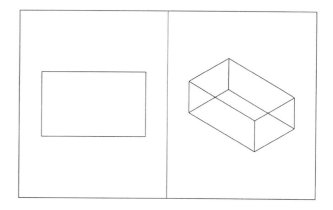

Center: Allows you to draw a box by first locating its center.

Cube: Allows you to draw a cube by specifying the length of one side.

Length: Allows you to draw a box by specifying its length (X), width (Y), and height (Z).

Sphere

Step 4. Draw a solid sphere, **3/8** radius (Figure 14-9), as described next:

Prompt	Response
Type a command:	**Sphere** (or type **SPHERE <Enter>**)
Specify center point or [3P 2P Ttr]:	Type **2-3/4,7-3/4 <Enter>**
Specify radius or [Diameter]:	Type **3/8 <Enter>**

Figure 14-9
Draw a solid sphere

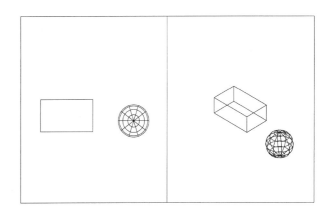

Wedge

Step 5. Draw a solid wedge, **3/4 × 1-1/4 × 1/2** height (Figure 14-10), as described next:

	WEDGE
Ribbon/ Modeling Panel	
Modeling Toolbar:	
Menu Bar:	Draw/ Modeling/ Wedge
Type a Command:	WEDGE

Prompt	Response
Type a command:	**Wedge** (or type **WE <Enter>**)
Specify first corner or [Center]:	Type **3-3/4,7-1/2 <Enter>**
Specify other corner or [Cube Length]:	Type **@1-1/4, 3/4 <Enter>**
Specify height or [2Point]<1/2″>:	Type **1/2 <Enter>**

Figure 14-10
Draw a solid wedge

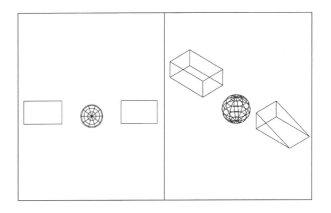

Cone

CONE	
Ribbon/ Modeling Panel	
Modeling Toolbar:	
Menu Bar:	Draw/ Modeling/ Cone
Type a Command:	CONE

Step 6. Draw a solid cone, **3/8** radius, **3/4** height (Figure 14-11), as described next:

Prompt	Response
Type a command:	**Cone** (or type **CONE <Enter>**)
Specify center point of base or [3P 2P Ttr Elliptical]:	Type **1-1/4,6-1/2 <Enter>**
Specify base radius or [Diameter]<0'-3/8">:	Type **3/8 <Enter>**
Specify height or [2Point Axis endpoint Top radius] <0'-0 1/2">:	Type **3/4 <Enter>**

Figure 14-11
Draw a solid cone

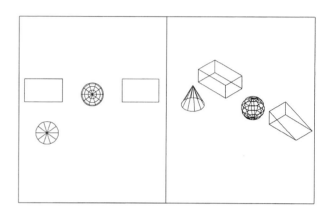

Cylinder

CYLINDER	
Modeling Toolbar:	
Ribbon Modeling Panel	
Menu Bar:	Draw/ Modeling/ Cylinder
Type a Command:	CYLINDER
Command Alias:	CYL

Step 7. Draw a solid cylinder, **3/8** radius, **1/2** height (Figure 14-12), as described next:

Prompt	Response
Type a command:	**Cylinder** (or type **CYL <Enter>**)
Specify center point of base or [3P 2P Ttr Elliptical]:	Type **2-3/4,6-1/2 <Enter>**
Specify base radius or [Diameter] <default>:	Type **3/8 <Enter>**
Specify height or [2Point Axis endpoint]<default>:	Type **1/2 <Enter>**

Figure 14-12
Draw a solid cylinder

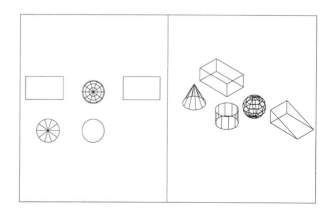

TORUS	
Ribbon/ Modeling Panel	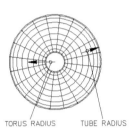
Modeling Toolbar:	
Menu Bar:	Draw/ Modeling/ Torus
Type a Command:	TORUS
Command Alias:	TOR

Torus

Step 8. Draw a solid torus (a 3D donut), **3/8** torus radius, **1/4** tube radius (Figure 14-13), as described next:

Prompt

Type a command:
Specify center point or [3P 2P Ttr]:
Specify radius or [Diameter]:
Specify tube radius or [2Point Diameter]:

Response

Torus (or type **TOR <Enter>**)
Type **4-3/8,6-1/2 <Enter>**
Type **3/8 <Enter>**

Type **1/4 <Enter>**

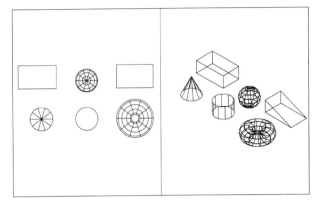

Figure 14-13
Draw a solid torus

Figure 14-14
Radius of the tube and radius of the torus

The radius of the torus is the distance from the center of the 3D donut to the center of the tube that forms the donut. The radius of the tube is the radius of the tube forming the donut (Figure 14-14).

EXERCISE 14-1
Part 2, Using Extrude to Draw Extruded Solids

Draw an Extruded Circle

Step 9. Draw a circle (Figure 14-15), as described next:

Figure 14-15
Extruding and tapering a circle

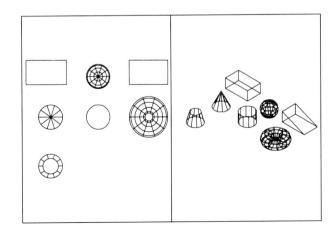

Prompt	Response
Type a command:	Type **C** **<Enter>**
Specify center point of circle or [3P 2P Ttr (tan tan radius)]:	Type **1-1/4,5** **<Enter>**
Specify radius of circle or [Diameter]:	Type **3/8** **<Enter>**

Step 10. Extrude the circle, **1/2** height, **15°** extrusion taper angle (Figure 14-15), as described next:

<table>
<tr><th>EXTRUDE</th><th></th></tr>
<tr><td>Ribbon/
Modeling
Panel</td><td>◻</td></tr>
<tr><td>Modeling
Toolbar:</td><td>◻</td></tr>
<tr><td>Menu Bar:</td><td>Draw/
Modeling/
Extrude</td></tr>
<tr><td>Type a
Command:</td><td>EXTRUDE</td></tr>
<tr><td>Command
Alias:</td><td>EXT</td></tr>
</table>

Prompt	Response
Type a command:	**Extrude** (or type **EXT** **<Enter>**)
Select objects to extrude or [MOde]:	Click the circle
Select objects to extrude or [MOde]:	**<Enter>**
Specify height of extrusion or [Direction Path Taper angle Expression]:	Type **T** **<Enter>**
Specify angle of taper for extrusion or [Expression] <0'-1">:	Type **15** **<Enter>**
Specify height of extrusion or [Direction Path Taper angle Expression] <0'-1">:	Type **1/2** **<Enter>**

Draw an Extruded Polygon

Step 11. Draw a polygon (Figure 14-16), as described next:

Prompt	Response
Type a command:	**Polygon** (or type **POL** **<Enter>**)
Enter number of sides <4>:	Type **6** **<Enter>**
Specify center of polygon or [Edge]:	Type **2-3/4,5** **<Enter>**
Enter an option [Inscribed in circle Circumscribed about circle <I>]:	Type **C** **<Enter>**
Specify radius of circle:	Type **3/8** **<Enter>**

Figure 14-16
Extruding a polygon

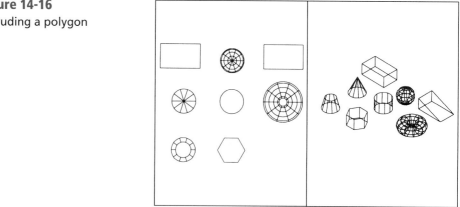

<table>
<tr><th>PRESSPULL</th><th></th></tr>
<tr><td>Ribbon/
Modeling
Panel</td><td>◻</td></tr>
<tr><td>Modeling
Toolbar:</td><td>◻</td></tr>
<tr><td>Type a
Command:</td><td>PRESSPULL</td></tr>
</table>

Step 12. Extrude the polygon, **1/2** height, using the **PRESSPULL** command (Figure 14-16), as described next:

Prompt	Response
Type a command:	**Presspull** (or type **PRESSPULL** <Enter>)
Select object or bounded area:	Click any point inside the polygon (in the **SE Isometric** viewport)
Specify extrusion height or [Multiple]:	
Specify extrusion height or [Multiple]:	Move your mouse up and Type **1/2 <Enter>**

Draw an Extruded Rectangle

Step 13. Draw a rectangle (Figure 14-17), as described next:

Prompt	Response
Type a command:	**Rectangle** (or type **REC <Enter>**)
Specify first corner point or [Chamfer Elevation Fillet Thickness Width]:	Type **4-1/4,4-1/2 <Enter>**
Specify other corner point or [Area Dimensions Rotation]:	Type **@1/4,7/8 <Enter>**

Figure 14-17
Extruding a rectangle

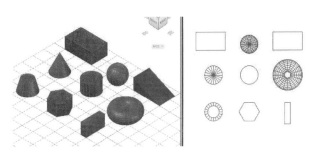

Step 14. Extrude the rectangle, **1/2** height, **0°** extrusion taper angle (Figure 14-17), as described next:

Prompt	Response
Type a command:	**Extrude** (or type **EXT <Enter>** or use **PRESSPULL**)
Select objects to extrude or [MOde]:	Click the rectangle
Select objects to extrude or [MOde]:	**<Enter>**
Specify height of extrusion or [Direction Path Taper angle Expression] <0'-1">:	Type **1/2<Enter>**

Draw an Extruded Structural Angle

Step 15. Draw the outline of the cross section of a structural angle (Figure 14-18), as described next:

Figure 14-18
Extruding a structural steel
angle

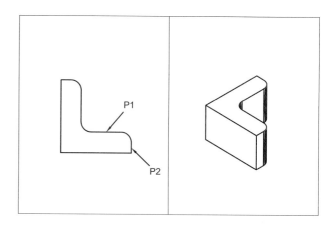

Prompt	Response
Type a command:	Type **L <Enter>**
Specify first point:	Type **1,3 <Enter>**
Specify next point or [Undo]:	Type **@7/8,0 <Enter>** (or turn **ORTHO** on and use direct distance entry)
Specify next point or [Undo]:	Type **@0,1/4 <Enter>**
Specify next point or [Close Undo]:	Type **@-5/8,0 <Enter>**
Specify next point or [Close Undo]:	Type **@0,5/8 <Enter>**
Specify next point or [Close Undo]:	Type **@-1/4,0 <Enter>**
Specify next point or [Close Undo]:	Type **C <Enter>**

Step 16. Add a **1/8″**-radius fillet to the outline (Figure 14-18), as described next:

Prompt	Response
Type a command:	**Fillet** (or type **F <Enter>**)
Select first object or [Undo Polyline Radius Trim Multiple]:	Type **R <Enter>**
Specify fillet radius <0′-0 1/2″>:	Type **1/8 <Enter>**
Select first object or [Undo Polyline Radius Trim Multiple]:	**P1→** (use the **Zoom-Window** command if needed to allow you to pick the necessary lines)
Select second object or shift-select to apply corner:	**P2→**

> **TIP**
>
> Type **M <Enter>** before you select the first object for the fillet so you can fillet all corners without repeating the command.

> **TIP**
>
> After typing **M <Enter>**, specifying the radius, and clicking the first two objects, hold down the **<Shift>** key and click the next two lines to get a zero-radius fillet.

Step 17. Draw **1/8″**-radius fillets (Figure 14-18) at the other two intersections shown.

Step 18. Use **Edit Polyline (PEDIT)** to combine all the lines and fillets into a single entity (Figure 14-18), as described next:

Prompt	Response
Type a command:	**Edit Polyline** (or type **PE <Enter>**)
Select polyline or [Multiple]:	Click one of the lines forming the structural angle
Object selected is not a polyline Do you want to turn it into one? <Y>	**<Enter>**
Enter an option [Close Join Width Edit vertex Fit Spline Decurve Ltype gen Reverse Undo]:	Type **J <Enter>** (to select the **Join** option)
Select objects:	Type **ALL <Enter>**
Select objects:	**<Enter>**
8 segments added to polyline	
Enter an option [Open Join Width Edit vertex Fit Spline Decurve Ltype gen Reverse Undo]:	**<Enter>** (to exit the **PEDIT** command)

Step 19. Extrude the cross section of the structural angle, **1/2** height, **0°** extrusion taper angle (Figure 14-18), as described next:

Prompt	Response
Type a command:	**Extrude** (or type **EXT <Enter>**) or use **PRESSPULL**
Select objects to extrude or [MOde]:	Click the rectangle
Select objects to extrude or [MOde]:	**<Enter>**
Specify height of extrusion or [Direction Path Taper angle Expression] <0'-1">:	Type **1/2 <Enter>**

TIP

PRESSPULL works well for **EXTRUDE** in cases where the extrusion is just up or down. In addition, you do not have to have a single polyline.

Draw an Extruded Shape

Step 20. Draw the shape shown as Figure 14-19 in the approximate location shown in Figure 14-2. When you draw the shape, be sure that you draw only what is needed. If you draw extra lines, the **Edit Polyline** command cannot join the lines into a single polyline.

Step 21. Use the **Edit Polyline** command to join all lines and arcs into a single polyline or use **PRESSPULL** without joining all lines.

Step 22. Extrude the figure to a height of **1/2**.

FOR MORE DETAILS

See Chapter 15 for more on revolving.

Figure 14-19
Extruding a molding shape

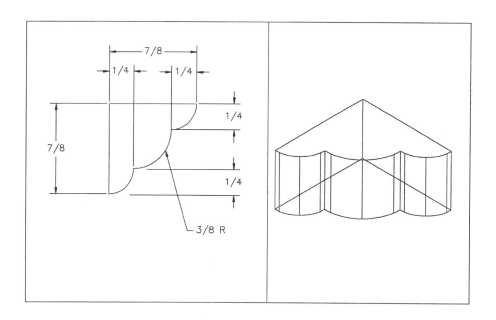

EXERCISE 14-1
Part 3, Using REVOLVE to Draw Revolved Solids; Using 3DROTATE to Rotate Solids about the *X*-, *Y*-, and *Z*-Axes

Draw Revolved Shape 1

Step 23. Draw two circles (Figure 14-20), as described next:

Prompt	Response
Type a command:	Type **C <Enter>**
Specify center point for circle or [3P 2P Ttr (tan tan radius)]:	Type **6-1/4,7-3/4 <Enter>**

Figure 14-20
Revolving a shape 90°

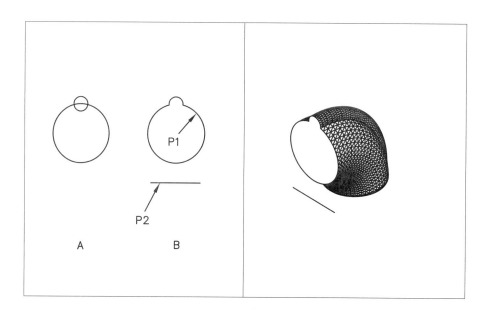

Prompt	Response
Specify radius of circle or [Diameter]:	Type **1/2 <Enter>**
Type a command:	**<Enter>**
Specify center point for circle or [3P 2P Ttr (tan tan radius)]:	Type **6-1/4,8-1/4 <Enter>**
Specify radius of circle or [Diameter] <0'-1/2">:	Type **1/8 <Enter>**

Step 24. Use the **TRIM** command to trim parts of both circles (Figures 14-20A and 14-20B), as described next:

Prompt	Response
Type a command:	**Trim** (or type **TR <Enter>**)
Select cutting edges...	
Select objects or <select all>:	**<Enter>**
Select object to trim or shift-select to extend or [Fence Crossing Project Edge eRase Undo]:	Trim the circles as shown in Figure 14-20A (use **Zoom-Window** to get in closer if needed) **<Enter>**

Step 25. Join all segments of the circles into one polyline (Figure 14-20B), as described next:

Prompt	Response
Type a command:	**Edit Polyline** (or type **PE <Enter>**)
Select polyline:	**P1→ <Enter>**
Object selected is not a polyline Do you want to turn it into one? <Y>	**<Enter>**
Enter an option [Close Join Width Edit vertex Fit Spline Decurve Ltype gen Reverse Undo]:	Type **J <Enter>**
Select objects:	Type **ALL <Enter>**
Select objects:	**<Enter>**
1 segment added to polyline Enter an option [Open Join Width Edit vertex Fit Spline Decurve Ltype gen Reverse Undo]:	**<Enter>** (to exit the **Edit Polyline** command)

Step 26. Draw the axis of revolution (Figure 14-20), as described next:

REVOLVE	
Ribbon / Modeling Panel	
Modeling Toolbar:	
Menu Bar:	Draw/ Modeling/ Extrude
Type a Command:	REVOLVE
Command Alias:	REV

Prompt	Response
Type a command:	**Line** (or type **L <Enter>**)
Specify first point:	Type **6,6-3/4 <Enter>**
Specify next point or [Undo]:	With **ORTHO** on, move your mouse to the right and type **5/8 <Enter>**
Specify next point or [Undo]:	**<Enter>**

Step 27. Use **REVOLVE** to form a revolved solid created by revolving a single polyline 90° counterclockwise about an axis (Figure 14-20B), as described next:

Prompt	Response
Type a command:	**Revolve** (or type **REV <Enter>**)
Select objects to revolve or [MOde]:	**P1→** (Figure 14-20B)

Prompt	Response
Select objects to revolve or [MOde]:	<Enter>
Specify axis start point or define axis by [Object X Y Z] <Object>:	<Enter>
Select an object:	**P2→** (be sure to click the left end of the line for counterclockwise rotation)
Specify angle of revolution or [STart angle Reverse EXpression]<360>:	Type **90 <Enter>**

Draw a Revolved Rectangle

Step 28. Draw a rectangle (Figure 14-21), as described next:

Prompt	Response
Type a command:	**Rectangle** (or type **REC <Enter>**)
Specify first corner point or [Chamfer Elevation Fillet Thickness Width]:	Type **7-3/8,7-3/8 <Enter>**
Specify other corner point or [Area Dimensions Rotation]:	Type **@7/8,7/8 <Enter>**

Figure 14-21
Revolving a rectangle

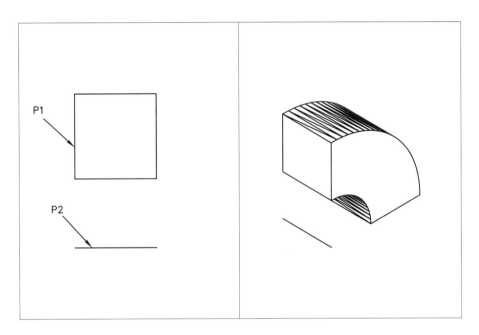

Step 29. Draw the axis of revolution (Figure 14-21), as described next:

Prompt	Response
Type a command:	Type **L <Enter>**
Specify first point:	Type **7-3/8,6-3/4 <Enter>**
Specify next point or [Undo]:	Move your mouse to the right and type **3/4 <Enter>** (be sure **ORTHO** is on)
Specify next point or [Undo]:	**<Enter>**

Step 30. Use the **REVOLVE** command to form a revolved solid created by revolving the rectangle 90° counterclockwise about an axis (Figure 14-21), as described next:

Prompt	Response
Type a command:	**Revolve**
Select objects to revolve or [MOde]:	**P1→ <Enter>**
Select objects to revolve or [MOde]:	**<Enter>**
Specify axis start point or define axis by [Object X Y Z] <Object>:	**<Enter>**
Select an object:	**P2→**
	(Click the left end of the line)
Specify angle of revolution or [STart angle Reverse EXpression]<360>:	Type **90 <Enter>**

Draw a Revolved Paper Clip Holder

Step 31. Draw the cross-sectional shape of the object shown in Figure 14-22 using the **LINE** and **ARC** commands in the left viewport in the approximate locations shown in Figure 14-2.

Figure 14-22
Revolving a paper clip holder

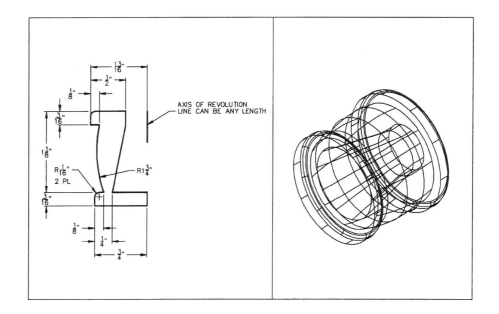

Step 32. Use the **Edit Polyline** command to join all entities of the shape into a single closed polyline.

Step 33. Locate the axis of revolution for the shape in the position shown.

Step 34. Use **REVOLVE** to revolve the shape full circle about the axis.

FOR MORE DETAILS

See Chapter 15 for more on extruding.

ROTATE3D

Step 35. Use **ROTATE3D** to rotate the paper clip holder **90°** about the X-axis so that it assumes the position shown in Figure 14-23, as described next:

Figure 14-23
Rotating an object
about the X-axis

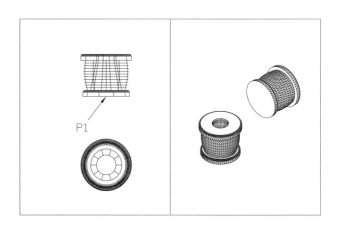

Prompt	Response
Type a command:	Type **ROTATE3D <Enter>**
Select objects:	Click the paper clip holder
Select objects:	**<Enter>**
Specify first point on axis or define axis by [Object Last View Xaxis Yaxis Zaxis 2points]:	Type **X <Enter>**
Specify a point on the X axis <0,0,0>:	**Osnap-Center**
of	**P1→**
Specify rotation angle or [Reference]:	Type **90 <Enter>**

EXERCISE 14-1
Part 4, Using CHAMFER and FILLET to Form Chamfers and Fillets on Solid Edges

Chamfer and Fillet the Top Four Edges of Two Separate Boxes

Step 36. Use **BOX** to draw two boxes measuring **1-1/4″ × 3/4″ × 1/2″** height each, in the approximate locations shown in Figure 14-2.

Step 37. Chamfer the top four edges of the first box (Figure 14-24), as described next:

Figure 14-24
Chamfering and filleting
solid edges

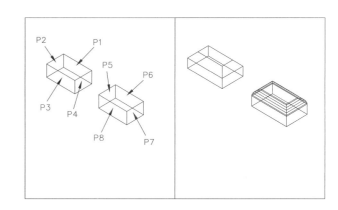

CHAMFER	
Ribbon/ Panel	Home/ Modify
Modify Toolbar:	
Menu Bar:	Modify/ Chamfer
Type a Command:	CHAMFER
Command Alias:	CHA

Prompt

Type a command:

(TRIM mode) Current chamfer Dist1 × 0'-0 1/2", Dist2 × 0'-0 1/2"

Select first line or [Undo Polyline Distance Angle Trim mEthod Multiple]:

Specify first chamfer distance <0'-0 1/2">:

Specify second chamfer distance <0'-0 3/16">:

Select first line or [Undo Polyline Distance Angle Trim mEthod Multiple]:

Base surface selection...

Enter surface selection option [Next OK (current)] <OK>:

Response

Chamfer (or type **CHA <Enter>**)

Type **D <Enter>**

Type **3/16 <Enter>**

<Enter>

P1→ (Figure 14-24)

If the top surface of the box turns dotted, showing it as the selected surface, continue. If one of the side surfaces is selected, type **N <Enter>** until the top surface is selected.

Prompt

Enter surface selection option [Next OK (current)] <OK>:

Specify base surface chamfer distance <0'-0 3/16">:

Specify other surface chamfer distance <0'-0 3/16">:

Select an edge or [Loop]:

Select an edge or [Loop]:

Response

<Enter>

<Enter>

<Enter>

P1→, P2→, P3→, P4→

<Enter>

Step 38. Fillet the top four edges of the second box (Figure 14-24), as described next:

Prompt

Type a command:

Current settings: Mode × TRIM, Radius × 0'-0 1/8"

Select first object or [Undo Polyline Radius Trim Multiple]:

Enter fillet radius <0'-0 1/8">:

Select an edge or [Chain Loop Radius]:

Select an edge or [Chain Loop Radius]:

Response

Fillet (or type **F <Enter>**)

P5→ (Figure 14-24)

Type **3/16 <Enter>**

P6→, P7→, P8→

<Enter>

Chamfer and Fillet on the Top Edge of Two Separate Cylinders

Step 39. Draw two cylinders using **CYLINDER** with a radius of **3/8** and a height of **3/4** in the approximate location shown in Figure 14-25 (in front of the two boxes).

Step 40. Chamfer the top edge of the first cylinder (Figure 14-25) using chamfer distances of **1/16**. Click **P1→** when you select edges to be chamfered.

FILLET	
Ribbon/ Panel	Home/ Modify
Modify Toolbar:	
Menu Bar:	Modify/ Fillet
Type a Command:	FILLET
Command Alias:	F

Figure 14-25
Chamfering and filleting cylinders

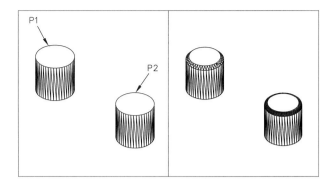

Step 41. Fillet the top edge of the second cylinder (Figure 14-25) using a fillet radius of **1/16**. Click **P2→** when you select edges to be filleted.

The edges of the cylinders should appear as shown in Figure 14-25.

EXERCISE 14-1
Part 5, Using UNION to Join Two Solids; Using SUBTRACT to Subtract Solids from Other Solids

Draw Solid Shape 1

Step 42. Draw solid shape 1 (the base of the shape) and a cylinder that will be the hole in the base (Figure 14-26) with UCS set to **World**, as described next:

Prompt	Response
Type a command:	Type **UCS <Enter>**
Specify origin of UCS or [Face NAmed OBject Previous View World X Y Z ZAxis] <World>:	**<Enter>**
Type a command:	**Box**
Specify corner of box or [Center] <0,0,0>:	Type **4-1/2,3/4 <Enter>**
Specify corner or [Cube Length]:	Type **@1,1 <Enter>**

Figure 14-26
Drawing a composite solid

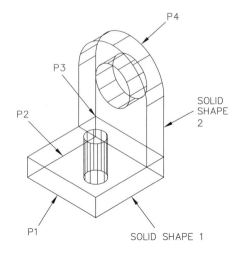

Prompt	Response
Specify height:	Type **1/4 <Enter>**
Type a command:	**Cylinder**
Specify center point of base or [3P 2P Ttr Elliptical]:	Type **.X <Enter>**
of	**Osnap-Midpoint**
of	**P1→**
(need YZ):	**Osnap-Midpoint**
of	**P2→**
Specify base radius or [Diameter]:	Type **1/8 <Enter>**
Specify height or [2Point Axis endpoint]:	Type **1/2 <Enter>** (make the height of the hole tall enough so you can be sure it goes through the model)

Draw Solid Shape 2

Step 43. Set the **UCS Icon** command to **ORigin** so you will be able to see the UCS icon move when the origin is relocated (type **UCSICON <Enter>**, then **OR <Enter>**).

Step 44. Rotate the UCS **90°** about the *X*-axis, and move the origin of the UCS to the upper left rear corner of the box (Figure 14-26), as described next:

Prompt	Response
Type a command:	Click the right viewport (so the UCS changes there and not in the left viewport)
Type a command:	Type **UCS <Enter>**
Specify origin of UCS or [Face NAmed OBject Previous View World X Y Z ZAxis] <World>:	Type **X <Enter>**
Specify rotation angle about X axis <90>:	**<Enter>**
Type a command:	Type **UCS <Enter>**
Specify origin of UCS or [Face NAmed OBject Previous View World X Y Z ZAxis] <World>:	Type **O <Enter>**
Specify new origin point <0,0,0>:	**Osnap-Endpoint P3→**

Step 45. Draw solid shape 2 (the vertical solid) and a cylinder that will be the hole in the vertical solid (Figure 14-26), as described next:

Prompt	Response
Type a command:	**Polyline** (or type **PL <Enter>**)
Specify start point:	Type **0,0 <Enter>**
Specify next point or [Arc Close Halfwidth Length Undo Width]:	With **ORTHO** on, move your mouse right and type **1 <Enter>**
Specify next point or [Arc Close Halfwidth Length Undo Width]:	Move your mouse up and type **3/4 <Enter>**

Prompt	Response
Specify next point or [Arc Close Halfwidth Length Undo Width]:	Type **A** **\<Enter\>**
Specify endpoint of arc or [Angle Enter CLose Direction Halfwidth Line Radius Second pt Undo Width]:	Move your mouse left and type **1 \<Enter\>**
Specify endpoint of arc or [Angle CEnter CLose Direction Halfwidth Line Radius Second pt Undo Width]:	Type **CL \<Enter\>**
Type a command:	**Extrude** (or type **EXT \<Enter\>**)
Select objects to extrude:	Click the polyline just drawn
Select objects to extrude:	**\<Enter\>**
Specify height of extrusion or [Direction Path Taper angle]:	Type **1/4 \<Enter\>** **\<Enter\>**
Type a command:	**Cylinder**
Specify center point of base or [3P 2P Ttr Elliptical]:	**Osnap-Center**
of	**P4→**
Specify base radius or [Diameter]:	Type **1/4 \<Enter\>**
Specify height or [2point Axis endpoint]:	Type **1/2 \<Enter\>**

The cylinder is longer than the thickness of the upright piece so you can be sure that the hole goes all the way through it.

Make sure the base of the cylinder is located on the back surface of the upright piece. If the cylinder is located on the front surface of the upright piece, move the cylinder **3/8** in the **negative Z** direction.

Union

UNION	
Ribbon / Solids Panel	⬭
Modeling Toolbar:	⬭
Menu Bar:	Modify/ Solids Editing/ Union
Type a Command:	UNION
Command Alias:	UNI

Step 46. Join the base and the vertical shape together to form one model, as described next:

Prompt	Response
Type a command:	**Union** (from **Modify-Solid Editing**) (or type **UNI \<Enter\>**)
Select objects:	Click the base (Shape 1) and the vertical solid (Shape 2).
Select objects:	**\<Enter\>**

Subtract

SUBTRACT	
Ribbon / Solids Editing Panel	⬭
Solids Editing Toolbar:	⬭
Menu Bar:	Modify/ Solids Editing/ Subtract
Type a Command:	SUBTRACT
Command Alias:	SU

Step 47. Subtract the holes from the model, as described next:

Prompt	Response
Type a command:	**Subtract** (from **Modify-Solid Editing**) (or type **SU \<Enter\>**)
Select solids, surfaces, and regions to subtract from...	

HIDE	
Render Toolbar:	
Menu Bar:	View/Hide
Type a Command:	HIDE
Command Alias:	HI

Figure 14-27
The completed model after a hide

SWEEP	
Ribbon/ Modeling Panel	
Modeling Toolbar:	
Menu Bar:	Draw/ Modeling/ Sweep
Type a Command:	SWEEP

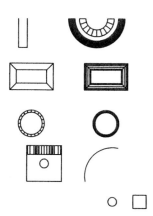

Figure 14-28
Draw an arc, a circle, and a square

Prompt	Response
Select objects:	Click any point on the model
Select objects:	**<Enter>**
Select solids, surfaces, and regions to subtract...	
Select objects:	Click the two cylinders
Select objects:	**<Enter>**

Hide

Step 48. Perform a **Hide** to be sure the model is correct (Figure 14-27), as described next:

Prompt	Response
Type a command:	**Hide** (or type **HI <Enter>**)

The model should appear as shown in Figure 14-27.

Step 49. Return to the World UCS.

EXERCISE 14-1
Part 6, Using SWEEP, HELIX, SUBTRACT, LOFT, Planar Surface, THICKEN, and POLYSOLID to Draw Solid Shapes

The commands in this part of Exercise 14-1 are extremely powerful. **SWEEP** and **SUBTRACT** are used in the first shape. **HELIX, SWEEP**, and **SUBTRACT** are used in the second shape.

Sweep

The **SWEEP** command gives you the ability to create a new solid by sweeping an object along a path. You have the options of selecting a base point, scaling the object as it is swept along the path, and twisting the object as it is swept.

Step 50. Draw an arc on the **3d-g** layer in the approximate location shown in Figure 14-28. It should be about 1-1/2″ long and approximately the shape shown and copy the arc in that exact location.

Step 51. Draw a **1/8″**-radius circle in the approximate location shown in Figure 14-28.

Step 52. Draw a **3/8″** square using the **RECTANGLE** command in the approximate location shown on the **3d-g** layer.

Step 53. Use the **SWEEP** command to create the shape shown in Figure 14-29, as described next:

Prompt	Response
Type a command:	**Sweep** (or type **SWEEP <Enter>**)
Select objects to sweep or [MOde]:	Click any point on the circle
Select objects to sweep or [MOde]:	**<Enter>**
Select sweep path or Alignment Base point Scale Twist]:	Click any point on the arc

Turn off the **3d-m** layer.

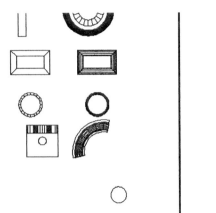

Figure 14-29
Sweeps with layers **3d-m** and **3d-g** on

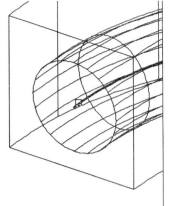

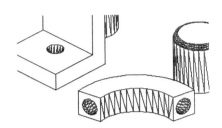

Figure 14-30
Use **SUBTRACT** to create a hole in
the swept square

Prompt	Response
Type a command:	**SWEEP**
Select objects to sweep or [MOde]:	Click any point on the square
Select objects to sweep or [MOde]:	**<Enter>**
Select sweep path or Alignment Base point Scale Twist]:	Click any point on the arc
Turn layer **3d-m** on and set it current.	

The sweeps appear shown in Figure 14-29.

Step 54. Use the **SUBTRACT** command to create a hole throughout the swept square and use the **HIDE** command to check the shape (Figure 14-30), as described next:

Prompt	Response
Type a command:	**Subtract** (or type **SU <Enter>**)
Select solids and regions to subtract from:	
Select objects:	Click any point on the swept square
Select solids and regions to subtract:	
Select objects:	Click any point on the swept circle
Type a command:	**Hide** (or type **HI <Enter>**)
Change the swept model to layer **3d-m**.	

Step 55. Use the **HELIX** command to make a helix, as described next:

HELIX	
Ribbon/ Draw Panel	
Modeling Toolbar:	
Menu Bar:	Draw/ Helix
Type a Command:	HELIX

Prompt	Response
Type a command:	**Helix** (or type **HELIX <Enter>**)
Specify center point of base:	Click a point in the approximate location shown in Figure 14-31
Specify base radius or [Diameter] <0'-0">:	Type **1/2 <Enter>**
Specify top radius or [Diameter] <0'-0 1/2">:	**<Enter>**
Specify helix height or [Axis endpoint Turns turn Height tWist] <0'-1/2">:	Type **T <Enter>**
Enter number of turns <3.0000>:	Type **6 <Enter>**
Specify helix height or [Axis endpoint Turns turn Height tWist] <0'-1">:	Type **1-1/4 <Enter>**

Figure 14-31
Draw the helix and
1/16″-radius and 1/32″-radius
circles on the helix endpoint

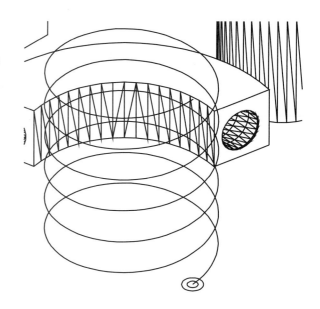

Step 56. Draw a **1/16″**-radius circle and a **1/32″**-radius circle on the end-point of the base of the helix (Figure 14-31).

Step 57. Use the **SWEEP** command to sweep the circles around the helix, as described next:

Prompt	Response
Type a command:	**SWEEP** (or type **SWEEP <Enter>**)
Select objects to sweep:	Click both the **1/16″**-and the **1/32″**-radius circles
Select objects to sweep or [MOde]:	**<Enter>**
Select sweep path or [Alignment Base point Scale Twist]:	Click any point on the helix

Step 58. Use the **SUBTRACT** command to subtract the inner swept circle from the outer swept circle (Figure 14-32), as described next:

Figure 14-32
Inner swept circle subtracted
from outer swept circle

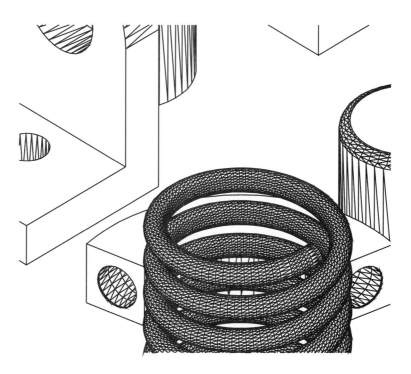

Prompt	Response
Type a command:	**SUBTRACT** (or type **SU <Enter>**)
Select solids and regions to subtract from...	
Select objects:	Click the **1/16″**-radius swept circle
	<Enter>
Select objects: Select solids and regions to subtract...	Click the **1/32″**-radius swept circle
Select objects:	**<Enter>**

Loft

LOFT	
Ribbon/ Modeling Panel	
Modeling Toolbar:	
Menu Bar:	Draw/Modeling Loft
Type a Command:	LOFT

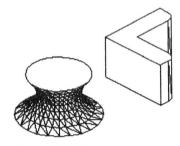

Figure 14-33
Draw 1/4″-, 3/8″-, and 1/2″-radius circles

The **LOFT** command gives you the ability to create a 3D solid or surface selecting a set of two or more cross-sectional areas.

If you select two or more closed cross-sectional areas, a solid is created.

If you select two or more open cross-sectional areas, a surface is created.

You cannot use both open and closed cross-sectional areas in a set. You have to choose one or the other.

When you make a lofted shape, you can use the **Loft Settings** dialog box to control the shape of the surface or solid.

Step 59. Draw three circles (**1/2″** radius, **3/8″** radius, and **1/4″** radius) in the approximate location shown in Figure 14-33.

Step 60. Move the **1/4″**-radius circle up **1/4″** in the **Z** direction. You may use the **MOVE** command and type **@0,0,1/4 <Enter>** for the second point of displacement or in the 3D view (with **ORTHO** on) click on the circle, click the center grip, move your mouse up, and type **1/4 <Enter>**.

Step 61. Move the **3/8″**-radius circle up **1/2″** in the **Z** direction.

Step 62. Use the **LOFT** command to create a lofted solid and use the **HIDE** command to check it (Figure 14-34), as described next:

Prompt	Response
Type a command:	**Loft** (or type **LOFT <Enter>**)
Select cross-sections in lofting order or [POint Join multiple edges MOde]:	Click the **1/2″**-radius circle (the one on the bottom)
Select cross-sections in lofting order or [POint Join multiple edges MOde]:	Click the **1/4″**-radius circle (the next one up)
Select cross-sections in lofting order or [POint Join multiple edges MOde]:	Click the **3/8″**-radius circle (the one on top)
Select cross-sections in lofting order or [POint Join multiple edges MOde]:	**<Enter>**
Enter an option [Guides Path Cross sections only Settings] <Cross sections only>:	**<Enter>**
Type a command:	**Hide** (or type **HI <Enter>**)

Figure 14-34
Lofted shape complete

Create a Bowl-Shaped Object

The **LOFT** command also enables you to create a bowl-shaped object, as described next:

Step 63. Draw three circles (**3/4″-radius**, **5/8″-radius**, and **1/2″-radius**) in the approximate location shown in Figure 14-35.

Step 64. Move the **1/2″-radius** circle up **1/8″** in the **Z** direction.

Step 65. Move the **5/8″-radius** circle up **1/2″** in the **Z** direction.

Step 66. Use the **LOFT** command to create the bowl, but pick the circles in a different order: click the one on the bottom first, the one on the top next, and the one in between the two others last.

Step 67. Use the **HIDE** command to check its shape (Figure 14-36).

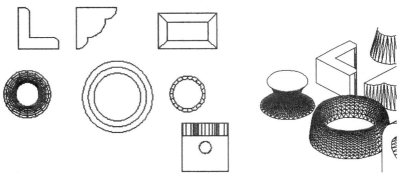

Figure 14-35
Draw 1/2″-, 5/8″-, and 3/4″-radius circles

Figure 14-36
Lofted bowl shape complete

Planar Surface

PLANAR	
Ribbon/ Panel	Surface/ Create
Modeling Toolbar:	
Menu Bar:	Draw/Modeling Surfaces/ Planar
Type a Command:	PLANESURF

You can use the **Planar Surface (PLANESURF)** command to make a surface using one of the following:

Select one or more objects that form an enclosed area.

Draw a rectangle so that the surface is created parallel to the rectangle.

Step 68. Draw a planar surface and thicken it (Figure 14-37), as described next:

Prompt	**Response**
Type a command:	**Planar Surface** (or type **PLANESURF** **<Enter>**)

Figure 14-37
Draw the planar surface and thicken it

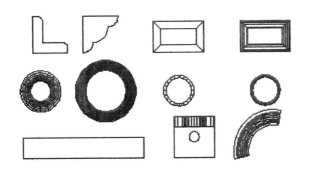

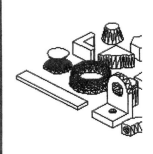

THICKEN	
Ribbon/ Solids Editing Panel	
Modeling Toolbar:	
Menu Bar:	Draw/Modeling 3D Operation/ Thicken
Type a Command:	THICKEN

POLYSOLID	
Ribbon/ Modeling Panel	
Modeling Toolbar:	
Menu Bar:	Draw/Modeling Polysolid
Type a Command:	POLYSOLID

Prompt

Specify first corner or [Object] <Object>:

Specify other corner:

Type a command:

Select surfaces to thicken:

Select surfaces to thicken:

Specify thickness <0'-0">:

Response

Click the lower left corner in the approximate location shown in Figure 14-37

Type **@3,1/2 <Enter>**

Thicken (or type **THICKEN <Enter>**)

Click the planar surface

<Enter>

Type **1/8 <Enter>**

POLYSOLID

You can use the **POLYSOLID** command to draw walls by specifying the wall width and its height. You can also create a polysolid from an existing line, polyline, arc, or circle. If the width and height have been set, clicking on an object from the polysolid prompt such as a line or an arc will change it to a polysolid that is the height and width of the polysolid setting.

Step 69. Draw a polysolid that has a height of **1/2"** and a width of **1/4"** (Figure 14-38), as described next. (Be sure you are in the World UCS.)

Prompt

Type a command:

Specify start point or [Object Height Width Justify] <Object>:

Specify height <0'-0">:

Response

Polysolid (or type **POLYSOLID <Enter>**)

Type **H <Enter>**

Type **1/2 <Enter>**

Figure 14-38

Draw a polysolid with a height of 1/2" and a width of 1/4"

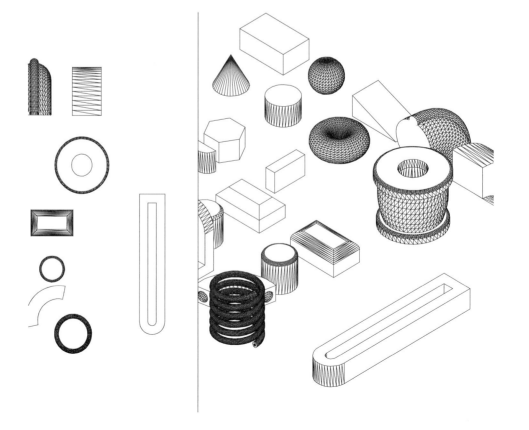

Prompt	Response
Specify start point or [Object Height Width Justify] <Object>:	Type **W** **<Enter>**
Specify width <0'-0">:	Type **1/4** **<Enter>**
Specify start point or [Object Height Width Justify] <Object>:	Type **8-1/2,4** **<Enter>**
Specify next point or [Arc Undo]: <Ortho on>	With **ORTHO** on move your mouse down and type **3** **<Enter>**
Specify next point or [Arc Undo]:	Type **A** **<Enter>**
Specify endpoint of arc or [Close Direction Line Second point Undo]:	Move your mouse to the left and type **1/2** **<Enter>**
Specify next point or [Arc Close Undo]:	
Specify endpoint of arc or [Close Direction Line Second point Undo]:	Type **L** **<Enter>**
Specify next point or [Arc Close Undo]:	Move your mouse up and type **3** **<Enter>**
Specify next point or [Arc Close Undo]:	Type **C** **<Enter>**
Type a command:	**Hide** (or type **HI** **<Enter>**)

EXERCISE 14-1
Part 7, Using INTERSECTION to Form a Solid Model from the Common Volume of Two Intersecting Solids

Drawing the solid model in Exercise 14-1, Part 7, demonstrates another powerful tool that can be used to form complex models.

In this exercise two separate solid shapes are drawn (in this case the same shape is copied and rotated so the two shapes are at right angles to each other) and moved so that they intersect. **INTERSECTION** is used to combine the shapes to form one solid model from the common volume of the two intersecting solids. Figure 14-39 shows the two separate solid

Figure 14-39

Two shapes and the shape formed from the intersected volume of the two shapes

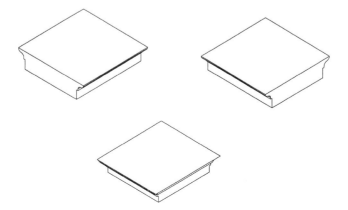

shapes and the solid model that is formed from the common volume of the two solid shapes.

This shape will also be used in Exercise 15-2 to form the cornices at the top of the columns (Figure 15-7).

Draw Two Extruded Shapes at Right Angles to Each Other

Step 70. Zoom out so you can draw the full-size shape shown in Figure 14-40 in the left viewport. In an open area of the screen, draw Figure 14-40 using **Polyline** and **FILLET** commands. Use **Polyline** to draw the shape with square corners shown in the top half of the figure, then use 1″-radius fillets to form the rounded corners.

Figure 14-40
Dimensions for the extruded shapes

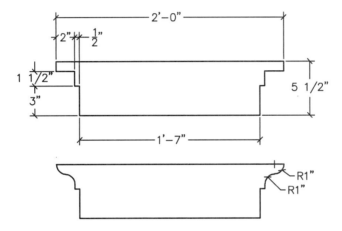

Step 71. Use the **SCALE** command to scale the polyline to **1/12** its size. (This is a scale of **1″ = 1′-0″**. In Exercise 15-2 you will scale this model to its original size.)

Step 72. In the right viewport, set UCS to **World**, copy the shape once, and use **ROTATE3D** to rotate both shapes **90°** about the X-axis.

Step 73. Use **ROTATE3D** to rotate the shape on the right **90°** about the Z-axis (Figure 14-41).

Step 74. Extrude both shapes **2′** (Figure 14-42) (or use **PRESSPULL** to extrude both shapes 2′).

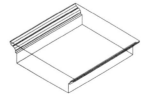

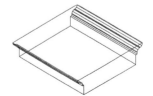

Figure 14-41
Two shapes rotated 90° to each other

Figure 14-42
Both shapes extruded

Step 75. Use the **MOVE** command to move the solid on the left to intersect with the other solid (Figure 14-43), as described next:

Figure 14-43
Moving one shape to intersect with the other

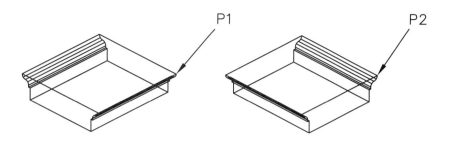

Prompt	Response
Type a command:	**Move**
Select objects:	Click the shape on the left
Select objects:	**<Enter>**
Specify base point or [Displacement] <Displacement>: of	**Osnap-Endpoint** **P1→**
Specify second point or <use first point as displacement>: of	**Osnap-Endpoint** **P2→**

INTERSECT	
Ribbon/ Solids Editing Panel	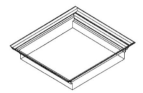
Solids Editing Toolbar:	
Menu Bar:	Modify/ Solids Editing/ Intersect
Type a Command:	INTERSECT
Command Alias:	IN

Intersect

Step 76. Use **INTERSECT** to form a solid model from the common volume of the two intersecting solids (Figure 14-44), as described next:

Prompt	Response
Type a command:	**Intersect** (from **Modify-Solid Editing**) (or type **IN <Enter>**)
Select objects: 2 solids intersected	Click both shapes **<Enter>**

The display should appear as shown in Figure 14-44.

Step 77. Perform a **Hide** to be sure the solid model is correct (Figure 14-45), as described next:

Prompt	Response
Type a command:	**Hide** (or type **HI <Enter>**)

The display should appear as shown in Figure 14-45.

Step 78. Return the UCS to **World** so you will not be surprised at the position the model will assume when it is inserted.

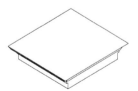

Figure 14-44
The shape formed from the intersected shapes

Figure 14-45
The intersected solid after a **Hide**

Wblock the Intersected Model

You should now Wblock the intersected model so you can use it in Exercise 15-2 to form the cornices at the tops of the columns (see Figure 15-7).

Step 79. Use **WBLOCK** to save the model to a disk (Figure 14-46), as described next:

Prompt	Response
Type a command:	Type **W <Enter>**
The **Write Block** dialog box appears:	Click the three dots to the far right of the **File name and path**: input box

Figure 14-46
Wblocking the intersected shape

Prompt	Response
	Locate the disk and folder where you store drawings and double-click the folder
The **Browse for Drawing File** dialog box appears:	Type **14-3** in the **File name**: input box, then click **Save**
	Click **Pick point**
Specify insertion base point:	Type **END <Enter>**
of	Click the bottom corner of the intersected shape using **Osnap-Endpoint**. It will be the lowest point on the display.
The **Write Block** dialog box appears:	Click **Select Objects**
Select objects:	Click the intersected shape
Select objects:	**<Enter>**
The **Write Block** dialog box appears:	If **Retain** is not on, click that option button
	Click **OK**

The shape now exists on your disk as 14-3.dwg, and it is also on the current drawing.

Complete Exercise 14-1

Step 80. Use the **MOVE** command to move the intersected shape to the approximate location shown in Figure 14-2.

Step 81. Use the **VPORTS** command to return to a single viewport of the 3D viewport (Figure 14-2).

Step 82. Click **Visual Styles Manager** (Figure 14-47) and double-click **Conceptual** to shade the drawing, as shown in Figure 14-48.

Figure 14-47
Visual Styles Manager

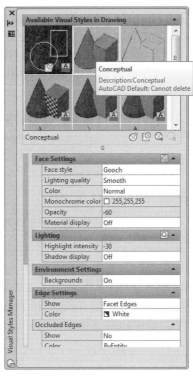

Figure 14-48
Rendered image of
Exercise 14-1

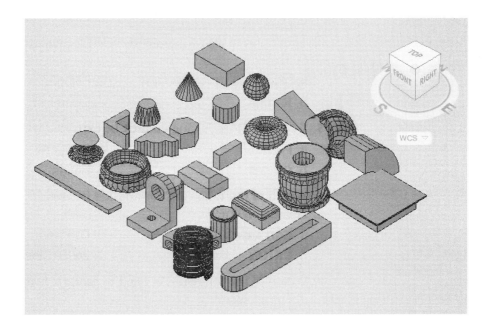

Step 83. Save the drawing in two places.

Step 84. Plot the 3D viewport from the **Model** tab on a standard size sheet of paper. Be sure to click **Conceptual** from the **Shade plot:** list in the **Plot** dialog box so the final plot appears as shown in Figure 14-48.

Chapter Summary

This chapter provided you the information necessary to set up and draw solid models. Now you have the skills and information necessary to produce solid models that can be used in interior design presentations, views of proposed spaces, contract documents, and other similar types of documents.

Chapter Test Questions

Multiple Choice

Circle the correct answer.

1. Which of the following is **not** a **SOLID** command used to draw solid primitives?
   - a. **BOX**
   - b. **CYLINDER**
   - c. **RECTANGLE**
   - d. **WEDGE**

2. Which of the following is used to make rounded corners on a solid box?
   - a. **FILLET**
   - b. **EXTRUDE**
   - c. **CHAMFER**
   - d. **ROUND**

3. Which is the last dimension called for when the **BOX** command is activated?
   - a. Height
   - b. Width
   - c. Length
   - d. First corner of box

4. Which is the first dimension called for when the **SPHERE** command is activated?
   - a. Segments in X direction
   - b. Radius
   - c. Segments in Y direction
   - d. Center of sphere

5. Which of the following **cannot** be extruded with the **EXTRUDE** command?
   - a. Polylines
   - b. Circles
   - c. Polygons
   - d. Solids

6. Which of the following commands is used to join several lines into a single polyline?
   - a. **Edit Polyline**
   - b. **UNION**
   - c. **OFFSET**
   - d. **EXTRUDE**

7. Which of the following is used to make a solid by revolving a polyline about an axis?
   - a. **REVOLVE**
   - b. **EXTRUDE**
   - c. **ROUND**
   - d. **FILLET**

8. Which of the following adjusts the smoothness of objects rendered with the **HIDE** command?
   - a. **SURFTAB1**
   - b. **SEGS**
   - c. **ISOLINES**
   - d. **FACETRES**

9. Which of the following allows you to rotate an object around an *X*-, *Y*-, or *Z*-axis?

   a. **ROTATE**

   b. **3DROTATE**

   c. **SOLROT**

   d. **OFFSET**

10. Which of the following sets the number of lines on rounded surfaces of solids?

   a. **FACETRES**

   b. **ISOLINES**

   c. **FILLET**

   d. **INTERFERE**

Matching

Write the number of the correct answer on the line.

a. Solid modeling _____

b. SteeringWheel _____

c. **Torus** _____

d. **Polysolid** _____

e. **INTERSECT** _____

1. A solid command used to create a solid from the common volume of two intersecting solids

2. A solid shape similar to a donut

3. A navigation tool

4. A method of drawing that allows you to view an object from any angle

5. A command used to draw a solid shape

True or False

Circle the correct answer.

1. **True or False:** Boxes made with the **BOX** command and combined with the **UNION** command cannot be made into a solid object.

2. **True or False:** A polysolid can have width and height.

3. **True or False:** A **torus** is a solid object.

4. **True or False:** Intersect is **not** a solid command.

5. **True or False:** SUBTRACT is the command used to subtract solids from other solids.

List

1. Five solid primitives.

2. Five key-in commands to create the above primitives.

3. Five methods for constructing surfaces or solids from other geometry.

4. Five solid creation commands under the **3D Solid** tab and **Solid/Boolean** panel.

5. Five drawing entities that can be can be used as a loft cross section.

6. Five drawing entities that can be can be used as a loft path.

7. Five commands containing **Rotate**.

8. Five prompts to answer when executing the **PolySolid** command.

9. Five commands/system variables to smooth the display of a 3D object.

10. Five view styles.

Questions

1. What is solid modeling and how is it used?

2. What are the settings that control how a solid is displayed?

3. What are the commands that can be used to create solid models?

4. When should solid models be rendered?

5. How should lights be placed when solid models are rendered?

Chapter Projects

Project 14-1: *Drawing Solid Models of Eight Objects* [BASIC]

1. Draw solid models of the eight objects shown in Figure 14-49. Use the dimensions shown in the top and front views of A through H:

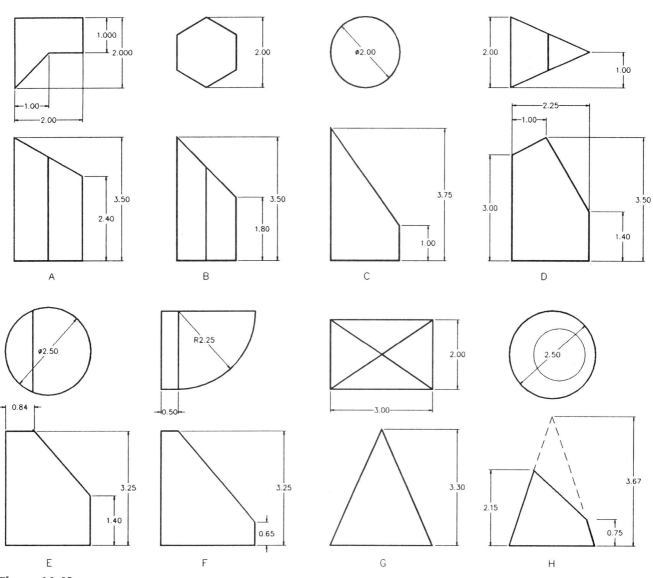

Figure 14-49
Project 14-1: Draw solid models of eight objects

Draw the top view, join it to form a continuous polyline, and extrude it to the height shown in the front view.

Rotate the UCS **90°** about the *X*-axis, draw a rectangle at the angle shown in the front view, extrude it, move it in the Z direction so it covers the area of the extruded top view that must be removed, and subtract it from the extruded top view.

2. Arrange the objects so that they are well spaced on the page and take up most of a **9″ × 7″** area on an **11″ × 8-1/2″** sheet. Use the **HIDE** command to remove hidden lines.

3. Your final drawing should show eight solid objects in a viewpoint similar to Figure 14-48 (Exercise 14-1).

4. Click **Layout1**, place your name in the lower right corner in **1/8″** letters, use **Shade plot - As displayed,** and plot or print the drawing on an **11″ × 8-1/2″** sheet at a scale of **1 = 1**.

5. Save your drawing in two places with the name **CH14-P1**.

Project 14-2: *Drawing a Solid Model of a Lamp Table* [INTERMEDIATE]

1. Draw a solid model of the lamp table shown in Figure 14-50. Scale the top and front views using a scale of **1″ = 1′-0″** to obtain the correct measurements for the model.

Figure 14-50

Project 14-2: Create a solid model of a table (scale: 1″ = 1′-0″)

2. Use **REVOLVE** for the table pedestal. Use **Polyline** and **EXTRUDE** for one table leg and duplicate it with **Polar Array.** The tabletop can be an extruded circle or a solid cylinder.

3. Use **Orbit** to obtain a perspective view of your final model and click **Layout1** before you plot.

4. Place your name in the lower right corner in **1/8″** letters using simplex or an architectural font.

5. Plot the drawing at a scale of **1 = 1** on an **11″ × 8-1/2″** sheet.

6. Return to the **Model** tab (World UCS current) and Wblock the lamp table to a disk with the name **TABLE**.

7. Save your drawing with the name **CH14-P2**.

Project 14-3: *Drawing a Solid Model of the Tenant Space Reception Seating* [BASIC]

1. Draw the chair coffee table and corner table with a series of boxes (Figure 14-51).

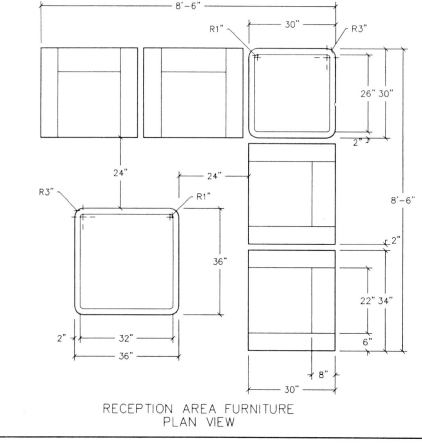

RECEPTION AREA FURNITURE
PLAN VIEW

CHAIR   COFFEE TABLE   CORNER TABLE

RECEPTION AREA FURNITURE ELEVATIONS

Figure 14-51
Project 14-3: Tenant space reception seating dimensions (scale: 3/8″ = 1′-0″)

2. Fillet the vertical edges of the coffee table and corner table.

3. Use the **RECTANGLE** command with **1″** fillets to draw the coffee table and corner table inlays. Extrude the rectangles **1″** and place them so they are flush with the top of the tables. Subtract the extruded rectangles from the tables and replace them with other extruded rectangles that are slightly smaller to form the inlays.

4. Use **Orbit** to obtain a perspective view of your final model and click **Layout1** before you plot.

5. Place your name in the lower right corner in **1/8″** letters using simplex or an architectural font.

6. Plot the drawing at a scale of **1 = 1** on an **11″ × 8-1/2″** sheet.

7. Save your drawing in two places with the name **CH14-P3**.

Project 14-4: *Drawing a Solid Model of a Lamp and Inserting It into the Lamp Table Drawing* [ADVANCED]

1. Draw the lamp and the shade from the dimensions shown in Figure 14-52. Use your 1/8″ architect's scale for any dimensions not shown.

Figure 14-52
Project 14-4: Overall dimensions of the lamp (scale: 1/8″ = 1′)

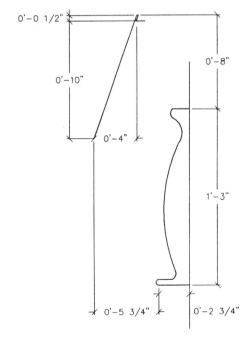

2. Revolve the two polylines to form the lamp.

3. Rotate the lamp **90°** about the X-axis so it is in an upright position.

4. With the World UCS current, Wblock the lamp to a disk with the name **LAMP**. Use the center of the bottom of the lamp as the insertion point.

5. Insert the lamp from the disk into the lamp table. Center the base of the lamp onto the tabletop as shown in Figure 14-53.

Figure 14-53
Project 14-4: Combine solid
models

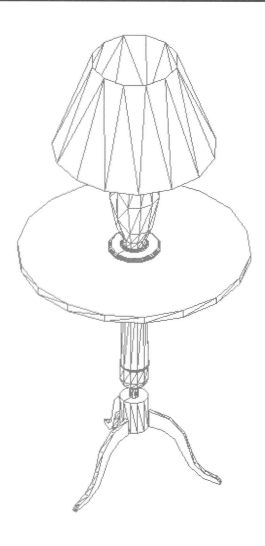

6. Use **Orbit** to obtain a perspective view of your final model and click **Layout1** before you plot.

7. Place your name in the lower right corner in **1/8″** letters using simplex or an architectural font.

8. Plot the drawing at a scale of **1 = 1** on an **11″ × 8-1/2″** sheet.

9. Save your drawing in two places with the name **CH14-P4**.

chapter fifteen

15 chapter

Advanced Modeling

CHAPTER OBJECTIVES

- Correctly use the following commands and settings:

  Animation　　　**LIGHT**
  BACKGROUND　　**MATERIALS**
  Landscape　　　**Materials Library**

  Orbit　　　　　　**RENDER**
  Print 3D models

- Use solid modeling commands to build solid models of rooms with furniture.
- Build solid models on your own from sketches.

Introduction

This chapter presents more complex models using the **Solids** commands from Chapter 14.

This chapter also covers the **RENDER** and **Animation** commands, which allow you to use lights, to attach materials, and to apply backgrounds so that a photo-realistic rendering of a 3D scene can be created and an animated file produced. Although there are many means of locating lights in a 3D scene, you will use the endpoints of lines and other objects in these exercises to place lights. You will use the existing materials in the materials library and existing backgrounds to begin using the **RENDER** commands.

You will also make a solid model of a room with furniture and build solid models from sketches.

The first two exercises, creating a chair and a patio, will give you the complex models needed to assign materials, place lights, render, and create an animated file.

Figure 15-1
Exercise 15-1 complete

EXERCISE 15-1
Creating a Solid Model of Chair 2

In this exercise you will create a solid model of a chair (Figure 15-1). This chair will be inserted into the structure that you will create in Exercise 15-2. The **Prompt/Response** format will not be used in this exercise. The steps will be listed with suggested commands for creating this model.

Step 1. Use your **3D** workspace to make the following settings:

1. Use **Save As...** to save the drawing on the hard drive with the name **CH15-EXERCISE1**.
2. Set drawing units: **Architectural**
3. Set drawing limits: **5',5'**
4. Set **GRIDDISPLAY: 0**
5. Set grid: **1**
6. Set snap: **1/4**
7. Create the following layers:

Layer Name	Color	Linetype
Fabric	magenta	continuous
Metal	green	continuous

8. Set layer **Fabric** current.
9. Use the **VPORTS** command to make two vertical viewports. Use **Zoom-All** in both viewports to start, then zoom in closer as needed. You will find it easier to draw in the left viewport and use the right viewport to determine whether the model is proceeding as it should.
10. Use **SW Isometric** to select a view for the right viewport.
11. Set **FACETRES** to **4**; set **ISOLINES** to **20**.

Step 2. Draw two **32″ × 5″** cushions using the dimensions from Figure 15-2.

Figure 15-2
Two construction lines, one horizontal 50″ and one vertical 51″; two 32″ × 5″ rectangles, one horizontal rotated −10° and one vertical rotated 20°

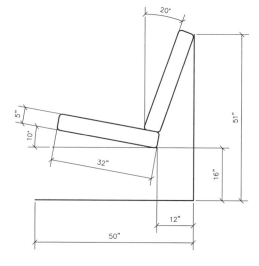

1. Draw two temporary construction lines near the bottom of your drawing in the left viewport. With **ORTHO** on, draw the first line **50″** to the right; draw the second line **51″** up (Figure 15-2).

2. Use **RECTANGLE** to draw the bottom cushion in a horizontal position **16″** above the temporary horizontal construction line and **12″** to the left of the vertical construction line. (Use the **From** option @-12,16 from the intersection of the construction lines. Draw the rectangle to the left and up @-32,5.) Use the **Fillet** option of the **RECTANGLE** command to create the **1″** fillet on all four corners at the same time.

3. Use **RECTANGLE** to draw the back cushion in a vertical position, and fillet all four corners.

4. Use **ROTATE** to rotate the bottom cushion –**10°** and the back cushion –**20°**.

5. Move the back cushion so it sits on the right endpoint of the bottom and use **STRETCH** to form the bottom of the back cushion so it fits flush against the bottom cushion.

Step 3. Draw chair legs and back support (Figure 15-3).

Figure 15-3
Draw three arcs; use
Polyline Edit to join the
two smaller arcs

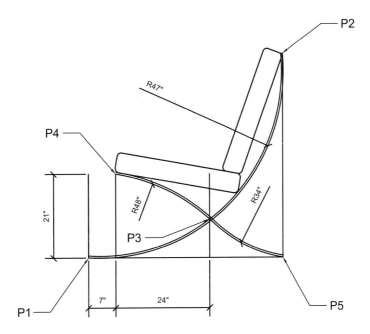

1. Set layer **Metal** current.
2. Draw temporary construction lines to locate the beginning and ending points of the three arcs; from the left end of the 50″ construction line, draw a **21″** line straight up, then offset it **7″** to the right. Offset that line **24″** to the right.
3. Use **Arc, Start-End-Radius** to draw the three arcs. First arc: start point **P1→**, endpoint **P2→**, radius **47″**. Second arc: start point **P3→**, endpoint **P4→**, radius **48″**. Third arc: start point **P3→**, endpoint **P5→**, radius **34″**.
4. Use **Edit Polyline** to join the arcs with the 34″ and 48″ radii.
5. Use **OFFSET** to offset the joined arcs **1/2″** up.
6. Use **OFFSET** to offset the arc with the 47″ radius **1/2″** to the left.
7. Use the **LINE** command to draw lines at the ends of all arcs so that the two metal legs have a thickness.
8. Use **Polyline Edit** to join all parts of each leg so they can be extruded.

Step 4. Draw chair supports.

1. Draw the three supports in Figure 15-4 in the locations shown.

Figure 15-4
Draw three 2″ × 1/2″
rectangles; move and rotate
them into position

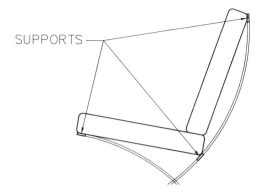

SUPPORTS

2. Use the **RECTANGLE** command to draw the **2″ × 1/2″** supports in either a vertical or horizontal position, as needed.
3. Use the **ROTATE** and **MOVE** commands to locate the supports in the positions shown.

Step 5. Extrude cushions, legs, and supports.

1. Set layer **Fabric** current so the extruded cushions will be on that layer.
2. Use the **EXTRUDE** command to extrude the two cushions **36″**.
3. Set layer **Metal** current.
4. Use the **EXTRUDE** command to extrude the polylines forming the legs **2-1/2″**.
5. Use the **EXTRUDE** command to extrude the supports **31″**.
6. Use the **HIDE** command so the drawing appears as shown in Figure 15-5.

Step 6. Move supports so they sit on top of the legs (Figure 15-6).

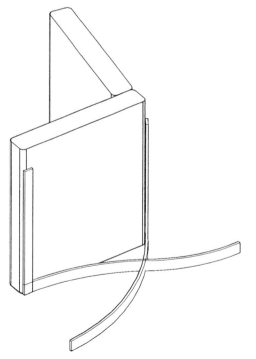

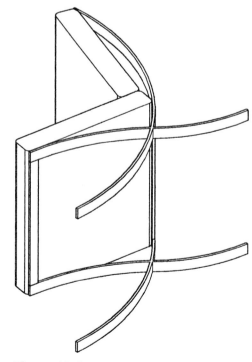

Figure 15-5
Extrude cushions 36″, legs 2-1/2″, and supports 31″

Figure 15-6
Supports moved, legs copied, and all metal parts joined with the **UNION** command

1. Use the **MOVE** command to move the three supports **2-1/2″** in the positive **Z** direction (second point of displacement will be **@0,0,2-1/2**).

Step 7. Join the extruded legs to form a single piece.

1. Use the **UNION** command to join the two extruded legs to form a single piece.

Step 8. Add the other set of legs and join legs and supports.

1. Use the **COPY** command to copy the legs **33-1/2″** in the positive **Z** direction (second point of displacement will be **@0,0,33-1/2**).
2. Use the **UNION** command to join both sets of legs and the three supports into a single object.

Step 9. Rotate the chair to the upright and forward position.

1. Use the **3DROTATE** command to rotate the chair **90°** about the X-axis. Click one of the lowest points of the end of one of the chair legs as the **Point** on the X-axis.
2. Use the **3DROTATE** command to rotate the chair **90°** about the Z-axis. Click one of the lowest points of the end of one of the chair legs as the **Point** on the Z-axis.

Step 10. Remove hidden lines.

1. Use the **HIDE** command to remove hidden lines so the chair appears as shown in Figure 15-1.

Step 11. Save the drawing as a wblock.

1. Use the **Wblock** command to save the drawing on a disk with the name **CH15-EXERCISE1**. Use the bottom of the front of the left leg as the insertion point. Click **Retain** to keep the drawing on the screen.
2. Make a layout in paper space. Use **PROPERTIES** to set a scale of **1/2″ = 1′-0″**.
3. Place your name in the upper right corner of the viewport **3/16″** high, simplex font.
4. Save the drawing as **CH15-EXERCISE1**.

Step 12. Plot.

1. Plot or print the drawing at a scale of **1 = 1** from paper space (the **Layout1** tab) in the center of an **8-1/2″ × 11″ sheet**. Click **3D Hidden** in the **Shade plot:** list. (If the **3D Hidden** option is gray, close the **Plot** dialog box, click the viewport boundary, and use the **PROPERTIES** command to change **Shade plot** to **3D Hidden**, then plot.)

EXERCISE 15-2
Creating a Solid Model of a Patio

In this exercise you will create a solid model of a patio area and insert your chair into it (Figure 15-7). The **Prompt/Response** format will not be used in this exercise. The steps will be listed with suggested commands for creating this model.

Step 1. Use your **3D** workspace to make the following settings:

1. Use **Save As...** to save the drawing on the hard drive with the name **CH15-EXERCISE2**.

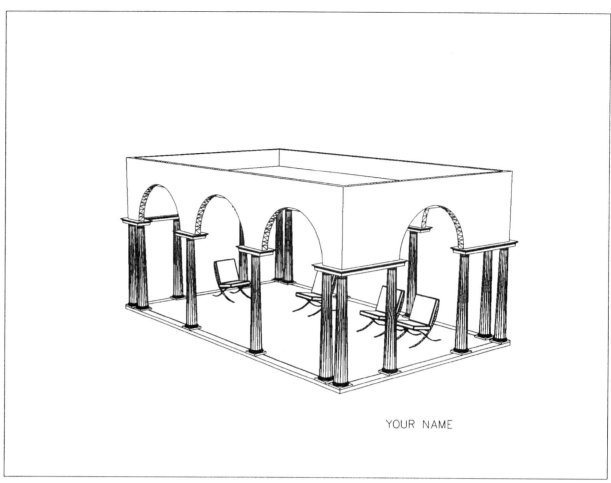

Figure 15-7
Exercise 15-2 complete

2. Set drawing units: **Architectural**
3. Set drawing limits: **50',40'**
4. Set **GRIDDISPLAY: 0**
5. Set grid: **2'**
6. Set snap: **6"**
7. Create the following layers:

Layer Name	Color	Linetype
Border	red	continuous
Column	white	continuous
Cornice	white	continuous
Roof	white	continuous
Pad	red	continuous

8. Set layer **Pad** current.
9. Use the **VPORTS** command to make two vertical viewports. Use **Zoom-All** in both viewports to start, then zoom in closer as needed. You will find it easier to draw in the left viewport and use the right viewport to determine whether the model is proceeding as it should.

10. Use **SE Isometric** to set a viewpoint for the right viewport.
11. Set **FACETRES** to **4**; set **ISOLINES** to **20**.
    Let's begin at the bottom and work up.

Step 2. Draw the concrete pad with a border around it.

The concrete pad and the border have to be two separate objects extruded to a height of **4″**. Draw the outside edge of the border and extrude it, then draw the inside edge, extrude it, and subtract it from the outside edge. Finally, draw the pad and extrude it (Figure 15-8).

EXTRUDE	
Ribbon/ Modeling Panel	
Modeling Toolbar:	
Menu Bar:	Draw/ Modeling/ Extrude
Type a Command:	EXTRUDE
Command Alias:	EXT

1. Use the **RECTANGLE** command to draw a rectangle measuring **39′ × 24′**. Start the first corner at absolute coordinates **6′,8′**.
2. Offset the first rectangle **1′** to the inside.
3. Use the **OFFSET** command to offset the **37′ × 22′** rectangle **1/2″** to the inside to form the concrete pad with a **1/2″** space between it and the border.
4. Use the **EXTRUDE** command to extrude all three rectangles **4″**.
5. Use the **SUBTRACT** command to subtract the inside of the border (the 1′-offset extruded rectangle) from the outside of the border. You will have to zoom a window so you can get close enough to pick the correct rectangle to subtract.
6. Put the border on the **Border** layer.

Step 3. Draw the base of the columns.

Draw the base of the columns on the lower left corner of the drawing. They will be copied after the columns are placed on them (Figure 15-9):

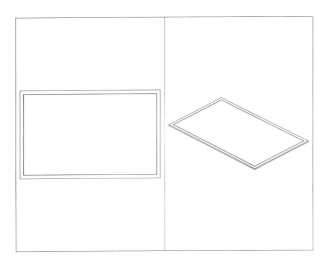

Figure 15-8
The concrete pad with a 1′ border

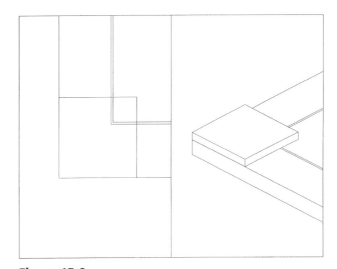

Figure 15-9
Draw the base of the column

1. Set layer **Column** current.
2. Zoom in on the lower left corner of the drawing, as shown in Figure 15-9, in both viewports.
3. Use **BOX** to draw the column base. The box measures **18″ × 18″ × 2″** height. Locate the corner of box on the lower left corner of the border as shown. Use **Osnap-Endpoint** to click the first corner, then **@18,18** to specify the other corner.

Step 4. Draw the columns.

Draw the column and rotate it so it sits on top of the base (Figures 15-10, 15-11, 15-12, 15-13, and 15-14):

Figure 15-10
Dimensions for drawing
the column

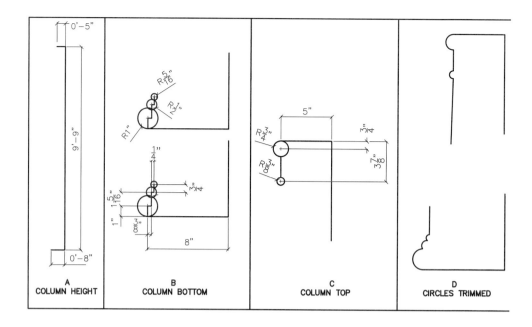

A
COLUMN HEIGHT

B
COLUMN BOTTOM

C
COLUMN TOP

D
CIRCLES TRIMMED

Figure 15-11
The column revolved

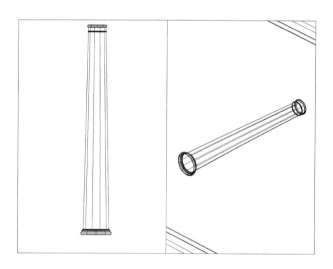

Figure 15-12
Move the UCS to the top
lower left corner of the base

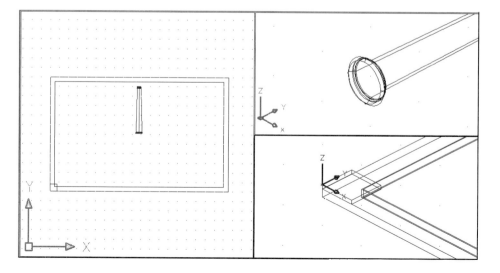

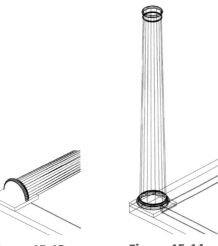

Figure 15-13
Move the column to
the center of the base

Figure 15-14
Rotate the column to
its upright position

1. Use the dimensions in Figure 15-10 to draw the column in an open area of your drawing. Use the **LINE** and **CIRCLE** commands to draw this figure. After you have drawn the circles and lines at the bottom and top of the column, draw a line from the quadrant of the lower circle on the top to the quadrant of the upper circle on the column bottom. Then, trim the circles to form the arcs.

> **TIP**
> Be sure to trim all parts of the circles so there are no double lines.

2. Use **Polyline Edit** to join all the parts of Figure 15-10 into a single polyline.
3. Use the **REVOLVE** command to create the solid column as shown in Figure 15-11. Select both ends of the vertical line using **Osnap-Endpoint** as the axis of revolution.
4. Use the **VPORTS** command to split the right viewport into two horizontal viewports **(three:left)** and zoom in on the bottom of the column and the box you drew as the column base, as shown in Figure 15-12 in both horizontal viewports. (You may need to adjust your view in the left viewport—type **PLAN <Enter>**.)
5. Use the **UCS** command to move your UCS to the lower left corner of the top plane of the base, as shown in Figure 15-12, in both right viewports.
6. Use the **MOVE** command to move the column to the center of the base, as shown in Figure 15-13. Use **Osnap-Center** as the base point and click the extreme bottom circular center of the column in the upper right viewport. Type **9,9** as the second point of displacement to move the column to the center of the base.
7. Use the **3DROTATE** command to rotate the column **90°** about the X-axis, as shown in Figure 15-14.
8. Use the **VPORTS** command to return the display to two vertical viewports.

Step 5. Add the cornice at the top of the column.

Insert drawing 14-3 (from Exercise 14-1, Figures 14-40 through 14-45) to form the cornice at the top of the column (Figures 15-15 and 15-16).

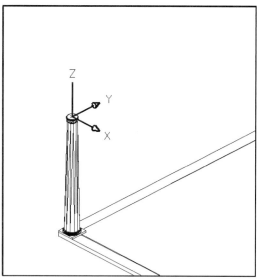

Figure 15-15
Move the UCS to the center of the top of the column

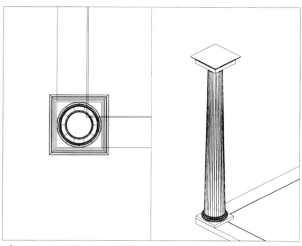

Figure 15-16
Inserting the cornice

1. Set layer **Cornice** current.
2. Use the **Move** option of the **UCS** command to move the UCS to the extreme top of the column as shown in Figure 15-15. Use **Osnap-Center** to locate the UCS at that point.
3. Use the **INSERT** command to insert drawing 14-3 onto the top of the column (Figure 15-16). Use the following:

> **TIP**
>
> Be sure the insertion point is positive **9-1/2**, negative **–9-1/2**. If you did not pick the correct insertion point when you Wblocked drawing 14-3, draw a line from a bottom corner to the diagonally opposite corner. Use the midpoint of that line to move drawing 14-3 to coordinates 0,0.

Insertion point: Type **9-1/2** in the **X:** box and **–9-1/2** in the **Y:** box. (Be sure to include the minus in the Y direction.) Leave **Z:** at 0. (The bottom of the cornice drawing measures 19″. Because you picked the endpoint of the lower corner as the insertion point when you Wblocked the shape, 9-1/2, –9-1/2 will place the center of the shape at the center of the column top. The shape must measure **24″ × 24″** when it is inserted. The arithmetic requires you to subtract 5″ from both measurements and divide by 2.)

After you have typed the insertion point in the **X:** and **Y:** boxes of **Insertion point**, type **12** in the **X: Scale** box and check **Uniform Scale**.

(The shape measures 2″ square, so an X scale factor of 12 will make the shape 24″ long.)

(The shape must also be 24″ in the Y direction, so **Uniform Scale** must be checked.)

(The height of the original shape was reduced to 1/12 of the 5-1/2″ dimension, so a scale factor of 12 will make it 5-1/2″ in this drawing.)

Leave **Rotation angle: 0**. Click **OK.**

4. Use the **EXPLODE** command to explode the inserted cornice so it can be joined to form longer cornices. **Explode it only once.** If you explode it more than once, you destroy it as a solid. If you are not sure whether you have exploded it, use the **LIST** command to find out. **LIST** should tell you it is a 3D solid, not a block.

5. Go to **3D Views-Front** (on the **View** menu) or use **ViewCube-Front** occasionally to be sure all parts are in the correct location, then return to the previous view.

Step 6. Draw the columns and cornices at the center and one corner of the structure.

Copy the column and cornice to create supports at the center of the structure (Figures 15-17 and 15-18):

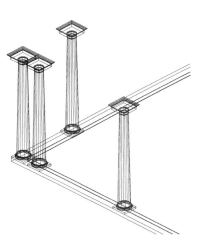

Figure 15-17
Copy the base, column, and cornice twice in the X direction and once in the Y direction

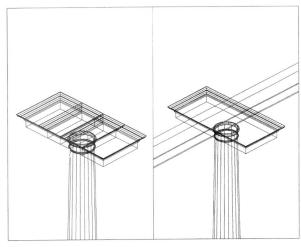

Figure 15-18
Copy the cornice in the positive X direction and the negative X direction and union the three cornice shapes

1. With **ORTHO** on, use the **COPY** command and direct distance entry to copy the column, its base, and cornice three times: **2′** and **12′9″** in the positive **X** direction, and once **6′2″** in the positive **Y** direction (Figure 15-17).

2. With **ORTHO** on, use the **COPY** command and direct distance entry to copy the cornice on the column that is to the far right **12″** in the positive **X** direction and **12″** in the negative **X** direction so that the cornice on this column will measure 48″ when the three are joined.

3. Use **UNION** to join the cornice and the two copies to form a single cornice that is 48″ long (Figure 15-18).

Copy the cornice and join all the cornice shapes on the three corner columns to create the L-shaped cornice at the corner of the structure (Figure 15-19).

1. With **ORTHO** on, use the **COPY** command and direct distance entry to copy the cornice on the corner column six times: **12″** and **24″** in the positive **X** direction and **12″**, **24″**, **36″**, **48″**, **60″**, and **72″** in the positive **Y** direction so that the cornice on the three corner columns will measure 48″ in the X direction and 96″ in the Y direction when all these shapes are joined.

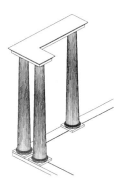

Figure 15-19
The L-shaped cornice after using the **UNION** and **HIDE** commands

2. Use **UNION** to join all the cornice shapes on the three corner
   columns to form a single L-shaped cornice (Figure 15-19).

Step 7. Draw all the remaining columns.
   Mirror the existing columns twice to form the remaining columns
(Figure 15-20).

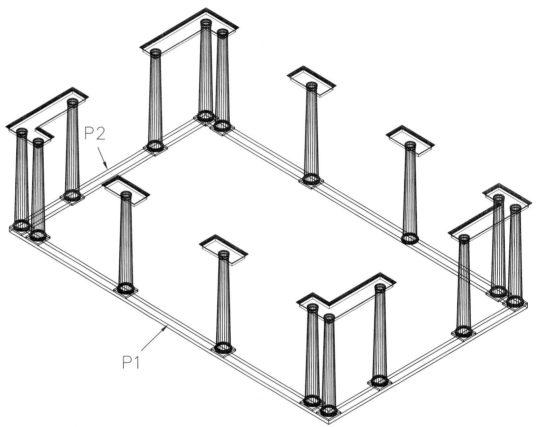

Figure 15-20
Copying the columns using the **MIRROR** command

1. Use the **UCS** command to return to the World UCS.
2. With **ORTHO** on, use the **MIRROR** command to form the
   columns on the right side of the structure. Select all existing
   columns, bases, and cornices. Press **<Enter>**, then using
   Osnap-Midpoint, click **P1→** (Figure 15-20) as the first point of
   the mirror line, then click any point directly above or below
   P1→. Do not erase source objects.
3. With **ORTHO** on, use the **MIRROR** command to form the columns
   on the back side of the structure. Select all existing columns,
   bases, and cornices. Press **<Enter>**, then using **Osnap-Midpoint**,
   click **P2→** (Figure 15-20) as the first point of the mirror line, then
   click any point directly to the left or right of **P2→**. Do not erase
   source objects.

Step 8. Draw the upper part of the structure.
   Draw the front and rear elevations of the upper structure
(Figure 15-21).

1. Set layer **Roof** current.
2. Use the **UCS** command to rotate the UCS **90°** about the X-axis.

Figure 15-21

Dimensions for the front and rear elevations of the upper structure

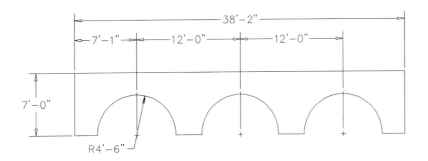

PRESSPULL	
Ribbon/ Modeling Panel	
Modeling Toolbar:	
Type a Command:	PRESSPULL

3. Draw the upper part of the structure in an open area. You will move it to its correct location after it is completed.
4. Use the dimensions from Figure 15-21 to draw that shape with the **RECTANGLE, CIRCLE**, and **TRIM** commands.
5. Use the **PRESSPULL** command to extrude the polyline **8″**. With **PRESSPULL** it is not necessary to have a closed polyline. Just click inside the boundary, move your extrusion in the direction you want, and type the distance **(8)**.
6. Use the **COPY** command to copy this shape **22′-6″** in the negative **Z** direction (*Base point:* click any point; *Second point of displacement:* type **@0,0,-22′6 <Enter>**).

Draw the left and right elevations of the upper structure (Figures 15-22 and 15-23).

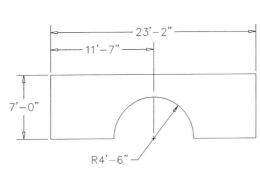

Figure 15-22

Dimensions for the left and right elevations of the upper structure

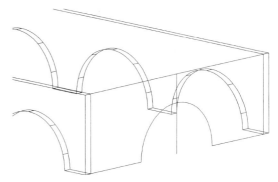

Figure 15-23

Draw the right elevation on the right ends of the front and rear planes

1. Use the **UCS** command to rotate the UCS **90°** about the *Y*-axis.
2. Use the dimensions from Figure 15-22 to draw that shape with the **RECTANGLE, CIRCLE**, and **TRIM** commands across the ends of the front and rear elevations.
3. Draw the right side of the structure on the right ends of the front and rear planes (Figure 15-23).
4. Use the **PRESSPULL** command to extrude the polyline **8″**.
5. Use the **COPY** command to copy this shape **37′-6″** in the negative **Z** direction (*Base point:* click any point; *Second point of displacement:* type **@0,0,-37′6 <Enter>** or move your mouse in the negative **Z** direction with **ORTHO** on and type **37′6 <Enter>**).

Draw the roof and complete the upper part of the structure (Figures 15-24, 15-25, 15-26, and 15-27).

1. Make the **Roof** layer current.
2. Use the **UCS** command to return to the World UCS.

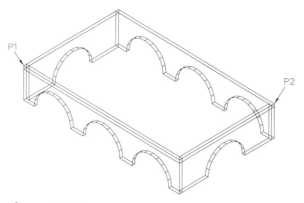

Figure 15-24
Draw a rectangle to form the roof

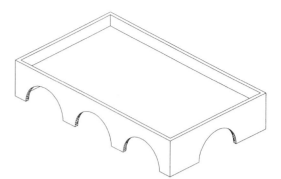

Figure 15-25
The completed upper structure

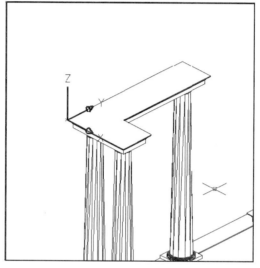

Figure 15-26
Move the UCS to the top of the cornice corner

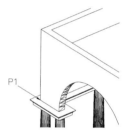

Figure 15-27
Move the upper structure into position

3. Use the **RECTANGLE** command to draw a rectangle to form the flat roof inside the upper part of the structure (Figure 15-24).

   First corner: **P1→**
   Other corner: **P2→**

4. Use the **EXTRUDE** command to extrude the rectangle **8″** in the negative **Z** direction.
5. Use the **MOVE** command to move the extruded rectangle **18″** in the negative **Z** direction (*Second point of displacement:* type **@0,0,-18 <Enter>**).
6. Use the **UNION** command to join all parts of the upper structure into a single unit.
7. Use the **HIDE** command to make sure your model is OK (Figure 15-25).
8. Use the **UCS** command to move the origin of the UCS to the endpoint of the lower left cornice (Figure 15-26).
9. Use the **MOVE** command to move the endpoint, **P1→** (Figure 15-27), of the lower right corner of the upper part of the structure to absolute coordinates **8,8,0**. Be sure you do not put the @ symbol in front of the coordinates.

Step 9. Insert chairs to complete the model.

Insert a chair at the correct elevation, copy it, rotate it, and complete Exercise 15-2 (Figures 15-28 and 15-29).

Figure 15-28
Move the UCS to the top of the border surrounding the pad

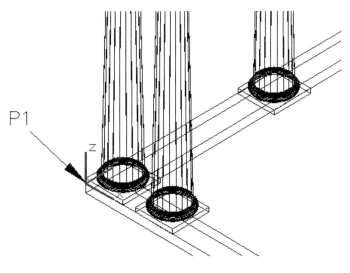

Figure 15-29
Locating the chairs

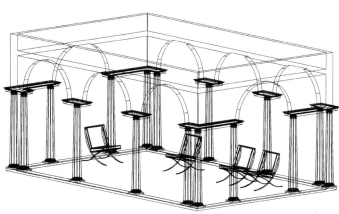

1. Use the **UCS** command to move the origin of the UCS to the top of the border surrounding the concrete pad, **P1→** (Figure 15-28).
2. Use the **INSERT** command to insert the chair drawing, **CH15-EXERCISE1**, at absolute coordinates **18′,14′,0**.
3. Explode the inserted chair **once**. If you explode it more than once, you will have destroyed it as a solid.
4. With **ORTHO** on, use the **COPY** command to copy the chair three times to the approximate locations shown in Figure 15-29.
5. Use the **ROTATE** command to rotate the chair on the far left **90°**.
6. Use the **Viewpoint Presets** dialog box to select a viewpoint of **315,10**.
7. Use **Orbit-Free Orbit** (right-click) with **Perspective** projection and **Visual Styles - 3D Hidden** to obtain a view similar to Figure 15-7.
8. With the right viewport active, use the **SIngle** option of the **VPORTS** command to return the display to a single viewport.
9. Click **Layout1** and place the viewport boundary on a new layer that is turned off.
10. Use the **Single Line Text** command (type **DT <Enter>**) to place your name in the lower right corner **1/8″** high in the simplex font. Your final drawing should appear as shown in Figure 15-7.

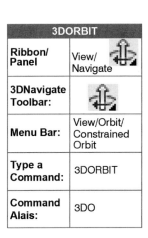

3DORBIT	
Ribbon/ Panel	View/ Navigate
3DNavigate Toolbar:	
Menu Bar:	View/Orbit/ Constrained Orbit
Type a Command:	3DORBIT
Command Alais:	3DO

11. Use the **Shade plot - As Displayed** option in the **Plot** dialog box to remove hidden lines when you plot.

Step 10. Use the **Save As** command to save your drawing in two places.

Step 11. Plot or print the drawing at a scale of **1 = 1**.

RENDER

The **Render** program uses objects, lighting, and materials to obtain a realistic view of a model.

Render Quality

There are five preset rendering quality options: draft, low, medium, high, and presentation. Draft produces very low-quality rendering but results in the fastest rendering speed. Presentation is used for high-quality, photo-realistic rendered images and requires the greatest amount of time to render.

Destinations

Render Window: Choosing **Render Window** as your render destination means the image will be displayed in the render window when processing is complete.

Save rendering to a file: Allows you to save the rendering to a disk with the file name you choose.

Viewport: Anything currently displayed in the viewport gets rendered.

Render in Cloud: Allows you to render to your Autodesk 360 account after you have created the account. You can create high-resolution final images in the cloud.

Lights

lights: Objects used in the RENDER command to light scenes. There are five types of lights that can be used to render a scene; sun, point, distant, spot, and photometric, also called web lights.

Render has five types of **lights** that are used to light any scene. They are as follows:

Sun: This light is present in all scenes and is used to lighten or darken all the images in the scene by the same amount. You can turn off the sunlight to simulate darkness and use only the other types of light to render the scene.

Point Lights: Point lights shine in all directions much like a common lightbulb. The intensity of a point light is controlled by selecting inverse linear, inverse square, or none for the attenuation. Inverse square has the highest intensity value; none has the lowest value.

Distant Lights: Distant lights shine as a parallel beam in one direction illuminating all objects that the light strikes. This light can be used to simulate the sun or another similar light source. You can use one or more distant lights and vary their intensity to achieve the result you want.

Spotlights: Spotlights shine in one direction in a cone shape. One of the settings for this light is the hotspot, at which the light has the greatest intensity. The other setting is the falloff, at which the light begins to decrease in intensity. Spotlights can be used in a manner similar to spotlights in a theater or to light a display.

Weblights: These lights are similar to those bought in a store: fluorescent, low-pressure sodium, incandescent, and high-intensity discharge.

AutoCAD has three lighting options: standard (generic), international (SI), and American. The default lighting for AutoCAD 2015 is a photometric based on American lighting units. This option is physically correct lighting. American differs from international in that illuminance values are measured in foot-candles rather than lux.

You can change the lighting option by typing **LIGHTINGUNITS <Enter>**, then changing the number to 0, 1, or 2:

0	Standard (generic) lighting
1	Photometric lighting in international SI units
2	Photometric lighting in American units

Photometric properties can be added to both artificial lights and natural lights. Natural lights are the sun and the sky.

You can create lights with various distribution and color characteristics or import specific photometric files available from lighting manufacturers. Photometric lights always attenuate using an inverse-square falloff and rely on your scene using realistic units.

Which of these options you use will depend on how your scene is constructed and what your preferences are.

Often, with photometric lights and the sun you will need to perform tone mapping. The **RENDEREXPOSURE** command allows you to adjust the tone mapping. Type **RENDEREXPOSURE <Enter>** to display the **Adjust Rendered Exposure** dialog box, which provides a preview and controls to adjust the tone mapping.

Materials

materials: Items that can be attached to solid shapes to give those shapes the appearance of metal, wood, brick, granite, textiles, or any one of a number of other materials. Materials are used in the RENDER command to make a scene.

AutoCAD has several palettes containing *materials* that can be attached to the surfaces of 3D objects in your drawing. You can also create new materials from scratch and modify existing materials and save them with a new name. In this exercise, only existing materials will be used. If you attach a material to an object and decide you do not like its appearance, the **Materials Browser** allows you to detach the material from that object.

Other Commands Available to Render, Animate, Attach Scanned Files, and Shade 3D Models

Orbit: As discussed in previous chapters, the **Orbit** command has several features that can be used to give a 3D model a photo-realistic appearance.

New View: Allows you to add a solid, a gradient, or an image background to your model.

Point Cloud: The **Point Cloud** command allows you to convert scanned pictures to a point cloud format that can be inserted into your drawing. The scanned pictures must be in one of these formats: PTG, PTS, PTX, LAS, XYZ, TXT, ASC, XYB, FLS, FWS, CLR, or CL3. The point cloud pictures are three-dimensional and can be placed in a 3D model to make a presentation.

The **Point Cloud Editor** is used to modify the point cloud; use it as a guideline for drawing, change its display, or apply color mapping to distinguish different features.

Render Environment: Allows you to simulate an atmosphere that enhances the illusion of depth. The color of the fog can be changed to create different visual effects.

Motion Path Animations...: Moves a camera along a path you choose.

3D Walk: Allows you to walk through your model controlling height and speed.

3D Fly: Allows you to fly through or around the model.

EXERCISE 15-3
Use Render Commands to Make a Photo-Realistic Rendering of the Solid Model in Exercise 15-2

In this exercise you will use the **Materials Browser** to select materials to attach to your model. You will then place lights in a manner that will illuminate your model. Next, you will give the model perspective projection, and finally, you will render the model using the **RENDER** command and the **Visual Styles Manager** (Figure 15-30).

Figure 15-30
Exercise 15-3 complete

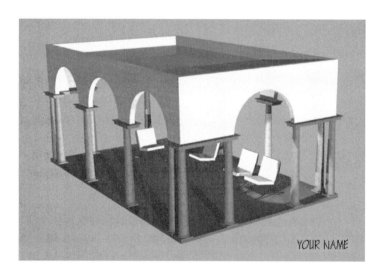

YOUR NAME

Step 1. Use your **3D** workspace to make the following settings:

1. Open drawing **CH15-EXERCISE2** and save it as **CH15-EXERCISE3**.
2. Click the **MODEL** tab to return to model space
3. Click in the right viewport to make it active and change the display to a single viewport if it is not already a single viewport.

Step 2. Move one of the chairs out of the patio so you can easily attach materials to its parts.

Step 3. Select the **White Canvas** material from the **Materials Browser** and place it onto the back and cushion of the chair you just moved, as described next:

Prompt	Response
Type a command:	**Materials Browser** (from the **View Palettes** panel)
The **Materials Browser** (Figure 15-31 appears)	Click **Autodesk Library**
The available materials appear:	Click **Fabric, Canvas White**
	Click the cushion and the back of the chair (you must select the object before you apply the material)
	Click **Canvas White** (That is it. The cushion and the back of all the chairs now have the white canvas material.) Be sure to click the **Add material** button to the far right of the material name.

Figure 15-31
The **Materials Browser**

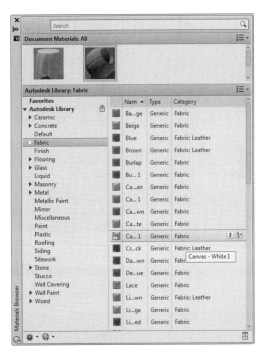

Step 4. Select the **Semi-Polished** material from the **Materials Browser** and place it onto the metal parts of the chair you just moved, as described next:

Prompt	Response
	Click **Metal-Aluminum, Semi-Polished**
	Click the metal parts of the chair
	Click **Aluminum, Semi-Polished**

Step 5. Check to be sure the material has been applied, as described next:

Prompt	Response
Type a command:	Type **RENDER** <Enter>
The chair (and the other parts of the drawing that have not had material applied) is rendered:	Close the **Render** dialog box.

Step 6. Move the chair back to the patio, erase the other chairs, and copy the chair with the material to replace the erased ones.

Step 7. Select the following materials from the **Materials Browser** and place them onto the specified objects. (Remember, you have to select the object before you attach the material.)

Prompt	Response
	1. **Masonry-Brick, Herringbone-Red** for the patio floor pad
	2. **Masonry-Brick, Common** for the border around the patio floor pad
	3. **Masonry-CMU, Sandblasted-Gray** for the columns and bases
	4. **Masonry-CMU, Sandblasted-Tan** for the roof
	5. **Masonry-CMU, Split Face-Running** for the cornices

Before the model is rendered with materials attached, look at the other parts of the **Materials Browser**.

Figure 15-32 shows the **Document Materials** options:

Show All: Shows all the materials that have been chosen for use in the current drawing (You can drag and drop materials from the list onto the document materials area.)

Show Applied: Shows all the materials that have been attached to objects

Show Selected: Shows all materials that have been selected

Show Unused: Shows all materials that have been chosen but not used

Purge All Unused: Used to purge all unused materials that have been chosen but not attached to objects

Figure 15-33 shows the right-click options that are available when you right-click on a material swatch.

Figure 15-32
Materials Browser - Document Materials

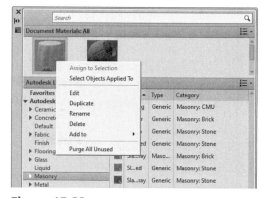

Figure 15-33
Right-click options for each material

Assign to Selection: Allows you to attach the material to an object that is already selected (It is grayed out because no object was selected before the right-click.)

Select Objects Applied to: Selects the objects to which this material has been attached

Edit: Opens the **Material Editor** and allows you to edit the material

Duplicate: Copies the material

Rename: Allows you to rename the material

Delete: Deletes the material from the document materials

Add to: Allows you to add this material to **My materials** or to an active tool palette

Purge All Unused: Deletes any document materials that are unused in the drawing

Figure 15-34 shows the **Libraries** drop-down list. This list allows you to create, open, or edit a user-defined library.

The drop-down list for how materials are displayed is shown in Figure 15-35:

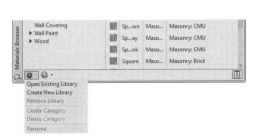

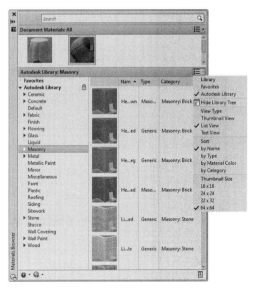

Figure 15-34
The **Libraries** drop-down list

Figure 15-35
The **Libraries** button

Grid View: The default and shows a swatch of the material with its title beneath

List View: Shows a swatch of the material with its category shown to the right

Text View: Does not show a swatch of the material and lists the material

Figure 15-35 shows the option that allows you to change the size of the swatch. When you click any of the sizes under **Thumbnail Size,** the size of the swatches changes.

The last button on the lower right displays the **Material Editor**. The **Material Editor** will be covered later in this chapter.

VISUAL STYLES	
Ribbon/ Panel	View/ Visual Styles
Visual Styles Toolbar:	
Menu Bar:	View/Visual Styles/Visual Styles Manager...
Type a Command:	VISUAL-STYLES

Step 8. Use the **Visual Styles Manager**, Figure 15-36, to render the model with the **Realistic** style.

Prompt	Response
Type a command:	**Visual Styles Manager**
	Double-click the **Realistic** style icon

The model is rendered as shown in Figure 15-36.

Now, lighting will be added, shadows turned on, the background selected, and the model rendered with the **RENDER** command to produce a realistic image.

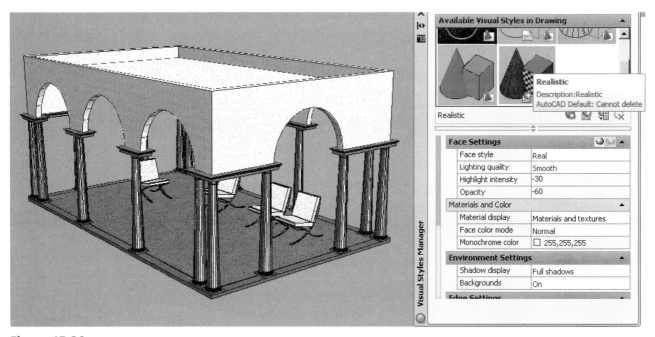

Figure 15-36
Realistic visual style

Step 9. Add distant lights using lines to locate the lights and targets.

1. With **ORTHO** on, use the **LINE** command to draw **30′** lines from the midpoints of the arches on the front and right side of the patio, as shown in Figure 15-37.
2. Draw a line from the midpoint of one side of the roof to the opposite side of the roof, then draw a **30′** line straight up with **ORTHO** on.

Prompt	Response
Type a command:	Type **LIGHT <Enter>** (you can also click **Distant Light** on the ribbon **Render** tab and skip the next prompt) (A warning regarding default lighting may appear. If it does, click **Turn off the default lighting.**)
Enter light type [Point Spot Web Targetpoint Freespot freeweB Distant] <Freespot>:	Type **D <Enter>**

Figure 15-37
Add lines for distant lights

Chapter 15

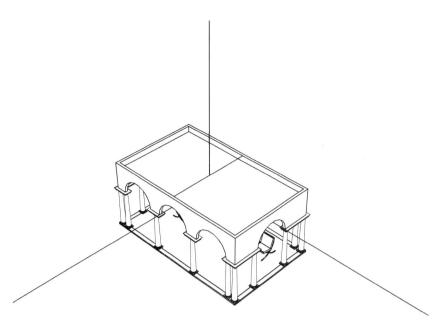

LIGHT	
Ribbon/ Panel	Point Spot Distant Weblight Render/ Lights
Light Toolbar:	Point Spot Distant Weblight
Menu Bar:	View/Render/ Lights
Type a Command:	LIGHT

Prompt	Response
Specify light direction FROM <0,0,0> or [Vector]:	**Osnap-Endpoint**; click the end farthest from the model of one of the 30′ lines
Specify light direction TO <1,1,1>:	**Osnap-Endpoint**; click the other end of the same line
Enter an option to change [Name Intensity Status shadoW Color eXit] <eXit>:	Type **N <Enter>**
Enter light name <Distantlight1>:	**<Enter>** (to accept the name **Distantlight1**)
Enter an option to change [Name Intensity Status shadoW Color eXit] <eXit>:	**<Enter>**

1. Add two more distant lights at the ends of the other two 30′ lines pointed toward the model.

2. Erase the construction lines locating the distant lights.

Distant lights shine uniform parallel light rays in one direction only. The intensity of a distant light does not diminish over distance; it shines as brightly on each surface it strikes no matter how far away the surface is from the light. Distant lights are used to light the model uniformly. You can change the intensity of a distant light if you want all surfaces on that side to be lighter or darker.

Step 10. Add spotlights to shine on the chairs.

Prompt	Response
Type a command:	**Spot** (or type **SPOTLIGHT <Enter>**)
Specify source location <0,0,0>:	Click an endpoint on the L-shaped cornice on the right side of the model, as shown in Figure 15-38
Specify target location <0,0,-10>:	Using **Osnap-Endpoint,** click a point on the two chairs closest together

Figure 15-38
Locate spotlights and point lights

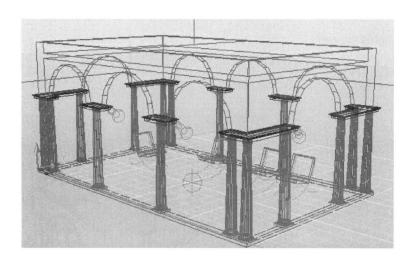

Prompt	Response
Enter an option to change [Name Intensity Status Hotspot Falloff shadoW Attenuation Color eXit] <eXit>:	Type **N** **<Enter>**
Enter light name <Spotlight4>:	**<Enter>**
Enter an option to change [Name Intensity Status Hotspot Falloff shadoW Attenuation Color eXit] <eXit>:	**<Enter>**

1. Add two more spotlights on the cornices of the two single columns on the front pointing to points on the other two chairs, as shown in Figure 15-38. Name the lights **Spotlight5** and **Spotlight6**.

A spotlight shines light in the shape of a cone. You can control the direction of the spotlight and the size of the cone. The intensity of a spotlight decreases the farther it is from the object. Spotlights are used to light specific areas of the model.

Step 11. Add a point light near the center of the patio.

Prompt	Response
Type a command:	Type: **POINTLIGHT<Enter>**
Specify source location <0,0,0>:	**Osnap-Endpoint**; click a point near the center of the floor of the patio
Enter an option to change [Name Intensity Status shadoW Attenuation Color eXit] <eXit>:	Type **N** **<Enter>**
Enter light name <Pointlight7>:	**<Enter>**
Enter an option to change [Name Intensity Status shadoW Attenuation Color eXit] <eXit>:	**<Enter>**

A point light shines light in all directions. The intensity of a point light fades the farther the object is from the light unless attenuation is set to **None**. Point lights are used for general lighting.

Step 12. Turn on the **Sun** light and adjust it to a summer month at midday. Click **Sun Status: OFF** to turn it on.

SUNPROPERTIES	
Ribbon/ Panel	Render/ Sun & Location
Light Toolbar:	
Menu Bar:	View/Render/ Light/Sun Properties...
Type a Command:	SUN PROPERTIES

Step 13. Type **Orbit <Enter>** or click **Orbit** (**View** tab), then right-click and click **Perspective** to change the view to a perspective view.

Step 14. Make advanced render settings.

Prompt	Response
Type a command:	**Advanced Render Settings...** (or type **RPREF <Enter>**) Set **Render quality** to **High** (Figure 15-39) (**Render quality** is at the top of the palette)
The **Advanced Render Settings** palette appears:	Set **Destination** to **Window** Set **Shadow map On** (in the middle of the first screen in this figure) Close this palette Click **Ground shadow** on the **Visual Styles Manager** (on the **View** tab) to turn shadows on; close this palette

Figure 15-39

Render quality high, render to a window, turn ground shadow on

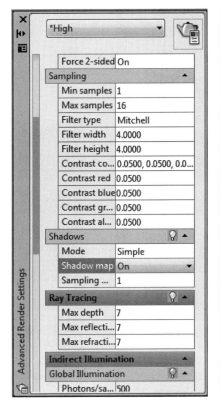
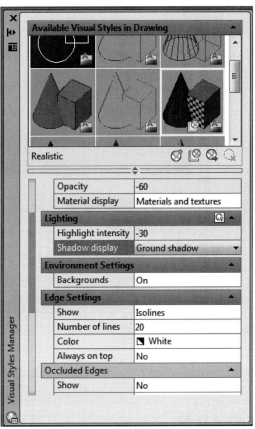

Step 15. Change the background to a color before rendering.

Prompt	Response
Type a command:	**Named Views...** (or type **V <Enter>**)
The **View Manager** appears:	Click **New...**
The **New View/Shot Properties** dialog box appears:	Type **VIEW 1** in the **View name:** input box Click **Default** (in the **Background** area), then Click **Solid**

VIEW	
View Toolbar:	(icon)
Menu Bar:	View/ Named Views...
Type a Command:	VIEW
Command Alias:	V

Prompt	Response
The **Background** dialog box appears:	Click **Color**: (the area beneath the word **Color**:)
The **Select Color** dialog box, Figure 15-40, appears:	Click the **Index Color** tab and click color **33**
	Click **OK**
The **Background** dialog box appears:	Click the **Type** list (Figure 15-41)

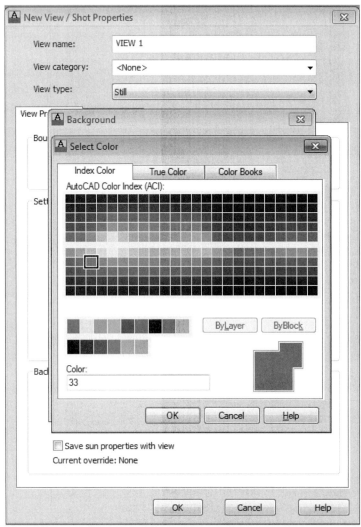

Figure 15-40
Set background color for rendering

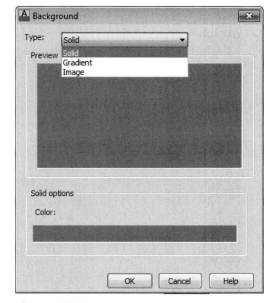

Figure 15-41
Background types

This list allows you to have a single-color background or a two- or three-color gradient background or to select an image file for the background of your rendering.

Prompt	Response
	Close the list with **Solid** selected and click **OK**
The **New View/Shot Properties** dialog box appears:	Click **OK**

Prompt	Response
The **View Manager** appears:	Click **VIEW 1** in the list to the left
	Click **Set Current**
	Click **OK**

Step 16. Render the drawing and insert it into a paper space viewport.

Prompt	Response
Type a command:	**Render** (or type **RENDER <Enter>**)
The rendered model appears similar to Figure 15-42.	Click **File-Save...** (if you like what you see; if not, add, erase, or change the intensity of lights, replace materials, and so forth)
The **Render Output File** dialog box appears:	Type **CH15-EXERCISE3** (in the **File Name**: input box)
	Select **TIF** in the **Files of type** input box
	Save the file on a disk and make note of the disk and folder
The **TIFF Image Options** dialog box appears:	Click **OK**
	Close the **Render** window
The drawing returns:	Click **Layout1**
The active model space viewport appears:	Click any point on the viewport border and erase the viewport
Type a command:	**Insert - Raster Image Reference...**
The **Select Reference File** dialog box appears:	
	Click the file **CH15-EXERCISE3** (on the disk where you saved it); you may need to make **Files of type:** read **All Image files**)
	Click **Open**
The **Attach Image** dialog box appears:	With a check in **Specify on Screen for Scale**
	Click **OK**
Specify insertion point <0,0>:	**<Enter>**

RASTER IMAGE REFERENCE	
Ribbon/ Panel	Insert/ Reference Attach
Reference Toolbar:	Attach
Menu Bar:	Insert/Raster Image Reference...
Type a Command:	IMAGEATTACH
Type a Command:	IAT

Figure 15-42
Exercise 15-3 complete

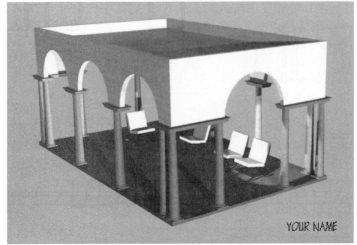

YOUR NAME

Prompt	Response
Specify scale factor or [Unit] <1>:	Drag the upper right corner of the image to fill the viewport, then click

The rendered image fills the viewport.

Step 17. Type your name **3/16″** high in the CityBlueprint font in the lower right corner of the drawing.

Step 18. Save the drawing in two places.

Step 19. Plot the drawing to fit on an **8-1/2″ × 11″** sheet, landscape.

EXERCISE 15-4
Create a Walk-Through AVI File for the Rendered 3D Patio

CAMERA	
Ribbon/ Panel	Render/ Camera
View Toolbar:	
Menu Bar:	View/ Create Camera
Type a Command:	CAMERA
Type a Command:	CAM

Step 1. Begin **CH15-EXERCISE4** on the hard drive or network drive by opening the existing drawing **CH15-EXERCISE3** and saving it as **CH15-EXERCISE4**.

Step 2. Make a new layer, name it **Path**, color white, and make the **Path** layer current.

Step 3. Split the screen into two vertical viewports and make the left viewport a plan view of the World UCS. (Type **UCS <Enter>**, then press **<Enter>** again to accept **World** as the UCS, then type **PLAN <Enter>**, then press **<Enter>** again to get the plan view of the World UCS.)

Step 4. Use the **Polyline** command to draw a path similar to Figure 15-43. The exact size and angle are not important.

Step 5. Make the settings for the camera.

Prompt	Response
Type a command:	**Create Camera** (or type **CAM <Enter>**)
Specify camera location:	Click **Osnap-Endpoint**, click **P1→**, Figure 15-43

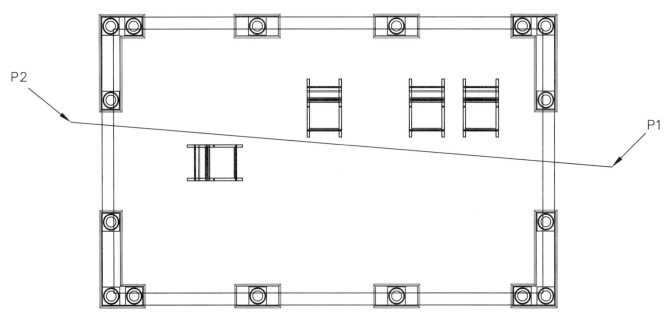

Figure 15-43
Draw a path and locate the camera and target

Prompt	Response
Specify target location:	Click **Osnap-Endpoint**, click **P2→**, (Figure 15-43)
Enter an option [? Name LOcation Height Target LEns Clipping View eXit] <eXit>:	Type **N <Enter>**
Enter name for new camera <Camera1>:	**<Enter>**
Enter an option [? Name LOcation Height Target LEns Clipping View eXit] <eXit>:	Type **H <Enter>**
Specify camera height <00>:	Type **6′ <Enter>**
Enter an option [? Name LOcation Height Target LEns Clipping View eXit] <eXit>:	Type **V <Enter>**
Switch to camera view? [Yes No] <No>:	Type **Y <Enter>**

The camera view should be similar to Figure 15-44.

Figure 15-44
Camera view

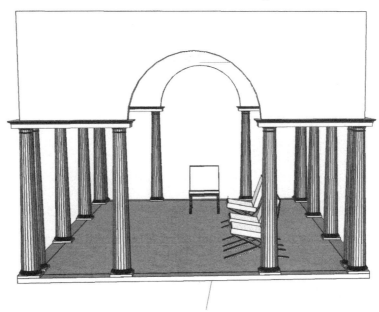

Step 6. Make walk and fly settings, as shown in Figure 15-45.

WALK AND FLY SETTINGS	
Ribbon/Panel	Render/Animations
Menu Bar:	View/Walk and Fly/Walk and Fly
Type a Command:	WALKFLY SETTINGS

Figure 15-45
 Walk and Fly Settings
dialog box

3D walk: A program that allows you to walk through a model controlling height and speed.

Step 7. Activate the ***3DWALK*** command and make an animation file.

Prompt	Response
Type a command:	**Walk** (or type **3DWALK <Enter>**)

To move forward, you can press and hold the up arrow or the **W** key. Similarly, use the left arrow or the **A** key to move left, down arrow or **S** to move back, and right arrow or **D** to move right. You can also hold down the click button on your mouse and move the display in the **Position Locator** palette, as shown in Figure 15-46.

Prompt	Response
Press **<Esc>** or **<Enter>** to exit: or right-click to display shortcut menu:	Hold your mouse over the drawing and right-click
The right-click menu appears:	Click **Animation Settings...**
The **Animation Settings** dialog box appears:	Make the settings as shown in Figure 15-47; click **OK** Hold your mouse over the drawing and right-click

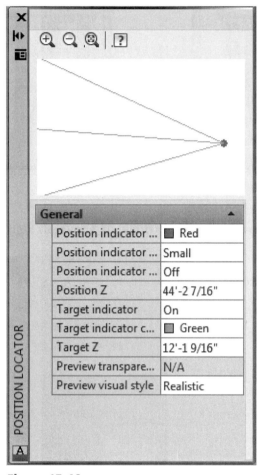

Figure 15-46
Use the mouse to move the camera through the walk

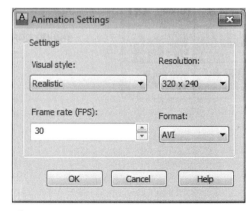

Figure 15-47
Animation Settings dialog box

Prompt	Response
The right-click menu appears:	Make any other necessary changes to your settings—you probably will not have to make any
	Click any point in the drawing to get rid of the right-click menu and right-click on the ribbon with the **Render** tab active to get the **Animations** panel
	Click **Animation Motion Path** on the ribbon
	Use the up, down, left, and right arrows to move the camera along the path, moving forward, back, left, and right
	When you have moved through the patio, click **Save Animation**
The **Save As** dialog box, Figure 15-48, appears:	Type **Walk1** in the **File name:** box
	Select: **AVI Animation (*.avi)** in the **Files of type:** box
	Be sure to save the file on a disk and in a folder where you can find it.

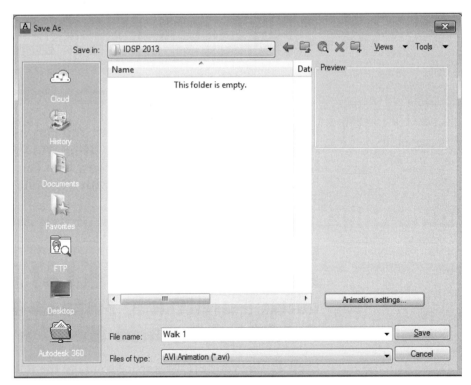

Figure 15-48
Save the animation file as an .avi file

TIP

If the **Animations** panel is not visible, right-click on a blank spot on the ribbon and click **Show Panels - Animations**.

Step 8. Preview the animation file, then exit the **3DWALK** command. Make changes if needed.

Prompt	Response
Press **<Esc>** or **<Enter>** to exit, or right-click to display shortcut menu:	Click **Play Animation**
The **Animation Preview** program appears:	View your animation (Figure 15-49)
	Close the **Animation Preview** box
	Press **<Esc>** or **<Enter>** to exit the **3DWALK** command

Figure 15-49

Play animation preview

If you like your animation, keep it. You can view it outside of AutoCAD by simply clicking on the .avi file using Windows Explorer. If you want to make lighting or material changes, you can do that easily and then do another 3D walk and save it with the same name to overwrite the original file.

EXERCISE 15-5
Build a Solid Model of a Living Room with Furniture, Attach Materials, Add Lights, and Render It

Step 1. Use your **3D** workspace to make the following settings (Figure 15-50 shows the completed drawing):

1. Use **Save As...** to save the drawing with the name **CH15-EXERCISE5.**
2. Set drawing units: **Architectural**
3. Set drawing limits: **45′,45′**
4. Set **GRIDDISPLAY: 0**
5. Set grid: **12**
6. Set snap: **3**

Figure 15-50
Exercise 15-5: complete
(Courtesy of Dr. David R.
Epperson, AIA)

7. Create the following layers:

Layer Name	Color	Linetype
Ceiling	white	continuous
Chair	green	continuous
Coffee Table	white	continuous
Couch	green	continuous
Couch cushions-back	yellow	continuous
Door	cyan	continuous
End Table	white	continuous
Floor	white	continuous
Glass	white	continuous
Picture	cyan	continuous
Rug	magenta	continuous
Supports	green	continuous
Standing Lamp	cyan	continuous
SL Shade	magenta	continuous
Table Lamp	red	continuous
T Shade	yellow	continuous
Walls	white	continuous
Woodwork	yellow	continuous

8. Set layer **Floor** current.

Step 2. Split the screen into two vertical viewports and make the left viewport a plan view of the world UCS. (Type **UCS <Enter>**, then press **<Enter>** again to accept **World** as the UCS, then type **PLAN <Enter>**, then press **<Enter>** again to get the plan view of the World UCS.) Set the right viewport to **SE Isometric**.

Step 3. Use the **RECTANGLE** and **EXTRUDE** commands to draw the floor.

1. The rectangle should measure **19′ × 21′**.
2. Extrude the rectangle **–4″** (be sure to include the minus).

Figure 15-51
Sheet 1 of 2, Furniture dimensions (Courtesy of Dr. David R. Epperson, AIA)

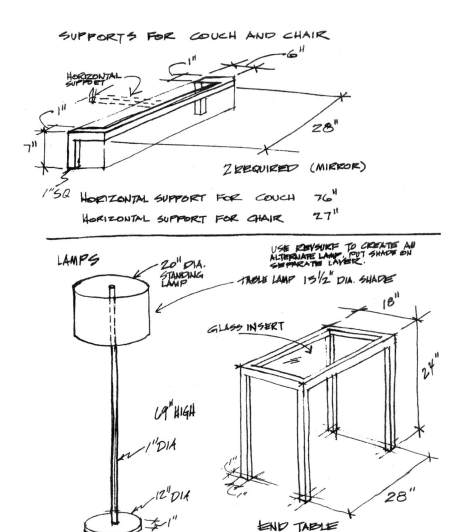

SUPPORTS FOR COUCH AND CHAIR

HORIZONTAL SUPPORT

1"

6"

1"

28"

7"

2 REQUIRED (MIRROR)

1"SQ   HORIZONTAL SUPPORT FOR COUCH   76"

HORIZONTAL SUPPORT FOR CHAIR   27"

LAMPS

20" DIA. STANDING LAMP

USE REVSURF TO CREATE AN ALTERNATE LAMP. PUT SHADE ON SEPARATE LAYER.

TABLE LAMP 15½" DIA. SHADE

GLASS INSERT

18"

24"

69" HIGH

1" DIA

12" DIA

1"

1"

1"

28"

END TABLE

Step 4. Use **RECTANGLE, EXTRUDE, 3DROTATE, COPY,** and **UNION** commands to draw the end table (Figure 15-51, Sheet 1).

1. Set layer **End Table** current.
2. Draw three **1″ × 1″** rectangles.
3. Extrude one **24″**, another **18″**, and the last one **28″**.
4. Use **3DROTATE** to rotate the extruded rectangles into position (Figure 15-52).
5. Copy the extruded rectangles from endpoint to endpoint to form the end table.
6. Use the **UNION** command to make all extruded rectangles a single object.
7. Set layer **Glass** current. Use the **RECTANGLE** command to draw the glass insert in the top of the end table and extrude it **−1/4″**.

Step 5. Use **RECTANGLE, EXTRUDE, 3DROTATE, COPY,** and **UNION** commands to draw the supports for the couch and chair (Figure 15-51, Sheet 2):

1. Set layer **Supports** current.
2. Draw three **1″ × 1″** rectangles.
3. Extrude one **7″**, another **6″**, and the last one **28″**.
4. Use **3DROTATE** to rotate the extruded rectangles into position (Figures 15-52 and 15-53).
5. Copy the extruded rectangles from endpoint to endpoint to form the support.

Figure 15-51
Sheet 2 of 2, Furniture
dimensions (Courtesy of
Dr. David R. Epperson, AIA)

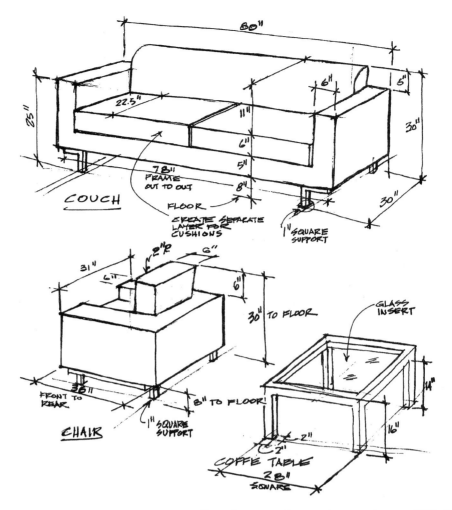

6. Draw two more **1″ × 1″** rectangles and extrude one **76″**, the other **27″**.
7. Use **3DROTATE** to rotate the extruded rectangles into position, and use **MOVE** to move those rectangles from midpoint to midpoint (Figure 15-54).
8. Use **MIRROR** to copy the supports to the other end of the 76″ and 27″ extruded rectangles (Figure 15-54).
9. Use the **UNION** command to make all extruded rectangles for the couch a single object and all the extruded rectangles for the chair another single object.

Figure 15-52
Use **3DROTATE** to rotate extruded
rectangles to form the end table

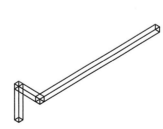

Figure 15-53
Use **3DROTATE** to rotate
extruded rectangles to
form the support

Figure 15-54
Rotate horizontal supports
and mirror supports to the
other end

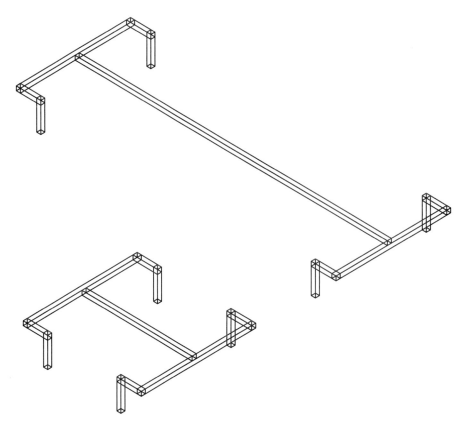

Step 6. Use the dimensions from the sketch (Figure 15-51, Sheet 2) to make
the solid model of the couch and place it on the couch support:

1. Set layer **Couch** current, rotate the UCS **90°** about the X-axis,
   and draw the U shape of the couch base and arms.
2. Extrude the U shape **30″**.
3. Set layer **Couch cushions - back** current and draw the cushions
   using the **BOX** command, or draw a rectangle and extrude it.
4. Rotate the UCS **90°** about the Y-axis, draw the back, and
   extrude it **68″**. Return to the World UCS.
5. Move all parts of the couch (Figure 15-55) so they fit together to
   form a couch as shown in the sketch. Use **Osnap-Endpoint** to
   select base points and second points of displacement.
6. Use **ViewCube** to change the 3D view to **Front,** then **Right**
   (Figure 15-56), and determine whether the couch must be
   moved to the right or left to center it on the supports. Be sure
   ORTHO is on when you move the couch, and do not use **Osnap,**
   so you can be sure the couch is moved correctly.
7. Return the model to an **SE Isometric** view and use the **HIDE**
   command to be sure the view is as it should be.

Step 7. Use the dimensions from the sketch, Figure 15-51, Sheet 2, to make
the solid model of the chair, and place it on the chair support.

1. Set layer **Chair** current, rotate the UCS **90°** about the X-axis,
   and draw the U shape of the chair base and arms.
2. Extrude the U shape **36″**.
3. Draw the cushion and the back using the **BOX** command, or
   draw rectangles and extrude them. Use the **UNION** command to
   make one object of the back, arms, and base. Do not include the
   cushion in the union.
4. Rotate the UCS **90°** about the Y-axis, draw the back cushion,
   and extrude it **19″**. Return to the World UCS.

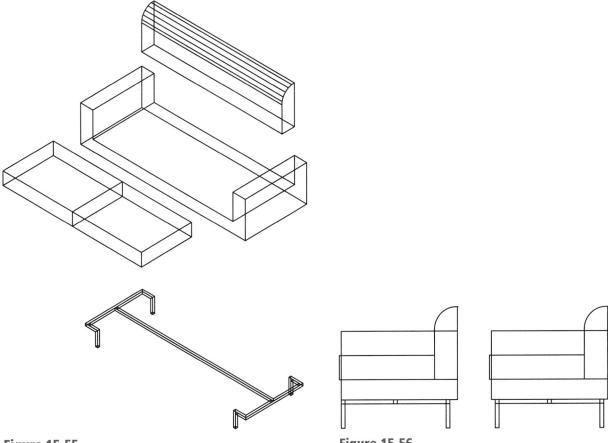

Figure 15-55
Pieces of the couch

Figure 15-56
Move the couch so it is centered on the supports

5. Move all parts of the chair (Figure 15-57) so they fit together to form a chair as shown in the sketch. Use **Osnap-Endpoint** to select base points and second points of displacement.

6. Change the 3D view to **Front**, then **Right** (Figure 15-56), and determine whether the chair must be moved to the right or left to center it on the supports. Be sure **ORTHO** is on when you move the chair, and do not use **Osnap**, so you can be sure the chair is moved correctly.

7. Return the model to an **SE Isometric** view and use the **HIDE** command to be sure the view is as it should be.

Step 8. Use **RECTANGLE, EXTRUDE, 3DROTATE, COPY**, and **UNION** commands to draw the coffee table (Figure 15-51, Sheet 2).

1. Set layer **Coffee Table** current.
2. Draw three **2″ × 2″** rectangles.
3. Extrude one **16″**, another **28″**, and the last one **28″**.
4. Use **3DROTATE** to rotate the extruded rectangles into position as you did for the end table.
5. Copy the extruded rectangles from endpoint to endpoint to form the coffee table.
6. Use the **UNION** command to make all extruded rectangles a single object.
7. Set layer **Glass** current. Use the **RECTANGLE** command to draw the glass insert in the top of the coffee table and extrude it **–1/4″**.

Step 9. Use **CYLINDER, LINE,** and **REVOLVE** commands to draw the floor lamp (Figure 15-51, Sheet 1).

Figure 15-57
Pieces of the chair

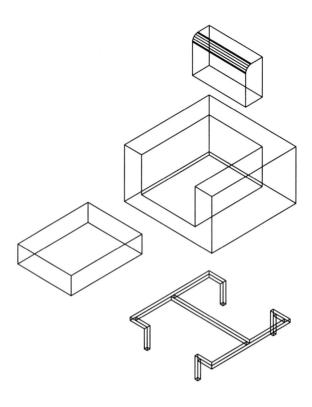

Figure 15-58
Draw the lamp shade

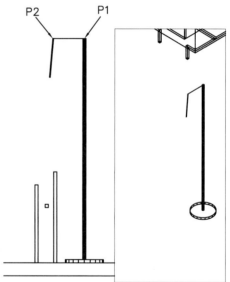

1. Set layer **Standing Lamp** current.
2. With UCS set to **World**, draw a cylinder, **6″** radius and **1″** high.
3. In the same center, draw another cylinder, **1/2″** radius and **69″** high.
4. Use the **UNION** command to make the two cylinders a single object.
5. Set UCS to **World**, then rotate the UCS **90°** about the *X*-axis.
6. Set layer **SL Shade** current.
7. Draw a line from **P1→** to **P2→** (Figure 15-58), **9-3/4″** long.
8. From **P2→**, draw a **12″** line and rotate it **−15°**.
9. Use the **REVOLVE** command to revolve the line **360°** around the 1/2″ cylinder to form a lamp shade.

Step 10. Use **POLYLINE, LINE,** and **REVOLVE** commands to draw the table lamp (Figure 15-59):

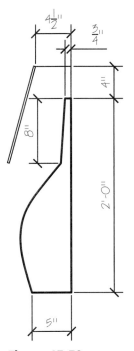

Figure 15-59
Dimensions for table lamps

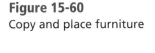

1. Set layer **Table Lamp** current.
2. Set UCS to **World**, then rotate the UCS **90°** about the *X*-axis in the left viewport and type **PLAN <Enter><Enter>** to see the plan view of the current UCS.
3. Use the **Polyline** command to draw the lamp without the shade. Draw the straight lines first and end the command, then draw short polylines to draw the curved line and end the command. Use **Polyline Edit** to smooth the curve and join all polylines into a single polyline.
4. Draw a **12″** line that is **4″** up and **4-1/2″** to the left of the lamp, as shown in Figure 15-59. Then, rotate the line **–15°**.
5. Use the **REVOLVE** command to revolve the polyline **360°** to form the lamp.
6. Set layer **T Shade** current.
7. Use the **REVOLVE** command to revolve the line **360°** to form the lamp shade.

Step 11. Copy the chairs and end tables, and place furniture in the room, as shown in Figure 15-60.

Step 12. Set layer **Rug** current. Use the **RECTANGLE** command to draw an **8′-0″ × 11′-0″** rug centered on the floor beneath the couch and chairs, and extrude it **1″**.

Step 13. Use the **POLYSOLID** command (**6″** width, **8′4″** height) to draw the back wall by selecting the endpoints of the back of the floor, then move the wall down **4″**.

Step 14. Change your UCS so it is parallel to the back wall as shown in Figure 15-61 and use the dimensions from Figure 15-62 to make openings in the back wall for the window and the door.

Step 15. Turn off all furniture layers if necessary, so you can draw more easily.

Step 16. Use the **POLYSOLID** command (**6″** width, **8′4″** height) to draw the side walls, move them down **4″**, then move them to the outside of the floor (**3″** to the right or left so they lie on the edge of the floor).

Figure 15-60
Copy and place furniture

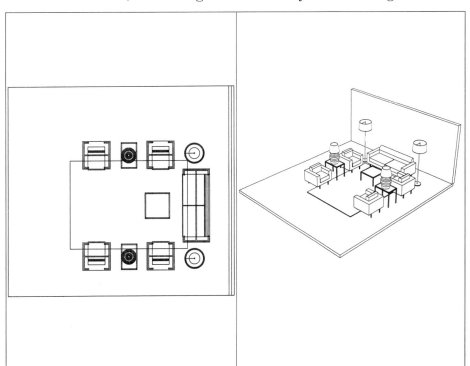

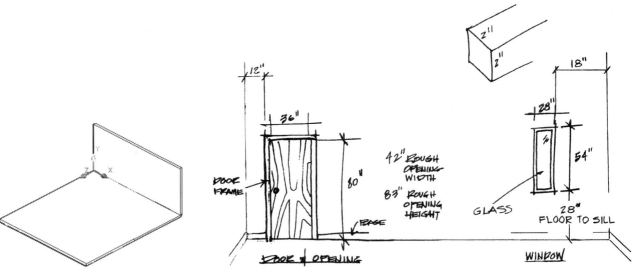

Figure 15-61
UCS parallel to back wall

Figure 15-62
Window and door dimensions (Courtesy of Dr. David R. Epperson, AIA)

Step 17. Draw windows (**2″ × 2″** sill and a rectangle for glass on the inside of the sill extruded **1/2″**), doors (**3″** jamb and header extruded **7″** and moved so they extend **1/2″** from the wall), and baseboards (make the baseboards **4″ × 1″**).

Step 18. Draw the ceiling and extrude it **4″**.

Step 19. Attach appropriate materials to all objects.

Step 20. Place point, spot, photometric, and distant lights in locations to obtain a lighting pattern similar to Figure 15-50.

Step 21. Set the view to **Perspective** projection with a view similar to Figure 15-63, set preferences using the **Advanced Render Settings** dialog box, and render the model.

Figure 15-63
Perspective view

Step 22. Save the rendering as a .jpg file and insert it into paper space **(Layout1)**.

Step 23. Put your name on the drawing and plot it to fit on an **11″ × 8-1/2″** sheet.

Step 24. Save the drawing in two places.

chapterfifteen

Chapter Summary

This chapter provided you the information necessary to build solid models of rooms with furniture, attach materials, light, render, and animate scenes. In addition you learned to use the materials library, make a background, and build solid models on your own from sketches. Now you have the skills and information necessary to produce complex solid models with materials, render those models, and make animations such as walk-throughs.

Chapter Test Questions

Multiple Choice

Circle the correct answer.

1. Which type of light is used to lighten or darken all the images in the scene by the same amount?
   a. Sun   c. Distant
   b. Point   d. Spotlight

2. Which type of light shines in one direction in a cone shape?
   a. Sun   c. Distant
   b. Point   d. Spotlight

3. Which type of light can be used as an incandescent lightbulb?
   a. Web   c. Distant
   b. Point   d. Spotlight

4. Which type of light shines in a parallel direction?
   a. Sun   c. Distant
   b. Point   d. Spotlight

5. Which of the following lights is **not** on the **Render** tab of the ribbon?
   a. Point   c. Distant
   b. Blue Point   d. Sun

6. When you select a new distant light, which of the following is the first prompt AutoCAD gives you?
   a. Locate distant light
   b. Click: First Point
   c. Specify light direction TO<1,1,1>:
   d. Specify light direction FROM<0,0,0>:

7. Which command is used to obtain a perspective projection of a solid model?
   a. **Shade**
   b. **Orbit**
   c. **Viewpoint**
   d. **Viewport**

8. Which of the following opens the **Advanced Render Settings** palette?
   - a. **ARS**
   - b. **Render**
   - c. **Render Pref**
   - d. **RPREF**

9. Which of the following is **not** a type of background that can be used in a rendering?
   - a. Solid
   - b. Image
   - c. Gradient
   - d. Picture

10. Which of the following is a panel on the **Render** tab of the ribbon?
    - a. **Modeling**
    - b. **Primitive**
    - c. **Mesh**
    - d. **Camera**

Matching

Write the correct answer on the line.

a. **Materials Browser** _____

b. **VPORTS** _____

c. **_POSITION LOCATOR** _____

d. **RPREF** _____

e. **VIEW** _____

1. A destination for a rendering
2. A dialog box that allows you to attach materials
3. A command that opens the **Advanced Render Settings** palette
4. A command that can be used to make a background
5. A dialog box that allows you to move a camera along a path

True or False

Circle the correct answer.

1. **True or False:** Materials cannot be detached after they are attached to a model.

2. **True or False:** The material preview uses several types of objects so you can see what the material looks like.

3. **True or False:** The size of the material image in the **Materials Browser** cannot be changed.

4. **True or False:** The object must be selected first before the material is applied.

5. **True or False:** The **Animation** panel on the **Render** tab of the ribbon can be turned on or off.

List

1. Five options of the polyline edit (**Pedit**) command.

2. Five options of the **UCS** command.

3. Five prompts when executing the **Box** command.

4. Five aspects of improved rendering due to material selection.

5. Five lighting options in rendering.

6. Five tools under the **Visualize** tab/**Animation** panel.

7. Five tools under the **Mesh** tab/**Mesh** panel.

8. Five materials available in the **Materials Browser**.

9. Five settings from the **Advanced Render Settings** palette.

10. Five steps to get to perspective view through the **Orbit** command.

Questions

1. In what situations would you use rendered solid models?

2. In what situations would you use an animation?

3. Are rendered solid models and surfaces as effective as 2D drawings for construction?

4. When should you use perspective projection versus isometric projection?

5. Where can you get more materials for use on solid models if you need them?

Chapter Projects

Project 15-1: *Make a Solid Model of the Picnic Table Shown in the Sketch. Use Render Commands to Make a Photo-Realistic Rendering of the Solid Model* [BASIC]

1. Draw a solid model of the picnic table shown in Figure 15-64.

Figure 15-64
Project 15-1: Picnic table

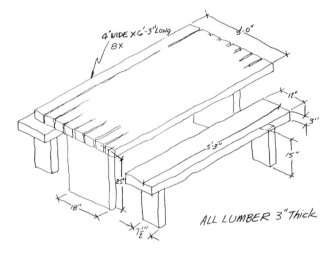

2. Attach the same wooden-appearing material to the entire drawing.

3. Position distant, point, or spotlights to illuminate the picnic table. Adjust the sunlight so the picnic table shows well.

4. Change the view to **Perspective** projection.

5. Use the **RENDER** command to render the scene in a single viewport.

6. Print the rendered drawing centered on an **11″ × 8-1/2″** sheet.

Project 15-2: *Make a Solid Model of the Chair Shown in the Sketch. Use Render Commands to Make a Photo-Realistic Rendering of the Solid Model* [INTERMEDIATE]

1. Draw a solid model of the chair shown in Figure 15-65.

Figure 15-65
Project 15-2: Chair

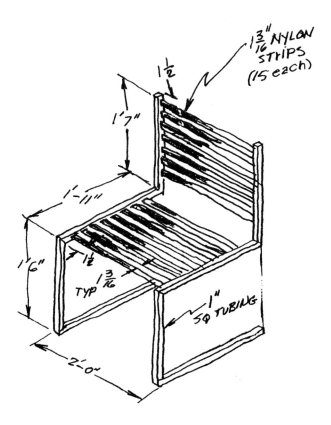

2. Attach appropriate materials to the legs, back, and seat. Use one material for the legs and another for the back and seat.

3. Position distant, point, or spotlights to illuminate the chair. Adjust the sunlight so the chair shows well.

4. Change the view to **Perspective** projection.

5. Use the **RENDER** command to render the scene in a single viewport.

6. Print the rendered drawing centered on an **11″ × 8-1/2″ sheet.**

Project 15-3: *Make a Solid Model of the Table Shown in the Sketch. Use Render Commands to Make a Photo-Realistic Rendering of the Solid Model* [ADVANCED]

1. Draw a solid model of the table shown in Figure 15-66. Estimate any measurements not shown.

Figure 15-66
Project 15-3: Table

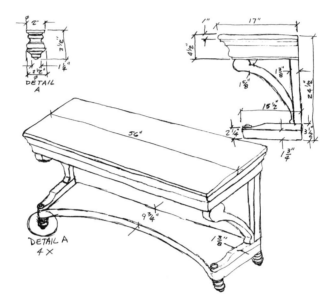

2. Attach the same wooden-appearing material to the entire drawing.

3. Position distant, point, or spotlights to illuminate the table. Adjust the sunlight so the table shows well.

4. Change the view to **Perspective** projection.

5. Use the **RENDER** command to render the scene in a single viewport.

6. Print the rendered drawing centered on an **11″ × 8-1/2″** sheet.

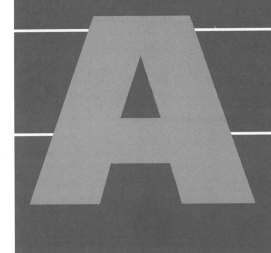

This appendix contains the AutoCAD command aliases (also called keyboard macros) that you can type to activate a command. Aliases and commands with a minus sign before the letters do not display a dialog box but instead show prompts at the command line.

3A	3DARRAY
3AL	3DALIGN
3DMIRROR	MIRROR3D
3DNavigate	3DWALK
3DO	3DORBIT
3DP	3DPRINT
3DPLOT	3DPRINT
3DW	3DWALK
3F	3DFACE
3M	3DMOVE
3P	3DPOLY
3R	3DROTATE
3S	3DSCALE
A	ARC
AA	AREA
AC	BACTION
ADC	ADCENTER
AECTOACAD	-ExportToAutoCAD
AL	ALIGN
AP	APPLOAD
APLAY	ALLPLAY
AR	ARRAY
-AR	-ARRAY
-AREDIT	ARREDIT
ARM	ACTUSERMESSAGE
-ARM	-ACTUSERMESSAGE
ARR	ACTRECORD

ARRAYRECT	RECTANGULAR ARRAY
ARS	ACTSTOP
-ARS	-ACTSTOP
AR/SELECTOBJECTS/P	PATH ARRAY
ARU	ACTUSERINPUT
ATI	ATTIPEDIT
ATE	ATTEDIT
-ATE	-ATTEDIT
ATT	ATTDEF
-ATT	-ATTDEF
ATTE	-ATTEDIT
B	BLOCK
-B	-BLOCK
BC	BCLOSE
BE	BEDIT
BH	HATCH
BO	BOUNDARY
-BO	-BOUNDARY
BR	BREAK
BS	BSAVE
BVS	BVSTATE
C	CIRCLE
CAM	CAMERA
CBAR	CONSTRAINTBAR
CH	PROPERTIES
-CH	CHANGE
CHA	CHAMFER
CHK	CHECKSTANDARDS
CLI	COMMANDLINE
COL	COLOR
COLOUR	COLOR
CO, or CP	COPY
CPARAM	BCPARAMETER
CREASE	MESHCREASE
CSETTINGS	CONSTRAINTSETTINGS
CT	CTABLESTYLE
CUBE	NAVVCUBE
CYL	CYLINDER
D	DIMSTYLE
DAL	DIMALIGNED
DAN	DIMANGULAR
DAR	DIMARC
DBA	DIMBASELINE
DBC	DBCONNECT
DC	ADCENTER
DCE	DIMCENTER
DCENTER	ADCENTER
DCO	DIMCONTINUE
DCON	DIMCONSTRAINT
DDA	DIMDISASSOCIATE
DDI	DIMDIAMETER
DED	DIMEDIT
DELCON	DELCONSTRAINT

DI	DIST
DIV	DIVIDE
DJL	DIMJOGLINE
DJO	DIMJOGGED
DL	DATALINK
DLI	DIMLINEAR
DLU	DATALINKUPDATE
DO	DONUT
DOR	DIMORDINATE
DOV	DIMOVERRIDE
DR	DRAWORDER
DRA	DIMRADIUS
DRE	DIMREASSOCIATE
DRM	DRAWINGRECOVERY
DS	DSETTINGS
DST	DIMSTYLE
DT	TEXT
DV	DVIEW
DX	DATAEXTRACTION
E	ERASE
ED	DDEDIT
EL	ELLIPSE
EPDF	EXPORTPDF
ER	EXTERNALREFERENCES
ESHOT	EDITSHOT
EX	EXTEND
EXIT	QUIT
EXP	EXPORT
EXT	EXTRUDE
F	FILLET
FI	FILTER
FREEPOINT	POINTLIGHT
FS	FSMODE
FSHOT	FLATSHOT
G	GROUP
-G	-GROUP
GCON	GEOMCONSTRAINT
GD	GRADIENT
GEO	GEOGRAPHICLOCATION
GR	DDGRIPS
H	HATCH
-H	-HATCH
HE	HATCHEDIT
HI	HIDE
I	INSERT
-I	-INSERT
IAD	IMAGEADJUST
IAT	IMAGEATTACH
ICL	IMAGECLIP
IM	IMAGE
-IM	-IMAGE
IMP	IMPORT
IN	INTERSECT

INF	INTERFERE
IO	INSERTOBJ
J	JOIN
JOG	DIMJOGGED
JOGSECTION	SECTIONPLANEJOG
L	LINE
LA	LAYER
-LA	-LAYER
LAS	LAYERSTATE
LE	QLEADER
LEN	LENGTHEN
LESS	MESHSMOOTHLESS
LI	LIST
LINEWEIGHT	LWEIGHT
LMAN	LAYERSTATE
LO	-LAYOUT
LS	LIST
LT	LINETYPE
-LT	-LINETYPE
LTS	LTSCALE
LTYPE	LINETYPE
-LTYPE	-LINETYPE
LW	LWEIGHT
M	MOVE
MA	MATCHPROP
MAT	MATERIALS
ME	MEASURE
MEA	MEASUREGEOM
MI	MIRROR
ML	MLINE
MLA	MLEADERALIGN
MLC	MLEADERCOLLECT
MLD	MLEADER
MLE	MLEADEREDIT
MLS	MLEADERSTYLE
MO	PROPERTIES
MORE	MESHSMOOTHMORE
MOTION	NAVSMOTION
MOTIONCLS	NAVSMOTIONCLOSE
MS	MSPACE
MSM	MARKUP
MT	MTEXT
MV	MVIEW
NORTH	GEOGRAPHICLOCATION
NORTHDIR	GEOGRAPHICLOCATION
NSHOT	NEWSHOT
NVIEW	NEWVIEW
O	OFFSET
OP	OPTIONS
ORBIT	3DORBIT
OS	OSNAP
-OS	-OSNAP
P	PAN

-P	-PAN
PA	PASTESPEC
PAR	PARAMETERS
-PAR	-PARAMETERS
PARAM	BPARAMETER
PARTIALOPEN	-PARTIALOPEN
PATCH	SURFPATCH
PC	POINTCLOUD
PCATTACH	POINTCLOUDATTACH
PCINDEX	POINTCLOUDINDEX
PE	PEDIT
PL	PLINE
PO	POINT
POFF	HIDEPALETTES
POL	POLYGON
PON	SHOWPALETTES
PR	PROPERTIES
PRCLOSE	PROPERTIESCLOSE
PRE	PREVIEW
PRINT	PLOT
PROPS	PROPERTIES
PS	PSPACE
PSOLID	POLYSOLID
PTW	PUBLISHTOWEB
PU	PURGE
-PU	-PURGE
PYR	PYRAMID
QC	QUICKCALC
QCUI	QUICKCUI
QP	QUICKPROPERTIES
QSAVE	QSAVE
QVD	QVDRAWING
QVDC	QVDRAWINGCLOSE
QVL	QVLAYOUT
QVLC	QVLAYOUTCLOSE
R	REDRAW
RA	REDRAWALL
RAPIDPROTOTYPE	3DPRINT
RC	RENDERCROP
RE	REGEN
REA	REGENALL
REC	RECTANGLE
REFINE	MESHREFINE
REG	REGION
REN	RENAME
-REN	-RENAME
REV	REVOLVE
RO	ROTATE
RP	RENDERPRESETS
RPR	RPREF
RR	RENDER
RW	RENDERWIN
S	STRETCH

SC	SCALE
SCR	SCRIPT
SE	DSETTINGS
SEC	SECTION
SET	SETVAR
SHA	SHADEMODE
SL	SLICE
SMOOTH	MESHSMOOTH
SN	SNAP
SO	SOLID
SP	SPELL
SPE	SPLINEDIT
SPL	SPLINE
SPLANE	SECTIONPLANE
SPLAY	SEQUENCEPLAY
SPLIT	MESHSPLIT
SSM	SHEETSET
ST	STYLE
STA	STANDARDS
SU	SUBTRACT
T	MTEXT
-T	-MTEXT
TA	TABLET
TB	TABLE
TEDIT	TEXTEDIT
TH	THICKNESS
TI	TILEMODE
TO	TOOLBAR
TOL	TOLERANCE
TOR	TORUS
TP	TOOLPALETTES
TR	TRIM
TS	TABLESTYLE
UC	UCSMAN
UN	UNITS
-UN	-UNITS
UNCREASE	MESHUNCREASE
UNHIDE	UNISLOATEOBJECT
UNI	UNION
V	VIEW
VGO	VIEWGO
-V	-VIEW
VP	DDVPOINT
-VP	VPOINT
VPLAY	VIEWPLAY
VS	VSCURRENT
VSM	VISUALSTYLES
-VSM	-VISUALSTYLES
W	WBLOCK
-W	-WBLOCK
WE	WEDGE
WHEEL	NAVSWHEEL
X	EXPLODE

XA	XATTACH
XB	XBIND
-XB	-XBIND
XC	XCLIP
XL	XLINE
XR	XREF
-XR	-XREF
Z	ZOOM
ZEBRA	ANALYSISZEBRA
ZIP	ETRANSMIT

Shortcut and Temporary Override Keys

This appendix contains a listing of the combination of keys that can be used to perform the described actions. For example, a shortcut key shown as **<Ctrl>+1** requires you to hold down the **<Ctrl>** key and press the **1** key while you continue to hold down the **<Ctrl>** key. This combination will display the **Properties** palette if it is not displayed or turn off the **Properties** palette if it is displayed.

    <F1> through **<F12>** keys are not used in combination with other keys to perform the stated functions. Just press the key.

<Ctrl>+A	Select all
<Ctrl>+C	Copy to the Windows Clipboard
<Ctrl>+D	Turns on and off **Dynamic UCS (DUCS)**
<Ctrl>+E	Cycles through isoplanes in isometric drawing
<Ctrl>+F	Turns **OSNAP** on and off
<Ctrl>+G	Turns **GRID** on and off
<Ctrl>+H	Toggles **PICKSTYLE**
<Ctrl>+I	Turns coordinates on and off
<Ctrl>+J	Repeat the last command
<Ctrl>+K	Insert a hyperlink
<Ctrl>+L	Turns **ORTHO** on and off
<Ctrl>+N	Start a new drawing
<Ctrl>+O	Open an existing drawing
<Ctrl>+P	Plot or print the current drawing
<Ctrl>+Q	Exit the AutoCAD program
<Ctrl>+R	Cycles through the viewports on the current layout
<Ctrl>+S	Save the current drawing
<Ctrl>+T	Turns **TABLET** on and off
<Ctrl>+V	Paste from the Windows Clipboard
<Ctrl>+X	Cut to the Windows Clipboard
<Ctrl>+Y	Redo last action
<Ctrl>+Z	Undo last action

\<Ctrl>+\<Shift>+C	Copy with base point
\<Ctrl>+\<Shift>+H	Toggles hide palettes
\<Ctrl>+\<Shift>+I	Toggles **Infer Constraints**
\<Ctrl>+\<Shift>+P	Turns on and off **Quick Properties**
\<Ctrl>+\<Shift>+S	**Save As...**
\<Ctrl>+\<Shift>+\<Tab>	Switch to previous drawing
\<Ctrl>+\<Shift>+V	Paste as block
\<Ctrl>+0	Toggles **Clean Screen**
\<Ctrl>+1	Displays and closes the **Properties** palette
\<Ctrl>+2	Displays and closes the **DesignCenter**
\<Ctrl>+3	Displays and closes the **Tool Palettes**
\<Ctrl>+4	Displays and closes the **Sheet Set Manager**
\<Ctrl>+6	Displays and closes the **dbConnect Manager**
\<Ctrl>+7	Displays and closes the **Markup Set Manager**
\<Ctrl>+8	Displays and closes the **QuickCalculator**
\<Ctrl>+9	Displays and closes the command line
\<F1>	Displays and closes Help
\<F2>	Displays and closes the text window
\<F3>	Turns **OSNAP** on and off
\<F4>	Turns **TABLET** on and off
\<F5>	Cycles through isoplanes in isometric drawing
\<F6>	Turns **Dynamic UCS** on and off (**DUCS**)
\<F7>	Turns **GRID** on and off
\<F8>	Turns **ORTHO** on and off
\<F9>	Turns **SNAP** on and off
\<F10>	Turns **POLAR** on and off
\<F11>	Turns **OTRACK** on and off
\<F12>	Turns **Dynamic Input (DYN)** on and off

appendix C

Floor Plans and Interior Elevations of a 15-Unit Condominium Building

The floor plans and interior elevations can be found as Figures C-1 through C-10, which are placed at the end of the book following the index.

All figures in Appendix C are courtesy of:

Kelly McCarthy
McCarthy Architecture
620 Main Street, Suite 100
Garland, Texas 75040

Figures C-1 and C-2

Figure C-1 is a floor plan of the first floor of the entire building. Notice that individual condos are labeled as Unit Types A through E. Unit E has a lower floor and an upper floor with an interior circular stairway. All other units are on either the lower floor or the upper floor. Notice that there are several Type A and Type B units on both floors. There are four stairways shown. These stairways lead to the second floor and are shown on both the first and second floor.

Figure C-2 is a floor plan of the second floor of the entire building. Here again the individual units are numbered as Type A through E units. Unit E shows the circular stairway leading to the lower floor. The second floor is almost identical to the first floor, with the exception of Unit E and the areas lying outside the dashed lines.

Figures C-3 Through C-8

Figures C-3 through C-8 are floor plans of the individual condos. Units on the first floor have a patio next to the storage area. Units on the second floor have a balcony next to the storage area.

Figures C-7 and C-8 are the lower and upper floors of the Type E unit.

These figures can be assigned as a project, with individual units drawn and attached as external references to the floor plans of the upper and lower floors of the entire building.

Figures C-9 and C-10

These figures show typical interior elevations of all the units. Many of the items are blocks that can be obtained from **Autodesk Seek** in the **DesignCenter**. The circular stairway shown as Item 31 in Figure C-10 is such a block.

Glossary

absolute coordinates: Coordinate values measured from an origin point or 0,0 point in the drawing.

annotation scale: A setting that controls how text and other annotative objects appear on the drawing.

annotative: A property that belongs to objects, such as text, dimensions, and hatch patterns, that are commonly used to annotate drawings.

annotative text: Text that has a property that allows it to change as the scale of the entire drawing changes.

array: A circular or rectangular pattern of objects.

attribute: A label that attaches data to a block. It consists of a tag and a value.

attribute definition: Text that is included in a block to store data. Attribute definition values can be predefined or specified when the block is inserted. Data from attributes can be extracted from a drawing and inserted into tables or other files.

axonometric: Forms of 2D drawing that represent 3D objects. The three axonometric drawing forms are isometric, dimetric, and trimetric.

block definition: A user-defined collection of drawing objects (and often attributes) that are assigned a base point and a name. A block can be inserted into a drawing multiple times. When a block is updated, all blocks in the drawing with the same name are automatically updated.

Cartesian coordinate system: A coordinate system that has three axes, *X*, *Y*, and *Z*. The *X*-axis value is stated first and measures left to right horizontally. The *Y*-axis value is stated second and measures from bottom to top vertically. The *Z*-axis value is stated third and is used in three-dimensional modeling.

chamfer: An angle (usually 45°) formed at a corner.

color-dependent plot style: A plot style that is organized by the AutoCAD Color Index (ACI) number. Color-dependent plot styles are automatically assigned by the color of the AutoCAD object and can be changed to plot any color specified. Color-dependent plot styles are often made to print all colors black.

command line window: The text area above the status bar used for keyboard input and prompts, and where AutoCAD displays messages.

data extraction: A method of extracting data such as attributes from drawings into a table or other file.

DesignCenter: A dialog box that allows you to use existing blocks that AutoCAD has provided. Drag and drop blocks, layers, linetypes, lineweights, text and dimensions styles, and external references from any existing drawing. Search for drawings and other files.

dimensioning variables: A set of numeric values, text strings, and settings that control dimensioning features.

direct distance entry: The process of specifying a second point by first moving the cursor to indicate direction and then entering a distance.

drawing limits: The user-defined rectangular area of the drawing covered by lines or dots (when specified) when the grid is on.

drawing scale: The scale at which drawings are made.

drawing template: A drawing used to ensure consistency by providing standard styles and settings.

dynamic block: The user-defined collection of drawing objects that can be changed without exploding the block.

external reference (xref): A drawing file that is inserted into another drawing. External references have the advantage that the primary drawing always contains the most recent version of the external reference.

font: A distinctive set of letters, numbers, punctuation marks, and symbols.

From: A command modifier that locates a base point and then allows you to locate an offset point from the base point.

gradient hatch: A method of rendering 2D drawings that is similar to air-brush rendering.

grid: An area consisting of evenly spaced dots or lines to aid drawing. The grid is adjustable. The grid lines or dots do not plot.

grips: Small squares, rectangles, and triangles that appear on objects you select when no command is active. After selecting the grip, you can move, stretch, rotate, scale, copy, add a vertex, convert a line to an arc, convert an arc to a line, and mirror the objects without entering commands.

hatch: The process of filling in a closed area with a pattern. Hatching can consist of solid filled areas, gradient filled areas, or areas filled with patterns of lines, dots, or other objects.

helix: An open 2D or 3D spiral.

isometric: A 2D drawing method that is used to give the appearance of three dimensions.

layer: A group of drawing objects that are like transparent overlays on a drawing. Layers can be viewed individually or in combination with other layers. Layers can be turned on or off, frozen or thawed, plotted or not plotted, and filtered.

layout: A two-dimensional page setup made in paper space that represents the paper size and what the drawing will look like when it is plotted. Multiple layouts can be created for each drawing.

lighting legend: A collection of symbols and text that identify lights and other lighting items such as switches.

lights: Objects used in the **RENDER** command to light scenes. There are five types of lights that can be used to render a scene: sun, point, distant, spot, and photometric, also called *web lights*.

linetype: How a line, arc, polyline, circle, or other item is displayed. For example, a continuous line has a different linetype than a hidden line.

lineweight: A width value that can be assigned to objects such as lines, arcs, polylines, circles, and many other objects that contain features that have width.

loft: A method of making a solid or surface by drawing it through a set of two or more cross-section curves. The cross sections make the profile (shape) of the resulting solid or surface.

materials: Items that can be attached to solid shapes to give those shapes the appearance of metal, wood, brick, granite, textiles, or any one of a number of other materials. Materials are used in the **RENDER** command to make a scene.

menu bar: The bar containing menus displayed when the **Quick Access** toolbar customization button is pressed; contains commonly used commands.

mesh model: A tessellated object type that is defined by faces, edges, and vertices. Mesh models can be smoothed to achieve a more rounded appearance and creased to introduce ridges.

Midpoint: An **Osnap** mode that helps you snap to the midpoint of a line or arc.

model: A two- or three-dimensional object.

model space: One of the two primary spaces in which objects are made.

multileader: A leader with multiple leader lines. These leaders can be customized to show index numbers inside circles, hexagons, and other polygons.

multiline: A method of drawing as many as 16 lines at the same time with or without end caps.

MVIEW: A command that operates only when **TILEMODE** is set to 0 (OFF) and is used to make and control viewport display in model space and paper space.

MVSETUP: A command that allows you to set units, scale, and paper size when **TILEMODE** is on. When **TILEMODE** is off, **MVSETUP** allows you to align, create, and scale viewports and insert title blocks.

named plot style: A plot style that is organized by a user-defined name. Named plot styles can be assigned to AutoCAD layers or to individual drawing objects.

navigation bar: An area in the AutoCAD user interface that contains navigation tools that are common across multiple Autodesk programs. The unified navigation tools include Autodesk ViewCube, SteeringWheels, ShowMotion, and 3Dconnexion.

Node: An **Osnap** mode that helps you snap to a point entity.

Orbit: A command that allows you to obtain a three-dimensional view in the active viewport.

Ortho: A setting that limits pointing device input to horizontal or vertical (relative to the current snap angle and the user coordinate system).

Osnap: An abbreviation of *object snap*, which specifies a snap point at an exact location on an object.

OTRACK: A setting that allows you to specify points by hovering your pointing device over osnap points.

page setup: A collection of plot settings that are applied to a drawing layout. Page setups can be used and shared among multiple drawings.

paper space: One of two spaces in which objects are made or documented. Paper space is used for making a finished layout for printing or plotting. Often, drawings are restored in paper space in a drawing title block and border.

Path Array: A command that allows you to make multiple copies along a path.

PDF (portable document format) files: Files of drawings that are made using the **Plot** dialog box. These files can be opened and read without the use of the AutoCAD program.

plot style: An object property that makes a collection of settings for color, dithering, gray scale, pen assignments, screening, linetype, lineweight, end styles, join styles, and fill styles. Plot styles are used at plot time.

plot style table: A collection of plot styles. Plot styles are made using plot style tables. They apply to objects only when the plot style table is attached to a layout or viewport.

point filters: A method of entering a point by which the X, Y, and Z coordinates are given in separate stages. Any one of the three coordinates can be first, second, or third.

Polar: The option of the **ARRAY** command that allows you to make multiple copies of an object in a circular array.

polar coordinates: Coordinate values that are entered relative to the last point picked. They are typed starting with an @ followed by a distance and angle of direction; the angle is preceded by a < sign.

polar tracking: A means of specifying points (similar to using **ORTHO** to constrain screen pointing motion) using your own increment angle.

POLYGON: Command that draws a polygon with 3 to 1024 sides.

polyline: A continuous line or arc composed of one or more segments, the width of which can be changed.

properties: All the attributes of an object such as color, layer, linetype, linetype scale, lineweight, and thickness.

Quick View: A command allowing you to preview and switch between open drawings and layouts.

raster image: An image consisting of dots that can be inserted into AutoCAD.

Rectangular Array: A command that allows you to make multiple copies in a rectangular pattern.

reflected ceiling plan: A drawing showing all the lighting symbols and other items such as exit signs that attach to the ceiling in their correct locations in the space. The plan also shows all the switching symbols needed to turn the lights on and off.

relative coordinates: Coordinates specified in relation to a previous point picked. Relative coordinates are entered by typing @ followed by the X and Y coordinates. For example, after a point is entered to start a line, typing and entering @1,0 will draw the line 1″ in the X direction and 0″ in the Y direction.

Render: A program that uses objects, lighting, and materials to obtain a realistic view of a model.

ribbon: The user interface below the **Quick Access** toolbar that comprises tabs and panels with flyouts used to access the commands for both 2D drawing and annotation and 3D modeling, viewing, and rendering.

sans serif: Any text font that does not contain serifs. Serifs are the small features at the ends of letters and numbers.

sheet set: An organized and named collection of sheets made from multiple drawing files.

SOLIDEDIT: A program allowing you to change solid objects by extruding, moving, rotating, offsetting, tapering, copying, coloring, separating, shelling, cleaning, checking, or deleting features such as holes, surfaces, and edges.

SteeringWheels: Icons that are divided into sections. Each section on the SteeringWheel is a tool that allows you to pan, zoom, or show the motion of the current view of the model.

surface model: A 3D model that is a thin shell. Surface models are formed using the commands **Surface Loft, Surface Sweep, Surface Offset, Surface Revolve, Surface Fillet, Surface Extend, Surface Trim** and **Untrim,** and **Surface Sculpt.**

table: A tool to make professional appearing tables such as door schedules, tables for drawing sets, tabular drawings, window schedules, and similar items. Tables often contain information about the materials needed for the construction of the building. In manufacturing they are often referred to as bills of materials or parts lists.

3D walk: A program that allows you to walk through a model controlling height and speed.

TILEMODE: A system variable that controls whether viewports can be made as layout viewports that can be moved or resized or as model viewports that lie side by side and do not overlap.

toolbar: A graphical interface containing icons that represent commands.

tracking: A means of reducing if not eliminating the number of construction lines you draw by specifying points.

transparency: A setting that makes an object more or less transparent.

transparent command: A command that can be used while another command is in progress.

units: A setting referring to drawing units. For example, an inch is a drawing unit. Architectural units utilize feet and fractional units. Decimal, fractional, engineering, and scientific units are also available in the **Drawing Units** dialog box.

user coordinate system: A user-defined variation of the world coordinate system. Variations in the coordinate system range from moving the default drawing origin (0,0,0) to another location to changing orientations for the X-, Y-, and Z-axes. It is possible to rotate the world coordinate system on any axis to make a UCS with a different two-dimensional XY plane.

user coordinate system icon: An icon showing the orientation of the X-, Y-, and Z-axes of the current coordinate system. In two-dimensional drawings only the X- and Y-axes are used. The UCS icon is located at the origin of the current UCS (0,0).

user interface: All the elements such as the AutoCAD screen that make up the interface between the user and the AutoCAD program.

ViewCube: A 3D viewing tool that can be used to switch from one view of a model to another.

viewports: Windows in either model space or paper space. Two types of viewports are available in AutoCAD, tiled and nontiled. Tiled viewports are those that exist in model space with **TILEMODE** on. Nontiled viewports exist in either model space or paper space with **TILEMODE** off.

voice/data/power plan: A drawing showing all symbols for telephones (voice), computers (data), and electrical outlets (power), and the locations of all these items.

workspace: A specific arrangement of user interface elements including their contents, properties, display status, and locations. Workspaces allow the user to quickly switch between specific arrangements of menus, toolbars, and dockable windows as well as many other settings previously specified.

zoom: The process of moving around the drawing. Zooming in shows you a close-up view of a drawing area. Zooming out shows you a larger viewing area.

Index